# CULTURES
# OF WAR

# CULTURES
# OF WAR

PEARL HARBOR / HIROSHIMA / 9-11 / IRAQ

## JOHN W. DOWER

W. W. NORTON / THE NEW PRESS

NEW YORK · LONDON

For information about permission to reproduce selections from this book,
write to Permissions, W. W. Norton & Company, Inc.,
500 Fifth Avenue, New York, NY 10110

For information about special discounts for bulk purchases, please contact
W. W. Norton Special Sales at specialsales@wwnorton.com or 800-233-4830

Manufacturing by RR Donnelley, Harrisonburg
Book design by Chris Welch Design
Production manager: Julia Druskin

Library of Congress Cataloging-in-Publication Data

Dower, John W.
Cultures of war : Pearl Harbor : Hiroshima : 9-11 : Iraq / John W. Dower. — 1st ed.
p. cm.
Includes bibliographical references and index.
ISBN 978-0-393-06150-5 (hardcover)
1. United States—History, Military—20th century. 2. United States—History,
Military—21st century. 3. United States—Military policy. 4. War and society—
United States. 5. Strategic culture—United States. 6. World War, 1939–1945.
7. September 11 Terrorist Attacks, 2001. 8. Iraq War, 2003– I. Title.
E745.D69 2010
355.00973—dc22
2010020395

W. W. Norton & Company, Inc.
500 Fifth Avenue, New York, N.Y. 10110
www.wwnorton.com

W. W. Norton & Company Ltd.
Castle House, 75/76 Wells Street, London W1T 3QT

The New Press, 38 Greene Street, 4th Floor, New York, N.Y. 10013

1 2 3 4 5 6 7 8 9 0

For Ashley and Cailey,
with love
and with the hope they will know
true cultures of peace

# CONTENTS

## PART I
## "PEARL HARBOR" AS CODE
### *Wars of Choice and Failures of Intelligence*

PART II
GROUND ZERO 1945 AND GROUND ZERO 2001
*Terror and Mass Destruction*

# PART III
# WARS AND OCCUPATIONS
*Winning the Peace, Losing the Peace*

# LIST OF ILLUSTRATIONS

# THE EVOLUTION
# OF AN INQUIRY

I began researching and writing this study shortly after September 11, 2001, when comparisons between Al Qaeda's surprise attack and Japan's at Pearl Harbor six decades earlier flooded the media in the United States. Japan and World War II in Asia have drawn my attention as a historian for many years, and analogies between the new conflict and that old one were provocative in unanticipated ways—increasingly so, as it turned out, as 9-11 spilled into the U.S.-led war of choice against Iraq, and that war and ensuing occupation in turn led to chaos and great suffering in a supposedly liberated land.

Bringing history and contemporary affairs together is never a one-way street. On the one hand—the more familiar hand—much that was associated with September 11 had an almost generic familiarity that accounts for the immediate analogies to Pearl Harbor and World War II: surprise attack, a colossal failure of U.S. intelligence, terror involving the targeting of noncombatants, the specter of weapons of mass destruction and "mushroom clouds," rhetoric of holy war on all sides. That the Islamist terrorists denounced the Judeo-Christian West and imagined a new caliphate cutting across the Middle East and South Asia deepened this resonance by evoking imperial Japan's earlier propaganda about a "White Peril" and vision of a Pan-Asian new order extending from Korea and Manchuria through China into Southeast Asia.

While light refracted from the past may help illuminate present-day conflicts, however, illumination also falls in the opposite direction. We see the past differently from the vantage of the present. This is what canards about the judgment of history imply, and what happened here: I found myself returning to old texts and arguments about Japan's war with China and the Western powers—and to all the clichés about the uniqueness of Japanese culture and peculiarities of its mid-century militarism and aggression—and asking new questions not merely about Japan and the United States and other Allied powers all those decades ago, but also about war as a culture in and of itself, and why it is always with us.

This is a departure from how we usually talk about culture in a world of conspicuous regional and national differences, and certainly a departure from what often goes on in the realm of so-called area studies with which I am sometimes associated by virtue of having spent many years studying Japan. "Culture" in the old-fashioned sense of distinctive societies bound together by shared beliefs, values, attitudes, and practices obviously is important. (My initial attraction to Japan as an undergraduate came in good part through traditional aesthetics, and the religious influences behind this.) Whether practiced by outsiders or insiders, however, such fixation on cultural uniqueness tends to end in postulation of an imagined "essentialism" suggesting that certain idealized values remain undiluted, undifferentiated, and fundamentally unchanged and unchallenged over time. Mythmaking of this sort leads to dwelling on differences rather than similarities when comparisons are made across regional or religious or ethnic boundaries. "What are the Blank like?" we ask; and the predictable answer invariably emphasizes the ways in which they are unlike Ourselves. Pushed to an extreme, we end up in Manichaean worlds where all is essentially black versus white and doomsday prophets embrace visions of a titanic clash of irreconcilable cultures.

It goes without saying that cultural differences matter; and we need only pick up the daily paper or go online or turn on a television to see how they can be manipulated to legitimize mayhem. Cultural determinism in the old-fashioned "clash of civilizations" sense, however, is of limited use in trying to comprehend the violence of our modern and contemporary world. The greater challenge is to bring comparative analysis to an understanding of the many cultures of modernity itself, one of which gives this book the title that came to mind in the wake of 9-11 and has remained unchanged: *Cultures of War*.

■

THE SUBTITLE ENVISIONED after September 11 was *Pearl Harbor / Hiroshima / 9-11*, and the expectation was that this could be thought out and written in a year or two, in five chapters or so. This turned out to be a dream once the U.S. war machine began girding to invade Iraq, which altered the scope and nature of any serious comparative study. Nonetheless, questions stimulated by the attacks on September 11 still frame much of the first two parts of the book. Thus, Part I takes up "'Pearl Harbor' as code" to examine the surprise attacks and disastrous failures of intelligence that took place on the U.S. side in 1941 and 2001. The parallels in the two cases—involving institutional, intellectual, and psychological pathologies—are sobering. Part I concludes with a brief rumination on how catastrophes like those that occurred on December 7 and September 11 also may turn out to be godsends to people in power—an outcome apparent early on for the Bush presidency that had precedent of a sort sixty years earlier for President Franklin D. Roosevelt. The great difference is that Roosevelt used his opportunity well, and Bush disastrously.

Part II takes terror bombing and the christening of Manhattan's devastated World Trade Center site as "Ground Zero" as a point of departure for reconsidering the emergence of terror bombing as standard operating procedure in the British and American air war of World War II. In most commentary on current affairs, certainly in the anti-Islamist camp, it is common to draw a sharp distinction between the terror tactics of Al Qaeda and other nonstate actors on the one hand, and state terror such as the World War II strategic bombing campaigns on the other. There are indeed significant differences, although the one embraced by Americans in the wake of 9-11—that the Islamists, and Muslims and Arabs more generally, do not value human life as Christians and Jews do—is absurd.

Deliberately targeting densely populated urban areas to undermine the morale of the enemy reached an apogee in the air raids against Germany and Japan. This marked a departure from "just war" practices that had been vocally proclaimed until then by the League of Nations and United States (which was not a member of the League). Once all-out war with the

Axis powers was engaged, such mass killing of noncombatants was rationalized not merely as inescapable when targeting enemy infrastructure,
but as integral to psychological warfare in an age of "total war." It was
defended with great moral fervor as necessary and just against a heinous
foe. And it was carried out with a vengeance. We will never possess precise death tolls, but somewhere around one million German and Japanese
noncombatants were killed in Allied bombing missions between 1943 and
1945. Baptizing the site of the World Trade Center atrocity as Ground
Zero, moreover, entailed appropriating a name originally associated with
the culmination of this rain of death from the skies: the atomic bombings
of Hiroshima and Nagasaki.

Two thoughts struck me upon observing the post–September 11 metamorphosis of Ground Zero into code for American victimization. First
was how quickly and nonchalantly the name was expropriated, without a
moment's self-reflection about its original association with the development and use of the atomic bomb. Second was the fact that although "terror bombing" was a familiar term in official and scholarly writings about
strategic bombing—a term historians like me had long used as a matter
of course, buried among innumerable other considerations about World
War II—I had never ventured to work out for myself precisely how this
applied to the bombing campaign that preceded Hiroshima and Nagasaki, in which sixty-four other Japanese cities were subjected to saturation
firebombing.

Over the last decade or so, the British and U.S. air war against Germany has drawn considerable attention. Here in Part II, I have built on
this research and commentary to examine the carryover to Japan—and,
building on this in turn, tried to rethink the use of the atomic bombs in
the context of our contemporary confrontation with annihilation. This
involves more than just acknowledging the pedigree and genealogy of the
weapons of mass destruction that threaten the world today. It also calls
attention to the post–World War II fixation of American military planners
on high-tech conventional warfare involving maximum violence—a fixation that reflects both hubris concerning the efficacy of undiluted force,
and insularity and delusion when it comes to appraising the nature, aspirations, and capabilities of less materially powerful adversaries. None of the
more limited wars that followed World War II—not even Vietnam, or the

Soviet debacle in Afghanistan, which helped precipitate the disintegration of the Soviet Union in 1991—weaned U.S. planners from their ultimate faith in annihilationist "shock and awe" strategies.

Nonstate actors differ from state actors, and terrorist attacks from declared wars involving formal armed forces, and miles-high bombers or miles-distant artillery from bombers who look their victims in the face and blow themselves up in the process. But, at the same time, terror is terror; the civilians and noncombatants killed are all dead; and the moral righteousness and even quasi-theological rationalization that accompany such terror tend to be cut of the same cloth. Part II concludes with the arguments and rhetoric Islamist apologists have employed to justify their own forms of terror—not to argue that all is same or relative, which is not the case, but to frame yet another facet of our cultures of war. The reasons we humans embrace violence and mass destruction are more convoluted than the war planners or most policy analysts acknowledge, and we ignore this complexity at our peril—however forbidding what this says about us as individuals and societies may be.

THE U.S. ENUNCIATION of a doctrine of "preemptive war" in June 2002 and invasion of Iraq in March 2003 expanded the parameters of thinking about "'Pearl Harbor' as code" in unanticipated ways. The Bush administration's "war of choice" now joined Japan's in 1941 and Al Qaeda's in 2001—a provocative notion in itself, but hardly the half of it. For at the same time, the failure of U.S. intelligence prior to 9-11 was compounded by a more confounding—almost criminally negligent—failure of intelligence evaluation vis-à-vis Iraq and the Islamist and terrorist challenge more generally. "Operation Iraqi Freedom" foundered quickly; and as Iraq spiraled into chaos, the subtitle of the inquiry elided into *Pearl Harbor / Hiroshima / 9-11 / Iraq*—and the prospect of a short book that might be wrapped up fairly quickly was abandoned.

The failures of intelligence and imagination exposed by the invasion of Iraq replicated 1941 and 2001 and at the same time were of a different order, for they were associated not with preventing a surprise attack but with planning an aggressive war. This debacle went beyond the issue of false or cooked intelligence about Iraq's possession of weapons of mass destruction, although this understandably has drawn particularly intense scrutiny. The larger intelligence failure pointed to a different and unexpected comparative perspective on Pearl Harbor: strategic imbecility. Like Japan's attack in 1941, America's war of choice against Iraq was tactically brilliant and strategically idiotic. In both cases, war planners ignored the psychology and capabilities of the enemy. In neither case did they give due diligence to evaluating risk, anticipating worst-case scenarios, formulating a coherent and realistic endgame, or planning for protracted conflict.

"Strategic imbecility" is a famous English-language phrase introduced in the 1950s to highlight the peculiar irrationality of the Japanese warlords who chose to attack Pearl Harbor and Western colonial possessions in Southeast Asia. I have spent many professional years observing the reiteration of this simplistic cultural critique, and the criticisms that later became directed against the Oval Office and Pentagon for failing to engage in serious planning for Iraq beyond the initiation of combat carried, to my ear, almost amusing vibrations. One could take the clichés about Japan's irrational warlords and Pearl Harbor that had circulated as conventional wisdom for over a half century and plug in "the United States," "the Bush administration," "Iraq" with few other changes—and the critique would seem perfectly reasonable. Wishful thinking trumped rational analysis in Tokyo in 1941 and Washington in the run-up to war with Iraq. Nor did delusion and reckless incompetence end there. Japanese war planners remained in their dream world long after disaster loomed—and so did President Bush and his top advisers.

This resonance between the strategic myopia of Tokyo's Pearl Harbor attack and Washington's invasion of Iraq undermines the mystique of "rationality" that gives so much pleasure to Westerners in general and Americans in particular in their postulations of a logical "West" pitted against an illogical "East." Put differently, the "herd behavior" and "groupthink" that Westerners tend to ascribe to most non-Western societies (notions that academics usually buttress with sociological exegesis extrapolated from Max Weber and others) turn out to be universal phenomena that became manifest with dire consequences in the war of choice against Iraq. This was true not only at the top ranks of war planners, but almost everywhere else in the United States until the invasion turned into a quagmire and criticism became fashionable: groupthink prevailed in the legislature, in the mainstream media, and across an electorate that returned George W. Bush to the presidency in the November 2004 election. According to the textbooks, such herd behavior is not what is supposed to take place in a functioning democracy, particularly one that prides itself on bedrock individualism.

Groupthink is not a simple pathology. Dissent always exists at some level in complex systems, and the routines of seemingly rational deliberation are always present in the formulation of grand policy. Despite the obsessive secrecy that accompanied the Bush administration's "war on terror," much of the backstage record has become accessible piecemeal in the form of official hearings and reports, declassified documents, books and articles by insiders, and first-rate investigative journalism based on extensive interviewing and occasional privileged access to classified materials. This is the stuff of a first draft of the history of the administration's strategic folly. Where I depart from most writers to date is in attempting to move, as a historian, through the concrete, and beyond the Bush administration per se, to sort out some of the broader dynamics and morbidities of our times and our modern and contemporary wars.

Where Japan's disastrous road to war is concerned, it is possible to reconstruct the basic thrust of policy making with similar confidence, even though there are many gaps in the record. Particularly valuable here is a set of detailed minutes of deliberations at the highest level from April to December 1941 that almost miraculously survived the war. As might be expected, the argument that war was both unavoidable and just was forcefully made even in top-secret sessions by Japan's leaders, as by America's six decades later. More tantalizing, it is also possible to compile a substantial list of seemingly reasonable arguments on why the risk seemed worth the gamble for Japan—why, that is, they might hope for some sort of favorable military outcome in the long run. Although this was a dream world, its furnishings seemed solid enough—as was also the case with the dream world in which the Bush administration and its supporters lived. Imperial Japan's strategic imbecility no longer seems so peculiar.

Neither does imperial Japan's authoritarianism. Japan was not a democracy, and the United States is. The differences are huge, but in terms of practical political power the decision-making processes in Tokyo in 1941 and Washington after 9-11 are not incommensurable. Here the resemblance is captured in a contradiction Americans frequently mention but rarely challenge in any meaningful way: between "democracy" and an "imperial presidency" unabashedly intent on aggrandizing and exercising executive authority, even in violation of existing law. Japan's wartime ideologues and propagandists made no bones about venerating the throne and scorning democracy, or about loyalty and patriotism being supreme virtues and dissent tantamount to treason, or about censoring what the media could say. At the same time, their emperor system was constitutionally defined, featured a parliament known as the Diet with an elective lower house, and held top leaders beneath the emperor accountable. (There were three Japanese prime ministers between the time of the Pearl Harbor attack and the atomic bombing of Hiroshima, and many ministerial changes.) The use and abuse of imperial power depended upon an acquiescent political class and populace that, here again, no longer seems peculiarly Japanese or alien to erstwhile democracies.

The political issue here goes beyond glib (but irresistible) comparisons between President Bush and Emperor Hirohito. The emperor was a hereditary monarch who sanctioned and symbolized rather than drove grand policy. His ministers borrowed his institutional charisma, much as Washington's top policy makers borrow the charisma of the presidency; the tight group that chose war in 1941 was no smaller than the so-called Oval Office cabal that turned combating terrorism into preemptive war against Iraq after 9-11; and, in interesting ways, Japan's warlords followed formal procedures of policy making more closely than President Bush and his war planners did. From different but mutually reinforcing perspectives, the emperor system and imperial presidency confront us with unsettling questions concerning authority and authoritarianism, competence and incompetence, responsibility and irresponsibility, and accountability and its absence at moments of transcendent consequence.

Beyond egregious negligence, the concrete acts of war unleashed by the emperor's warlords and the imperial presidency also invite comparative analysis of outright war crimes like torture and other transgressions. I touch on this controversial subject only in passing, but it is worth noting that both cases entail discussion of the Geneva Conventions. Imperial Japan's black deeds have left an indelible stain on the nation's honor and good name, and it remains to be seen how lasting the damage to America's reputation will be. In this regard, the Bush administration's war planners are fortunate in having been able to evade formal and serious investigation remotely comparable to what the Allied powers pursued vis-à-vis Japan and Germany after World War II in the name of both historical clarity and respect for the rule of law.

These various post–9-11 issues—addressed in the context of wars of choice and strategic folly—eventually became a substantial part of the Part I treatment of "'Pearl Harbor' as code."

AFTER IT BECAME clear that Iraq did not possess the weapons of mass destruction that had been offered as the rationale for launching war, a great deal of critical attention was devoted to the Bush administration's "cherry-picking" of intelligence. It did indeed harvest data and ostensible facts selectively, although how much this reflected Machiavellian manipulation and how much the self-delusion of finding only what one expects and wishes to find may never be resolved. Cherry-picking, in any case, was not confined to raw intelligence data. It extended to history as well, in both large and small ways. Among the smaller distortions of history was the administration's invocation of postwar Japan and Germany as attractive mirrors of the stability and democracy that could be anticipated in post-invasion Iraq.

This false analogy was first floated around October 2002, and it should have been obvious from the outset that this was whistle-stop history at its worst. What postwar Japan and Germany made clear was that virtually every factor that contributed to the reform and recovery of the two defeated Axis powers was missing or severely lacking in Iraq. Even long after occupied Iraq had become a nightmare, however, the president and his speechwriters continued to invoke the precedent of occupied Japan in particular as a template that offered hope for the future. (Racially, culturally, and religiously, Japan's non-Western nature made it more attractive than Germany as a purportedly pertinent model of successful post-conflict occupation and reconstruction.) Such allusions, and illusions, continued to the end of the Bush presidency.

Much of my research has dealt with occupied Japan, and as the tragedy in Iraq unfolded, "wars and occupations" inevitably became the third part of this inquiry. For all practical purposes, the O-word (occupation) was taboo in the U.S. circles that planned Operation Iraqi Freedom, for the mission was defined as "liberation." When occupation was formally and belatedly acknowledged with the creation of the U.S.-led Coalition Provisional Authority (CPA) in Baghdad in April 2003, Iraq lost its sovereignty and the United States lost almost all semblance of credibility. Although the CPA was dissolved in June 2004, de facto occupation continued; domestic violence and terror increased; occupation authorities remained largely confined to the grotesque fortified "Green Zone" in Baghdad; some two million Iraqis eventually fled the country, and more than this number were internally displaced. By the time Bush left office in January 2009, violence had decreased, but daily life remained harsh and precarious and the death toll since the invasion stood at many scores of thousands of Iraqis at the very least—more probably at hundreds of thousands of largely civilian deaths—and over four thousand U.S. military fatalities.

By contrast, no Allied military were killed in occupied Japan or occupied Germany. Although daily life remained difficult for several years, no Japanese died in violence triggered by the foreign presence. Japan endured over six years of occupation (from August 1945 to April 1952), mended quickly from its war wounds, and emerged whole. Iraq was denied such good fortune, and the question is, why? The answers lie in taking history more seriously than policy makers have time or inclination to do; and addressing this required some three long chapters in Part III.

The first of these chapters is more or less predictable: it sets the Japan and America of the late 1940s against the Iraq and America of the first decade of the twenty-first century, and attempts to sort out the differences that mattered. It goes without saying that Iraq was not Japan in too many critical ways (although this seems to have been lost upon the cherry-pickers of 2002 and afterwards). It takes some saying, on the other hand, to point out how different the contemporary United States is from the nation, government, and body politic that exited World War II prepared to take on "nation building" abroad.

It also, as it transpired, took some thought and more than a few words to clarify how occupied Japan and occupied Iraq are not simple binary opposites, a success story set against a tragedy. As the disaster in Iraq unfolded, I found myself drawn not merely to stark contrasts but also to "convergences of a sort" that complicate the study of wars and occupations. Defeated Japan's American overlords got away with prejudices and policies that proved disastrous in Iraq. They were largely unversed in Japanese language and culture, for example, and often ethnocentric and arrogant. They bent the law on occasion, not only in their war-crimes trials but even in the root-and-branch reformist agendas they introduced, which had no basis in international law as set forth most conspicuously in the Hague conventions. In another direction, with U.S. connivance the English, French, Dutch, and Chinese all retained Japanese military who surrendered overseas as labor after the war, sometimes for prolonged periods, and even forced Japanese units to participate in ongoing conflicts in Indochina (Vietnam), the Dutch East Indies (Indonesia), and on both sides in the civil war in China. Rather like the Bush administration, the Allied powers manipulated the labeling of enemy fallen into their hands to abet and presumably legitimize such abuses—or simply showed contempt for the rules of war.

Convergence of a sort also took place at the level of specific occupation policies, where agendas that proved disastrous in Iraq—most notably, the dissolution of the military and categorical purge of Baathist Party members—had seeming precedent of a sort, and smooth going, in Japan. In Japan, some two hundred thousand individuals were prohibited from holding public office, while demilitarization involved the top-to-bottom elimination of the Imperial Army and Navy. The devil is in the details, and exploring some of these details became, for me, still another new way of thinking about the United States, Japan, Iraq, and social engineering more generally.

Social engineering is the rubric we used to use in describing grand post–World War II undertakings such as the occupations of Japan and Germany, and this was undergirded by a number of basic assumptions. The state had a proper role to play abroad as well as at home. The military took care of its own business, including civil affairs in occupied areas. Lines of command were clear. Bipartisanship and serious interagency collaboration were essential to the success of overseas operations. Reconstruction in occupied areas had to come largely at the hands of the people occupied. And so on. Little of this carried over to George W. Bush's America, where social engineering had been renamed "nation building"—and nation building was ideologically anathema.

This ideological difference helps explain how and why the United States invaded Iraq with no serious planning for post-conflict contingencies and no capacity to respond to upheaval and insurgency. The twenty-first-century imperial presidency belittled nation building, venerated the rationality and efficiency of the market, outsourced huge portions of military and civilian planning and practice, and was intent on (and blithely optimistic about) seeing a post-Saddam Iraq become the Middle East showcase for its own ideology of "free market" fundamentalism. The U.S. military that invaded Iraq was not trained or equipped to stabilize and occupy the country, nor was it equipped to take care of many of its own needs. Such lack of common sense seems appalling in retrospect, and we know now that it was questioned and challenged at lower levels of the civilian and military bureaucracies. Under the imperial presidency, such challenges to the entrenched groupthink fell like water on stone.

Even as private contractors streamed into occupied Iraq beginning in 2003, and foreign mercenaries assumed major security functions there, the Coalition Provisional Authority made clear that extreme privatization was also the guideline for reforming and reconstructing the Iraqi state and economy. This reflected an arrogant indifference to the pride and immediate needs and desires of the Iraqis themselves—and amounted, in the process, to a gift to terrorists and insurgents. Privatization was a recipe for confusion, unaccountability, and disaster that outlived the short life of the CPA itself—an ostensible exercise in "rational choice" that in practice made America a symbol, to much of the world, of irrationality and irresponsibility.

AS WRITING ABOUT these issues unfolded, I found myself weaving other threads into the narrative. Holy war was one, for most wars—and certainly those addressed here—are rendered sacred by their participants. Hubris became another thread, both as the fatal arrogance of self-righteousness and as the extraordinary faith Americans in particular place in the efficacy of supposedly overwhelming military firepower. Evil, including the treacherous terrain of so-called necessary or lesser evils, drew more attention than I had anticipated. As titles and subtitles in some of the chapters indicate, I take evil seriously, even while exploring the fallacy of postulating a Manichaean world. Double standards and hypocrisy became another recurrent theme, the potent play of memory and grievance yet another. Tragedy is not a very popular concept in the social sciences, for (like ambiguity and irrationality) it does not model well. I came to doing history from the humanities; and tragedy, like evil, seems to me to be indispensible to understanding our cultures of war.

The use, misuse, and plain disregard of history became another subtext. This operates at several levels. The Japanese, Islamists, and Americans all called on "history" to propagandize their crusades—picking up the shards of a usable past while ignoring whatever did not suit their purposes. More interesting than what they cherry-picked, however, is what they ignored at their peril concerning both their chosen enemies and themselves. Where the twenty-first-century American war planners are concerned, this whitening out of an inconvenient past includes not merely the U.S. role in developing and using weapons of mass destruction and targeting civilians to destroy morale, and not just the entire post–World War I history of the Western powers in the Middle East, but also concrete post–World War II lessons about asymmetrical war, insurgency, national and transnational pride, "smart" versus hard power, and the many ways in which, sooner or later, arrogance and negligence lead to blowback, quagmires, incalculable suffering and harm.

And one final thread: language. War words saturate this analysis—to convey as vividly as possible why participants in these holy wars fight, but even more to illuminate how easily such rhetoric can become a trap, making exit from war far more difficult than starting war in the first place. The other side of the battle cries, however, is the language of peace, freedom, and justice. This was true of the Japanese in the Asia-Pacific War. It is woven throughout the screeds of Islamist holy warriors like Osama bin Laden. It is the lifeblood of America's patriotic oratory. And it is more than cynical propaganda. This—the possibility for shared cultures of peace and reconciliation—is the distant shore that lies opposite the cultures of war.

■

MULLING AND WRITING up these themes was largely completed by the time the Bush presidency entered its closing months. As I turned to drafting a conclusion, however, the big picture was again altered by stunning developments: in this case, the financial meltdown that began on

Wall Street and shook global capitalism to its foundations. Although this crisis in the cultures of money came as a shock, many of the underlying pathologies of the private sector quickly revealed themselves to be of a piece with the faith-based thinking and organizational pathologies associated with Washington's war culture. Secular priesthoods; herd behavior; cherry-picking data; incompetent risk assessment; wishful thinking garbed as rationality; extraordinary failures of imagination concerning both history and contemporary affairs; absence of transparency, accountability, and plain common sense—these and other points of convergence pointed to disconcerting overlap between the fools' errands of the ostensibly hard-nosed and rational war makers on the one hand, and the fools' gold of the money makers, with their complex "instruments" and ultrasophisticated computer models, on the other.

*Cultures of War* ends with this juxtaposition of fools' errands and fools' gold, and with reflections that go beyond specific policy issues and beyond war and war cultures per se. It ends, that is, with the beginnings of what would be another inquiry, in this case concerning behavioral and organizational pathologies that also amount to cultures in themselves.

*A note on Japanese names:* Japanese names are rendered throughout in Western order, namely, the given name followed by the surname. Thus, Isoroku Yamamoto refers to Admiral Yamamoto, Hideki Tōjō to General and Prime Minister Tōjō. I have adopted this policy with some reservations, for there is an element of cultural presumptuousness in reversing the order by which Japanese identify themselves and know each other: Yamamoto Isoroku and Tōjō Hideki in these two cases. My rationale for the reveral is practical. The names of Japanese who write in languages like English, or are translated into them, for example—scientists, social scientists, and novelists among them—are generally rendered in Western order to avoid confusing non-Japanese readers. Going one way with some Japanese names, and another way with others, is confusing. This reversal of order is jarring to my own eye and ear. Nonetheless, it seems desirable to ensure consistency and optimal clarity.

*A note on illustrations:* The illustrations have been selected with several considerations in mind. One is that certain images are so familiar as to deserve being called iconic: they shaped popular consciousness when first seen, and remain immediately recognizable to later generations. A second, related criterion for selection is that many visual images, certainly of a historical nature like those introduced here, must be regarded as "texts" in themselves. They do not just duplicate or reinforce what has been laid out in words. Rather, they can open windows to different ways of understanding the past or present. Sometimes the effect is multiplied by direct (or even implicit) juxtapositions. Often the impact derives from being the opposite of iconic—from being unexpected and unfamiliar, even jarring. Overlapping the iconic and the incisive or jarring graphics is a category of images that might loosely be called generic, in that they seem genuinely representative of the repetitive visual world people experienced at the time; they are, in their distinctive ways, visual tropes. Be this as it may, selecting the graphics turned out to be an exploration in itself, and whittling them down was a challenge.

# ACKNOWLEDGMENTS

In pursuing this unfolding inquiry, I found that my most precious resource was time to read, write, and rewrite. My greatest debt is to two generous institutions that made such time available: the Andrew W. Mellon Foundation and my university, the Massachusetts Institute of Technology. A multiyear Mellon grant enabled me to focus more attention on this (and one other) project, and Harriet Zuckerman at the foundation was a particularly gracious source of encouragement. The Institute initiated the Mellon grant and, ever since I joined its faculty almost two decades ago, has been supportive of the attempt to balance research and teaching. Through all this, I have had the good fortune of being associated at MIT with a collegial department, History, in a forward-looking School of Humanities, Arts, and Social Sciences.

The extensive notes reveal my great debts where the substance of the inquiry is concerned. One reason these are so long is that I tend to use notes as a kind of "supplementary commentary" to elaborate on cryptic observations. Beyond this, however, the notes should convey how much I have learned and borrowed from other writers and writings. We historians tend to be addicted to "primary" sources—documents, government publications and hearings, memoirs, diaries, contemporary popular discourse, and the like—and I have tapped these. So have others before me, however, and I hope I have succeeded in conveying how much I have benefitted from their research.

This debt to other writers exists at several levels. One involves several generations of scholarship focused on World War II—and, more specifically, on the road to war in Asia and the Pacific, the Pearl Harbor attack, strategic bombing and the decision to target noncombatants and ultimately to use the atomic bombs, and the postwar occupation of Japan. As a longtime academic, I was familiar with much of this literature but revisited it with new comparative questions in mind.

These questions stemmed, of course, from September 11 and the invasion and occupation of Iraq that followed. The Web has made resources available in ways undreamed of when I began doing history in the 1960s: documents, reports, speeches, interview transcripts, articles, and polemics are all much more easily accessible. At the same time, however, books and articles in the traditional print media have flourished. I have drawn on declarations, insider reports, and memoirs from a range of perspectives, but wish to call particular attention to my indebtedness to the many investigative journalists who also are frequently cited in the notes. They have been indefatigable, and must be seen as the invaluable oral historians of our time—asking hard questions close to the events, and recording answers that otherwise would be lost to history. The notes also reveal my debt to the writings of a number of insightful analysts of terror and counterterrorism, as well as of Islam and the Middle East crisis more generally.

*Cultures of War* carries the joint imprint of W. W. Norton and The New Press, and I am grateful for the unstinting support of Edwin Barber and Andre Schiffrin at these two distinguished publishing houses. They, along with my agent, Georges Borchardt, have been patient with my sense of an evolving inquiry and consequent disregard of projected deadlines. Kana Dower and Ken Dower helped guide me through computer challenges, and Margo Collett tracked down many hard-copy and online materials. Bedross Der Matossian and Hamid Rezai clarified the writings in Middle East languages that appear in some of the illustrations. As *Cultures of War* moved into production, I received invaluable assistance from a range of individuals, and am pleased to have the opportunity to thank them here: Mary Babcock for copyediting; Elyse Rieder for clearing illustration permissions, Chris Welch for producing a display-page design that incorporates my interest in visuals, and the strong support staff at W. W. Norton— Julia Druskin, Nancy Palmquist, and especially Melanie Tortoroli, who kept everything on track.

Finally, as always, I thank my wife, Yasuko, for her support and patience. This time around I filled a sizable portion of our living room in Boston with books and papers, and more or less took up permanent residence there. This is called colonization when undertaken by bodies larger and more formally constituted than me, and I will remain forever impressed by, and thankful for, her grace in refraining from mentioning this.

July 5, 2009

# PART I
# "PEARL HARBOR" AS CODE

*Wars of Choice and Failures of Intelligence*

# INFAMY AND THE CRACKED MIRROR OF HISTORY

S hortly after noon on December 8, 1941, President Franklin Roosevelt
appeared before a joint session of Congress to deliver one of history's most famous war messages. These were his opening words:

> Yesterday, December 7, 1941—a date which will live in infamy—the
> United States of America was suddenly and deliberately attacked by
> naval and air forces of the Empire of Japan.

*A date which will live in infamy*—the phrase quickly became an indelible
part of American history. Little known is the fact that this fine rhetoric
was an editorial afterthought.

The Japanese had deliberately chosen Sunday, a quiet day, for their attack; their first wave of planes swooped in from six aircraft carriers just before eight o'clock in the morning. Three hours later, around five in the evening Washington time, the president summoned his secretary and began to dictate his message to the nation. No speechwriters were involved. The words were Roosevelt's own, and we still possess the typed text that was made from this session—heavily marked in pencil with the president's subsequent revisions. In the original version, the message began as follows: "Yesterday, December 7, 1941, a date which will live in world history . . ."[1]

What a difference a second draft can make.

## "Pearl Harbor" as Code

Immediately, "infamy" became American code for "Pearl Harbor," as well as code for Japanese treachery and deceitfulness—a stab in the back that cried out for retaliation and would never be forgotten. When the September 11 terrorist attacks occurred in New York and Washington just a few months short of six decades later, "infamy" was the first word many American commentators summoned to convey the enormity of these crimes. Pundits and politicians and appalled Americans everywhere almost reflexively evoked "Pearl Harbor." Past and present were momentarily fused, like a flashback in a film.

I was in Vermont on September 11. The next day's banner headline on one newspaper read simply "Infamy!" On the other local paper it was "Day of Infamy!" My hometown newspaper, the *Boston Globe*, headlined its September 12 issue "New day of infamy." The weekly edition of the *Washington Post*, which arrived a few days later, filled its front cover with President Roosevelt's exact quote: "A Date Which Will Live in Infamy."

President George W. Bush seized the same historical analogy when dictating to his diary on the night of September 11. "The Pearl Harbor of the 21st century," he recorded, "took place today." At the opposite end of the political spectrum, the liberal columnist Paul Krugman, reflecting on the first anniversary of 9-11, wrote, "It was natural to think of Sept. 11 as the moral equivalent of Pearl Harbor, and of the struggle that began that day as this generation's equivalent of World War II."[2]

What Krugman was evoking was the other side of infamy: the moral

*1. USS* Arizona *burning on Battleship Row. Japan's surprise attack on the Pacific Fleet at Pearl Harbor killed 2,345 military personnel and fifty-seven civilians, sank four battleships and damaged four others, and destroyed 188 aircraft while damaging another 155. The battleship* Arizona, *depicted above, sank with a loss of 1,177 sailors and became the final resting place of 1,102 of them. The memorial commemorating the attack, dedicated in 1962 and visited by over a million people annually, spans the sunken hull of the* Arizona.

*2. Flak and billowing smoke at Pearl Harbor.*

*3. A rescue boat approaches the USS* West Virginia.

4. USS Shaw *exploding.*

5. *A broken B-17, caught on the ground at Hickam Field.*

REMEMBERING DECEMBER 7

*6–9. "Remember Pearl Harbor," the single most potent of wartime slogans, assumed new meaning in the wake of 9-11. As these posters reveal, contrary to Japanese hopes that the*

outrage and thirst for revenge against a shameless foe that the crime of September 11, like that of December 7, triggered. "Remember Pearl Harbor," far and away the most popular rallying cry in America's war against Japan, ended only three years and eight months later, after the atomic bombing of Hiroshima and Nagasaki. (In the U.S. military, the slogan was sometimes rendered more graphically as "Remember Pearl Harbor—Keep 'em Dying.") After the destruction of the World Trade Center and attack on the Pentagon, the ubiquitous slogan was "9-11—We Will Never Forget."[3]

The similarity of these battle cries was not mere coincidence. Like the language of "infamy," the call for everlasting remembrance of September 11 was all the more effective because most adult Americans immediately grasped—or grasped at—the resonance between the two catastrophes. As a billboard on the Kennedy Expressway in Chicago made clear, no one needed footnotes. *Never forget!* exhorted the legend in the middle, flanked right and left by two dates: *December 7, 1941,* and *September 11, 2001.*[4]

*surprise attack would demoralize the Americans, the searing memory of December 7 went hand in hand with a fierce thirst for revenge.*

Poor Japan: so many postwar years devoted to burying the past and proving itself a peaceful nation and devoted ally of the United States—and suddenly nineteen suicidal Islamist terrorists in hijacked airplanes had resurrected searing memories of the old and ostensibly bygone war. "Infamy" and "Remember Pearl Harbor" turned out to be but opening notes in an expansive rhetorical interplay of past and present. The attacks on Manhattan and the Pentagon also became likened to kamikaze attacks, even though these Japanese suicide tactics were not adopted until late 1944 and had nothing to do with Pearl Harbor or, indeed, with targeting civilians. The devastated World Trade Center site itself was christened "Ground Zero," a name originally associated with the nuclear destruction of Hiroshima and Nagasaki in 1945. Transparently evoking the famous posed photograph of Marines raising the Stars and Stripes on Mount Suribachi on Iwo Jima in early 1945, a photo of firemen raising a flag amidst the smoldering ruins in Manhattan received wide circulation as a symbol of

America's heroic resolve to crush the enemy and fight through to victory. These iconic images of GIs in 1945 and New York City firemen in 2001 were frequently reproduced side by side.

The president and his speechwriters lost few opportunities to cast the new crisis in the mold of the old war. Just as Roosevelt had declared war on Japan with a memorable speech, Bush moved quickly to declare a "war on terror." Lost in the process were vast differences between 2001 and 1941. Unlike Japan and Germany, with their formidable military machines, the new antagonists were transnational, crudely armed, loosely organized, and committed to ad hoc "asymmetric" tactics of confrontation and destruction. They materialized and disappeared like phantoms. Politically, however, what mattered more than such differences was the opportunity to brand and empower President Bush, like Franklin Roosevelt and Harry Truman before him, as a war president.[5]

Two months after September 11, the president evoked, more obliquely, another provocative World War II allusion: Nazi genocide. Terrorists, he told the UN General Assembly on November 10, were "searching for weapons of mass destruction, the tools to turn their hatred into holocaust." Soon after, in his January 29, 2002, State of the Union address, the World War II analogy was ratcheted to another level when the president coupled Iraq, Iran, and North Korea as an "axis of evil." This transparent allusion was to the "Axis" alliance of Nazi Germany, fascist Italy, and imperial Japan that had been formalized in the so-called Tripartite Pact of September 1940, culminating some five years of increasingly close relations.

The Axis alliance of World War II involved a formal military pact among three powerful nation-states hell-bent on conquest. By contrast, Iraq, Iran, and North Korea had no comparable great-power stature, no comparable formal (or informal) ties, no comparable armies and arsenals, no comparable expansionist plans. In this case, the forced analogy rested on the argument that the three nations possessed weapons programs, including missiles and existing or imminent nuclear capabilities, which could fall into the hands of Al Qaeda or other terrorists. Hand in hand with such evocations, from early on until the very end of the Bush presidency, critics of the conduct of the war on terror were routinely tarred with replicating the most craven and discredited of pre–World War II responses to the Axis threat: "appeasement."[6]

Pearl Harbor, the Axis, even the Holocaust—such plundering from the last "good war" was natural, irresistible, almost addictive, and took on a certain momentum all its own. On May 1, 2003, for example, after the war against terror had been escalated into "preemptive" war on Iraq, the president famously celebrated victory over Saddam Hussein's motley forces with a dramatic "Mission Accomplished" appearance on the aircraft carrier *Abraham Lincoln*. More subtle than other official exercises in ransacking recent military history, Bush's triumphal setting reprised General Douglas MacArthur's receipt of Japan's formal surrender on the battleship *Missouri* in Tokyo Bay on September 2, 1945. Even the language carried echoes. MacArthur had taken that grand moment to announce that "the Holy Mission has been completed."[7]

More overt and sustained was the use and misuse of history to frame what would supposedly follow the overthrow of Saddam Hussein and his despotic Baathist regime. This campaign looked to the Axis not in war, but in defeat. Before the invasion, high officials invoked the "success story" of postwar Japan as a reassuring preview of what could be anticipated in Iraq: cordial welcome of the conquerors, followed by impressive accomplishments in reconstruction and democratization. And they continued to belabor this analogy long after the Bush-as-MacArthur moment had evaporated and the putative liberation of Iraq turned into protracted occupation of a violent, fractured land. (Occupied Germany was less useful as a positive precedent, since that defeated Axis nation had been divided into U.S., British, French, and Soviet zones of occupation and soon fell into the Cold War partition we know as East and West Germany.) On August 30, 2005, for example, Bush devoted almost an entire speech at the North Island Naval Air Station in California to this particular variant of the Japan code.

The historical touchstone for this widely publicized address was the sixtieth anniversary of "V-J Day." (Victory over Japan—"V-J"—signaled the end of World War II and actually had two anniversary dates. The Japanese emperor announced Japan's capitulation on August 14, 1945, while the formal surrender ceremony took place on the *Missouri* on September 2.) Invited audience included World War II veterans, and the president took care to mention by name Americans fighting in Iraq whose grandfathers "came together to join a mighty force that defeated the Japanese empire."

Such personalized touches were characteristic of Bush's public presentations in general, but the V-J Day address was an especially blatant— and, by this date, desperate—attempt to emphasize the intimate, generational "sacred bond" among "patriots past and present who have worn the nation's uniform." At the same time, painstaking care was taken to place Bush himself in the hallowed light of Franklin Roosevelt. Although Roosevelt and his liberal New Deal policies were reviled by the administration where domestic policy was concerned, the speech amounted to a paean to the wisdom, vision, and resolution of Roosevelt ("and later President Truman") as a leader in war.

One can almost picture White House speechwriters working from a crib on World War II highlighted with a magic marker. Pearl Harbor and the "dark days" that followed received the usual emphasis. More insistently, however, the V-J Day speech lingered on the hard struggles and decisive moments of victory that followed, including the Battle of Midway in mid-1942 and "the flag-raising of Iwo Jima" over two years later. (Iwo Jima, where U.S. forces began to take heavier losses as they drew closer to victory, was mentioned many times.) The ferocious Japanese enemy was exhumed—"kamikaze pilots on suicidal missions, soldiers who fought to the last man, commanders animated by a fanatical belief that their nation was ordained to rule the Asian continent." So too were the ghosts of Jimmy Doolittle (who led "the daring first attack on Japanese soil") and General MacArthur (who "sixty years ago this Friday . . . accepted the Japanese surrender aboard the USS Missouri in Tokyo Bay").

There was a double lesson in all this. First, history had come full cycle:

As we mark this anniversary, we are again a nation at war. Once again, war came to our shores with a surprise attack that killed thousands in cold blood. Once again, we face determined enemies who follow a ruthless ideology that despises everything America stands for. Once again, America and our allies are waging a global campaign with forces deployed on virtually every continent. And once again, we will not rest until victory is America's and our freedom is secure.

10–11. *For Americans, combat in the Pacific and rescue operations at the World Trade Center each produced a single photograph that surpassed all others in conveying heroism and patriotism. After 9-11, Thomas Franklin's color photograph of three firemen raising the Stars and Stripes in the ruins of the World Trade Center was often set alongside the most famous counterpart image of World War II: Joe Rosenthal's black-and-white photograph of five marines raising the flag on Mount Suribachi on Iwo Jima on February 23, 1945 (described in one commentary as "the most reproduced photograph in the history of photography"). A post–9-11 website captured the prevailing sentiment with this legend running across the paired images: "Different times, different enemy, same flag, same feeling . . ."*

*Both iconic images were cropped and reproduced as postage stamps. The Iwo Jima stamp appeared in July 1945 in response to public demand and congressional pressure, overturning a long-standing Post Office policy that living persons could not be depicted on postage. For many years, this was the best-selling stamp in U.S. postal history, with well over one hundred million sold. The firemen image, bearing the words "Heroes USA 2001," was issued in March 2002.*

And second, looking to the future, one could find hope and inspiration in Japan in defeat. "American and Japanese experts claimed that the Japanese weren't ready for democracy," the president declared. (This was, indeed, largely true in conservative American and Japanese circles at war's end in 1945.) But they were wrong, he emphasized, and this would prove to be the case in Iraq as well—so long as Americans did not lose heart and abandon the good fight.[8]

## The Boomerang of "Pearl Harbor"

Words matter. History matters. Freedom and democracy matter. But the V-J Day speech, coming as it did more than two years after the "Mission Accomplished" celebration, rang hollow. Osama bin Laden was still at large. The trumpeted rationale for invading Iraq—its supposed weapons of mass destruction and putative support of Al Qaeda—had long been discredited. Occupied Iraq was almost into a free fall of murderous chaos. Although White House ghostwriters were obsessively and perhaps sincerely drawn to making comparisons to World War II, most of the analogies they belabored were misleading. History misused is a cracked mirror, and tragedy can ensue from failing to recognize this. In this case, it did.

Even a cracked mirror throws back recognizable reflections, however, and the rough correspondence between September 11 and December 7 that most American adults instinctively perceived was provocative. As touchstone or code, "Pearl Harbor" signifies many things—negative and positive, infamous and catalyzing, ultimately deeply disturbing. On September 11, for example, it captured not merely moral outrage and a furious desire for swift and thoroughgoing retaliation, but also deep shock at the nation's unpreparedness. All the "while we slept" imagery that followed the surprise assault on Pearl Harbor—all the horrified realization that Fortress America was actually vulnerable to attack by determined enemies—suddenly returned.

Like December 7, the shock of September 11 prompted fevered analysis of the failure of U.S. intelligence. And, as it turned out, such analysis—particularly in the official form of joint congressional committee hearings in 2002 and the widely praised 2004 report of the 9-11 Commission—generally came up with diagnoses of "system failure" and recommendations for organizational reform comparable to the official response to the Pearl Harbor debacle over a half century earlier. Bureaucracies change but do not change, and much the same can be said of committees appointed to investigate them. Both are predictable, and the former can be counted on to undercut or circumvent whatever of substance the latter may recommend.

The same also can be said of human psychology, error, and folly. For "Pearl Harbor" turns out to be code for other things as well—myths of American innocence, victimization, and "exceptionalism," for example, as well as failures of both imagination and common sense. Prejudice and preconceptions skew assessment of the intentions and capabilities of potential enemies more than is usually acknowledged by those who focus on structural failure—especially where differences of race, culture, and religion are involved. By the same measure, such biases impede comprehension of the grievances that enable antagonists to mobilize support.

Failure of imagination goes far to explain why officials in Washington and commanders in Hawaii were unprepared for the surprise attack in December 1941, despite the fact that Japan's leaders were clearly poised for war. The imaginative failure is even more flagrant in the case of September 11. The first terror attack on the World Trade Center occurred eight years before 9-11. Osama bin Laden and other Islamist militants had issued a fatwa, or religious injunction, declaring holy war against "the Judeo-Christian alliance" and calling on Muslims in every country "to kill the American[s] and their allies—civilian and military" more than three and a half years before the attacks in 2001. This was the very opposite of a secret agenda, but analysts outside the inner sanctum of Washington policy planning struggled in vain to elevate terrorist threats to the homeland on the agenda of national security priorities before it was too late.[9]

A major study chaired by two former senators, released in January 2001 under the title *New World Coming: American Security in the 21st Century*, for example, predicted that "states, terrorists, and other disaffected groups will acquire weapons of mass destruction and mass disruption, and some will use them. Americans will likely die on American soil, possibly in large numbers." Later bipartisan investigations disclosed that between the time of that January report and September 10, counterterrorism specialists in the Central Intelligence Agency and National Security Council made urgent presentations on the threat ("the system was blinking red"); the president himself received over forty top-secret President's Daily Briefs with entries related to bin Laden; a dozen or so concrete leads to the 9-11 plot were not vigorously pursued; and there had been at least a dozen warnings about the possibility of using planes as weapons. Signals and warnings pointing to an impending attack on U.S. soil were far more numerous than in the case of Pearl Harbor, although they were not absent in the latter case.[10]

No one at top levels of the Bush administration, however, had the imagination to take these warnings seriously. The president's handlers prevented one of the coordinators of the *New World Coming* study from even meeting with the president, for example, and a canceled policy address on "the threats and problems of today and the day after, not the world of yesterday" scheduled for the evening of September 11 by national security adviser Condoleezza Rice did not mention bin Laden, Al Qaeda, or Islamist extremists. The primary focus was on promoting missile defense, and terrorism was mentioned in passing only in the context of rogue states. In strategic-planning circles, a considerable portion of pre–9-11 energy was devoted to identifying China as the great pending threat to American hegemony. In domestic policy projections, terrorism was not even included among the "top-ten" priorities established for the Justice Department by Attorney General John Ashcroft. "9-11" surpassed the Pearl Harbor debacle in exposing negligence and inability to think outside the box at the highest levels.[11]

Pearl Harbor analogies did not end with 9-11, moreover. On the contrary, they became greater and more provocative thereafter, as both the locus of "infamy" and failure of intelligence and imagination became compounded by the war of choice against Iraq. March 19, 2003—the date the U.S. military initiated "Operation Iraqi Freedom," its code name for the invasion of Iraq—joined December 7 and September 11 as the decisive marker of an unprovoked act of aggression. The octogenarian scholar of U.S. history Arthur Schlesinger Jr. introduced this jarring perception in an anguished response to the invasion. "The president has adopted a policy of 'anticipatory self-defense' that is alarmingly similar to the policy that imperial Japan employed at Pearl Harbor on a date which, as an earlier American president said it would, lives in infamy," Schlesinger wrote.

"Franklin D. Roosevelt was right, but today it is we Americans who live in infamy."[12]

This was a decidedly minority opinion among Americans at a moment when patriotic passion ran high, the high-tech extravaganza of the opening "shock and awe" assault dominated the media, and the fatal myopia of relying on sheer military might to combat terrorism had not yet been exposed by Iraq's subsequent descent into chaos. Outside the United States, Schlesinger's critique of the so-called Bush Doctrine would have been unexceptional. Within the nation, it was heresy—albeit less so as time passed, the rationales for invasion were discredited, and the promised liberation turned into bloody and seemingly interminable occupation of a broken land.

As it became clear that Operation Iraqi Freedom was a tactical success and strategic disaster, "Pearl Harbor" took on symbolic meaning at yet another level, unimagined even by those who shared Schlesinger's concern that the United States was violating the very principles it professed to uphold. The code here was psychological and practical rather than moral or legalistic—a matter of strategic folly or, put differently, of irrationality, wishful thinking, and groupthink at the highest levels.

Collective irrationality is the diagnosis most commentators have offered to explain imperial Japan's disastrous decision to take on the United States and Allied powers. Pearl Harbor was but one of scores of Japanese attacks launched throughout Southeast Asia and the Pacific in December 1941. In the long run it was an ephemeral "mission accomplished," a Pyrrhic victory indeed. The most acid (and probably most quoted) judgment on Japan's decision for war was delivered by the American naval historian Samuel Eliot Morison in his semiofficial history of the war at sea. In his view, the Pearl Harbor attack,

> far from being a "strategic necessity," as the Japanese claimed even after the war, was a strategic imbecility. One can search military history in vain for an operation more fatal to the aggressor. . . . On the strategic level, it was idiotic. On the high political level it was disastrous.[13]

After the U.S. invasion and occupation of Iraq, those who search military history for a strategic imbecility comparable to December 7, 1941, will no longer come up dry. But what are we to make of this? Hitherto, the accepted explanation for imperial Japan's disastrous policy making, particularly by Americans and Europeans, was simple: for reasons of history, culture, and perhaps even ethnicity, the Japanese simply did not think rationally as Westerners did.

Here, too, we have some almost canonized observations—often by Joseph Grew, who served as U.S. ambassador to Tokyo from 1931 through Pearl Harbor (and was one of the authorities Morison quoted in advancing his thesis of Japan's "imbecile" behavior). As one of the State Department's highest officials after his repatriation from Japan in 1942, Grew spoke frequently and published prolifically about the thought and behavior of the enemy. His often lengthy dispatches to Washington before the outbreak of the war filled many pages in a massive 1943 State Department publication that reproduced many originally secret diplomatic papers from the decade leading up to Pearl Harbor. In 1944, these in-the-belly-of-the-beast views reached an even broader general public when Grew published a widely reviewed trade book based on his official communiqués and the detailed diary/journal he had maintained during his eventful years in Tokyo.

Grew's caricatures were all of a piece. A lengthy dispatch recycled in the wartime publications, for example, read as follows in the original cable sent September 29, 1941:

> The Ambassador stresses the importance of understanding Japanese psychology, fundamentally unlike that of any Western nation. Japanese reactions to any particular set of circumstances cannot be measured, nor can Japanese actions be predicted by any Western measuring rod. This fact is hardly surprising in the case of a country so recently feudalistic.

Another Grew character sketch (picked up in the postwar congressional Pearl Harbor hearings as well as by later commentators) held that "Japanese sanity cannot be measured by our own standards of logic."[14]

This is the formulaic language of "civilizational" differences and Western superiority. The irrational, nonwhite foreigner was a stock figure in the rhetoric of European and American imperialist and colonial expansion, and the Asia-Pacific War triggered countless English-language variations on Grew's perception of the Japanese as a race and people alien to any Western measuring rod. Brigadier General Bonner Fellers, MacArthur's chief of intelligence and a putative expert on Japanese psychology, for example, was especially proud of a pre–Pearl Harbor report in which he concluded that "in methods of thought, the Japanese and the Americans are today as different as if each had always lived on different worlds, separated by hundreds of *light years*."[15]

After World War II, irrationality was passed on like a candle flame to burn one nonwhite adversary after another—the Chinese, Koreans, peoples of Southeast Asia, and Muslims and Arabs. Speaking about the Chinese in 1955, for example, President Dwight Eisenhower channeled Joseph Grew in observing that "we are always wrong when we believe that Orientals think logically as we do."[16] L. Paul Bremer III, the U.S. viceroy in occupied Iraq in 2003 and 2004, commented similarly about one of the most admired of local leaders, the Ayatollah Sistani (who demanded that popular elections be held before the U.S.-led Coalition Provisional Authority pushed through a new constitution and other drastic reforms). "Unfortunately developments in Iraq were not always logical," Bremer wrote in the memoir of his year in Iraq. "Certainly Ayatollah Sistani operated on a different rational plane than we Westerners."[17]

Turned about, this stereotype of the irrational Oriental reflects an abiding assumption that the Enlightenment ideals of reason, order, and civilized behavior do indeed guide modern Western thought and behavior. Sometimes they do. Just as often they do not, and this is nowhere more apparent than in the modern history of war and peace. Even if we were to set moral issues aside, technological and technocratic sophistication all too often go hand in hand with wishful thinking, delusion, and herd behavior at top levels. This was true of Japan's military planners in 1941—and true in many comparable ways of the U.S. planners and war enthusiasts who promoted the invasion of Iraq over six decades later. Rereading the detailed minutes of the top-secret Japanese policy-making sessions that culminated in Pearl Harbor is sobering. The Japanese deliberations are procedurally more formal than what we know of decision making in the Bush Oval Office. They involve articulate civilian and military officials engaged in ostensibly rational discussion. And, in the upshot—as in official Washington in the wake of 9-11—neither wisdom nor common sense prevail.

Consider the similar rationales and rhetoric of Japan's war of choice in 1941 and America's in 2003. Both rest on a combination of deep anxiety about national security and a professed goal of bringing about "liberation" overseas as prelude to establishing a lasting peace. Control of strategic resources abroad enters the picture in each case. Preoccupation with planning the initial attack overwhelms all other considerations in both Tokyo and Washington. Pushed aside is any truly serious evaluation of the nature, resources, and likely psychological response of the enemy. To question the justness of a preemptive or preventive war is taboo, and all criticism of the war plans on practical grounds is condemned as defeatism and close to treason. Ultimately, both wars of choice released forces of destruction beyond control and caused unspeakable suffering.

In a now-classic analysis of the Pearl Harbor debacle published in 1962, the social scientist Roberta Wohlstetter expressed wonder at "the paradox of pessimistic realism of phrase coupled with loose optimism in practice" where the U.S. response to imperial Japan's looming threat was concerned.[18] This observation turns out to work well as a generality. It can be applied to the imbecility of Japan's leaders opting to take on the Allied powers without engaging in serious long-range planning. It fits well the casualness of the Roosevelt administration in anticipating Japanese aggression while failing to give serious scrutiny to the actual mindset of Japan's leaders and capabilities of its armed forces. And it captures the paradox of the Bush administration's rush to war with Iraq—apocalyptic forebodings about the target nation's arsenals and inclinations, and the menace of terror worldwide, coupled with a nonchalance regarding post-invasion contingency planning that bordered on the criminally negligent. Had the Oval Office planners been Japanese, a legion of white pundits would have materialized to explain that they simply did not think logically, as Westerners do.

Perhaps the greatest boomerang effect that arose out of the pervasive Pearl Harbor and World War II analogy was the fatal assumption that terrorism, like the old Axis enemies, could be defeated by brute force. Almost everyone at top levels in Washington bought into this, no one more so than the president. For years after embracing the role of "war president" and invading Iraq, Bush ignored the roots of anti-Americanism and insurgency and kept asking his commanders for body counts of killed enemy.

An attack by a small nonstate organization was equated with an assault by a formidable nation-state. What should have been recognized as a fundamentally criminal challenge, calling for a broad range of multilateral responses, was addressed as a threat to be met, first and foremost, with conventional military force. More than undiscerning and counterproductive, this response was a disaster.[19]

Obviously, the differences between World War II and the "war on terror" are compelling. At the same time, it is well to keep in mind that code words—and the use and misuse of history more generally—can be political and ideological triggers. Thus, among power brokers, "Pearl Harbor" is also code for useful catastrophes. A full year before September 11, conservatives committed to radical revision of U.S. foreign and military policies who later became influential in shaping the Bush administration's foreign policy were already ruminating on "some catastrophic and catalyzing event—like a new Pearl Harbor" that might facilitate military expansion and a more aggressive policy in the Middle East, particularly against Iraq. They did not wish this horror upon the nation, but it served their strategic purposes well.

Prophecies may be self-fulfilling, as we constantly learn and forget, and catastrophes godsends for the agile and cynical.[20]

# THE FAILURE OF INTELLIGENCE

## *Prelude to Pearl Harbor*

By all conventional measures of power and peril, the Japanese threat in 1941 and that of Al Qaeda and Islamist terror in 2001 had very little in common. Imperial Japan was a nation-state with a huge, highly mechanized army and navy. Beginning in 1933 it had increasingly isolated itself from the international community after being condemned by the League of Nations for seizing Manchuria and, in angry response, withdrawing from that world organization. Since 1937, it had been mired in all-out war with China—occupying that country's vast, populous seaboard while tied down by Nationalist and Communist forces in the interior. Japan's decision to "move south" and take over colonized Southeast Asia (French Indochina, the Dutch East Indies, British Hong Kong, Malaya and Burma, the U.S.-controlled Philippines)—the fatal decision that prompted the preemptive attack on Pearl Harbor—was motivated primarily by a need for guaranteed access to strategic resources necessary to carry on the war in China.

Initially, Japan's aggression against China relied heavily on imports of steel, fuel, and the like from the United States. (Japan rather than China was America's major Asian market.) As the war dragged on and pro-Chinese domestic pressures forced the Roosevelt administration, in conjunction with other colonial powers, to incrementally tighten restrictions on such exports, the Japanese responded with cries of "economic strangulation" and "ABCD encirclement" (American, British, Chinese, and Dutch). While it might seem the epitome of perversity to argue that China was encircling Japan, this notion seemed plausible in Japanese eyes—where the "C" in ABCD could just as well have stood for "communism." Much Japanese war propaganda in the 1930s focused on the rise of communist influence in China. Where Americans and Europeans placed Japanese expansion in the context of a "Yellow Peril," Japanese ideologues were fixated not merely on the "White Peril" of European and American imperialism, but also the "Red Peril" of Soviet-led international communism.

Even after the outbreak of open war between Japan and China, the anticommunist exhortation had considerable appeal among Western diplomats and policy makers. Ambassador Grew in Tokyo was so insistent in stressing the importance of Japan as a "stabilizing power" in Asia, for example, that he was eventually forced to defend himself against accusations of appeasement. China—still saddled in 1941 with unequal treaties and foreign concessions associated with nineteenth-century European, American, and Japanese imperialism—*was* unstable and in turmoil when all-out war broke out in 1937. Revolutionary change was in the air, and antiforeign sentiment animated both Communist forces under Mao Zedong and the Guomindang (Kuomintang) under Jiang Jieshi (Chiang Kai-shek). In this turbulent ideological struggle, virtually all parties in China rallied support under the flag of "liberation."

Although Japan's relations with the United States were severely strained and worsening by 1941, on the eve of Pearl Harbor the two nations were still talking in Washington in an attempt to resolve their differences. From the U.S. perspective, the most critical issues were Japan's aggression in China, its expansionist ambitions in Southeast Asia, and its alliance with Germany and Italy, dating from September 1940. The Japanese, on their part, demanded that the United States abandon its embargoes on strategic exports and stop supporting the Chinese resistance led by the Nationalist regime operating out of Chongqing (Chungking), deep in China's unconquered interior.[21]

By late November, both sides concluded that these negotiations had failed. In a soon-famous diary entry on November 27, Secretary of War Henry Stimson recorded that Secretary of State Cordell Hull informed him he had broken off talks with Japan. "I have washed my hands of it," he quoted Hull saying, "and it is now in the hands of you and [Secretary of the Navy Frank] Knox—the Army and the Navy."[22] Two days earlier, the Japanese attack force had already set out for Pearl Harbor from its secret training base in the Kurile Islands. The armada numbered some sixty warships, including six aircraft carriers, and maintained strict radio silence—a ghost fleet embarked on a mission U.S. war planners had long talked about and even planned for but no one actually took seriously.

While high U.S. officials recognized that war was imminent, they expected it to take the form of an invasion of Western colonies in Southeast Asia—particularly the Dutch East Indies (Indonesia), probably British holdings in Malaya including Singapore, and possibly America's own Asian enclave, the Philippines. Within Japanese officialdom, the Pearl Harbor attack plan itself was a well-guarded secret but not—as made clear by Gordon Prange, who devoted several decades to historical study of the attack—a "supersecret." As the actual date of attack drew near, an increasing number of naval officers on the task force itself had to be brought in on the secret. So did navy and army officers engaged in planning the complex and simultaneous "Southern Operation" aimed at seizing all of Southeast Asia, including the Philippines. In the cabinet, the highest organ in Japan's executive branch, on the other hand, knowledge of the Pearl Harbor plan was highly restricted. Although Prime Minister Hideki Tōjō (an army general who served simultaneously as minister of war) knew of it, he later claimed he was not privy to the actual operational details. The emperor was briefed beforehand. The Foreign Ministry was not, nor by extension were the envoys negotiating with the State Department in Washington.[23]

It was Japan's intention to inform the United States that it was breaking off relations moments before the attack. Admiral Isoroku Yamamoto, who conceived and oversaw the Pearl Harbor operation, insisted on this as a matter of honor. With this in mind, the negotiators in Washington were given strict instructions about exactly when this final message should be delivered. As fate would have it, with its propensity for mixing small mischief with great catastrophes, clerical ineptitude in the Japanese embassy delayed the decryption, translation, and delivery of this note. It was conveyed to Secretary of State Hull shortly after the Pearl Harbor attack was underway. While announcing termination of relations, the note said nothing about war.

In practice, this bungled communication did not matter. The United States had cracked Japan's diplomatic code in August 1940 (but, prior to December 7, 1941, not its basic army and navy codes).[24] Top-level officials thus already knew that relations were being broken off and Japan was poised to embark on a new stage of military expansion. Precisely *where* the next attacks would come was the question; and on this—on who in the top ranks of U.S. civilian and military leadership really knew or should have known what, and why the military was caught so disastrously unprepared—oceans of ink would be spilled in the years and decades to come.

Japan's objective in the Pearl Harbor attack was to cripple the U.S. Pacific Fleet and thereby thwart an immediate response to the advance into Southeast Asia. This was but one of many offensive actions in a breathtakingly complex, "phase one" coordinated strike on some twenty-nine separate targets with an initial force of two thousand aircraft, 160 surface ships, and over sixty submarines.[25] Any psychological considerations of how the Americans might be expected to respond usually emerged as marginal afterthoughts. Thus, in a letter dated January 7, 1941—when he was still urging adoption of his audacious proposal to attack Pearl Harbor, well before any concrete planning had been initiated—Admiral Yamamoto put his case to the navy minister in these terms:

> The most important thing we have to do first of all in a war with the U.S., I firmly believe, is to fiercely attack and destroy the U.S. main

fleet at the outset of the war, so that the morale of the U.S. Navy and
her people goes down to such an extent that it can not be recovered.

Casual and shallow as such thinking may have been, it became enshrined
in basic planning. The major document outlining projections for "has-
tening the end of the war," approved a few weeks before Pearl Harbor
(on November 15), expressed hope that Japan's early military successes
would "destroy the will of the United States to continue the war." What
Samuel Eliot Morison later ridiculed as the "strategic imbecility" of the
Pearl Harbor attack was thus present start to finish in this blissful retreat
into wishful thinking.[26]

Personally, Yamamoto opposed initiating hostilities with the United
States. A charismatic veteran of the old navy (as a young officer, he was
wounded in the celebrated Battle of Tsushima in 1905, when Japan
destroyed the Russian fleet in the Russo-Japanese War), he had spent time
at Harvard after World War I and two terms as a naval attaché in Washington in the 1920s. He opposed tightening Japan's relations with Germany between 1936 and 1940 on the grounds that this would lead to war
with America, and as late as October 1941 was still writing privately that
the decision for war "was entirely against my private opinion." On more
than one occasion, Yamamoto made it clear that the best one could hope
for was to keep U.S. forces at bay for six months or a year while Japan
consolidated control over the southern region.[27]

As an officer and a loyal subject of the emperor, however, Yamamoto
accepted the decision to launch war if diplomacy failed—and devoted
himself to making that war a success. Against strong internal opposition
(particularly from the old-guard "battleship admirals"), he persuaded his
superiors that a preemptive strike against the U.S. fleet from aircraft carriers was not only essential to buy time, but also feasible; and, on the latter
score, the stunning tactical success at Pearl Harbor proved him correct.
In war games conducted in September 1941, the Japanese navy had concluded that they might well lose two or three of their six carriers. Seamen
and pilots in the attack force anticipated dying and wrote wills and farewell messages to kin and loved ones on shipboard on the eve of the attack.
As it turned out, Japanese losses amounted to only twenty-nine aircraft,

five midget submarines, and sixty-four men (fifty-five pilots and nine sub-mariners), who were killed in action.[28]

Tactically brilliant as it may have been, Yamamoto's brainchild was a psychological blunder of fatal proportions. Contrary to weakening American morale, it mobilized the country under the "Remember Pearl Harbor—Keep 'em Dying" war cry that resonated until Japan's navy had been sunk, its great cadre of experienced pilots killed, its army destroyed or simply stranded to starve on isolated Pacific islands, and its homeland torched, first with firebombs and finally with nuclear weapons.

## Prelude to 9-11

All this stands in sharp contrast to 9-11. Japan was a major power engaged in conventional warfare. Its targets were purely military, and psychological considerations at best an afterthought—in contrast to their central place in the terrorist agenda. Hawaii itself was marginal in American consciousness at the time: a remote, exotic territory annexed in 1898 that did not become a U.S. state until 1959. It was not until the spring of 1940 that Pearl Harbor even became the major base of the Pacific Fleet, which until then had been berthed in San Diego.

"Weapons of mass destruction" were certainly available in superabundance to the protagonists in World War II. One need only consider the toll of the war globally—at least sixty million dead—to be reminded that mass slaughter did not require nuclear weapons. But arsenals of the time were nonetheless rudimentary when compared to the aircraft, warships, missiles, "smart weapons," nuclear devices, and chemical and biological weapons of the twenty-first century. Similarly, codes and code breaking did play an important role in intelligence gathering prior to Pearl Harbor, and much more so during the war that followed—but, again, at levels that seem elemental when compared to the technological sophistication of present-day intelligence gathering and the gargantuan security agencies that have grown like dark forests around this. It was in considerable part the debacle of December 7 that focused attention on elevating the collection and analysis of foreign intelligence after World War II. As William Casey, director of the Central Intelligence Agency in the 1980s, put it, the CIA was created in 1947 "to ensure there will never be another Pearl Harbor."[29]

Unlike imperial Japan with its racial homogeneity, fierce nationalism, and ponderous war machine, Al Qaeda was a loose network that crossed national and ethnic boundaries. Although its base in Afghanistan was important for training terrorists, the organization did not rely on state sponsorship. Possessing neither army nor navy nor massive firepower, its warriors were volunteers driven by the political and religious fervor of jihad, or holy war. Operating out of remote and hidden places, Osama bin Laden exploited satellite television and cyberspace to convey his messages not merely to terrorist operatives, but also to the Arabic-speaking world at large. He issued his first "Declaration of Jihad against the Americans Occupying the Land of the Two Holy Sanctuaries" (Mecca and Medina in Saudi Arabia) in August 1996, and in February 1998 joined four other Islamist radicals in declaring a second fatwa against "the soldiers of Satan, the Americans, and whichever devil's supporters are allied with them."[30]

Since 1991, the 1998 screed charged, "America has occupied the holiest parts of the Islamic lands, the Arabian peninsula, plundering its wealth, dictating to its leaders, humiliating its people, terrorizing its neighbors and turning its bases there into a spearhead with which to fight the neighboring Muslim people." The fatwa singled out Iraq, where "over one million" had already died as a consequence of U.S.-led economic sanctions imposed through the United Nations after the first Gulf War, as the major target of future U.S. aggression. Predictably, this declaration of war went on to declare that the religious and economic objectives of the Americans also served "the interests of the petty Jewish state, diverting attention from its occupation of Jerusalem and its murder of Muslims there."

Following the February 1998 fatwa, bin Laden elaborated on why the United States had been singled out for attack and told an ABC television reporter, "We anticipate a black future for America." Shortly after this, on August 7, Al Qaeda directed simultaneous suicide-bombing attacks on the U.S. embassies in Kenya and Tanzania, killing over two hundred people. These were the first anti-American atrocities unequivocally connected to Al Qaeda, and the Clinton administration retaliated by launching cruise missiles against a training camp in Afghanistan where bin Laden was thought to be, and subsequently offering a $5 million reward for information leading

*12. September 11: Flight 175, the second hijacked plane, approaches the burning World Trade Center.*

to his capture. The code name of the unsuccessful missile strike was, in retrospect, a fair reflection of superpower hubris in a new world of asymmetric conflict: "Operation Infinite Reach." Two years later, in October 2000, suicide bombers in a small boat severely damaged the destroyer USS *Cole* berthed in Aden, Yemen, killing seventeen American seamen.[31]

U.S. counterterrorism analysts, collaborating with Saudi Arabia, first discovered the size, shape, and name of bin Laden's operation in the spring of 1996, shortly before the first fatwa. As Richard Clarke, head of the National Security Council's interagency Counterterrorism Security Group

*13. The flaming moment of impact at the south tower of the World Trade Center.*

from 1992, later wrote, this network was perceived by its organizers to be "the necessary base for the edifice that would become a global theocracy, the great Caliphate."[32] With the 1998 fatwa, bin Laden and his confederates publicly turned their focus onto America as the primary enemy, and U.S. intelligence in turn placed Al Qaeda's leader clearly in its sights.

Even Al Qaeda's subsequent flamboyant attacks on the U.S. diplomatic and military presence overseas, however, offer scant analogy to imperial Japan and its road through China to Pearl Harbor. Al Qaeda remained organizationally fragile and torn by internal disagreements as the mil-

*14. Richard Drew's "Falling Man" photograph captured the double shock of seeing people throw themselves from the burning towers to escape the inferno.*

lennium approached and passed. And the theocratic empire bin Laden vaguely imagined, and modes of violence at his command, differed in almost every way from Japan's territorial objectives and war-making capabilities. The stunning, almost freakish success of the 9-11 attacks changed all this, giving the bin Laden network both notoriety and an appeal among many disaffected Muslims and Arabs that it never previously possessed. Where Pearl Harbor marked the beginning of the end for imperial Japan, September 11 signaled the end of the beginning for Al Qaeda.

Unlike Pearl Harbor, the targets of the terrorists—the World Trade

15. *A fireman in the ruins of the World Trade Center on September 15 signals for ten more rescue workers.*

Center, the Pentagon, and probably the White House or Congress (by the fourth, unsuccessful hijacked plane)—were not conventional military targets. Although the numbers killed in 1941 and 2001 were fairly close (some twenty-four hundred at Pearl Harbor and slightly more than three thousand on September 11), those who perished in 2001 were largely civilians and represented, as Lawrence Wright has reminded us, some sixty-two countries and "nearly every ethnic group and religion in the world."[33]

Although Al Qaeda's war of choice was as audacious in its way as that of the Japanese aggressors six decades earlier, it was not preemptive in a strict military sense and had nothing to do with buying time. The September 11 attack was an unprecedented exercise in psychological warfare that struck not at the periphery of the United States, but at its heartbeat in New York and Washington. It targeted not only the symbolic institutional essence of the American state—finance, the military establishment, and democratic government—but the nation's core values as well. Bin Laden, always chillingly direct, made this clear in interviews shortly after September 11, in which he predictably placed the attacks in the context of "self-defense," of revenge, and of overthrowing the secular values of the infidel West itself.

In a video scheduled for broadcast on Al Jazeera television on October 7, when retaliatory U.S. bombardment of Al Qaeda training camps in Afghanistan commenced, for example, bin Laden declared that "what America is tasting today is but a fraction of what we have tasted for decades. For over eighty years our *umma* [Islamic nation or community] has endured this humiliation and contempt. Its sons have been killed, its blood has been shed, its holy sanctuaries have been violated, all in a manner contrary to that revealed by God, without anyone listening or responding." Several weeks later, he gave a long interview to Al Jazeera (not aired until January 2002) in which his scorn for "this Western civilization, which is backed by America" was filtered through the ruins of the World Trade Center: "The immense materialistic towers, which preach Freedom, Human Rights, and Equality, were destroyed."[34]

In almost every imaginable way, 9-11 shocked, mesmerized, and electrified the world—abetted by technologies of mass communication that were undreamed of in 1941. Apart from a few photographs of dark clouds of smoke billowing from crippled warships, no one outside Pearl Harbor itself really "saw" the attack. Even later "documentary" film footage, such as in John Ford's 1943 Academy Award–winning *December 7th*, was mostly contrived. By contrast, almost everyone in the developed world was able to bear eyewitness—over and over and over again—to September 11.

Despite such substantive differences, Pearl Harbor and September 11 pose the same question: why was the United States caught by surprise? The hostility of both adversaries was amply clear beforehand, and had deep roots. In each instance, codes had been broken and intelligence experts were reading secret communications. It was obvious in both cases that *something* spectacular was going to happen, and soon. The only question was, where?

The most persuasive explanations as to why the United States was so woefully unprepared in both cases turn out to be similar. They involve, first, bureaucratic structures and procedures that abetted human error, and, second, a profound failure of imagination.

### Postmortems: Pearl Harbor

In the wake of Pearl Harbor, Americans did what people usually do in response to man-made catastrophes. They focused on the immediate disaster (rather than the deeper causes that drove events to this pass), singled out scapegoats, played partisan politics to a greater or lesser degree, launched official investigations, drew largely predictable conclusions, and proposed bureaucratic reorganization.

Between December 1941 and July 1946, the United States conducted no less than nine investigations aimed at determining responsibility for the intelligence failure. Seven were initiated by the executive branch during the war and one just afterwards; these inquiries were conducted by or in close collaboration with the military. The most extensive investigation involved hearings sponsored by both houses of Congress after Japan's surrender. Running from November 15, 1945, to July 15, 1946, the hearings resulted in a transcript that totaled roughly a million words and was issued in forty parts. The final report, well over five hundred pages long, included a majority opinion endorsed by eight committee members and a minority report submitted by two members. These documents quickly became a basic source for subsequent commentaries.[35]

The first and last investigations involved scapegoating of a particularly harsh nature. In January 1942, the navy and army commanders in Pearl Harbor, Admiral Husband Kimmel and Lieutenant General Walter Short, were found guilty of "dereliction of duty"—a grievous charge that momentarily deflected scrutiny away from personal and procedural failures in Washington. (General MacArthur, who let his air force in the Philippines be caught on the ground nine hours *after* Pearl Harbor, unaccountably escaped such disgrace and went on to command the Army's Pacific campaigns.)[36] Although the charge against Kimmel and Short was tempered in the majority report of the postwar hearings, which found them guilty of "errors of judgment and not derelictions of duty," their careers and reputations were ruined.

Politically, the postwar hearings offered the out-of-power Republican Party a conspicuous opportunity to repudiate the bipartisanship that had lasted until near the end of the war and to argue that President Roosevelt (who died in April 1945, four months before Japan's defeat) and his "war cabinet" bore heavy responsibility for the disaster. In magnified form, these arguments have persisted to the present day. In the early postwar years they inspired a body of writings identified as Pearl Harbor "revisionism," or the "backdoor to war" thesis, arguing that Roosevelt desired war in order to come to the aid of England against Nazi Germany. To this end, the argument proceeds, he deliberately provoked the Japanese and ignored their overtures to work out some sort of modus vivendi. In 1982, the popular author John Toland published a bestseller titled *Infamy* that turned Roosevelt's famous phrase on its head by elaborating on this revisionist thesis and suggesting that the United States had possessed hitherto neglected intelligence explicitly pointing to Pearl Harbor. More than Japan, in Toland's view, it was America's behavior in 1941 that was shameful.[37]

The backdoor-to-war thesis is a dense and contentious subject and deserves attention, but such conspiracy theories are not persuasive. Despite their partisan undercurrents, even the congressional hearings identified the larger problem to be one of institutional structures and procedures, within which individual failures took place. This argument has been embellished at length in the writings of academics such as Roberta Wohlstetter and Gordon Prange, the latter of whom conducted prodigious bilingual research on the attack. As Prange's research associates summed it up (Prange died in 1980 before his exhaustive studies saw the light of publication), his conclusion after decades of research was this: "There were no Pearl Harbor villains; there were no Pearl Harbor scapegoats. No one directly concerned was without blame, from Roosevelt on down the line. They all made mistakes." Wohlstetter, whose dry approach focused more tightly on systems analysis, argued that these mistakes occurred because the entire apparatus of intelligence gathering, analysis, and dissemination was flawed.[38]

One of Wohlstetter's key concepts in explaining the difficulties inherent in making order out of a torrent of competing intelligence signals was "noise." (One chapter in her influential 1962 study is titled "Noise in Hawaii" and another "Signals and Noise at Home.") At one point she borrows someone else's phrase to describe the cacophony of ambiguous signals as "buzzing and blooming confusion." In current discourse the essentially

synonymous buzzword for noise is "chatter." Condoleezza Rice, serving
as the national security adviser in 2001, for example, blamed the failure to
identify warnings of the 9-11 attacks partly on the fact that there was "a
lot of chatter in the system." We founder in words; and the more words
intercepted, the greater the prospects of being overwhelmed.[39]

Monday-morning quarterbacking, the noise argument holds, enables
us to revisit collected intelligence and single out signals or messages
belatedly known to be significant. It certainly enables us to ignore the
fact that in the weeks leading up to Pearl Harbor, "almost everyone"
in the U.S. government from Roosevelt down was primarily absorbed
in developments "in the Atlantic and European battle areas"—just as in
the weeks and months prior to 9-11 the Bush administration was preoccupied with a range of strategic priorities other than terrorism, led by
missile defense and relations with China, Russia, Europe, and Eastern
Europe.[40] Much of the heated debate over responsibility for the failure
at Pearl Harbor focused on such exhumed, decoded messages. Why were
they not pursued more vigorously? Was it not clear what they portended?
(Usually, it was not.)

What impedes effective analysis, absent the benefit of hindsight, however, goes beyond noise in the mere sense of volume per se. In the uncertain and rapidly changing world of 1941, signals often reflected indecision,
vacillation, or rapid change in the enemy's policy process itself, and thus
might be inherently contradictory and confusing. Even more problematic, the bureaucratic system through which information was processed
in 1941 was not only rigid and compartmentalized, but also riddled with
turf wars. The majority report that emerged from the congressional hearings in 1946, for example, called attention to "supervisory, administrative,
and organizational deficiencies" in general and focused on the "pitfalls of
divided responsibility" within the military in particular. "The whole story
of discussions during 1941 with respect to unity of command," the majority found, "is a picture of jealous adherence to departmental prerogatives
and unwillingness to make concessions in the interest of both the Army
and Navy."[41]

The minority report, which directed its harshest criticism at the president and his top aides, concluded along similar lines that "the failure of
Washington authorities to act promptly and consistently in translating

intercepts, evaluating information, and sending appropriate instructions to the Hawaiian commanders was in considerable measure due to delays, mismanagement, non-cooperation, unpreparedness, confusion, and negligence on the part of officers in Washington." "Dysfunction" was not part of the operative jargon of those immediate postwar years, but, as with the majority report, the minority's summary conclusion was generic and could be applied to the September 11 catastrophe with little change: "The tragedy at Pearl Harbor was primarily a failure of men and not of laws or powers to do the necessary things, and carry out the vested responsibilities. No legislation could have cured such defects of official judgment, management, cooperation, and action as were displayed by authorities and agents of the United States in connection with the events that culminated in the catastrophe at Pearl Harbor on December 7, 1941."[42]

Later postmortems of the Pearl Harbor attack concurred with this picture of organizational disarray. There was "no single person or agency in Washington," Wohlstetter concluded, "that had all the signals available at any one time." Communication between Washington and Hawaii was "rudimentary." Frequently—most significantly, at the critical moment in late November when the State Department was breaking off negotiations with Japan—Secretary of State Hull acted "without consulting the Army or Navy." The Army and Navy themselves maintained "respectful and cordial, but empty, communication" between one another, both in Washington and in Hawaii. Such interservice impediments to analysis and communication, moreover, were also to be observed in "intraservice" rivalries.[43]

Beyond this, secrecy itself was a double problem. On the Japanese side, Pearl Harbor was an ultrasecret operation to which the vast majority of even top-level military officers and civilian officials were not privy. The Foreign Ministry as a whole was out of the loop; and since the only major Japanese code American cryptographers had broken in 1940 was the diplomatic code (known as "Purple"), intercepted materials pertinent to the military's plans were at best oblique. They involved, that is, instructions to diplomats in Washington, Hawaii, Berlin, or elsewhere that Foreign Ministry officials in Tokyo had been asked to make but did not fully comprehend themselves.

More problematic, however, was the conundrum inherent in handling secret intercepts, for to share such sensitive materials threatened to expose the biggest secret of all: the fact that the United States was reading Japan's diplomatic traffic. The more the decoded intercepts were disseminated within the government and acted upon, that is, the greater the danger that the Japanese would figure out that "Purple" had been broken—and proceed to change the code. The name of the U.S. code-breaking (and translation) operation was "Magic"—and one did not casually share the fruits of such magic with others. The congressional majority report of 1946 called attention to this with a rare touch of irony. "So closely held and top secret was this intelligence," the report observed, "that it appears the fact that the Japanese codes had been broken was regarded as of more importance than the *information* obtained from decoded traffic." Wohlstetter reached a similar conclusion in noting that "the effect of carefully limiting the reading and discussion of MAGIC, which was necessary to safeguard the secret of our knowledge of the code, was thus to reduce this group of signals to the point where they were scarcely heard." Secrecy, in an ultra-clandestine world, easily becomes a trap.[44]

## *Postmortems: 9-11*

These postmortems of unpreparedness for Pearl Harbor foreshadow the analysis of intelligence failure offered in *The 9/11 Commission Report*, which was released with fanfare in July 2004. The devil may be in the details, and the details in both cases are engrossing. When it comes to recommended reforms, however, the diagnosis of the September 11 disaster falls back on much the same generic critique of system dysfunction compounded by negligence that runs through the literature on Pearl Harbor.

The 2004 report, which included a table of fifteen major intelligence agencies, commented harshly about inter- and intra-agency rivalries among and within the CIA, FBI, National Security Agency (NSA), and Defense Department "behemoth." Its indictment touched all the familiar bases associated with bureaucratic compartmentalization: "duplication of effort," "civilian-military misunderstandings," administrative "stovepipes" and "turf" wars, "structural barriers to performing joint intelligence work," "divided management of intelligence analysis." As with Pearl Harbor, the 9-11 intelligence failure also was attributed to the culture of secrecy. The

NSA, for instance, was condemned for "almost obsessive protection of sources and methods," but the problem again was system-wide—rooted in "the culture of agencies feeling they own the information they gathered"; in the problems posed by "a 'need-to-know' culture of information protection"; in "overclassification and excessive compartmentalization of information among agencies"; in "human or systemic resistance to sharing information"; in a milieu in which "security agencies' personnel and security systems reward protecting information rather than sharing it."

Unsurprisingly, the 9-11 Commission's investigation itself was impeded by the secrecy game. Bureaucratic "stonewalling" by the White House and others blocked access to critical resources—a problem also encountered by the congressional investigators in 1945–46. The investigation also was constricted by agreement to exclude assessment of individual negligence and accountability in the *use* of intelligence at the highest levels. From its inception, the commission was committed to producing a unanimous "bipartisan" report, which may have been politically understandable but amounted to a recipe for sanitization.[45]

Still, even without pursuing the who and why of negligence at top levels, the findings of the bipartisan report were damning. As summarized by Thomas Powers, an incisive analyst of intelligence operations, the commission found that in the nine months preceding September 11, intelligence personnel "had warned the administration as many as forty times of the threat posed by Osama bin Laden, but that is not what the administration wanted to hear, and it did not hear it."[46]

Beginning around 2004, a cottage industry of accounts by investigative journalists and angry mid-level officials emerged to supplement the 9-11 Commission's postmortem and throw sharper light on the distraction and disarray that characterized negligence at the highest levels. Immediately after the Bush administration took office in January 2001, for example, the National Security Council's counterterror czar Richard Clarke told top incoming officials (including Vice President Dick Cheney, National Security Adviser Condoleezza Rice, and Secretary of State Colin Powell) that Al Qaeda was at war with the United States, had sleeper cells in the country, and was about to launch a major offensive. On January 25, within a week of the president's inauguration, Clarke formalized his concern in a letter to his superiors asking "urgently" for a cabinet-level meeting to review this threat. Not until April, however, did the NSC even convene a lower-level "deputies" meeting on the subject—at which Deputy Secretary of Defense Paul Wolfowitz dismissed the urgency of the avowed threat. (Clarke quotes Wolfowitz referring to bin Laden as "this little terrorist in Afghanistan.") The "principals" meeting requested on January 25 did not take place until September 4, exactly a week before the 9-11 attacks, and left Clarke chagrined at what he regarded as "largely a nonevent."[47]

Other attempts to focus White House attention on the Al Qaeda threat were similarly stillborn. On July 10, CIA director George Tenet and his counterterrorism chief Cofer Black, alarmed by an increase in intercepts suggesting an approaching "Zero Hour" offensive by Al Qaeda, held an "out of cycle" session with the NSC's Rice but left this meeting feeling they had not been taken seriously. On August 6, President Bush, vacationing at his ranch in Texas, received a later-notorious President's Daily Brief from the CIA titled "Bin Laden Determined to Strike in U.S." that, again, simply dissolved into the general chatter that held little interest for top officials.[48]

In the prelude to Pearl Harbor, dysfunction, distraction, and gross negligence at high levels also went hand in hand, but the difference from the Bush administration's level of inattention is still notable. Roosevelt and his top aides were at least paying attention to intercepted cables and other intelligence pointing to Japan's war preparations. There was no counterpart in 1941 to the clear signals of impending attack on the United States that were so plentiful in 2001. No alarmed intelligence specialists were begging in vain to be heard in the weeks and months prior to Pearl Harbor, or delivering stark warnings to the president himself. Still, when all is said and done, what remains etched in the historical record is the occurrence of two similar disastrous failures of U.S. intelligence.

THE FINAL CHAPTER of the 9-11 Commission's report acknowledged resonance between Pearl Harbor and 9-11:

> "Surprise, when it happens to a government, is likely to be a complicated, diffuse, bureaucratic thing. It includes neglect of responsibility, but also responsibility so poorly defined or so ambiguously

delegated that action gets lost." That comment was made more than 40 years ago, about Pearl Harbor. We hope another commission, writing in the future about another attack, does not again find this quotation to be so apt.[49]

Ironically, that quotation was already apt once again when the commission's report was published, for by July 2004 the United States was mired in a tragedy of its own making in Iraq. Little had been learned from 9-11 about the nature and roots of anti-American grievances and terrorism in the Middle East. "Surprise" had happened again, with a vengeance, as a consequence of this obtuseness. In the aftermath of 9-11, the U.S. government managed to bring about what seemed inconceivable in September 2001: to simultaneously diminish global respect and support for the United States; turn blood-stained bin Laden into a David fighting an armed-to-the-teeth Goliath; inflame Muslim rage throughout the world by precipitating chaos and carnage in Iraq; and, by its extraordinary incompetence, shatter the myth of military invincibility and "infinite reach" that hitherto had buttressed the mystique of American power.

This stupefying accomplishment reflected intensification rather than rectification of the generic intelligence failures that allowed 9-11 to happen in the first place. Turf wars, "stovepiping," obsessive secrecy, and plain individual arrogance and irresponsibility were only part of the problem, however, and not necessarily the most critical part. Like the unpreparedness of September 11 and December 7, the intelligence fiasco of March 2003 that resulted in tearing apart rather than liberating Iraq also reflected a monumental failure of imagination—a failure that became magnified rather than reduced in the months that followed September 11.

# THE FAILURE OF IMAGINATION

## *"Little yellow sons-of-bitches"*

In all the many volumes of documents, testimony, and commentary about the intelligence failure of 1941, there are no more telling words than an informal confession made by Admiral Kimmel while the congressional hearings of 1945–46 were taking place.

Although the commanders in Pearl Harbor had received a "war warn-ing" message from Washington on November 27, ten days before the attack, when the first wave of Japanese planes swept in, General Short was caught with his air force tightly bunched on the ground, most of his ammunition locked away, and major airfields such as Hickam without any antiaircraft guns. Admiral Kimmel's Pacific Fleet (except the carriers, which by sheer good fortune had put out for maneuvers) was peacefully at anchor in the harbor. These were the shocking failures that led the first post–Pearl Harbor investigation to charge the two officers with dereliction of duty, later tempered in the findings of the congressional inquiry to grave errors of judgment.

Both Short (who died in 1949) and Kimmel (who passed away in 1968, at eighty-six) argued that Washington failed to share all the information about Japanese plans it had gleaned through the still-secret Magic code-breaking operation. Never, they claimed, were they explicitly instructed to prepare for an actual attack. The two officers were given the opportunity to defend themselves in the postwar hearings, where Short read a 61-page typed statement and Kimmel's prepared statement ran to 108 pages. The disgraced admiral's most cryptic and persuasive explanation of why he had been caught by surprise, however, came in a lunch-break conversation with Edward Morgan, a lawyer who eventually drafted the majority report. As Morgan recalled it years later, the exchange went as follows:

> *Morgan*: Why, after you received this 'war warning' message of November 27, did you leave the Fleet in Pearl Harbor?
> *Kimmel*: All right, Morgan—I'll give you your answer. I never thought those little yellow sons-of-bitches could pull off such an attack, so far from Japan.[50]

Although unvarnished language like this did not make it into the transcript of the hearings, the majority report did take care to argue that "had greater imagination and a keener awareness of the significance of intelligence existed . . . it is proper to suggest that someone should have concluded that Pearl Harbor was a likely point of Japanese attack." Failing to think outside the box is a theme that surfaces and resurfaces in the serious general literature. Gordon Prange, for example, speaks of "psychological unpreparedness"; Roberta Wohlstetter, of "the very human tendency to pay attention to the signals that support current expectations about enemy behavior."[51]

Admiral Yamamoto, like his American navy counterpart, also put the

American failure in plain language—in his case, in two personal letters written shortly after the attack. On December 19, he wrote this to a fellow admiral:

> Such good luck, together with negligence on the part of the arrogant enemy, enabled us to launch a successful surprise attack.[52]

Two days later, writing to the student son of a personal friend, Yamamoto made a bit clearer what he had in mind in speaking of American arrogance. This letter, in its entirety, read as follows:

> 22 December 1941
>
> My dear Yoshiki Takamura,
>
> Thank you for your letter. That we could defeat the enemy at the outbreak of the war was because they were unguarded and also they made light of us. "Danger comes soonest when it is despised" and "don't despise a small enemy" are really important matters. I think they can be applied not only to wars but to routine matters.
>
> I hope you study hard, taking good care of yourself.
>
> Good-bye,
>
> Isoroku Yamamoto[53]

Yamamoto obviously misread American psychology disastrously when expressing hope that the surprise attack would strike a crippling blow at morale. The Americans, however, also disastrously misread and underestimated the Japanese. Can there be a more precise confirmation of Yamamoto's perception of Japan being "despised" and made light of as a "small enemy" than Kimmel's frank reference to "those little yellow sons-of-bitches"?

In a rational world, this should not have been the case. American perceptions of Japan as a potential foe traced back to the turn of the century, when Japan startled the world by defeating China and Tsarist Russia in quick succession (in the Sino-Japanese War of 1894–95 and Russo-Japanese War of 1904–5), thereby joining the Western, Caucasian, and Christian expansionist nations as one of the world's few imperialist powers. Financiers in New York and London had helped finance the Russo-

Japanese War, and many Western observers expressed admiration for the doughty "Yankees (or Brits) of the Pacific," but such support and praise were hardly unalloyed. The obverse side of support and respect for Japan and its spectacular accomplishments in "Westernization" was fear of the "Yellow Peril"—fear, that is, that Asia's masses would acquire the scientific skills and war-making machinery hitherto monopolized by the West.[54]

From the 1890s to the eve of Pearl Harbor, influential U.S. media such as the Hearst newspapers relentlessly editorialized that Japan posed a direct threat to the United States. Concurrent with Japan's formal surrender in September 1945, the Hearst syndicate ran a two-page advertisement in *Business Week* proudly itemizing how "for more than 50 years, the Hearst Newspapers kept warning America about JAPAN." The spread reproduced "a startling prophetic cartoon" from 1905 depicting a Japanese soldier standing in Korea with the sun behind him and his shadow falling across the Pacific onto the west coast of the United States. It boasted about how "the Hearst Newspapers first pointed out the 'Yellow Peril' of Japan to U.S. aims and interests in the Pacific" in the 1890s; how in 1898 it had "urged the annexation of the Hawaiian Islands by the United States as a defense measure against growing Japanese power in the Pacific"; how in 1912 the paper had "focused national attention on Japanese attempts to colonize Lower California"; and on, and on, up to 1941, when "the Hearst Newspapers, right up to the time that bombs fell on Pearl Harbor, were still hammering for increased naval appropriations and for strengthened fortifications in the Pacific."[55]

Here, it would seem, was imagination and "psychological preparedness" in abundance; and the United States did, in fact, adopt strategic policies that took the rise of Japan into consideration. Hawaii was annexed in 1898, and from 1905 Navy planners identified Japan as the major hypothetical enemy in the Pacific; there was, of course, no other candidate. In the color-coded contingency plans the Navy introduced before World War I, war plans vis-à-vis Japan were coded "Orange." It has been calculated that, over ensuing decades, officers at the Naval War College tested and refined the Orange plan at least 127 times.[56]

In May 1940, the clarity of Japan's intent to advance into Southeast Asia and the South Pacific led to transfer of the U.S. Pacific Fleet from the west coast of the United States to Hawaii, as a more visible "deterrent."

Several months prior to the Pearl Harbor attack, this ostensible deterrent was augmented by carefully leaked plans to strengthen U.S. forces in the Philippines with advanced B-17 "Flying Fortress" bombers. (In October 1941, Secretary of War Stimson expressed hope that the threat of these bombers would suffice to keep Japan from going after Singapore "and perhaps, if we are in good luck, to shake the Japanese out of the Axis.") Three times in 1941—in June, July, and October—the army and navy in Hawaii were placed on alert during particularly tense moments in the deteriorating relationship between the two countries.[57]

Beyond this deep history of mistrust and fear, it might have been expected that the plain nuts-and-bolts of military developments—the huge buildup of warships, aircraft, and ground forces that took place in the years preceding Pearl Harbor—would have made it apparent that Japan would be a formidable foe. This was not the case, and as a consequence it was more than just the unexpected attack that shocked Americans. Even more unnerving was the competence of the Japanese military.

This, at least, should not have come as a surprise. Japan had been working toward a capability for waging "total war" since the early 1930s. (Such thinking dated back to lessons drawn from World War I, which stimulated military strategists everywhere to consider how to mobilize the total resources of the nation in the eventuality of another great war.)[58] Isolation from the world community after the takeover of Manchuria in 1931 accelerated these plans, and from 1932 on the military establishment dominated the Japanese government. The nation had been at war with China for over four years at the time Pearl Harbor was attacked; and while the interminable nature of this conflict could be taken as a sign of military shortcomings and overextension, the other side of the coin was that the China war had created an experienced fighting force and spurred major advances in military technology.

These developments were not hidden, but even the experts failed to see them clearly—or, at least, to see them whole. Thus, the list of Japan's military capabilities that caught the Americans by surprise seems quite astounding in retrospect. Their torpedoes were more advanced than those of the Americans. (It was last-minute development of an airplane-launched torpedo with fins, capable of running shallow, that made the Pearl Harbor attack so deadly.) Their sonar, which the Americans believed inferior, was four to five times more powerful than what the U.S. military had at the time. Although the high-speed Mitsubishi "Zero," introduced to combat in China in August 1940, was more effective than any U.S. fighter plane at the time, the Americans underestimated its range, speed, and maneuverability.

The list goes on. According to testimony introduced at the congressional hearings, the Japanese had "better material in critical areas such as flashless powder, warhead explosives, and optical equipment." Japan's monthly output of military aircraft by December 1941 was more than double what the Americans estimated it to be. Their pilots, intensively trained and also seasoned by combat in China, were among the best in the world. As noted in an authoritative history of the U.S. air forces in World War II, "the average pilot in the carrier groups which were destined to begin hostilities against the United States had over 800 hours" of flying experience. The "first-line strength" of the imperial air forces "gave them a commanding position in the Pacific."[59]

In Prange's emphatic estimation, on December 7, 1941, "Japan stood head and shoulders above any other nation in naval airpower." The British military historian H. P. Willmott concludes that "in December 1941 the Imperial Japanese Navy possessed clear superiority of numbers in every type of fleet unit over the US Pacific and Asiatic fleets"; that it had "superiority over its intended prey" in the crucial category of aircraft carriers; and that in tactical technique, it was "second to none" at the opening stage of the war. Willmott also observes that the land-based Betty medium bomber developed by the Japanese in the 1930s "possessed a range and speed superior to any other medium bomber in service anywhere in the world." Other sources call attention to the Imperial Navy's exceptional skill in night gunnery, and its initial advantage in launching torpedoes from cruisers. As the audacious December 7 attack made painfully obvious, the ability of Japan's naval officers to plan and execute an exceedingly bold and complex operation—particularly one involving carriers—was simply beyond imagining. Except, of course, that the Japanese had imagined it down to the last detail.[60]

What accounts for this American failure of imagination?

Racism is part of the answer, but only part. The Japanese were not merely "sons-of-bitches." They were "little," and they were "yellow." In

16. *Japanese crew cheer a torpedo plane taking off from the* Shokaku, *one of six aircraft carriers in the attack force.*

17. *An officer watches the takeoff. The chalked message exhorts the crew to do their utmost in performing their duty.*

*18. Attack planes revving up.*

*19. A Japanese photograph of the first torpedo bombs hitting U.S. warships on Battleship Row.*

the American vernacular, the phrase "little yellow men" had become so common that it almost seemed to be a single word. To be "yellow" was to be alien as well as threatening (as in the "Yellow Peril"); but the reflexive adjective "little" was just as pejorative, for it connoted not merely people of generally shorter physical stature, but more broadly a race and culture inherently small in capability and in the accomplishments esteemed in the white Euro-American world.

Such contempt was not peculiar to Americans. It was integral to the conceit of a "white man's burden" and sneering animus of white supremacy that invariably accompanied Western expansion into Asia. When, after Pearl Harbor, the Japanese swept in and conquered their supposedly impregnable outpost in Singapore, the British also expressed disbelief (and engaged in the same sort of racial invective). Wherever and whenever objectivity overrides prejudice, it is usually the exception that proves the rule.[61]

Still, racial blinders alone do not adequately account for the failure to anticipate Pearl Harbor. The Americans also were unable to imagine what it was like to look at the world from Tokyo. From the Japanese perspective, the entire globe was in turbulent flux and grave crisis. The nation's situation was desperate. Its cause was just. And things had come to such a pass that there was no alternative but to take whatever risk might be necessary.[62]

### Rationality, Desperation, and Risk

The top-secret policy meetings that took place at the highest level in Japan from the spring of 1941, including "Imperial Conferences" at which diplomatic and military decisions were approved by the emperor, are provocative in retrospect because of the generic, rather than uniquely Japanese, outlook they reveal. It was unthinkable for the nation's leaders to question the assumption that China, including Manchuria, was Japan's economic lifeline, or that the war there was not merely essential to national survival but also moral and just. Indeed, with Japan having already "sacrificed hundreds of thousands of men" in invading and occupying China, it was all the more inconceivable to consider military withdrawal from the continent as the United States had demanded in pre–Pearl Harbor negotiations. It also was taken for granted that the nation could not break the military stalemate in China without access to the strategic resources of Southeast Asia, and time was running out. "Our Empire's national power," explained the head of the Planning Board at one critical meeting, "is declining day by day." The argument that creation of a "Greater East Asia Co-Prosperity Sphere" would ensure not only the "security and preservation of the nation" and well-being of all Asia, but ultimately "world peace," went unchallenged.[63]

This was not propaganda intended for domestic or international consumption. It was what these men believed—the assumptions and emotions that guided their deliberations and decisions. And so, in the end, the policy makers agreed there was no choice but to break off relations with the United States and "move South." To give in to U.S. demands would be "national suicide." "I fear," Prime Minister Tōjō stated at a critical meeting in early November, "that we would become a third-class nation after two or three years if we just sat tight."[64]

The fateful decision to secure their nation's position in Asia by pursuing a war of choice against the United States and other Allied powers was reinforced by a number of seemingly sane and rational projections. These included German victory in Europe, particularly against England and the Soviet Union; U.S. difficulties in fighting a two-front war; the strength of isolationist sentiment in the United States, and consequently probable domestic opposition to a protracted war in the Pacific; and the fact that there was a current of thinking in U.S. ruling circles, exemplified by Joseph Grew, that saw a constructive role for Japan as a "stabilizing force" against "chaos and communism" in China. Additionally, it was argued that while Japan lacked the industrial potential of the United States, its army and navy were huge; its forces, including air forces, were seasoned by combat in China; and the esprit de corps of the emperor's loyal soldiers and sailors was superior to whatever fighting spirit the Americans could hope to marshal. (In a casual conversation a few months after arriving in defeated Japan, General MacArthur told a British diplomat he "would have given his eyeballs to have such men" as the Japanese forces he encountered in the Philippines.) Given such considerations, it did not seem unreasonable to hope that the war would end in some sort of negotiated settlement with the United States, with both sides cooperating in maintaining peace in Asia.[65]

Counterfactual rumination (the "what if" school of history) also helps illuminate the misplaced optimism of Japan's war planners. That Japan was able to drag out the war for over three and a half years after Pearl Harbor was due in considerable part to the priority the United States gave to the European theater. At the same time, with a little more luck and operational shrewdness Japan might have prolonged the war even longer. For example, *what if*: (1) Germany had not attacked the Soviet Union while the Japanese were descending their slippery slope to war, thus leaving resistance to U.S. and British forces stronger on the European front; (2) the U.S. carriers had been berthed at Pearl Harbor at the time of the attack, and had not been by sheer chance at sea; (3) the Pearl Harbor attack force had launched a third wave of strikes and destroyed repair facilities and critical fuel sources; (4) the Japanese had changed their military code in 1942, thus thwarting major post–Pearl Harbor U.S. breakthroughs in cryptanalysis that proved critical not only in decisive battles such as Midway but also in the ongoing decimation of Japanese warships and merchant vessels by American submarines; (5) Japanese naval commanders had been less timid at decisive battles such as Midway and the Solomons? (The counterfactual question that trumps all others is *what if* Japan had excluded Pearl Harbor and the Philippines from the December 1941 offensive? This would have eliminated the "Remember Pearl Harbor" rage that solidified the nation behind retaliation, and forced the Roosevelt administration to decide whether or not to declare war in the face of continuing isolationist opposition.)

There is almost no end to the "what ifs" of history, and perhaps military history in particular. (Hitler's folly in deciding to attack the Soviet Union is the great strategic *what if* where the war in the West is concerned.) Be that as it may, Japan's desperation and consequent willingness to take extreme risks also enter the strategic equation. It was irrational to miscalculate the psychological impact the Pearl Harbor attack would have among Americans, and hope instead that demoralization would be the result. By the same measure, however, the U.S. leadership was grievously negligent in ignoring the possibility of direct attack once it became clear the Japanese had concluded they could not retreat in China and, unless the Western powers lifted their embargoes on strategic exports, had no alternative but to move into Southeast Asia.

Military men, like politicians, cherish cherry-picked history and the symbolism and rhetoric of past challenges and glories. When MacArthur took
the Japanese surrender on the *Missouri* in September 1945, the flag raised
at Morning Colors was the same Stars and Stripes that had flown over the
Capitol in Washington on December 7, 1941, while the bulkhead overlooking the ceremony displayed the thirty-one-star flag Commodore Matthew Perry had flown on his flagship in 1853, when he initiated the gunboat
diplomacy that forced Japan to abandon its feudal seclusion. In the surprise
attack of December 7, the Japanese engaged in similar symbolism. As the
attack force approached Pearl Harbor, the flagship *Akagi* ran up the "Z" flag
signal that had been hoisted more than thirty-five years earlier by Admiral
Heihachirō Tōgō in the decisive 1905 Battle of Tsushima, in which Tōgō's
modern warships destroyed a huge Russian armada that had sailed all the
way from the Baltic, thereby assuring Japan's emergence as a great power.
The signal read, "The rise and fall of the Empire depends upon this battle;
everyone will do his duty with utmost efforts."

Shortly before this, the commander of the Pearl Harbor attack fleet
read an "imperial rescript" to his men that had been prepared earlier by
the emperor. "The responsibility assigned to the Combined Fleet is so
grave that the rise and fall of the Empire depends upon what it is going
to accomplish," the message said. Japan's sovereign placed his trust in the
fleet to accomplish what it had long been training for, "thus destroying
the enemy and demonstrating its brilliant deed throughout the whole
world."[66]

One side's infamy was the other's brilliant deed, on which the very fate
of the empire depended.

### Aiding and Abetting the Enemy

Al Qaeda commanded no military machine on September 11. It had been
engaged in no negotiations with the United States, nor could it have
been, not being a nation-state. Although Osama bin Laden's ambitions
had grown ever more expansive over the years since Al Qaeda's founding in 1988, and although U.S. intelligence specialists took seriously his
vision of a "great Caliphate," he was not engaged in an escalating quest
for autarky—for military and economic domination of a formal, secure,

and self-sufficient sphere of influence—comparable to the quest that had obsessed Japan ever since its takeover of Manchuria in 1931.[67]

Even here, however, certain points of comparison merit attention. A full decade of mounting tensions preceded Pearl Harbor, beginning with the impasse over Manchuria. In the case of Islamist terrorism, the first attack in the United States took place in 1993, when the World Trade Center suffered extensive damage from explosives detonated in a parked van. Although later intelligence connected this to Al Qaeda, this was not clear for a number of years. A National Intelligence Estimate distributed in July 1995 predicted future terrorist attacks against and in the United States, but the 9-11 Commission concluded that Al Qaeda itself was not identified in a conspicuous manner until around 1999—three years after the NSC's Richard Clarke dates this "discovery," eleven years after the organization was founded, six years after the first attack on the World Trade Center, and only two years before the September 11 attack.[68]

Where the actual attack plans for 1941 and 2001 are concerned, both were quite long in the hatching. The Pearl Harbor operation was conceived by Admiral Yamamoto at the end of 1940, probably in December, and the first draft of an operational plan was drawn up the following March (by Commander Minoru Genda and Rear Admiral Takijirō Ōnishi, who in late 1944 would become the prime mover behind the kamikaze attacks). By April, the project had been moved into command channels, and training in activities such as aerial torpedo practice commenced in May and June. War games for the entire "Southern Operation," including Hawaii, were carried out in Tokyo over a ten-day period beginning September 11.

The "Operation Hawaii" plan was accepted in principle by the navy chief of staff in mid-October, and Emperor Hirohito was briefed on this at the imperial palace some time between October 20 and 25. "Dress rehearsals" by the fleet began in October, and the plan received final approval by the navy general staff in early November. On November 17, vessels assigned to the attack force began making their way to Hitokappu Bay in the Kurile Islands (under Japanese control since the Russo-Japanese War), from where—on November 25 (November 26, Japan time)—the fleet would depart for the attack. In Al Qaeda's case, where there is less information, the 9-11 Commission simply concluded that the complex September 11 operation was "the product of years of planning."[69]

It is also provocative to note that collusion or at least mixed signals between the American side and the enemy preceded both catastrophic surprise attacks. In U.S.–Japanese relations, this took several forms. Despite the fact that the 1937 invasion and occupation of China provoked fairly widespread sympathy for China and condemnation of Japan in the United States, until around mid-1940 pressures to appease Japan came from many directions. For all practical purposes, isolationists associated with "Fortress America" and "America First" activities often found themselves on the same page with peace and antiwar groups. Both desired that the United States isolate itself from foreign conflicts and avoid provoking Japan in any way that might lead to hostilities. As late as October 1941, one informal council devoted to "prevention of war" that included several well-known scholars of Far Eastern relations was still urging the government to "make a deal" with Japan. At both official and public levels, attention focused far more on Europe than on Asia, particularly after Germany unleashed its blitzkrieg in 1939; to some degree, this fixation on the war in Europe strengthened popular opposition to any involvement in the conflict in Asia.[70]

Japanese leaders, naturally attentive to such sentiments, found them in more explicitly governmental circles as well, where officials like Ambassador Grew were cautiously receptive to the argument that Japan could be a bulwark against both domestic chaos in China and Soviet-led international communism. Although Grew became increasingly critical of Japan's actions beginning in mid-1940, as late as September 1941 he was still urging "constructive conciliation."[71]

Just as encouraging, if not more so, was the attitude within U.S. business circles. The dollar value of U.S. exports to Japan in 1937 was more than five times that of the export trade with China, and in 1940 still amounted to roughly three times the China trade. A major portion of these exports consisted of strategic materials such as aviation fuel, crude and refined oil, scrap iron, and steel—all critical to the Japanese war machine. A fair indication of sentiment in the business community emerged in a survey published in *Fortune* magazine in September 1940, allegedly tapping the views of some "15,000 businessmen" including directors of the 750 largest American corporations. Forty percent of respondents chose to "appease" the Japanese, and another 35 percent to "let nature take its course."[72]

The United States did not begin to impose serious controls over exports until mid-1940, when Japan, following the fall of France to the Nazis, moved troops into the northern half of French Indochina and began the courtship that would culminate in the Axis alliance in September. Part of the U.S. concern involved old-fashioned colonial interests—namely, fear that losing Southeast Asia would deprive Britain of critical resources. The scenario that unfolded thereafter became an all-too-familiar tit-for-tat game: the more the U.S. government tightened economic screws to deter Japanese aggression, the more persuaded Japanese leaders became that their empire faced disaster and there was no alternative but to "move South."

Although there was no comparable economic dimension in the rise of Islamist terrorism, there was an analogous prehistory of support and appeasement prior to September 11. In the closing decade of the Cold War, U.S. strategic planners embraced the prospect of an anticommunist "arc of Islam" stretching east from the Middle East along the underbelly of the atheistic Soviet Union. The policy birthed by such thinking took the form of covert collaboration with Pakistan and Saudi Arabia in recruiting, training, and arming radical mujahideen for the war against Soviet forces in Afghanistan between 1979 and 1989. President Ronald Reagan posed for a photograph with mujahideen leaders in the White House in 1986, and at one point CIA director William Casey, a devout Catholic, sponsored a translation of the Qur'an for dissemination to Uzbek-speaking holy warriors. More striking is the weaponry provided to these anti-Soviet zealots by true believers in Washington who were persuaded that a shared monotheism made Christians and radical Islamists kindred souls. As itemized by Steve Coll, these weapons included "antiaircraft missiles, long-range sniper rifles, night-vision goggles, delayed timing devices for plastic explosives, and electronic intercept equipment." Also part of this covert support were Japanese-made pickup trucks, Chinese and Egyptian rockets, Milan antitank missiles, and somewhere between 2,000 and 2,500 heat-seeking Stinger missiles. Although material U.S. aid was directed primarily to the Afghan resistance forces rather than volunteer Arab fighters (like bin Laden), the U.S. government looked favorably on the latter.[73]

Benazir Bhutto, the Pakistani political leader assassinated in 2008, dwelled on this shortsighted Realpolitik in a book completed only days before her death. In her view, the blowback from covert engagement in the anti-Soviet Afghanistan war (which involved close U.S. collaboration with Bhutto's political adversaries in Pakistan) was by no means an exceptional instance of myopic Western policies in the Middle East. On the contrary, the United States and European powers had a long history of engaging in "double standards" by preaching freedom and development while in actual practice supporting both dictators and, in Afghanistan, the most radical and oppressive Islamist fundamentalists. Over the course of decades, she concluded, the West had "unintentionally created its own Frankenstein's monster." These were harsh words and more than a little disingenuous, since while she was prime minister of Pakistan from 1993 to 1996, her own government—alarmed by the civil strife that followed the Soviet withdrawal from Afghanistan in 1989—had provided covert financial support, supplies, and military advisers to the extremist Taliban who later provided a haven for bin Laden.[74]

Monsters commonly have multiple creators, but this does not diminish the U.S. role in helping to promote Islamist radicalism early on. Like the Japanese soldiers and sailors who became seasoned veterans in the war against China and initially benefitted materially from U.S. support through trade in strategic goods, the mujahideen—once proxy soldiers for the U.S. government and romanticized "freedom fighters" in Washington and the U.S. media—emerged from Afghanistan as hardened fighters primed for new missions. It fell to Al Qaeda, birthed in Afghanistan in 1988, to define that mission for them.

### "This little terrorist in Afghanistan"

The stunning "asymmetrical" victory of Afghan and Muslim fighters over the Soviet Union emboldened Islamist radicals to believe they could prevail over U.S. military power as well. In a television interview more than three years before 9-11, bin Laden boasted that the victory of lightly armed holy warriors in Afghanistan "utterly annihilated the myth of the so-called superpowers." (This interview was rebroadcast on Al Jazeera nine days after 9-11.) By contrast, U.S. policy makers drew few if any counterpart lessons. With the collapse of the Soviet Union, the politicized zealotry they had encouraged in Afghanistan no longer attracted top-level attention. Even within the U.S. military, the effectiveness of Islamist insurgency and terror did not prompt serious attention to counterinsurgency doctrine.[75]

This was true when the Soviet Union withdrew its humiliated forces from Afghanistan in 1989 and official Washington proceeded to remove the latter nation from its radar. It was still true in 2001, when the United States invaded Afghanistan and routed the Taliban in the wake of the 9-11 attacks. And, despite belated attention to counterinsurgency tactics in Iraq beginning around 2006, it would remain largely true where Afghanistan was concerned to the end of the Bush presidency, when the Taliban were on the upsurge and again helping shelter bin Laden. At the beginning of 2009, as a new administration assumed power in Washington, Russia's ambassador to NATO looked back on the twentieth anniversary of the Soviet withdrawal and held this up as a mirror to the beleaguered U.S. military mission in Afghanistan. "They have repeated all our mistakes," he observed, "and they have made a mountain of their own."[76]

Why did top military and civilian leaders fail to take asymmetrical threats from Al Qaeda and the Islamists seriously? As with the earlier failure to take Japanese military capabilities seriously, part of the answer lies in racial arrogance and cultural condescension. When Charles Freeman, the U.S. ambassador to Saudi Arabia at the time of the first Gulf War in 1991, tried to draw attention to the mujahideen after the Soviet withdrawal from Afghanistan, for example, he found no one interested, including top leaders at the CIA. "Part of the attitude in Washington," he recalled, "was, 'Why should we go out there and talk to people with towels on their heads?'"[77]

Michael Scheuer, who headed the CIA's "bin Laden unit" until being cashiered in 1999, tells a similar story in even grittier language. Washington's top personnel and policy makers, he declared, are "so full of themselves, they think America is invulnerable; cannot imagine the rest of the world does not want to be like us; and believe an American empire in the twenty-first century not only is our destiny, but our duty to mankind, especially to the unwashed, unlettered, undemocratic, unwhite, unshaved, and antifeminist Muslim masses." One could only describe this hubris as "arrogance (or is it racism?)," Scheuer went on. The elites simply could not fathom that "a polyglot bunch of Arabs wearing robes, sporting scraggly beards, and squatting around campfires in Afghan deserts and mountains could pose a mortal threat to the United States."[78]

This was the "little yellow men" mindset transferred to the Middle East. As in 1941, civilian and military planners underestimated the enemy and failed to grasp both the depth of their self-righteousness and their willingness to take enormous risk as well as heavy losses. Most disastrously, they were unable to imagine this enemy possessing the cunning and competence to pull off a complex and imaginative act of aggression. None of his peers challenged Deputy Secretary of Defense Wolfowitz when, five months before 9-11, he dismissed bin Laden as "this little terrorist in Afghanistan."

Once again, as with system breakdown and leadership negligence, the diagnostic language in postmortems of the failure of imagination exposed on September 11 is essentially the same as that which analysts have long used in describing the disbelief that greeted Pearl Harbor: *psychological unpreparedness, prejudices and preconceptions, gross underestimation of intentions and capabilities.* There is a sense of encountering a pathologist's repetitive case book, glossing near-identical cases. Thus, to crib from Roberta Wohlstetter: prior to September 11, American analysts (with some marginalized exceptions) and decision makers simply were unable "to project the daring and ingenuity of the enemy." To borrow from Admiral Yamamoto's letter to a young student: Bush administration planners were undone by the arrogance of despising a small enemy. To appropriate Admiral Kimmel's pithy words: no one in a position of command thought that those little Muslim sons-of-bitches could pull off such a spectacular attack, so far from home.

In this ethnocentric world, terrorists of the twenty-first century were "little men" in a compound sense—little because they were racially, ethnically, culturally, and religiously alien; and little because, unlike Japan sixty years earlier, and unlike the Soviet Union or China or even Iraq, Iran, and North Korea, they were not a nation-state. When Richard Clarke criticized the Bush administration's disregard of the Al Qaeda threat, and its subsequent misguided response to September 11, his most vivid revelations concerned the immediate response—and disbelief—of the president's inner circle of advisers:

> On the morning of the 12th, DOD's [the Department of Defense's] focus was already beginning to shift from al Qaeda. CIA was explicit

now that al Qaeda was guilty of the attacks, but Paul Wolfowitz, Rumsfeld's deputy, was not persuaded. It was too sophisticated and complicated an operation, he said, for a terrorist group to have pulled off by itself, without a state sponsor—Iraq must have been helping them.

On the same day, September 12, Clarke went on to record, President Bush "grabbed a few" intelligence experts including himself: " 'Look,' he told us, 'I know you have a lot to do and all . . . but I want you, as soon as you can, to go back over everything, everything. See if Saddam did this. See if he's linked in any way.' "[79]

These responses, revealed after the invasion of Iraq, can be interpreted as genuine or Machiavellian (already preparing to use the 9-11 outrage to initiate a long-desired war against Iraq)—but in all likelihood they were both. Ensuing use of the "war on terror" to invade Iraq, with all the distortion of intelligence data this involved, *was* duplicitous; but the prior failure to take Al Qaeda or the terrorist threat really seriously reflected a lingering Cold War mindset. The 9-11 Commission singled out "imagination" as one of "four kinds of failures" revealed by the attacks of September 11. (The other three were "policy, capabilities, and management.") The commission even went so far as to recommend remedying this by "institutionalizing imagination"—an oxymoron one could easily imagine the bureaucratic behemoth taking seriously to heart by forming committees, preparing flow charts, and perhaps even creating a supersecret NIA (National Imagination Agency).[80]

IN A PASSING comment, the 9-11 Commission also took note of what happens when, after unexpected catastrophe, erstwhile little men prove to be formidable adversaries:

> Al Qaeda and its affiliates are popularly described as being all over the world, adaptable, resilient, needing little higher-level organization, and capable of anything. The American people are thus given the picture of an omnipotent, unslayable hydra of destruction. This image lowers expectations for government effectiveness.

What the commission was evoking was what one U.S. counterterrorism official called "the superman scenario." The shocking success of the little Muslim men abruptly endowed them with hitherto undreamed-of powers and capabilities—to the extent of precipitating a declaration of a global war on . . . *what*? On a tactic (terror). On a worst-case scenario where Al Qaeda or other terrorists might obtain weapons of mass destruction. Eventually, this paranoia reached such a level that deflating hyperbole became almost a category in itself in the burgeoning popular literature on terrorism. As another counterterrorism expert put it, writing specifically about Al Qaeda, "by failing to understand the context of the organization, its very strengths and weaknesses, we magnified our mental image of terrorists as bogeymen." Yet another posed the rhetorical question "Are they ten feet tall?" and deemed it necessary to answer this. "They're not," he assured his audience.[81]

A comparable cognitive dissonance took place after Pearl Harbor. In American eyes, the Japanese foe morphed, overnight, from little men into supermen. Until 1943 or even 1944, when the war turned unmistakably against Japan, the cartoon rendering of the enemy was often a monstrously huge figure. Like the 9-11 Commission, more sober commentators responded by warning of the danger of exaggerating the enemy's resources and capabilities to the point where this became demoralizing. A typical essay in the Sunday *New York Times Magazine* in March 1942, for example, might have served as a draft for post–September 11 warnings about being carried away by the specter of an unslayable hydra of destruction. It was titled "Japanese Superman? That, Too, Is a Fallacy."[82]

# INNOCENCE, EVIL,
# AND AMNESIA

*Catastrophe and the Transfer of Innocence*

In 1942, the admired Hollywood director John Ford cobbled together a dreadful black-and-white "documentary" film titled *December 7th* that, in its first incarnation, came in at eighty-two minutes. Drastically pruned to thirty-four minutes before its release in the theaters, *December 7th* won the Academy Award for Best Documentary Short Subject in 1943.

*December 7th*, particularly in the uncut version, is unusually raw and revealing. It opens in a comfortable bungalow in Hawaii with a sleepy, dreamy, idealistic figure representing Uncle Sam debating a cynical, ruefully head-shaking figure called "C," who represents Sam's "conscience."

The date is December 6, 1941. Sam gushes on at length about the beauty and serenity of Hawaii, its thriving commerce (pineapples, sugar cane, trading companies, etc.) and wonderful demographic diversity. A gamut of ethnic backgrounds, many of them Asian, are itemized at one point, each represented by a smiling young woman who speaks, or lisps, her ethnicity to the camera.

"C" responds by calling Sam a sentimental fool who fails to recognize that 37 percent of these residents are Japanese with hyphenated souls. To all outward appearances they seem Americanized and completely loyal to the United States. We see Boy Scouts, Girl Scouts, charming youngsters reciting the Pledge of Allegiance, and listen at length to an earnest community leader delivering a red-white-and-blue speech in flawless English. In practice, however, "C" tells Sam, they maintain Japanese-language schools, believe in pagan "so-called religions" like Shinto, and accept it as their duty to worship both their ancestors and the Japanese emperor. "If that's Americanism," Sam's conscience tells him, "it's very hyphenated."

As "C" speaks, always calmly and rationally, Ford's camera lingers on a spectrum of ethnic Japanese in Hawaii, all operating as spies: a gardener at the naval officers' club, a fisherman in his small boat, a taxi driver, a young woman working in a barbershop, a pretty girl chatting with a lonely white sailor in a dance hall, ordinary families living suspiciously near U.S. military installations. We see a neatly dressed family at home, clustered around the radio listening to a Japanese-language broadcast. Shop signs written in Japanese ideographs flicker across the screen. The cacophonous music of gongs breaks into the soundtrack.

Something may happen in the Philippines or Singapore, Sam says in response to his nagging conscience, but surely not here. He natters on about the melting pot. The camera pans idyllic beach scenes and we hear a voice singing "Aloha," before Sam dozes off to nightmares of a world at war. When he wakens, it is early Sunday morning, December 7.

Although presented as if actual documentary footage, Ford's depiction of the surprise attack itself was almost entirely staged. Unlike September 11, there was no real-time film to draw on. We see the Pacific Fleet anchored in the harbor, planes lined up in rows on Hickam Field, sailors tossing a baseball, a white-haired Catholic priest conducting an open-air Mass for servicemen standing under palms by the sea. He has just told his congregation not to forget to send presents to their loved ones for Christmas when the first wave of Japanese airplanes appears—out of nowhere, "like tiny locusts." The drone of the approaching planes goes on and on. And then, the narrator intones, "All hell broke loose. Man-made hell—made in Japan."

The re-creation of the surprise attack in *December 7th* is extraordinary for its time. It is excruciating. Even in the edited version, it is as if Ford became mesmerized by chaos and carnage and could not bring himself to stop the camera. Enemy planes swoop in for so long and from so many directions it seems they will never cease coming. American fighting men caught unawares or rushing to their stations are gunned down over and over and over. The camera moves from airfield to airfield, warship to warship, observing them wracked with explosions and consumed in flames. Roosevelt's famous phrase is repeated: a date which will live in infamy. The narrator speaks of bitter, grievous sorrow. The total number of the dead, viewers are told, is 2,343.

With this, the scene shifts to a cemetery. The dead are mourned, and we are slowly introduced to portrait photographs of seven men killed in the attack. As they identify themselves, we see brief film clips of their silent survivors back home—parents, a wife and a newborn son the dead man never lived to see (born on his birthday and named after him). The dead come from many places and walks of life; they reflect America's social and ethnic diversity, although without an ethnic Asian among them. The same narrative voice speaks for them all, however, and explains why. It is because "we *are* all alike. We are all Americans."

As a bugle plays taps, the camera pans to palm trees against the sky, then cuts to the screeching voice of a Japanese propagandist crowing about his nation's spectacular victory. The narrator tells "Mr. Tōjō" he is wrong, and a series of sharp cuts follows. Against rousing music, we see the great efforts at salvage and repair underway at Pearl Harbor. We see Hawaii girding for war, with rolls of barbed wire on its beaches and little schoolchildren in grotesque gas masks engaged in air-raid drills. We are reminded that "all they that take the sword shall perish by the sword." And, finally, we are transported to a rolling cemetery with endless rows of white crosses, where two uniformed men walk together engaged in debate. Both are ghosts—one of a sailor killed on December 7, the other of a soldier killed in World War I. The soldier says he has seen it all before: no one ever learns; there will be war after endless war. The young sailor says: not this time. They talk in metaphors drawn largely from baseball, and after the many flags of the Allied powers have fluttered across the screen, we end with more planes in the sky—this time American fighters flying in "V" (for Victory) formation—and the comforting assurance that this war will end with a World Series pennant called "Peace."

It would be difficult to find a more graphic, grieving, emotional, racist, idealistic, hopeful, and conflicted contemporary response to Pearl Harbor than the uncut version of *December 7th*. Ford's obsession with "sabotage" by the "hyphenated" Americans captures perfectly the fixation on an internal threat from Japanese Americans that deflected the attention of Admiral Kimmel and General Short from the real threat from Japan itself; but that is just the half of it. Perhaps more powerfully than any other single source, *December 7th* conveys the racist climate that resulted in the incarceration in 1942 of some 110,000 Japanese Americans living on the West Coast of the continental United States (but not in Hawaii)—an act that Congress and the executive branch formally apologized for only in 1988. The making of Ford's uncut film, like the incarceration itself, took place after it had become known there was not a single act of sabotage by the Japanese community.[83]

In the wake of September 11, cautionary articles on the shameful treatment of Japanese Americans after Pearl Harbor appeared in the press, and President Bush took care to appear publicly with Muslim and Arab spokesmen and emphasize that the enemy was Islamist terrorists and not the Islamic community or peoples of or from the Middle East as a collectivity. In this regard, a liberal and salutary lesson was drawn from the earlier surprise attack. There was no persecution of Muslims or ethnic Arabs comparable to the collective abuse of Japanese Americans.

The larger lesson supposedly acknowledged in 1988, however, was not just disregarded but almost wantonly cast aside. After 9-11, "terrorism" replaced "sabotage" as justification for violating the very bedrock of a genuinely democratic society in a time of perceived crisis. Civil liberties, human rights, individual rights, constitutional checks-and-balances, habeas corpus, the rule of law itself—all were undermined, both openly and covertly, by a government panicked by the specter of future attacks. In the years to come, "war on terror" legislation and related "homeland security" provisions and

20. *A Japanese American youngster in California waits with her family's belongings before being bused to an assembly center where the processing for incarceration took place, April 1942.*

revisionist legal interpretations (including the permissibility of torture) may well be judged a more sweeping and malignant abuse of justice and democracy than the notorious "Executive Order 9066" under which Roosevelt set in motion contravention of the rights of Japanese Americans.[84]

THE PROTRACTED RACIAL hysteria of Ford's rough cut did not survive the final edit. The mayhem and killing of his reconstructed attack scenes did survive; and even more than a half century later, in a world where violence rules screens large and small, this pandemonium is remarkable. Although the assault is interspersed with heroic Americans manning guns and shooting down a Japanese plane or two, this does not offset the overwhelming impression of a slaughter of innocents.

In a surprising way, the killing in *December 7th* is more graphic than anything widely seen in the wake of 9-11, and the destruction of the World

21. *Dust storm at California's Manzanar internment camp for Japanese Americans, July 1942.*

Trade Center in particular, where heart-stopping photos of men and women leaping from the towers to escape the flames appeared only briefly in the press, soon to all but disappear, and corpses in the wreckage were rarely shown. Despite his impassioned pretence of verisimilitude, Ford's lambs being slaughtered were mostly generic sailors and soldiers. That, presumably, is why he could venture to dwell so long and excruciatingly on them.

Where *December 7th* more closely foreshadows the response to 9-11 is in its rage (the very opposite of Japan's fatuous hope that the surprise attack would "destroy the will" of Americans)—and, more subtly, in mourning individual victims in the closing minutes of the film. The latter takes the form of funeral ceremony and, more intimately and effectively, introduction of real people. We see their photo portraits. We are given their names, told where in the United States they were from, view brief silent footage of their surviving kin. This is deeply moving, for it transcends abstract fatality numbers and staged scenes of gunned-down servicemen and restores indi-

viduality to each victim. Simultaneously—this at a time of Jim Crow laws
and rigid segregation that extended to the armed services—the "we are all
Americans" portrait sequence celebrates the great myth of the melting pot
as if it were reality. This became a cherished theme in Hollywood battle
films during the war, conveyed most commonly in the form of what film
historians refer to as "the multi-ethnic platoon."[85]

In the wake of 9-11, many media outlets eulogized the victims of the terrorist attacks in similar manner. The *New York Times*, for example, printed
portrait photos and brief biographical vignettes of the World Trade Center
victims in a series that necessarily extended over many weeks. All, again,
were individuals going about their job on a day that had dawned clear and
bright. All had something to live for. Despite their differences, in the end
all spoke—as did the victims in *December 7th*—with a single voice.

The impact of such intimate portraits is heartbreaking; and in both
1941 and 2001 the sense not merely of loss but of extraordinary innocence and victimization is intensified by the physical setting—Hawaii as
paradise on a pristine Sunday morning, Manhattan as the thriving center
of urban élan and world commerce. In the case of 9-11, with the attack
striking a civilian community in the very heart of the nation, the sense of
violation is even greater.

In such graphic ways, "9-11," like "Pearl Harbor," became code for
American innocence.

### Evil and the Transfer of Evil

On September 11, the deputy secretary of state, Richard Armitage, met with
the head of Pakistan's Inter-Services Intelligence directorate, who happened
to be in Washington. "History begins today," Armitage told the intelligence
chief and later repeated on national television. This amounted to a cliché in
Washington power circles. Past was not prologue. Everything started anew
when those planes destroyed the World Trade Center and crashed into the
Pentagon. Richard Perle, a former defense official who exercised exceptional influence in conservative and neoconservative foreign-policy circles,
later moved this observation directly into the Oval Office. "Nine-eleven
had a profound effect on the president's thinking," he told an interviewer.
"The world began on nine-eleven. There's no intellectual history."[86]

Even while ransacking World War II for political purposes, the administration closed off serious engagement with the modern history of Western interaction with the Middle East. President Bush was the rhetorical point man. Addressing Congress on September 20, he declared the nation was attacked without warning or reason or plausible cause or explanation beyond the evil nature of the perpetrators. One White House speechwriter (David Frum) later lavished particular praise on this address, emphasizing that it "was remarkable equally for what it did not say and for what it did say. Here is the most important thing it did not say: It did not accept—it did not even deign to acknowledge—the argument that the United States somehow brought the terror attacks on itself."[87]

The most-quoted words in this celebrated speech were "they hate our freedoms," and this too became a mantra—applied not merely to Al Qaeda but terrorists in general. The president's refusal to "whine" or engage in critical reflection about U.S. policies and practices—his adamant declaration of national innocence confronted by purblind evil—was praised domestically as a reflection of political clarity and moral strength. This black-and-white polarity shaped the "war on terror" that followed. There was no need to look beyond evil and hating America's freedoms to understand the enemy.

This was the unwobbling pivot of the administration's worldview. "Our responsibility to history," the president declared on a "National Day of Prayer and Remembrance" three days after 9-11, "is already clear: to answer these attacks and rid the world of evil." In an exchange with journalists two days later, on September 16, he provoked an international uproar by characterizing his war on terror as a "crusade"—language that incited Muslims and Arabs to recall the medieval Christians who invaded and devastated their homeland. The president's phrasing had, again, been prefaced with evil. September 11, he told the journalists in this unscripted exchange, was a warning that "there are evil people in this world . . . evil folks still lurk out there."[88]

The argument that Al Qaeda was a reactionary and murderous organization was irrefutable: 9-11 was the logical product of the organization's basic doctrinal tracts (authored by Sayyid Imam al-Sharif, known by the nom de guerre Dr. Fadl), which called for the indiscriminate killing even of Muslims who did not conform to the most extreme fundamentalist beliefs.

22. *This popular broadside was photographed in Manhattan's financial district one week after the terrorist attack.*

The false corollary argument that radical Islamists had no legitimate grievances, on the other hand, blocked any serious attempt to understand the appeal of anti-Western polemics throughout much of the Middle East. This argument that "no act of ours invited the rage of the killers" (from a later presidential address) was already gospel in conservative circles well before September 11. Following Al Qaeda's bombings of U.S. embassies in Kenya and Tanzania in August 1998, for example, L. Paul Bremer III, then a State Department ambassador-at-large for counterterrorism during the Reagan administration, advanced this argument on television in words that could have served as a draft for the president's September 20 speech three years later. "In the case of people like bin Laden," Bremer observed, "there really is . . . nothing we can do politically to satisfy him. There's no point in addressing the so-called root causes of bin Laden's despair with us. We are the root cause of his terrorism. He doesn't like America. He doesn't like our society. He doesn't like what we stand for. He doesn't like our values. And short of the United States going out of existence, there's no way to deal with the root cause of his terrorism."[89]

Following 9-11, many of the administration's most persuasive public

23. *Eighteen months after Al Qaeda's attack, this patriotic artwork served as background for an April 15, 2003, address to his sailors by the commander of the Fifth Fleet, Vice Admiral Timothy J. Keating. The fleet was deployed in support of Operation Iraqi Freedom, the invasion of Iraq undertaken in the name of a global war on terrorism.*

supporters placed this hate-our-freedoms argument center stage. The military historian Victor Davis Hanson, for example, entered the fray nine days later with an itemization of "war myths" that had to be repudiated in combating "the present evil." "Nothing could be further from the truth," he emphasized, than the argument that the United States had incurred legitimate hatred in the Arab world. On the contrary, America's radical antagonists were "wedded to a medieval world of perpetual stasis," and Al Qaeda's adherents in this most recent atrocity were "driven to murder by hatred and envy, not hunger or exploitation."

Hanson's conclusion was unqualified: "These terrorists hate us for who we are, not what we have done." It was a myth to think that "war has never solved anything." On the contrary, "the three greatest scourges of the 20th century—Nazism, Japanese militarism, and Soviet Communism—were defeated through war or continued military resistance." Hanson approvingly quoted Heraclitus's observation that war is "the father of us all" (a sentiment imperial Japan's warlords also cherished). To eradicate the present evil, the United States thus had to be prepared, if necessary, to take the moral high ground and "act alone."[90]

These clarion calls for military assertiveness heralded a transfer of evil from the loose transnational networks exemplified by Al Qaeda to targets top policy makers were more comfortable with: namely, nation-states. This was the thrust of the January 2002 State of the Union address, in which the president linked the terror threat to an "axis of evil" composed of Iraq, Iran, and North Korea. Some months later, in a graduation speech at West Point, the "Bush Doctrine" of preemptive war was articulated publicly for the first time and combating evil was established as the centerpiece of U.S. policy. In a world of "shadowy terrorist networks with no nation or citizens to defend" and "unbalanced dictators with weapons of mass destruction," the president declared, "Cold War doctrines of deterrence and containment" could no longer be relied on. After September 11, nothing less than quasi-scriptural rhetoric could adequately describe the threat facing the world:

> There can be no neutrality between justice and cruelty, between the innocent and the guilty. We are in a conflict between good and evil, and America will call evil by its name.

In such a conflict, the United States had no choice but to "take the battle to the enemy" in its struggle to attain a safe, just, and peaceful world.

The Bush Doctrine took militarized and militaristic policies to unprecedented levels. The United States would not hesitate to use force where diplomacy was faltering; would reject or withdraw from entangling international agreements where these might be constricting; would act unilaterally and take preemptive military action against perceived foes whenever deemed necessary; would place increasingly greater reliance on clandestine operations by top-secret "special forces," even in the countries of nonbelligerents; would explore the possibility of first-strike use of nuclear weapons as well as tactical use of enormously powerful "bunker busters" and even "mini-nukes"; would rearrange and expand a global web of long-term military bases (already numbering upwards of seven hundred overseas installations); would extend and secure the nation's military hegemony in outer space; and, to the extent possible, would implement abroad the peculiar vision of "democracy" that was central to neoconservative ideology: extreme privatization and market economies wide open to foreign and particularly U.S. capital. In the apt phrase of James Carroll, it

24. *Karachi, Pakistan, October 7, 2001.*

25–26. *London, September 18, 2001, and Jakarta, Indonesia, September 21, 2001. The Arabic banner reads, "There is no god but Allah, Muhammad is the Messenger of Allah."*

27. *An Afghan boy looks at posters of bin Laden in the Pakistan border city of Chaman on the third anniversary of 9-11.*

was to these ends that the Bush administration unleashed its own crusade of "sacred violence."[91]

This was the prelude to invading Iraq in March 2003, and there was no looking back. History was about to begin again.

## Amnesia and Frankenstein's Monster

The Oval Office theology of refusing to accept or "even deign to acknowledge" grievances against the United States repelled reality like stone repelling water. Three years after 9-11—eighteen months after Iraq was invaded—a task force commissioned by the Pentagon deemed it necessary to repudiate the politicization of evil and stress that "Muslims do not 'hate our freedom,' but rather, they hate our policies." The report agreed that terrorist networks were "symptomatic of a broader transformation within Islam and a continuation of the 20th century conflict between tolerance and totalitarianism," and took care to emphasize that "we must understand the United States is engaged in a generational and global struggle about ideas, not a war between the West and Islam." At the same time, the report itemized grievances that extended beyond just the anger, instability, and suffering caused by the post–9-11 invasions of Afghanistan and Iraq. "The overwhelming majority," it observed, "voice their objections to what they see as one-sided support in favor of Israel and against Palestinian rights, and the longstanding, even increasing support for what Muslims collectively see as tyrannies, most notably Egypt, Saudi Arabia, Jordan, Pakistan, and the Gulf states."[92]

Months later, in January 2005, "supporting papers" to a report on the crisis in Iraq submitted to the Pentagon's Defense Science Board expressed even harsher criticism of the insularity and self-righteousness of the administration's war planners. "To put it bluntly," this task force concluded, "they never possessed an understanding of the political and religious nature of their opponent." Nor, the report continued, did they even understand themselves and their own country:

> The only way to understand the motivations of an opponent is by having a real understanding of the historical and religious framework that has molded his culture. It is clear that Americans who

waged the war and who have attempted to mold the aftermath have had no clear idea of the framework that has molded the personalities and attitudes of Iraqis. Finally, it might help if Americans and their leaders were to show less arrogance and more understanding of themselves and their place in history. Perhaps more than any other people, Americans display a consistent amnesia concerning their own past, as well as the history of those around them.[93]

Historical amnesia is what Benazir Bhutto dwelled on in her last published words in 2008: the United States and other powers led by England and France neither practiced what they preached nor faced up to their deserved reputation for hypocrisy. Bhutto was unrestrained in condemning Islamist fundamentalism and terror, but saw this as inseparable from the West's own practices, tracing back to European colonialism prior to World War II and intensified through the four-plus decades of the Cold War. "The shadow between Western rhetoric and Western actions has sowed the seeds of Muslim public disillusionment and fanaticism," she observed. "The double standards have fueled extremism and fanaticism," and accounted "at least in part, for the precipitous drop in respect for the West in the Muslim world."[94]

All this is what Bhutto had in mind when she accused the United States itself of helping to create a "Frankenstein's monster" in the Middle East. The chasm between paeans to "freedom" and a history of supporting authoritarian regimes and Islamist fanatics when power politics made this expedient was for all practical purposes obscured by the history-begins-today smog that settled over official Washington in the wake of 9-11. This cynical reading of modern history did not go ignored elsewhere in the world. Nor was it peculiar to the Middle East, or to the new age of global terror.

FRANKENSTEIN'S MONSTER WAS both a time traveler and a global traveler. The exogenous forces that battered the Middle East—beginning in the nineteenth century and intensifying exponentially in the twentieth— also shaped the international milieu imperial Japan's ideologues and policy makers had declared unacceptable. Like the geographically expansive

CELEBRATING JAPAN'S NEW ORDER IN ASIA

*28–31. The mighty-hand poster promotes an exhibition titled "Toward the Advance of a Scientific Japan," celebrating innovations in military technology. "Rise of Asia," a vividly colored leaflet dating from 1943, depicts Japan liberating Asia from its U.S.- and U.K.-led oppressors and breaking the chains of "ABCD" (American, British, Chi-*

---

Islamist dream of a "new caliphate," Japan's earlier propagandizing of a "Greater East Asia Co-Prosperity Sphere" gained credibility from contrasting what the Western powers espoused and what they actually practiced. While mid-century Pan-Asianism lacked a religious core, it resembled Pan-Islamic agitation in incorporating intellectual strains associated with the West even while reacting against Western strategic and cultural intrusion.[95]

The double standards of the United States and European powers were an easy target on the eve of Pearl Harbor. Roosevelt might extol the "four freedoms" (of speech and religion, from want and fear) and join Prime Minister Winston Churchill in the vaunted Atlantic Charter of August 1941 (proclaiming respect for "the right of all peoples to choose the form of government under which they will live"), but the Japanese had no dif-

*nese, Dutch) domination. "Crush Anglo-Americans," a 1943 poster directed at the occupied Philippines, combines "new order" rhetoric with the virulent anti-Anglo sentiment that was inseparable from this. The multi-flag poster celebrates the anniversary of the December 1941 attacks that inaugurated Japan's so-called Greater East Asia Co-Prosperity Sphere.*

---

ficulty dismissing this as transparent hypocrisy. Just look, their propagandists exclaimed, at the areas the emperor's soldiers and sailors were "liberating" from the White Peril: French Indochina, the Dutch East Indies, the U.S.-ruled Philippines, and British colonial possessions including Hong Kong, Malaya, and Burma—as well as a China still burdened with unequal treaties and foreign concessions. Neither the Japanese then nor Islamists later, of course, paused to reflect on their own hypocrisies. Self-righteous missions do not accommodate self-reflection.

We usually identify the West-born and West-driven developments to which the Pan-Asianists, and later Pan-Islamists, were responding in terms of "isms"—beginning, for the modern world, with capitalism, imperialism, and colonialism. Although the victory of the Allied powers in World War I ushered in an intensified rhetoric of liberalism and internationalism, the inequitable old global order survived in both familiar and new guises. At the same time, Bolshevism thrust itself on the stage and a firestorm of other "isms" followed: communism and anticommunism; nationalisms inspired by anti-imperialism and anticolonialism; militarism accelerated by technology-driven arms races; economic protectionism in response to the global depression that began in the late 1920s; totalitarianism in the forms of Stalinism, Nazism, fascism, and Japan's peculiar emperor-centered national socialism. White racism was ubiquitous, provoking antiwhite racisms in return, as well as intensified hierarchies of race, tribe, and sect in the non-Western world. "Anti-Westernism" itself originated as a product of European thought, reflecting opposition to the oppressiveness and perceived banality of modern mass society.

This upheaval, rather than samurai values or a history "so recently feudalistic" (in Joseph Grew's often-quoted phrase), is the milieu that prompted imperial Japan's leaders to choose war, however foolhardy that choice may have been. In counterpart ways, Islamist fundamentalism and terror came to a boil in a global cauldron, and not sui generis out of some "medieval world of perpetual stasis." Recognizing this does not mean exonerating evil deeds, as those who equated denying grievances with moral clarity declared. Rather, it means trying to better understand the enemy as well as oneself. Legacies and causalities are a mare's nest in a world of vulnerable borders and gross disparities of power, but policy makers court disaster when they refuse to "deign to acknowledge" complexity in the form of deep-seated conflicts and complaints.

■

OFTEN, PRECEDENTS THAT help illuminate the present are scarcely apparent at first glance. Take, for example, the simultaneous emergence of the United States and Japan as expansionist Pacific powers between 1895 and 1905. This turn-of-the-century burst of U.S. imperialism led to the acquisition of Hawaii and the Philippines, the territorial holdings that propelled Japan's attacks on Pearl Harbor four decades later. It provided the United States with a gulag (Guantánamo, acquired in 1901 following the Spanish-American War) and a notorious practice (waterboarding, done by both sides during the conquest of the Philippines) that became enormously controversial after September 11. And it established a righteous expansionist vocabulary that was played like chimes by the Bush administration. Much of the boilerplate about innocence, virtue, and "our freedoms" that encased the war on terror and invasion of Iraq as rhetorical armor was hammered out a century earlier, when the United States seized the Philippines as a prize during its war with Spain and found itself embroiled in a violent struggle against native resistance that lasted from 1898 into 1902.[96]

Some of this burnished language required mild editing in later decades, but the key words and overall thrust of the rhetoric remained intact— "benevolent assimilation" (President William McKinley's phrase), "the white man's burden" (poeticized by Rudyard Kipling in explicit support of U.S. annexation of the Philippines), a civilizing mission, a Christian duty to "our little brown brothers" (as William Howard Taft, the first civilian governor-general and later U.S. president, famously called the Filipino elites with whom he dealt). Senator Albert Beveridge greeted news that the United States had defeated a Spanish fleet in Manila Bay on the first day of May 1898 with a particularly exuberant (and enduring) vision of Mars, Mammon, and God wrapped in the Stars and Stripes:

> We will establish trading-posts throughout the world as distributing points for American products. We will cover the ocean with our merchant marine. We will build a navy to the measure of our greatness. Great colonies governing themselves, flying our flag and trading with us, will grow about our posts of trade. Our institutions will follow our flag on the wings of commerce. And American law, American order, American civilization, and the American flag will plant themselves on shores hitherto bloody and benighted, but by those agencies of God henceforth to be made beautiful and bright.

Another senator urged acquisition of the Philippines on grounds that "those who believe in Providence see, or think they see, that God has placed upon this government the solemn duty of providing for the people of these islands a government based upon the principle of liberty no matter how many difficulties the problem may present." Religious publications endorsed conquest of the Philippines as a "righteous war," while others such as Secretary of War Elihu Root spoke in more secular terms of establishing a colonial administration that would promote "happiness, peace and prosperity." The Philippines, it was said, would become a "showcase of democracy."[97]

These were the ghosts behind the ghostwriters behind George W. Bush. In the run-up to the invasion of Iraq, and for years thereafter, the president's wordsmiths and supporters added little that was truly new to such effusions. "Benevolent global hegemony" replaced "benevolent assimilation." Paternalistic rhetoric like "white man's burden" was shorn of overt racism and became simply America's "burden." "Empire" became "empire lite"—but the mystique of a unique goodness, mission, and manifest destiny remained.[98] Personally, the forty-third president even emerged as a kindred spirit to McKinley when it came to knowledge about the world. Although McKinley had difficulty locating the Philippines on a map, this did not deter him from declaring that the United States was annexing that country for "liberty and law, peace and progress." Much like Bush, who spoke frequently of being guided by God as a war president, McKinley also famously (and possibly apocryphally) was said to have told a delegation of Methodists visiting the White House that he "went down on my knees and prayed Almighty God for light and guidance," and God told him "that there was nothing left for us to do but to take them all, and to educate the Filipinos, and uplift and civilize and Christianize them, and by God's grace do the very best we could by them, as our fellow-men for whom Christ also died." (McKinley was unaware that many Filipinos had converted to Christianity under the Spanish, much as Bush rushed into war with Iraq ignorant of and incurious about Islam in general, let alone Sunni-Shiite schisms.) Governor-General Taft, apparently without divine counsel, agreed that the United States had a "sacred duty" to Americanize the Filipinos.[99]

Led by Emilio Aguinaldo, many Filipinos chose not to be uplifted by annexation. Guerrilla resistance was tenacious before U.S. forces succeeded in crushing what they called the "Philippine Insurrection" and the native opposition called a revolutionary struggle for independence.[100] The fighting was vicious. An official U.S. report belatedly made public in April 1902 observed that "almost without exception, soldiers, and also many officers, refer to the natives in their presence as 'niggers', and the natives are beginning to understand what 'nigger' means." (Such racism had a more muted pre– and post–9-11 incarnation in slurs deriding Arabs as "sand niggers," "desert niggers," "sand monkeys," and the like.) Testimony that quoted a U.S. general in the field identifying anyone over the age of ten as a potential enemy capable of bearing arms, and ordering his men to "kill and burn" and turn the contested area in which they were fighting into a "howling wilderness," provoked outrage among anti-imperialists but a certain savage pride among at least some participants. Years later, in a memoir published in 1939, Admiral Yates Stirling almost boastfully recalled fighting near a rural river in 1899, early in his career. "We certainly did a good job on the river," he wrote. "After we had finished up, there was little left to speak of. We burned the villages; in fact, every house for two miles from either bank was destroyed by us. We killed their livestock: cattle, pigs, chickens, and their valuable work animals, the carabaos. It seemed ruthless; yet it was after all war, and war is brutal."[101]

Both sides committed atrocities, and at one point use of the "water cure" or "Chinese water torture" by U.S. troops came under particular criticism in the United States. McKinley's successor as president, Theodore Roosevelt, spoke vigorously about the unacceptability of torture or other inhumane conduct on the part of the military—while observing in a personal letter that "nobody was seriously damaged" by this "old Filipino method of mild torture." Even private discourse tended to identify such abuse as Asian—in this case the "Chinese" or "Filipino" water torture—ignoring the fact that this particular form of interrogation was common practice in the Spanish Inquisition.[102]

In the Philippines conquest, as in the war on terror a century later, the official response to accusations of atrocity on the part of the U.S. military was twofold. Such behavior was dismissed as rare and aberrant. Secretary of War Root declared that "the war in the Philippines has been conducted by the American Army with scrupulous regard for the rules of civilized warfare, with careful and genuine consideration for the prisoner and non-combatant, with self-restraint and with humanity, never surpassed, if ever equaled, in any conflict, worthy only of praise and reflecting credit upon the American people." What else was a public official supposed to say? At the same time, viciousness was rationalized (again in Root's words) as an inevitable and "not incredible" response to "the barbarous cruelty common among uncivilized races." As Edmund Morris has concisely documented, Roosevelt reassured one of his generals that he realized "sporadic cases" of abuse of prisoners were inevitable in war, as the general himself well knew from the battle at Wounded Knee (in 1890) when "troops under your command killed squaws and children as well as unarmed Indians." Governor-General Taft, who would succeed Roosevelt as president in 1909, publicly extolled America's "moral mandate" while expressing solicitous concern for the "little brown brothers." Privately, he dismissed even the educated Filipinos with whom he dealt as being "ambitious as Satan and quite as unscrupulous." They would "need the training of fifty or a hundred years before they shall even realize what Anglo-Saxon liberty is."[103]

In the final reckoning, over five thousand U.S. military, twenty thousand native soldiers, and at least two hundred thousand Filipino civilians were killed in the Philippines war. Some accounts put civilian deaths as high as one million, deriving from war-caused famine as well as the atrocities committed by both sides. Like all subsequent U.S. wars on foreign soil, even the conservative estimate reflects a strikingly disproportionate ratio between American military fatalities and enemy military and civilian deaths. When the Bush presidency ended, U.S. military fatalities in Iraq totaled over four thousand. The number of "violent" or "excess" deaths among Iraqis caused directly or indirectly by the invasion, while contested, was in the hundreds of thousands.[104]

Nothing during the bloody conquest of the Philippines or in the years and decades that followed—including over thirty U.S. military interventions in Central America and the Caribbean—undermined mainstream American belief in the innocence and benevolence of its activities abroad.[105] When President Bush visited the Philippines in October 2003, seven months after the invasion of Iraq, he offered another of his trademark lessons from history. "Together our soldiers liberated the Philippines from colonial rule," he declared. "Together we rescued the islands from invasion and occupation." The reference, as usual, was to World War II ("Bataan, Corregidor, Leyte, Luzon"); and the message was that postwar democracy in the Philippines demonstrated that, contrary to what doubters might say, non-Western nations like Iraq could adopt and sustain the institutions of democracy. The *New York Times* covered this under the headline "Bush Cites Philippines as Model in Rebuilding Iraq."[106]

TO ARGUE A line of "causality" from turn-of-the-century imperialism to Pearl Harbor, let alone to 9-11 and Iraq, is patently absurd—just as denying evil in the world is, or ignoring the constructive interactions that have accompanied Western expansion and domination. It is just as absurd to ignore the dense texture of the past, however, and the legacies and potent memories this has created. Launching a "war on evil" as the Bush administration did—with contempt for the grievances or opinions of others, ignorance of the nature and capabilities of the enemy, and of how and why that enemy attracted recruits, and only a cherry-picker's regard for history—carried tragic consequences. This made it impossible to comprehend why non-Western peoples may simultaneously embrace and repudiate Western contacts and influences, and why rallying cries about humanitarian intervention and the like may be dismissed as the latest refrain of an old imperialist song.

The longtime Middle East journalist Robert Fisk put it well in introducing his sad and lengthy observations on "The Great War for Civilization" (the ironic title of his book taken from World War I): morality becomes "hitched like a halter round the warhorse" on all sides, and the upshot is death and devastation. This is not moral relativism or denial of just war, but a lament for the loss of perspective that accompanies arrogant self-righteousness. Bin Laden also hitched a Manichaean halter round his warhorse with a ritualized litany about leading "forces of faith" against "the evil forces of materialism."[107]

Despite its distinctive sanctimoniousness, the rhetoric of American benevolence has many antecedents. Shakespeare reminds us of how hoary some of this language is in *Julius Caesar*, where Brutus exclaims, "Let's all cry 'peace, freedom, and liberty!'" England and the European powers routinely cloaked hegemony and domination in the rubric of a civilizing mission. Upon seizing Alexandria in 1798, Napoleon told the Egyptians he had come "for the purpose of restoring your rights from the hands of the oppressors," and those who declared otherwise were but "slanderers." Well over a century later, when defeat of the Ottoman Turks in World War I enabled Britain to occupy Iraq and seize control of its oil, the British officer in charge (Major General Sir Stanley Maude) offered similar reassurance. "Our armies do not come into your cities and lands as conquerors or enemies," he declared, "but as liberators." This practice of gilding power politics with fine rhetoric persisted through the Cold War, when the struggle between the United States and Soviet Union carried into the Middle East and Washington deemed it expedient to support authoritarian and repressive regimes including, to the end of the 1980s, Saddam Hussein's Baathist Party in Iraq.[108]

Bin Laden's speeches and writings both before and after 9-11 refer to the Crusades as well as European plunder and occupation after World War I, and are suffused with denunciation of infidel Christians and Jews. From the outset, however, much of his propaganda addressed contemporary issues: the plight of the Palestinians; establishment of U.S. military bases on the sacred soil of Saudi Arabia in the wake of the first Gulf War in 1990–91; Western control over Middle East energy resources and support of corrupt and repressive regimes in Saudi Arabia, Egypt, and elsewhere; and so on. Western "double standards" is a leitmotif in his polemics, just as it is in the laments of outspoken opponents of Islamist fundamentalism and terror like Benazir Bhutto, whose pro-Western credentials were unquestioned. To ignore such perceptions and grievances played into terrorists' hands before and after 9-11, and—remarkably—even for years after the disastrous failure of Operation Iraqi Freedom.[109]

It is difficult to exaggerate how elemental and theocratic this moral righteousness was. It saturated the Oval Office, made the Bush Doctrine's premise of "a conflict between good and evil" unchallenged gospel, and expedited the transfer of evil from the perpetrators of 9-11 to an "axis of evil" personified by Saddam Hussein. Even as the administration took care to say it was not engaged in a crusade against Islam, top-secret Pentagon reports personally delivered to the White House by Secretary of Defense Donald Rumsfeld in March and April 2003, as the invasion unfolded, were dramatically highlighted with biblical quotations. The coversheet to the "Worldwide Intelligence Update" for March 31, for example, reproduced these lines from Ephesians against a color photograph of a tank silhouetted against a blood-red sky: "Therefore put on the full armor of God, so that when the day of evil comes, you may be able to stand your ground, and after you have done everything, to stand." The coversheet quotation for April 3, paired with a triptych of color photographs of U.S. troops,

## BIBLICAL QUOTATIONS
## ON TOP-SECRET REPORTS TO THE PRESIDENT
## DURING THE INVASION OF IRAQ

32. The attack on Iraq began on March 19, 2003, and U.S.-led forces occupied Baghdad on April 9. During these three weeks the president received a regular "Worldwide Intelligence Update" from the secretary of defense, the cover sheets of which featured biblical quotations along with color photographs. As presented to the president, these scriptural passages included the following:

| | |
|---|---|
| *March 17:* | "Whom shall I send, and who will go for us?"<br>"Here I am, Lord. Send me." [Isaiah 6:8] |
| *March 19:* | If I rise on the wings of the dawn,<br>if I settle on the far side of the sea,<br>even there your hand will guide me,<br>your right hand will hold me fast, O LORD. [Psalm 139:9–10] |
| *March 20:* | "Their arrows are sharp, all their bows are strung;<br>their horses' hoofs seem like flint, their chariot wheels<br>are like a whirlwind." [Isaiah 5:28] |
| *March 31:* | "Therefore put on the full armor of God, so that when the<br>day of evil comes, you may be able to stand your ground,<br>and after you have done everything, to stand." [Ephesians 6:13] |
| *April 1:* | Commit to the LORD whatever you do,<br>and your plans will succeed. [Proverbs 16:3] |
| *April 3:* | "Have I not commanded you? Be strong and courageous.<br>Do not be terrified; do not be discouraged, for the LORD<br>your God will be with you wherever you go." [Joshua 1:9] |
| *April 7:* | It is God's will that by doing good you should<br>silence the ignorant talk of foolish men. [1 Peter 2:15] |
| *April 8:* | Open the gates that the righteous nation may enter,<br>The nation that keeps faith. [Isaiah 26:2] |
| *April 9:* | "Suddenly the fingers of a human hand appeared & wrote on the plaster of the wall, near the lampstand in the royal palace. The king watched the hand as it wrote . . . This is what these words mean:<br>Mene: God has numbered the days of your reign & brought it to an end.<br>Tekel: You have been weighed on the scales & found wanting.<br>Peres: Your kingdom is divided . . ." [Daniel 5:5–28] |

armored vehicles, and a jet fighter, came from Joshua: "Have I not commanded you? Be strong and courageous. Do not be terrified; do not be discouraged, for the LORD your God will be with you wherever you go." On April 8, accompanying a photo of military vehicles rumbling beneath the monumental crossed-swords archway in Baghdad, the biblical passage of the day came from Isaiah: "Open the gates that the righteous nation may enter, / The nation that keeps faith."[110]

The crude and abusive conduct of the occupation that followed conformed to this holy-war dichotomy. After as well as before the invasion, the Iraqi populace essentially became flattened and divided into an evil minority who opposed the Americans and a great and good majority who welcomed them. When opposition to occupation proved unexpectedly widespread, the military response was characteristically Manichaean. U.S. forces adopted a "kill or capture" policy of kicking down doors and indiscriminately targeting Iraqi "MAMs" (military-age males). Iraqis killed in firefights were almost automatically identified as "Al Qaeda." At one point as many as twenty-six thousand "suspects" were incarcerated, in most cases arbitrarily and in many cases abusively. All this was deemed, again in Army lingo, an appropriate "kinetic" approach to an evil, monolithic adversary. That many Iraqis and their Muslim and Arab neighbors could agree that Saddam Hussein's regime was despicable but still find it unacceptable to unleash a foreign war machine to destroy it was not deemed worthy of serious consideration—nor was the mounting rage that kill-or-capture practices provoked. Even as nationalism was pumped to fever pitch in the United States—always under the name of "patriotism" rather than "nationalism"—the nationalism or group identity and pride of others was ignored.[111]

Viewed through such absolute either/or lenses, America's perceived enemies thus were largely denied diversity, complexity, autonomy, history and historical consciousness, legitimate fears and grievances, and the possibility of being contained or dealt with constructively short of ultimatums and brute force. This was true also of potential allies. "You're either with us or against us in the fight against terror," the president famously declared at a press conference on November 6, 2001—much as bin Laden had thrown down the gauntlet a few weeks earlier. In a long interview with Al Jazeera television on October 20, bin Laden declared that "everyone that supports Bush with one word, even without offering help and aid, and whatever else that is described as facilities, is nothing but a traitor." September 11, in his chilling formulation, was simply a step in the direction of evening out "a balance of terror."[112]

## Evil Where the Price Is Worth It

Bin Laden's denunciations of Western double standards were hypocritical and themselves a double standard. From around 1996, for example, he frequently invoked the atomic bombing of Japan as an example of American inhumanity—a "terrorist act" whose victims included "women, children, and elderly people." At the same time, he had no compunction against calling for a "Hiroshima" in the United States. The doctrinal interpretations of jihad that Al Qaeda advanced before 9-11 to justify holy violence amounted to a license to kill anyone, including Muslim "apostates," who did not endorse the most extreme interpretation of the Qur'an.

After 9-11, even as the jihad against "the West" intensified, most victims of Al Qaeda's terror were other Muslims. And after the U.S. occupation of Iraq triggered a bloodbath of Muslim-versus-Muslim killing, even Islamists who applauded 9-11 and remained critical of Western policies in the Middle East began to turn bin Laden's rhetoric against him. Around the sixth anniversary of 9-11, for example, a Saudi cleric admired by bin Laden framed this as a direct question: "My brother Osama, how much blood has been spilt? How many innocent people, children, elderly, and women have been killed . . . in the name of Al Qaeda? Will you be happy to meet God Almighty carrying the burden of these hundreds of thousands or millions [of victims] on your back?"[113]

Where the West was concerned, bin Laden was chillingly direct about his balance-of-terror theology. "We treat others like they treat us," he told Al Jazeera shortly after 9-11. "Those who kill our women and our innocent, we kill their women and innocent, until they stop doing so." This was "good terrorism" as opposed to the "ill-advised terrorism" practiced by the United States and Israel, and killing Americans and Jews was "among the most important duties and most pressing things" in jihad. On one occasion, bin Laden presented the 9-11 attacks as a matter of almost literal reciprocity. In a videotape made available in October 2004, just before the U.S. presidential election, he recalled his shock at witnessing the destruction of Beirut in 1982, "when America allowed the Israelis to invade Lebanon with the help of its third fleet . . . bombing, killing, and wounding many, while others fled in terror." Looking at "those destroyed towers in Lebanon," he went on, "it occurred to me to punish the oppressor in kind by destroying towers in America, so that it would have a taste of its own medicine and would be prevented from killing our women and children. On that day I became sure that the oppression and intentional murder of innocent women and children is a deliberate American policy. It seemed then that 'freedom and democracy' are actually just terror, just as resistance is labeled 'terrorism' and 'reaction.'"[114]

Bin Laden did not conceal his contempt for Saddam Hussein, referring to him at one point as "a thief and an apostate." Iraq, on the other hand, held a place in his polemics in ways that antedated the Bush administration and, again, highlighted how ambidextrous the concept "evil" can be. Beginning around 1996, his litany of the "ill-advised terrorism" of the United States and others called attention to a recent and ongoing development: the drastically higher mortality rate among Iraqi infants and very young children caused by economic sanctions imposed during and after the short Gulf War. This was adroit propaganda, for it pointed to a human tragedy that already attracted concern and condemnation worldwide.[115]

IN "OPERATION DESERT STORM," the decisive final phase of the first Gulf War—which began with Iraq's invasion of Kuwait in August 1990 and extended through February 1991—forty-three successive days of bombardment by U.S. manned bombers, cruise missiles, and laser-guided explosives decimated Iraq's civilian infrastructure, much as Anglo-American forces had done in the air war against Germany and Japan many decades earlier. The devastation, involving some seven hundred sites, included electric power stations and telecommunication centers; dams, pumping stations, water-purification facilities, and sewage-treatment plants; transportation networks including railways, highways, bridges, and ports; oil and petrochemical facilities; and factories producing everything from metals and textiles to medical supplies.

Pentagon analysts estimated that the country's electrical generating capacity, critical to everything from water purification to sewage treatment to hospital functioning, was reduced to the level Iraq possessed in 1920. A UN report issued in March 1991 described the results of the bombing as "near apocalyptic." "Most means of modern life support have been destroyed or rendered tenuous," this report observed, and the country had been "relegated to a pre-industrial age but with all the disabilities of post-industrial dependency on an intensive use of energy and technology." Two years after the war, the Arab Monetary Fund placed the cost of destroyed Iraqi infrastructure at around a quarter-trillion dollars.[116]

Official spokesmen for Operation Desert Storm emphasized that unlike earlier wars these high-precision attacks kept civilian casualties to a minimum. This was dishonest, for such claims focused on deaths caused directly by the bombing and obscured the larger objective of creating what air-war strategists call "strategic paralysis" or "system paralysis" by destroying dual-use infrastructure. Additionally, the disclaimers ignored the long-term, post-combat economic campaign aimed at further disabling Iraqi society and thereby, it was hoped, undermining "civilian morale" and establishing "long-term leverage" over Saddam. A lengthy internal U.S. military document issued near the start of the Gulf War bombing campaign, for example, explicitly acknowledged that destroying water-treatment facilities and cutting off access to equipment and chemicals necessary to purify Iraq's poor-quality water supplies would "result in a shortage of pure drinking water for much of the population. This could lead to increased incidences, if not epidemics, of disease and to certain pure-water-dependent industries becoming incapacitated, including petro chemicals, fertilizers, petroleum refining, electronics, pharmaceuticals, food processing, textiles, concrete construction, and thermal power plants."[117]

In unguarded moments, American military spokesmen even suggested that Iraqis bore some responsibility for Saddam's invasion of Kuwait, and so deserved to suffer. "The definition of innocents gets to be a little bit uncertain," a senior air force officer observed in one Gulf War briefing. "They do live there, and ultimately the people have some control over what goes on in their country." Later—still several years before 9-11—bin Laden offered a comparable explanation regarding his declaration of jihad against the United States. The American people were not exonerated from responsibility for U.S. crimes in Palestine, Lebanon, Iraq, and elsewhere, he argued, "because they chose this government and voted for it despite their knowledge of its crimes."[118]

■

THE FIRST GULF WAR occurred during the administration of the forty-first president, George H. W. Bush, and was prologue to the war of choice launched by his son, George W. Bush, twelve years later. It bears recollection since much that took place then and later was obliterated by the history-begins-today amnesia that followed 9-11. The carefully considered arguments advanced in 1991 against trying to take the fighting to Baghdad and overthrow Saddam were dismissed a decade later with scarcely a second thought. Brushed aside at the same time was the devastating impact of the economic sanctions imposed on Iraq in the wake of the Gulf War, which among other things caused a dramatic spike in infant mortality. With this latter development, "innocence and evil" again took center stage—in ways that exacerbated anti-American and anti-Western sentiments. Saddam predictably pointed to the embargo as one more example of "the courses of evil coming from outside Iraq." Washington and London, just as predictably, argued that all suffering was due to the dictator's refusal to cave in to the sanctions and allow arms inspectors to confirm that Iraq had abandoned all production of weapons of mass destruction. Bin Laden, in turn, lost no opportunity to single out the devastating effect of the sanctions as one more example of the "terror" of America and its allies.[119]

The arguments that persuaded top U.S. leaders to reject overthrowing Saddam by force in 1991 assumed a certain poignancy as touchstones of an abandoned pragmatism after the 2003 invasion spiraled into chaos. Colin Powell, chairman of the Joint Chiefs of Staff during the first Gulf War and secretary of state when the later invasion took place, for example, opposed advancing to Baghdad in 1991 after drawing a provocative lesson from Pearl Harbor. In a 1995 memoir, Powell devoted several pages to how he was influenced at the time by a book documenting "the scant thought the Japanese had given to how the war they started would end." General Norman Schwarzkopf, who commanded Desert Storm, retrospectively placed his endorsement of not invading Baghdad in a different historical context. There was the problem of "legitimacy" in the court of international and domestic opinion, he observed, a lesson painfully learned earlier in Vietnam. Had his forces gone on to Baghdad, "I think we'd still be there. We'd be like a dinosaur in a tar pit. We could not have gotten out and we'd still be the occupying power and we'd be paying 100 percent of all the costs to administer all of Iraq." The first President Bush joined his strategic adviser Brent Scowcroft in offering a similar retrospective explanation in 1998. "Trying to eliminate Saddam," they argued, "would have incurred incalculable human and political costs. . . . Had we gone the invasion route, the United States could conceivably still be an occupying power in a bitterly hostile land. It would have been a dramatically different—and perhaps barren—outcome."[120]

The secretary of defense at the time of the first Gulf War couched the issue firmly in the language of Vietnam's great lesson: *quagmire*. "I think for us to get American military personnel involved in a civil war inside Iraq would literally be a quagmire," he explained to a nationwide television audience. "Once we got to Baghdad, what would we do? Who would we put in power? What kind of government would we have? . . . I do not think the United States wants to have U.S. military forces accept casualties and accept the responsibility of trying to govern Iraq. I think it makes no sense at all." The defense secretary was Dick Cheney, who as vice president to the second President Bush ignored these arguments and became a major force behind the decision to bring about Iraqi "regime change" by force. Several years after occupied Iraq had become the quagmire he once warned about, Cheney was asked how to reconcile what he argued in 1991 and disregarded later. "Well, I stand by what I said in '91," he replied. "But look what's happened since then—we had 9/11."[121]

Ignoring the human costs of post–Gulf War sanctions on Iraq amounted to amnesia of a different sort, albeit with equally costly consequences when it came to failing to take account of widely held perceptions in the Muslim and Arab world. One of the earliest reports addressing infant and child mortality appeared in a 1992 issue of the *New England Journal of Medicine* and came to this widely cited conclusion: "These results provide strong evidence that the Gulf war and trade sanctions caused a threefold increase in mortality among Iraqi children under five years of age. We estimate that an excess of more than 46,900 children died between January and August 1991." Subsequent studies as well as emotional personal observations indicated that this morbidity was accelerated by the continuation of the embargoes. Politically decisive in drawing public attention was a letter by two UN-affiliated researchers published in the British medical journal *Lancet* in December 1995, which concluded that "since August, 1990, 567,000 children in Iraq have died as a consequence" of the UN-sanctioned embargo.[122]

Such high numbers—and their causes—were challenged from various directions, and the 1995 estimate was eventually lowered by other investigators, as well as by the authors of the original letter. But the tragedy remained. Numerous follow-up studies generally concurred that "excess deaths" among Iraqi children under five in the 1990s were more than double that of the 1980s. Figures endorsed by a reputable researcher for the entire period from 1991 to 2002, for example, placed the probable range of deaths from the war and subsequent sanctions at between 343,900 and 529,000. Neither official Washington nor official London challenged these inexact but enormous numbers. The political task was how to spin them, and Britain's Prime Minister Tony Blair gave perfect voice to the agreed-upon line in a joint press conference with the second President Bush at Camp David on March 27, 2003, as Operation Iraqi Freedom was underway. "Over the past five years," he observed, "400,000 Iraqi children under the age of five died of malnutrition and disease, preventively, but died because of the nature of the regime under which they are living. Now, that is why we're acting."[123]

The most notorious moment in the sanctions debate took place seven years earlier, in a televised exchange with Madeleine Albright, then serving as ambassador to the United Nations. Albright was interviewed in May 1996, when the high estimate of December 1995 was attracting great attention, and described the U.S. position as follows:

> *Interviewer*: We have heard that a half a million children have died. I mean, that's more children than died in Hiroshima. And—and, you know, is the price worth it?
>
> *Ambassador Albright*: I think this is a very hard choice, but the price—we think the price is worth it.

Albright later attempted to retract these careless words and place responsibility entirely on Saddam Hussein. She had "fallen into the trap" by the questioning, she claimed, but the episode did her no harm domestically. Seven months later she was approved to be secretary of state by the Senate. During her confirmation hearings, she stood fast in support of "maintaining tough UN sanctions against Iraq unless and until that regime complies with relevant Security Council resolutions."[124]

Opinion outside the United States was less complacent. In his 1998 New Year's greeting to diplomats at the Vatican, Pope John Paul II called attention to "our brothers and sisters in Iraq, living under a pitiless embargo," and called for placing compassion above political, economic, and strategic considerations. "The weak and innocent," the pope declared, "cannot pay for mistakes for which they are not responsible." Later that year Denis Halliday, the Irish "humanitarian coordinator" for the United Nations in Iraq, resigned because he no longer wished to be part of a situation in which sanctions were "starving to death 6,000 Iraqi infants every month, ignoring the human rights of ordinary Iraqis and turning a whole generation against the West." He was unwilling, he said, "to administer a program that satisfies the definition of genocide." Halliday's successor Hans von Sponeck, a German national, resigned early in 2000, declaring that sanctions had created a "true human tragedy."[125]

By the late 1990s, criticism of the sanctions came from many directions. On the one hand, the humanitarian crisis posed a "moral dilemma" for the United Nations and all who supported this policy (the phrase is from Kofi Annan, the UN secretary-general). On the other hand, rather than undermining Saddam's hold on power, the embargo helped strengthen it—while simultaneously ruining Iraq and intensifying anger throughout the Middle East. An essay in a military journal published by the U.S. Army War College shortly after 9-11 drew these moral and pragmatic arguments together concisely, noting that the sanctions had strengthened the Iraqi government's control of the economy, increased poverty nationwide, triggered emigration by members of the professional classes, and "retarded the emergence of a middle class and civil society."[126]

CREATING HAVOC AND suffering from a safe distance stunts the imagination. Morality as well as sensitivity to the psychology of others becomes dulled; so does plain practical comprehension of destruction so far away that it becomes abstract. This was certainly the case in the Pacific War. Almost to a man, Americans setting foot in defeated Japan in 1945, after a U.S. bombing campaign that leveled over sixty urban areas, expressed astonishment at discovering that great cities had been turned into rubble and millions made homeless. Much the same reaction characterized the Americans who occupied Baghdad in the spring of 2003 and were astonished not only to find no lethal arsenals, but also to discover that a dozen years of strategic policy aimed at creating "system paralysis" had indeed paralyzed the system almost beyond repair. This was precisely the response of L. Paul Bremer, who became head of the occupation government in May 2003. Nothing in the "frantic round" of briefings he received in Washington before leaving for Iraq, Bremer later recalled, had given him "a sense of how utterly *broken* this country was."

Bremer, on the other hand, had no doubts about what caused this: a combination of Saddam's brutality and corruption, and the dictator's "cockeyed socialist economic theory" that "had all but destroyed the country's middle class and private sector." Decades of chronic mismanagement under "the Baathist command economy" had left the economy devastated—crippled by "state monopolies" and strangled by "distorting subsidies" that kept prices artificially low. No one could deny the widespread malnutrition and premature death among destitute Iraqi children the invaders of 2003 encountered, but to argue that the sanctions had caused this, Bremer declared, was nothing more than "the official Baathist propaganda line."[127]

As Robert Fisk put it, when the Operation Iraqi Freedom liberators settled into the vacated palaces in Baghdad, sanctions "were 'ghosted' out of the story. First there had been Saddam, and then there was 'freedom.'"[128]

# WARS OF CHOICE AND STRATEGIC IMBECILITIES

## *Pearl Harbor and "Operation Iraqi Freedom"*

Nine hours after the Japanese caught Admiral Kimmel's fleet by surprise at Pearl Harbor and pounded the fighter planes General Short had ordered grouped in the middle of airfields as defense against sabotage by Japanese Americans, they attacked General MacArthur's forces in the Philippines. MacArthur's planes, too, were caught on the ground and became sitting targets. Just the day before, the general had explained that the Philippines were beyond the range of any possible Japanese air attack. Immediately after the assault, MacArthur among others reported that white men had been seen piloting some of the attacking aircraft. They were presumably Germans.[129]

That MacArthur survived and prospered after such negligence while his counterparts in Hawaii were cashiered and disgraced is one of the better examples we have that the Fates, along with politicians and military establishments, engage in whimsy. Six decades later, such whimsy had a second act of sorts as the president and his closest advisers concluded that Iraq must be piloting Al Qaeda. This was the implication of Deputy Secretary of Defense Wolfowitz's immediate response that the September 11 attacks were "too sophisticated" for a terrorist group and had to have a "state sponsor."[130]

MacArthur's delusion came and went in a moment, however, whereas the Bush administration's attempt to weld terrorism to state sponsorship became the core of its war on terror. Ultimately, this argument rested on more than assumptions of a link between 9-11 and Iraq. It tapped already existing fears about Saddam's megalomania and Iraq's potential for producing chemical, biological, and nuclear weapons; conflated one Middle East evil with another; and made politically feasible what many conservatives had advocated since the early 1990s: bringing about "regime change" in Iraq.

Whatever the exact mix of hard analysis, ideological fervor, apocalyptic fantasy, and sheer purblind panic, this shift of focus from an elusive non-state menace to a single nation had dire consequences. Instead of concentrating on running bin Laden and Al Qaeda to the ground in Afghanistan, attention and resources were diverted to overthrowing Saddam's police state. Instead of learning from the failure of imagination exposed by 9-11, Washington's war planners compounded this by continuing to ignore circumstances—like foreign occupation, one of bin Laden's favorite rhetorical targets—that helped exacerbate grievances and draw recruits to terrorism in the first place. Instead of confronting and ending the bureaucratic turf wars and personality clashes so rife before 9-11, internecine discord became even more intense. In his rush to war with Iraq, and for years to come, Bush presided over an administration and bureaucracy that was fractious and ultimately incompetent to an extreme.[131]

The war of choice against Iraq rested on more than mere disregard of the fact that Great Power heavy-handedness had inflamed anti-Western sentiment in the first place. It also reflected a perverse refusal to acknowledge the lesson bin Laden had learned from the Soviet defeat in Afghanistan: that even so-called superpowers were vulnerable to "asymmetrical" resistance. Despite the fact that Al Qaeda and the threat terrorism posed bore no resemblance to the massed enemies faced in World War II, the president and his war planners were drawn, like moths to flame, to deploying overwhelming force and sophisticated hardware in "lean" but essentially conventional ways. That was easier and more exciting to plan, and held out greater promise of individual glory for a self-described "war president" and his commanders.

Like MacArthur, the president and his advisers were allowed to soldier on. Even after the reasons given for initiating war had been proved false, and after Iraq had fallen into chaos, the U.S. electorate returned Bush to office for a second term. But the comparison only goes so far. Three years and nine months after his debacle in the Philippines, MacArthur stood on the battleship *Missouri* in Tokyo Bay as a conquering hero. World War II had ended with unconditional surrender of the last of the Axis powers. After a much longer stretch of time had followed Operation Iraqi Freedom, Bush and his speechwriters and supporters, so enamored of drawing analogies to World War II, could only look at the Middle East and weep. The president left office five years and nine months after U.S. forces entered Baghdad, with Iraq still torn and ravaged and Islamist holy warriors again on the rise in Afghanistan.

AT FIRST GLANCE it seems outlandish to compare the invasion of Iraq to Japan's attack on Pearl Harbor and its advance into Southeast Asia. Prior to the launch of Operation Iraqi Freedom, no one asked if or where the United States was preparing to strike. Rather, the prelude to war against Iraq was a carnival of saber rattling, and the question was simply "when?" The only thing surprising about the invasion when it came was the absence of preparation for post-hostilities stabilization and occupation—the absence, that is, of serious contingency planning and a carefully considered endgame. That in itself, however, is a striking point of comparison.

Like Japan's war of choice in December 1941, Operation Iraqi Freedom was a tactical military success and strategic disaster. Top-level policy makers in both cases underestimated the psychology and resourcefulness of their adversary and plunged into a conflict they could not control. In the inner sanctums of the state, people of reason were timid in pressing their reservations, loyal to authority rather than driven by the courage of their convictions, quickly co-opted, or abruptly marginalized. Ideology, emotion, and wishful thinking overrode rationality at the highest level, and criticism was tarred with an onus of defeatism, moral weakness, even intimations of treason once the machinery of war was actually set in motion. This was true of Tokyo, and no less true of Washington six decades later.

The strategic failure of these wars is not the only measure of comparison. The basic issue was launching a war of choice—and doing so based on questionable arguments of peril and transparent disdain for international law and opinion, as well as for any truly serious pursuit of alternatives short of military force. As Arthur Schlesinger and a small number of other critics remarked even before things fell apart in Iraq, "Pearl Harbor" abruptly became code for something very different from what it had signified after September 11—namely, unpreparedness, victimization, a stab in America's back by a treacherous foe. By initiating war against Iraq, the Bush administration had placed the stigma of "infamy" not just on Al Qaeda and Islamist terror, but now on the United States as well.[132]

From this perspective, even before the administration's basic arguments for invasion (weapons of mass destruction and close Iraq–Al Qaeda links) turned out to be unfounded, the U.S. war of choice undercut the laws and values America claimed to be upholding. This was a practical, and not just moral, issue. The unilateral choice of war dissipated much of the global support that followed 9-11, played into the hands of those already primed to accuse the United States of double standards, and undermined the intangible aura of legitimacy that helps buttress power and authority.

To critics of such criticism, comparing this war of choice to Japan's in 1941 was and remains a preposterous analogy. Unlike imperial Japan, the rebuttal runs—indeed, unlike any empire or initiator of hostilities the world has ever seen—America's reasons for choosing war were both defensive and humane, its intentions were idealistic and constructive, and its deployment of power was restrained. Saddam Hussein's "republic of fear" can in no way be compared to the American democracy Japan attacked in 1941. By the same measure, it borders on defamation to place the ghosts of the emperor and his warlords in the same room as President Bush and his hard-line but still well-intentioned advisers.[133]

Fundamental differences between imperial Japan and the conservative America of the Bush administration are indeed plentiful. Japan was a constitutional monarchy, after all, and not a republic—its populace "subjects" rather than "citizens." Every schoolchild was taught the myth that Hirohito was the 124th emperor in a dynasty dating back to 660 BCE (making 1940 the 2,600th anniversary of unbroken imperial rule). Under the Meiji Constitution of 1889, the throne and its occupant were "sacred and inviolable," and the rallying cry under which the emperor's subjects were mobilized for war beginning in the late 1930s was defense of the "Imperial Way" (Kōdō). The political ideals of "freedom," "democracy," and "free markets and free trade" that the Bush administration evoked in defending its preemptive war were anathema to Japan's wartime ideologues. Japan's expansive slogan was "co-existence and co-prosperity" in Asia. Its more specific goal in China was preserving economic lifelines with the continent by enforcing "stability" in a chaotic world of warlords, nationalists, communists, and "bandits" (the guerrilla resistance).[134]

Differences are just as striking when it comes to power, prosperity, and vulnerability. Japan was militarily dwarfed by the adversaries it chose to take on in attacking the United States and European colonial powers in Southeast Asia. As a consequence, the element of perceived risk in its war of choice in 1941 was vastly greater than it appeared to be for the United States in attacking Saddam's rickety police state. Japan was also a relatively poor nation, whose people were called on to sacrifice, literally, everything for the holy war. A few weeks after 9-11, President Bush urged Americans to restore confidence in the airline industry by flying and enjoying "America's great destination spots," visiting "Disney World in Florida," enjoying life with their families "the way we want it to be enjoyed"— a message he never abandoned. More than three and a half years after invading Iraq, in a press conference during the 2006 Christmas holidays, the president's words were "I encourage you all to go shopping more." By contrast, one of the drumbeat slogans in wartime Japan was Zeitaku wa teki: "Extravagance is the enemy." Another, after U.S. bombing of the home islands commenced, was the exhortation that all of the emperor's loyal subjects be prepared to die like the kamikaze (Ichioku tokkōtai). Every Japanese family eventually felt the bite of war, materially and in kin and acquaintances lost.[135]

Differences diminish, however, when we set the emperor and his minis-ters, generals, and admirals against the president and his intimate advisers and observe them unleashing the dogs of war. The language they speak in each instance is similar in its nationalism and righteousness. The geo-political vision in both cases is radical in its willingness to break the mold of the existing international order (and domestic order as well: these went hand in hand).[136] Like the Bush administration moving inexorably into war, Japan's leaders were obsessed with threats to national security and never questioned the justness of their cause: they would simultaneously defend the nation and bring stability and prosperity to Asia. Their secret deliberations were laced with concrete information and ostensibly rea-sonable arguments, as well as genuflection to the goal of creating a more stable world. They were, in their own eyes, moral and rational men. That the nation's actions, and their own, so often belied their words did not trouble them or even register upon them.

At this cloistered level of strategic planning, the most conspicuous differences between the Japanese and Americans lay in the realms of confidence and modus operandi. As a rule, decision making on the Japa-nese side took place in a more formal and regular manner than was the case in Bush's rush to war with Iraq. Hardball politics ran rampant in the Pentagon and White House, and individuals close to the president seem to have spent considerable time trying to read his "body language." The risk of taking on the United States gave Japan's leaders such seri-ous pause that for a while they clung feebly to the hope that Wash-ington could be persuaded to appease Japan's "reasonable" demands in Asia, particularly in China. As late as early November, Prime Minis-ter Tōjō was still telling subordinates he hoped talks with the United States would succeed. Conversely, there is little evidence that desire for a diplomatic solution with Iraq seriously influenced Bush and his war planners, despite their reluctant acquiescence in bringing the United Nations into the picture.[137]

To compare the decision making that led to these two very different wars of choice is to enter a veritable hall of cracked mirrors. Still, what is reflected quite clearly is a process and mindset antithetical to the ratio-nality both sides believed themselves to be exercising: shortsighted, dog-matic, delusory, a tragic exercise in "groupthink" by individuals of broad experience and considerable shrewdness who turned out to be careless and lacking in wisdom.

The two wars of choice also reinforce old lessons one would have expected military planners to know by heart: that once war preparations have been set in motion, they quickly reach a point at which there is no turning back; and most wars, easy to initiate, prove difficult and costly to end. Language and rhetoric themselves become a prison, and the machinery of destruction has its own momentum.

## The Emperor System and Imperial Presidency

In imperial Japan the decision for war was made within a constitutional monarchy that included a bicameral parliament, the Diet, which exercised control over the budget. Composed of a House of Peers and elective House of Representatives, the Diet essentially served as a rubber stamp for the nation's war policies. "Peace preservation" legislation dating back to the 1920s, which equated criticism of national policy with *lèse-majesté*, led to imprisonment of outspoken critics of the government, and at the time of Pearl Harbor many hundreds of unrepentant and mostly left-wing individuals remained incarcerated. (Most Japanese communists recanted and threw themselves behind "revolution under the brocade banner" of the imperial system—a subject of anguished debate in leftist circles after the war.) Formal censorship existed, but the media largely censored itself.

There was no legislative counterpart in imperial Japan to the congressional resolution of October 2002 that authorized President Bush to use military force against Iraq, and less public criticism overall to the government's policies than occurred in post–9-11 America. Military officers and politicians who criticized the war policy in China or the decision to attack the United States and European colonial powers were censured. (The best-known examples are the firebrand general Kanji Ishiwara, who played a central role in the Manchurian Incident in 1931 but opposed taking on America, and the Diet member Takeo Saitō, who was expelled from the parliament by his fellow party politicians in February 1940 for criticism of policy in China deemed "blasphemy against the holy war.") One harsh, reasonable appraisal by Japanese academics concludes that after 1931 the political parties in the parliament "seemed cast almost in

the role of a court fool whose antics were at the service of those in power."
The Republican-controlled Congress that endorsed the Bush administration's war policies between 2001 and 2006 did not descend to the level of
entirely silencing dissent.[138]

Despite such differences, however, the Japanese and U.S. cases hardly
amount to sharply contrasting examples of authoritarian rule versus democratic checks and balances. Congress did not seriously challenge the
rush to war, or investigate the deceptions that accompanied this and were
quickly exposed. Nor did Congress move to end practices that violated
international and domestic laws, such as torture and arbitrary detention
of prisoners. For all practical purposes, the legislative branch was passive
and complaisant and the mainstream media a mouthpiece for executive
policies presented in the name of national security. Particularly in times
of crisis and overseas conflict, the "obedient herd"—that most popular of
dismissive English-language phrases for the Japanese at war—turns out to
brand American behavior as well.

Under the Meiji Constitution, the emperor's prerogatives as a constitutional monarch essentially detached him from the policy-making process
itself. Even while designating him the head of state and nominal supreme
commander, the constitution made clear that "the Emperor exercises the
legislative power with the consent of the Imperial Diet." While he had the
right to issue imperial ordinances, "no Ordinance shall in any way alter
any of the existing laws." The dividing line between reigning and ruling
was porous, and the emperor ultimately threw his weight and enormous
symbolic authority behind the militarists. Unlike the president, however,
he did not initiate and drive high policy.

At the leadership level beneath the monarch, Japan's parliamentary
system actually resulted in more give-and-play—more holding leaders to
account for policy failures—than within the presidential system under the
Bush administration. Japan saw three prime ministers and scores of different cabinet ministers between Pearl Harbor and the end of the war
in August 1945. Prime Minister Tōjō, who also held the war minister's
portfolio, lost his job in July 1944, thirty-one months after Pearl Harbor,
when the debacle of his war of choice became clear. His successor, Kuniaki
Koiso, was forced to step down early in April 1945, following the loss of
the Philippines and commencement of urban bombing by U.S. air forces.

No single individual, not even the emperor, wielded decision-making power commensurate to the authority President Bush exercised; and no Japanese advisers exerted influence on the emperor or prime minister as great as that exercised by the few individuals who had the president's ear. In practice, the imperial presidency under George W. Bush was in certain critical respects more absolute, inviolate, impenetrable, and arbitrary than the militaristic government that took imperial Japan to war.

The top-level decision making that culminated in Pearl Harbor and Japan's "move South" took place in regular meetings of a so-called Liaison Conference composed of six civilian and military officials: the prime minister, war (army) and navy ministers, army and navy chiefs of staff, and foreign minister. Under constitutional stipulations concerning the "right of supreme command," the military establishment was responsible only to the emperor—giving it the ability, among other things, to make and break cabinets by its control over the military-service appointments. Major decisions reached in Liaison Conferences were formally approved in infrequent Imperial Conferences conducted in the presence of the emperor and involving additional high-level civilian and military officials. The emperor spoke only rarely, but all decisions required his formal approval. Between mid-April and early December of 1941, the government convened fifty-seven Liaison Conferences and four Imperial Conferences. Minutes from these meetings that survived Japan's defeat enable us to reconstruct with considerable precision how and why the nation's leaders chose war.[139]

No comparable secret records are available for the Bush administration. Quite likely they never will be in full; but certain comparisons to the Japanese war planners can be ventured. In the U.S. case, the tidy flow charts of the decision-making process suggest a rationalized structure analogous to the Liaison and Imperial Conferences. In theory, that is, deliberations and recommendations within U.S. civilian and military agencies moved up the ladder through a hierarchy of interagency committees ultimately culminating in the National Security Council, whose regular attendees were the president, vice president, national security adviser, and secretaries of state, defense, and treasury. Other high officials also routinely participated in NSC meetings, including the chair of the Joint Chiefs of Staff, director of the Central Intelligence Agency, White House chief of staff and legal counsel, and others. When the NSC met without the president, it was

called the Principals Committee. The top non–cabinet-level policy committee below this was the Deputies Committee, whose chief participants
were deputy or under secretaries and their military counterparts.[140]

However orderly this may appear on paper, insider accounts reveal that
the bureaucratic process was largely broken in practice. Analyses and recommendations by specialists at lower levels were often ignored; turf wars
and intensely personalized disagreements crippled the procedure at higher
levels; and the president himself was not interested in serious or protracted
policy debates. On the contrary, President Bush took pride in being a
"big-picture" executive who relied primarily on his "gut" instincts—and,
as it transpired, on the advice of a coterie led by Vice President Cheney,
Defense Secretary Rumsfeld, and to a lesser degree National Security
Adviser Rice. All leaders rely on intimate advisers, but the modus operandi in this administration was particularly arbitrary and perverse.

Even admirers of Bush and Rumsfeld like Douglas Feith—the Pentagon's under secretary of defense for policy, who contributed to formulating
the rationale for preemptive war—later targeted the "lack of clarity" of "the
interagency decision-making process" as responsible for the fiasco in Iraq.
"Interagency discord," he argued, began before 9-11 and "confounded the
President's Iraq policy from the outset of the Administration." Feith was
particularly incensed by friction over planning post-invasion policy that
grew ever more intense between the Defense and State departments, but
his partisan horror story of bureaucratic discord was more shotgun than
rifle, targeting turf wars within the Defense Department and extending
to Pentagon clashes with the CIA, NSC, CENTCOM (military Central
Command responsible for Operation Iraqi Freedom), and the Coalition
Provisional Authority that was ultimately established in Iraq.[141]

Feith's account adds intimate detail to what the 9-11 Commission and
almost every other commentary on the September 11 disaster pointed out:
turf wars, fiefdoms, impenetrable administrative walls, and other organizational obstacles to communication and collaboration made coherent
policy making close to impossible. Personal rivalries, which Feith gnaws
like a bone, likewise played a destructive role in planning circles after Al
Qaeda's attack, as was the case before it. Where war planning vis-à-vis Iraq
is concerned, however, these institutional and personal pathologies take
on a different light, for in this case the intelligence failure involved offen-

sive rather than defensive planning. The United States, as the aggressor, controlled the planning routines and timetables—and the failure of the flow charts to reflect the realities of war planning involved more than just "interagency discord." Underlying all was a concerted effort to strengthen executive power in theory and exercise it almost unilaterally in practice—if necessary, by simply gaming the system.[142]

In the legalistic jargon of the Oval Office, this aggrandizement of presidential power was known as the concept of the "unitary executive." In more familiar lay terms, it amounted to an attempt to restore and enhance an "imperial presidency" that, in conservative eyes, had been seriously weakened after the Watergate scandal and resignation of Richard Nixon in 1974. Put even more strongly, this strengthening of presidential prerogatives, at the expense of Congress and the judiciary, amounted to what Americans call authoritarian governance when practiced by others, even dictatorship of a sort. The political scientist Sheldon Wolin goes so far as to analyze this as a form of "inverted totalitarianism." Turf wars without question impeded rational policy formulation, but those who controlled power at the center, led by the Office of the Vice President, were not interested in the opinions of lower-level analysts and officials. They concluded early on that war with Iraq was necessary, and heard what they wished to hear. They did not wish to hear warnings of disaster.[143]

Early in the Bush administration, a few top officials gave themselves the half-humorous, half-pretentious nickname "the Vulcans." Composed of Cheney, Rumsfeld, Rice, Secretary of State Powell, Deputy Secretary of Defense Wolfowitz, and Deputy Secretary of State Armitage, the group's early cohesion soon disintegrated over the big question of going to war with Iraq and the smaller issue of whether the United States should support a major role for Iraqi exiles in the post-invasion transitional period. Cheney and the Pentagon deemed "the externals" essential to a quick invasion and withdrawal of U.S. forces; the State Department argued that U.S. imposition of such a transitional government would lack legitimacy; and the national security adviser did nothing to resolve that disagreement or focus the president's attention on it. In the end, the Vulcans proved incapable of forging a coherent policy, and their impasse and negligence abetted an imperial presidency more fixated on waging war than planning peace or addressing the root causes of terror and insurgency.[144]

Once the debacle of the invasion and occupation became clear, many formerly loyal insiders took to publicly describing the administration's decision-making process in ways as damning as anything usually used to describe Japan's so-called warlords and *gunbatsu*, or "military cliques." Five secretive and inordinately influential lawyers in the White House and Justice Department who devoted themselves to eliminating obstacles to the exercise of executive power, it was learned, had styled themselves the "War Council." It was their shoddy legal opinions that later came to public notice as the shameful "torture memos" authorizing brutal interrogation of prisoners. This, however, was but one of countless manifestations of executive imperiousness. Journalists as well as players like Feith, for example, went further to reveal that actual policy formulation frequently took place in the process of writing presidential speeches, with the president and his ghostwriters operating on the assumption that they could either "take or leave" what had been decided in the formal interagency process.[145]

The rationale for an imperial presidency rests on the seemingly reasonable argument that, particularly in time of peril, the executive branch must be unencumbered in acting swiftly based on its superior access to classified information. Numerous insider accounts, however, concur that in practice this authority was wantonly abused. Paul Pillar, the CIA's national intelligence officer for the Near East and South Asia at the time, went public in 2006 to argue that although the CIA was wrong on weapons of mass destruction, the Bush administration "went to war without requesting—and evidently without being influenced by—any strategic-level intelligence assessments" on other pertinent issues regarding Iraq. A year later, he expanded on this. "There was no meeting, no policy-options paper, no showdown in the Situation Room where the wisdom of going to war was debated or the decision to do so made," he reported. "And this meant scant opportunity to inject judgments, invited or uninvited, that should have been central to the decision." "Cherry-picking," "sugarcoating," "politicization of intelligence," "policymaker self-deception"—all emphasized in Pillar's indictment—became staples of insider commentaries. Richard Haass, head of the State Department's Policy Planning Staff at the time, who supported the decision to go to war with reservation, later reinforced such revelations in describing his own experience. "There was no meeting or set of meetings," Haass wrote, "at which the pros and cons were debated and a formal decision taken."[146] The administration essentially slithered into war like the rattlesnake on old American flags bearing the motto "Don't tread on me."

The most scalding early public criticism of this modus operandi by an insider came from Lawrence Wilkerson, a retired army colonel who served as chief of staff to Secretary of State Powell. In a widely cited presentation in October 2005, Wilkerson offered this denunciation of what he called an "Oval Office cabal":

> The case that I saw for four-plus years was a case that I have never seen in my studies of aberrations, bastardizations, perturbations, changes to the national security decision-making process. What I saw was a cabal between the vice president of the United States, Richard Cheney, and the secretary of defense, Donald Rumsfeld, on critical issues that made decisions that the bureaucracy did not even know were being made. And then when the bureaucracy was presented with the decisions to carry them out, it was presented in such a disjointed, incredible way that the bureaucracy often didn't know what it was doing as it moved to carry them out.[147]

The detailed minutes of the 1941 Liaison and Imperial Conferences suggest that Japan's war planners, delusory and clique-riddled as they were, were at least relatively conventional and imperturbable by comparison when it came to following established procedures.

WHERE PERSONAL EXECUTIVE style is concerned, President Bush was indisputably more assertive and actively engaged in choosing war than Emperor Hirohito. The emperor's position was hereditary, and he reigned for life. While his authority as sovereign was constitutionally "sacred and inviolable," and he was nominally (like the U.S. president) supreme commander of the armed forces, his charisma was largely institutional and his input into decision making largely passive. War-related proclamations known as imperial rescripts were issued in his name, and from the beginning of open aggression against China in the late 1930s he appeared in public in military uniform as the preeminent symbol of the war state and its ineffable Imperial Way values. Emperor Hirohito placed his enormous prestige behind both the China war and subsequent expanded hostilities, and conveyed support and displeasure to underlings in various ways. At the same time, however, he did not lead in any conventional sense. Until the very end of the war, when he announced Japan's capitulation on the radio, the emperor never addressed a single spoken word directly to his subjects.[148]

President Bush, like most other modern and contemporary leaders, never ceased to use the podium as a bully pulpit; nor was this the only way in which he displayed a personality antithetical to that of the austere and reticent emperor. It is unclear whether the president actually read important documents with any care, as opposed to relying on oral briefings and short written summations. What *is* clear is that he took pride in leaving details to others, was notoriously incurious about international affairs, exercised regularly, went to bed early, read the Bible upon awakening, was as Manichaean as his nemesis bin Laden in expostulating about good and evil, vacationed frequently, and had no hesitation in making decisions based on his instincts or intuition. As he told a reporter, "I'm not a textbook player; I'm a gut player."[149]

Hirohito, by contrast, was intensely interested in the minutia of policy, particularly regarding military affairs, in which he had been intimately educated as heir apparent. He was briefed in depth and sometimes ventured tactical queries and observations. His sense of decorum, including the peculiarly stilted courtly language he used both verbally and in formal proclamations, was also worlds apart from the president's style. The emperor, for example, is not recorded as ever yelling, "I don't care what the international lawyers say, we are going to kick some ass," as President Bush did in his first meeting with top advisers following the September 11 attack, or to have used language equivalent to the president's "Fuck Saddam. We're taking him out"; and the president never read a poem by his grandfather to his advisers, as Hirohito did at one critical Imperial Conference.[150]

At the same time, however, the president and emperor shared in common both institutional charisma and an inability to acknowledge and rectify error. Scholarly literature on Japan at war has long singled out the prolonged failure of Hirohito and his high command to accept that the war could not be won and to seriously seek a way out. Instead, long after the tide of battle turned in mid-1942, and even after the enemy had established bases within striking range of the home islands in late 1944, the response was simply more military madness: the suicidal kamikaze, the ghastly battles of Iwo Jima and Okinawa, exhortations that the entire populace be prepared to die "like a shattered jewel." Decision making came to resemble agitated sleepwalking, and proposals urging drastic reconsideration of the war policy fell on deaf ears.

Hirohito was the most eminent of the sleepwalkers—naturally distressed as the enemy approached and air raids began, but paralyzed, almost catatonic, when it came to responding constructively. Belatedly, some high advisers did vainly urge him to support a change of course— the most famous such entreaty was made in February 1945, before the firebombing of Japanese cities began—but most were awed by the throne and told the sovereign what he wished to hear: that fighting on remained the best policy. The pertinent academic phrase in this regard is "proximity to the throne"; such proximity conferred special authority, and at the same time inhibited speaking truth to power. Advisers hesitated to tell the sovereign that his holy war had become a debacle. Rather, they put the most optimistic gloss possible on reports of military disasters, arguing that ever greater sacrifice and bloodletting would eventually persuade the Americans to seek a compromise peace. As the war in Iraq dragged on for year after year, aspects of this "Imperial Palace" scenario almost seemed to have been transposed to the White House: denial, paralysis, evasion of accountability, the awed circle of court sycophants.[151]

The picture that emerges from such observations, for both imperial Japan and the United States decades later, is contradictory: contention and factionalism on the one hand, conformity and abject acquiescence on the other. In the popular anthropology of "East and West," it is a commonplace to emphasize the group orientation of the Japanese and the particular emphasis they place on harmony. "The hundred million" (*ichioku*) was the formulaic way Japan's ideologues framed this, as in "a hundred million hearts beating as one" (*ichioku isshin*; the actual population of wartime Japan was around seventy million). In Western parlance, such alleged harmony was turned into pejorative metaphors that tended to come from the insect or animal world. Bees (the "swarm," with the emperor as "the queen bee in a hive") and ant colonies were popular, for example, along with sheep and the obedient herd. Equally popular was depicting Japanese behavior as "tribal," with all the connotations this carried of being not merely narrowly group-oriented but also backward and even primitive. The contrast to Anglo-style individualism and the glorified Western hero who follows the dictates of his conscience could not have been drawn more starkly.[152]

This dichotomy, too, does not withstand close scrutiny. The shape-shifting notion of consensus—whether regarded as myth, reality, or curse—can indeed be useful in helping to understand Japan's war follies. "Consensus" is often just propaganda. Conversely, it may reflect negotiated understanding and rational compromise. Yet again, what is presented as consensus and mutual agreement may be little more than camouflage covering fundamental differences. This was standard operating procedure in the course of imperial Japan's march to war, where incompatible army and navy priorities and material demands, for example, were buried in official verbiage. A prize-winning study of Hirohito and the road to war, for example, emphasizes that Japan's bureaucratic elites tended to "line up their respective positions, side by side, in vague official texts that could be interpreted to suit the convenience of their drafters," thus "papering over their differences."[153]

There is nothing peculiarly Japanese or "non-Western," however, about engaging in a pretense of bureaucratic harmony. In the run-up to war with Iraq, much the same practice characterized U.S. policy making at the National Security Council level, where Condoleezza Rice tended to view disagreement as dysfunction, and took care to craft "bridging proposals" that buried interagency discord under a facade of unanimity. Such false appearance of agreement became a catastrophe when the United States had to actually execute post-invasion policy in Iraq. The nuts and bolts of who would bear responsibility in the "liberated" nation, and how and for how long, ripped away any illusion of consensus among the Pentagon, State Department, CENTCOM, and other parties. Feith, for one, argued that Rice's refusal to bring "clear-cut, mutually exclusive options" directly to the president amounted to "an approach that tended to paper over, rather than resolve, important differences of opinion. Her pursuit of harmony came, at times, at the expense of coherence." When American power brokers elevate "harmony" in this manner, it is treated as idiosyncratic and aberrant rather than a reflection of national character or a familiar technocratic slight of hand. To suggest otherwise challenges one more myth about American "exceptionalism."[154]

As agonizing over the failure to anticipate 9-11 spilled into agonizing over the recognition that Iraq did not possess weapons of mass destruction, and that the United States had no serious plans for what to do once it had overthrown Saddam, commentators across a broad spectrum moved en masse to blame *groupthink* for such colossal blundering. How else could one explain how, despite serious warnings at lower levels, an ill-planned war of choice ultimately became endorsed by the White House, Pentagon, State Department, National Security Council, intelligence community, Congress, mass media, U.S. populace at large, and faithful U.S. allies like the leaders of Great Britain and Japan? Groupthink had a largely buried history in American discourse dating back to the 1950s; and, as it happened, the resurrected popularity of the concept was reinforced by parallel shocks in the private sector—notably the succession of financial disasters that began with the collapse of Enron at the very end of 2001, mere months after 9-11.

The metaphoric obedient herd, like a slow-motion, soul-stealing, demonic reincarnation of the fleet that attacked Pearl Harbor, almost seemed to have crossed the Pacific and taken over America, unnoticed until too late. And when it came to spelling out what such American "groupthink" entailed, the traditional literature on Japan at war also provided a sister pejorative: *denial.*[155]

## Choosing War

When Ambassador Grew cabled Washington shortly before Pearl Harbor to warn that "Japanese sanity cannot be measured by American standards of logic," and this was only to be expected in a recently feudal society, he drew on ten years of experience dealing with Japan's ruling elites. Looking back on the secret minutes of the Japanese policy sessions that led to war in 1941, it is easy to agree that common sense was in short supply—but more provocative to observe that the outward forms of logical discussion were preserved. It is not difficult to imagine participants in the Liaison Conferences and Imperial Conferences looking in on President Bush and his cadre of Oval Office advisers and finding the tenor of discourse largely familiar, however jarring the cruder, more colloquial expressions of national purpose and resolve might be.

Like Bush and his advisers, Japan's military and political leaders were resilient individuals seasoned in wielding power. That is how they got to the top. All were obsessed with national security, believed the homeland imperiled, and never questioned that control over China was essential to Japan's well-being—and control over the resources of Southeast Asia, in turn, essential to resolve the stalled war in China. Like the planners of the Iraq war, they made at least a pretense at pursuing diplomacy while preparing for war; and, again similarly, they soon found themselves in a situation where the war preparations dictated the timetable and direction of policy making. Among other considerations, Japanese war plans were influenced by the impending onset of the monsoon season in Southeast Asia; the counterpart concern on the U.S. side was seasonal conditions in the desert combined with the need to wear heavy protective gear against possible chemical or biological weapons. Of greater impact in driving events was the buildup and priming of the massive attack forces themselves.

In the United States, the "principle of preemption" is usually traced back to the early 1990s, when this became an influential concept in the neoconservative intellectual circles that would come to exert inordinate influence in the Bush administration. After 9-11, this became public policy. When the president introduced the war-of-choice concept at West Point on June 1, 2002, he raised the specter of weapons of mass destruction falling into the hands of terrorists and declared that "we must take that battle to the enemy, disrupt his plans and confront the worst threats before they emerge." Americans, he went on to applause, must be "ready for pre-emptive action when necessary to defend our liberty and to defend our lives. . . . In the world we have entered, the only path to safety is the path of action. And this nation will act." This became formal policy almost exactly a year after 9-11 (on September 17, 2002) when it was incorporated in the "National Security Strategy of the United States of America."[156]

By this date the United States was firmly on the road to war. Although the point of no return occurred earlier, precisely when is a matter of dispute. Unlike in Japan, the ultimate decision lay in the hands of a single individual, the president; and he and his secretary of defense, among others, immediately conflated Iraq and Al Qaeda, Saddam Hussein and bin Laden. Five hours after terrorists crashed American Airlines Flight 77 into the Pentagon, when evidence already pointed to Al Qaeda, Rumsfeld's response, in the scribbled notes of an aide, was "judge whether good enough hit S.H. [Saddam Hussein]@ same time—Not just UBL [Usama—that is, Osama—bin Laden]. . . . go massive—sweep it all up—Things related and not." Going massive suited the president's temperament, and Bush called for preparation of a major new war plan for Iraq two months later, on November 21—some fourteen months before the invasion was launched. By early 2002, or mid-year at the latest, any number of military and civilian insiders had conclued that the president's commitment to war was unshakable.[157]

On the Japanese side, the first serious operational plans for attacking Pearl Harbor were drawn up in the spring of 1941, several months after Admiral Yamamoto first conceived of the plan. The first war games took place in September—shortly after an Imperial Conference on September 6 at which the emperor approved a document titled "Essentials for Carrying Out the Empire's Policy," which called for war unless, as seemed unlikely, a diplomatic solution could be reached with the United States. Thereafter, the war plans were virtually impossible to stop, although the Imperial Navy did not formally approve the Pearl Harbor attack until mid-October and the decisive rupture in diplomatic conversations between Tokyo and Washington did not occur until the final week of November. The attack force itself rendezvoused off the Kurile Islands on November 22 and set off on its mission several days later.

While there was no precise articulation of a "doctrine" of preemptive war on Japan's part—certainly not for public consumption—the transcripts of the policy conferences that preceded and followed the Imperial Conference on September 6 are peppered with essentially the same language of impending crisis that governed U.S. war planners after 9-11: "seize the initiative," "our nation . . . stands at a crossroad," "time is running out," "the time for war will not come later," and so on. The September 6 document itself enshrined the rationale for a war of choice in a mantra both generic and portable: "self-defense and self-preservation."[158]

As the inevitability of war became clear, Japan's leaders rode a rollercoaster that plunged to depths of anxiety and rose to heights of overconfidence—the inevitable adrenaline rush, perhaps, of most warlords girding for combat. In the heady moments of last-stage preparations, Japanese military planners even contemplated later campaigns against additional targets, most notably a "move North" against the Soviet Union in the spring of 1942 to secure Siberian resources. (This seemed feasible, and exceptionally tempting, after Germany launched "Operation Barbarossa," its massive invasion of the Soviet Union, in June 1941.) After their unexpectedly easy opening victories against U.S. and British forces, some of Japan's most zealous strategists even contemplated returning to seize and occupy Hawaii. In this regard, the strategic fantasizing of Japan's leaders was comparable to that of the most hawkish of the Bush administration's planners and supporters, who initially rhapsodized over the prospect of following a quick knock-off of Iraq with operations against the rest of the "axis of evil" (Iran and North Korea) and possibly a "five-year campaign" against at least five additional major targets (Syria, Lebanon, Libya, Somalia, and Sudan.)[159]

The military offensives of 1941 and 2003 also reflected a certain "high-tech" infatuation. The Iraq operation was promoted as a showcase for cutting-edge "smart weapons" and the "lean" military posture espoused by Rumsfeld—developments that reflected the "revolution in military planning" that had been promoted in defense circles since the early 1990s. Somewhat similarly, the Pearl Harbor attack amounted to a demonstration and apparent vindication of the radical "naval airpower" concepts advocated by Admiral Yamamoto in defiance of the Imperial Navy's old-school "battleship admirals."

Once hostilities were initiated, moreover, these strategies appeared to have been brilliantly conceived. The U.S. military campaign up to the occupation of Baghdad on April 9 impressed everyone inclined to be awed by massive firepower deployed with precision. Japan's battle plan was even more complex and impressive, involving almost three-score offensive operations in Southeast Asia and, six thousand miles distant, Hawaii—mostly against U.S. and British forces that could and should have been formidable. The parallel can be taken only so far, however. Whereas the Japanese proved scientifically, technologically, and industrially incapable of building on their early success, the twenty-first-century U.S. military machine never lost its overwhelming superiority in sophisticated war fighting. The U.S. problem, in Afghanistan as well as Iraq, was that brute force, no matter how technologically sophisticated, was inappropriate and counterproductive when it came to fighting elusive enemies embedded in complex communities.[160]

## Strategic Imbecilities

When Samuel Eliot Morison described Japan's war of choice against the United States as "strategic imbecility," he was lending his authority as one of America's best-known military historians to conventional opinion. Hand in hand with their immediate explosion of rage, in the immediate wake of Pearl Harbor commentators across America also took it for granted that the Japanese had gone mad. The *New York Times* ruminated editorially about "a military clique in Tokyo whose powers of self-deception now rise to a state of sublime insanity." While eschewing sublimity, the *Philadelphia Inquirer* similarly observed that "Army jingos in Tokyo threw reason to the winds and went berserk in an insane adventure that for fatalistic abandon is unsurpassed in the history of the world." The *Los Angeles Times* described the attack as "the act of a mad dog," while the *Chicago Tribune* saw war forced on America "by an insane clique of Japanese militarists who apparently see the desperate conduct into which they have led their country as the only thing that can prolong their power." The *Chicago Times*, postulating Nazi Germany behind the attack, spoke of "a mad military clique in Tokyo that made this war against us on orders of a madder military cabalism in Berlin."[161]

Winston Churchill, speaking before a joint session of the Congress on December 26, drew prolonged applause when, with his usual articulateness, he meshed intimation of Japanese insanity with promise of thoroughgoing retaliation. "When we consider the resources of the United States and the British Empire, compared to those of Japan, when we remember those of China, which has so long and valiantly withstood invasion, and when also we observe the Russian menace which hangs over Japan," the prime minister observed, "it becomes still more difficult to reconcile Japanese action with prudence, or even with sanity. What kind of a people do they think we are? Is it possible they do not realize that we shall never cease to persevere against them until they have been taught a lesson which they and the world will never forget."[162]

After Operation Iraqi Freedom turned into a fiasco, the accusatory language of strategic folly or imbecility was directed against U.S. war planners, eventually leading to Rumsfeld's resignation in December 2006. In one such critique, Rumsfeld and by extension his Pentagon's policy were denied even the virtue of tactical acumen. Calling for the secretary's resignation early in 2006, a retired general who had served in the opening stages of the Iraq invasion (Paul D. Eaton) declared that Rumsfeld had "shown himself incompetent strategically, operationally and tactically." Military officers and civilian bureaucrats who recognized this, he went on, were quickly cowed after the few who ventured countervailing views were ignored or forced to resign.[163] In short time, Operation Iraqi Freedom, initially lauded as a state-of-the-art military operation, became a subject of ridicule. ("Plan A was to get in and out quickly. Plan B was to hope Plan A worked.")

"Imbecility" and "fiasco" are descriptive rather than explanatory terms, and beg the question of how and why ostensibly rational civilian and military officials promoted such follies. Hideki Tōjō, who led Japan to war, was nicknamed "the Razor" because of his sharp military and bureaucratic intelligence. Donald Rumsfeld, sixty-nine years old when 9-11 occurred, had an exceptionally successful career in the private and public sectors and more than a few admirers who lavished praise on his competence and probing intellect. Even if one posits some fatal arrogance in these and other top leaders, this does not explain how they managed to carry entire governments and nations into disaster with them. For this, one must look to some of the shared cultures and psychologies of war making itself.

What was intoxicating for Japan's war planners in 1941 was also intoxicating for the American president and his military advisers after 9-11: offensive planning. By the same measure, negligible meaningful planning was devoted to closure or an endgame. This does not mean potentially ominous scenarios were ignored. Admiral Yamamoto was openly pessimistic about Japan's prospects in a long war, and the stunning success of the Pearl Harbor attack was greater than the war planners had anticipated insofar as loss in men, aircraft, and warships was concerned. Right up to the very moment of attack, more than a few high navy and army officers expressed reservations about Japan's logistical capability to engage in protracted hostilities, and (like the emperor) murmured their apprehensions before going along with the decision for war.[164]

33. *March 22, 2003: A Tomahawk Land Attack Missile launched from an offshore guided missile destroyer in the opening "shock and awe" stage of the Iraq war. Operation Iraqi Freedom became the code name of the invasion after the initially chosen name, Operation Iraqi Liberation, was recognized as producing an unfortunate acronym (OIL). The war began with a nighttime strike on a presidential residence on March 19. Formal invasion operations extended from March 20, when U.S. and British forces poured in from Kuwait, to May 1, when President Bush announced the end of major combat in his famous "Mission Accomplished" speech. Coalition forces entered Baghdad on April 5, and the capital was formally occupied four days later.*

34. *March 21: Baghdad burning.*

35. *March 29: A British marine encounters an Iraqi woman while on patrol in the port city of Umm Qasr in southern Iraq.*

*36. March 31: A hooded Iraqi taken prisoner during heavy fighting in the holy city of Najaf comforts his four-year-old son in a U.S. "regroupment center" for POWs.*

*37. April 9: U.S. marines cover one another with assault weapons as they take over one of Saddam Hussein's palaces in Baghdad. The inscription on the wall is a quotation from the Qur'an.*

*38. April 9: The statue of Saddam Hussein in Firdos Square is toppled from its pedestal by the first U.S. marines to reach the center of Baghdad. The square was closed off and almost empty of local people, and the event was stage-managed by American "psyops" personnel who supplied the armored vehicle and equipment used to pull the statue down. This was publicized in the United States and Britain as the spontaneous act of a joyous Iraqi crowd. More truly spontaneous and indicative of things to come was the orgy of looting and destruction of government buildings that followed the dictator's fall.*

U.S. war planners similarly raised questions in passing on many problems that could arise in attacking Iraq. Five months before the invasion, for example, Rumsfeld and a small group of aides produced a list of potential crises that eventually grew to some twenty-nine items. Grimly nicknamed the "Parade of Horribles" by Feith, the list was sobering by any standards. Possible calamities itemized included sabotage of oil production; humanitarian disasters (displaced persons, refugees, epidemics, and the like); higher-than-expected collateral damage; ethnic strife among Kurds, Sunnis, and Shia "as had happened before," and the possible fracture of the nation into two or three pieces; escalation into regional conflict including a possible Arab-Israeli war; a spike in terrorist recruiting as a result of the

*39. April 9: A U.S. marine covers the face of the statue of Saddam Hussein with the Stars and Stripes moments before the forty-foot figure is toppled—an impromptu and hastily corrected act that, to the acute embarrassment of war planners in Washington, gained lasting notoriety as a symbol of occupation and incisive expression of American arrogance.*

invasion; and even a protracted post-Saddam process of stabilization and reconstruction that (in Feith's summary) "could take not two to four years, but eight to ten years, absorbing U.S. leadership, military, and financial resources."[165]

The issue is not whether red flags were noted but whether they were taken seriously. They were not. A few years after stepping down as secretary of state in November 2004, Colin Powell ruminated about how Rumsfeld "had written a list of the worst things that could happen, but we didn't do the contingency planning on what we would do about it." Powell himself played no small role in letting this happen. In the course of a year and a half of war talk and serious war planning, he personally ventured only one truly serious attempt (in August 2002) to ask the president if he and Rumsfeld and their Pentagon team had "really thought through the after-

*40. April 16: A soldier weeps at a memorial service in Baghdad for Americans killed in Operation Iraqi Freedom.*

math." They had not, and did not; and that was the end of it. "That was the big mistake," Powell ruefully observed—an understatement indeed. What had happened to the "Pearl Harbor" lesson he had dwelled on at some length in his 1995 memoir in explaining his rationale for not invading Baghdad in 1991? What had become of Cheney's earlier premonition of a Vietnam-like "quagmire"? Taking worst-case scenarios seriously, as had been done in the first Gulf War, was now essentially taboo—evidence not of sobriety but of defeatism.[166]

The planning that culminated in both Pearl Harbor and the invasion of Iraq thus reflected a curious schizophrenia. The perceived threats that dictated a war of choice were framed apocalyptically: demise as a great nation with a secure and self-sufficient sphere of influence in Asia in Japan's case, Iraq-produced weapons of mass destruction in the hands of terrorists worldwide where the professed rationale for invading Iraq was concerned. Despite having conjured a formidable foe, however, when it came to concrete planning at the topmost level, neither the Japanese in 1941 nor the Americans after 9-11 gave serious attention to the long-term challenges that lay ahead.

■

AFTER JAPAN'S DEFEAT, this lack of a practical war plan was offered—even by many chastened Japanese—as evidence of a cultural propensity for irrational behavior. The major grand strategy document produced for consideration by the Liaison Conference a mere three weeks before Pearl Harbor (on November 15) amounted to a masterpiece of wishful thinking. "We will endeavor to quickly destroy American, British, and Dutch bases in the Far East, and assure our self-preservation and self-defense," the document began, and "at the same time to hasten the fall of the Chiang regime [in unoccupied China] by taking positive measures, to work for the surrender of Great Britain in cooperation with Germany and Italy, and to destroy the will of the United States to continue the war." The document anticipated that "at the appropriate time, we will endeavor by various means to lure the main fleet of the United States [to Pacific waters near Japan] and destroy it." Nothing else in this relatively short document was any more concrete than this.[167]

Immediately after their surrenders, the United States Strategic Bombing Survey sent researchers to Germany and Japan to assess the road to war and, in particular, the role of the air war in bringing about defeat of the two Axis powers. The Survey produced more than one hundred detailed reports on Japan alone, one of which opens by observing the discrepancy between Japan's war potential and its decision to initiate war with the United States: "The dividing line between erroneous calculations and adventurous irrationality in the conduct of national affairs is always difficult to draw. Considering retrospectively the policies which ultimately led Japan to the catastrophe of 7 December, it would be tempting to dismiss them summarily as expansionist megalomania of the Japanese war lords and to abandon all search for a rational scheme which could have guided the Japanese military and economic planners."

Such an opening note would seem to invite an explanation of Japan's folly along the lines of Joseph Grew's observations about semifeudal backwardness and inability to think logically. The Survey, however, warned (surely with the Grew-school pundits in mind) that such a facile explanation "would render an understanding of Japan's strategy impossible." No one could deny that Japan's rulers had committed grave mistakes over the preceding decade and a half, the gravest of them all being the war against the United States.

> Nevertheless, it was not "insanity" which drove them into disaster, nor can the fault be attributed solely to specific individuals in responsibility—it was a considered national policy whose pitfalls, however, were insufficiently appreciated—whose chances of success were inadequately gauged.[168]

An economist affiliated with the U.S. occupation forces reached a similar conclusion after analyzing the reams of data that became available after Japan's surrender. The nation's war plans, he wrote, were "characterized by . . . early confidence . . . lack of planning, poor administration and . . . internal conflict of interest." Policy makers were, in a word, "singularly lacking in foresight." George Sansom, who spent decades as chief analyst of the Japanese economy for the British Foreign Office, concurred that Japan's leaders "not only misjudged the strength of the enemy, but they prove to have overestimated their own power." Still, Sansom went on, "examined in retrospect their policy turns out to have been based upon mistaken assumptions and executed with insufficient foresight, but at the time when their decision was taken it was not irrational." Politically, they simply miscalculated that Germany would defeat Britain and Russia, and a compromise peace with the United States would then be possible.[169]

Such observations are all the more striking in the wake of the war of choice against Iraq. One can change Japan to the United States, Japan's leaders to U.S. leaders, December 1941 to March 2003, and these generalizations stand up just as well. Along this same line, an authoritative analysis of the air war in World War II published in the 1950s concluded that despite their high level of efficiency as of 1941, "the Japanese air forces were not prepared for a war of long duration. . . . Confident of an early victory, they discounted the potential strength of their enemies." Overconfidence in one's own capability, underestimating the enemy, and failing to prepare for a more protracted conflict: these, again, are essentially the explanations commonly offered to explain America's fiasco in Iraq.[170]

This is unsettling because the differences between Japan in 1941 and the United States in the twenty-first century are obvious: a second-rate power as opposed to a superpower, a militaristic and supposedly only superficially "modern" regime in contrast to a purported democracy. Neither stage of development nor "cultural" differences in the traditional sense, however, adequately account for the irrationality of ostensibly rational actors.

## Deception and Delusion

Mendacity and deception are standard operating procedure in the cultures of war, as in politics more generally. Legions of wordsmiths and crafters of visual imagery earn their keep by churning out truths, half-truths, imagined truths, iconic images, catchphrases, euphemisms, exaggerations, evasions, and outright lies—invariably, where war is at issue, with an eye on both foreign and domestic audiences. Imperial Japan's propagandists were masterly at playing this game in an age of pretelevision and pre-Internet mass communications. Radio, the print media, photography, and film were all exploited to promote overseas expansion and aggression.

Manchuria, for example, was seized in 1931 after rogue militarists in Japan's own Kwantung Army blew up a section of the Japan-controlled South Manchurian Railway and blamed it on anti-Japanese Manchurian leaders. A plot against Japan is how Japanese back home heard the story. Expanding Japan's sphere of influence on the continent was glossed as an "Asian 'Monroe Doctrine'" and "Greater East Asia Co-Prosperity Sphere"; replacing European and American colonial regimes with puppet governments under Japanese control was called liberation; and war photographs, newsreels, and feature films naturally portrayed brave Japanese fighting men rather than invaders engaged in oppression and atrocity. Propagandists continued to preach certain victory after the war turned against Japan and battles took place ever closer to the home islands.

Such propaganda and delusion continued to war's end, even after 1944 bled into 1945 and firebombs began destroying city after city. When the emperor addressed his subjects by radio in August 1945 to announce Japan's capitulation, words such as "defeat" and "surrender" were not mentioned. "The war situation has developed not necessarily to Japan's advantage," was the sovereign's euphemistic phrasing, "while the general trends of the

world have all turned against her interest." The enemy, Hirohito continued, had begun to employ "a new and most cruel bomb" that could "lead
to the total extinction of human civilization." The emperor was ordering
Japan's armed forces to lay down their arms not only to save his loyal subjects but also to save mankind.

Where the Bush administration is concerned, even the president's
former press secretary, Scott McClellan, later confessed to becoming
enmeshed in a "culture of deception." By the time of this mea culpa (in
2008), the administration's deceptions already had been exposed and
documented at great length. The intelligence expert Thomas Powers calculated early on that the ostensibly definitive official case for invading
Iraq—Secretary of State Powell's February 5, 2003, address to the United
Nations—advanced twenty-nine claims about Iraqi "weapons, programs,
behaviors, events, and munitions" that, almost without exception, proved
to be false or unverifiable in the months following the invasion. Frank
Rich of the *New York Times* drew together several years of his writings on
the subject in a 2006 collection titled *The Greatest Story Ever Sold*. In 2008,
the Select Committee on Intelligence in the Senate published a lengthy
report documenting the extent to which "the Administration's public
statements were NOT supported by the intelligence." Like the emperor's
loyal subjects, however, most Americans believed what their leaders told
them and supported the invasion. And like the Japanese or any other people, once the nation's troops had been placed in peril, it was regarded as
unthinkable not to support them no matter how duplicitous the originally
proclaimed *casus belli* had been.[171]

The administration's litany of lies is a dreary topic. The greater challenge is to understand the groupthink by which "spin" and deception
became indistinguishable from self-deception and outright delusion on
high—and how this in turn became accepted at all levels of society. In
the case of imperial Japan, the conventional wisdom is clear: censorship
and self-censorship, indoctrination, traditional cultural emphasis on "harmony" and "consensus," and the rudimentary nature of democratic institutions explain the obedient herd. But what, then, can be said about deception in war-of-choice America: that its vaunted individualism, democracy,
checks and balances, and rigorous "fourth estate" of independent investigative journalism are themselves delusions of a sort?

■

AFTER "LIBERATION" OF Iraq devolved into occupation, and occupation into savage violence, many specialists in the U.S. military and civilian bureaucracies revealed that they had attempted in vain to call attention to obstacles that made this particular war of choice exceptionally risky insofar as post-invasion stabilization and reconstruction were concerned. Their futility echoed the experience of counterterrorism experts in the CIA and National Security Council who were ignored prior to 9-11: top leaders listened only to what they were predisposed to hear. A secret British intelligence memorandum to Prime Minister Blair dated July 23, 2002, certainly reinforced this impression of rigidity. A sensation when brought to light after the invasion, this so-called Downing Street Memorandum concluded that "military action was now seen as inevitable" in Washington; that "Bush wanted to remove Saddam, through military action, justified by the conjunction of terrorism and WMD [weapons of mass destruction]"; that "the intelligence and facts were being fixed around the policy"; and that "there was little discussion in Washington of the aftermath after military action." General Wesley Clark had the same impression months later where postwar planning was concerned. "As I went through the Pentagon to check facts before my Senate testimony in September 2002," he recalled, "I was disappointed to learn that no more than a few discussions had taken place on postwar matters. 'Not a popular subject on the third floor [where Defense Department policy is decided by civilian leaders],' I was informed."[172]

The unpopularity of discussing "the aftermath of military action" looms large in explanations of the invasion fiasco, since so much of that debacle seemed to arise out of neglect of the most elemental of contingencies: immediately ensuring law and order. Iraqi exiles visiting Washington as early as August 2002 warned Cheney and Rumsfeld personally of the likelihood of looting once the Baathist regime was overthrown. This did not require exceptional imagination, for such lawlessness had erupted more than a decade previously in parts of Iraq where Saddam's control was temporarily weakened during the first Gulf War. The diplomat Peter Galbraith, who knew Iraq well, tendered the same warning months later, in January 2003, while serving as a professor at the Defense

Department's National War College. "Rapid collapse is much more likely than prolonged resistance," Galbraith predicted in a presentation that was subsequently published. "Based on the experience of 1991, however, I see chaos as more likely than an orderly surrender." It was his discouraging experience, however, that Pentagon planners shared the administration's fixation on making a political case for the war and were less interested in consulting him about what might happen after an invasion than they were in having him "talk about the evils of Saddam Hussein's regime, including the gassing of the Kurds." Where thinking beyond the invasion per se was concerned, little had changed at top levels in the half year that followed the writing of the Downing Street Memorandum.[173]

Galbraith's experience was typical. In December 2002, a month before his warning, for example, a two-day session at the Army War College involving some two dozen officers, diplomats, and Middle East experts resulted in a report that zeroed in on the familiar cliché about winning or losing the peace. "The possibility of the United States winning the war and losing the peace is real and serious," the report stated, offering this thinly disguised rebuke to those planning hostilities: "Thinking about the war now and the occupation later is not an acceptable solution." Much the same alarm was reiterated in two studies initiated at the urging of the CIA's Paul Pillar and prepared and circulated by the State Department's Policy Planning Staff in January 2003.

One of these studies, titled "Principal Challenges in Post-Saddam Iraq," began by observing that the "building of an Iraqi democracy would be a long, difficult and probably turbulent process, with potential for backsliding into Iraq's tradition of authoritarianism." The report went on to predict that "a post-Saddam authority would face a deeply divided society with a significant chance that domestic groups would engage in violent conflict." It also emphasized that, despite its oil resources, economic options were "few and narrow" and reconstruction would require measures comparable to the Marshall Plan for Europe after World War II.

The companion study, titled "Regional Consequences of Regime Change in Iraq," warned that "a U.S.-led war against and occupation of Iraq would boost political Islam and increase popular sympathy for some terrorist objectives, at least in the short term." As Pillar later observed— just as the Downing Street Memorandum predicted and Galbraith and countless others also later confirmed—there was no delusion that these assessments would "derail the policy train," since "the war-makers consistently and assiduously tuned out all types of expert and professional input (except when it suited their purposes). . . . On Iraq, the Bush Administration instead used the intelligence community to provide material to sell the public a foregone conclusion."[174]

Tuning out warnings requires that they be audible in the first place— and in fact many of these dire predictions *did* make it into high-level presentations and papers in one form or another. As early as July 2002, departmental and NSC papers began to become salted with warnings about the danger of the United States becoming seen as "an occupying power." Two months before the invasion, many of the points emphasized in Rumsfeld's October "Parade of Horribles" list made it into a briefing to the Principals Committee on "potential post-war challenges." A fourteen-page "action memo" prepared by the Pentagon for CENT-COM five weeks before the invasion stressed the importance of "maintaining public order," reiterated the possibility that the United States could "win the war but lose the peace," and predicted "some degree of civil disorder—ranging from common lawlessness to ethnic/religious reprisals to regime-generated acts that cause major disorder and harm." An "inter-agency rehearsal and planning conference" conducted roughly a month before Operation Iraqi Freedom was unleashed included a fifty-two-page PowerPoint briefing that began with a section titled "Assumptions about the World," which emphasized that "maintaining law and order will be necessary from Day 1."[175]

Nothing in the available record, however, indicates that the president and his key advisers paid attention to these warnings or produced anything in the way of concrete long-range plans that was much more substantial than the nostrums expressed in Japan's vacuous November 15 Liaison Conference document. They did produce a quantity of paperwork about creating some sort of U.S.-led "interim Iraqi government," but this amounted to next to nothing. Indeed, the Japanese, by contrast, at least managed to quickly install stable occupation regimes throughout Southeast Asia including the Philippines.

On the critical big picture, however—the endgame—the similarities are again striking. What fascinated the president and his war planners, almost to the point of mesmerizing them, were the challenges of offensive force deployment and target selection (and the Lorelei of getting victory on the cheap). Like the emperor's warlords, they became carried away by "best-case" scenarios and—as earlier U.S. studies of Japan's folly concluded—"discounted the potential strength of their enemies."

■

WHILE THE DECEPTION and self-deception of the war advocates were acute, it is misleading to see this as peculiar to the Bush White House. The extent to which delusion and denial were ingrained in the system was exposed when it became known that the U.S. military had not merely invaded Iraq unprepared to respond to insurgency, but in fact had neglected such "irregular" military challenges in internal planning and training sessions for decades. This stunning failure of both imagination and common sense traced back to the Vietnam War.

Although defeat by materially inferior forces in Vietnam in the late 1960s and early 1970s never ceased to haunt planners and policy makers, their response to this humiliation was counterintuitive. Rather than intensify counterinsurgency training, the military closed its eyes. In 2006, a retired officer who served during both the Vietnam and Iraq operations (Jack Keane, a former vice chief of staff of the army) spoke of this in almost surreal terms. "After the Vietnam War," he observed, "we purged ourselves of everything that had to do with irregular warfare or insurgency, because it had to do with how we lost that war. In hindsight, that was a bad decision."[176]

This was more than a bad decision. It amounted to a purge of rational thinking and planning that carried through other insurgencies in other lands: El Salvador, for example, and the Palestinian intifadas. Most striking was the psychological suppression of the obvious lesson of Afghanistan after Soviet forces were defeated there in the late 1980s. Despite covert U.S. support for the mujahideen for almost a decade—and despite the spectacle of lightly armed native and foreign fighters taking enormous losses but still besting the huge Soviet machine, and the extraordinary postscript of the collapse of the Soviet Union immediately afterwards—no serious top-level attention was given to the military significance of the

Soviet defeat. "Counterinsurgency" remained all but ignored in military training. When David Kilcullen, an Australian expert on irregular warfare and counterterrorism, was assigned to work with a small military team of maverick U.S. colleagues on these matters months *after* the Coalition Provisional Authority was disbanded amidst chaos, he found that these ideas "were too subversive even to write down when we first began talking about them in late 2004," and only became "accepted wisdom (or at least, the object of institutional lip-service)" around the end of 2005. When the Army and Marine Corps finally issued a *Counterinsurgency Field Manual* with fanfare in December 2006, more than three and a half years after the invasion of Iraq, official announcements acknowledged that work on this did not even begin until 2004, and "it had been 20 years since the Army published a formal field manual devoted to counterinsurgency operations, and 25 years since the Marine Corps published its last manual on the subject." West Point, the public learned in the midst of all this, had exorcised counterinsurgency from its curriculum after the Vietnam War.[177]

Why did top military and civilian leaders fail to take asymmetrical threats seriously? Part of the answer lies in the racial arrogance and cultural blindness regarding "people with towels on their heads" that persisted in spite of the victory of Afghan fighters and foreign mujahideen in Afghanistan—and, indeed, in spite of 9-11. Another part of the answer, as suggested by the West Point exorcism, lies in the suffocating cultural politics of Vietnam War memory in the United States: the increasingly effective conservative argument that politicians and a weak-kneed American public lost the war, rather than the Vietnamese resistance winning it. And part of the answer has to do with technological (and corporate) imperatives: Cold War and post–Cold War fixations on massive destruction and a high-tech "revolution in military affairs." Despite the many low-intensity conflicts and insurrections that followed World War II— and despite the deeper history of guerrilla warfare and the like that preceded this, tracing back even to ancient military classics like Sun Tzu's *The Art of War*—the institutional culture of the U.S. military and glory dreams of armchair commanders like Bush and Rumsfeld remained fixated on attaining victory by destroying the enemy through application of overwhelming firepower.[178]

Where such intellectual and psychological denial becomes systemic and sustained, deception and delusion must be regarded as part of a larger psychopathology. Collectively blocking out insurgency (and counterinsurgency) in core military thinking, for example, had a perverse analog in the administration's and intelligence community's thinking about torture. The practice was euphemistically neutered ("enhanced interrogation techniques," etc.); its moral repugnance was minimized; existing legal restraints and conventions against it were dismissed as anachronistic and "quaint." But beyond this, practical arguments against torture also were exorcised. One was the loss of moral standing and legitimacy in the eyes of much of the world. Another was the fact that torture is likely to produce false or misleading information geared to what the interrogators wish to hear. Even putting morality aside, the costs in reputation and misinformation exceed the benefits.

Like the revelation that the military had by and large purged teaching about irregular warfare and "how we lost that war" in Vietnam, exposure of this pathology of forgetting regarding torture became another unexpected by-product of the Iraq war. This drew attention in 2008 when it became known that beginning in December 2002 American torturers at Guantánamo had been using a checklist of methods that appeared in a 1957 Air Force study of "brainwashing" of U.S. soldiers taken prisoner by the Chinese during the Korean War. Excised from this grim pedagogy was the point of the original article: that the GI victims of such torture said what their captors wished them to say—in this case regarding U.S. war crimes in Korea.[179]

Unanticipated revelations such as these are most often left freestanding as discrete, sporadic events. They are better seen as jigsaw pieces, misshapen and irregular but fitting a larger pattern.

## Victory Disease and the Gates of Hell

Before the military roof fell in on the Japanese (in mid-1942) and the Americans (shortly after entering Baghdad in April 2003), both sides waxed rapturous at the success of their immediate military mission. Even after weeks of widespread looting and violence in Baghdad, an atmosphere of denial and almost giddy back-slapping permeated the White House and Pentagon—as if someone had indeed released one of those chemical weapons the administration had been warning about, and it turned out to be laughing gas.

The euphoria and triumphalism that marked the Japanese response to initial victories in 1941 and early 1942 were all the more striking because they replaced a mood of foreboding that had permeated the nation as the war in China bogged down and relations with the United States deteriorated. Popular response to reports of smashing victories at Pearl Harbor and in Southeast Asia and the Philippines was captured in ubiquitous clichés along the lines of the sun breaking out from behind dark clouds. Later, this ephemeral euphoria became sardonically known as the "victory disease"—the metaphor of disease carrying psychological connotations of ultranationalism, delirium, delusion, and to some degree sheer blood lust.

Preinvasion forebodings also existed in the United States. As zero hour for war with Iraq approached, however, such pessimism was offset by a rush of confidence bordering on complacency. It is easy to understand this overconfidence. Even apart from history's traditional empires, modern times provide many examples of strong states imposing their will on others with the help of native collaborators. Germany did this in Europe beginning in 1939, the Soviet Union in Eastern Europe after World War II, Japan in Manchuria after 1931, in great reaches of China after 1937, and in Southeast Asia after 1941. None of these states was as overwhelmingly powerful as the United States after the Cold War, and none as liberal in its professed intentions. Where good intentions coupled with successful postwar collaborations were concerned, moreover, the war-of-choice advocates could—and earnestly did—point to defeated Germany and especially defeated Japan after World War II.[180]

At the same time, the president's own militant impulses were reinforced by numerous voices from outside his inner circle. These included Middle East experts, Iraqi exiles and expatriates, other Arab and Muslim friends of the United States, bellicose supporters of Israel, liberal supporters of humanitarian intervention, and foreign allies led by England's Prime Minister Blair. It was Iraqi exiles who, in a White House meeting on January 10, 2003, assured Bush that U.S. forces entering Baghdad would be greeted with "sweets and flowers." The exiles found that the president, even at this late date, knew next to nothing about religious, ethnic, and political tensions in Iraqi society—but they assured him that religious schism between the ruling minority Sunnis and majority Shiites had been exaggerated by people outside Iraq. Similarly, it was the expatriates who persuaded the Pentagon and Office of the Vice President (but not the State Department or CIA) that Iraqis who had long suffered under Saddam's despotism would welcome a provisional government dominated by exiles who had spent these years abroad—a roseate reading of the domestic climate in Iraq, of the fractious expatriate community itself, and of politics and human nature more generally.[181]

It was this world of wishful expectations that lower-level officials and military officers attempted to challenge by pointing out that recent history and current circumstances fairly screamed the perils of attempting to invade and occupy foreign lands, let alone implant "democracy." It did not require access to secret information about Iraq or Islamist terrorism to present compelling case studies that made clear the imperative of exercising extreme caution before choosing to invade and occupy a volatile foreign land: Vietnam; the festering wound of Israel's post–1967 occupied territories; the fatal Soviet invasion and occupation of Afghanistan from 1979 to 1989; the mounting difficulties of America's own post–9-11 incursion in Afghanistan.

Indeed, much the same lesson about failing to take seriously the nationalistic pride of others could be drawn from imperial Japan's strategic folly in China prior to the "imbecility" of Pearl Harbor. In 1937, Hirohito's war minister assured him that China would succumb in six months at best. In September 1941, the same officer, now chief of the army general staff, told him, "We intend to end it [war with the United States] in about three months." On the latter occasion, the emperor reminded the general of his earlier prediction; but such moments were fleeting and rare. The emperor did not revisit this, and in the scores of planning conferences that culminated in Japan's war of choice against the United States, no one else dared whisper "China" as a cautionary reminder. Fervid nationalism induces an almost willful myopia regarding the national or group pride of others.[182]

SHORTLY BEFORE THE invasion of Iraq, an Arab League spokesman warned that such an attack would "open the gates of hell." *Typical Middle*

*East hyperbole* was the generic dismissive response to such voices. Against such warnings, scoffers could cite the counterarguments of select Middle East experts, and one argument in particular: that, more than anything else, Arabs respect force and power. The eminent historian Bernard Lewis, whose counsel and support were especially prized by those advocating war against Iraq, was often paraphrased to this effect. Brent Scowcroft, an establishment insider and agonized critic of the administration's unilateral militancy, concluded that after 9-11 Lewis's influence on hawks like Vice President Cheney reinforced the White House commitment to war. "It's the idea that we've got to hit somebody hard," Scowcroft observed. "And Bernard Lewis says, 'I believe that one of the things you've got to do to Arabs is hit them between the eyes with a big stick. They respect power.'"[183]

Such arguments, extremely popular in pro-war circles, were part and parcel of the broader mindset of refusing to "deign to acknowledge" Arab and Muslim historical grievances against the Western powers. An article in the April 2002 issue of the *National Review*, the flagship of conservative commentary, captured some of the almost bantering crudeness of such thinking by paraphrasing a well-known pundit: "Every ten years or so, the United States needs to pick up some small crappy little country and throw it against the wall, just to show the world we mean business."[184] It is instructive to see high doctrine and noble rhetoric boiled down to its practical essence—and to follow this by imagining how such throw-them-against-the-wall or hit-them-between-the-eyes swagger sounds to others. To targets of such contempt, a long history of European and U.S. practices confirmed that Westerners were undeniably accomplished in hitting Middle East peoples between the eyes with a big stick. Power rather than idealism was always the name of the game.

This bullyboy swagger found consummate expression in some of the more flamboyant phrasemaking that ricocheted back to haunt the war advocates. One was the argument that imposing America's will on Iraq would be a "cakewalk"—little more than a jaunty strut on the global stage. Another widely cited instance of provocative rhetoric carried the "history begins today" outlook to its logical conclusion. In the summer of 2002, as the bandwagon for war against Iraq picked up speed, one of the president's senior advisers advanced this death-of-history outlook with almost breath-

taking arrogance. Critics of the president and his policies, he told the former *Wall Street Journal* writer Ron Suskind, operated "in what we call the
reality-based community," where people "believe that solutions emerge
from your judicious study of discernible reality." That, however, was "not
the way the world really works anymore." The new reality was this:

> We're an empire now, and when we act, we create our own reality.
> And while you're studying that reality—judiciously, as you will—
> we'll act again, creating other new realities, which you can study
> too, and that's how things will sort out. We're history's actors . . .
> and you, all of you, will be left to just study what we do.

Apart from its world-class fatuousness (and resemblance to the "New
Order" hubris of imperial Japan's most arrogant ideologues), this soon-
notorious comment had the added attraction of being forthright and
unwittingly accurate. The Bush administration did create new realities,
and in the process left the world with yet another tragedy to study.[185]

In the end, the gates-of-hell scenario proved more rational than the
cakewalk. This was not an exceptional prediction, but rather followed
the conclusion militant Islamists had drawn earlier from the defeat of
Soviet forces in Afghanistan. As bin Laden put it late in 1998, men with
"very few RPGs [rocket-propelled grenade launchers], very few anti-tank
mines, and very few Kalashnikovs . . . managed to destroy the myth of the
largest military machine ever known to mankind and utterly annihilated
the idea of the so-called superpowers. We believe that America is much
weaker than Russia." This, too, was wishful thinking of a sort; but 9-11
reflected such thinking, and the incompetent U.S. conduct of the "war on
terror" surpassed even bin Laden's wildest dreams. The immediate U.S.
military response to the September 11 attacks killed close to 80 percent of
Al Qaeda's forces in Afghanistan by the end of 2001—but redirection of
the war on terror to Iraq replenished them and, in effect, turned that new
battleground into something akin to what Afghanistan had been to the
Soviets. As bin Laden observed early in 2006, "Iraq has become a point
of attraction and restorer of [our] energies," inspiring the mujahideen to
extend the holy war against America and its allies even to Europe.[186]

In time, 9-11 and the wholesale murder of innocents preached by Al

Qaeda and other militants split the ranks of the jihadi themselves and even became regarded as "a catastrophe for Muslims." It was, of course, more than this: a catastrophe for the entire world that was compounded by the U.S. response. This was apparent even in the Bush administration's war before the war in Iraq—in Afghanistan—where U.S. forces also soon became bogged down. Observing the scene in the summer of 2002, a contributor to a Middle East Internet journal commented that the U.S. administration "did not proceed from a careful and in-depth study of the enemy it was about to face. Instead, it proceeded from a hysterical state that made its position lack the basic scientific rules that ought to be considered when making a decision."[187]

Joseph Grew's canards about rationality and measuring rods of logic had been turned upside down.

# "PEARL HARBOR"
# AS GODSEND

Political and ideological code words often swing on a two-way hinge. For most Americans, "Pearl Harbor" calls to mind infamy, vulnerability, drastic failure of military intelligence, rage, and revenge. It is code for wars of choice, and for aggression that ricochets against the aggressor. At the same time, however, December 7, 1941, was also a political godsend for President Roosevelt—much as September 11 proved to be a windfall for President Bush. Near the end of Bush's second term, his longtime *éminence grise* Karl Rove obliquely acknowledged this. "History has a funny way of deciding things," Rove told an audience of university students. "Sometimes history sends you things, and 9/11 came our way."[188]

As godsend, "Pearl Harbor" signifies a traumatic incident that, however terrible in itself, may open the gate to enactment of desired but hitherto thwarted policies. By much the same measure, the Pearl Harbor code also is a potent scare word that can be exploited to promote draconian military change in the name of both self-preservation and assertive offensive capabilities and policies. Both the godsend and the scare word were imbedded in the geopolitical agenda that the Bush administration embraced.

The perception that, for all its horrors, December 7 was also a blessing did not come as delayed hindsight. On the contrary, the positive impact of the Japanese attack was emphasized immediately by a range of American commentators. The *New York Herald Tribune* captured this sentiment in its December 8 editorial: "Since the clash now appears to have been inevitable, its occurrence brings with it a sense of relief. The air is clearer. Americans can get down to their task with old controversies forgotten." Newspapers in Chicago joined the chorus. "Thanks now to Japan, the deep division of opinion that has rent and paralyzed our country will be swiftly healed," the *Chicago Daily News* proclaimed. "It cannot be otherwise. Once more we shall be a united people, firm in a single determination—to maintain our liberties by the complete and utter defeat of our foes." The *Chicago Herald-American* celebrated the fact that "we are all Americans now, united and strong and invincible," while the *Chicago Times* rejoiced that "already the bitterest isolationists have announced their unswerving support of the Nation's defense."

These references to deep divisions pertained to bitter foreign-policy disputes pitting "America First" isolationists against a more interventionist Democratic administration. And in the Capitol, too, December 7 dispelled this tension. Politicians filled the *Congressional Record* with short statements along the lines of "America has been a sleeping giant. This attack by the Japanese has awakened us. We are no longer divided. We are one people." The *Washington News* echoed this in an editorial on December 8 that began by quoting Kipling about "the drumming guns that have no doubts" and proceeded to celebrate the fact that "many problems have been solved on a Sabbath day. Chief of these is the problem of national unity. . . . America now turns, as Kipling said, 'a keen, untroubled face home, to the instant need of things.'" The attack on Hawaii, the *News* went on, "united America in a common horror and in a common resolve—a unity as grim and complete as if Japan had struck individually at 180,000,000 Americans. She has thereby eliminated our chief dangers—indifference and division."[189]

In time, as the war drew near closure in 1944 and early 1945, political and ideological feuding resumed and the "old controversies" were resurrected. Remembering Pearl Harbor became a trigger for fractiousness rather than unity, as conservatives reassessed December 7 as a catastrophe that simply enabled Roosevelt to do what he desired: take the nation into war against the Axis powers, particularly the German juggernaut that had engulfed Europe and threatened England. In its severest form, this "backdoor to war" argument accused the Democratic president and his aides of conspiring to invite Japan's attack. As more and more of the backstage record became accessible, the argument gained legs in Republican and conservative circles. This is a controversy that will not go away.

Among the pieces of purported evidence that the Roosevelt administration desired war is a diary entry Secretary of War Stimson made on November 25, one day *before* an "ultimatum" to the Japanese by Secretary of State Hull effectively ended the efforts of the two nations to reach some sort of diplomatic resolution of their differences. Referring to a meeting held at noon that day, Stimson recorded that Roosevelt "brought up the event that we were likely to be attacked perhaps next Monday, for the Japanese are notorious for making an attack without warning, and the question was what we should do. The question was how we should maneuver them into the position of firing the first shot without allowing too much danger to ourselves." Two days later, the War Department sent a cable to MacArthur in the Philippines reflecting the same sentiment:

> Negotiations with Japan appear to be terminated to all practical purposes with only barest possibilities that Japanese Government might come back and offer to continue period Japanese future action unpredictable but hostile action possible at any moment period If hostilities cannot comma repeat cannot comma be avoided the United States desires that Japan commit the first overt act period.[190]

Much of this secret record was introduced in the joint congressional investigation conducted immediately after the war. The majority report that came out of these hearings (endorsed by eight committee members) did chastise the leadership in Washington for failing to communicate adequately with army and navy commanders in Hawaii. It went on to emphasize, however, that "the committee had found no evidence to support the charges, made before and during the hearings, that the President, the Secretary of State, the Secretary of War, or the Secretary of Navy tricked, provoked, incited, cajoled, or coerced Japan into attacking this Nation in order that a declaration of war might be more easily obtained from the Congress. On the contrary, all evidence conclusively points to the fact that they discharged their responsibilities with distinction, ability, and foresight and in keeping with the highest traditions of our fundamental foreign policy." The majority's criticism focused on how "the Hawaiian commands failed."[191]

This gingerly treatment of top leaders foreshadowed the failure of the 9-11 Commission to address leadership delinquency on the part of the Bush administration prior to September 11. And it did not go unchallenged. The minority report (by Republican Senators Homer Ferguson and Owen Brewster) also called attention to the failures of Admiral Kimmel and General Short in Hawaii, but leveled its harshest criticism against Roosevelt and his "war cabinet": Secretary of State Stimson, Secretary of the Navy Frank Knox, General and Army Chief of Staff George Marshall, Admiral and Chief of Naval Operations Harold Stark, and Major General Leonard Gerow, the assistant chief of staff of the War Plans Division. Although the dissenting senators paid particular attention to intercepted Japanese cables and top-level deliberations in the ten days or so that preceded the surprise attack (following the November 26 ultimatum), they went so far as to argue that "the possibility, indeed the probability of a Japanese attack on Pearl Harbor had entered into the calculations of high authorities in Washington and the commanders at Pearl Harbor for years, months, and days before December 7."

This picture of Roosevelt and his aides poring over intercepted Japanese messages and anticipating imminent hostilities poses a sharp contrast to the Bush administration's disengagement from intelligence warnings about Al Qaeda. That U.S. leaders knew Japan was poised to commence "hostile action" is indisputable, and their failure to ensure the military was thoroughly briefed and prepared for this eventuality is inexcusable. To argue as the minority report did that "the probability of a Japanese attack on Pearl Harbor" had long been clear to Roosevelt and his advisers, however, is another matter entirely. Military planners had conducted war games predicated on such an attack for many years; alerts were issued in Hawaii on several occasions in 1941; but the prevailing mindset remained that of Admiral Kimmel: no one really took seriously the possibility that the little yellow sons-of-bitches could pull off such an audacious operation so far from home. It was not Japan's war of choice that was a surprise, but rather the fact that their war plans actually included Hawaii.

Whether the United States and Japan could have worked out their differences is a serious issue, for it raises questions about both the causes of war and the perils of appeasement. But the backdoor-to-war conspiracy thesis does not hold water well. If leaders in Washington *had* known that Pearl Harbor was targeted, there was no reason for them to let the Pacific Fleet be attacked. They could, and surely would, simply have ordered the commanders in Hawaii to take preemptive action against the advancing attack force. The *casus belli* would have been persuasive enough to persuade most isolationists to support retaliation against the Axis powers collectively, and the nation would have rallied behind the president— although it would not have remembered Pearl Harbor in the same searing way. In this alternative scenario, there would have been no humiliating intelligence failure and no trauma of innocence betrayed comparable to what did take place—but the rousing "date which will live in infamy" and "Remember Pearl Harbor" rhetoric would not have been entirely absent. Roosevelt still would have had his godsend: his united citizenry and good war against the Axis menace.[192]

IN 2001, THERE was no anticipation of an impeding Al Qaeda attack on U.S. soil on the part of the president and his key advisers, although there should have been. CIA leaders tried in vain to impress National Security Adviser Rice with the urgency of the Al Qaeda threat in the opening days of July, and Bush received the soon-notorious secret President's Daily Brief titled "Bin Laden Determined to Strike in US" a month later, on August 6.[193] However one may interpret the administration's failure to respond to these warnings (the president spent most of that August at his ranch in Texas), the attack proved a double godsend.

First, 9-11 rescued a first-term presidency that had begun in disarray.

The presidential election of November 2000 ended in virtual stalemate, with slightly more than half the popular vote going to the Democrat's candidate (Al Gore) and contested electoral returns (and the decisive Electoral College vote) in Florida being decided in Bush's favor only after controversial intervention by the Supreme Court. The September 11 attacks thus came as a boon for a presidency that lacked a clear mandate and rested on shaky ground. Like Roosevelt before him, Bush donned the mantle of a president at war and pulled a fractured body politic solidly behind him. His rating in opinion polls soared at one early point to a remarkable 90 percent, and the lingering aura of being an unwavering war leader sufficed to carry him to a second term, even after the war in Iraq had become, in the eyes of most of the world, a disaster.

Second, and less well known to the general public at the time, 9-11 enabled the conservatives who served as the president's key advisers to put into effect a radical foreign and military policy they had advocated since before the 2000 election. Among other recommendations, this called for major increases in the defense budget, across-the-board transformation of the armed forces to exploit "the revolution in military affairs," repositioning of U.S. forces abroad, removing Saddam Hussein from power, and asserting the political leadership of the United States rather than the United Nations in international peacekeeping.

These proposals, long in gestation, were formulated most concisely by the Project for the New American Century (PNAC), an exceptionally articulate lobby founded in 1997. They were itemized in a PNAC report titled *Rebuilding America's Defenses: Strategy, Forces, and Resources for a New Century*, which was released in September 2000, shortly before the presidential election. Support for such drastic escalation of the military agenda could not be expected to come all at once, the report noted in a chapter titled "Creating Tomorrow's Dominant Force." Thus:

> the process of transformation, even if it brings revolutionary change,
> is likely to be a long one, absent some catastrophic and catalyzing
> event—like a new Pearl Harbor.

Almost exactly one year later, this is what they got. September 11 was the "new Pearl Harbor" that enabled President Bush to take the nation in a desired military direction. This, rather than any serious intelligence information linking Al Qaeda to Iraq, is why the president and those who now had greatest influence on U.S. military policy—led by Vice President Cheney, Defense Secretary Rumsfeld, and Deputy Secretary of Defense Wolfowitz, all of whom had signed the PNAC report—diverted the focus of attention and hostility from Al Qaeda to Iraq without a moment's hesitation. The "catastrophic and catalyzing event" had occurred, and they were primed to take it in predetermined directions.[194]

While both Roosevelt and Bush played domestic politics adroitly, however, the latter differed from his predecessor in notable ways. For one, he was incurious to the point of psychological aversion when it came to detailed knowledge about the outside world, and even about the actual on-the-ground situation in his chosen battlefields. He and his inner circle also chose to exploit fear itself as a political windfall—to strengthen his and the Republican Party's control of domestic politics by never failing to emphasize the imminent threat of catastrophe, and how any criticism of the administration's response to this placed the nation in peril. There was a great deal of political (and personal) opportunism in these scare tactics— but also a deep current of genuine, abiding, almost paranoid fright. By contrast, one of Roosevelt's most remembered statements to the American people was that "the only thing we have to fear is fear itself." Although he said this in the depth of the Great Depression in 1933, in the opening sentences of his first inaugural address, it set the tone for his successive administrations and later war leadership.

History surely will take special note of the Bush administration's fearmongering, particularly as this played out in the Iraq war and the abuses of law that accompanied the war on terror in general. An administration that went to war trumpeting its humanitarian mission to liberate Saddam Hussein's "republic of fear" ended up strengthening the forces of instability and terror around the world and turning America itself into a republic riddled with fear and an economy where enormous fortunes were made by ensuring that fear stayed center stage. Nor was this confined to home consumption. A disenchanted State Department participant in the administration's high-level deliberations (Richard Armitage) was later quoted as observing that "since 9/11 our principal export to the world has been our fear."[195]

■

IN THIS MILIEU of unremitting insecurity and panic, the "new Pearl Harbor" did not just open the door to war against Saddam Hussein. It was a godsend, more broadly, for those who advocated directing vastly greater resources to the enhancement of sophisticated military hardware. This extended to a revised agenda for nuclear weapons as well as a grand vision of militarizing outer space.

This, too, was foreshadowed in the PNAC report, which called for resuming nuclear testing and developing "a new family of nuclear weapons" including bunker busters capable of destroying deep underground facilities. The PNAC strategists also gave particularly strong emphasis to the need to control the new "international commons" of space and cyberspace, and to this end even proposed creating a military service tentatively titled "U.S. Space Forces."

Militarizing outer space was President Ronald Reagan's old "Star Wars" agenda, which took its nickname from the 1977 Hollywood film that also provided Reagan with the "evil empire" label he attached to the Soviet Union. Pentagon planners had devoted increasing attention to controlling real and virtual space since the revolution in communications technology took off in the 1980s, and this preoccupation was accelerated by the role of electronic warfare in the first Gulf War. These projections, like all others, rested on the assumption of America's unique role as a force for good—not merely in the world, but in the heavens as well. Although the military might of the United States was roughly equivalent to that of the major nations of the rest of the world combined, it was argued that the country was still vulnerable. And the code for such vulnerability—even in outer space—was again Pearl Harbor.

This emerged explicitly in a report submitted to Congress on January 11, 2001—just before Bush's inauguration, and precisely nine months before 9-11—by the Commission to Assess United States National Security Space Management and Organization. The commission was chaired by Donald Rumsfeld from its inception until his nomination as secretary of defense a few weeks before the report was released. Rumsfeld's committee warned not once or twice but six times of the danger of a "Space Pearl Harbor" if the United States did not hasten to consolidate its control over space. One version of the drumbeat warning was this:

> The question is whether the U.S. will be wise enough to act responsibly and soon enough to reduce U.S. space vulnerability. Or whether, as in the past, a disabling attack against the country and its people— a "Space Pearl Harbor"—will be the only event able to galvanize the nation and cause the U.S. Government to act.[196]

Language was adroitly manipulated in these visions of new frontiers and new challenges in warfare—"space control," for example, was an oblique way of repudiating "arms control"—and September 11 paved the way for accelerated planning for both new uses of nuclear weapons and establishing control of outer space. Thus, in early January of 2002, three weeks before Bush introduced the "axis of evil" notion in his first State of the Union address, the Pentagon released lengthy excerpts from a classified *Nuclear Posture Review* that posited possible use of nuclear weapons in "immediate, potential, or unexpected contingencies" involving North Korea, Iraq, Iran, Syria, Libya, and China (particularly in a "military confrontation over the status of Taiwan"). The review called for giving serious consideration to whether the United States should "develop an entirely new [nuclear] capability—one that is not a modification of an existing weapon." It endorsed undertaking "new missions" such as using nuclear weapons to penetrate and destroy "hard and deeply-buried targets" (HDBTs) like underground bunkers, command centers, and biological and chemical weapons facilities. And it frankly observed that to maintain the nuclear stockpile and develop new capabilities, continuing to adhere to a moratorium on nuclear testing (observed since 1992) "may not be possible for the indefinite future."[197]

The "Space Pearl Harbor" mindset found striking expression in October 2003, when the administration's ongoing wars in Afghanistan and Iraq made the centrality of satellites, drones, and the like in U.S. high-tech warfare clear even to the general public. On this occasion, the Air Force Space Command issued a twenty-five-year "strategic master plan" bristling with expressions that made previous projections seem almost restrained by comparison: "ownership" of the new "high ground" of space; "full spectrum space command"; optimal capability to "control space and ensure Space Superiority"; dedication to the mission of deterring adversaries by continuing "to pursue lethal or nonlethal effects such as the use of deception, disruption, denial, degradation, and destruction of space capabilities"; and so on. This master plan coincided with a moment in the Iraq war when early overconfidence about a swift "shock and awe" victory was giving way to premonitions of a long and brutal slog; and the militancy of the language was so provocative that it had to be tempered in subsequent published plans.[198]

LIKE THE CULT of secrecy and the labyrinth of bureaucratic proliferation, the Pearl-Harbor-as-godsend mindset can become a trap. This, in part, helps explain the failure of the Bush administration's war on terror, which amounted to a mixture of acute paranoia on the one hand and, on the other hand, confidence that possessing the most sophisticated weapons of mass destruction imaginable would ensure success in deterring or defeating all enemies, real or imagined. Pearl Harbor, in this sense, became a code, symbol, or synecdoche for Big War. This is the outlook that a standard military history written in the 1970s refers to as "the strategy of annihilation," which became "characteristically the American way in war" long before World War II. It is the mindset that made Rumsfeld's immediate response to 9-11 ("go massive—sweep it all up—Things related and not") seem perfectly natural.

Big War, however, was not what combating terrorism or insurgency demanded.[199]

# PART II

# GROUND ZERO 1945 AND
# GROUND ZERO 2001

*Terror and Mass Destruction*

# "HIROSHIMA" AS CODE

hortly after the destruction of the World Trade Center on September 11, a little-noticed newspaper article reported that prior to the attack the CIA had "intercepted a cryptic but chilling message . . . from a member of Al Qaeda, who boasted that Osama bin Laden was planning to carry out a 'Hiroshima' against America."[1]

Like Pearl Harbor, "Hiroshima" is code of a sort for placing 9-11 in historical perspective. Among Americans, both the surprise attack of December 7, 1941, and the ensuing war's cataclysmic end with the birth of the nuclear age in August 1945 seemed to be compressed, merged, resurrected in the hellfire that raged in Manhattan and mesmerized the world. Even the post–Cold War American superpower was suddenly exposed as being vulnerable to weapons of mass destruction—not in the hands of another great power, but in the possession of ragtag fanatics. The connection between September 11 and Hiroshima was locked in place when politicians and the media almost immediately baptized the ravaged site of the World Trade Center's twin towers "Ground Zero."

As with Pearl Harbor and "infamy," Hiroshima and Ground Zero turned out to have multiple levels and layers. For Americans, September 11 presented the awful spectacle of a few terrorists in a few planes bringing devastation to a great and peaceful metropolis. For bin Laden and Al Qaeda's zealots, "Hiroshima" similarly meant using just a few aircraft to inflict harm on the United States—but with an entirely different interpretation of what this symbolized. Beginning around five years prior to September 11, the dropping of atomic bombs on Hiroshima and Nagasaki "with their entire populations of children, elderly, and women" became a staple in bin Laden's public recitations of U.S. crimes against humanity: the starting point, in his polemic, of a post–World War II agenda of coercive global hegemony that became ever more oppressive in the Middle East. From this perspective, condemnation of Islamist terror by Americans and others "set a double standard," and the jihadi holy warriors of 2001 were appropriately to be seen as righteous agents of retribution.[2]

In a sardonic message "to the Americans" delivered a little more than a year after September 11 (on October 6, 2002), Al Qaeda's leader played on this theme of double standards and just punishment with particular relish:

> That which you are singled out for in the history of mankind is that you have used your force to destroy mankind, more than any other nation in history; not to defend principles and values, but to hasten to secure your interests and profits. You dropped a nuclear bomb on Japan, even though Japan was ready to negotiate an end to the war. How many acts of oppression, tyranny, and injustice have you carried out, O callers to freedom?[3]

While bin Laden was singling out Hiroshima and Nagasaki as symbols of American destructiveness and injustice, President Bush and those who spoke for him were turning the nuclear devastation of 1945 into the touchstone of why a preemptive war against Iraq was essential. In this campaign, the code word was "mushroom cloud." In a widely quoted television interview on September 8, 2002, Condoleezza Rice declared that "we don't want the smoking gun to be a mushroom cloud." A month later (October 7), the president picked up the refrain. "Facing clear evidence of peril," he declared in a major speech on Iraq's alleged weapons of mass destruction, "we cannot wait for the final proof—the smoking gun—that could come in the form of a mushroom cloud."[4]

As the countdown to the war of choice against Iraq began in earnest, a third and more subtle coded evocation of Hiroshima and Nagasaki became popular in planning circles and the media: "shock and awe." This was the catchphrase journalists, pundits, and the general public savored in imagining the awesome military assault the United States would direct against Iraq, paving the way for swift removal of Saddam Hussein and the equally swift emergence of a more democratic Iraqi state. As time would quickly prove, what this catchphrase actually caught was the fatal flaw embedded in the administration's embrace of World War II analogies, and of Bush personally being a "war president" akin to Roosevelt and Truman: naïve faith in the efficacy of overpowering force to combat a threat utterly unlike Japan or Germany.

"Shock and awe" was more than a passing phrase, for the jargon derived from a strategic battle plan that had been influential in U.S. military circles since the mid-1990s. This scenario for "rapid dominance" emphasized "delivery of instant, nearly incomprehensible levels of massive destruction directed at influencing society writ large," and it drew much of its inspiration from the nuclear bombs used against Japan a half century earlier. The 1996 *urtext* of the doctrine makes this clear:

> Theoretically, the magnitude of the Shock and Awe [that] Rapid Dominance seeks to impose (in extreme cases) is the non-nuclear equivalent of the impact that the atomic weapons dropped on Hiroshima and Nagasaki had on the Japanese. The Japanese were prepared for suicidal resistance until both nuclear bombs were used. The impact of those weapons was sufficient to transform both the mindset of the average Japanese citizen and the outlook of the leadership through this condition of Shock and Awe. The Japanese sim-

ply could not comprehend the destructive power carried by a single airplane. This incomprehension produced a state of awe.

We believe that, in a parallel manner, revolutionary potential in combining new doctrine and existing technology can produce systems capable of yielding this level of Shock and Awe. In most or many cases, this Shock and Awe may not necessitate imposing the full destruction of either nuclear weapons or advanced conventional technologies but must be underwritten by the ability to do so.[5]

Shock and awe was the high-tech, strategy-wonk, book-length version of hitting the enemy between the eyes with a big stick; and it throbbed like a vital pulse in conservative and neoconservative prescriptions about how to deal with Arabs in particular and adversaries in general. It also turned Hiroshima as code for horror on its head. Much as bin Laden evoked using the dropping of atomic bombs on Japan as an American crime against humanity and then proceeded to endorse inflicting a "Hiroshima" upon Americans, so U.S. strategists horrified by the specter of a mushroom cloud in the United States glorified Hiroshima and Nagasaki as demonstrating how to anticipate and prevent such nuclear catastrophe. Even while emphasizing that the psychological lessons to be derived from these two incinerated cities did not necessarily require the use of nuclear weapons, the apostles of shock and awe did not rule this out. On the contrary, they ruled it in, and called for resumption of nuclear testing and development of a new generation of nuclear weapons such as mini-nuke "bunker-busters."

Reality did not validate the shock-and-awe prognostications, for the most shocking aspect of the invasion of Iraq was that deployment of awesome, cutting-edge military force did not in fact drive "society writ large" into abject submission. On the contrary, it destroyed infrastructure, decapitated an authoritarian regime without replacing it, opened the gates to lawlessness and eventually insurrection, and seeded the ground for more brutal and widespread terrorism than before. At the dawn of the twenty-first century, the preeminent case study of shock and awe truly traumatizing a society was September 11 and involved a few commercial airplanes, nineteen men armed with box cutters, and an estimated outlay by Al Qaeda of a half-million dollars.

THE PSYCHOLOGICAL AND strategic miscalculations of the war of choice against Iraq will be analyzed and debated for years to come. Where the cultures of war more generally are concerned, both 9-11 and the Iraq war raise historical and moral questions that deserve equally sustained debate. Those who politicize the grief and horror of lower Manhattan's Ground Zero, for example—drawing alarming word-pictures of mushroom clouds, and rhapsodizing over the positive shock-and-awe lessons to be drawn from Hiroshima and Nagasaki—rarely look squarely at the original Ground Zeroes. They avert their gaze from what actually took place beneath the mushroom clouds in August 1945—and from the almost inexorable logic that led to the U.S. decision to obliterate these two densely populated cities, and what all this might tell us about the emergence of a world in which the line between soldier and civilian, combatant and noncombatant, has ceased to exist.

This is not a matter of moral equivalence or relativism (the instinctive nationalistic response to undertaking any inquiry that might cast doubt upon the "exceptionalism" of America's own morality, or the wisdom and necessity of using the atomic bombs in August 1945). Rather, it is to ask how far we can meaningfully pursue the linkage between 9-11 and Hiroshima / Ground Zero that is already established in popular consciousness. The moral questions are, as the textbooks and encyclopedias of philosophy tell us, "as old as war itself."[6] They raise the issue of just war (*justum bellum*), and more precisely the legitimacy or justice of a war (*jus ad bellum*) and the observance or violation of fair, acceptable, "proportionate" conduct in war (*jus in bello*). While Japan's attack on China and later Pearl Harbor, and the Bush administration's war of choice against Iraq, raise the former issue (*jus ad bellum*), the crimes against humanity seen in 9-11 and terrorism more generally involve a practice widely condemned as violating the concept of *jus in bello*, namely, the deliberate targeting of civilians.

In the wake of 9-11, the moral strictures underlying traditional *jus in bello* thinking became a bell Americans rang with passion. This was used, moreover, to highlight the chasm separating the United States (and "Western civilization" more generally) from the terrorists—and from Saddam Hussein as well. When the Bush administration coined the term "war on terror," care was taken to call attention (here in Douglas Feith's words) "to differences between us and our enemies on the issue of respect for human life." The sanctity of the distinction between combatants and innocent noncombatants was emphasized, and with this the observation that "terrorists are reprehensible precisely because they negate that distinction, by purposefully targeting civilians." In the January 2002 State of the Union address in which the "axis of evil" term was introduced, the president's indictment of "the Iraqi regime" included the charge that "this is a regime that has already used poison gas to murder thousands of its own citizens—leaving the bodies of mothers huddled over their dead children."[7]

To anyone familiar with the graphic visual record of what took place beneath the mushroom clouds of 1945, the president's choice of imagery is doubly disturbing: for the incinerated mother huddling over a dead child is one of the most iconic images of Ground Zero in Hiroshima and Nagasaki. Targeting civilians and noncombatants has been familiar practice since the Western powers introduced aerial bombing in World War I—and became standard operating procedure in World War II, when British and U.S. air forces introduced the doctrine and practice of indiscriminate bombing of "urban areas." Hiroshima and Nagasaki represented a dramatic change in the nature and efficiency of such operations, but the moral as well as strategic Rubicon was crossed before the birth of the nuclear age. Deliberately killing noncombatants is hardly new to war, but in World War II it became part and parcel of a new age of "total war" and ostensibly sophisticated "psychological warfare."[8]

Modern war breeds its own cultures, and incinerating civilians is one of them.

■

IT IS TESTIMONY to the impressive defense mechanisms of popular consciousness in general, and patriotism in particular, that most Americans managed to embrace the resurrected images of Ground Zero, the mushroom cloud, and shock and awe without giving much if any thought to the contradictions among them, or to the fact that it was the United States itself that, in the final five months of the war against Japan, perfected the policy and practice of destroying cities and enemy populations with weapons of mass destruction.

*41. In this photograph from 1965, a crude "Ground Zero" sign in the desert near Alamogordo, New Mexico, marks the hypocenter of the first explosion of a nuclear weapon in the "Trinity" test conducted on July 16, 1945.*

In the wake of September 11, there was a brief moment in the United States when it seemed possible that Al Qaeda's crime against humanity might help foster a popular consciousness and imagination concerning air war and terror bombing in general, past as well as present and future, that transcended patriotic parochialism and a reflexive thirst for retaliation in near-kind. This did not happen. On the contrary, the rubric of Ground Zero was appropriated—*expropriated*, really—without serious discussion or thought about its origins at the dawn of the nuclear age. "Zero" was the code used to identify the hypocenter of the explosion in the desert in Alamogordo, New Mexico, where the United States tested the world's first nuclear weapon on July 16, 1945. "Point zero" and "zero area" became common references in early accounts of the test and subsequent bombings of Hiroshima and Nagasaki, and by 1946 "ground zero" had become a familiar term in the mass media—ominously and inseparably linked to the nuclear weaponry only the United States possessed at that point in time. The hypocenter of the test site in New Mexico used to be identified by a crude sign bearing these forbidding words. For decades, the label was attached to Hiroshima and Nagasaki in particular, although as time passed, its usage became more generically associated with the epicenter of great violence and turbulence in general.[9]

The spectacle and language of terror bombing, on the other hand, became commonplace earlier. Italy shocked the world when it invaded Ethiopia in late 1935 and greeted 1936 with a New Year's Day bombing that targeted, among other things, a conspicuously marked Swedish Red Cross hospital there. The Italians dropped eighty-five tons of bombs on Ethiopia all told, as well as a rain of mustard gas that poisoned pastures and waterways as well as humans and animals. (Mussolini's son Bruno, one of the pilots, later recalled that "it was all most diverting. . . . After the bomb racks were emptied I began throwing bombs by hand. . . . It was most amusing.") Germany honed its air-war skills in support of Francisco Franco's fascists during the Spanish civil war that began in 1936. Here, the bombing of one small Basque village became a global symbol of the horror of terror from the sky when the Spanish Pavilion at the World's Fair in Paris in 1937 exhibited Pablo Picasso's disturbing mural *Guernica*.[10]

Japan's most shocking contribution to the spectacle of bombing cities and killing civilians from the air came with its invasion of China in 1937. When an attack in late August not only killed many Chinese but also wounded the British ambassador, the British Foreign Office issued a protest declaring that "such events are inseparable from the practice, illegal as it is inhumane, of failing to draw that clear distinction between combatants and noncombatants in the conduct of hostilities, which international law, no less than the conscience of mankind, has always enjoyed." *Life* magazine branded the horror of Japan's air attacks on Chinese cities on the mind's eye of its many readers with a photograph of a bawling infant sitting amidst the rubble of a bombed-out railway station in Shanghai. This memorable image—which the journalist Harold Issacs later called "one of the most successful 'propaganda' pieces of all time"—was actually extracted from a newsreel by a Chinese cameraman working for the Hearst syndicate. By late 1938 *Life* itself estimated that, in one form or another, the image probably had been seen by as many as "136 million" people worldwide. Newsreels—the most compelling expression of wartime "realism" in this pretelevision era—as well as headlines, official condemnations, and graphic photographs all rein-

*42. This August 28, 1937, scene of a baby crying in the rubble after Japanese aircraft bombed Shanghai's South Station was originally caught on film by a Chinese cameraman working for Hearst Metrotone News. The movie frame was quickly isolated and reproduced in newspapers and magazines, including* Life, *whose readers voted it one of the ten "Pictures of the Year." Such depictions of the civilian victims of Japanese and German air attacks provoked moral revulsion and widespread condemnation in the late 1930s and very early 1940s, led by the League of Nations and American and British leaders.*

forced the argument that deliberately bombing civilians was beyond the pale of civilized behavior.[11]

Beginning in 1937, the U.S. government strenuously condemned such practices. When World War II erupted in Europe with Germany's invasion of Poland on September 1, 1939, President Roosevelt immediately issued an appeal "to the Governments of France, Germany, Italy, Poland and his Britannic Majesty" that read in full as follows:

> The ruthless bombing from the air of unfortified centers of population during the course of the hostilities which have raged in various quarters of the earth during the past few years, which has resulted

in the maiming and in the death of thousands of defenseless men, women, and children, has sickened the hearts of every civilized man and woman, and has profoundly shocked the conscience of humanity.

If resort is had to this form of inhuman barbarism during the period of the tragic conflagration with which the world is now confronted, hundreds of thousands of innocent human beings who have no responsibility for, and who are not even remotely participating in, the hostilities which have now broken out, will lose their lives. I am therefore addressing this urgent appeal to every government which may be engaged in hostilities publicly to affirm its determination that its armed forces shall in no event, and under no circumstances, undertake the bombardment from the air of civilian populations or of unfortified cities, upon the understanding that these same rules of warfare will be scrupulously observed by all of their opponents. I request an immediate reply.

In response, the British and French, and even the Germans, declared their intention to eschew targeting civilians and cultural property and bomb only military targets. In the months that followed, similar denunciations of deliberate bombing of civilians were issued in Washington, London, and Geneva (where the League of Nations was based). Early in 1940, Winston Churchill—then First Lord of the Admiralty, and soon to become prime minister—denounced the bombing of civilians as "a new and odious form of attack."[12]

Such moral outrage was short-lived, however, and as World War II unfolded, it was England and the United States rather than the Axis powers that refined the theory, legitimization, and practice of firebombing densely populated targets. The strategic bombing campaign that the Royal Air Force initiated in Germany in 1942 and the U.S. Army Air Forces perfected against Japan in 1945 was routinely described as terror bombing in later academic studies and textbooks. In the prelude to Hiroshima and Nagasaki, B-29 "Superfortress" bombers—new on the scene and used only in the Pacific theater—conducted massive incendiary raids against sixty-four Japanese cities. British air-war planners had euphemized their raids against German cities as "dehousing" (which to more than a few keen-eared speakers of English surely must have resonated with "delousing"), and this soon entered the plans and reports of their American counterparts. U.S. air crews targeting the cities of Japan eventually came to refer to their own missions as "burn jobs." While the urban-area raids against Japan were awesome operations that filled the sky with hundreds of Superfortress bombers, antiaircraft resistance was sporadic and feeble from the start and virtually nonexistent at the end. (Mechanical failure was a far greater cause of B-29 losses.) Both the Hiroshima and Nagasaki bombings involved only a single B-29 accompanied by two observer planes and preceded by unescorted weather planes.[13]

As always in such large-scale destruction, there is variation in the estimated death tolls. All told, it is calculated that between 400,000 and 600,000 civilians were killed in the air war against Germany, where almost all major cities were targeted. Including Hiroshima and Nagasaki, the total number of Japanese civilians killed in "urban area" attacks appears to have been comparable to this: close to 120,000 died in Tokyo alone, and 210,000 or more in Hiroshima and Nagasaki combined, with fatalities in the remaining sixty-three bombed cities numbering over 100,000. (An estimated 100,000 to 150,000 civilians also were killed in the battle of Okinawa.) It is thus reasonable to conclude that at least 800,000 civilians, and possibly one million or more, were killed in the Anglo-American air raids in World War II. By war's end, deliberately targeting men, women, and children in congested residential areas with "saturation" or "carpet" or "obliteration" bombing had been firmly established as strategically desirable and, certainly among the victorious Allied powers, morally acceptable.[14]

After September 11, this World War II history largely fell away. Ground Zero became code for America as victim of evil forces—alien peoples and cultures who, "unlike ourselves," did not recognize the sanctity of human life and had no compunctions about killing innocent men, women, and children. Such Islamist barbarism was offered as prima facie evidence of a clash of civilizations—the clearest imaginable illustration of a profound difference between Western and non-Western values. To an extent almost impossible to exaggerate, "Ground Zero 2001" became a wall that simultaneously took its name from the past and blocked out all sightlines of from what and where that name came.

# AIR WAR AND TERROR BOMBING IN WORLD WAR II

## *Ghost Cities*

One of the first Americans to set foot in defeated Japan was the talented photographer John Swope, who arrived with the U.S. Navy on August 28, 1945. Swope's assignment was to record the liberation of prisoners from POW camps, most of which were located outside the metropolitan areas. He did not visit Hiroshima or Nagasaki, and only passed hastily through ruined cities like Tokyo, Nagoya, Hamamatsu, Kawasaki, and Sendai. Along the way, Swope interacted with a variety of Japanese struggling to recover from the war. Although he was the first representative of the enemy most of these men and women encountered after the hostilities, Swope went about his business armed with only his camera and was almost always cordially received—an experience that prompted him to reflect about the madness of the conflict that had just ended. In the course of his several weeks in Japan, he managed not only to photograph ordinary Japanese as well as liberated POWs but also to type a thoughtful long journal, framed as a letter to his wife.[15]

Swope's description of Japan's featureless cityscapes would in one form or another be echoed by almost every representative of the victorious powers who saw the country in these immediate postwar days. Although two weeks elapsed between the emperor's announcement of capitulation and actual arrival of the victors, Tokyo remained to all appearances "a dead city." So did the other once-congested metropolitan areas Swope saw: all had become "cities bombed into nothingness," "ghost cities," "stinking ruins" peppered with "tin shanty shelters."

What Swope added to this picture that was unique among non-Japanese observers was the comparative perspective of someone accustomed to viewing war's devastation through the camera's eye. In Germany, as well as in parts of Nazi-occupied France, the aftermath of Allied bombing was rubble spiked with the skeletal remains of once-sturdy stone-and-mortar buildings, and sometimes the still-towering steeples of churches. (One need only think of the photographs of Cologne, with its great cathedral spires still reaching toward heaven.) War-ravaged urban Japan was another story:

> There is really no way to describe a bombed-out city—there is simply nothing left—that's all there is to it. I thought Le Havre [in Nazi-occupied France] . . . was badly hit, but it was nothing compared to Tokyo and the other Jap cities that have had it. It is also very hard to photograph this type of destruction. Whereas in Germany there were walls standing and many of the houses were shells, here there is nothing standing, and not even any bomb craters or piles of wreckage—it is just flat, the whole city has gone up in smoke.[16]

In retrospect, these words help explain what may seem puzzling: why the photography of bombed-out Germany tends to be more dramatic and memorable than the visual record that came out of defeated Japan. The

*43 and 44. Two of the few images John Swope recorded of the obliterated "ghost cities" he encountered everywhere upon arriving in Japan in late August 1945. Swope observed that there was almost nothing left to photograph.*

strength of Swope's own photographs lies in the record he provides of people rather than devastated places. Essentially, much of urban Japan simply burned to the ground.

■

THAT THERE WAS little left standing in these bombed cities was due to the flimsy construction of Japanese structures in general, particularly when it came to crowded residential, commercial, and industrial areas. The first aerial attack on Tokyo (and Nagoya) was the daring, one-shot "Doolittle raid" of April 18, 1942—launched from a single aircraft carrier and undertaken exclusively for its psychological impact within Japan and among Americans and other members of the Allied alliance. U.S. air forces operating out of unoccupied China also launched a score or so attacks against Japanese industrial and military targets (including Yawata and Nagasaki) in 1944, with less-than-satisfactory results.

The little-remembered attack on Nagasaki, in early August 1944, involved a small nighttime mission of twenty-four bombers dropping firebombs. Like the Doolittle raid, this was undertaken partly "for psychological reasons." At the same time, it also was regarded as a test of the effective-

ness of incendiary attacks on Japan's inflammable cities, as opposed to relying primarily on so-called precision targeting with high-explosive bombs.
The first major air raid on Tokyo, conducted by bombers operating out of
the fiercely fought-for island redoubts in the Pacific (in this case, Saipan),
did not take place until November 24, 1944. The major effect of this high-
altitude raid was also fundamentally psychological. Few bombs hit their
intended targets, but the attack brought home to the Japanese populace
that their forces were incapable of holding off the foe.[17]

Throughout the air war, U.S. planners consistently defined their
objectives in terms of destroying Japan's industrial and economic capability to wage war. At the same time, the definition of what comprised this
capability was elastic. It extended from the factories, arsenals, refineries,
shipyards, docks, and other installations where the machinery of war was
produced and concentrated to the workforce that kept this war machine
operating—and from the workforce to the populace in general, whose
patriotic morale and support enabled the leadership to continue flogging
their doomed cause. There were no clear categorical boundaries at this
level of warfare. Killing workers could be justified as just as much of a
blow at the enemy as killing soldiers and sailors. Killing women, children,

elderly people—civilians in general—obviously would demoralize both the workforce and the fighting force, and—at least in theory—undercut the government's appeals to fight to the bitter end. It was all too easy to argue that, in one way or another, everyone was a combatant.

## Extirpating "Noncombatants"

The disappearance of "noncombatants" had its genesis in the Anglo-American air war in Europe. As early as July 1941, England's Bomber Command issued a directive explicitly identifying "destroying the morale of the civil population as a whole and of the industrial workers in particular" as one of the objectives of aerial attacks against Germany. In the opening stage of this campaign (when planning the destruction of the medieval wooden city of Lübeck early in 1942), Air Marshal Arthur Harris argued for an optimal combination of incendiaries and high-explosive bombs on these grounds: "What we want to do in addition to the horrors of fire is to bring the masonry crashing down on top of the Boche, to kill Boche, and to terrify Boche." (*Boche* is derogatory French slang for the Germans, dating from World War I.) The British made no distinction between soldier and civilian in their air war on Germany, and neither did the Americans when they turned to Japan. The biggest difference in Japan was that there was not a great deal of masonry.[18]

Obliterating the distinction between fighting men and noncombatants could be rationalized by calling attention to the Axis enemy's own policies and propaganda, for Japan's leaders and ideologues, like Germany's, also declared that every one of the emperor's subjects or the Führer's *Volk* was an integral part of their nation's military mission. "One-hundred-million hearts beating as one," "the hundred million as a single bullet," the hundred million as a "shattered jewel" or a "Special Suicide Force" ready to fight to the bitter end—such rabid sloganeering on the Japanese side also turned every man, woman, and child into a combatant. Mobilization for total war touched every corner and member of society, on every side. Even as Japan's leaders were self-righteously condemning U.S. attacks on civilian populations, moreover, their naval engineers were launching the huge *Sen Toku* I-400-class "submarine aircraft carriers" it was hoped would deliver bacteriological bombs on U.S. cities; their aeronautic engineers were fiddling with blueprints for a six-engine long-range bomber nick-named "Mount Fuji" that would be capable of carrying out a one-way attack on American cities, possibly even including New York; and their scientists were looking into the possibility of developing nuclear weapons (and concluding this was theoretically possible but technically improbable in the near future). On every side, as "morale" entered the picture, moral-ity exited.[19]

At the same time, it is also true that the vision of killing Japanese (and other peoples of color) wholesale had deeper roots in the Anglophone world. Although it is correct to argue that "precision bombing" of explicit, conventional military targets was a mantra among those who directed the U.S. air war prior to 1945, the image of Japan's cities and their inhabitants going up in smoke had mesmerized the apostles of aerial bombardment—as well apocalyptic Caucasian dreamers of a race war between East and West—almost from the very beginning of the age of air power. In the mid-1920s General William (Billy) Mitchell, America's outspoken vision-ary in these matters, was already describing Japan as an "ideal target" where a U.S. air offensive would be "decisive," given the congested nature of cities built from "paper and wood or other inflammable structures." By the early 1930s, Mitchell was speaking with little restraint of a war against the "yellow military peril" in which Japan's "wood and paper" cities and towns would provide "the greatest aerial targets the world has ever seen. . . . Incendiary projectiles would burn the cities to the ground in short order." To polish off the task, Mitchell proposed accompanying this with "an attack by gas."[20]

Although the systematic incendiary bombing of congested Japanese urban areas did not begin until March 1945, and although "precision bombing" remained on the agenda of the air war until Japan's surrender, U.S. strategic planners were already discussing how easy it would be to ignite Japan's tinderbox cities before the Pearl Harbor attack. In 1939, for example, an instructor at the Army's Air Corps Tactical School directed attention to the devastating 1923 Kanto earthquake, in which flames from simple household braziers ignited collapsed dwellings and caused a conflagration that destroyed the greater part of Tokyo and Yokohama. The 1923 disaster, students were told, called attention to the "flimsy and highly inflammable materials" that constituted most urban construction in Japan, and "bears witness to the fearful destruction that may be inflicted by incendiary bombs." At the same time, however, the instructor reminded his class that "humanitarian considerations" ruled out engaging in this sort of warfare.[21]

Two years later, such reservations had been put aside. In the months immediately preceding Pearl Harbor, the prospect of torching Japanese cities not only was on the minds of U.S. military planners but even entered their wishful calculations as a deterrent to Japanese aggression. Thus, on November 15, 1941, Army Chief of Staff General George Marshall confidentially briefed seven senior journalists in Washington about the planned dispatch of additional B-17 "Flying Fortress" bombers to the Philippines, where they would more than triple what was already "the largest concentration [of B-17s] anywhere in the world" and possibly be in a position to bomb Japan itself using landing fields in the Soviet Union and perhaps China. "The U.S. is on the brink of war with the Japanese," minutes of this secret briefing read in summarizing Marshall's presentation, and "our position is highly favorable in this respect."

Marshall distributed a detailed map illustrating the numerous airfields from which Japan might be bombed, and noted that the buildup in the Philippines would be "allowed to leak" to the Japanese leadership but not the public at large. Even if this failed to serve as a deterrent, the record of the briefing paraphrased Marshall as promising that "if war with the Japanese does come, we'll fight mercilessly. Flying fortresses will be dispatched immediately to set the paper cities of Japan on fire. There won't be any hesitation about bombing civilians—it will be all-out." On November 19, four days later, Marshall instructed his staff, again in graphic language, to investigate plans for "general incendiary attacks to burn up the wood and paper structures of the densely populated Japanese cities."[22]

The media was attuned to such scenarios even before Marshall's ostensibly confidential projections. The October 31 issue of the weekly *United States News*, for example, featured a dramatic two-page topological map of "Bomber Lanes to Japan," with arrows indicating how "Japan is today within range of bomber attacks from seven main points." These ranged from Vladivostok in the Soviet Union (440 miles away) to Cavite in the Philippines (1,860 miles) to Singapore (3,250 miles). Tokyo, Yokohama, and Osaka were identified as prime targets, with the capital being typically identified as a "city of rice-paper and wood houses." Lurid illustrations of terrified Japanese being pounded from the air had actually appeared in U.S. periodicals years earlier. It was no doubt partly in response to this sort of speculation that, in the weeks before Pearl Harbor, almost half of Americans polled anticipated that any future conflict with Japan would be "comparatively easy" to win.[23]

U.S. military planners actually began tentatively identifying potential bombing targets in Japan in the spring of 1941, and were funneling this intelligence to MacArthur in the Philippines. Prior to the day of infamy, the general had received photographs and maps identifying some six hundred prospective targets in Japan. As usual, these reports described Japan's cities as "a lucrative target for bombardment aviation." Although much of this speculation stretched the actual capacity of the bombers available at the time, and depended on undependable ties with other nations (especially the Soviet Union, and the hope that it would provide bases in Siberia), it was taken seriously and proved prophetic. Once the United States entered the war in the wake of Pearl Harbor, such planning was naturally ratcheted to entirely new levels. In the immediate wake of Pearl Harbor, the U.S. government mobilized an impressive range of academics and corporate consultants explicitly to offer technical advice on the development of incendiary weapons. Long before the all-out firebombing of Japanese cities was launched in 1945, the U.S. Army Air Forces had planned and seriously practiced the art of incendiary urban attacks in the European theater of operations.[24]

As frequently happens in such matters of high policy with deadly consequences, popular fantasizing and top-level secret planning developed side by side where the doctrine of bombing enemy populations was concerned. In July 1943, as the Anglo-American air war against Germany intensified, the Walt Disney Studio rushed to produce a seventy-minute animated feature film titled *Victory Through Air Power*, based on a best-selling book of that title by the Russian strategist Major Alexander P. de Seversky, which first appeared in bookstores six months after Pearl Harbor. Animation was interspersed with interviews with de Seversky, and Disney's illustrators introduced viewers to ever more sophisticated warplanes, along with bombs that grow ever larger in size, eventually dwarfing the humans who stand next to them.

In a much commented-upon closing sequence, *Victory Through Air Power* ends with animated bombers attacking Japan from bases in Alaska. City streets are seen through opened bomb-bay doors; bombs fall; explosions destroy factories, machinery, and naval yards. The scene then dissolves into a high-altitude view of the Pacific with a fierce eagle repeatedly plunging its talons into a grotesque octopus representing Japan, its tentacles extending over nearby territories—a scene one commentator described as "a prolonged sequence of orgiastic destruction." In a final, triumphal image, the slain octopus dissolves into burned ruins, the sky clears, the sun rises, and against the soundtrack of "America the Beautiful" the eagle soars and alights on a realistic Stars and Stripes rippling in the wind as the film's title and final words, "VICTORY THROUGH AIR POWER," appear on the screen. Although much of the Disney treatment dealt with Germany, the final minutes of the film—released well before the German defeat—dwelled exclusively on long-range bombers pulverizing Japan.

Powerful, technologically advanced, efficient both economically and militarily, as well as in obliterating enemy evil and saving Allied lives—strategic bombing, to judge from this paean, had the added attraction of eliminating human terror and misery as well. As the film critic James Agee observed at the time, "there were no suffering and dying enemy civilians under all those proud promises of bombs; no civilians at all, in fact." Agee found "the gay dreams of holocaust at the end" particularly offensive. (The *New York Times*, by contrast, praised "Mr. Disney" for "a delightful and stimulating combination entertainment-information film"; rhapsodized about "eyes glued on the screen with exciting shots" that end with "dropping bomb after bomb until Japan is consumed in a roaring blaze"; and concluded that "if 'Victory Through Airpower' is propaganda, it is at least the most encouraging and inspiring propaganda that the screen has afforded us in a long time.") As the story goes, in any case, Disney sent a copy of the film to Roosevelt and Churchill while they were meeting in Quebec in August 1943, and an impressed Roosevelt passed it on to his Joint Chiefs. It was at this important conference on grand policy that the United States presented "An Air Plan for the Defeat of Japan," which included among its objectives, in contorted bureaucratic language, "the dislocation of labor by casualty."[25]

## *"Increasing the Terror" in Germany*

It is conventional wisdom that in the Anglo-American air war in Europe, the Royal Air Force (RAF) focused on firebombing German cities while the U.S. Army Air Forces (USAAF) devoted itself primarily to high-altitude "precision bombardment" of specific military and industrial targets. Even the particularly shocking February 1945 destruction of Dresden—whose architectural beauty and cultural heritage had led it to be called Germany's "Florence on the Elbe," and whose population was swollen by refugees fleeing the advancing Soviet army—seemed to confirm the precision-bombing rule where the Americans were concerned. While the British concentrated on obliterating the old city in a typical nighttime incendiary attack, the complementary U.S. raid focused on railroad marshaling yards.

While the British and U.S. air commands did adhere to such a general division of labor against Germany, however, in practice the USAAF also engaged in extensive indiscriminate bombing of its own, deliberate as well as inadvertent. Explicit targets such as rail yards, for example, were commonly located in the middle of urban areas. In addition, the frequency of dense cloud cover made U.S. bombers heavily reliant on a recently developed "radar blind bombing device" (known as "H2X"). A scrupulous analysis of Eighth Air Force mission records by Richard G. Davis, a senior Air Force historian, for example, reveals that in the last eighteen months of the air war against Germany the USAAF carried out at least sixty-nine missions explicitly targeting the "city area" of twenty-five different cities. Each of these attacks involved at least one hundred heavy bombers, and all together they dropped 60,000 tons of bombs. Thirty-five percent of this bomb load was incendiaries, whose "one function" was to destroy so-called soft targets such as houses, commercial buildings, and government offices.[26]

The bombing of Dresden conformed to this pattern. On the night of February 13, the RAF carried out "a technically perfect fire-raising attack" that unloaded 2,700 tons of bombs on the heart of the city, of which incendiaries comprised some 40 percent. The following day, the USAAF followed with a "blind" daytime raid of over three hundred B-17s ostensibly directed against Dresden's rail yards, dropping 771 tons of bombs in which the percentage of incendiaries was, again, 40 percent. Estimates of the number of civilians killed in the Dresden raids vary greatly, and will

*45. The first major air raid by the Royal Air Force was directed against the medieval city of Lübeck, on the Baltic Sea, on March 2, 1942.*

never be certain; many reliable sources now place the probable total at around thirty-five thousand.[27]

Although internal Eighth Air Force mission reports frequently identified "city areas" and "towns and cities" as targets in 1944 and the opening months of 1945, such straightforward language was rarely shared with the public and was deleted from most official U.S. accounts in the immediate postwar period. In the wake of the unexpectedly controversial bombing of Dresden, the importance of such obfuscation was reemphasized. As a top-level internal cable on USAAF press policy put it, "Public relations officers have been advised to take exceptional care that the military nature of targets attacked in the future be specified and emphasized in all cases. As in the past the statement that an attack was made on such and such a city will be avoided; specific targets will be described." Consistent with this policy, official postwar surveys of Eighth Air Force targeting scrubbed the "city area" terminology that appeared in mission reports and replaced it with the lexicon of specific military targets ("marshaling yards," "industrial areas," "port areas," etc.).

In a massive study published under Air Force auspices in 1993, Davis

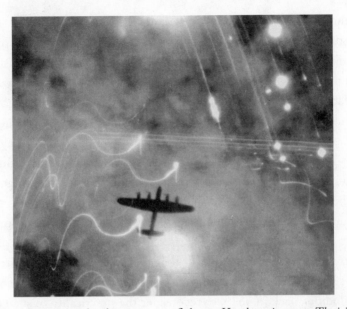

*46. A British Lancaster bomber encounters flak over Hamburg in 1943. The joint British and U.S. incendiary bombing of the city—in a massive attack codenamed "Operation Gomorrah" that extended over three nights in July—created a firestorm that resulted in fatalities variously estimated at between thirty thousand and fifty thousand residents.*

offered a graphic description of the difference between precisely labeled military targets and the actual nature of the U.S. raids: "a well-hit marshaling yard meant a well-hit city, with block upon block of residential areas gutted, families left homeless, small businesses smashed, and workers and others—including women and children—blown to bits or, more likely, burned or crushed by the hundreds, if not thousands." In actual practice, he concluded, "'marshaling yards' undoubtedly served as a euphemism for city areas." This was a euphemism that, for sometimes complex psychological reasons, many war planners themselves long persisted in accepting at face value.[28]

The destruction of Dresden so near the end of the war against Germany momentarily drew public attention to the concept of "terror" itself. To the consternation of both the British and U.S. high commands, the Associated Press paraphrased an RAF briefing officer to the effect that "Allied Air Chiefs" had made "the long awaited decision to adopt deliberate terror bombing of German population centers as a ruthless expedient to hasten Hitler's doom." Although military spokesmen hastened to deny this, and the comment was quickly suppressed in the British—but not U.S.—media, by this date terror was firmly established as central to the everyday practice of the air war in Europe. Certainly on the British side, the old-fashioned notion that *jus in bello* still should reflect "proportionality" and constrain the means chosen to attain a desired military end had long since gone out the window. As Air Marshal Harris put it in an internal memorandum after the controversy over Dresden erupted, "Attacks on cities like any other act of war are intolerable unless they are strategically justified. But they are strategically justified in so far as they tend to shorten the war and pre-serve the lives of Allied soldiers." Dresden, Harris declared, "was a mass of munitions works, an intact government centre, and a key transportation point to the East. It is now none of these things."[29]

Still, Dresden and the criticism that followed prompted Churchill, a strong supporter of area bombing despite his condemnation of such prac-tices as odious back in 1940, to reconsider the practicality of such tactics at this late stage of the war in Europe. (Among Churchill's concerns was the impending victory of the Soviet Union, as well as material problems in a devastated postwar Germany.) On March 28, a few weeks before Ger-many's capitulation, the prime minister dashed off this minute to his mili-tary staff:

It seems to me that the moment has come when the question of bombing of German cities simply for the sake of increasing the ter-ror, though under other pretexts, should be reviewed. Otherwise we shall come into control of an utterly ruined land. We shall not, for instance, be able to get housing materials out of Germany for our own needs because some temporary provision would have to be made for the Germans themselves. The destruction of Dresden remains a serious query against the conduct of Allied bombing. I am of the opinion that military objectives must henceforward be more strictly studied in our own interests rather than that of the enemy.

The Foreign Secretary has spoken to me on this subject, and I feel the need for more precise concentration upon military objec-tives, such as oil and communications behind the immediate battle-zone, rather than on mere acts of terror and wanton destruction, however impressive.[30]

## Targeting Japan

*Bombing . . . simply for the sake of increasing the terror, though under other pretexts.* No one combined unsentimental realism and linguistic acrobatics more fluently than Churchill, and his confidential observation adroitly captures this where area bombing was concerned: one planned and practiced terror and wanton destruction from the sky under other names. In this instance, indeed, the language was too clever by half, for on April 1 the prime minister withdrew his memorandum of four days earlier at the urging of his air staff and replaced it with a more discreet note that eliminated all references to wanton terror.[31]

In military parlance itself, the most benign of names and pretexts entailed identifying targets as "marshaling yards" and the like, even where incendiaries comprised a large percentage of the bomb loads and the air raids themselves were usually carried out in weather that demanded blind bombing. More accurate, although still in its own way euphemistic, was the straightforward identification in Eighth Air Force mission records of "city areas" and "towns and cities" as targets. A more composite euphemism enshrined at the highest levels of secret wartime U.S. planning from an early date called for targeting "urban industrial areas." It was not until the air war shifted to Japan, however, that the United States—like the RAF in Germany—made this the absolute focus of its bombing policy. Even then, moreover, the policy affirmed in public remained the same: that the basic intent of these missions was to destroy explicitly military targets.

Serious selection of bombing targets in Japan began in February 1943— before the cutting-edge long-range B-29 heavy bombers had come off the production lines and been debugged and actually dispatched to Asia, and before the key Pacific islands that would serve as their primary bases were captured. Central to the strategic thinking behind these developments was the argument that the peculiar industrial demography of Japan made urban-area bombing especially desirable, since a great deal of military-related manufacturing was concentrated in cities and took place in small establishments and "feeder" or "home" enterprises. Among other initiatives, the military's studies involved the construction of clusters of model Japanese (and German) working-class houses at the Dugway Proving

Ground in Utah, and their demolition with various kinds of firebombs. The mock Japanese residences were built as twelve wooden duplex units positioned in four rows (the German counterpart was a large brick duplex structure divided into apartments).[32]

The demolition tests, which began in May 1943 and extended into 1944, provide a snapshot of cultural knowledge at war. The architect chosen to design the models of Japanese housing was Antonin Raymond, who had lived in Japan and was deeply influenced by its architectural aesthetics. Raymond accepted the assignment after concluding that bombing was the most effective way to terminate the war quickly, and proceeded to apply his knowledge meticulously. Commercial researchers were enlisted to ensure the closest approximation to Japanese building materials. Sitka spruce was selected as the nearest American counterpart to the Japanese cypress (*hinoki*) used in construction. Southwest adobe took the place of the mud plaster used in Japanese walls. *Tatami* straw mats were shipped in from Hawaii. A prefabrication factory was established near Fort Dix in New Jersey, and the parts were shipped by truck to Utah over a thousand miles away and replaced as earlier shipments were destroyed in the tests. Raymond's description of his contribution was almost affectionate in its intimate detail: "The buildings were fully furnished with 'futon,' 'zabuton' and everything that one finds usually in a Japanese house. They even had 'amado' (sliding shutters), and bombarding was tried at night and in the daytime, with the 'amado' closed or open." Although the RAF did not participate in the air war against Japan, at this early stage the British also built "some Japanese structures" and subjected them to bombing trials. (Raymond saw their design plans and dismissed them with scorn as having been "copied from some books" and being "more in the design of temples with large timbers, and completely misleading.")[33]

"Incendiary attack" had been explicitly added to the USAAF itemization of targets in May 1943 (when the mock workers' homes project was initiated), and by October the engineers, scientists, and strategic planners had finalized a report that unsurprisingly confirmed what common sense as well as several decades of apocalyptic pulp literature had already suggested: that Japan's population as well as war industry was densely concentrated in a small number of cities, and these cities were tinderboxes waiting to be ignited. Titled "Japan, Incendiary Attack Data," this report listed, on

47. *Beginning in 1943, mock German and Japanese urban residences were constructed at the Dugway Proving Ground in Utah for use as experimental targets in the testing of new incendiary weapons. The brick-and-stone German residences are on the right, and wooden Japanese homes, meticulously re-created right down to interior furnishings, on the left.*

its first page, four reasons why Japanese cities were even more attractive targets than German cities for incendiary attack: greater inflammability of residential construction; greater congestion; proximity of factories and military objectives to residential construction; and the concentration of war industry in a few major cities.

The report also called attention to the complementariness of "direct effects" of incendiary bombing (on production facilities, military establishments, storage facilities, etc.) and "indirect effects" (in the form of reduced worker efficiency, casualties among workers, damage to transportation and public utilities, diversion of resources to reconstruction, and lowered Japanese morale). This was the planning process that lay behind the "dislocation of labor by casualty" scenario introduced at the Quebec Conference two months previously as being integral to defeating Japan. In the final version of "Japan, Incendiary Attack Data," submitted to the U.S. high command on November 11, "*urban industrial areas*, vulnerable to incendiary attacks" were listed as one of six "profitable aviation target systems."[34]

These evolving targeting plans quickly took on a momentum of their own. By June 1944, planners had focused attention on destroying the six most important urban areas on the main island of Honshu: Tokyo, Nagoya, Osaka, Kobe, Yokohama, and Kawasaki. By September, they had worked out plans estimating that such attacks might result in over a half-million

fatalities. As one internal planning report by the Army Air Forces intelligence division (A–2) put it, "The subcommittee considered an optimum
result of complete chaos in six cities killing 584,000 people." By October,
the list of prospective urban targets had been expanded to twenty-two cities. Earlier arguments that Japan's war industry was concentrated in just
"a few major cities" were already being brushed aside in the excitement of
contemplating the new capabilities of aerial mass destruction.[35]

Although the chillingly elegant four-engine B-29s were not deployed
against Japan until 1944, their inception and development dated back to
1939. Despite the early identification of urban-area targets, however, and
despite the precedent of firebombing German cities, prior to March 1945
the missions U.S. crews flew from bases in China and subsequently the
Marianas (notably Guam, Saipan, and Tinian) involved daytime attacks
on specific military-industrial complexes from altitudes of around 30,000
to 35,000 feet. U.S. losses on these early missions amounted to over 5
percent of bombers airborne, and photo reconnaissance revealed that the
results of this so-called precision bombardment campaign were highly
imprecise and unsatisfactory.

The reasons for these unsatisfactory results were numerous, not least
among them the fact that the jet stream high above Japan was exceptionally strong and turbulent, sometimes amounting to winds in the neighborhood of two hundred miles per hour or more. Encountered as a tailwind,
the jet stream propelled bombers over their projected targets at speeds too
fast for precision bombing. Hit by the jet stream from the side, the B-29s
often drifted as much as forty-five degrees, which was usually too much for
the bombsights to compensate for. Confronted as a headwind, the speed
of the planes dropped to a point where they became easier targets for antiaircraft defenses. As over Germany, moreover, the cloud cover over Japan
was more often than not dense, making visual targeting impossible.[36]

Plans for carpet bombing Japanese cities, in any case, were already on
the books long before this actually became standard operating procedure—
and not only on the books but also on the calendar. As early as May 1944,
U.S. planners had concluded that the best weather for delivering incendiary attacks would occur in March and September. Thus, a kind of meteorological imperative meshed with other considerations (long-established
anticipation of urban-area attacks, acquisition of Pacific bases from which

the B-29s could easily reach Japan, persistent difficulties and shortcomings in the "precision-bombing" raids) to prompt a stunning new strategy that changed the nature of America's air war—and in certain ways, perhaps, the nature of America itself.[37]

### Firebombing the Great Cities

On March 9, 1945—much as the weathermen had been recommending—General Curtis E. LeMay, commander of the Twentieth Air Force, dispatched his B-29 crews on a massive, low-altitude, radar-guided, nighttime, incendiary raid that burned the heart of Tokyo to the ground. Among other considerations, going in at low altitude at night placed less strain on the engines and decreased the effectiveness of Japan's already overwhelmed antiaircraft (fighter plane and ground fire) defenses. With the latter consideration in mind, LeMay also boldly stripped the bombers of much of the defensive guns, gunners, ammunition, and armor they had carried on high-altitude flights, thus greatly increasing the bomb load each Superfortress could carry by as much as 25 percent (or roughly three-thousand additional pounds of incendiaries).[38]

In theory—and in the sanitized coverage of the air war in the U.S. media—war-related industry remained the primary target of this and subsequent raids on Japan's major and minor cities. In practice, as Thomas Searle has carefully documented, there was little attempt in military circles to disguise the fact that civilians were being deliberately killed en masse. In the "Target Description" for the March 9 raid, titled "Tokyo Urban Industrial Area" and distributed to officers of the bomber crews, it was noted that "within this target area of approximately 10 square miles, the average population is 103,000 people per square mile, an average probably not exceeded in any other modern industrial city in the world." Pilots were thus explicitly informed that they would be firebombing an area with an estimated population of around one million people. Under "Importance" of the mission, the Target Description explained, among other things, that "employment at scores of war plants throughout Tokyo and environs would be directly affected by casualties, movement of workers out of the area, use of manpower in reconstruction, and probably lowered worker morale." Lieutenant General Ira C. Eaker, deputy commander of

*48. Charred corpses of a mother and child killed in the great Tokyo air raid on the night of March 9, 1945. (Her back, where she was carrying the child while attempting to flee the conflagration, is less burned.) The firestorm killed close to one hundred thousand residents and was a prelude to the incendiary bombing of sixty-three additional cities and towns prior to the dropping of the atomic bombs on Hiroshima and Nagasaki five months later.*

the USAAF from March 1945 on, later paraphrased this for a postwar interviewer. "It made a lot of sense," he explained, "to kill skilled workers by burning whole areas."[39]

Until Hiroshima, this first Tokyo air raid remained the most devastating single aerial attack delivered against Japan. LeMay's force, numbering 334 bombers, dropped two thousand tons of bombs from altitudes ranging from roughly 5,000 to 9,000 feet on a target area that actually measured some four by three miles. An authoritative early postwar account records that "the bombs-away message set the pattern for future reports: 'Bombing the target visually. Large fires observed. Flak moderate. Fighter opposition nil.'" B-29 crews returning home could still see the conflagration from 150 miles away, and post-attack photo reconnaissance calculated that the destruction amounted to 15.8 square miles burned out, including "18 per cent of the industrial area, 63 per cent of the commercial area, and the heart of the congested residential district."

The violence of the firestorm created by this first all-out incendiary

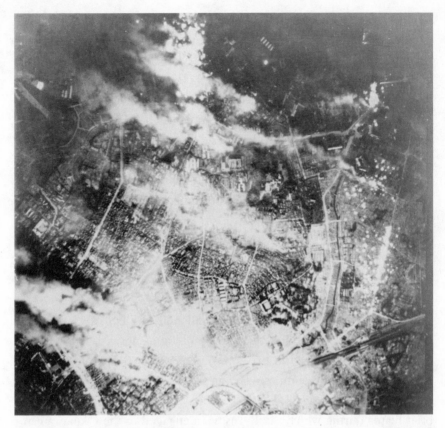

*49.  Aerial view of Tokyo engulfed in flames during an air raid on May 26, 1945. By war's end, fifty-two square miles of the capital city had been destroyed.*

raid on Japan was not replicated until Hiroshima five months later. Winds generated by the conflagration are estimated to have ranged from twenty-eight to over fifty-five miles per hour, carrying "burning brands" out to sea and creating—if we can believe the official postwar U.S. reports—turbulence approximating a Hollywood spectacle within the attacking force itself. "Pilots reported," one Strategic Bombing Survey report has it, "that the air was so violent that B-29s at 6,000 feet were turned completely over, and that the heat was so intense, even at that altitude, that the entire crew had to don oxygen masks." Imagine, as few wished to do, what it was like for men, women, and children on the ground—what it was like, as did happen, for example, for a mother fleeing the ferocious firestorm with an infant strapped on her back to discover that her child was aflame.

Japanese officials themselves, who after as well as before the surrender usually underestimated their losses (and proved unreliable with statistics in general), calculated that this first Tokyo air raid destroyed around 267,000 buildings, about one-quarter of Tokyo's total. It took the police twenty-five days to remove all the corpses, some of which clogged the city's canals; individuals attempting to flee the flames had often sought refuge in these waterways, and then been scalded to death when the heat from the firestorm brought the water to a boil. Radio Tokyo called the disaster "slaughter bombing," and the human toll was awesome by anyone's reckoning. Japanese authorities put the number of fatalities at the impossibly exact number of 83,793, which is now regarded as conservative; the estimated number of injured ranges from half to twice that number. Over a million individuals were left homeless. In his postwar memoirs, LeMay blandly described victims of this historic air raid as being "scorched and boiled and baked to death."[40]

In the ten days following the Tokyo air raid, the USAAF launched a concentrated campaign of saturation bombing against Nagoya (around 5 square miles destroyed in two raids), Osaka (over 8 square miles), and Kobe (close to 3 square miles)—giving a total of roughly 32 square miles of dense urban landscape demolished between March 9 and 19. After a brief hiatus during which the B-29s were engaged in the Okinawa campaign, the bombers returned to urban-area targeting in the home islands in mid-April. (Estimates of civilian fatalities in Okinawa, not reckoned as part of the air war since USAAF support there was largely tactical, range from less than 100,000 to as high as 150,000.) Successive attacks on Tokyo on April 13 and 15 destroyed an additional 17 square miles of the capital (although on explicit orders from Washington, pilots were briefed to avoid bombing the imperial palace, "since the Emperor of Japan is not at present a liability and may later become an asset"). Nagoya was subjected to additional raids. Yokohama and Kawasaki, the last two of the big-six major cities, came next. In the latter part of May, the B-29s revisited Tokyo, again inflicting massive physical damage but with a far smaller number of casualties than on March 9.[41]

U.S. officials put the total urban area of Japan's six major industrial cities at 257 square miles. By mid-June of 1945, it was calculated that over 105 square miles of this total had been destroyed. This was, in fact, very close to the "planned target areas" in the six cities, which added up to some 113 square miles. In the sprawling capital city alone, total physical destruction amounted to 56 square miles, slightly over half of the metropolis.[42]

Although casualties in these subsequent bombings of the capital and other major cities never came close to the appalling level of March 9 and 10, that was not the impression Americans back home were given. On the contrary, on May 30, 1945, the *New York Times* carried a three-line, three-column, front-page headline reading as follows: MARINES CRASH INTO SHURI, WIN ALL NORTH PART OF NAHA; TOKYO ERASED, SAYS LEMAY. The independent article on the erasure of Tokyo took second place to the military advance in Okinawa, and received its own two-column, two-tier subhead:

> *51 Square Miles Burned Out*
> *In Six B-29 Attacks on Tokyo*

---

> *LeMay Backs Figures With Photos of Havoc*
> *—1,000,000 Japanese Are Believed*
> *to Have Perished In Fires*

The accompanying article, datelined from LeMay's headquarters in Guam, spoke of "miles and miles of rubble . . . all that was left of what had been important arsenals, electric plants, engine plants and the home factories that figured so largely in the Japanese economy." It gave the reasonable estimate of 51 square miles of Tokyo destroyed, and only in the eleventh paragraph, on an inside page, did it get to the astonishing estimate of fatalities—and suggest that the subhead may in fact have been restrained. "It is possible," the *Times* reported, "that 1,000,000, or maybe even twice that number of the Emperor's subjects, perished." The remainder of the article focused on the dates of the six raids and number of B-29s lost.

The fatality estimate for Tokyo was exaggerated by a factor of ten or twenty, but more suggestive in retrospect is how casually such a staggering number of projected Japanese civilian deaths could be reported, and tucked away, by this date. It did not even qualify as the lead story. Suggestive, too, is how nonchalantly even a paper at the respected level of the *Times* could report that one or perhaps two million "of the Emperor's subjects" had been killed in an attack on arsenals, electric plants, engine plants, and home factories—and leave it at that.[43]

### "Burn Jobs" and "Secondary Targets"

In the reports that laid the groundwork for urban-area incendiary raids, U.S. planners emphasized that one of the features of Japan's economy that made such raids particularly desirable was that war industry was concentrated in a few large cities. As it turned out, the bombing of the country's six major urban areas was but a prelude to an intensified campaign that ultimately targeted sixty additional cities.

Beginning in mid-June, and prior to the dropping of the atomic bombs on Hiroshima and Nagasaki in early August, LeMay's command firebombed fifty-eight "secondary cities" with populations ranging from an estimated 31,000 (Tsuruga) to 400,000 (Isezaki). In twenty of these cities, the population was less than 75,000, and in another twenty between 75,000 and 150,000. Twelve of the firebombed "secondary cities" had populations between 150,000 and 250,000. In terms of "square miles destroyed," the crudest index of effectiveness, it was calculated that ten of these secondary cities were between 40 and 49 percent destroyed; six, between 50 and 59 percent destroyed; eleven, between 60 and 69 percent destroyed; and nine, between 70 and 79 percent destroyed. In four cities—Fukui, Hachioji, Numazu, and Toyama—the firebombing destroyed 80 percent or more of the built-up urban area. The destruction in Toyama, with a population of 128,000, was put at an astonishing 99.5 percent. (An American radio operator in the Toyama raid wrote this in his journal: "The drop was made, no flak no fighters were encountered—a milk run, intelligence was correct.") The cumulative area destroyed in the so-called secondary cities came to around 64 square miles, bringing the estimated total of urban-area destruction prior to the dropping of the atomic bombs to close to 170 square miles. When the photographer John Swope spoke of dead cities and ghost cities and cities bombed into nothingness, he was engaging in only the slightest hyperbole.[44]

The lavishly staffed postwar U.S. Strategic Bombing Survey concluded that "the urban area incendiary attacks eliminated completely the residential and smaller commercial and industrial structures in the affected areas and a significant number of important plants." Including Hiroshima and Nagasaki, "approximately 30 percent of the entire urban population of Japan lost their homes." Compared to the air war against Germany, Japan's cities proved to be a cost-efficient target indeed: the total tonnage of bombs dropped on Japan proper came to a mere 8.4 percent of that dropped on Germany, with two-thirds of this bomb load—and three-quarters from May 1945 on—being firebombs.[45]

There are a number of explanations for why the total number of casualties from this wholesale targeting of urban areas was not much larger. For one, firestorms of the sort that devastated Tokyo in early March depended on a rare confluence of conditions that was not repeated until the atomic bombing of Hiroshima. (Only two target cities in the air war against Germany, Hamburg and Dresden, experienced firestorms.) Additionally, once the air raids began, most cities tore down houses to create firebreaks ranging from 100 to 300 feet wide. While saturation bombing ignited both sides of these breaks, some nonetheless provided avenues of escape. Civil defense measures, including homemade ditches and makeshift backyard shelters as well as public shelters, were inadequate but helped to a degree in decreasing casualties. Also, large numbers of schoolchildren were evacuated to the countryside—although many adolescents remained behind to help create firebreaks, work in factories, and provide other kinds of low-skill assistance to the increasingly desperate war effort.[46]

In designating "secondary targets" once the six major urban areas had been decimated, the number-one consideration of planners was "congestion and inflammability" or "combustibility" (followed, in the formal listing of priorities, by incidence of war-related industry, transportation facilities, size and population, and adaptability to radar bombing). In practice, as the Strategic Bombing Survey observed, "certain of the cities attacked had virtually no industrial importance," and "the preponderant purpose appears to have been to secure the heaviest possible morale and shock effect by widespread attack upon the Japanese civilian population." Chronologically, most of the targeted cities that had populations under 100,000 were bombed in the final month of the war—that is, beginning around mid-July. They were chosen for destruction primarily because they were highly combustible and still standing. They were, in a word, simply targets of opportunity. These were the missions that were referred to as "burn jobs" as well as "milk runs," and Japanese opposition to them, as an official postwar U.S. account observed of the very first of the secondary-city raids, was "almost nil."[47]

As U.S. forces advanced on Japan, psychological warfare operatives in the Office of War Information and the Army produced a variety of leaflets to drop on soldiers in the field and the emperor's subjects back home, all urging them in one way or another to cease resistance in the face of impending annihilation. Many of these leaflets, particularly those per-taining to the bombing campaign, featured lengthy messages in Japanese on one side and doomsday graphics on the other. Boldly drawn arma-das of warships and bombers closed in on the home islands. Bomb loads tumbled from B-29s. Several grim colored leaflets featured artists' ren-derings of Japanese workers and city dwellers consumed in flames. One, a woodcut colored bright red, depicted a crowd of Japanese fleeing the conflagration—their features distended like the disturbed and disturbing figure on the bridge in Edward Munch's famous painting *The Scream*.

"Every day of added resistance will bring greater terror upon you," read the text on one such leaflet. "Bombs will blast great holes in your cities. Bombs directed at factories will also destroy your homes while you scurry desperately for a place of shelter, which does not exist. Incen-diary bombs will start conflagrations, which will envelop you and con-sume you in flames. Every plane will leave horror in its wake. You cannot escape. You cannot hide. Resistance means a horrible death. Demand an end to such hopeless resistance. This is the only way to save the nation."

In the final days of July 1945, LeMay's command introduced the most famous of the bombing leaflets, featuring a blue-tinted photo of five B-29s in profile dropping their payloads. Twelve cities were named in circles at the bottom of the image, and several-score cities all told received these warnings. The message on the reverse side declared that the main tar-gets of air raids which would soon hit some of the itemized cities were military installations, workshops, and factories. "Unfortunately," the text continued, "bombs have no eyes. So, in accordance with America's well-known humanitarian policies, the American Air Force, which does not wish to injure innocent people, now gives you warning to evacuate the cities named and save your lives." America's goal was to free the Japanese people from the oppression of the military clique and bring about "the emergence of a new and better Japan." All the cities itemized on these leaflets were small and of negligible strategic importance. Neither Hiroshima nor Nagasaki nor Kokura (a third projected atomic-bomb target) were included among them.[48]

## Morale, Shock, and Psychological Warfare

In official and semiofficial accounts of the air war, "morale and shock effect" tend to be buried beneath exhaustively detailed accounts of operational planning and physical damage, but they are never neglected. Only one of the Strategic Bombing Survey's 100-plus studies of the Pacific Theater addressed "the effects of strategic bombing on Japanese morale"— but this report was a substantial one, and concluded that those effects were considerable. (There was no intensive official inquiry beyond this into the immediate and longer-term human costs of Japan's war. Certain considerations that would interest researchers today, such as post-traumatic stress, went unexamined and were rarely addressed even in passing.)

In the exceedingly brief summation of these findings that appeared in the Survey's overall summary report, it was observed that in "scientifically" conducted post-surrender polls, "sixty-four percent of the population stated that they had reached a point prior to surrender where they felt personally unable to go on with the war. Of these, less than one-tenth attributed the cause to military defeat, one-quarter attributed the cause to shortages of food and civilian supplies, the largest part to air attack." Because an estimated 8.5 million urban residents (or more) left the cities for the countryside after air raids or to escape them, their demoralization and defeatism rubbed off on the rural population as well.[49]

In fact, morale was a double-edged consideration throughout the bombing campaign—a simple fact that often is buried when discussing psychological warfare in this new age of total war. Terror bombing was not aimed only at destroying enemy will. The devastating urban-area raids simultaneously provided an enormous boost to American morale as the Pacific War entered its ferocious endgame against a fanatical enemy now engaged in kamikaze tactics and suicidal last stands like Saipan, Iwo Jima, and Okinawa. As one internal military report put it after the great

50. *The ideographs on this 1944 leaflet, printed entirely in red ink, read "America's Overwhelming Sea and Air Power." Japanese text on the reverse side typically warns that resistance is futile.*

51. *Titled "Living Hell of the Bombs," this multicolored leaflet dropped in 1945 dwells in detail on how "every day of added resistance will bring greater terror upon you," and "every plane will leave horror in its wake."*

52. *This scene of mass panic, flame red in color, is accompanied by a reverse-side text describing the destructiveness of U.S. airpower as "a thousand times greater" than the 1923 Kanto earthquake. This "American style of earthquake," the warning continues, will destroy homes, cause factories to vanish, and kill "your family."*

53. *Fully and almost delicately colored, this rendering of a broken, burning man carries a very long description of the advanced bombers and new incendiary weapons the United States has developed "to kill and destroy," against which resistance is hopeless.*

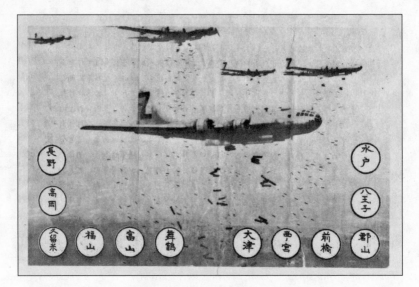

長野　高岡　久留米　福山　富山　舞鶴　大津　西ノ宮　前橋　郡山　水戸　八王子

*54. On July 27, July 30, and August 3, 1945, U.S. aircraft dropped many hundreds of thousands of "twelve-city" leaflets on over thirty prospective bombing targets, warning of possible impending destruction. The cities itemized were of negligible strategic significance apart from psychological considerations, and neither Hiroshima nor Nagasaki was among them.*

incendiary raid on Tokyo in early March, the astounding success of the new bombing policy "salvaged the morale and fighting spirit" of LeMay's crews and persuaded them that the B-29 was "an efficient and reliable aircraft."[50] Beyond this, of course, news that war had finally come home with a vengeance to Japan, and the emperor's loyal subjects were being "erased" in a wholesale manner, was uplifting to virtually everyone on the Allied side—not only in the theaters of battle but also on the home fronts of the Anglo-American powers and, to the extent such information could be disseminated, in China and much of the rest of occupied Asia as well.

On the more usually observed side of the coin, the final year of the war saw a severe decline in both Japanese industrial productivity and living conditions, including nutrition levels. To what extent the air war deserves credit for this remains an ongoing debate, however, in which the effects of direct bombing must be set against the U.S. Navy's destruction of Japan's merchant marine and the combined sea-air blockade that cut off vital resources to the home islands. In one extreme line of argument, it was the

*55. The strategic-bomber-in-profile leaflet introduced at the end of the air war against Japan became a psyops fixture in subsequent U.S. bombing campaigns in Korea, Vietnam, the first Gulf War, and Kosovo. This leaflet juxtaposing a B-52 and Osama bin Laden was first dropped on Afghanistan on October 15, 2001, one week after the United States began bombing that country for providing a haven for Al Qaeda. The text warns, ironically in retrospect, that there is no possibility of hiding or escaping.*

cutting off of resources rather than the strategic bombing campaign that was the precipitating factor behind Japan's surrender.[51]

A parallel debate surrounds how to measure the demoralization that undeniably grew ever greater as city after city was incinerated. No one denies that most Japanese were emotionally exhausted before Hiroshima and Nagasaki, but almost no one doubts that the great majority would have fought tenaciously to defend their country if it faced invasion. At the same time, the records of the Japanese secret police and others keenly attuned to popular sentiments reveal great anxiety on the part of the ruling groups that shattering defeat itself might well tip popular sentiment in the direction of revolutionary and even "communistic" internal upheaval—a perception that ultimately made the queasy elites, including advisers close to the throne as well as Emperor Hirohito himself, increasingly anxious to find a way out of their mounting crisis before it was too late.[52]

What is not controversial is that urban-area bombing brought the war home to the general populace in the starkest manner conceivable, amounting not merely to physical ruin but to psychological warfare of the most brutal sort: amounting, in a word, to terror.

IN THE WAKE of 9-11, many horrified Americans reverted to the moral mindset of the late 1930s, when it was assumed that deliberately targeting civilians was something that only barbaric others did. This is unsurprising, but it involved excising from memory much of the culture, psychology, and practice of warfare that came out of World War II. "Terror" was not a term the Americans and English bandied around loosely at that time, for there was always the danger that such frankness would blur the enormous differences between the democracies and the Axis enemy. As Churchill had privately acknowledged, one practiced terror and wanton destruction "under other pretexts." At the same time, however, neither during the war nor after was such straightforward labeling buried. Thus, a multivolume study of U.S. Army Air Forces in World War II, written under official auspices and published in the 1950s, concludes that "the all-out B-29 attack" that followed destruction of the six major urban areas had a profound effect on Japanese morale, "as the terror which had earlier been confined to a few great cities was spread throughout the country."[53]

Other accounts were less restrained. In the midst of the euphoria over Japan's shattering defeat, for example, the USAAF itself issued a celebratory public-relations release titled "Highlights of the Twentieth Air Force" that rhapsodized over the "fiery perfection" of "jellied fire attacks" that "literally burned Japan out of the war." Prepared by the military's Office of Information Services in New York, the release reiterated the then-standard approximate casualty estimates (in this case 310,000 Japanese civilians killed, 412,000 injured, and over 9 million rendered homeless) and found patriotic joy in imagining how for "five flaming months . . . a thousand All-American planes and 20,000 American men brought homelessness, terror, and death to an arrogant foe, and left him practically a nomad in an almost cityless land."[54]

This was, of course, good terror—delivered against an atrocious enemy that, in the Japanese case, showed no mercy to its own fighting forces and civilian populace, let alone to other Asians like the Chinese or Fili-

*56. "Should there be air raids," this dramatic poster reads, "they will not be aimed at destroying our homeland, but at breaking our morale. Are we to let them demoralize our Yamato Spirit?"*

もし、空襲があるならば
それは日本本土の爆破を目的とはしてゐない
諸君の心を破壊しようとしてゐるのだ
そんなことで僕等の大和魂が挫ぐものか

pinos or Indonesians, or to their own colonial subjects like the Koreans, or to Caucasian adversaries in the field. From their own perspective on the other side of the battle line, Allied fighting forces were as familiar as the Japanese themselves with the suicidal indoctrination that exhorted the "hundred million" to choose death before dishonor. (This prompted the black war-zone joke that the Japanese had been taught it was their duty to die for the emperor, and it was the Americans' duty to see that they did.) Had Japan's leaders been courageous enough to seek some kind of early surrender, they could have ventured to explore the possibility of capitulating at any time. That is what former prime minister Konoe had vainly urged the emperor to do in February 1945, before the horrendous Tokyo air raid. Even sixty-three additional devastated cities later, the emperor and his high command remained paralyzed.

Such considerations inevitably color any debate concerning whether targeting densely populated residential areas with napalm and other incendiaries explicitly designed to incinerate civilians violated the *jus in bello* provisions of traditional understandings of just war. Obviously, many would argue, the indiscriminate U.S. air attacks on civilian populations were "proportionate" to the ferocity, fanaticism, and frequent atrocious-ness of Japan's own war conduct. In the end, this argument proceeds, urban-area targeting and terror bombing shortened the war and saved uncountable Allied lives—including the lives of Chinese, who were still being killed in great numbers in 1945. As an afterthought, it is sometimes added that by helping precipitate Japan's capitulation in August 1945, these terror tactics also saved the lives of countless thousands of Japanese fighting men in the field, as well as civilians who would have perished in any Allied invasion of the home islands.

On the other hand, even bland recitation of the unfolding stages in the air war against Japan reveals an incremental callousness and almost casual-ness regarding human slaughter, accelerating from precision targeting of explicit military-related installations to targeting "urban industrial areas" in the abstract, then identifying "a few major cities" that were critical to military production, then aiming at crowded commercial and residential areas more generally—and from this in turn, once the major citie https://mail.google.com/mail/?shva=1#inbox s had been destroyed, proceeding to "all-out" bombing of medium-sized cities and towns prioritized as tar-gets based, first and foremost, on their "congestion and inflammability." Technological capability drove the war tactics, and simultaneously altered the very definition of "proportionate" and acceptable behavior. Area bombing, incendiary bombing, firebombing, carpet bombing, saturation bombing, obliteration bombing, "dehousing" the urban workforce with "jelly" bombs (that is, napalm)—all these euphemisms meant deliberately targeting and terrorizing civilian men, women, and children.

The burn jobs and milk runs that characterized the air war prior to Hiroshima and Nagasaki also represented—and this is another controver-sial story in itself—a decision not to concentrate on destroying Japan's fuel and food supplies by crippling the internal transportation system, espe-cially railroads. Given the intense, sustained concentration on destroying residential and commercial areas, it is startling to learn that after Hiro-shima was bombed, residents still struggling to survive in faraway cities like Tokyo were almost immediately able to travel by train directly to that devastated city to see whether family or relatives there had survived. That, of course, was the same transportation system that fed the industrial war machine that was purportedly the major target of the air war. In this regard, the Strategic Bombing Survey provocatively speculated, almost in passing, that had bombing priorities been directed against the railway system, there is good reason to believe that such attacks "might have brought about a very rapid capitulation."[55]

◾

IN ITS OWN way, the psychological and moral quantum leap from denouncing deliberate targeting of civilians as "inhuman barbarism" (President Roosevelt's phrase in 1939) to embracing this as the very essence of realism by 1943 was as great as the technological leap from "conventional" weapons of mass destruction to nuclear bombs. That it received less public attention—both at the time and subsequently—is not surprising: patriotic gore always trumps moral self-reflection, and sensational mass destruction is more captivating than incremental mayhem. As the casual *New York Times* article of May 30, 1945, suggested, by the time the war against Japan entered its endgame, "erasing" one of the world's most populous cities and killing a (mis)estimated million or two Japanese civilians did not warrant a banner headline or even lead-article attention, let alone provoke moral outrage. In the first issue of *Fortune* published after the war ended, the magazine's editor contributed a feature article about "the air war on Japan" that had ushered in a new age of warfare in which atomic bombs were merely the capstone. This was, he wrote, "the first unlimited war in the air," characterized by "routine obliteration of one city after another."[56]

Equally worthy of note, however, is the quiet fact that the profound challenge to the very idea of *jus in bello* that preceded Hiroshima and Nagasaki did trouble some if not a great many participants in the war against German and Japanese aggression. Such critical thoughts were usually relegated to confidential exchanges, as in an internal memorandum by General Bonner Fellers, MacArthur's intelligence chief in the Philippines. Writing on June 17, 1945—the very day, as it happens, that the campaign against the fifty-eight secondary Japanese cities was inaugurated—Fellers characterized the U.S. air war as "one of the most ruthless and barbaric killings of non-combatants in all history."[57]

Over a half century later, one of General LeMay's then-young bombing planners suggested that even the hard-boiled architect of the all-out incendiary bombing of Japan's cities was sensitive to the moral and legal ambiguity of his actions. In an Academy Award–winning documentary film, Robert McNamara (who served as secretary of defense during the Vietnam War) recalled his superior's thinking right after the war, and placed it in the context of his own retrospective rumination:

> LeMay said, "If we'd lost the war, we'd all have been prosecuted as war criminals." And I think he's right. He—and I'd say, I—were behaving as war criminals. LeMay recognized that what he was doing would be thought immoral if his side had lost. But what makes it immoral if you lose and not immoral if you win?[58]

The answer to McNamara's rhetorical question is not far to seek. Victors control the history books, and rewrite the moral codes as well.

# "THE MOST TERRIBLE BOMB IN THE HISTORY OF THE WORLD"

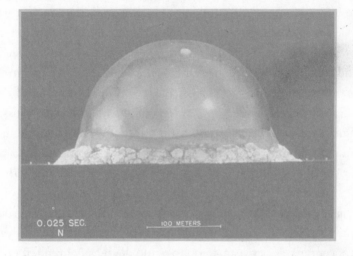

## *Ground Zeroes, 1945*

By August 1945, only a handful of Japanese cities had escaped the B-29s and their rain of fire from the sky. Such apparent good fortune was misleading. While U.S. target selection in Japan as in Europe had been left largely to planners in the military theaters, there was one great exception in the air war against the Japanese homeland. Following instructions from Washington, General LeMay's command left several cities off its lengthy list of "secondary" targets. These were to be held in reserve for a qualitatively new level of terror.

The new level of terror was the atomic bomb, and the cities selected as potential targets by the top-secret "Interim Committee" that decided whether and how to use the new weapon were Kyoto, Hiroshima, Kokura, Niigata, and, belatedly, Nagasaki. Kyoto—Japan's ancient capital and the site of many of its greatest religious, cultural, and architectural treasures—was later dropped from the list at the urging of Secretary of War Henry Stimson. Stimson had visited and been charmed by the old capital in the 1920s, and also feared that attacking a city that held such a hallowed place in Japanese consciousness would prove counterproductive, stiffening resistance and hardening anti-American sentiments. Against strenuous opposition, he won his case for removing Kyoto from the target list in late July by taking it directly to President Truman.[59]

The United States successfully tested the world's first nuclear weapon in the desert in Alamogordo, New Mexico, on July 16. Truman received the news in Potsdam, Germany, where he was meeting with the leaders of England and the Soviet Union to discuss the future of postwar Europe and conduct of the ongoing war against Japan. By the beginning of August, the U.S. military possessed two nuclear bombs based on the fission of two significantly different isotopes (uranium 235 and plutonium 239). The uranium bomb, nicknamed "Little Boy," was dropped by parachute directly over Hiroshima at 8:15 a.m. on August 6—coinciding with a time of day when many people were outdoors on their way to work or other morning activities, and timed to explode some 1,900 feet above ground so that the blast would wreak the most havoc. The thermal heat released at the hypocenter was between 5,400 to 7,200 degrees Fahrenheit (3,000 to 4,000 degrees Centigrade). Apart from tens of thousands of victims who were immediately incinerated, serious flash burns were experienced by unshielded individuals within a radius of 1.9 miles (3 kilometers), while lesser burns were incurred as far away as 2.8 miles (4.5 kilometers). The simultaneous eruption of fires all over the stricken area caused an inrush of "fire wind" that over the next few hours attained velocities of thirty to forty miles per hour, creating a firestorm comparable to that which devastated Tokyo in the March 9 incendiary raid.

Three days later, after heavy cloud cover forced Kokura to be abandoned as the target of the second bomb (nicknamed "Fat Man" because of its bulbous shape, and apparently also with the jocular innuendo of resembling England's portly Prime Minister Churchill), Nagasaki was bombed. In this case, the bomb was dropped at 11:02 a.m. and fell approximately two miles northwest of the planned hypocenter. Fat Man exploded at an altitude of some 1,500 feet above a section of Nagasaki called Urakami, and the scope of the blast and ensuing conflagration were confined by surrounding hills. The fires were less intense than in Hiroshima, and the radius of utter destruction was smaller. It is possible, at least for those so inclined, to see a certain symbolism in the fact that the Nagasaki bomb exploded close to the imposing Catholic cathedral in Urakami, and the Hiroshima bomb directly above a large hospital.[60]

Early postwar estimates of the damage inflicted by the two nuclear weapons were accurate when it came to the extent of devastation in the "zero area" of each target: approximately 4.4 square miles in Hiroshima and 1.8 square miles in Nagasaki were obliterated. Fatalities, however, were greatly understated. Relying on data provided by the Japanese, the U.S. Strategic Bombing Survey reported in June 1946 that it "believes the dead at Hiroshima to have been between 70,000 and 80,000, with an equal number injured; at Nagasaki over 35,000 dead and somewhat more than that injured seems the most plausible estimate." These early calculations, recycled in innumerable subsequent publications, lie behind the persistent but misleading argument that the first incendiary air raid on Tokyo killed more people than the atomic bombs. More recent and generally accepted estimates put the probable number of fatalities at around 130,000 to 140,000 in Hiroshima and 75,000 in Nagasaki, with most deaths occurring by the end of 1945. Some generally responsible (but less persuasive) sources place the total number of deaths from the two bombs as high as 250,000 in Hiroshima and 140,000 in Nagasaki. These latter exceptionally high fatality estimates amount to roughly 50 percent of the populations in the two cities.[61]

We will never know for certain how many men, women, and children were killed. Given the turmoil of the times, with people evacuating cities and troops moving into or passing through them, the population actually resident in the two targets in early August is unclear. Entire neighborhoods and residential areas were totally destroyed, including the paper records that might enable survivors to reconstruct who might once have lived there. To prevent spread of disease, corpses had to be disposed of quickly. Some survivors cremated their dead spouses, children, neighbors, and co-workers on their own; schoolchildren gathered a few days after

*The Hiroshima bomb, dropped on August 6, probably killed around 140,000 people. The death toll from the Nagasaki bomb three days later—which exploded some distance off target over the Catholic cathedral in the Urakami district—was around 75,000.*

57. *The mushroom cloud over Hiroshima.*

58. *Crossroad in the Hiroshima wasteland.*

59. *The mushroom cloud over Nagasaki.*

60. *The nuclear wasteland near the Urakami Cathedral in Nagasaki.*

the explosions to see dead classmates consumed in this eerie rekindling of fires; massive pyres of unidentified victims were hastily constructed and set aflame. Years later, some survivors remained haunted by the sight of this second round of deliberate fires, where in Hiroshima in particular the devastated nighttime landscape seen from a distance was pinpricked with the orange-red glow of cremations everywhere. Afterwards, people continued to die without necessarily being identified as bomb victims. For some survivors, and some kin of those who perished, to have been singled out for such a horrendous fate was a stigma to be concealed.

Most fatalities were caused by flash burns from the nuclear explosions, "secondary blast effects" including falling debris, and burns suffered in the ensuing fires. In the clinical language of the Strategic Bombing Survey, "many of these people undoubtedly died several times over, theoretically, since each was subjected to several injuries, any one of which would have been fatal." The majority of deaths occurred immediately or within a few hours, but many victims lingered in agony for days, weeks, and months before perishing. There was virtually no medical care or even ointments, medicines, or painkillers initially (most doctors and nurses had been killed, and most medical facilities destroyed), and woefully inadequate care in the prolonged aftermath of the bombings. Deaths from atomic bomb–related injuries and diseases continued to occur over the course of ensuing years and even decades.

Apart from flash burns, the most unique cause of death came from exposure to gamma rays emitted by the fission process. Among survivors of the initial blast who had been near the centers of the explosions, the onset of radiation sickness usually occurred within two or three days. Individuals who had been exposed at greater distances, and who often initially appeared to have survived unscathed, did not show severe symptoms until one to four weeks later. In addition to fever, nausea, diarrhea, vomiting blood, discharging blood from the bowels, and bloody urine, these symptoms included (in the Strategic Bombing Survey's summation) "loss of hair, inflammation and gangrene of the gums, inflammation of the mouth and pharynx, ulceration of the lower gastro-intestinal tract, small livid spots . . . resulting from escape of blood into the tissues of the skin or mucous membrane, and larger hemorrhages of gums, nose, and skin." Autopsies "showed remarkable changes in the blood picture—almost complete absence of white blood cells, and deterioration of bone marrow. Mucous membranes of the throat, lungs, stomach, and the intestines showed acute inflammation."

Years afterwards, a man who survived the Hiroshima bombing drew a picture of the pillowed face of his younger brother on his death bed, dying from the mysterious plague that was only identified as radiation sickness much later. Blood spilled from his nose and mouth, and a bowl filled with blood lay by the pillow. Text written on the picture explained that the brother had been demolishing buildings for firebreaks when the bomb was dropped, and was then recruited to help respond to the catastrophe. "He returned home on August 20, walking and apparently healthy, but around August 25 his nose began bleeding, his hair started falling out, small red spots appeared all over his body. On August 31 he died while vomiting blood." Many thousands of other survivors could have drawn similar family portraits.[62]

In the Strategic Bombing Survey's 1946 estimate, "no less than 15 to 20 percent of the deaths were from radiation," a calculation that later sources tend to endorse. At the same time, the American researchers also speculated that "if the effects of blast and fire had been entirely absent from the bombing, the number of deaths among people within a radius of one-half mile from ground zero would have been almost as great as the actual figures and the deaths among those within 1 mile would have been only slightly less. The principal difference would have been in the time of the deaths. Instead of being killed outright as were most of these victims, they would have survived for a few days or even 3 or 4 weeks, only to die eventually of radiation sickness."

The effects of residual radiation are difficult to evaluate, but it is possible that some individuals who entered the stricken cities within a hundred hours after the bombings were exposed to this. Although the weather was clear in Hiroshima and overcast in Nagasaki when the bombs were dropped, the explosions altered the atmosphere, causing moisture that condensed on the rising ash and dust to return as radioactive "black rain" in both cities. In the years that followed, the so-called late effects of radiation poisoning and other atomic bomb–related injuries took the form of statistically abnormal incidences of cataracts, blood cancers such as leukemia and multiple myeloma, and malignant tumors including thyroid cancer, breast cancer, lung cancer, stomach cancer, salivary gland cancer, and malignant lymphoma. Burn victims often found their wounds healing in the form of particularly unsightly protuberant scars known as keloids.

Radiation, compounded by other atomic-bomb effects, also affected reproduction among survivors. Shortly after the bombings, sperm counts among males within 5,000 feet of the epicenter of the Hiroshima explosion showed severe reduction. More starkly visible was the harm to pregnant women and their unborn. The Survey summarized this as follows:

> Of women in various stages of pregnancy who were within 3,000 feet of ground zero, all known cases have had miscarriages. Even up to 6,500 feet they have had miscarriages or premature infants who died shortly after birth. In the group between 6,500 and 10,000 feet, about one-third have given birth to apparently normal children. Two months after the explosion, the city's total incidence of miscarriages, abortions, and premature births was 27 percent as compared to a normal rate of 6 percent.

Scores of women who had been in the first eighteen weeks of pregnancy when exposed to the radioactive thermal blasts gave birth to congenitally malformed offspring. Microcephaly, a condition characterized by abnormally small head size and sometimes accompanied by mental retardation, was observed in some sixty children who had been in utero at the time of the bombings. In later years, as these infants grew into adolescents and adults, they became one of many sad symbols of the enduring legacy of the bombs.[63]

Until more than a decade had passed, the general public in as well as outside Japan rarely asked or cared to see or hear what it was like to be permanently maimed, scarred, or otherwise disfigured; or to live wondering if one's blood had been poisoned by radiation or, where such poisoning was assumed, if this would be passed on to children and generations yet unborn. The psychological trauma and social stigma of victimization by the atomic bombs—sometimes referred to in the newborn Japanese lexicon of nuclear affliction as "leukemia of the spirit" and "keloids of the heart"—were unquantifiable. Many survivors suffered lasting guilt that they had lived while so many around them, including loved ones, perished without their being able to help them. For many, life after August 1945 entailed what the psychiatrist Robert Jay Lifton later characterized as a "permanent encounter with death."[64]

## Anticipating Zero

Described in this clinical manner, the human effects of the atomic bombs seem almost preternaturally malevolent. They could have been imagined beforehand; and, in certain almost strangely detached ways, they were. The 509th Composite Group that was established in September 1944 to train the air crews selected for the nuclear mission, for example, focused on precision bombing from an exceptionally high altitude (as high as 30,000 feet, or between five to six miles); according to one account, "dropped a hundred and fifty-five Little Boy and Fat Man [non-nuclear] test units in the desert"; and devoted countless hours to perfecting banking sharply after release of a bomb to ensure not being taken down by the anticipated atomic blast. The projected danger area was within five miles of the explosion, and the targeted "distance-away" for the B-29 was double this.

As early as mid-May, two months before the new bomb was ready for testing, J. Robert Oppenheimer, the scientific director of the "Manhattan Project" that secretly developed the weapon under Army auspices, addressed the unique peril to the bombing crew from a different direction. The minutes of his presentation to military planners "on the radiological effects of the gadget" summarized its basic recommendations as follows: "(1) for radiological reasons no aircraft should be closer than 2½ miles to the point of detonation (for blast reasons the distance should be greater) and (2) aircraft must avoid the cloud of radio-active materials." ("Gadget" was the widely used code word for the prototype bomb.) On a later occasion, Oppenheimer informed the Interim Committee that radioactivity in all likelihood "would be dangerous to . . . a radius of at least two-thirds of a mile."[65]

These scrupulous precautions concerning the safety of the bombers themselves extended to the mid-July Trinity test in the desert of New Mexico, where around 150 military officers and scientists viewed the explosion from slit trenches three feet deep, seven feet wide, and twenty-five feet long at a "base camp" located nine miles from Zero. The closest

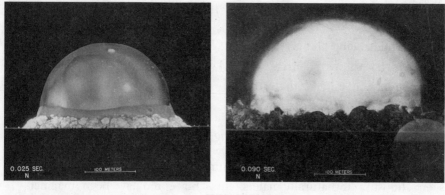

TRINITY

*61. The Trinity fireball at .025 second.*      *62. The fireball at .090 second.*

observation points, including the control center, were some 10,000 yards (5.7 miles) from where the bomb was sited on a hundred-foot steel tower, and involved shelters reinforced with cement and buried under thick layers of earth. Even observers positioned as far as twenty miles away were instructed that when a siren signaled "two minutes to zero," they were to "lie prone on the ground immediately, the face and eyes directed toward the ground and with the head away from Zero." They were given dark welder's glass through which to view the spectacle following the blinding initial flash, and told to remain prone for two minutes to avoid harm from flying debris. They also were instructed to make sure car windows were open to avoid being shattered by the blast.

Every living creature within a radius of a mile from the Trinity hypocenter—every reptile, animal, and insect—was exterminated, and the dazzling light from the explosion in the night sky was powerful enough to cause temporary blindness. (When the crews selected to bomb Hiroshima and Nagasaki were briefed about their actual mission for the first time on Tinian island, they were given special polarized goggles and the alarming warning—as one airman recorded—that "a soldier stationed twenty miles away sitting in a tent was blinded by the flash" during the test of the bomb.) The elite cadre of American, British, and European émigré scientists who planned and carried out the development and use of the bombs, and ushered in a new age of mass destruction in the process, thus did so with eyes protected but wide open—except when it came to imagining precisely whom they were killing, and how casually, and how great the slaughter

63. *Mushroom cloud forming at 2 seconds.*    64. *The mushroom cloud at 10 seconds.*

would actually be. On the latter score, Oppenheimer ventured the modest guess of perhaps twenty thousand Japanese fatalities from one bomb.[66]

At the same time, however, American and British leaders, including the scientists, immediately recognized the new weapon's potential for world-transforming catastrophe. Before Hiroshima and Nagasaki confirmed that a single bomb could now destroy an entire city as thoroughly as the earlier raids against Germany and Japan, which had required hundreds of planes carrying huge bomb loads; before anyone saw aerial photographs of the obliterated "zero areas" of the two pulverized Japanese cities, let alone beheld the destruction firsthand; before the Strategic Bombing Survey produced its influential report on "the effects of the atomic bombs on Hiroshima and Nagasaki"; before the technicians produced a "Standardized Casualty Rate" calculation that Little Boy had been 6,500 times more efficient than an ordinary high-explosive bomb in producing death and injury—before any of this, the language of Apocalypse had already been introduced to war talk.[67]

In an eyewitness report on the July 16 test, for example, Brigadier General Thomas Farrell immediately turned to thoughts of divinity, transgression, and doom. "The strong, sustained, awesome roar," he wrote, "warned of doomsday and made us feel that we puny things were blasphemous to dare tamper with the forces hitherto reserved to The Almighty." The Harvard chemist and explosives expert George Kistiakowsky found himself haunted by the same image, describing the Trinity spectacle as "the nearest thing to Doomsday that one could possibly imagine." "I am sure," the only journalist at the test recorded Kistiakowsky saying, "that at the end of the world—in the last milli-second of the earth's existence—the last man will see what we saw!" When news of the successful test reached Potsdam, Churchill characterized the new weapon as "the Second Coming—in wrath." Truman similarly turned to biblical prophecy to express his thoughts. In a handwritten diary scribbled on loose sheets of paper at Potsdam, the president wrote, on July 25, that "we have discovered the most terrible bomb in the history of the world. It may be the fire destruction prophesied in the Euphrates Valley Era, after Noah and his fabulous Ark."[68]

Oppenheimer too summoned ancient doomsday theology, in this case the Hindu tradition, to find adequate expression for what he and his colleagues felt when they opened the door to an unprecedented capacity for mass slaughter. "We knew the world would not be the same," he famously recalled when asked to describe what it felt like to harness the destructive forces of the atom. "A few people laughed, a few people cried. Most people were silent. I remembered the line from the Hindu scripture, the Bhagavad Gita; Vishnu is trying to persuade the Prince that he should do his duty, and to impress him, takes on his multi-armed form and says, 'Now I am become death, the destroyer of worlds.' I suppose we all thought that, one way or another."[69]

## Becoming Death

Despite such visions of Apocalypse, the policy makers, scientists, and military officers who had committed themselves to becoming death managed to dress and soften their doomsday visions with garments of euphemism and cocoons of comforting denial. They never seriously considered not using their devastating new weapon. They did not talk about turning mothers into cinders or irradiating even the unborn. They brushed aside discussion of alternative targets, despite the urging of many lower-echelon scientists that they consider this. They gave little if any serious consideration to whether there should be ample pause after using the first nuclear weapon to give Japan's frazzled leaders time to respond before a second bomb was dropped. Rather, the theoretical scientists, weapon designers, bomb builders, and war planners adopted the comfortable, dissembling language of destroying military targets that already had been polished to high gloss in the saturation bombing campaign that devastated sixty-four cities prior to Hiroshima and Nagasaki.

The Interim Committee had established the criteria for being selected as a prospective atomic-bomb target by the end of April. Although this preceded LeMay's initiation of the incendiary bombing of "secondary" Japanese cities by several months, the priorities for determining desirable nuclear targets were much the same. As recapitulated by General Leslie Groves, the key military coordinator of the Manhattan Project, the "governing factor" in choosing targets was that they "should be places the bombing of which would most adversely affect the will of the Japanese people to continue the war." Military considerations in the form of command posts, troop concentrations, or war-related industry were secondary to this. Overarching this were the practical provisos of any thoroughgoing experiment: that the target city should have escaped prior bombing and "be of such size that the damage would be confined within it, so that we could more definitely determine the power of the bomb."[70]

Secretary of War Stimson, one of Truman's major links to the military planners and a man widely admired for seriously engaging moral issues, provides an excellent example of this peculiar exercise in evasive ratiocination. On May 31, he recorded that the Interim Committee had reached the decision "that we could not give the Japanese any warning; that we could not concentrate on a civilian area; but that we should seek to make a profound psychological impression on as many of the inhabitants as possible." Stimson agreed with the suggestion of James Conant, another Interim Committee member and since 1933 the president of Harvard, "that the most desirable target would be a vital war plant employing a large number of workers and closely surrounded by workers' houses." Boston Brahmins and ivory-tower intellectuals—and every other statesman at the Interim Committee's planning table—apparently saw no contradiction between targeting a crowded blue-collar residential area with the most deadly weapon ever made and claiming to "not concentrate on a civilian area."[71]

It was through such rhetorical gymnastics—through what Kai Bird and Martin Sherwin nicely call "such delicate euphemisms," and Gerard DeGroot characterizes as "window dressing to assuage the guilt of those who found terror bombing unpalatable"—that the decision was made to obliterate two densely populated cities while denying that this meant deliberately targeting civilians. Stimson's diary entries and casual observations to others are as tortuous on this score as his more formal public utterances, and the fantasizing he engaged in while planning the destruction of worlds obviously rubbed off on his commander in chief. In the same "Potsdam diary" entry for July 25 in which Truman wrote of possessing "the most terrible bomb in the history of the world," the president also wrote this:

> This weapon is to be used against Japan between now and August 10th. I have told the Sec. of War, Mr. Stimson, to use it so that military objectives and soldiers and sailors are the target and not women and children. Even if the Japs are savages, ruthless, merciless and fanatic, we as the leader of the world for the common welfare cannot drop this terrible bomb on the old capital or the new [that is, on Kyoto or Tokyo].
>
> He and I are in accord. The target will be a purely military one and we will issue a warning statement asking the Japs to surrender and save lives. I'm sure they will not do that, but we will have given them the chance. It is certainly a good thing for the world that Hitler's crowd or Stalin's did not discover this atomic bomb. It seems to be the most terrible thing ever discovered, but it can be made the most useful.[72]

In the Potsdam Declaration of July 26, the United States, United Kingdom, and China called on the Japanese government to submit to terms amounting to unconditional surrender or face "prompt and utter destruction." This was the extent of the "warning statement," and its vagueness amounted in practice to the Interim Committee's no-warning decision of May 31. More striking, however, is the president's characterization of the nuclear targets as "purely military" and excluding women and children. In a radio broadcast following the dropping of the atomic bomb on Hiroshima, Truman persisted in describing the target as "a military base . . . because we wished in this first attack to avoid, insofar as possible, the killing of civilians," and in his memoirs he characterized Hiroshima similarly as a "war production center of prime military importance."

What the diary suggests—along with the table talk of the bomb planners more generally—is that this mythmaking was more than willful misrepresentation. It is better understood in terms of the self-deception, psychological avoidance, and moral evasion that almost necessarily accompanied the so-called strategic air war in general. (Truman's "Potsdam diary" was a spontaneous record of the president's daily thoughts, and for decades remained buried among the papers of a minor functionary at the Potsdam conference and unknown to researchers.) Faith in one's own and one's nation's righteous cause, and to some degree personal sanity itself, required closing off any genuinely unblinking and sustained imagination of what modern warfare had come to.[73]

Like all large Japanese cities, Hiroshima and Nagasaki were undeniably involved in the military effort. In addition to war-related factories and the presence of troops, Hiroshima in particular was a major command center and point of departure for fighting men embarking for the continent and points south. By August 1945, however—with the Japanese navy and merchant marine at the bottom of the ocean, Okinawa in Allied hands, the nation cut off from outside resources, six major cities and fifty-eight "secondary" cities and towns already pulverized by incendiary bombing, and the Japanese leadership known to be groping for an exit strategy—it was meaningless to speak of these two targets as "military objectives" in any conventional sense. They were psychological-warfare targets—an entirely new level of terror "under other pretexts."

As the Strategic Bombing Survey put it, "The two raids were all-Japan events and were intended so: The Allied Powers were trying to break the fighting spirit of the Japanese people and their leaders, not just of the residents of Hiroshima and Nagasaki." Oppenheimer came to the same conclusion after the event, and put it in even stronger terms as he contemplated the world his contribution to the Manhattan Project had ushered in. "The pattern of the use of atomic weapons was set at Hiroshima," he wrote less than four months after the war. "They are weapons of aggression, of surprise, and of terror. If they are ever used again it may well be by the thousands, or perhaps by the tens of thousands; their method of delivery may well be different, and may reflect new possibilities of interception, and the strategy of their use may well be different from what it was against an essentially defeated enemy. But it is a weapon for aggressors and the elements of surprise and terror are as intrinsic to it as are the fissionable nuclei."[74]

In the years after his presidency ended, Truman often garnered praise bordering on adulation for his plain speaking and common sense. That such a pragmatic man, placed in the cauldron of war and at the very highest level of authority, could approve targeting densely populated cities on one day, and speak of his terrible new weapon as the fire destruction prophesied in the Old Testament on another, and still imagine "women and children" would be largely excluded from harm is testimony to the extent to which psychological warfare had become inseparable from psychological denial and delusion.

## Ending the War and Saving American Lives

Denial and delusion went hand in hand with a clear, concrete concern that understandably dominates mainstream analysis of the decision to obliterate the two Japanese cities: to end the war quickly and save American lives. The analogue to this preoccupation after September 11 was equally compelling, albeit ironic. In August 1945, the professed goal was to save American lives by unleashing the most terrible weapons of mass destruction in the history of the world. The goal after 9-11 was to save American lives by preventing the ghastly spawn of the Hiroshima and Nagasaki bombs from being unleashed by stateless or state-sponsored terrorists.

After Japan's surrender, the question of how many American lives were saved by dropping the atomic bombs and precipitating Japan's capitulation without having to invade the home islands became a fiercely contested subject. Truman spoke at one point in his memoirs of anticipating a half-million casualties and at another point a half-million deaths. (Deaths, nonfatal battle injuries of varying severity, and non-battle casualties like illness or psychological disability from combat stress were easily conflated or confused in wartime projections and, much more so, in postwar recollections.) In a public exchange at Columbia University many years later, he typically and defiantly asserted that he had no second thoughts about his decision to drop the atomic bombs, and offered an even larger projection of lives spared: "It was merely another weapon in the arsenal of righteousness," he declared, and "saved millions of lives. . . . It was a purely military decision to end the war."[75] Churchill retrospectively suggested at one point that the atomic bombs saved 1.2 million Allied lives (1 million of them American), and justified using them with characteristic eloquence in the final volume of his acclaimed history of World War II: "To avert a vast, indefinite butchery, to bring the war to an end, to give peace to the world, to lay healing hands upon its tortured peoples by a manifestation of overwhelming power at the cost of a few explosions, seemed, after all our toils and perils, a miracle of deliverance."[76]

Other participants in the decision to use the bombs similarly emphasized their overriding concern with the mounting human cost of the campaign against Japan and the heavy U.S. losses this portended in any projected invasion. No responsible military or civilian leader could possibly have thought otherwise. As Stimson, the always reflective (but not always consistent or forthcoming) former secretary of war put it in a widely discussed article published in *Harper's* in 1947, "My chief purpose was to end the war in victory with the least possible cost in the lives of the men in the armies which I had helped to raise."[77] Former Army chief of staff George Marshall, another military leader admired for his moral integrity, similarly recalled the ferocity of Japan's no-surrender policy as seen in Okinawa, and coupled this with the apparent resilience of Japanese morale even after the devastating Tokyo air raid and all the incendiary urban air attacks that followed this. "So it seemed quite necessary, if we could, to shock them into action" by using the atomic bombs, he recalled. "We had to end the war; we had to save American lives."[78]

These were not rationalizations after the event, nor did they reflect a misreading of Japan's fanatical no-surrender policies. It was the hope of Japan's leaders that the suicidal defensive battles that began with Saipan in mid-1944 and extended to Iwo Jima and Okinawa would discourage the Allied powers from pursuing thoroughgoing victory and persuade them to negotiate some sort of compromise peace. Essentially, the warlords in Tokyo were still beguiled by the same sort of wishful thinking about the psychological weakness and irresolution of the American enemy that led them to attack Pearl Harbor in the first place. When Emperor Hirohito ignored advice to end the war in early 1945, he threw his support instead behind the advocates of an all-out defense of Okinawa, which it was hoped would convince the United States that Japan was willing to fight to the bitter end. (This vision of a decisive land battle calls to mind the earlier misguided faith of the Japanese "battleship admirals" that the

65. *This scene of three dead American soldiers on Buna Beach in Papua, New Guinea, marked a turning point in U.S. media coverage of the Pacific War when it appeared as a full-page picture in the September 20, 1943, issue of* Life. *The photograph, taken by George Strock seven months earlier, was initially withheld from release under the official U.S. policy of accentuating the positive and not showing graphic images of dead or gravely injured Americans. Publication of this and similar stark images marked the formal end of such censorship and the beginning of a rising crescendo of horror at the human costs of the war and rage at the Japanese responsible for this.* Life *devoted a long editorial to the Buna Beach photograph, describing the dead men as "three fragments of that life we call American life: three units of freedom." To the end of the conflict, the faces, names, and unit insignia of photographed American corpses remained concealed. They became emblematic victims, symbols of the war's terrible toll.*

enemy might be thoroughly demoralized and defeated through a single decisive battle at sea.) The basic plan for a final defense of the homeland, code-named *Ketsu-Go* (literally, Decisive Operation), was approved and disseminated to field commanders in early April. This called for suicidal resistance beginning with kamikaze attacks against the invading fleet, continuing with intense military resistance at the beachheads, and extending

66. Life *featured another iconic rendering of the war in the Pacific on the cover of its April 9, 1945, issue—here, a cropped version of W. Eugene Smith's photograph of a marine demolition team destroying a Japanese blockhouse and fortified cave on "Hill 382" on Iwo Jima. Hill 382, nicknamed "Meat Grinder," was overrun only after five previous attempts had failed. Iwo Jima "conveyed a sullen sense of evil to all the Americans who saw it for the first time,"* Life *told its readers, and "seemed like a beachhead on hell." In its archive of "Great War Photos," the magazine described this as "one of the most starkly violent cover photos in LIFE's long history," and the lengthy cover story itself also included a full-page picture by Smith of a cemetery of white crosses, representing a fraction of the more than 6,800 U.S. fighting men who were killed taking the island. This was the atmosphere in which the U.S. Army Air Forces carried out their campaign of systematically firebombing Japanese cities.*

if and when necessary to the active self-sacrifice of all the emperor's loyal adult subjects, women and men alike. It was reasonable to anticipate that "Okinawa" would have been replicated in mayhem many times over in any projected invasion, and the internal record on the U.S. side confirms how deeply this weighed on the minds of the war planners.[79]

Casualty projections were at best reasoned guesses, and U.S. planning

for an invasion of the home islands not only was subject to constant reevaluation but also was a generally compartmentalized procedure, involving
many branches and subunits of the military. There was, however, one
rough calculation that seems to have generally influenced military thinking from the fall of Saipan in early July 1944 through the spring of 1945.
Known as the "Saipan ratio," this was formulated as follows in a Joint
Chiefs of Staff planning document dated August 30, 1944: "In our Saipan
operation, it cost approximately one American killed and several wounded
to exterminate seven Japanese soldiers. On this basis it might cost us half
a million American lives and many times that number wounded . . . in the
home islands." Right up to the dropping of the bombs, most formal military plans anticipated that the conflict, including a projected two-stage
invasion, would continue well into 1946.[80]

Inevitably, these estimates fluctuated over time. U.S. intelligence did not
have access to *Ketsu-Go*, but it did not require code breaking to decipher
the thrust of enemy thinking. Japan's suicidal policies—including the cal-
lous sacrifice of civilian populations as well as fighting men on its own side
(shockingly displayed on Saipan in mid-1944 and Okinawa in the spring
of 1945) and desperate deployment of kamikaze (beginning in October
1944)—meshed with other considerations to heighten U.S. visions of how
costly an invasion would be. Knowledge that Japan had reserved army
forces several-million strong to defend the home islands was one such consideration. Japanese edicts in the spring of 1945 mobilizing all adult men
and women into a ragtag but nonetheless alarming homeland defense force
reinforced the prospect of truly tenacious resistance, accompanied as it was
by increasingly hysterical rhetoric exhorting the "hundred million" to die
gloriously in defense of the nation and its emperor-centered "national polity." The high human costs of the Allied endgame against Germany also
influenced U.S. planners, who among other considerations were well aware
that Soviet forces had taken the brunt of these casualties, whereas any invasion of Japan would fall almost entirely on U.S. forces. It was with the war
against Japan in mind that the U.S. Selective Service upped its monthly
draft quotas in early 1945.[81]

This was the atmosphere in which, in May 1945, former president
Herbert Hoover submitted an alarming estimate of projected casualties to Stimson and Truman, suggesting that if peace could be arranged

with Japan, "America will save 500,000 to 1,000,000 lives" (which would extrapolate to a total number of casualties of between two and four million). On June 4, the War Department, with General Marshall concurring, dismissed these estimates as "entirely too high." General MacArthur, who would have commanded the projected invasion, also projected confusing but drastically lower casualty estimates for the first ninety days. By mid-June, the "Saipan ratio" had been supplanted by other models (such as casualties in the Leyte and Luzon campaigns, as well as Iwo Jima and Okinawa), and projections of initial American fatalities lowered to the tens of thousands. Still, the dire grand figures retained their mesmerizing, almost emblematic attraction. After the war, General Dwight D. Eisenhower recalled meeting with Stimson during a break in the Potsdam Conference in late July 1945 and finding the secretary of war "still under the influence of a statement from military sources who figured it would cost 1,000,000 men to invade Japan successfully."[82]

While military planners reworked their projections of invasion fatalities and revised them downwards, in some cases to as little as a tenth or twentieth of what the alarmists were predicting, what remained unchanged was the overriding vision of unacceptable potential losses. The "1.2 million," "million," "half million" numbers amounted to a kind of numerological shorthand for "huge"—rather like the exaggerated evocation of the "hundred million" that the Japanese used when referring to the emperor's loyal subjects, and not entirely different from wildly inflated references to "one-million" and possibly "two-million" fatalities in bombed-out Tokyo that the *New York Times* so casually reported on May 30, 1945, based on what the military was telling it. The fundamental difference, of course, was that American lives were precious.[83]

Whatever the number might be, it was to be avoided at all costs. On June 16, for example, the top-level "Science Panel" that advised the Interim Committee endorsed immediate use of nuclear weapons on the grounds that "we recognize our obligation to our nation to use the weapons to help save American lives in the Japanese war."[84] At a key meeting at the White House two days later—on June 18, three days before it was announced that the fighting on Okinawa had finally come to an end—General Marshall expressed the common view that an invasion "would be much more difficult than it had been in Germany." Truman took the occasion to state his hope

*67. Six kamikaze pilots pose for a group portrait before departing on their missions.*

*68. A kamikaze about to hit the USS Missouri off Okinawa, April 11, 1945. Less than five months later, Japan's formal surrender took place on the Missouri in Tokyo Bay.*

*69. A kamikaze bursts into flame upon hitting the USS* Intrepid *in the Philippines, November 25, 1944.*

*70. U.S. sailors killed in a kamikaze attack on the USS* Hancock *are buried at sea off Okinawa, April 9, 1945.*

"that there was a possibility of preventing an Okinawa from one end of Japan to the other."[85] At the Trinity test one month later, General Farrell's first words to General Groves were, "The war is over," to which Groves recalled replying, "Yes, after we drop two bombs on Japan." When Colonel Paul Tibbets, the pilot of the *Enola Gay*, the B-29 that dropped the atomic bomb on Hiroshima, briefed his crew prior to takeoff, he spoke of the honor of being chosen to conduct the raid and predicted it might shorten the war by six months or more. "And you got the feeling," one of his crew recorded in his diary, "that he really thought this bomb would end the war, period."[86]

In a report on the Potsdam Conference broadcast on August 9, Truman concluded with reference to "the tragic significance of the atomic bomb" dropped on Hiroshima and eschewed the exaggerated slaughterhouse projections that later came to dominate postwar rationalizations, including his own, for using it. He stated that the bomb had been used "in order to shorten the agony of war, in order to save the lives of thousands and thousands of young Americans." In a message to Congress on atomic energy on October 3, he spoke similarly about how the bomb had "saved the lives of untold thousands of American and Allied soldiers who would otherwise have been killed in battle."[87]

*Thousands and thousands. Untold thousands.* This in itself was indicative rhetoric, synonymous with far-too-many. At the same time, it also was indicative of how far American war planners had traveled from moral considerations that preoccupied many of them only a few years earlier— when pre–Pearl Harbor statesmen like Franklin Roosevelt were still able to declare that "ruthless bombing from the air . . . which has resulted in the maiming and in the death of thousands of defenseless men, women, and children, has sickened the hearts of every civilized man and woman, and has profoundly shocked the conscience of humanity"; and when, in the earliest years of the ensuing air war, American advocates of precision bombing still spoke seriously about the moral imperative of avoiding, as much as possible, untold thousands of casualties among enemy noncombatants.

Those days were gone forever. With their passing, and in their stead, a model had been established for future exercises in psychological warfare, terror, reliance on deployment of maximum and virtually indiscriminate force, and the obsessive development of weapons of ever more massive destructive capability.

# THE IRRESISTIBLE LOGIC
# OF MASS DESTRUCTION

## *Brute Force*

When we roll out clichés like "time will tell" or "the judgment of history," we are of course playing with language. Time does not speak, nor does history judge. Rather, commentators including historians acquire perspective as time passes—regard the past with greater detachment, knowledge of long-term legacies, and the fuller understanding that derives from accounts by participants and access to private papers and hitherto secret documents. Bias may color judgments, and controversy is predictable, but in any case knowledge becomes thickened and understanding altered.

In the triumphal narrative of Hiroshima and Nagasaki, the bombs mark the end of a horrendous war. In narratives that place tragedy alongside triumph, neither the horror of the war, nor the fight-to-the-bitter-end fanaticism of the Japanese, nor the desire to end the conflict quickly and save lives are ignored. At the same time, however, the war that culminated in Hiroshima and Nagasaki also is recognized as the onset of an epoch in which slaughter from the air became routine. More noncombatants were killed in America's subsequent wars in Korea and Indochina than in the Allied bombing in World War II. Nuclear weapons spread to other nations and were stockpiled in the tens of thousands in the United States and Soviet Union at the peak of the Cold War, awaiting only the cloud, once again, over congested cities.[88]

In our oblique, coded manner, we often fall back on place names and localized references to symbolize the violence that threads through modern times to the present day. Almost any such list will include Verdun and the Somme, Nanjing, Pearl Harbor, Stalingrad, Auschwitz, Dresden, Algiers, "Siberia" in Stalin's murderous Soviet Union, the Cultural Revolution in China, My Lai in Vietnam, September 11, and more. Any such list also will include Hiroshima/Nagasaki. Developing and using the bombs had a momentum of its own—propelled by multiple forces in a world where notions of "total war," including undermining enemy morale, obsessed planners on all sides. In turn, the Ground Zeros of 1945 accelerated the quest for ever more sophisticated ways to deliver death and destruction short of resorting to nuclear devastation.

This continuum of resort to brute force defies simple explanation, but the dynamics behind use of the first nuclear weapons against Japan provide a window on the interplay of political, institutional, and psychological imperatives that contribute to impelling such policies. It is possible to see a terrible logic in the use of the bombs that is unique to the circumstances of that moment and at the same time not peculiar at all. This logic still begins with (1) ending the war and saving American lives. It no longer ends there, however, but extends to additional considerations, including the following: (2) fixation on deploying overwhelming force, as opposed to diplomatic or other less destructive alternatives including, most controversially, an unwillingness to back off from demanding Japan's unconditional surrender; (3) power politics in the emerging Cold War, notably playing the new weapon as a "master card," as Stimson put it, to intimidate the Soviet Union in eastern Europe as well as Asia; (4) domestic political considerations, in which using the bomb was deemed necessary to prevent partisan post-hostilities attacks on Truman and the Democratic administration he inherited from Roosevelt for wasting taxpayers' money on a useless project—and simultaneously to build support for postwar nuclear and military projects; (5) scientific "sweetness" and technological imperatives—coupled with (6) the technocratic kinetics of an enormous machinery of war—which combined to give both developing and deploying new weaponry a vigorous life of its own; (7) the sheer exhilaration and aestheticism of unrestrained violence, phenomena not peculiar to modern times but peculiarly compelling in an age of spectacular destructiveness; (8) revenge, in this instance exacted collectively on an entire population in retaliation for Pearl Harbor and Japan's wartime atrocities; and (9) "idealistic annihilation," whereby demonstrating the appalling destructiveness of an atomic bomb on real, human targets was rationalized as essential to preventing future war, or at the very least future nuclear war.

Other factors that in one way or another help illuminate our attraction to mass destruction also animated the rush to use the bombs. Flattening combatants and noncombatants into a collective whole, rhetorically dehumanizing them, and literally standing, sitting, or flying great distances away from the targeted men, women, and children all abetted wholesale killing. So did the emotional counterpoise to this: patriotic fervor and, among fighting men, the intimate bonding of battlefront camaraderie. Psychological drives that may run deeper than group identity or thirst for collective revenge enter the picture, such as constructs of masculinity or the compelling attractiveness of "limit experiences." Ultimately we confront human nature, with its deadly as well as noble compulsions and inclinations.

Throbbing like a pulse through the development and use of the atomic bombs is still another vital force, bordering on megalomania: the abiding sense of a concentrated moment in which mortals found themselves playing God, both destroyer and creator. Sudden possession of awesome power was accompanied by sentiments of wrath and mercy combined—an almost giddy sense that becoming death would usher in a life-giving and redemptive world order dominated by America's unprecedented power and magnanimous ideals. The euphoria of victory over Japan, and of the end of the struggle against Axis fascism and aggression more generally, was extraordinary.

It was also fragile and ephemeral. The underside of triumph was profound anxiety—a presentiment that making and using the atomic bomb had birthed not peace but vulnerability of a sort inconceivable just a few years earlier. Although this fear never was dispelled, in time it became sublimated or turned into a kind of spectator sport and celluloid thrill in the mode of science-fiction and Hollywood disaster films. When the twin towers of the World Trade Center were taken down on September 11, this suppressed or diluted dread erupted, certainly among Americans, as full-blown collective trauma.[89]

When Truman scribbled in his Potsdam diary (on July 25) that "this atomic bomb . . . seems to be the most terrible thing ever discovered, but it can be made the most useful," he captured the contradiction inherent in developing and using the bombs. He might just as easily have turned his phrasing around and written "the most useful, but possibly the most terrible." More than a few American military and civilian leaders did quickly declare that the latter way of weighting the scale was more accurate. Admiral William Leahy, who served as chief of staff to both Roosevelt and Truman, for example, emerged as a particularly quotable representative of this position. "The lethal possibilities of atomic warfare in the future are frightening," Leahy wrote in his memoirs, published in 1950. "My own feeling was that in being the first to use it, we had adopted an ethical standard common to the barbarians of the Dark Ages. I was not taught to make war in that fashion, and wars cannot be won by destroying women and children." The distinguished physicist and Manhattan Project participant I. I. Rabi, reflecting on the Trinity test in New Mexico, put the sense of foreboding in more prophetic terms: "Suddenly the day of judgment was the next day and has been ever since."[90]

These multiple considerations and impulses are not necessarily of equal weight, nor are they watertight; some spill over into others. All together, in any case, they tell us something about how pressures and fixations multiply in the cauldron of enmity and war; how reason, emotion, and delusion commingle; how blood debts can become blood lust, and moral passion can bleed into the practice of wanton terror—into what Leahy regarded as regression to barbarism, and Oppenheimer, in his inimitable way, came to speak of as intimate knowledge of sin.[91]

## August 1945 and the Rejected Alternatives

Neither Colonel Tibbets and his crew, nor scientists in the Manhattan Project (up to and including Oppenheimer), nor outside commentators on probable casualties in an invasion like former president Herbert Hoover were privy to the military's actual long-term planning for invading Japan. When these plans became known after the war, they complicated the argument about saving lives by revealing that no invasion of the home islands was contemplated in August, or September, or even October. The plans called for an initial assault on the southernmost island of Kyushu commencing around November 1 (code-named "Olympic"), to be followed by a major assault on the Kanto area where Tokyo and Yokohama are located beginning around March 1, 1946 (code-named "Coronet"). The overall U.S. invasion plan carried the code name "Downfall," and revelation of its timetable inevitably raised new questions about the atomic bombs: why the extreme haste in using them, given this breathing space before untold thousands of American lives would be in jeopardy? As MacArthur had observed in mid-June, when projected invasion casualty figures were being scrutinized and revised downwards, "The several preceding months will involve practically no losses in ground troops."[92]

A partial—but only partial—answer lies in the simple fact that, by this stage in the war, reliance on overwhelming force was both gospel and second nature. This was the essence of the incendiary air war against Japan, where the primary criteria for selecting cities to bomb had already devolved into their congestion and combustibility rather than military or industrial significance. When the possibility of *not* using the new weapon in a surprise attack on a crowded city was addressed, almost in passing, at an extended meeting of the Interim Committee on May 31, the persuasive counterargument, as recalled by one participant, appears to have been that the "number of people that would be killed by the bomb would not be greater in general magnitude than the number already killed in fire raids" on Tokyo. May 31, as it happened, was the day the *New York Times* carried its wildly exaggerated report about "one-million" and possibly as many as twice that number of Japanese killed in the air raids on Tokyo.[93]

In addition to the delayed and staggered timetable for the projected invasion, other postwar revelations also prompted reconsideration of the necessity of using the bombs. Prominent among these disclosures was that, as long urged by the United States and Britain, the Soviet Union had promised to join the war against Japan within three months of Germany's defeat—which put its projected date of entry in early August. (Germany signed unconditional-surrender terms on May 7, and the United States and European Allies declared May 8 "Victory in Europe Day.") Stalin had confirmed this at the Yalta Conference in February 1945, and again at Potsdam, where he informed Truman that Soviet forces were deploying and would require an extra week beyond the "three month" promise. Truman recorded this dramatically in his diary on July 17: "He'll be in the Jap War on August 15th. Fini Japs when that comes about." Beginning soon after Pearl Harbor, U.S. and British planners repeatedly emphasized the shattering impact a Soviet declaration of war would have on Japan's leaders—forcing them to open a new front in northeast Asia, threatening the very heart of their empire on the Asian continent, and confronting them with the most alarming bogey of all: the Red Peril. Why, then, were the bombs rushed into use before the shock of a Soviet declaration of war could be tested?

This question was compounded when it was learned that, in the months and weeks preceding Hiroshima and Nagasaki, U.S. policy makers had addressed the possibility of trying to persuade Japan's leaders to capitulate by offering an essentially diplomatic inducement. In this scenario, the major impediment to ending the war short of invasion was the "unconditional surrender" policy Roosevelt and Churchill had endorsed ever since January 1943—a policy steadfastly adhered to in Germany's capitulation. From the Japanese perspective, unconditional surrender placed the very essence or "national polity" (*kokutai*) of the nation—the imperial system and "sacred and inviolable" emperor—in dire peril. U.S. and British intelligence were keenly attuned to Japanese dread in this regard. It was, analysts agreed, the single greatest consideration behind Japan's fanatical commitment to fight to the bitter end.

The possibility of a conditional Japanese surrender entered public debate after the war when several concrete developments in the final months of the conflict were disclosed. Beginning in late May 1945, Joseph Grew, the former ambassador to Japan then serving as under secretary of state, had strongly and repeatedly recommended that the surrender terms be revised to guarantee the continued existence of the imperial "dynasty." In mid-July, intercepted and decoded diplomatic cables from Tokyo to the Japanese embassy in Moscow indicated that "it is His Majesty's heart's desire to see the swift termination of the war," but "as long as America and England insist on unconditional surrender, our country has no alterna- tive but to see it through in an all-out effort for the sake of survival and the honor of the homeland." And in the Potsdam Declaration of July 26, which demanded Japan's capitulation and threatened "prompt and utter destruction" if it did not comply with the terms of surrender articulated in the ultimatum, a key sentence in the twelfth paragraph of the working draft—reflecting Grew's view and assuring the Japanese that their future government "may include a constitutional monarchy under the present dynasty"—had been deleted at close to the last moment. Since subsequent U.S. policy in defeated and occupied Japan not only retained the imperial system but also exonerated Emperor Hirohito personally from any war responsibility, the critical postwar query went, why was assurance of the continuation of the throne rejected before the bombs were used?[94]

ONCE ALLIED OCCUPATION forces actually set foot in defeated Japan, firsthand observation of the material devastation of the nation and exhaus- tion of the populace—the ghost cities that made such a strong impres- sion on John Swope and every other foreigner who saw the vanquished country in the immediate postwar months—prompted further reflection on whether the bombs had been necessary. More than a few observers were thus primed to be receptive when the Strategic Bombing Survey speculated in mid-1946 that Japan "certainly" would have been forced to surrender by the end of 1945, and "in all probability" prior to November, even *without* the atomic bombs, Soviet entry into the war, or an Allied invasion.

This counterfactual conjecture, impossible to prove (and challenged by a number of postwar critics), called into question the reliability of wartime intelligence projections anticipating Japanese resistance well into 1946 and possibly even longer. Even as the Survey was advancing this provocative opinion, moreover, individuals such as Oppenheimer already were engaging in public soul-searching about how the United States and Britain, "the two nations which we like to think are the most enlightened and humane in the world . . . used atomic weapons against an enemy which was essentially defeated."[95]

As the Cold War intensified and it became obvious that the world faced the plague of ever-increasing numbers of ever more devastating weapons, many other American military and civilian leaders publicly questioned the use of the atomic bombs. Some even indicated that they had expressed reservations before the bombs were used. This roster of critics was not predictable. It included, for example, General LeMay, the architect of incendiary bombing of Japan's cities, and Admiral William Halsey Jr. (who had famously exhorted his men to "kill Japs, kill Japs, kill more Japs," and in a 1944 newsreel enthused about the "pleasure" of "drowning and burning the bestial apes all over the Pacific"), as well as General Eisenhower, who had supported incendiary bombing in the European theater, and Admiral Leahy. Leahy was among the wartime insiders who endorsed the argument that unconditional surrender was unnecessary and undesirable.[96]

Halsey's postwar criticism of the use of the bomb was as harsh as Leahy's comparison to the barbarism of the Dark Ages. In 1949, he told Congress that "bombing—especially atomic bombing—of civilians is morally indefensible," and went so far as to refer to this as "extermination theory." This was not a spur-of-the-moment opinion on the part of the notoriously abrupt admiral. Three years earlier, Halsey dismissed the first atomic bomb as "an unnecessary experiment" on the grounds that "it killed a lot of Japs, but the Japs had put out a lot of peace feelers through Russia long before." Unlike Leahy but like the vast majority of high-ranking officers, Halsey had been excluded from the small circle informed about the atomic-bomb project, but he did not hesitate to put the onus of the unnecessary experiment on the scientists, who "had this toy and . . . wanted to try it out, so they dropped it." What went unmentioned in this philippic was that many scientists also were troubled by use of their handiwork—and had, in fact, expressed their concerns strongly but confidentially before the bombs were dropped. Oppenheimer's was the most famous postwar voice within the scientific community, but his agonizing came later than that of many of his colleagues and tended to focus on the threat he and his fellow scientists had helped unleash.

Concern among scientists associated with the Manhattan Project found formal expression on several occasions. A lengthy "Prospectus on Nucleonics" finalized in November 1944 (and more popularly known as the Jefferies Report), for example, endorsed continued U.S. domination in nuclear energy, including vigorous postwar collaboration between the government and private scientific and industrial sectors, but expressed concern that failure to promote international cooperation and establish "an international administration with police powers which can effectively control at least the means of nucleonic warfare" would result in these new weapons becoming "the destroyer of our civilization."[97]

Fear of a future nuclear arms race was expressed in even greater detail seven months later, a little over a month before the mid-July Trinity test, in an internal report by seven scientists associated with the Manhattan Project's Metallurgical Laboratory (Met Lab) in Chicago. Titled "The Political Implications of Atomic Weapons," this became popularly known as the Franck Report after the committee's chairman James Franck, a German émigré who had been awarded the Nobel Prize in 1925 for his work on atomic theory. This *cri de coeur*, prepared after considerable discussion among Met Lab scientists and submitted confidentially to the War Department, was prefaced with the dramatic observation that "all of us, familiar with the present state of nucleonics, live with the vision before our eyes of sudden destruction visited on our own country, of a Pearl Harbor disaster repeated in thousand-fold magnification in every one of our major cities." Like the Jefferies Report, apprehension concerning a future "race for nuclear armaments" with Russia, and possibly other nations as well, prompted Franck and his colleagues to urge immediate attention to creating an efficient "international authority which would make all resorts to force in international conflicts impossible." It would be foolhardy, the scientists declared, to hope that the United States and England could keep their scientific findings secret "for more than a few years" or rely on their superior industrial capacities to ensure future security and protection "from sudden attack."

What did this specter of a future nuclear holocaust have to do with the immediate question of whether or how to use the bomb against Japan? As the Franck Committee saw it: everything. The key to preventing a nuclear arms race was the immediate establishment of "mutual *trust*" between the Anglo powers and other nations; and "from this point of view, the way in which the nuclear weapons now being secretly developed in this country are first revealed to the world appears to be of great, perhaps fateful importance." The use "of the very first available atomic bombs in the Japanese war" was a profoundly political and not just military issue, as the report's title emphasized, and if carried out suddenly and without warning, it could easily provoke mistrust on the part of Russia and other countries excluded from even cursory knowledge of the existence of the nuclear project.

"It may be very difficult to persuade the world that a nation which was capable of secretly preparing and suddenly releasing a weapon as indiscriminate as the rocket bomb [deployed by Germany] and a million times more destructive," the scientists predicted, "is to be trusted in its proclaimed desire of having such weapons abolished by international agreement." It thus followed that

> *From this point of view, a demonstration of the new weapon might best be made, before the eyes of representatives of all the United Nations, on the desert or a barren island.* The best possible atmosphere for the achievement of an international agreement could be achieved if America could say to the world, "You see what sort of a weapon we had but did not use. We are ready to renounce its use in the future if other nations join us in this renunciation and agree to the establishment of an efficient international control."

If such a demonstration failed to persuade Japan's leaders to capitulate, subsequent military use might follow conditional on international support and preceded by something along the order of an ultimatum to Japan and a warning to evacuate certain regions "as an alternative to their total destruction."[98]

The distinguished scientists who signed the Franck Report emphasized that the urgency of laying the ground for effective international control made "early use of nuclear bombs against Japan" undesirable "quite independently of any humanitarian consideration," and would help ensure "the saving of American lives in the future." While the Franck Report was submitted through formal channels to nuclear planners in the War Department, scientists also expressed their concerns in other ways in the weeks preceding the Trinity test. A petition drafted by the physicist Leo Szilard, addressed to President Truman, and eventually signed by around sixty-nine Manhattan Project scientists urged,

> First, that you exercise your power as Commander-in-Chief to rule that the United States shall not resort to the use of atomic bombs in this war unless the terms which will be imposed upon Japan have been made public in detail and Japan, knowing these terms, has refused to surrender; second, that in such an event the question whether or not to use atomic bombs be decided by you in the light of the considerations presented in this petition as well as all the other moral responsibilities which are involved.

In a separate poll conducted on July 12 and involving 150 scientists in Chicago, 46 percent favored "a military demonstration in Japan to be followed by renewed opportunity for surrender before full use of the weapons is employed"; 26 percent supported "an experimental demonstration in this country, with representatives of Japan present; followed by a new opportunity for surrender before full use of the weapon is employed"; 13 percent opposed military use in the present war; and only 15 percent endorsed using the bombs "in the manner that is from the military point of view most effective in bringing about prompt Japanese surrender at minimum human cost to our armed forces."[99]

THESE, THEN, WERE the alternatives to relying on overwhelming force that were on the table before the first atomic bomb was dropped on Hiroshima. The new weapon could be introduced in a noncombat demonstration or against an exclusively military target before being used against cities, should such prior demonstration fail to persuade Japan's leaders to capitulate. The surrender terms could be modified and clarified in a manner that might encourage Japan's leaders to sue for peace, as opposed to rigid adherence to the unconditional surrender demanded by the United

States and Britain since 1943. The Soviet Union could be brought into the picture in ways that would not only shock even the hardest-line Japanese militarists but also hopefully contribute to the "mutual trust" the Franck Committee and many other scientists believed essential to avert a postwar nuclear arms race. Since no invasion was scheduled for several months, there would seem to have been ample opportunity to explore such options during an interlude when, as MacArthur had noted, no conspicuous losses in ground troops were anticipated.

After the war, some American officers and officials argued—much as the Strategic Bombing Survey had done—that simply continuing the existing air and naval blockade of Japan, along with conventional air raids, would have forced Japan's leaders to cave in sooner rather than later. As the window opened on the top-secret wartime deliberations, moreover, it also became known that it was not just idealistic scientists who supported some form of information sharing or preliminary nuclear demonstration short of targeting civilians. At one fleeting moment prior to the Trinity test, on May 31, for example, General Marshall mused about the possibility of inviting Russian scientists as witnesses and also broached using the first bomb "against straight military objectives such as a large naval installation."

A month after Marshall's musings, still several weeks before Trinity, Under Secretary of the Navy Ralph Bard submitted a top-secret "Memorandum on the Use of S-1 Bomb" expressing his growing misgivings about the direction plans were taking, and what this implied for "the position of the United States as a great humanitarian nation" whose people respected "fair play." Bard ventured that the Japanese were looking for some way to surrender, and suggested that perhaps it could be arranged to clandestinely "contact representatives from Japan somewhere on the China Coast and make representations with regard to Russia's position and at the same time give them some information regarding the proposed use of atomic power, together with whatever assurances the President might care to make with regard to the Emperor of Japan and the treatment of the Japanese nation following unconditional surrender." After the war, the influential diplomatic historian Herbert Feis, who ultimately endorsed the decision to use the bombs, embellished on the vague idea of sharing information about the new weapon by suggesting that things might have turned out differently if the United States had chosen to fully reveal—for Japan's leaders as well as "the whole world"—the results of the Trinity test itself as soon as persuasive photographs and data were available.[100]

In the end, secrecy coupled with an unwavering reliance on brute force ruled the day. "Let there be no mistake about it," Truman recorded in his memoirs, "I regarded the bomb as a military weapon and never had any doubt that it should be used." Churchill made much the same point, declaring in his own recollections that "there never was a moment's discussion as to whether the atomic bomb should be used or not." "The historic fact remains, and must be judged in the after-time," he went on, "that the decision whether or not to use the atomic bomb to compel the surrender of Japan was never even an issue. There was unanimous, automatic, unquestioned agreement around our table; nor did I ever hear the slightest suggestion that we should do otherwise."[101]

### Unconditional Surrender

Here in the after-time, it is apparent that Churchill was being less than honest. He was well aware, for example, of grave misgivings in the scientific community, just as Truman was well informed about the argument of Grew and others that guarantees concerning the future of the imperial system might overcome Japan's reluctance to surrender. In any case, the voices of caution and alternative courses had no chance. Groupthink prevailed at top levels—much as would occur a half century later in the Bush administration's rush to war with Iraq.

The "demonstration" argument, for one, was quickly gunned down by the Interim Committee: this would eliminate the critical "spectacular" element of surprise and outright shock; it might be a dud, and thereby even embolden the enemy; it would not replicate exact battle conditions, such as being dropped from a plane or destroying buildings and their inhabitants; if conducted in an isolated or noncombat setting, Japan's fanatical militarists would be unlikely to be impressed; given prior warning of prospective targets in or around Japan, the Japanese could mobilize antiaircraft resistance and might well move prisoners of war into the areas identified; the United States would have only a few bombs in hand at the outset, and could not afford to waste them; and so on.

On this issue, Oppenheimer, while supporting advising "Russia, France, and China" about the progress made in developing nuclear weapons, unequivocally endorsed the Interim Committee's preordained consensus. On June 16, a month prior to the Trinity test, his small "Science Panel" subcommittee completely undercut the arguments of their concerned colleagues by declaring that "we can propose no technical demonstration likely to bring an end to the war; we see no acceptable alternative to direct military use."[102]

Grew's argument that Japan's leaders might be persuaded to capitulate if the surrender terms were modified to give assurance that this would not mean elimination of the imperial dynasty enjoyed a more extended incubation before being aborted. As Gar Alperovitz and other scholars have documented in detail, between Grew's presentation of this proposition to Truman on May 28 and the mid-July elimination of the "paragraph twelve" proviso to this effect from the Potsdam Declaration, an impressive number of civilian officials and military officers conveyed to the president their support for such clarification of the "unconditional surrender" formula. These included the Joint Chiefs of Staff (at least intermittently), the secretary and assistant secretary of war, the secretary and under secretary of the navy, the president's special legal counsel as well as his chief of staff (Admiral Leahy), representatives of the State Department led by Grew, as well as informal advisers such as former president Herbert Hoover. At Potsdam, Churchill and the British chiefs of staff also indicated they were receptive to clarifying the surrender terms so as to give the Japanese "some show of saving their military honour and some assurance of their national existence."[103]

After the war, Grew reiterated his belief that language to this effect might have hastened Japan's capitulation, among other places in an often-cited letter to Stimson. His explicit premise was that a nascent "peace movement" among men within Japan's elite circles whom he called moderates would be greatly and possibly decisively strengthened if the Allied powers offered a clear guarantee that they would "not molest the person of the emperor or disestablish the institution of the throne," and that the Japanese would be "permitted to determine for themselves the nature of their future political structure."[104] His implicit premises, which are questionable and often downplayed in postwar treatments supportive of this argument, were several: that indications of a desire to get out of the war constituted a serious peace movement within Japanese ruling circles; that Hirohito personally and the imperial institution in general were not deeply implicated in the rise of Japanese authoritarianism, militarism, and aggression, or in the actual conduct of the war; and that offering some vague assurance about preserving the emperor system would not open the door to a barrage of Japanese demands for detailed clarification of precisely what this meant.

The so-called Grew line also reflected a conservative position associated with an articulate coterie of State Department diplomats known as the "Japan Crowd," who were persuaded that ordinary Japanese were inherently incapable of governing themselves and would fall into chaos or communism without the stabilizing presence of the throne. These "old Japan hands"—and many of the U.S. officials and uniformed officers who supported them—envisioned a relatively short post-hostilities occupation devoted primarily to disarming the defeated foe, rehabilitating the old-guard civilian "moderates," introducing modest reforms, promoting "reeducation," and establishing international controls against future Japanese aggression. Admiral Leahy captured the essence of this outlook at a critical White House meeting in mid-June, where the minutes record him as saying he "feared no menace from Japan in the foreseeable future, even if we were unsuccessful in forcing unconditional surrender."[105]

Critics of this position, sometimes loosely identified as the "China Crowd," looked upon the unconditional-surrender demand less in terms of its impact on ending the war than as the necessary foundation for assuring a peaceful and less authoritarian postwar Japan. That, after all, was the spirit in which this principle was first articulated by Roosevelt and Churchill in 1943, and it had been adhered to in taking Germany's surrender. Where Japan was concerned, these opponents of the Grew line argued that the emperor system lay at the heart of Japanese militarism and domestic oppression. Assistant Secretary of State Archibald MacLeish conveyed this critique concisely, early in July, in challenging the conciliatory "paragraph twelve" language in the working draft of the Potsdam Declaration:

What has made Japan dangerous in the past and will make her dangerous in the future if we permit it, is, in large part, the Japanese

cult of emperor worship which gives the ruling groups in Japan—
the *Gumbatsu* [that is, *gunbatsu* or "military clique"]—the current
coalition of militarists, industrialists, large land owners and office
holders—their control over the Japanese people. As Mr. Acheson
[Assistant Secretary of State Dean Acheson, a later secretary of state]
pointed out in the Staff Committee, the institution of the throne is
an anachronistic, feudal institution, perfectly adapted to the manipulation and use of anachronistic, feudal-minded groups within the
country. To leave that institution intact is to run the grave risk that
it will be used in the future as it has been used in the past.[106]

It followed, from this contrary perspective, that for Japan to become a
peaceful and reasonably democratic nation in the future it was essential
that the victors be completely free to promote a root-and-branch agenda
of reform without any restrictions once hostilities ended—an agenda that
later generations would call "nation building," and a still later generation
influential in the Bush administration would reject out of hand as inappropriate when planning the invasion of Iraq. Opponents of modifying
the unconditional-surrender policy were sanguine that ordinary Japanese
were capable of becoming responsible citizens (as opposed to acquiescent
subjects of the emperor). They also were skeptical of both the authoritarianism inherent in the imperial system and the inclinations and influence
of the so-called moderates in whom the Japan Crowd rested hope, up to
and including Hirohito personally—these individuals having been neither
prewar supporters of democracy nor effective opponents of militarism as
it gathered the momentum that culminated in aggression against China
and the Allied powers. From this perspective, unconditional surrender
was essential if the United States was to have the political clout and legal
authority necessary to seriously attempt to "demilitarize and democratize"
a defeated Japan.

To the more elitist and ethnocentric Japan Crowd, such liberal idealism
was ludicrous: in their view, neither history nor culture made popular sovereignty feasible in Japan. Although critics of the Grew line like MacLeish
and Acheson were out of the loop where knowledge of the atomic bomb
was concerned, in the wake of Japan's capitulation it was their influence
and outlook—and not that of Grew and his conservative colleagues—that

was decisive in finalizing the radically reformist agenda General MacArthur actually followed as unchallenged overlord of occupied Japan.[107]

IT DID NOT require ten years of living in Japan, as Grew had done up to and through Pearl Harbor, to deduce that Japan's leaders including the emperor were desperate to escape the predicament they had brought upon themselves. How could they not be? Their vaulting ambitions and unbridled violence had come home with a vengeance. It did, however, take considerable wishful thinking to imagine that a cryptic statement along the proposed "paragraph twelve" lines—vaguely declaring that Japan's future government "may include a constitutional monarchy under the present dynasty"—would tip the scales toward capitulation in any simple way in the small "Supreme War Leadership Council" that decided grand policy.

It is clear from the record on the Japanese side that, particularly after the fall of Okinawa in June, Hirohito personally was deeply alarmed by the possibility of threats to the emperor system. He perceived this peril as emanating not merely from the Allied powers but also from his own ostensibly loyal subjects, whom he began to fear might choose to engage in "revolution from below" rather than embrace death like shattered jewels. Although it may have become, at long last, his "heart's desire" to see the quick termination of the war, as the intercepted cable of July 12 phrased it, this still did not translate into clarity as to *how*. The so-called peace feelers to Russia in July were, as the unusually blunt Japanese ambassador in Moscow put it, little more than "loose thinking which gets away from reality"—a muddled and bizarrely oblique signal of desperation to end the war, to be sure, but as strategically and psychologically inept, in its own way, as the foolish decision making that had preceded Pearl Harbor.[108]

No one can say with certainty what the Japanese response would have been if the conciliatory language had been retained in the Potsdam Declaration—or, indeed, tendered earlier as an explicit retreat from the unconditional-surrender formula, as Grew initially hoped it would be. It is reasonable to conjecture, however, that this would have prompted, at best, Japanese demands that Emperor Hirohito be explicitly guaranteed exemption from any future war-crimes trials; that he be assured that he, and not just his "dynasty," remain on the throne; and that the entire constitutional and institutional structure that established and policed his status and pre-rogatives as "sacred and inviolable," and defined the Japanese people as "subjects" rather than citizens, be guaranteed. Because the United States and Britain had from the outset coupled their demands for unconditional surrender of the Axis powers with equally unqualified prescriptions for "complete and permanent" disarmament (the Potsdam Declaration simply reiterated this), it is likely that the Japanese militarists would have insisted on clarification and qualification of this as well. Beyond this, it would have been natural for the nation's beleaguered leaders to seize upon any open-ing for a conditional or contractual surrender to raise concrete questions concerning the projected occupation of the defeated nation, the conduct of war crimes trials in general, and the postwar retention of a Japanese pres-ence in Korea and Formosa, and possibly also Manchuria.[109]

IN THE WAKE of the dropping of the atomic bombs on August 6 and 9, together with the Soviet declaration of war in the interim, Hirohito broke a deadlock among the six members of the Supreme War Leadership Council by endorsing acceptance of the Potsdam Declaration. This was conveyed to the United States on August 10, "with the understanding that the said declaration does not comprise any demand which prejudices the prerogatives of His Majesty as a Sovereign Ruler." The ensuing "Byrnes Note" responding to this stipulation—approved by Britain, China, and the Soviet Union and transmitted under the name of Truman's new sec-retary of state James Byrnes on August 11—is often described as a de facto guarantee of the throne comparable to the paragraph-twelve lan-guage that had been deleted from the proclamation—thus prompting the question of why this could not have been offered before the bombs were dropped. But this reply did not constitute a conditional surrender. On the contrary, it involved weasel language—or, put more delicately, evasion and adroit ambiguity. It did not resurrect the deleted paragraph-twelve language about "constitutional monarchy" and the "present dynasty," or offer any assurance concerning the person of the emperor—did not, indeed, actually respond to the "imperial prerogatives" issue at all.

Following introductory caveats, the five-paragraph reply began with the declaration that "from the moment of surrender the authority of the

Emperor and the Japanese Government to rule the state shall be subject to the Supreme Commander of the Allied Powers who will take such steps as he deems proper to effectuate the surrender terms." The presumed response to the specific issue of imperial prerogatives constituted the penultimate paragraph and simply read, "The ultimate form of government of Japan shall, in accordance with the Potsdam Declaration, be established by the freely expressed will of the Japanese people." Among other things, under Japan's existing emperor-centered constitution there was no "freely expressed will" of the people. The Japanese let all this ride, simply announcing on August 14 (Washington time) that they had accepted "the provisions of the Potsdam Declaration" and Byrnes's August 11 reply.

Truman's immediate public announcement of Japan's acceptance of the Byrnes Note began by emphasizing that he deemed this "a full acceptance of the Potsdam Declaration which specifies the unconditional surrender of Japan." This was reflected in the orders cut for MacArthur on August 13, even before the Japanese acceptance arrived, which affirmed the general's supreme authority as commander of the occupation forces. When MacArthur actually set up shop in defeated Japan several weeks later, and wishful emissaries from the Japanese side attempted to argue that the capitulation had actually been contractual and thus governance and decision making should be shared, they were sent packing in no uncertain terms. MacArthur's authority was, literally as well as nominally, supreme. For all practical purposes defeated Japan had a new, Caucasian, emperor.[110]

As it transpired, the fate of both Hirohito and the throne in general remained in limbo for many months after the surrender. This uncertainty was of incalculable value to MacArthur and his staff, for it provided a tacit (and sometimes crude) bargaining chip vis-à-vis Japan's conservative postwar leaders: they expedited initial reformist policies more readily than they might otherwise have done in order to save the throne and protect Hirohito personally. It was not until early 1946 that Allied authorities made explicit that the emperor would not be indicted as a war criminal or required to abdicate; and it was only then that the structure and prerogatives of the imperial system were revamped—in ways that astonished the ruling elites and would have been anathema, not to mention *lèse majesté*, if even whispered while the war was still in progress.

Under a new postwar constitution, which MacArthur essentially imposed in draft form upon a thunderstruck Japanese government in February 1946, popular sovereignty replaced imperial sovereignty and the formerly sacred and inviolable emperor became a mere "symbol of the State and the unity of the people, deriving his position from the will of the people with whom resides sovereign power." If the Japanese government did not promote this draft charter as its own, essentially whole cloth, MacArthur's aides made clear that they could not guarantee the future security of either Hirohito personally or the imperial institution. In the workaday world of practical politics, the protracted uncertainty of the fate of Hirohito and his dynasty, coupled with the authority MacArthur's supreme command exercised by virtue of the unconditional surrender, thus enabled occupation authorities to introduce precisely the sort of radical "democratization" agenda that Grew and the Japan Crowd deemed inane and impossible. The emperor system survived, but in ways no Japanese could have imagined, or endorsed, prior to August 1945.[111]

From the beginning of the occupation, Japanese at all levels of society—liberated from the institutionalized authoritarianism of the emperor-centered state and the straightjacket of "Imperial Way" indoctrination—showed themselves receptive to pacifist and democratic ideals, often embracing and promoting them in home-grown ways. As the Cold War intensified, however, the United States backed away from its initial radical agenda. By 1948, reconstruction replaced democratization as a primary objective and reformist policies were rolled back, particularly where capital and labor were concerned. In 1950, Japan began rearming under U.S. encouragement and control. When the occupation ended in 1952, the political economy was largely dominated by conservative old-guard civilians; war-crimes trials had punished a few scapegoats before being abandoned; the ideal of complete and permanent disarmament had been dismissed as the folly of a naïve interlude; Japan had been dragooned as a partner in containing the great new menace in Asia, Red China; politicians and others purged for supporting the war machine were poised to return to public life; and Hirohito was able to report the successful outcome of events to his divine ancestors. A mere fifteen years had elapsed since imperial Japan launched war on the continent in the name of suppressing chaos and communism in China, stumbling from there into Pearl Harbor four years later. The nearer past already seemed unreal.

One can thus argue that compromising the demand for unconditional surrender in a way that even die-hard militarists could have accepted in 1945 might have opened the door to a negotiated capitulation before the bombs and Soviet Union descended upon Japan simultaneously—and that this, measured in terms of Cold War Realpolitik, would have served the United States just as well. But MacArthur would have been a conspicuously diminished figure in this case; the grassroots participation his early radical reforms made possible would likewise have been diminished; and the grand ideals of "demilitarization and democratization" that many Japanese continued to cherish after the reversal of policy would never have found such unequivocal expression and institutionalized protections. Postwar Japan would have been a different place.

## Power Politics and the Cold War

Prior to the Potsdam Conference, U.S. military projections almost formulaically emphasized how decisive a Soviet declaration of war might be in ending the conflict in Asia. The minutes to an important meeting involving Truman in mid-June are typical: "the impact of Russian entry on the already hopeless Japanese may well be the decisive action levering them into capitulation at that time or shortly thereafter if we land in Japan." A month later, when Stalin confirmed at Potsdam that Soviet forces would be ready to move into Manchuria by August 15, Truman's spontaneous "Fini Japs when that comes about" diary response still reflected this assumption. At the same time, however, the president failed to inform Stalin about the atomic bomb, apart from (in his own words) "casually" mentioning "that we had a new weapon of unusual destructive force." And the United States proceeded to move in great haste to drop both available bombs before the long-solicited and imminent Soviet entry. (Stalin hastily declared war on Japan on August 8, in response to the Hiroshima bombing.) Why the rush to drop the bombs before the Soviet entry?[112]

The answer is: power politics. No one around the planning tables was so simplistic as to believe that dropping the bombs was a military response to a fanatical foe pure and simple, although this became a staple argument in subsequent justifications. Those knowledgeable about the new weapon had relations with the Soviet Union in mind from an early date: counterintelligence surveillance on the Manhattan Project focused obsessively on communist or "extreme liberal" sympathies or affiliations dating back to the 1930s among participating scientists, and the obsessive secrecy of the project was thought of almost exclusively in terms of the Soviet ally rather than the Nazi enemy. As the bomb became a reality, this anti-Soviet fixation naturally moved from abstraction to concreteness.[113]

The Franck Committee approached these "political implications" from one direction by urging that the existence of the new weapon be revealed in a manner that paid scrupulous heed to promoting "mutual trust" internationally. The decision makers opted for exactly the opposite approach: using the bomb essentially without warning in a manner that would shock and awe the Russians every bit as much as the Japanese— and, in the process, ideally deter them from their territorial ambitions in eastern Europe while simultaneously undercutting them in Asia. The geopolitical consideration in Asia per se reflected belated recognition of the strategic downside of Soviet entry into the war—a sudden fear, that is, that even moderately prolonged Russian engagement with Japanese forces would strengthen the postwar Soviet position in Manchuria, the rest of China, and northeast Asia generally, including Korea, while simultaneously enhancing Moscow's ability to demand a meaningful share (and territorial "zone," as in occupied Germany) in the occupation of Japan.

The wartime intelligence projections about how profoundly a Soviet declaration of war would affect Japan's leaders were accurate. While American accounts of Japan's capitulation usually focus almost exclusively on the impact of the bombs, Japanese commentary commonly couples the bombs with the Soviet declaration of war just before Nagasaki was decimated. This, for example, was the blunt immediate response of Admiral and Navy Minister Mitsumasa Yonai, a former prime minister who sat on the Supreme War Leadership Council, was deeply alarmed by the "domestic situation" of mounting discontent, and supported ending the war as quickly as possible. "The term is perhaps inappropriate," Yonai confided to a fellow admiral on August 12, a few days before the imperial broadcast announcing capitulation, "but the atomic bombs and the Soviet entry into the war are, in a sense, gifts from the gods (*tenyū*)." Former prime minister Konoe used similar words on being informed of the Soviet invasion. Many other high-ranking Japanese, including the most militant diehards, regarded the Soviet attack as the true tipping point, sufficient in itself to prompt immediate surrender.[114]

Would the Soviet declaration of war alone have been decisive? We will never know. The more formal record from these critical days is mixed. The emperor's radio address of August 15 (Japan time) announcing capitulation, for example, mentioned only the "cruel new bomb." On the other hand, an August 12 cable by the Army General Staff to military attachés in neutral countries, intercepted and immediately decoded by the Americans, stated simply that "as a result of Russia's entrance into the war, the Empire . . . is faced with a struggle for the existence of the nation." Similarly, the critical "Imperial Rescript to the Soldiers and Officers" of August 17 that ordered Japanese military forces to lay down their arms ignored the atomic bombs and mentioned only the Soviet entry. In a careful analysis of Japanese records between August 6 and August 17, the historian Tsuyoshi Hasegawa found only two statements (out of twelve) referring to the impact of the bombs alone; the rest emphasized both the bombs and Soviet action, or Soviet action alone. In Hasegawa's own estimation, the Soviet entry rather than atomic bombs was the determining factor in forcing Japan's hand.[115]

The roads not taken by U.S. policy makers in this instance are, in any case, several. Stalin could have been informed more explicitly of the existence of the new weapon, as well as plans to use it. (As it happened, he already knew about the atomic bomb through spies in the Manhattan Project.) Consideration might have been given to bringing the Soviet Union in as the fourth Great Power endorser of the Potsdam Declaration in late July—alongside the United States, Great Britain, and China—thus making unmistakably clear that Tokyo's pathetic peace feelers to Moscow were futile and the "five year" Soviet-Japanese neutrality pact but a piece of paper. The use of the bombs could have been delayed, at least for a few weeks, to see if Russia's entry into the war did indeed prove to be "the decisive action levering them into capitulation."[116]

These alternatives were not pursued because the World War II Soviet ally had become identified as an adversary before the war in Asia ended. The contention that the atomic bombs were used as the "first major operation" of the Cold War was forcefully expressed a few years after the war by the British physicist and 1948 Nobel laureate P. M. S. Blackett, who was involved in wartime military developments but found his views on postwar nuclear policy diverging sharply from those of the U.S. and British governments. In a 1948 book published under the title *Fear, War, and the Bomb* in its American edition, Blackett succinctly articulated many of the arguments that still roil this debate:

> So we may conclude that the dropping of the atomic bombs was not so much the last military act of the second World War, as the first major operation of the cold diplomatic war with Russia now in progress. The fact, however, that the realistic objectives in the field of *Macht-Politik*, so well achieved by the timing of the bomb, did not square with the advertised objective of saving "untold numbers" of American lives, produced an intense inner psychological conflict in the minds of many English and American people who knew, or suspected, some of the real facts. This conflict was particularly intense in the minds of the atomic scientists who rightly felt a deep responsibility at seeing their brilliant scientific work used in this way. The realization that their work had been used to achieve a diplomatic victory in relation to the power politics of the post-war world, rather than to save American lives, was clearly too disturbing to many of them to be consciously admitted. To allay their own doubts, many came to believe that the dropping of the bombs had in fact saved a million lives. It thus came about that those people who possessed the strongest emotional drive to save the world from the results of future atomic bombs, had in general a very distorted view of the actual circumstances of their first use.[117]

Does the record that has become available over the half century since Blackett was writing support this harsh indictment? No and yes. Those who made the decision to reject the Franck Committee's recommendations about building trust—who chose instead to reveal the destructiveness of the new weapon in the most shocking manner possible, while simultaneously hoping to preempt Soviet entry into the war—did not, as Blackett suggests, see a contradiction between saving lives by ending the war quickly and using the bomb as a form of diplomatic intimidation vis-à-vis the Russians. Thinking about ending the war against Japan and thinking about the Soviet Union overlapped. The plain-speaking Vannevar Bush, who served as director of the Office of Scientific Research and Development from mid-1941 through the end of the war, expressed this succinctly when he was later asked what significance he attached "to the delivery of the A-bomb on time":

> It saved hundreds of thousands of casualties on the beaches of Japan. It was also delivered on time so that there was no necessity for any concessions to Russia at the end of the war. It was on time in the sense that after the war we had the principal deterrent that prevented Russia from sweeping over Europe after we demobilized. It is one of the most magnificent performances of history in any development to have that thing on time.[118]

The documentary as well as anecdotal evidence that "atomic diplomacy" extraneous to Japan per se was never far from the minds of the war planners is in any case voluminous. On April 13, the day after Truman's abrupt ascension to the presidency following Roosevelt's death, for example, Byrnes briefed him about the secret weapons project ("capable of wiping out entire cities and killing people on an unprecedented scale"), and went on to add "that in his belief the bomb might well put us in a position to dictate our own terms at the end of the war." When Stimson gave the president his first detailed report on the project two weeks later, the secretary of war also paired dire imagery ("modern civilization might be completely destroyed") with utopian hopes of handling the new weapon in such a way that "we would have the opportunity to bring the world into a pattern in which the peace of the world and our civilization can be saved."[119]

Truman learned about the success of the Trinity test while at Potsdam; and although this forced the issue, the fact that the U.S.-Soviet relationship was absolutely central to dictating the patterns of a postwar nuclear world was clear before Trinity and even before Germany's capitulation. The Polish-born physicist Joseph Rotblat, who worked on the bomb in England before joining scientists in Los Alamos in 1944, for example, attended a social occasion in March of that year at which General Groves casually observed, "You realize of course that the main purpose of this project is to subdue the Russians."

Rotblat was shocked. "Until then," he recalled, "I had thought that our work was to prevent a Nazi victory." That this was not false memory on Rotblat's part was implicitly confirmed after the war by Groves himself, who stated in sworn testimony, "I think it is important to state—I think it is well known—that there was never from about 2 weeks from the time I took charge of this project [in September 1942] any illusion on my part but that Russia was our enemy and that the project was conducted on that basis. I didn't go along with the attitude of the country as a whole that Russia was a gallant ally. I always had suspicions and the project was conducted on that basis. Of course, that was so reported to the President."[120]

Other scientists gleaned the same message from other high officials. Thus, when Leo Szilard, the Nobel laureate Harold Urey, and another scientist colleague visited Byrnes in late May of 1945 to emphasize the impossibility of maintaining a nuclear monopoly and warn of the danger "that our 'demonstration' of atomic bombs will precipitate a race in the production of these devices between the United States and Russia," Byrnes brushed them off. Truman's future secretary of state brought up the Soviet military presence in Hungary and Rumania, and suggested (as Szilard summarized the colossal mis-meeting of minds) "that Russia might be more manageable if impressed by American military might, and that a demonstration of the bomb might impress Russia." Szilard, a Hungarian émigré, was hardly naïve about the Soviet projection of power in eastern Europe following Germany's collapse, but nonetheless found himself "completely flabbergasted by the assumption that rattling the bomb might make Russia more manageable."[121]

These anti-Soviet considerations colored decision making both explicitly and metaphorically, as Stimson's conversations and ruminations at the time reveal with particular vividness. In his diary entry for June 6, for example, the secretary of war recorded discussing with the president "further quid pro quos which should be established for our taking them [the Soviet Union] into partnership," leading the two men to agree that once the bomb had been used against Japan the United States would be in a stronger position to pursue "the settlement of the Polish, Rumanian, Yugoslavian, and Manchurian problems." On other occasions, Stimson and his colleagues fell back on gaming metaphors. On May 14, for example, the secretary's diary records conversations with General Marshall and

Assistant Secretary of War John J. McCloy about dealing with Russia, in which Stimson emphasized the need to "let our actions speak for words . . . and perhaps do it in a pretty rough and realistic way." He proceeded to paraphrase his argument as follows: "This was a place where we really held all the cards. I called it a royal straight flush and we mustn't be a fool about the way we play it. They can't get along without our help and industries and we have coming into action a weapon which will be unique."

The following day's diary entry records a meeting concerning when to schedule the Potsdam Conference, relates this explicitly to the "S–1 secret" (that is, the Manhattan Project) and desirability of postponing the conference until the bomb had been tested, and—in a line often quoted after the diary became accessible—goes on to observe that "it seems a terrible thing to gamble with such big stakes in diplomacy without having your master card in your hand." A day later (May 16), in a meeting with the president, the card-playing language was repeated ("We shall probably hold more cards in our hands later than now") and reinforced with the metaphor of ball playing ("We must find some way of persuading Russia to play ball").[122]

The Potsdam Conference, at which Truman met Stalin for the first time, was devoted to postwar policies in general rather than the situation in Asia alone. The desire not to attend such a meeting until the United States had its "master card" in hand explains both why the projected conference date was repeatedly pushed back and why Oppenheimer's bomb makers were placed under greater pressure than ever before to finish and test their product—the clear understanding being that a successful test would be followed as swiftly as possible by deployment on crowded Japanese cities. Some of the ambiguity of Truman's fascinating Potsdam diary, and his postwar memoirs as well, reflects the bridge nature of that moment when he learned that Trinity was a resounding success—and the desire for Soviet entry into the war ("Fini Japs") was replaced by confidence that this could be preempted by using the new weapon quickly.

Looking back on all this later for the public record, the president skated over the "quid pro quo" and "master card" gaming that colored discussions of this exercise in what Blackett reasonably identified as *Macht-Politik.* At the same time, however, Truman did in his own way frankly acknowledge the power politics of the new game in northeast Asia itself.

"Our dropping of the atomic bomb on Japan," he observed in his memoirs, "had forced Russia to reconsider her position in the Far East." More specifically: "I was determined that I would not allow the Russians any part in the control of Japan. Our experiences with them in Germany and in Bulgaria, Rumania, Hungary, and Poland was such that I decided to take no chances in a joint setup with the Russians." And again: "I did not want divided control or separate zones. I did not want to give the Russians any opportunity to behave as they had in Germany and Austria."[123]

Byrnes also acknowledged, somewhat vaguely, that Soviet actions in eastern Germany and eastern Europe had led him to look with alarm on Soviet entry into the war in Asia. "I believed the atomic bomb would be successful and would force the Japanese to accept surrender on our terms," he wrote in memoirs published in 1947. "I feared what would happen when the Red Army entered Manchuria. Before it left Manchuria, my fears were realized." The rough record kept by one of Byrnes's aides at Potsdam was more graphic on this score, noting "JFB still hoping for time, believing after atomic bomb Japan will surrender and Russia will not get in so much on the kill, thereby being in a position to press for claims against China."[124] What was actually involved, as the broader record reveals (and individuals like Vannevar Bush and General Groves were more frank in acknowledging), however, was more than "Manchuria" or "China" or "control of Japan" alone. The perceived game was nothing less than global domination at the dawn of a nuclear age.

## Partisan Politics

Dramatic violence serves vested interests, and the new practices of air warfare were inescapably political domestically as well as internationally. Bureaucratic competition within the military establishment helped propel the conventional strategic-bombing policy that culminated in the B-29 offensive: demonstrating their awesome capacity to bring ruination upon the enemy (and arguing that *this* was the decisive factor in bringing about Japan's capitulation, like Germany's earlier) contributed immeasurably to ensuring a postwar political commitment to air power and the creation of an independent air force. Using the atomic bombs as flamboyantly as possible not only complemented this agenda but also introduced a new one by helping to ensure broad support for a post-hostilities commitment to developing nuclear energy. This is not *why* the bombs were used, but it helps illuminate the milieu in which proposed alternatives to their use fell on deaf ears.

Electoral party politics also entered the picture. As seasoned Democratic Party politicians, both Truman and Byrnes were keenly aware that the congressional bipartisanship forged by the war was ephemeral and already fraying—and, more specifically, that the costly top-secret Manhattan Project would be a particularly vulnerable target for postwar attack by Republicans unless it could be shown to have been money well spent. As a committee chairman in the Senate prior to becoming vice president following the presidential election of 1944, Truman himself had cast a skeptical eye on these highly classified expenditures, and the political vulnerability of the project was addressed on various occasions thereafter.

Negotiations with the British in 1943 concerning collaborating on the bomb, for example, were framed in terms of the need to "avoid at all costs the President's being accused of dealing with hundreds of millions of taxpayers' money improvidently or acting for purposes beyond the winning of the war." Congressional leaders warned the War Department in early 1945 that "as soon as the war is over Congress will conduct a most thorough inquiry into the project," and Groves was cautioned to keep scrupulous records of all expenditures. Byrnes, then director of the Office of War Mobilization, sent a memo to Roosevelt in early March, the month prior to the president's death, calling attention to expenditures approaching two billion dollars and warning that "if the project proves a failure, it will then be subjected to relentless investigation and criticism."[125]

The Franck Report of mid-June referred almost matter-of-factly to this political consideration. "Another argument which could be quoted in favor of using atomic bombs as soon as they are available," the report observed critically, "is that so much taxpayers' money had been invested in the Projects that the Congress and the American public will demand a return for their money." This, indeed, had been one of the several discouraging conclusions that Szilard and his colleagues came away with after their miserably unsuccessful attempt to persuade Byrnes that hasty use of the bomb would be internationally disastrous. As Szilard recalled it, Byrnes essentially told the scientists what he had confidentially told

Roosevelt a few months earlier: that "we had spent two billion dollars on developing the bomb, and Congress would want to know what we had got for the money spent." Szilard also quoted the cagey former senator as relating this consideration to future appropriations for nuclear research, which the scientists were eager to ensure. "How would you get Congress to appropriate money for atomic energy research," he recalled Byrnes saying, "if you do not show results for the money which has been spent already?"[126]

Blackett, writing a few years later, found it appalling that such partisan considerations might have influenced the decision to use the bomb—but also probable, given the frequency with which this was mentioned after the war. If indeed true, he predicted, what this portended was ominous: "If the United States Government had been influenced in the summer of 1945 by this view, then perhaps at some future date, when another two billion dollars had been spent, it might feel impelled to stage another Roman holiday with some other country's citizens, rather than 120,000 victims of Hiroshima and Nagasaki, as the chosen victims. The wit of man could hardly devise a theory of the dropping of the bomb, both more insulting to the American people, or more likely to lead to an energetically pursued Soviet defense policy."[127]

Blackett's professed shock notwithstanding, politicians play politics. In the critical moments when the reply to Japan's "imperial prerogatives" demand was being drafted, Byrnes remarked to one of his aides that had he simply gone along with the Japanese request, this (as recorded in the aide's diary) "would have led to crucifixion of [the] President." Byrnes almost certainly was referring to politics and public opinion. A fair indication of popular sentiment on these matters was conveyed in a Gallup Poll published on the front page of the *Washington Post* on June 29, just days after the Potsdam ultimatum was issued. In response to the question "What do you think we should do with the Japanese Emperor after the war?" the largest number of respondents (33 percent) supported "Execute him." Seventeen percent endorsed "Let court decide his fate"; 11 percent, "Keep him in prison the rest of his life"; 9 percent, "Exile him"; 4 percent, "Do nothing—he's only a figurehead for war lords"; and only 3 percent, "Use him as a puppet to run Japan."[128]

# SWEETNESS, BEAUTY, AND
# IDEALISTIC ANNIHILATION

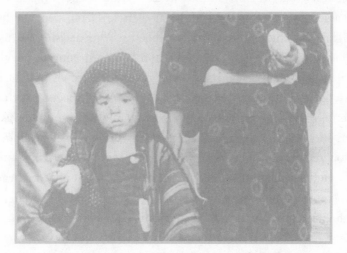

The military and political considerations behind the decision to drop atomic bombs on Hiroshima and Nagasaki—ending the war quickly, intimidating the Soviet Union, and preempting partisan political criticism at home—are well documented. How this is sorted and weighed is another matter, and in the United States disagreement between supporters and critics of the decision has become more rather than less pointed as time passes. Nothing revealed this more sharply than the controversy that erupted in 1994 and 1995 over plans by the Smithsonian Institution's Air and Space Museum for a fiftieth-anniversary exhibition featuring the *Enola Gay*, the B-29 that dropped the Hiroshima bomb. Those who would simply celebrate the mushroom cloud that, in their view, ended the war were challenged by curators and historians who were more interested in calling attention to internal debates, the physical and human destruction at Ground Zero itself, and the strategic and nuclear legacies of August 1945. In the end, political pressure thwarted what might have been a rare public engagement with tragic complexity.

Beyond decision making per se—that is, when we move from the formal records of war planners to essentially psychological and institutional dynamics—understanding why mass destruction possesses an almost irresistible momentum becomes even more challenging and provocative. We enter territory that lies beyond the formal written and testimonial record, beyond assumptions of rational choice at every level and step, and beyond any single case study. From this perspective, the decision to use the atomic bombs is exemplary in calling attention to driving forces that lie beneath the surface—or, perhaps better phrased, were visible but barely acknowledged. The scientific thrill of playing Faust was one such force; the technological imperative to develop and deploy ever more devastating weapons another; the relentless technocratic thrust of war machinery set in motion yet another. Mass destruction itself was mesmerizing—horrific from the victim's perspective, but attractive to the point of being beautiful, even rapturous, if one was the victimizer instead. Thirst for revenge naturally influenced behavior. So did idealism—albeit an idealism in which traditional just-war considerations were discarded and replaced by rationalizations and delusions about engaging in a lesser evil. One killed the many to save the more.

### Scientific Sweetness and Technological Imperatives

In his acclaimed study of the making of the atomic bomb, Richard Rhodes quotes a simple query from a Hiroshima survivor who was a fourth-grade student when the bomb was dropped. "Those scientists who invented the . . . atomic bomb," she asked—"what did they think would happen if they dropped it?"[129]

The simple answer is that, with some exceptions, they did not think much about this until the project neared completion; and, even then, they thought mostly about international repercussions rather than the people who would be on the ground at "point zero." What motivated many scientists initially was the belief they were in a race with Nazi Germany to make a nuclear weapon, as Joseph Rotblat stated in explaining why he left the Manhattan Project at the end of 1944 when it had become obvious this was no longer the case. What sustained them, and soon overrode this initial sense of urgency, was the sheer sweetness of the undertaking. Rotblat was the rare participant who was not seduced by wedding science to power and power to forces of annihilation never before released by man. He later recalled that when he asked colleagues at Los Alamos—many of whom were European émigrés like him—why they were staying on even after Germany was defeated, "the most frequent reason given was pure and simple scientific curiosity—the strong urge to find out whether the theoretical calculations and predictions would come true."[130]

Decades later, the physicist Victor Weisskopf looked back on his participation in the Manhattan Project and confessed he was "ashamed to say that few of us even thought of quitting." To his knowledge, only two scientists had done so. Why? "It was the attraction of the task," Weisskopf explained. "It was impossible to quit at that time. . . . It was 'technically sweet'." Viewed from the summer of 1945, he went on, there were four options. The first, not to use the new weapon, was out of the question, for "it was unthinkable in a time of war for the military not to use its most potent weapon." The second option, demonstrating the bomb over an uninhabited area, was simply dismissed. The third option, using the bomb on a purely military target, was rejected because this was not deemed big enough to demonstrate the new weapon's power, and because it would probably be difficult afterwards to distinguish prior damage from the nuclear damage. Oppenheimer's rationale, as Weisskopf recalled it, was that "if the bomb is to make war impossible, it must have a very strong effect." Thus, Hiroshima. And Nagasaki? That, in Weisskopf's view, was simply "a crime."[131]

The sweetness of the undertaking—particularly at Los Alamos, where Oppenheimer held sway and the knotty challenges of actually making the bomb work continued to the very end—was communal as well as intellectual. "Here at Los Alamos," the English physicist James Tuck exclaimed, "I found a spirit of Athens, of Plato, of an ideal republic." Edward Teller giggled, in a light moment, about being "a big happy family." Oppenheimer himself described wartime Los Alamos as "a remarkable community, inspired

71. *"The gadget," as the first nuclear explosive was called, being installed at the top of the Trinity test tower, just prior to detonation on July 16, 1945.*

by a high sense of mission, of duty and of destiny, coherent, dedicated, and remarkably selfless." The schoolgirl in Hiroshima who asked what the scientists were thinking would surely find little reason for forgiveness in this, but the sense of participating in a rare community of men of high purpose and exceptional talent was widely shared. This aura of intellectual challenge and common cause was, in fact, so seductive that most of the scientists who agonized over the dropping of the bombs in 1945 nonetheless continued to work on advanced nuclear weaponry after the war—including development of "the super," as the hydrogen or thermonuclear bomb that dwarfed the spawn of the Manhattan Project was called.[132]

This intimate bonding was comparable to the "band of brothers" cama-raderie experienced by men in combat on every side—by the kamikaze pilots, for example, whose sense of identification ultimately came to focus on their small unit, just as the crew of a B-29 came to see themselves as family and focus on the collective performance and well-being of their tight

72. *J. Robert Oppenheimer and General Leslie Groves revisit Ground Zero of the Trinity explosion in September 1945.*

and interdependent little group. At the same time, however, the atomic-bomb scientists were intellectual, elitist, and history-minded in unique ways. Oppenheimer, as he so often did, put this in particularly quotable ways. Looking back in 1954 (in government hearings that stripped him of his security clearance), he first framed this in a general way:

Almost everyone realized that this was a great undertaking. Almost everyone knew that if it were completed successfully and rapidly enough, it might determine the outcome of the war. Almost everyone knew that it was an unparalleled opportunity to bring to bear the basic knowledge and art of science for the benefit of his country. Almost everyone knew that this job, if it were achieved, would be

part of history. This sense of excitement, of devotion and of patriotism in the end prevailed.

Later, in the same proceedings, he introduced the simpler, succinct language Victor Weisskopf used decades afterwards:

> It is my judgment in these things that when you see something that
> is technically sweet, you go ahead and do it and you argue about
> what to do about it only after you have had your technical success.
> That is the way it was with the atomic bomb. I do not think anyone
> opposed making it; there were some debates about what to do with
> it after it was made.[133]

In November 1945—closer to the event and in the company of a newly
formed "Association of Los Alamos Scientists"—Oppenheimer spoke as
"a fellow scientist" about the "organic necessity" that underlies scientific
inquiry in general:

> But when you come right down to it the reason that we did this
> job is because it was an organic necessity. If you are a scientist you
> cannot stop such a thing. If you are a scientist you believe that it
> is good to find out how the world works; that it is good to find out
> what the realities are; that it is good to turn over to mankind at large
> the greatest possible power to control the world and to deal with it
> according to its lights and its values.
>     . . . It is not possible to be a scientist unless you believe that it is
> good to learn. It is not good to be a scientist, and not possible, unless
> you think that it is of the highest value to share your knowledge,
> to share it with anyone who is interested. It is not possible to be a
> scientist unless you believe that the knowledge of the world, and
> the power which this gives, is a thing which is of intrinsic value to
> humanity, and that you are using it to help in the spread of knowl-
> edge, and are willing to take the consequences.[134]

This was noble rhetoric, the other side of Oppenheimer's more mor-
bid "Death, the destroyer" ruminations. There were, of course, additional
kinds of sweetness in being the deliverer of "the greatest possible power to

control the world" that anyone had ever imagined. Playing God was one—and, more modestly and American, playing the Wild West hero another. Oppenheimer may have thought of the Bhagavad Gita upon witnessing Trinity, but as one of his colleagues later recalled, after the spectacular explosion he strutted from his bunker at the base camp like Gary Cooper in *High Noon*. A terser and less romantic rendering of the "organic necessity" argument was provided by Enrico Fermi, the Italian Nobel laureate who led the Chicago team that created the first controlled chain reaction in December 1942. As the story goes, the often irascible Fermi was well known for exclaiming, "Don't bother me with your conscientious scruples! After all, the thing's superb physics!"[135]

*Superb physics! Willing to take the consequences.* But what consequences? A guilty or conflicted conscience hardly compared to the consequences the schoolgirl in Hiroshima witnessed.

## Technocratic Momentum and the War Machine

When Admiral Halsey opined that the scientists "had this toy and they wanted to try it out, so they dropped it," he was speaking recklessly. The scientists did not drop the bomb. They were, on the contrary, cogs in a war machine and had no control over how their product was used. That, indeed, was the realization that prompted the belated, futile activism reflected in the Franck Report and Szilard-inspired petitions, as well as the soul-searching that found organized expression in the postwar "scientists' movement" led by politically concerned atomic scientists. When Weisskopf addressed colleagues and students about the sweetness and shame of developing the bomb, he deemed it necessary to emphasize that scientists must think beyond the attractiveness of the subject and give serious consideration to the applications of their work. This was not a lesson every scientist endorsed, or wished to hear—nor was it a lesson that all who preached it necessarily consistently practiced themselves.

By the summer of 1945, in any case, the desire to see the product work was irresistible; and the argument that followed as a matter of course was that to see how it *really* worked—and simultaneously demonstrate this to the world in general, and the Russians in particular—required using it against a crowded city that had as yet few if any war scars. In April

1945, several months before the Trinity test, Stimson noted in his diary that the bomb "has this unique peculiarity: that, although every prophecy thus far has been fulfilled by the development and we can see that success is 99% assured, yet only by the first actual war trial of the weapon can the actual certainty be fixed." Early in June, he discussed the bomb project with Truman at length and recorded, "I was a little fearful that before we could get ready the Air Force might have Japan so thoroughly bombed that the new weapon would not have a fair background to show its strength. He [Truman] laughed and said he understood." This was close to the reasoning that prompted Oppenheimer and his small Science Panel to conclude a few months later, "We see no acceptable alternative to direct military use." (That the two bombs available as of early August differed technically—Little Boy involving enriched uranium and Fat Man plutonium, like the bomb detonated in the Trinity test—surely enhanced the attractiveness of giving both a war trial, but there seems no evidence that this was discussed.)[136]

These internal dynamics or momentums—military, political, scientific, technological, and technocratic—help explain how the very purpose of the bomb shifted seamlessly from the original urgency at being in a "race against the Germans" (Truman's words in his memoirs) to preempt Nazi possession of such a ghastly weapon, to the unquestioned assumption that it could and should be used as an offensive weapon against Japan. Such thinking actually surfaced at an early date: before Germany's surrender in May 1945; before U.S. intelligence had determined with absolute certainty (in the "Alsos" operation in November 1944) that the Germans were not building a bomb; before the United States had begun bombing Japan from China in mid-1944; even before U.S. forces were fully launched on their island-hopping advance against the Japanese homeland. The official history of the development of the atomic bombs as seen from the British side notes flatly that British intelligence experts had concluded the Germans were not developing atomic energy in a serious way "by the beginning of 1944," and that while the German threat had not been completely dismissed, "during the last eighteen months or so [of the war] it ceased to be the driving force of the Manhattan Project."[137]

On April 23, 1945, with Germany's collapse imminent, Groves told Stimson that "the target is and was always expected to be Japan." This was hyperbole, but only slightly so. On May 5, 1943, more than two years before Germany's capitulation, the Military Policy Committee of the Manhattan Project discussed use of "the first bomb" and rejected Tokyo as the first target but agreed that it might be best used "on a Japanese fleet concentration" in the Pacific, where a dud bomb would be difficult to salvage." "The Japanese were selected," the minutes of this meeting continue, "as they would not be so apt to secure knowledge from it [a retrieved bomb] as would the Germans." The official history of the Atomic Energy Commission records that later in 1943 "Groves approved arrangements to modify a B-29 for operations with nuclear weapons. The choice of the B-29 over the British Lancaster, the only other plane sufficiently large, reflected the disposition to use the bomb against Japan." Following a meeting at Roosevelt's retreat at Hyde Park in mid-September of 1944, the president and Churchill signed a short, secret, and subsequently often-quoted *aide-mémoire* affirming that their collaborative nuclear research should remain a matter "of the utmost secrecy; but when a 'bomb' is finally available, it might perhaps, after mature consideration, be used against the Japanese, who should be warned that this bombardment will be repeated until they surrender." Germany was not mentioned.[138]

Although Japan had several accomplished nuclear scientists, and both the Imperial Army and Imperial Navy launched small projects looking into the feasibility of making nuclear weapons, the infrastructure to do this was lacking and there was never any apprehension in U.S. circles of being in a race with the Japanese. Yet unborn, the bomb conceived in fear and horror that the Nazis might make and use it very quickly assumed the identity of a desirable offensive weapon—and more. Japan replaced Germany as the projected target. Once Germany capitulated, Oppenheimer's team in Los Alamos was placed under intense pressure to complete the bomb and have this "master card" in hand before Truman met with Churchill and Stalin at Potsdam. And once the Potsdam ultimatum had been issued, the rush was on to use the two bombs then available as soon as possible. Underlying all this was a vast machinery devoted to possessing and using the bomb; and once Germany was out of the war, this machinery moved into high gear. The obverse side of science at war was modern war as science—a highly rationalized, bureaucratized, compartmentalized undertaking in which the answer to the query "what were they thinking" was essentially the same almost anywhere one looked: "they" were thinking about their jobs, the demanding and particularistic tasks immediately before them.[139]

WHEN THE CRITIC James Agee tried to explain why the Disney Studio's 1943 rendering of *Victory Through Air Power* seemed to him "queasy, perhaps in an all-American sense" characteristic of Disney in general, he spoke of "antiseptic white lies" that failed to confront "human terror, suffering, and death." He then moved to a different level of figurative expression, characterizing the film version of de Seversky's bestseller as amounting to the simplistic morality of "victory-in-a-vacuum," of "machine-eat-machine." Such machine imagery is evocative. At the most elemental level, it calls to mind the literal machinery of the war that was not even known to the public when Agee was writing: the spectacular B-29s, for example, as well as "the gadget" itself.[140]

Beyond this, machine-eat-machine places men at war, whether on the battlefront or home front, within an enormous bureaucratic and technocratic apparatus—not just focused on their jobs, but more often than not unable or disinclined to see things whole. Wilbur Morrison, a thoughtful B-29 airman who ended the war with the rank of major and was among those who did reflect on the horrors of the business, instinctively turned to the machinery idiom to describe how routinized the incendiary air raids had become by the month or so before Hiroshima. "The missions," he wrote, "were run off on a production-line basis." The production-line operations he witnessed personally were, in fact, but a small part of a huge operation set in motion by men and forces never seen and rarely even contemplated.[141]

The suprapersonal mega-machine is also a reminder of literal distancing or abstraction, especially in modern, high-tech warfare: how the majority of military men in World War II never actually saw an enemy face-to-face; how high above the target the bombers were when they dropped their explosives and incendiaries (a mile or more even in the so-called low-altitude raids); how relying on aerial reconnaissance photos of "square miles destroyed" helped sanitize the actual horror of urban-area bombing; how many thousands of miles distant from "human terror, suffering, and death" the planners in Washington and bomb makers in Los Alamos, Chicago, Oak Ridge, and Hanford resided. It followed that distancing became figurative too—involving individual and small-group subordination and self-absorption that amounted, in the grand picture, to isolation, alienation, and surrender of individual autonomy in an institutional climate inhospitable to questioning and completely intolerant of dissent.

The thrust of the machine was conveyed in the almost offhand observation by leaders like Truman, Churchill, Stimson, and Groves that they always assumed the bomb would be used. "President Roosevelt particularly spoke to me many times of his own awareness of the catastrophic potentialities of our work," Stimson wrote in his famous 1947 article justifying using the bomb. "I therefore emphasize that it was our common objective, throughout the war, to be the first to produce an atomic weapon and use it. The possible atomic weapon was considered to be a new and tremendously powerful explosive, as legitimate as any other of the deadly explosive weapons of modern war. The entire purpose was the production of a military weapon; on no other ground could the wartime expenditure of so much time and money have been justified." Groves, on his part, acknowledged that "when we first began to develop atomic energy, the United States was in no way committed to employ atomic weapons against any other power. With the activation of the Manhattan Project, however, the situation began to change." Like Stimson, Groves emphasized the costliness of the work, in terms of both money expended and interference with other aspects of the war effort: "As time went on, and as we poured more and more money and effort into the project, the government became increasingly committed to the ultimate use of the bomb, and while it has often been said that we undertook development of this terrible weapon so that Hitler would not get it first, the fact remains that the original decision to make the project an all-out effort was based upon using it to end the war. . . . Certainly, there was no question in my mind, or, as far as I was ever aware, in the mind of either President Roosevelt or President Truman or any other responsible person, but that we were developing a weapon to be used against the enemies of the United States."[142]

Oppenheimer, who was attracted to what he called the exciting adventure of constructing a bomb even before Pearl Harbor, later recalled that while scientists in Chicago belatedly came to question using the weapon, there was little talk about this at Los Alamos: "We always assumed, if they [the bombs] were needed, they would be used." When asked about the step-up in tempo at Los Alamos after Germany was out of the war, Oppenheimer acknowledged that "we were still more frantic to have the job done and wanted to have it done so that if needed, it would be available. In any case, we wanted to have it done before the war was over, and nothing much could be done. I don't think there was any time where we worked harder at the speedup than in the period after the German surrender and the actual combat use of the bomb." This captures, with unusual and perhaps unintended sharpness, the double-edge nature of the enterprise: that the bomb was desirable to end the war, but also that there was an almost frantic effort to have the bomb and use it before the war ended.[143]

In this relentless machinery, the Interim Committee set up by Stimson in early May, ostensibly to coordinate atomic-bomb matters and advise the secretary of war on what to recommend to the president, was more ornament than indispensible part—as was true of counterpart groups like the Consultative Council on the British side. Arthur Compton, a 1927 Nobel laureate in physics who headed the bomb project in Chicago and was a member of the Science Panel that advised the Interim Committee, later wrote that "it seemed to be a foregone conclusion that the bomb would be used. It was regarding only the details of strategy and tactics that differing views were expressed."

Preparation for combat operations to deliver the bomb was initiated in the spring of 1944, a year before Groves was really certain "that we could produce an atomic explosion." The 509th Composite Group established specifically to drop the new weapon was formed in September and already practicing over-water flights (out of Cuba) by December. The first selection of atomic-bomb targets was made in late April of the following year (although Kyoto would be dropped from the list later, and Nagasaki added), and Groves had begun setting up on-the-ground military preparations for launching the missions out of Tinian a month previously. The 509th Group's B-29s began deploying to Tinian in May (before the Interim Committee held its key meetings, on May 31 and June 1), and the physicist Luis Alvarez was dispatched to Tinian to prepare for readying the bombs some two and a half months before Hiroshima was destroyed, well before the Alamogordo test. The British gave their assent to U.S.

plans to use the bomb (as stipulated in a prior agreement between Roosevelt and Churchill) on July 4, almost two weeks before it was tested; and when Truman set sail for Europe and the Potsdam Conference two days later, the Americans were carrying with them not only the working draft of the three-power ultimatum to Japan but also a statement for the president to deliver after the first bomb was dropped.[144]

By the time of the Trinity test on July 16, as Alice Kimball Smith observed in her highly regarded study of the atomic scientists, "the whole machinery for using the bomb had been set in motion." The official British history of these developments concluded similarly that "the project had taken on a momentum of its own" by early 1944. As it happened, at the moment the plutonium weapon was being tested in the predawn desert in Alamogordo (where the old Spanish name of the site was *Jornada del Muerto*, or Journey of Death), the uranium bomb assembly that would be dropped on Hiroshima was being loaded onto the heavy cruiser *Indianapolis* in San Francisco for transfer to Tinian; it was unloaded at its destination on July 26, the day the Potsdam ultimatum was released. The reports and appeals of concerned insiders like the Chicago scientists amounted to little more than grit that fell into this machinery and disappeared, all but unnoticed.[145]

MICHAEL SHERRY HAS addressed the "sociology" of the air war against Germany and Japan in compelling detail, with particular attention to the emergence of "civilian militarism" and the relentless dynamics of what he calls "technological determinism" and "technological fanaticism." (Sherry notes, among other things, that the air force alone employed some 500,000 civilians by war's end, and documents how, in the eyes of the technocrats, the "dehumanized rhetoric of technique reduced the enemy to quantifiable abstractions" and led Japan to be viewed as little more than "a vast laboratory in destruction.")[146]

The Manhattan Project provides a discrete case study of technical imperatives and technocratic momentum within this vast bureaucracy—and, beyond this, an illustration of the socialization, indoctrination, and plain intellectual numbing that accompanied this. The "Manhattan Engineer District" (the formal name of the project) was huge in itself—employing some 130,000 individuals by war's end, with sprawling secret sites producing uranium 235 in Oak Ridge, Tennessee, and plutonium in Hanford, Washington. General Groves, the military superintendent of the entire undertaking—an engineer by training and outstanding administrator by almost any standards—deemed *compartmentalization* desirable for maximum efficiency, and essential for optimum security. Apart from the scientists, few of these tens of thousands of employees even knew they were working on a nuclear weapon. (Colonel Tibbets's bomb crews were not briefed on the exact nature of their mission until just prior to takeoff for Hiroshima.) The unchallenged principles that defined this hierarchical and rigidly partitioned structure were to trust the leaders, serve the state, know your place, accept authority and the chain of command without question.[147]

The elite scientists caused Groves some grief by resisting extreme compartmentalization within their community, arguing that the nature and process of cutting-edge inquiry required free give-and-take. When scientists like Szilard and the Franck Committee went further, late in the game, and expressed concerns and reservations of a political nature, however, Oppenheimer politely but firmly attempted to bring them back in line by endorsing the ethos of acquiescence to higher and wiser authority. Edward Teller, for example, later recalled (and regretted) how Oppenheimer persuaded him to disregard Szilard's petition by expressing "in glowing terms the deep concern, thoroughness, and wisdom with which these questions were being handled in Washington. Our fate was in the hands of the best, the most conscientious men of our nation. And they had information which we did not possess." Years later, when at the height of the Cold War Oppenheimer's loyalty and trustworthiness were challenged, he reiterated the same position regarding knowing one's proper place. "I did my job which was the job I was supposed to do," he declared. "I was not in a policy-making position at Los Alamos. I would have done anything that I was asked to do, including making the bombs in a different shape, if I had thought it was technically feasible."[148]

Where the atomic bombs were concerned, compartmentalization and the secrecy that accompanied this were extreme. Truman's personal experience reflected this, being kept in ignorance about the nature of the project until he assumed the presidency upon Roosevelt's death. Outside the War Department, most of the cabinet was similarly kept in the dark. So was most

## SCIENTIFIC AND TECHNOLOGICAL SWEETNESS

*The ultrasecret Manhattan Project—shorthand for the "Manhattan Engineer District," run by the U.S. Army Corps of Engineers—extended to some thirty research and production sites in the United States, Canada, and United Kingdom, and employed around 130,000 people. It included three major "secret cities" in the United States. Facilities in Oak Ridge, Tennessee, covered more than sixty thousand acres and focused on uranium enrichment. The Hanford plant in the state of Washington, engaged in plutonium production, eventually spread over a thousand square miles. Basic research, design, and testing were conducted at Los Alamos, New Mexico. The mammoth undertakings at Oak Ridge and Hanford, where employees remained ignorant of the purpose of their work, never drew the retrospective attention that Los Alamos and its contingent of charismatic scientists attracted.*

73. *Workers load uranium slugs into the X-10 graphite reactor in Oak Ridge.*

74. *The four-story K-25 gaseous diffusion plant in Oak Ridge measured roughly a half-mile long and a thousand feet wide, making it larger than the Pentagon. This is where uranium 235 was separated from uranium 238.*

75. *The B reactor in Hanford was one of three reactors built along the Columbia River that produced plutonium for the Trinity test and Nagasaki bomb. The reactors used water as a coolant, drawing about seventy-five thousand gallons per minute from the river.*

76. *"Calutron" operators at control panels in the Y-12 plant in Oak Ridge, where uranium ore was refined into fissile material. Rotating shifts kept the plant operating twenty-four hours a day, seven days a week.*

77. *An electromagnetic "racetrack" used for uranium enrichment at the Y-12 plant. Three two-story buildings were required to accommodate nine such first-stage "alpha" racetracks, each of them measuring 122 feet long, 77 feet wide, and 15 feet high.*

of the military—including even the Joint Chiefs of Staff and Combined (U.S. and British) Chiefs. Where special arrangements were necessary to further developmental work or set up procedures for the actual bombing missions, they were done with an absolute minimum of "need to know" divulgence of information. Although Truman could have vetoed using the bombs upon becoming president, this was never a real possibility. As Groves put it, "As far as I was concerned, his [Truman's] decision was one of nonin-terference—basically a decision not to upset the existing plans."[149]

In or out of uniform, everyone had to be a good soldier. This was not difficult to do in the good war against Nazism, fascism, and Japanese aggression: one accepted one's role as a cog in the machine in the name of patriotism, loyalty, security, trust in the leaders, belief in the cause. It was only when non-Americans displayed good-soldier loyalty to the group or state or supreme leadership that this was to be understood in terms of lack of individualism, lack of adherence to universal principles of morality, herd behavior, aversion to genuine freedom and democracy and independence of mind, plain totalitarian brainwashing.

## The Aesthetics of Mass Destruction

Elting Morison, Stimson's admiring biographer, touched in different but compatible language on the psychology of individuals drawn into the process by which using the bomb became virtually preordained. "The Secretary, like everyone else who had to do with the making of the bomb," he wrote, "was engaged in a developing process. Any process started by men toward a special end tends, for reasons logical, biological, aesthetic or whatever they may be, to carry forward, if other things remain equal, to its climax. Each man fully engaged over four years of uncertainty and exertion in the actual making of the weapon was moved, without perhaps a full awareness, toward a predictable conclusion by the inertia developed in the human system. . . . In a process where such a general tendency has been set to work it is difficult to separate the moment when men were still free to choose from the moment, if such there was, when they were no longer free to choose."[150]

Militarists and romantics have always extolled—and realists and humanists called into question—the so-called glory of war. As a young congressman in 1848, Abraham Lincoln condemned President James

Polk's arguments for war against Mexico on these very grounds, accusing him of "fixing the public gaze upon the exceeding brightness of military glory—that attractive rainbow, that rises in showers of blood—that serpent's eye, that charms to destroy."[151] This seems the very opposite of depersonalized mega-machinery, but Morison's passing reference to aesthetic reasons that may carry men toward a certain technocratic end, even one as destructive as making and using the atomic bomb, reminds us that both the rainbow of military glory and the creation of an awesome military machine possess a seductive beauty. What the atomic-bomb scientists called sweetness was a form of aestheticism. So was the satisfaction that came from operating a mammoth political and industrial bureaucracy, whatever its purposes might be. When the purposes were deemed noble, such technocratic seductiveness might be heightened, but these gratifications also were intensified by the serpent's eye of unrestrained violence itself. Visualizing hell on earth does not preclude finding it attractive. It may even invite drawing closer.

In the wake of World War I, Sigmund Freud was drawn to explore what he eventually called the death wish or death instinct. After World War II, Erich Fromm spoke of a more positive embrace of "ecstatic destructiveness," present in primitive blood rituals as well as modern "technotronic" society. Analytical approaches to attraction to extreme experiences that court and precipitate violent death run the gamut: psychological and psychiatric sensitivity to dark forces of the unconscious, anthropological attentiveness to rituals involving the "life force," historical sensitivity to the mystique of "regenerative violence," feminist critiques of muscular masculine identity, post-structuralist attraction to the compelling "limit experience" of death or near death, animal-behavior studies of hard-wiring for violence, and so on. Early-twentieth-century Anglophone writers of pulp fiction thrilled their readers by setting the world aflame, ultimately wiping out entire races with still-imaginary "superweapons" and thereby ensuring the survival of white men's virtue.

Seemingly worlds apart from the thrill of pulp fiction on the literary spectrum was the "Trinity" code name under which the atomic bomb was first tested in the desert of New Mexico; yet this also reflected a potent inheritance from the world of imagined and rapturous violence. Oppenheimer dismissed the name as "just something suggested to me by John

Donne's sonnets, which I happened to be reading at the time," but the specific ecstatic poem that inspired him was hardly "just something." Its famous four opening lines read as follows: "Batter my heart, three-person'd God; for you / As yet but knocke, breathe, shine, and seeke to mend; / That I may rise, and stand, o'erthrow mee,' and bend / Your force, to breake, blowe, burn and make me new." Knowing all we know about the bomb, the precious narcissism of Oppenheimer's aestheticism seems almost breathtaking: *breake, blowe, burn and make me new*—when, in fact, it was by advancing the art of literally breaking, blowing away, and burning others that he imagined himself transformed.[152]

Like any piece of complex engineering, the war machine itself could be perceived as a marvelously functioning system deserving of aesthetic appreciation. Edward Bowles, an MIT professor of electrical communications who made important wartime contributions in radar and electronics, for example, captured this sense of technocratic and technological elegance when he visited Saipan in conjunction with the air war against Japan. He expressed deep admiration for America's ability to conduct operations "on a big scale" and for the "great silence and seriousness" of men taking off in their Superfortress bombers, all of which conveyed to him "the thrill and the satisfaction that real achievement carried with it." Here was a sense of organizational beauty every bit as compelling as the sweetness of work at the frontiers of science. Thus Bowles (quoted by Michael Sherry) enthused about the "spirit of this enterprise, its magnitude and beauty" that was capable of carrying him "into the realm of enchantment so long as one can throw into the distance the dread and the horror of war." And casting horror aside did not prove difficult.[153]

Beyond such technical and technocratic enchantment, air warfare possessed a beauty peculiarly its own, coupling as it did graceful flying machines, seas of flame and pillars of smoke, the nighttime crisscross of searchlights that made the planes glisten—an aura, almost, of touching heaven and hell simultaneously. "It was like looking through the keyhole of the gates to hell," Wilber Morrison recalled of peering through a break in the clouds during an attack on Nagoya. Much the same scene recurred on a subsequent raid—"the clouds parted and we were looking into a glowing red sea of flames that was once the city of Okayama"—but this did not take away the stunning fireworks of the night sky, where "clusters, set to burst at five thousand feet, looked like Roman candles as the prima cord exploded, and each cluster tore apart and descended as liquid fire."[154]

Even Japanese who witnessed the air raids from relative security were sometimes taken by their beauty. The French journalist Robert Guillain, who was in Tokyo during the great March 9 raid but lived in a neighborhood that escaped the conflagration, recalled the B-29s shining "golden against the dark roof of heaven or glittering blue, like meteors, in the searchlight beams spraying the vault from horizon to horizon," while "bursts of light flashed everywhere in the darkness like Christmas trees lifting their decorations of flame high into the night, then fell back to earth in whistling bouquets of jagged flame." The burning city became a "huge borealis," and the glinting wings of the bombers cut through columns of smoke "sharp as blades." All the Japanese in his neighborhood, Guillain observed, were standing in their gardens or peering out of home shelters and "uttering cries of admiration . . . at this grandiose, almost theatrical spectacle." A retrospective journalistic account of the Tokyo raid quotes Japanese describing the bombers as "translucent, unreal, light as fantastic glass dragonflies," and the shower of bombs as descending like a "cascade of silvery water." Two Japanese who were teenagers at the time and later became well-known cultural figures—the composer Tōru Takemitsu and photographer Shōmei Tōmatsu—reminisced about the deep and lasting aesthetic impression these deadly raids made on them. If even the bombed could be captivated, how much more so the bombers.[155]

THE CONCEIT THAT there was something particularly pure about air war and destruction from the sky crystallized in World War I and was articulated by Admiral Alfred von Tirpitz as early as 1914, when aerial bombardment was still a rudimentary business. "Single bombs from flying machines are wrong; they are odious when they hit and kill old women, and one gets used to them," the German military theorist (better known for his naval policies) declared. If, however, "one could set fire to London in thirty places, then what in a small way is odious would retire before something fine and powerful." Thirty places. Three decades later, the admiral seemed a cautious prophet indeed; but he was correct about the allure, and prescient about the peculiar way in which mass death from the air would somehow make the dead old women invisible and acquire the luster of being not merely less odious, but heroic and even civilized and refined. Although happenstance, it is nonetheless suggestive that the only B-29 that participated in both the Hiroshima and Nagasaki bombings, tasked with scientifically measuring the blast effects, was named by its crew *The Great Artiste*.[156]

From the moment of Trinity, the tremendous spectacle of the nuclear explosion sent observers searching for words to describe the indescribable. Horror and attraction commingled; the light, the coloration, the sound seemed to defy description. Breathtaking, said one well-known scientist, at an obvious loss for words. Like opening curtains to the sun, said another. The flash would be like ten suns, the crew of the *Enola Gay* was told when warned to wear dark goggles. "Brighter than a thousand suns" became a famous descriptive phrase. Perhaps the most effective attempt to capture the spectacle, and the emotions it engendered, was written hastily and confidentially by General Farrell, whose lengthy eyewitness account was included in the top-secret "Report on Alamogordo Atomic Bomb Test" completed on July 18 by General Groves and sent to Truman at Potsdam:

> The effects could well be called unprecedented, magnificent, beautiful, stupendous and terrifying. No man-made phenomenon of such tremendous power had ever occurred before. The lighting effects beggared description. The whole country was lighted by a searing light with the intensity many times that of the midday sun. It was golden, purple, violet, gray and blue. It lighted every peak, crevasse and ridge of the nearby mountain range with a clarity and beauty that cannot be described but must be seen to be imagined. It was that beauty the great poets dream about but describe most poorly and inadequately. Thirty seconds after the explosion came first, the air blast pressing hard against the people and things, to be followed almost immediately by the strong, sustained, awesome roar which warned of doomsday and made us feel that we puny things were blasphemous to dare tamper with the forces heretofore reserved to The Almighty. Words are inadequate tools for the job of acquainting those not present with the physical, mental and psychological effects. It had to be witnessed to be realized.[157]

For public consumption, description of the wondrous beauty of the bomb as dropped on a real target was assigned to William Laurence, the *New York Times* science writer who doubled behind the scene as "Special Consultant to the Manhattan Engineer District." Laurence was invited to witness the Trinity test, and later to fly as the only press representative on the Nagasaki mission. (No journalists accompanied the Hiroshima bombing.) In typically American report-from-the-battlefront style, he devoted many paragraphs to giving the name, age, hometown, and even street address of each crew member—an almost perfectly individualized and asymmetric counterpoint to the anonymous Japanese who were about to be obliterated miles below. Although photographs and replicas as well as its "Fat Man" nickname reveal how squat and ungainly the plutonium bomb dropped on Nagasaki was (seven feet eight inches in length and five feet in diameter, more than twice as wide as the "Little Boy" uranium bomb dropped on Hiroshima), Laurence offered his exclusive audience a different impression. "It is a thing of beauty to behold, this 'gadget,'" he wrote in the opening paragraphs of his dispatch. "In its design went millions of man-hours of what is without a doubt the most concentrated intellectual effort in history. Never before had so much brain-power been focused on a single problem."

In Laurence's telling, the bombing mission itself was "our odyssey," marked at the outset by darkness and storm and the spectacular static electricity known as St. Elmo's Fire. ("The whirling giant propellers had somehow become great luminous discs of blue flame. The same luminous blue flame appeared on the plexiglass windows in the nose of the ship, and on the tips of the giant wings it looked as though we were riding the whirlwind through space on a chariot of blue fire.") When dense cloud cover ruled out the original target city (Kokura), which Laurence left nameless, "Destiny chose Nagasaki as the ultimate target." And when the thing of beauty detonated above Destiny's choice, and the crew and observers removed their dark welder's goggles, they saw "a giant ball of fire rise as though from the bowels of the earth," followed by "a giant pillar of purple fire, 10,000 feet high, shooting skyward with enormous speed." Within forty-five seconds, it had reached their altitude of more than six miles above the target: "Awe-struck, we watched it shoot upward like a meteor coming from the earth instead of from outer space, becoming ever more alive as it climbed skyward through the white clouds. It was no longer smoke, or dust, or even a cloud of fire. It was a living thing, a new species of being, born right before our incredulous eyes."[158]

The concluding five paragraphs of Laurence's exclusive account of the explosion—issued by the War Department for release on September 9, exactly one month after the bombing—were almost indistinguishable from the apocalyptic aesthetics popularized in the early years of the twentieth century by writers anticipating a climactic global war in which white Westerners emerged triumphant. Decades before the discovery of nuclear fission in the late 1930s, these prophets of mass destruction already had lavished purple prose on "battles of annihilation," "aerial monsters of war," warfare relying on "atomic bombs" and "atomic energy" among other superweapons, even the "great mushroom of smoke" that grew and billowed above a bombed "city of doom." In most of this literature, ultimate victory was attained through the genius of Western science and particular virtues of American character and industry. One contribution to this morbidly ecstatic literature—published coincidentally with the outset of World War I in 1914, titled *Armageddon*, and bearing the inspired catchall subtitle *A Tale of Love, War, and Invention*—frankly described the destruction wrought by its imagined superweapon as "beautiful, but with the beauty of terror."[159]

Laurence's report read as if he were channeling these earlier voluptuaries of mass destruction, the major difference being that this was no longer imaginary. His description of the bombing of Nagasaki ended theatrically, still miles high and miles away from ground zero, still mesmerized by the spectacular mushroom cloud:

At one stage of its evolution, covering millions of years in terms of seconds, the entity assumed the form of a giant square totem pole, with its base about three miles long, tapering off to about a mile at the top. Its bottom was brown, its center was amber, its top white. But it was a living totem pole, carved with many grotesque masks grimacing at the earth.

Then, just when it appeared as though the thing has [*sic*] settled down into a state of permanence, there came shooting out of the top a giant mushroom that increased the height of the pillar to a total of 45,000 feet. The mushroom top was even more alive than the pillar, seething and boiling in a white fury of creamy foam, sizzling upwards and then descending earthward, a thousand Old Faithful geysers rolled into one.

It kept struggling in an elemental fury, like a creature in the act of breaking the bonds that held it down. In a few seconds it had freed itself from its gigantic stem and floated upward with tremendous speed, its momentum carrying into the stratosphere to a height of about 60,000 feet.

But no sooner did this happen when another mushroom, smaller than the first one, began emerging out of the pillar. It was as though the decapitated monster was growing a new head.

As the first mushroom floated off into the blue it changed its shape into a flowerlike form, its giant petal curving downward, creamy white outside, rose-colored inside. It still retained that shape when we last gazed at it from a distance of about 200 miles.

This was the most intimate early "eye-witness" impression of the dropping of the bomb released by the U.S. government and disseminated by the American press. In 1946, Laurence was awarded a Pulitzer Prize for his coverage of nuclear issues.[160]

## Revenge

Laurence's firsthand account of the Nagasaki bombing dwelled almost entirely on the brave crew and numinous aesthetics of the mission. Almost casually, however, he offered this reflection on the faceless, nameless populace about to be bombed:

Somewhere beyond these vast mountains of white clouds ahead of me there lies Japan, the land of our enemy. In about four hours from now one of its cities, making weapons of war for use against us, will be wiped off the map by the greatest weapon ever made by man. In one-tenth of a millionth of a second, a fraction of time immeasurable by any clock, a whirlwind from the skies will pulverize thousands of its buildings and tens of thousands of its inhabitants. . . .

> Does one feel any pity or compassion for the poor devils about to
> die? Not when one thinks of Pearl Harbor and of the Death March
> on Bataan.

The "making weapons of war for use against us" rationale was familiar dissembling: Nagasaki was not selected because it was a major military target, but because it was a congested city relatively unscarred in
prior bombings and thus suitable, first, for the psychological impact of
its obliteration, and second, for its technical usefulness for after-action
study. More striking in Laurence's rendering, however, is the satisfaction of retribution—and the specificity of this. The bombs dropped on
Hiroshima and Nagasaki were not rationalized only in terms of saving
American lives. This consummate act of violence was also retrospective
and vindictive—returning to the beginning of the conflict on December
7, 1941, and avenging all the American lives lost then and thereafter. This
was wrath and retribution in the biblical sense already seen in responses to
the Trinity test, but now made more explicit: the Japanese as a collectivity
were being punished for Pearl Harbor and subsequent atrocities against
American fighting men, and justly so.

This keen, almost gnawing hatred of the Japanese went beyond anything seen in the war against Japan's Axis partners Germany and Italy. In
part, this reflected the naked racism already pumped up over the course of
a half century of fictional scenarios of cataclysmic conflict between white
and nonwhite peoples and cultures. In immeasurable part, too, however,
this particularly virulent hatred toward the Japanese as a collectivity—in
which there were no "good Japanese," and consequently no line drawn
between militarist leaders and ordinary people, or between fighting men
and civilians—was triggered by the particularly shocking and unforgetta-
bly iconic, almost cinematic, nature of the Pearl Harbor attack.

Polls made public a mere three days after December 7 indicated that 67
percent of Americans supported unqualified bombing of Japanese cities,
while only 10 percent flatly opposed this (3 percent supported bombing
"if military objectives," and 13 percent "if they bomb us"). The Marines
put the thirst for revenge succinctly in their slogan "Remember Pearl
Harbor—Keep 'em Dying," and many fighting men took this at face
value. Well into the war in the Pacific, a poll conducted among American

78. *The thirst for revenge that followed Pearl Harbor was intensified by belated official revelation of Japanese atrocities including the Bataan death march in the opening stage of the war. This poster was issued by the U.S. Army.*

men in combat found a great percentage of them defining their objective not as being to defeat Japan, or to gain victory, but simply to "kill Japs." As the Pacific War entered its endgame in mid-1944, moreover, vindictiveness was intensified by two developments in particular: the suicidal fanaticism of Japanese resistance, and belated revelation of Japanese atrocities against prisoners. While horrors such as the Bataan death march took place early in the war, during Japan's fleeting interlude of military triumph, the general public in the United States and United Kingdom was not informed of such war crimes until much later. When news of the Bataan atrocity was belatedly released in January 1944, the popular response was predictably furious. Hollywood captured this outrage—and the near-genocidal emotions that often accompanied it—with particular vividness. In *Objective, Burma!* (starring Errol Flynn), for example, a scene that actually provoked intense internal controversy among the film's writers and producers has an American reporter, a voice of reason to this point, coming upon unseen U.S. soldiers tortured and killed by the Japanese foe. "Degenerate, moral idiots," he erupts. "Stinking little savages. Wipe them out, I say. Wipe them off the face of the earth. Wipe them off the face of the earth."[161]

More extended and graphic yet was the treatment of atrocity in *The Purple Heart*, a film that imagined the eight U.S. airmen captured after the Doolittle raid of 1942 being abused and brought to trial in a grotesque court proceeding. (Three were actually executed, and a fourth died before the war ended.) The climactic speech of one prisoner was pitch-perfect in conveying the righteous fury that endorsed obliterating Japanese men, women, and children in general:

> It's true we Americans don't know very much about you Japanese, and never did—and now I realize you know even less about us. You can kill us—all of us, or part of us. But if you think that's going to put the fear of God into the United States of America and stop them from sending other flyers to bomb you, you're wrong—dead wrong. They'll come by night and they'll come by day. Thousands of them. They'll blacken your skies and burn your cities to the ground and make you get down on your knees and beg for mercy. This is your war. You wanted it. You asked for it. You started it. And now you're going to get it. And it won't be finished until your dirty little empire is wiped off the face of the earth!

*The Purple Heart*, produced in 1943, was released in February 1944, almost exactly one year before the formal planning process for the air war caught up and the systematic practice of burning Japanese cities to the ground was initiated with the firebombing of Tokyo, on March 9, 1945.[162]

Where such visceral emotions held sway, embracing Nemesis quickly dispelled any lingering notion that bombing noncombatants was barbaric and odious—and any inclination to hold on to old-fashioned *jus in bello* ideals of "proportionality." The Old Testament injunction of "an eye for an eye" metamorphosed into numberless Japanese eyes for every American one closed forever by the atrocious foe. This reprisal peaked in the atomic bombs. Even while official pronouncements were establishing the argument that dropping the bombs was motivated simply and exclusively by the clear-cut military goal of ending the war quickly and saving American lives, the element of revenge was rarely suppressed.

On August 7, for example, when the reflective General Marshall cautioned against celebrating the successful mission against Hiroshima excessively, given the large number of Japanese casualties, General Groves responded (and proudly recorded later in his memoirs) that he "was not thinking so much about those casualties as I was about the men who had made the Bataan death march." General Henry (Hap) Arnold, commander of the Army Air Forces, Groves reported, later slapped him on the back and exclaimed, "I am glad you said that—it's just the way I feel." Similarly, when Truman addressed the American public by radio on August 9, when the results of the Hiroshima bombing were in hand, he declared, even before speaking of saving "thousands and thousands of young Americans" and shortening the agony of war, that "having found the bomb we have used it. We have used it against those who attacked us without warning at Pearl Harbor, against those who have starved and beaten and executed American prisoners of war, against those who have abandoned all pretense of obeying international laws of warfare."[163]

In a private communication at almost the very same time (August 11), the president fell back on the same measure-for-measure sentiments. Responding to a telegram from the general secretary of the Federal Council of Churches that began with the declaration that "many Christians [are] deeply disturbed over use of atomic bombs against Japanese cities because of their necessarily indiscriminate destructive efforts and because their use sets extremely dangerous precedent for future of mankind," Truman defended his decision in these words:

> Nobody is more disturbed over the use of Atomic bombs than I am but I was greatly disturbed over the unwarranted attack by the Japanese on Pearl Harbor and their murder of our prisoners of war. The only language they seem to understand is the one we have been using to bombard them.
>
> When you have to deal with a beast you have to treat him as a beast. It is most regrettable but nevertheless true.

But who, really, was "him"? Who, in actuality, were "those" who attacked Pearl Harbor and committed unspeakable atrocities after this?[164]

This desire to wreak vengeance on an entire people for the transgressions of their leaders and those fighting men who had committed atrocities carried through the atomic bombings and into the early months of the occupation, when the victors had occupied Japan. While the Japanese leadership was still fumbling for acceptable language in the final terms of capitulation, for example, General Arnold hastened to marshal the largest airborne armada ever assembled by the Americans to bomb Tokyo one more time—a vindictive last hurrah involving 1,014 aircraft. There was not a single loss, and the last B-29s were still returning when Truman announced Japan's unconditional surrender. According to one calculation, some 15,000 Japanese were killed in conventional incendiary air raids between the time of the Nagasaki bombing and the end of the war five days later—a small number compared with the civilian death toll from urban-area bombing overall, but largely gratuitous, and greater than the total number of fatalities suffered by U.S. fighting men in the horrendous months-long battle of Okinawa.[165]

The bombs pleased a great many of Japan's foes not merely because they contributed to ending the war, but also because they inflicted such

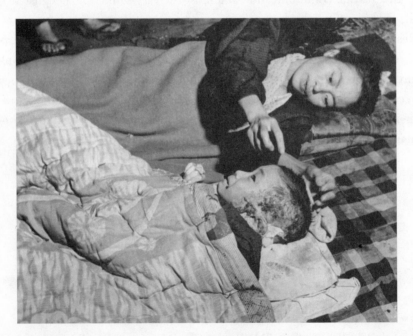

79. Life's *caption for this photograph of an injured mother and child in Hiroshima ended by noting that the photographer said they reminded him of burned victims he had seen following the Pearl Harbor attack.*

widespread suffering. A poll conducted several months after Japan's capit-ulation, for example, found over 22 percent of Americans agreeing that "we should have quickly used many more of them [atomic bombs] before Japan had a chance to surrender." Even after the enormity of the human toll in Hiroshima and Nagasaki began to sink in, the U.S. mass media and public at large found it difficult to transcend the satisfaction of collective punishment. Two months after the bombings, for example, *Life* magazine published a rare photograph of a mother lying beside her young son in Hiroshima. His face is burned, his expression pained; injured herself, she is extending her hands and tenderly placing a compress on his wounds. The photo is humane and moving—and the caption takes this all away. "Mother and child, burned by the blast, rest on bank's floor," it reads. "Photographer Eyerman reported their injuries looked like those he had seen when he photographed men burned at Pearl Harbor."[166]

Such visceral equations were the balm that enabled men and women to valorize indiscriminate terror.

## *Idealistic Annihilation*

To call attention to personal, organizational, and psychological impera-tives, extending even to the blood lust of wholesale revenge, is not to deny the simultaneous presence of humane impulses. Truman himself, for all his affirmations of certitude, was conflicted. Even as he claimed Hiroshima and Nagasaki were routine military targets, and even as he collapsed all Japanese into a single beast, he was troubled by the enormity of his decision. As a now well-known diary entry by Commerce Secretary Henry Wallace tells us, in a cabinet meeting on August 10 "Truman said he had given orders to stop atomic bombing. He said the thought of wip-ing out another 100,000 people was too horrible. He didn't like the idea of killing, as he said, 'all those kids.' "[167]

This, however, was afterthought. A more pervasive strain of human-istic concern, bordering on utopianism, actually came into play as the gears meshed to hasten completion of the first bomb and deliver the new weapon to the bombers. Victor Weisskopf touched on this when he recalled, in his own words, Oppenheimer's rationalization for immedi-ate use against Japan: "if the bomb is to make war impossible, it must have

*80. This photograph of survivors in Hiroshima was taken in December 1945, four months after the bomb was dropped. The victimized Japanese mother and child became perhaps the most familiar symbol of the horrors of nuclear war.*

a very strong effect." This was an integral part of the reasoning behind the Science Panel's rejection, on June 16, of proposals to delay using the new weapon on cities before first demonstrating its destructiveness in other ways. As this small elite coterie of scientists phrased it in their recommendation to the Interim Committee, they sided with those who believed that immediate use "will improve the international prospects, in that they [members of the Science Panel] are more concerned with the prevention of war than with the elimination of this specific weapon."

*Prevention of future war.* Weisskopf found this persuasive, and so did other scientists, particularly at Los Alamos where Oppenheimer's influence was, by all accounts, charismatic. Edward Teller articulated the disagreement on these matters with exceptional clarity in a letter to Leo Szilard dated July 2, explaining why he had decided not to sign the petition against hasty use of the bomb that Szilard was circulating:

> First of all let me say that I have no hope of clearing my conscience. The things we are working on are so terrible that no amount of protesting or fiddling with politics will save our souls. . . .
>
> But I am not really convinced of your objections. I do not feel that there is any chance to outlaw any one weapon. If we have a slim

282

*81. A mother and child clutch rice balls received from an emergency relief party in Nagasaki on August 10. This now well-known photograph, together with many others taken by the military photographer Yōsuke Yamahata, was withheld from the public during the U.S. occupation that extended into 1952.*

chance of survival, it lies in the possibility to get rid of wars. The more decisive the weapon is the more surely it will be used in any real conflicts and no agreement will help.

Our only hope is in getting the facts of our results before the people. This might help to convince everybody that the next war would be fatal. For this purpose actual combat-use might even be the best thing.[168]

Arthur Compton, who encouraged the Chicago scientists to put their concerns in writing, sided against them when he forwarded the Franck Report to the Department of War. His rationale amounted to the same sort of rudimentary deterrence theory that Oppenheimer and Teller were intimating. "The [Franck] report," Compton explained later, "while it called attention to difficulties that might result from the use of the bomb, did not mention the probable net saving of many lives, nor that if the bomb were not used in the present war the world would have no adequate warning as to what was to be expected if war should break out again." According to Stimson, the same line of reasoning lay behind Harvard president James Conant's endorsement of using the bombs immediately. Conant had written him, Stimson told a journalist in 1947, "that one of the principal rea-

283

sons he had for advising me that the bomb must be used was that that was the only way to awaken the world to the necessity of abolishing war altogether. No technological demonstration, even if it had been possible under the conditions of war—which it was not—could take the place of the actual use with its horrible results. . . . I think he was right and I think that was one of the main things which differentiated the eminent scientists who concurred with President Conant from the less realistic ones who didn't."[169]

Incinerating Hiroshima and Nagasaki was thus, from this perspective, not only realistic but idealistic in the broadest manner imaginable: "actual use with its horrible results" would warn the world of the folly of war in the future. P. M. S. Blackett, writing in 1948 when the United States still retained its nuclear monopoly and proposals for international control had proved to be a chimera, summarized this coil of so-called realism and idealism or "progressively minded" thinking with his typical incisiveness:

> There were undoubtedly, among the nuclear physicists working on the project, many who regarded the dropping of the bombs as a victory for the progressively minded among the military and political authorities. What they feared was that the bombs would *not* be dropped in the war against Japan, but that the attempt would be made to keep their existence secret and that a stock pile would be built up for an eventual war with Russia. To those who feared intensely this latter possible outcome, the dropping of the bombs and the publicity that resulted appeared, not unplausibly, as far the lesser evil.[170]

In the cultures of modern and contemporary conflict, this is yet another seductive mantra: that deployment of extreme force is the necessary evil or "lesser evil" that will bring about peace and even help pave the way to a future world without war. (*Necessary Evil* was the name its crew gave the third B-29 that participated in the Hiroshima bombing, charged with photographing the explosion.) Using the indiscriminate new weapon as spectacularly and devastatingly as possible before the war against Japan ended was thus desirable for reasons that transcended the immediate conflict and went beyond even the complicated forebodings about future relations with the Soviet Union to which Blackett called attention. "Proportionality" in the traditional *jus in bello* sense was lifted from the war at hand to imagined conflagrations that might eventually destroy the United States and Western world itself; and from this perspective, the sacrifice of unnumbered Japanese men, women, and children was a small price to pay.[171]

AFTER THE *fait accompli* of Hiroshima and Nagasaki, concerned nuclear scientists in Chicago mobilized to warn the world of the nuclear peril and to "work unceasingly for the establishment of international control of atomic weapons, as a first step toward permanent peace." They took the occasion of the fourth anniversary of the Pearl Harbor attack to issue their inaugural statement; and their forebodings, as it turned out, were unduly pessimistic in the short run but prescient in the long view. The statement opened as follows:

> On the fourth anniversary of the Pearl Harbor attack, American public opinion seems to be much more concerned with assessing the responsibility for the disaster which occurred four years ago, than with preventing a future "Pearl Harbor" on a continental scale, which may occur four years from now. Three thousand Americans— mostly members of our Armed forces—lost their lives in the Japanese sneak attack. Thirty million Americans—civilians, women, and children—may be doomed to perish if a sneak attack on our cities by atomic bombs ever comes to pass. This catastrophe will be inevitable if we do not succeed in banishing war from the world. Our own better preparedness could have saved Pearl Harbor—but in a world of atomic bombs, preparedness can only give us the power to retaliate— to smash in our turn the cities of the nation which attacked us.[172]

Their cautionary words in December 1945 were as unavailing as they had been before the atomic bombs were dropped. They survive, rather, as a kind of timeworn boundary marker between the old age of destructiveness and the new one—and as a reminder of the truly revolutionary transformation not merely in technology, but also in moral consciousness, rationalizations about "proportionality," and plain acceptance and even endorsement of terror that had taken place in the forty-four months that transpired between December 7, 1941, and August 6, 1945.

# NEW EVILS IN THE WORLD:
## 1945/2001

### *Evil beyond Recall*

Twenty years after the atomic bombing of Hiroshima and Nagasaki, Aver-ill A. Liebow, a professor of pathology at Yale University School of Medi-cine, published an expanded version of his "Medical Diary of Hiroshima, 1945." Liebow had been a lieutenant colonel in the Army Medical Corps in 1945. He was stationed on Saipan during the battles of Iwo Jima and Okinawa, tending casualties, expanding hospital facilities, and on many evenings watching, as he wrote in introducing the diary, "fleets of B-29 bombers making a rendezvous with their kind from neighboring Tinian and Guam to carry death and destruction to Iwo and Japan."

Like everyone around him, Dr. Liebow only learned about the atomic bombs when the news reports came in. For months, however, there had been expectation that something big was about to happen. As he recalled it, as early as the spring of 1945 "wagers that the war would end by August 15 were being freely made by airmen who, with enigmatic smiles, even offered substantial odds." Canny gamblers indeed, if this is true: right down to the month and day.

In mid-September, Liebow arrived in Japan as part of a medical team that collaborated with Japanese counterparts under the name Joint Commission for the Investigation of the Effects of the Atomic Bomb in Japan. He thus had the opportunity to observe the human toll of idealistic annihilation at Ground Zero. His first impression of Hiroshima from the arriving airplane was tersely expressed in the diary: "devastated, cold—an ash." There was no real airport, no tower, no landing lights at the airfield—only a wind sock—and the first victims he encountered upon alighting were "some horribly scarred children including a boy who told us in understandable English of his experience. He seemed to know how far he had been from the center of the explosion."

The diary, which records Liebow's research and social activities until he departed at year's end, was published in a scientific journal under the title "Encounter with Disaster." In his retrospective introductory observations, he wrote this:

> When, at 8:14 on the morning of August 6, 1945, on command from Washington, the hand aboard the Enola Gay loosed beyond recall a new evil in the world, we had no knowledge of how our lives, in fact the lives of all men, would be changed.[173]

Liebow would have endorsed Oppenheimer's wartime observation (upon learning of the death of President Roosevelt) that "we have been living through years of great evil and great terror," here referring to the evil of the Axis menace. Like virtually all Americans and most other members of the Allied camp, he would have had no quarrel with Truman's August 16, 1945, "day of prayer" proclamation solemnly commemorating "victory in the East." "The cruel war of aggression which Japan started eight years ago to spread the forces of evil over the Pacific has resulted in her total defeat," the president observed. "This is the end of the grandiose schemes of the dictators to enslave the peoples of the world, destroy their civilization, and institute a new era of darkness and degradation. This day is a new beginning in the history of freedom on this earth." Victory, the president went on, "has come with the help of God, Who was with us in the early days of adversity and disaster, and Who has now brought us to this glorious day of triumph."

Some two weeks later, in a radio address designating September 2 "V-J Day" in commemoration of Japan's formal signing of "the terms of unconditional surrender," Truman spoke similarly. "The evil done by the Japanese war lords can never be repaired or forgotten," he declared, and again thanked Almighty God for enabling the victors "to overcome the forces of tyranny that sought to destroy His civilization." Regardless of whether or not one shared the president's religious belief, the worldwide sense of a triumph over evil was palpable. And yet, in the eyes of many, this good war had ended with a new evil loosed "beyond recall" by the victors themselves.[174]

Looking back, Dr. Liebow found it easy to sympathize with "the physicists who bore the real responsibility for the development of the atomic bomb and who suffered genuine torment of conscience" after it was used. He confessed that "when we saw the pitifully crippled and maimed we felt both guilt and shame," and asked of himself and his fellow medical researchers, "Were we, even in the aftermath, accessories to a crime against mankind?" But he also asked whether the absence of apparent resentment on the part of his Japanese scientific colleagues and collaborators in Hiroshima might go beyond just stoicism or discipline and reflect a sense of guilt on their own part. And he answered his rhetorical query about complicity, at least in part, by concluding that it was necessary to measure the full force and radiation effects of the new weapon; that nuclear energy also could be harnessed to constructive ends; and that "in performing this work, we could then, not merely unthinkingly obey orders, but make a partial and uneasy peace with conscience."[175]

When Dr. Liebow published his Hiroshima diary in 1965, thermonuclear weapons bristled in the arsenals of the United States and Soviet Union. Little Boy and Fat Man were regarded as crude and primitive; the new evil in the world was widely perceived to be Soviet-led communism or

American-led capitalism, depending on where one stood in the Cold War; and a new generation of strategists and policy makers was promoting ever more powerful weapons of mass destruction as the key to "deterrence"— essentially diverting the utopian notion of idealistic annihilation that had been expressed immediately before and after the first atomic bombs were used in the perverse direction of proliferation rather than abolition or control. Clearly, the legacy of Hiroshima and Nagasaki had been world altering in alarming ways anticipated at the time, but only by a powerless few.

How much more difficult, then, to look ahead and imagine the guise of future evil—the forms it might take by the twenty-first century. The Jefferies Report, issued by concerned scientists in November 1944, had contained forebodings anticipating not only an arms race with the Soviet Union but also some of the apocalyptic prospects later associated with the war on terror. Nuclear weapons, this report warned, might be "produced in small hidden locations in countries not normally associated with a large scale armaments industry, thus evading surveillance"; and such weapons "could easily be smuggled in by commercial aircraft or even deposited in advance by the aggressor." In the decades that followed, however, no one of influence took this seriously, as both the Cold War arms race and abrupt awakening of September 11 revealed. Who could really imagine a world of stateless zealots and terrorists challenging the greatest nuclear power of all, and possibly capable of using weapons of mass destruction anywhere they chose?[176]

## Arrogating God

We have language that attempts to capture such catastrophic unfolding of human affairs: megalomania, hubris, tragedy, fate, Nemesis, Faustian bargains by collective entities as well as individuals, the iniquity of fathers visited on later generations (from Exodus 20:5 and 34:6–7; Deuteronomy 5:9). The New Testament observation that "whatsoever a man soweth, that shall he also reap" (Galatians 6:7) had a more dire counterpart in the Old Testament warning that "they that plow iniquity, and sow wickedness, reap the same" (Job 4:8). In 1944, the British Christian pacifist Vera Brittain drew attention (and harsh criticism) in England and the United States with a small publication titled *Seeds of Chaos: What Mass Bombing Really Means*, which took its title from Alexander Pope's *The Dunciad*: "Then rose the seed of Chaos, and of Night, / To blot out order and extinguish light."[177]

Truman himself underscored what is perhaps the most eloquent expression of mortal folly and self-destructiveness ever written when, sometime after his presidency, he underlined these lines from Horatio's speech in *Hamlet*, which were quoted at the end of a book about the atomic bomb:

> . . . let me speak to th' yet unknowing world
> How these things came about. So shall you hear
> Of carnal, bloody, and unnatural acts,
> Of accidental judgements, casual slaughters,
> Of deaths put on by cunning and forced cause;
> And, in this upshot, purposes mistook
> Fall'n on th' inventors' heads. . . .
> But let this same be presently performed,
> Even while men's minds are wild, lest more mischance
> On plots and errors happen.[178]

The atrocity of 9-11 also must be numbered among history's carnal, bloody, and unnatural acts—deaths put on by cunning, and a plot by men whose minds were wild. Here the stage was not Shakespeare's little theater The Globe, but a postmodern world with an audience that was literally global. September 11 was not a Hiroshima or Nagasaki where only the victims, or rare foreigners like Dr. Liebow, really saw the horror at Ground Zero. The entire world looked on in real time.

Al Qaeda's terror was miniscule in scale compared to the incendiary and nuclear bombing of World War II, and did not involve weapons of mass destruction in any conventional sense. Yet 9-11 also changed the world beyond recall—in immeasurable part because of the revolution in communications technology that gave it an impact beyond anything anticipated even by the perpetrators. To much of the world, the spellbinding collapse of the World Trade Center towers became the emblem of evil in a new century—infernos caught by cameras on a real stage with real victims and survivors and heroes; skeletal girders looming out of a ghostly place that (like Dr. Liebow's first impression of Hiroshima) had been made "devastated, cold—an ash"; and all replayed times beyond counting for the world to see and see again. This horror became magnified exponentially, certainly in the eyes of planners in Washington, when the prophecy buried in the Jefferies Report suddenly could no longer be ignored: that even puny aggressors might obtain and "smuggle in" nuclear weapons.

ALTHOUGH THE DESTRUCTION of 9-11 was shocking, collective trauma was nowhere more protracted than among Americans: partisan politics and media frenzy feasted on fear for year after excruciating year. The new enemy was equated with the old enemies of World War II and the Cold War. "We have seen their kind before," the president told Congress on September 20, 2001. "They are the heirs of all the murderous ideologies of the twentieth century. By sacrificing human life to serve their radical visions—by abandoning every value except the will to power—they follow in the path of fascism, and Nazism, and totalitarianism." "Islamofascism" became a popular albeit contested catchphrase. The "war on terror" itself underwent a succession of name changes, but constant throughout this naming and renaming was perception of a renewed struggle between good and evil—and with this the arrogation of God.

Truman had thanked Almighty God for enabling the victors to defend "His civilization" against the evil of the Japanese warlords. So had General MacArthur and countless other Christian leaders in the Allied camp. President Bush, however, carried both this faith and the perception of America and Americans as more virtuous than others to a level beyond the Christian rhetoric and plain patriotism of World War II. In his anniversary "Address to the Nation" on September 11, 2006, for example, he reminded his audience that the enemy "are evil and they kill without mercy—but not without purpose," and coupled this with a remarkably provincial affirmation of the exceptional virtue of Americans ("On 9/11, our nation saw the face of evil. Yet on that awful day, we also witnessed something distinctively American: ordinary citizens rising to the occasion, and responding with extraordinary acts of courage"). Typically, he concluded his address by expressing "faith in a loving God who made us to be free," and calling on that God to bless the American people.

Where Bush went beyond his Christian brethren of the World War II generation was in using language that placed him—and by extension the

United States—firmly in the most fundamentalist Christian camp. Some of this language was overt, as when, conversing with conservative journalists in the Oval Office, he associated himself with a rising tide of devotion in the United States; reaffirmed that "a lot of people in America see this as a confrontation between good and evil, including me"; and went on to speak of this religious revival as a "Third Awakening," a concept popular among evangelical Americans. On this occasion, the president summoned Abraham Lincoln to his side. Many of Lincoln's strongest supporters were religious people "who saw life in terms of good and evil" and believed slavery was evil, he observed, and he and his supporters looked at the war against international terror similarly.[179]

More covertly, the president turned to coded language to convey his born-again beliefs to his evangelical political base. Thus, in the State of the Union address delivered on January 28, 2003, less than two months before the invasion of Iraq, he called attention to deep national problems such as homelessness and addiction, and went on to exclaim, "Yet there's power, wonder-working power, in the goodness and idealism and faith of the American people." Apart from the cadence of revivalism, what the speechwriters had imbedded here was allusion to a hymn titled "There Is Power in the Blood," dating from 1899 and beloved of evangelicals. The blood, also referred to as "Calvary's tide," is the blood of "Jesus your King," and the oft-repeated lines of the hymn are established in the opening stanzas: "Would you be free from the burden of sin? / There's power in the blood, power in the blood; / Would you over evil a victory win? / There's wonderful power in the blood. / There is power, power, wonder working power / In the blood of the Lamb; / There is power, power, wonder working power / In the precious blood of the Lamb."[180]

This was the State of the Union address in which the president laid out the later-discredited case for war against Iraq, including Saddam Hussein's possession of an advanced nuclear weapons development project along with biological and chemical arsenals, plus his support and protection of terrorists including members of Al Qaeda. When he typically concluded this address by placing trust "in the ways of Providence" and "confidence in the loving God behind all of life, and all of history," and entreating God to "continue to bless the United States of America," his fellow evangelicals understood this God was inseparable from the blood of the Lamb.

The president's deep faith gave him great comfort and confidence, and reinforced a Manichaean mindset that allowed for little in the way of complexity or nuance or even plain curiosity about others. As became clear after 9-11, this outlook went hand in hand with faith-based thinking in secular affairs: perception that the terrorists were *simply* evil, and could be successfully combated by declaring war and unleashing overwhelming force.

This faith-based outlook, simultaneously religious and secular, blocked seeing Islamist terrorism in ways that clarified its differences from earlier state enemies. It impeded any understanding of how and why this new evil had erupted at this juncture in history. And it discouraged genuinely serious attention to measures beyond relying on force to slay the evil adversary. As time passed, it became notorious that the president was inordinately interested in the numbers and names of enemy killed—to the point of keeping a list of terrorist leaders in his desk in the White House, and crossing out each name when their deaths were reported to him. Until almost four years after his invasion of Iraq, he retained abiding faith in the wonder-working power of military force exercised by the Lamb's chosen people—all the while remaining in denial about disasters on the ground and how and why his holy war was faltering. Postulating absolute evil became an intellectual passport for ignoring the circumstances that bred terror and insurgency, turned Iraq into a new cauldron of mayhem and murder, allowed the Taliban to regain influence in Afghanistan, and spawned a new generation of radical Muslims and Islamists.

Osama bin Laden rallied his core supporters under a comparably theocratic vision of good and evil, and similarly embroidered every pronouncement with obeisance to "the grace of God Almighty," or "the will of God Almighty," or the like. When he joined other terrorist leaders in declaring global jihad against Americans and "the Judeo-Crusader alliance" in February 1998, Al Qaeda's leader and his confederates repeatedly invoked God and his prophet Muhammad. The closing line of their fatwa was "God Almighty also said: 'Do not lose heart or despair—if you are true believers you will have the upper hand.'"

Bin Laden's public statements after 9-11 also typically began and ended with God. On September 24, for example, before he had publicly acknowledged Al Qaeda's responsibility for the attacks, he opened an address to "brothers in Pakistan" with the declaration that "those who believe in God and his messengers are the truthful ones who will bear witness before their Lord: they will have their reward and their light." This message ended with a quote from the Qur'an to the effect that "if God helps you, no one can overcome you; if He forsakes you, who else can help you?" Early the next month, still before taking responsibility for the attacks, bin Laden released a statement that again formulaically began and ended with God. "Praise be to God" were the opening words. "We beseech Him for help and forgiveness. We seek refuge in God from the evil of our souls and our bad deeds. He whom God guides will not go astray, and he whom He leads astray can have no guide. I testify that there is no god but God alone, Who has no partners, and that Muhammad is His slave and messenger."

In this latter declaration, September 11 was presented as retribution for past American atrocities. These included the atomic bombs that killed "hundreds of thousands, young and old" in Japan—as well as the more predictable argument that "what America is tasting today is but a fraction of what we have tasted for decades. For over eighty years our *umma* [the Muslim community worldwide] has endured this humiliation and contempt. Its sons have been killed, its blood has been shed, its holy sanctuaries have been violated, all in a manner contrary to that revealed by God." This justification of responding to terror with terror and slaughter with slaughter ended with that most consoling of divine supplications: "Peace be upon you and all God's mercy and blessings.[181]

### *Holy War against the West:* Seisen *and* Jihad

One of the effective early propaganda films commissioned by the U.S. Army immediately after Pearl Harbor, titled *Prelude to War* and directed by Frank Capra, contained a scene of Japanese forces marching down Pennsylvania Avenue in Washington while a shrill voice speaking stilted English proclaimed Japan's intention to conquer the world. *Prelude to War* won the 1943 Academy Award for Best Documentary, and the narration in the film at this particular point relied on a quote wrenched out of context. Japan's ideologues did preach the superiority of the Imperial Way, and after the astounding early success at Pearl Harbor and throughout

Southeast Asia some of the nation's wilder military planners did briefly propose returning to occupy Hawaii and possibly even California. The real goal was ambitious enough: to establish an autarkic bloc in East and Southeast Asia.

Bin Laden and Al Qaeda offered the world blood-curdling declarations about killing Christians and Jews, and vaguer intimations about establishing the "righteous caliphate of our *umma*" prophesied by Muhammad.[182] In practice, the political and military capabilities of the terrorists were more constrained although, again, ambitious enough: to eliminate foreign intrusion in Muslim lands and restore the practices of an austere Islam. The deeply religious thrust of the Islamist jihad has no real counterpart in Japan's *seisen*, or holy war. Where telling parallels lie is in the secular and territorial fixations of both wars against the Western powers, and in their litanies of grievances.

Imperial Japan was polytheistic. Although Shinto and Buddhism were exploited to mobilize the populace for war, neither God nor good nor evil as such were fixations. Japanese did speak of being favored by divine Providence (*tenyū shinjo*), or enjoying the protection of the indigenous Shinto gods (*kami no kago*) or Shinto and Buddhist deities together (*shinbutsu no kago*). Fighting men and officers involved in the Pearl Harbor attack, including Admiral Yamamoto, routinely invoked the gods' protection and heaven's favor. As the tides of war turned and it became clear that heaven had withdrawn its favor, vague notions of an afterlife were conveyed in the fatalistic parting phrase "see you at Yasukuni," referring to the great shrine in Tokyo where the soul of each and every "departed hero" (*eirei*) who died fighting for the emperor was enshrined.

The colloquial term "kamikaze" (more formally, *shinpū*) literally meant "divine wind" and referred to typhoons that protected Japan from invasion by destroying Mongol fleets on two occasions in the thirteenth century. Despite such intimations of divine favor, however, propagandists and ideologues mainly focused on Japan's ineffable Imperial Way, and framed their holy war in terms of purity versus impurity—the corruption and moral degeneracy, that is, that were said to be rooted in Western core values like egoism and materialism and blatantly manifest in threats like European and American imperialism, as well as Soviet-led communism. Still, September 11 provoked compelling points of comparison between the jihad of Islamist suicide bombers and the socialization for death that took place on the Japanese side in the Pacific war—the kamikaze, banzai charges, and no-surrender battles like at Saipan, Iwo Jima, and Okinawa.[183]

The greatest distinctions between Japanese and Islamist socialization for death lie, first, in state organization and coercion on the Japanese side as opposed to religious identification and a more genuine volunteerism on the part of Islamist holy warriors; and second, in the Japanese focus on killing military antagonists rather than noncombatants. Despite such huge differences, however, there are similarities between the Japanese and Islamist cults of martial martyrdom that can help sharpen comprehension of why individuals may give their lives in causes hostile to "Western civilization"—why, that is, men may be driven to carnal, bloody, and unnatural acts by more than just abandonment of "every value except the will to power," as President Bush declared. Sincere belief in the morality of one's own cause enters the picture. So, at the intellectual level, does a repudiation of Enlightenment values that often tapped polemical strains in the West's own critical intellectual tradition. Recognizing such motivations has nothing to do with endorsing the crimes they inspire, but a great deal to do with responding effectively.[184]

Death unleashed is both piercing and numbing, and the killing cycle is relentless. In Japan's war, grief at the death of compatriots and comrades kindled sentiments of blood debt and thirst for revenge, just as it did on the part of Japan's Allied adversaries. We now know, for example, that many and perhaps most kamikaze pilots tended to identify particularly closely with their own small unit, and to feel an obligation to follow those who already had sacrificed their lives—and guilt if, by chance, the war ended before they had an opportunity to fly their fatal missions. Camaraderie, revenge, and atonement were closely linked.

As the war intensified and Japanese casualties escalated, it also became easier to persuade young men (and for them to persuade themselves) that the alternative to martyrdom was to die a dog's death. This belief was, in fact, largely true for the airmen assigned to kamikaze units: by war's end, most regular pilots were gunned down without inflicting harm on the enemy. "Immortality" did not require visions of paradise in the hereafter. One's name could live on as a martyr who gave his life in the bloom of youth—a cult cultivated by Japan's militarists, no less than by the older Islamists who recruit and train young terrorists for death missions.

The mythology of Japan at war, perpetuated by Japanese nationalists and taken at face value by most foreigners, holds that Japanese fighting men almost unanimously embraced death out of devotion to the emperor and Imperial Way. This, too, does not withstand scrutiny; and if we take this challenge to orthodox interpretations seriously as another small window on why men and women may give their lives, it again throws a different slant of light on suicide terror. The last communications of kamikaze, as well as postwar testimony by survivors, for example, suggest that many of the men who seemed to court death were driven primarily by love of family and native place. As best we can tell, the thoughts of young men on the eve of their one-way sortie, or gasping their dying words on the battlefield, were more often directed to their mothers rather than their sovereign. And where, as often, these last thoughts also embraced native place, this was sometimes expressed as "Japan" but often in more localized terms of one's native village or beloved mountains, rivers, and fields. The natural analogue to this was visceral enmity toward those who threatened to occupy this precious soil.[185]

Perhaps the most subtle and evocative public expression of this love of native place in wartime Japan involved not fighting men in the field but rather fictional young women laboring in a factory. It appeared in *The Most Beautiful* (*Ichiban Utsukushiku*), a 1944 feature film directed by Akira Kurosawa. Kurosawa's protagonists are engaged in making optical lenses for military aircraft; his style is semi-documentary; and his theme, in his own retrospective words, is "self-sacrificing service to one's country" and "the vitality and beauty of people at work." The walls of the factory are plastered with patriotic slogans, including exhortations to follow the example of those who have died in battle: "Follow our military gods" (*gunshin*, another euphemism for heroic war dead), for example, and "Follow Admiral Yamamoto" (who was killed in 1943). Kurosawa's most brilliant touch, however, lies in capturing the wellspring of such patriotic ardor in the simple faith that defending the nation means protecting one's cherished local community and beloved parents and siblings.

As was true throughout industrializing Japan, Kurosawa's factory workers are largely young women in their mid or late teens who have been recruited from the countryside. They were asked to bring a packet of soil when they first arrived, and these were mixed into the vegetable garden at the factory dormitory. All Japan is commingled here. Workers can stand in the garden and be literally in touch with home. A signboard by the garden plot, titled "Earth of Our Native Place" (*Furusato no Tsuchi*), spells this out:

> This is the very earth the blood of my ancestors flows through,
> the earth where I was born.
> On this same earth, today again, my parents and elder brothers and
>     sisters
> must be tirelessly plowing and cultivating.
> On this earth, my younger brothers and sisters
> must be playing without a care,
> the dog must be happily running around,
> the horse must be neighing loudly, in high spirits.
> At the scent of this earth, I recall scenes from long ago
> and cherish memories of childhood.
> And when I stand barefoot on this earth,
> I always feel the warmth of my mother's skin
> and return in a flash to the home of my soul.
> This is the very earth the blood of my ancestors flows through,
> the earth where I was born.[186]

However romanticized this may be, it is a very different kind of attachment to sacred ground and sacred community than Japan's emperor-worshipping ideologues emphasized—more secular than spiritual, concrete and even tactile rather than abstract. Much the same distinction is often emphasized in studies of contemporary terrorist "martyrs." In the latter case, the evocation of occupied lands is also concrete, embracing past and present as well as the premonition of impending foreign encroachment that obsessed so many Japanese. The speeches of bin Laden and his fellow terrorists never failed to marry paeans to God and denunciation of Christian and Jewish infidels with worldly place names and explicit shards of recent history that tell a story of Western intrusion in Muslim lands.

Such points of likeness and difference in holy wars against the West, past and present, would require another book to pursue.[187]

## Ground Zeroes: State and Nonstate Terror

Most observers would agree that, borrowing Dr. Liebow's phrase, Al Qaeda and the terrorism of September 11 marked the advent of a new evil in the world. At the same time, September 11 also reflected the accuracy of his dark presentiment of evil "beyond recall"—something very different indeed from the defeated, shattered evils of fascism, Nazism, and Japanese militarism. He had written his diary, after all, as witness to the development, use, and consequences of unprecedented weapons of mass destruction by his own country. He published this, two decades later, when it was clear that postwar states and scientists and entrepreneurs had created war machines that gave the continued perfection and proliferation of such weapons irresistible momentum. Confronted by Ground Zero 2001, the same leaders who kept the machinery of lethal weaponry in high gear suddenly became almost paranoid believers in Nemesis.

The devastation of the World Trade Center also represented another evil beyond recall: the World War II legacy of terror bombing and deliberately targeting noncombatants. Unlike the atomic bombs, which marked the closing pages of a merciless war between formal adversaries, 9-11 inaugurated a seemingly interminable struggle between a superpower armed to the teeth and decentralized, lightly armed "substate" antagonists who crisscrossed national boundaries and materialized and disappeared like shadows. At the same time, it stimulated an approach to terror bombing among Anglophone analysts that is willfully neglectful when it comes to placing the massacre of civilians in the historical context of psychological warfare. Lethal shock tactics aimed at undermining the spirit and will of the enemy reflect an embrace of "total war" and a repudiation of old-fashioned morality that was locked in place as standard operating procedure in the air war against Germany and Japan. There is nothing peculiarly Islamist or un-Christian or non-Western or un-American about killing ordinary men, women, and children. They are simply the flesh and blood of that great abstract target "enemy morale."[188]

Islamist terror tactics are innovative for reasons other than their atrociousness: the intimate physical proximity of bombers and bombed; willful self-sacrifice of those delivering death; low-tech nature of the operations, coupled with the possibility they might move into possession of weapons of mass destruction. For Americans, what was truly original in the horror of September 11 was the spectacle of being the bombed rather than the bomber. "Pearl Harbor," for all its resonance as code for strategic vulnerability, still involved an attack on a military target thousands of miles off the coast of the continental United States. Cold War fears of a nuclear exchange with the Soviet Union were undeniably terrifying, but remained largely abstract.

Fundamentally, terror is the state of mind both terrorists and high-tech strategic planners seek to create in the collective consciousness of their adversaries, demoralizing masses and prompting leaders to change their policies. "Shock and awe" is not just the catchphrase for a lesson strategists in Washington drew from Hiroshima and Nagasaki and incorporated in the "revolution in military affairs" that became the *idée fixe* of Rumsfeld's Pentagon. It is also a practical weapon of the weak. The Japanese played at this when they attempted to deter the U.S. advance on their homeland by adopting the suicidal policies of the kamikaze and no-surrender defense of island redoubts. The objective was to unnerve U.S. forces and shock the U.S. leadership into some form of negotiated peace settlement short of unconditional surrender. Although this ultimately backfired, the fear these tactics instilled among the fighting forces that had to confront them was enormous.[189]

September 11, by contrast, was a stunningly successful exercise in psychological warfare at an almost incomparably lower level of violence: Americans almost literally lived in terror through the remaining seven-plus years of the Bush presidency, and their government and way of life became altered for the worse. This objective of disorienting and unsettling the enemy through a signal act of destruction is the import of the disregarded pre–9-11 warnings that Al Qaeda was planning a "Hiroshima" in the United States. As it turned out, it was not the terrorists but rather the planners in Washington—who seized on the same example of Hiroshima and Nagasaki to elevate "shock and awe" to the level of doctrine, and predicted that this would shock Iraq and the Iraqi people into complaisant "regime change"—who turned out to be dreaming.

The loose, nonstate nature of Al Qaeda upended conventional state-oriented thinking in Washington, and the response was simultaneously hubristic and panicked—almost exactly what the terrorist psychological warriors had hoped for, but more extreme than they dreamed actually possible. Rumsfeld's immediate reaction to the September 11 attacks ("sweep it all up—Things related and not") epitomized the faith in overwhelming force that remained one of the abiding but anachronistic legacies of World War II and the Cold War. At the same time, the elusive nature of bin Laden's organization and other terrorist groups was seized upon as pretext for discarding conventional rules governing conduct in war, and repudiating due process more generally. Both extreme responses—war making and law breaking—caused immeasurable harm both abroad and at home.[190]

Even staunch allies on the British side were appalled. Late in 2008, in the waning months of the Bush presidency, two British counterterrorism experts criticized U.S. policy with unusual frankness for high officials. Stella Rimington, the former head of MI5, England's domestic intelligence agency, described the response to 9-11 as "a huge overreaction" and the declaration of a "war on terror" as a great mistake that "got us off on the wrong foot, because it made people think terrorism was something you could deal with by force of arms primarily. And from that flowed Guantanamo, and extraordinary rendition," and ultimately "Iraq." Sir Ken Macdonald, the outgoing head of the Crown Prosecution Service, delivered a farewell address to his agency which similarly argued that terrorism can be most effectively countered by being treated as a criminal problem. In contrast to "the Guantanamo model," he praised Britain for having staunchly held fast to "a relentless prosecutorial struggle against terrorism" that was "absolutely grounded in due process and pursued with full respect for our historical norms and for our liberal constitution. We have not feared fairness. . . . The best way to face down those threats is to strengthen our institutions rather than to degrade them."

These were strong words, and Macdonald's implicit warning to the United States, a full seven years after September 11, was stark: "We need to take very great care not to fall into a way of life in which freedom's back is broken by the relentless pressure of a security State."[191]

## Managing Savagery

Despite their enormous differences, the Ground Zeroes of 1945 and 2001 share more in common than is usually acknowledged. Both draw attention, for example, to the ways modern men at war rationalize violence, terror, and the targeting of noncombatants or acceptance of deaths casually brushed away as "collateral damage." (This euphemism emerged within the U.S. military during the Vietnam War, where the death toll among Vietnamese eventually came to several million.) Both reflect the cycle of now almost naturalized crimes against humanity perpetuated by implacable antagonists who share rage and righteousness in common, and have no doubt that reason, morality, destiny, and divine Providence itself all stand on their side. Once again, this is not a matter of moral relativism but rather a matter of understanding why, apart from coercion, men may choose to fight and die.

In the eyes of those who perpetuated or applauded the crimes of 9-11, such terror in the name of God is neither immoral nor unusually murderous. Rationalizations are numerous and tediously verbose, and many of the modes or categories of justification dovetail more than might be expected with arguments and imperatives that helped drive the decision to use the atomic bombs. Saving lives—even defending "freedom" itself— by relying primarily on brute force, including terror aimed at destroying the morale of the enemy writ large, is one such correspondence. Coupling annihilation with hymns of praise to justice and mercy, and violence with paeans to peace, is another.

Islamist exaltations about revenge and retribution for specific past and present Western aggression and atrocities offer a rough counterpart to the "Pearl Harbor"/"killing our prisoners"/"dealing with a beast" incantation that is the ground bass in much of the justification for incinerating Hiroshima and Nagasaki. (After 9-11 and the invasion of Iraq, terrorist recruitment was greatly abetted by the rage and thirst for revenge that crystallized in response to a flood of online accounts of what was occurring at Guantánamo, alongside ghastly graphic images of what happened at Abu Ghraib and what Americans routinely refer to as "collateral damage" but rarely dwell on in their own online and on-screen imagery.) Similarly, defending the *umma* amounts to an Islamist analogue to what Truman phrased as protecting and saving "His civilization." Much as the decision makers of 1945 placed using the atomic bombs in the context of multiple enemies (Japan, the Soviet Union, partisan politicians at home), bin Laden and his confederates always made clear that they were engaged in simultaneous battle with "far enemies" (the West, the Americans, the "Crusaders and Jews") and "near enemies" (corrupt and authoritarian Middle East governments; Islamic "apostates" from their own skewed interpretation of the Qur'an).

Both the "sweetness" of advanced (as well as simple) technology and the beauty of adept technocratic organization also fascinate Islam's holy warriors. It did not take long after 9-11 for the world to learn that the terrorists are master manipulators of new information technology and the Web; proud craftsmen of improvised explosives capable of wreaking havoc on an enemy that relies on sophisticated weaponry; avid consumers, at higher levels, of Western business-school texts and literature in the social sciences; shrewd bureaucrats in the fine art of compartmentalization; slick public-relations mavens in the eminently *au courant* world of "branding." Brutal violence itself is aestheticized in modern and even postmodern ways. In the eyes of Islamist fundamentalists and many of their fellow travelers, the flaming twin towers in Manhattan were as awesome and beautiful as the billowing, multicolored pillars of nuclear smoke and fire that carried American observers of the earliest nuclear explosions to transports of near rapture.

A graphic example of the technocratic fascination of terrorist intellectuals was posted online after the U.S. invasion of Iraq, under the title (in Arabic) *The Management of Savagery: The Most Critical Stage Through Which the Umma Will Pass*. "Savagery" in this case refers to situations where infidel foreign powers and apostate regimes repress the Muslim community, and the text naturally draws on traditional Islamic sources. Overall, however, it reads like a combination of an American business-school casebook and military manual. The author emphasizes the necessity of following "correct scientific method," and describes his wide-ranging tactical and strategic proposals as a product of "careful reflection using pure human reason." His basic concern is "the advancement of managerial groups" and "mastery of the art of management," and to this end it is essential to be knowledgeable about political theory, history, psychology, sociology, military strategy, and information technology including—a subject that receives particularly close attention—manipulation of the media. Ruthless revenge ("paying the price") is identified as psychologically important in deterring future aggression and breaking the morale of the enemy.

Although temporary reconciliation with "the regions of savagery" may be possible, only thoroughgoing and unconditional victory—the great watchwords of the Anglo-American powers in World War II—is acceptable in the end, however long and blood-stained the road to this end may be.[192]

<br>

■

<br>

AMONG ISLAMIC SCHOLARS as well as less learned polemicists like bin Laden, paying the price stimulated an outpouring of what amounts to "just war" commentary. Radicals exhumed passages in the Qur'an and its accompanying *hadith* or commentaries that, in their interpretation, legitimized the new terror. They also drew intellectual sustenance and religious inspiration from the extraordinarily influential writings of the Sunni fundamentalist Sayyid Qutb, hanged and martyred by the Egyptian government in 1966. Qutb's unrelenting vision of "the whole earth in evil, in chaos and in servitude to lords other than God" cited the Qur'an (3:110) to buttress the call to violence ("You are the best community raised for the good of mankind. You enjoin what is good and forbid what is evil, and you believe in God").

In his influential book *Milestones*, published two years before his execution, Qutb acknowledged the "marvelous works in science, culture, law, and material production" that emanated from the genius of medieval Europe, but went on to argue that both Christianity and Judaism had promoted "false and distorted beliefs" that ultimately elevated the secular above the sacred and spawned the corruption of both capitalism and communism. Following a brief passage describing his alienating experience at a small college in Colorado in 1948–50 (during which he earned a master's degree in education), Qutb typically segued into praise of the "logic, beauty, humanity and happiness" of true Islam and utter contempt for "this rubbish heap of the West" and "the evil and dirty materialism of the East" that resulted from contamination by Western filth.[193]

The furniture of theological, ideological, and pathological declarations that distinguished Qutb's writings carried over to Islamist discourse in the wake of what jihadists called "the blessed Tuesday" (September 11), always with the same varnish of logical as well as moral reasoning. Much of this appeared in essays on the Internet. Typically, for example, in the spring of 2003—possibly at the request of Al Qaeda—the Saudi cleric Nasir bin Hamid al-Fahd published a carefully argued *Treatise on the Legal Status of Using Weapons of Mass Destruction Against Infidels*. While providing theological justification for future terror on a massive scale, this simultaneously sanctioned the terror to date. In al-Fahd's presentation, Western treaties banning the proliferation and use of so-called weapons of mass destruction are skewed to permit using devastating conventional explosives, and at the same time are designed to ensure perpetuation of the long-standing Western monopolization of chemical, biological, and nuclear weaponry. This hypocrisy, the treatise argues—with, as it happens, explicit reference to August 1945—is plain to see:

> Those who speak so pretentiously about combatting the spread of weapons of mass destruction, America and Britain for example, were the first to have used these weapons: Britain used chemical weapons against the Iraqis in the World War I; America used nuclear weapons against Japan in World War II; and their arsenals—and those of the Jews—are full of such weapons!

Like bin Laden and others, al-Fahd elicited the Ground Zeroes of 1945 not only as a particularly conspicuous atrocity in a long continuum of Western violence but also as characteristic behavior that must be resisted and avenged—and may be responded to in kind.

In developing this logic, al-Fahd deployed the familiar argument that the self-serving laws of the infidels have "no standing in Islamic law, because God Almighty has reserved judgment and legislation to Himself." It follows from Islamic law, in turn—as he presented it—that killing must be in accordance with the teachings of the Prophet: "If people of authority engaged in jihad determine that the evil of the infidels can be repelled only by their means, they [weapons of mass destruction] may be used. The weapons of mass destruction will kill any of the infidels on whom they fall, regardless of whether they are fighters, women, or children. They will destroy and burn the land. The arguments for the permissibility of this in this case are many."

In explicit defense of attacks on America, the treatise then proceeds to cite three passages from the Qur'an:

God has said: "And if you chastise, chastise even as you have been chastised." (16:126) God says: "Whoso commits aggression against you, do you commit aggression against him like as he has committed against you." (2:194) And God says: "And the recompense of evil is evil the like of it." (42:40) Anyone who considers America's aggressions against Muslims and their lands during the past decades will conclude that striking her is permissible merely on the basis of the rule of treating as one has been treated. No other arguments need be mentioned. Some brothers have totaled the number of Muslims killed directly or indirectly by their weapons and come up with a figure of nearly ten million. As for the lands that their bombs, explosives, and missiles have burned, only God can compute them.

Such reasoning is chilling but, apart from the Qur'anic scaffolding, unexceptional. This is the ethos of retribution that resonates through the Old Testament. At the same time, it also reflects a line of strategic reasoning—expressed elsewhere in the treatise as "there is no prohibited thing where there is necessity"—that was put into practice with less overt theorizing in the Anglo-American air war in World War II, and was essentially endorsed by the Bush administration after 9-11, when its self-styled "War Council" lawyers concluded that the exigencies of the war on terror necessitated a "unitary presidency" or "unitary executive" freed from the constraints of both traditional and more recent international laws.

In the Islamists' war culture, as in everyone's, responding harshly and in kind thus becomes a necessary evil. Al-Fahd acknowledged that "the Prophet forbade the killing of women and children," but argued that closer analysis makes it "apparent that the prohibition is against killing them intentionally. If they are killed collaterally . . . there is nothing wrong with it. Jihad is not to be halted because of the presence of infidel women and children." Many pages of the treatise are devoted to buttressing "the permissibility of setting fire to enemy lands and destroying their homes if the jihad requires it" with statements by other Islamic scholars, but al-Fahd also could have assembled supporting quotations by innumerable infidels had he chosen to do so.[194]

In the dream palace of noble objectives, necessary evils are lesser evils—even "good," even "merciful." Such assurances, whether pragmatic or ostensibly theological, are a narcotic that blunts inherent restraints against killing.

IN AN INTERVIEW with a reporter from Al Jazeera conducted on October 20, 2001, bin Laden was asked if he supported the idea of a "Clash of Civilizations" and responded that "there is no doubt about this."[195] Sayyid Qutb, who died before this particular phrase became fashionable, would have concurred. The venom of these representative attacks on the West—even where, as with Qutb, Western civilization is acknowledged to have made admirable long-ago contributions—is unadulterated.

With the usual qualifications, much the same can be said about the anti-Western hatred that accompanied Japan's holy war. No compromise was possible with the "demonic Anglo-Americans"—just as, on the Allied side, no compromise was possible with the Japanese beasts. Yet apart from the extreme fringes (like the novelist Yukio Mishima, who killed himself in 1970), for all practical purposes imperial Japan's suicidal ultranationalism became a spent force once the war ended—much as Nazism did in Germany and communism in Russia after the collapse of the Soviet Union. And despite the Allies' wartime insistence on unconditional surrender, postwar Japan proceeded to fashion a new sort of "imperial democracy" that accommodated pluralism and did not disrupt amity among the erstwhile enemies.

The "clash of civilizations" postulated by extremists on both sides in the post–9-11 world does not offer promise of such a smooth metamorphosis. There can be no abrupt surrender or collapse on the Islamist side, since there is no state to capitulate or disintegrate. The political and territorial grievances in the Middle East that succor terror have no prospect of an easy solution, particularly given the self-righteousness that prevails on all sides. Religious zealotry is more intractable than political fanaticism, or at least seems to be. Vested official, political, and economic interests guarantee the continued proliferation of weapons of mass destruction. The "security State" may yet break freedom's back. When Dr. Liebow wrote about a new evil "beyond recall" in his Hiroshima journal in 1945, he foreshadowed a despair that found new incarnations in 2001 and after.

The other side of such despair is hope in shared, nonviolent ideals, of course—and, more subtly, hope in the malleability of language. After World War II, great numbers of Japanese who had been prepared to die for the state found it possible to repudiate militarism without feeling they were jettisoning their ideals. The ideals, after all, had been expressed in grand and noble terms—so grand that they were essentially nonspecific, and thus could be given new interpretations or, like large but empty valises, new content. Peace, for example, or coexistence, or coprosperity.[196]

Islamist radicals are practiced hands at giving old concepts new meaning: this is what they have done with jihad, the core concept in their jeremiad. What is striking when their polemics are set alongside U.S. rhetoric in the war on terror is not just the shared articulation of a clash of civilizations or crusade against evil, but also the repetitive, abstract expression of what is good. Some of this derives from a shared monotheism. The God of the Qur'an is merciful and compassionate as well as almighty—this is enshrined in the hallowed Arabic phrase *Bismilláh ir-rahmán ir-rahúm* (In the name of Allah, the Beneficient, the Merciful)—just as the Christian God to whom presidents Truman and Bush paid homage is loving and merciful. The surface resonance of abstract ideals goes beyond this, however, and extends to the political as well as theological—to freedom and justice on earth, that is, as well as in the hereafter.

Thus the writings of Sayyid Qutb—the "philosopher of Islamic terror" in Western appraisals—sometimes read in translation as if many key words and ideals might have come from a catechism of non-Islamic values. Throughout *Milestones*, for example, Qutb evokes virtues and visions like these: escaping "the suffering of mankind"; committing oneself "to abolish all injustice from the earth"; striving towards "true social justice," "true human progress," "true freedom to mankind"; nourishing the "human" characteristics of "freedom and honor, family and its obligations, morals and values"—or, again, of "dignity, purity and cleanliness, modesty and piety, and a desire for good deeds"; attaining "freedom from tyranny" and "from servitude to other men" (by serving God alone); realizing the true "dignity of man."

Qutb presents his theology as a "proclamation of universal freedom," with the realization of such freedom coming from adherence to the "universal law" of *sharia* as prescribed in the Qur'an and *hadith*. Eternal bliss in the hereafter may be the ultimate reward of struggling to realize such ideals, but the path to such immortality lies in never ceasing to struggle for "the good of mankind." This is what it means to be "truly civilized." Such language is formulaic, but no less potent for that reason. The same noble rhetoric ("universal law," "oppose tyranny and seek justice," "liberate the earth," etc.) permeates even such practical Islamist texts as *The Management of Savagery*.

It is human nature to judge others by their deeds and ourselves by our words or professed ideals; or, at least, to sift through our deeds and romanticize them. Qutb—like bin Laden, Al Qaeda, the Taliban, the whole bloody vanguard of terror in the name of God—was explicitly a foe of democracy, individualism, secular law and concepts of human rights, secularized institutions in general. He envisioned a theocracy based on the truth revealed by Muhammad, and what he and his spiritual disciples mean by "justice" or "universal freedom" or "universal law" bears little relation to what these phrases signify in liberal democracies. Intolerance, oppression, and violence followed from the radical rendering of these prescriptions.

Still, abstract values of a common coinage—or, perhaps better stated, of a shared root and resonance—can move masses when they are articulated persuasively. Qutb is a powerful writer. Bin Laden's pronouncements are distinguished by their rhetorical polish. Language can be both a path to different places and a bridge to reconciliation, and believers in a more moderate Islam ("apostates" to the fundamentalists) are able to use the same scriptural sources as the extremists, and the same devotion to *sharia*, to disavow violence and promote the more pluralistic modernism the militant Islamists so vehemently condemn.

At least, again, in theory. As it transpired, the stunning success of the 9-11 attacks energized the extremists, and the equally stunning recklessness of the U.S. response seemed to confirm the image of a corrupt and hypocritical enemy. Islamist holy war found a new cadre of articulate spokesmen and strategists, all elaborating in one way or another on the old watchwords of reason, morality, and mass destruction in the name of a merciful God.

# PART III
# WARS AND OCCUPATIONS

*Winning the Peace, Losing the Peace*

# OCCUPIED JAPAN
# AND OCCUPIED IRAQ

## *Winning the War, Losing the Peace*

Shortly after Japan's surrender, Shigeru Yoshida, who would eventually serve as prime minister for more than six years between 1946 and 1954, attempted to put an optimistic gloss on his country's predicament. History provides examples of losing in war but winning the peace, he reminded his compatriots, and that is what the nation had to set its collective will to accomplishing. Years later, after Japan emerged as an economic power in the 1970s, many commentators concluded this had happened. The occupation of the defeated nation ended with a conservative government firmly in power. A capitalist phoenix rose from the ashes, staunchly allied with the United States. And the crusty Yoshida became, in retrospect, a minor prophet.[1]

In the spring of 2007, close to the fourth anniversary of President Bush's "Mission Accomplished" performance announcing that "major combat operations in Iraq have ended," Ali Allawi, a longtime exile in London who returned to Iraq to hold several ministerial positions after the invasion, delivered a speech in the United States titled "The Occupation of Iraq: Winning the War, Losing the Peace." He was promoting his insightful and mournful book of the same title. Iraq had long since plunged into chaos, the occupation had become one of the most disgraceful overseas failures in U.S. history, and mere mention of "victory" evoked sorrow, cynicism, and scorn. Iraq had become hell of a different kind than under Saddam Hussein, with no good exit in sight. No more striking contrast to the U.S.-Japan precedent of war and occupation could be imagined.[2]

There are few rhetorical old saws more timeworn than winning the war but losing the peace; and although precisely this warning was issued with some urgency in government circles in the months preceding the Iraq invasion, it was not taken seriously at top levels.[3] Nor were the real lessons of post–World War II occupations taken seriously. Although few critics anticipated the quotidian incompetence of U.S. post-invasion planning and performance in Iraq, it was clear before war was launched that occupied Japan should have been a red light. To think otherwise—to evoke Japan as some sort of assurance that the United States could easily win the peace once it had been victorious in the combat phase of Operation Iraqi Freedom, and that "democracy" would follow fairly naturally in another land that was neither Western nor Christian nor largely Caucasian—was to engage in false analogy and magical thinking.

Beginning in the second week of October 2002—as a small piece in the propaganda campaign about weapons of mass destruction, "mushroom clouds," and Saddam's alleged support of Al Qaeda that mobilized American sentiment behind the impending war—the White House ventured to strengthen its case by floating the putative success stories of postwar Japan and Germany. From the outset Japan was the more attractive model of the two, since Germany had been divided into U.S., British, French, and Soviet zones of occupation and ended up in the Cold War partition known as West and East Germany. By contrast, although occupied Japan was nominally under the control of the victorious Allied powers, in practice the United States ran the show. Even years later, as violence continued to consume Iraq, the "postwar Japan" analogy remained cherished by the White House. When a surge in troop numbers was introduced to stave off outright defeat in the summer of 2007, for example, the president's speechwriters still deemed it effective to cite defeated Japan as reason for maintaining hope in the emergence of a democratic Iraq.[4]

Where discrepancy between labels and realities is concerned, occupied Iraq followed the pattern established in Japan. "Coalition" replaced "Allied" as the nominal cover of the undertaking, while for all practical purposes the United States exercised unilateral authority. There were other points of similarity or partial congruity as well, many of them highly suggestive, as will be seen; but fundamentally the two occupations were as different as night and day. Both the victors and losers in World War II won the peace in Japan. In Iraq, there was no peace.[5]

Using defeated Japan to paint a positive picture of what to anticipate in Iraq was perverse, for the two nations differed enormously and so did the wars and occupations being addressed. Beyond this, the U.S. government in the opening years of the twenty-first century bore only shadow resemblance to that of 1945—not merely in ideological orientation (beneath a deceptive common rhetoric of "freedom and democracy") but also in operational procedures. Even the most rudimentary checklist of why the occupation of Japan unfolded without violence and jump-started a functional postwar democracy provided a sobering reminder of what would *not* be present in any imaginable post-hostilities Iraq. Evocation of postwar Japan as a reassuring precedent was not simply a misreading of the past. It was bowdlerization: another example of wishful thinking compounded by delusory "cherry-picking"—in this case, ransacking not raw intelligence data but history itself.

## Occupied Japan and the Eye of the Beholder

Defeated Japan did not regain sovereignty until April 1952, making the period of U.S. control almost three years longer than the Pacific War itself. The world order was tumultuous during this period, and by 1949 Asia had become a cauldron of Cold War tensions. The Soviet Union tested its first nuclear weapon that year; the Chinese Communists took Beijing and extended their control over the entire country; Southeast Asia was aflame with anticolonial revolutions (ignited by imperial Japan's rout of the European powers). War erupted in Korea in June 1950. In this tumult, occupation policy in Japan passed through several stages, beginning with a radical agenda of "demilitarization and democratization" and ending in a "reverse-course" campaign to crush the political left, reconstruct a "self-sufficient" export-oriented economy, promote Japanese rearmament, ensure the indefinite retention of U.S. military bases on Japanese soil, detach Okinawa from the rest of Japan as a major strategic (and nuclear) garrison, and lock Japan economically and diplomatically as well as strategically into the "containment" of communism, particularly vis-à-vis China. (This last policy lasted until the Nixon-Kissinger rapprochement with China in 1972.) Seen whole, start to finish, the occupation reveals a certain schizophrenia.

Problems rooted in these years plagued Japan into the twenty-first century, when the occupation was being singled out as an encouraging beacon for Iraq. Okinawa remained a grotesquely militarized U.S. outpost. Electoral politics remained warped by a canny and corrupt conservative hegemony that traced back to a decisive electoral victory under Prime Minister Yoshida in early 1949 and was not seriously upended until 2009, after the Bush presidency ended. Economic growth was hindered by entrenched practices of government intervention that had roots in the war years and had been reinforced during the occupation. Ideologically, conservative and right-wing attempts to sanitize imperial Japan's war crimes were stronger than ever a half century after the defeat, reflecting both festering resentment at the "victor's justice" aspects of the postwar war-crimes trials conducted by the Allied powers and chagrin at still being constrained by a postwar constitution that prohibited Japan from dispatching military forces overseas—to Afghanistan and Iraq, for example—like a "normal" nation.[6]

From a Japanese perspective, there was an ironic, bitter twist to watching Americans invoke the "success" of occupied Japan to brighten the picture of what might be anticipated in postwar Iraq. While the Japanese government threw wholehearted support behind the Bush administration's war policy (playing the role, as it were, of the England of Asia), Japan's own experience of being occupied was regarded by many as a humiliating chapter in the nation's history—more dishonorable even, some would have it, than the war years. Transcending or escaping "the postwar" was a mantra among Japanese conservatives—and "postwar" (*sengo*) was code for a litany of negative rather than positive legacies of the occupation era, during which the nation had no sovereignty and was ruled by foreigners. Military emasculation was one such regretted legacy; the one-sided "victor's justice" judgments of the Tokyo trials another, particularly as regurgitated by liberals and leftists on the one hand and foreigners on the other; lingering suspicion of flag-waving and anthem-singing patriotism another (U.S. occupation authorities had banned both); being constrained in paying official homage to the several million "departed heroes" (*eirei*) of the Asia-Pacific War who were enshrined in Tokyo's Yasukuni Shrine another; still having as the basic law of the land a constitution originally drafted in English yet another.[7]

Rose-colored invocations of occupied Japan by Americans gearing up for war with Iraq thus fell in place with the other uncomfortable Japan-related images that poured out in the wake of September 11: Pearl Harbor and "infamy"; kamikaze and terror bombing; Japan's membership alongside Nazi Germany and Fascist Italy in the original "Axis" of evil; Ground Zero as transplanted code for American rather than Japanese victimization; all-out war against an Islamist enemy as fanatical as the emperor's soldiers and sailors had been; the Stars and Stripes triumphantly raised at Iwo Jima; and so on. In theory, evoking Japan's "American interlude" and postwar rebirth as a democratic and prosperous nation was—certainly in the eyes of Americans—benign and complimentary. In practice, being occupied and dictated to by foreigners, no matter how far in the past, is a wound to pride. In Japan's case, moreover, reopening this wound called attention to one of the more subtle but malignant legacies of the long-ago occupation—the nation's lingering image as an American client state.

Despite postwar Japan's hard-earned status as a major economic power, the unabated fixation of Japanese leaders on currying American goodwill cast a pall of psychological as well as structural dependency over the nation's accomplishments. Unqualified support of the Iraq war became but the latest manifestation of this. For reasons of its own, postwar Germany escaped such obsequiousness—and the open criticism of the Bush administration's rush to war with Iraq by German leaders only served to highlight this difference. Nor was dependency and subordination just a slur leveled by cynical foreigners. "Client state" was also a self-disparaging perception in the same conservative constituencies that called for a new nationalism transcending the Americanization of the occupation period—even while simultaneously remaining America's most deferential supporters through the Cold War and into the so-called war on terror. A half century after the occupation ended in 1952, many Japanese were still wrestling with an identity crisis that traced back to these immediate postwar years. In this situation, casual references to the Japanese precedent in conjunction with invading and occupying Iraq were at best discomforting.[8]

None of these tangled considerations mattered in Washington, of course, when it came to plucking grand models from recent history. Postwar Japan was peaceful, prosperous, capitalist, and compliant; and advocates of war against Iraq understandably found this useful in embellishing the scenario of a swift overthrow of Saddam's Baathist regime followed by smooth transition to a democratic nation friendly to the United States. Apparent parallels were, on the surface, quite striking. Imperial Japan had been authoritarian and militaristic, oppressive within its borders and atrocious outside them. Unlike Germany, Japan was a non-Western culture and power that denounced "the West" fiercely when animosity was at its peak, but at the same time—again superficially like Iraq—it also had enjoyed periods of amity and collaboration with the United States and European powers. Who could resist drawing encouraging lessons from Japan's grand postwar transformation from authoritarianism and aggression to a civil and prosperous society that posed no threat to others—not to mention its role as a secure base for projecting U.S. military power in a strategically critical part of the world? Who could resist the argument—and as time passed this became a particular favorite of President Bush—that Japan was proof positive that "democracy" did not require a Western milieu to take root?

## Incommensurable Worlds

Attentive students of history could resist these arguments, for one, as well as even casual observers looking for insight rather than ammunition. Before the war of choice against Iraq was unleashed, critics pointed out that the occupation of Japan succeeded largely for reasons that were, or would be, almost entirely absent in Iraq.[9]

Conspicuous among these differences was the virtually uncontested moral *legitimacy* of the United States venturing to occupy a defeated Japan. Japan had initiated the war, and the emperor himself announced its beginning, announced its end, and gave his full consent to the formal terms of surrender. None of America's allies questioned the dominant role of the United States in a nominally Allied occupation; even the Soviet Union went along, after initial sputtering. (Stalin regarded U.S. control in Japan as essentially a quid pro quo for Soviet control in Eastern Europe.) Japan's savaged Asian neighbors and victims, led by China, were happy to see the humbled and ruined nation under America's iron hand.

Led by their suddenly supremely pragmatic sovereign, the Japanese people themselves by and large also accepted the unconditional nature of the surrender, the legitimacy of the occupation, and the inevitability and even desirability of following the dictates of the victor, however emotionally painful surrender itself might be. In his radio address on August 15 (Japan time) announcing acceptance of the terms of surrender, Emperor Hirohito exhorted his subjects to follow his lead in "enduring the unendurable and bearing the unbearable, to pave the way for a grand peace for all generations to come." Two days later, he issued a separate rescript to the armed forces praising their gallantry, grieving over their losses, mentioning the entry into the war by the Soviet Union (but not the atomic bombs) as a major reason for laying down arms, and concluding by linking compliance with his August 15 message to the highest form of patriotism. "We charge you, the members of the armed forces," this August 17 message read, "to comply faithfully with Our intentions, to preserve strong solidarity, to be straightforward in your actions, to overcome every hardship, and to bear the unbearable in order to lay the foundations for the enduring life of Our nation."[10]

On August 25—with occupation forces still a few days away from actually setting foot in Japan—yet another imperial message endorsed orders for all army and navy personnel to demobilize in similar terms: "Turn to civilian occupations as good and loyal subjects, and by enduring hardships and overcoming difficulties, exert your full energies in the task of postwar reconstruction." Two days later the minister of war, who had faced and overcome resistance to the surrender orders by a few small groups of officers, issued a final appeal to the army that also turned capitulation into a demonstration of patriotism. "We must behave prudently, taking into consideration the future of the nation," he declared. "Do not become excited and conceal or destroy arms which are to be surrendered. This is our opportunity to display the magnificence of our nation." The emperor's loyal subjects complied—and a great many of them went on to embrace the surrender and occupation as a liberation from death and a welcome opportunity to eliminate the forces and institutions that had driven them into their disastrous war.[11]

Given the criticism the Bush administration provoked as it deflected the war against Al Qaeda into plans to attack Iraq, it was obvious that occupying Iraq would find no comparable approbation in the world at large or within the United States or the invaded country itself. The speed, arrogance, and indifference with which Washington dissipated the global sympathy and support that followed September 11 is breathtaking in this regard. Failure to impose control and security following the fall of Baghdad in April 2003, coupled with revelation that Iraq did not possess the arsenals that had been offered as the major reason preemptive war was necessary, precipitated the ultimate shredding of U.S. credibility—but that most critical of intangibles, "legitimacy," was absent from the start. Critics who raised this issue before the war agreed Saddam was a brutal dictator, but this did not suffice to give the so-called lesser evil of invading and occupying his country legitimacy.[12]

Also predictably lacking in any projected post-Saddam Iraq was an essential component in the operational efficiency of the occupation of Japan: the carryover of *competent administrative machinery*. Emperor Hirohito was the most prominent symbol of this institutional continuity and stability, and his disciplined military establishment was retained long enough to carry out an orderly demobilization before being disestablished. Truly essential to the transition from war to peace, however, was the fact that while the military disarmed and demobilized, governing structures remained intact and administrators and technocrats remained at their jobs top to bottom, from Tokyo to the remotest town and village. Even before widely criticized U.S. policies in Iraq such as dissolution of the military and the purge of top-level Baath Party members from public office were introduced, it was clear to critics that the Iraqi state—with its head decapitated and no obvious government capable of maintaining order—would not be remotely comparable to Japan once the dictator and his minions had been overthrown.

Further reason for pessimism in this regard was the impressive *social cohesion* that held Japan together during the difficult years required to win the peace. Political and ideological differences certainly existed in defeated Japan; early on, they found expression in the emergence of a militant but nonviolent labor and left-wing movement. To anyone who seriously placed the Japan of 1945 side by side with the Iraq targeted by America, however, this third realm of contrast seemed, again, simply enormous. No explosive schisms lurked just beneath the thick skin of the Japanese state. Religion posed no threat whatsoever in this polytheistic culture, apart from how it had been temporarily manipulated in the cause of a militaristic modern nationalism. There was, on the contrary, a compelling and carefully nurtured "Yamato race" history that traced back over a millennium to the earliest written chronicles of the eighth century. Twentieth-century ideologues had turned this sense of racial, cultural, and national solidarity in the direction of militarism and war, but postwar pragmatists like Yoshida could just as easily direct it toward peaceful reconstruction.

In Iraq, shared history was short. The Iraqi nation itself, after all, only dated back to British and French machinations in the wake of World War I. What ran perilously deep, on the other hand, were religious, ethnic, tribal, and regional fault lines. "Iraqi nationalism" was not a myth: the nation's solidarity through eight years (1980–88) of ferocious war with Iran was proof of this. Such cohesion under Saddam's police state was, at the same time, misleading. Like India at the time of partition in 1947, and Yugoslavia after Tito, and the Soviet Union in the wake of its fatal incursion into Afghanistan, absent force the center could not hold in Iraq.

The center did more than just hold in post-surrender Japan. It proved receptive to and capable of promoting much of the democratization agenda the Americans promoted in the first few years of occupation. This was possible because a resilient *civil society* had emerged prior to the rise of the militarists in the 1930s. This was a fourth realm of striking difference that advocates of the Iraq war chose to ignore. Japan's Meiji Constitution of 1889 established a constitutional monarchy with an elective parliament

that had remained in operation through the war years; party-led governments first appeared on the scene in 1918, and universal male suffrage
was endorsed by the legislature in 1925. Starting around the turn of the
century, and accelerating exponentially during the years Hirohito's father
occupied the throne (1912–26) and into the early 1930s, a variety of social
and political developments took place that scholars weigh heavily (under
the rubric "Taishō democracy") in assessing the roots of Japan's postwar
pluralism. Electoral politics flourished; labor and women's movements
emerged; capitalist entrepreneurship took off after World War I; cosmo-
politanism penetrated the ever more populous cities and towns that the
B-29s would later incinerate; consumerism and "modernity" seeped into
the countryside.

All this was fertile soil for the development of a more democratic Japan
once the emperor's holy war failed and the militarists were removed. Nor
were the years of mobilization for "total war" that began in the 1930s and
continued to 1945 necessarily retrogressive in this regard. Freedom was
repressed, but creativity and social transformation flourished in ways that
also bore positive legacies for postwar reconstruction. With sixty-six cities bombed, its Asian empire cut off at a stroke, and roughly one-quarter
of the national wealth destroyed, Japan was to all outward appearances
ruined when the fighting ended in August 1945. Until around 1948 or
1949, most urban dwellers struggled just to survive day to day. What mattered in the longer run, however, was that the human resources essential for reconstruction at both technological and technocratic levels were
vastly greater at war's end than they had been when the militarists gained
control over a decade earlier.[13]

Iraq was a highly literate society that once possessed one of the most
developed industrial economies in the Middle East. Many Iraqis, too,
were skilled professionals who to one degree or another supported democratic ideals. Again, however, the Japanese case pointed more to deficiencies than similarities. No one could speak with heartfelt assurance of a
truly promising experience with the values and practices of civil society
prior to Saddam's police state. The post–Gulf War decade of crippling
economic sanctions against Iraq, moreover, compounded by the repression and ineptitude of Saddam's corrupt rule, had undermined rather
than accelerated enhancement of human resources. Much of the Iraqi

leadership that war advocates counted on to lead "regime change" after Saddam was eliminated resided in a largely secular community of exiles and expatriates who had lived abroad for most of their adult lives and had no strong constituencies on their native soil. Civil society had been hollowed out in Iraq.[14]

A fifth seemingly obvious difference also failed to give pause to those who evoked postwar Japan as a heartening example: Japan's *isolation*. This was both spatial and temporal. Japan was an archipelago with no porous contiguous borders. Until around 1947, moreover, no one in the larger world cared much about what was taking place there so long as it was not threatening. The nations and peoples of Japan's short-lived empire—China, Korea, Southeast Asia—were consumed with their own conflicts. Europe and the Soviet Union were preoccupied with reconstruction, and where foreign policy was concerned they and the United States were fixated on nuclear issues and challenges in Eastern and Western Europe. There were no hostile outside forces or supra-state movements gathered around Japan viewing it as a potential prize—no counterparts, that is, to the Islamist fundamentalists and terrorists perched on Iraq's borders.

Deprived of sovereignty, utterly lacking in critical natural resources, and dismissed for the moment as a fourth-rate power or worse, Japan in defeat was initially, apart from Okinawa, of slight strategic interest. The American reformers ensconced in Tokyo had the luxury of being able to introduce their reform agenda without much outside attention or intervention. Absent this cocoon of place and time, the occupation surely would have unfolded differently—as happened next door in the strategically contested Korean peninsula, for example, as well as in Okinawa. Both of the latter were subjected to militaristic U.S. policies from the outset, and neither has ever been evoked as a model of enlightened and successful occupation.

It is difficult to exaggerate the importance of this early breathing space. In all likelihood postwar Japan would have become democratic and pro-Western without the occupation, but in substance as well as form it would have become a different state with a different collective ethos. When the Cold War intruded and the United States turned against some of the more progressive reforms it originally sponsored, the old-guard conservatives led by Yoshida naturally were pleased. This, after all, was what the old man himself had in mind when he spoke early on about winning the peace. His satisfaction, however, was not unalloyed. Many *fait accompli* (like land reform, constitutional revision, thoroughgoing demilitarization, and promotion of progressive educational ideals) could not be undone easily. As Yoshida himself later ruefully put it, "There was this idea at the back of my mind that, whatever needed to be revised after we regained our independence could be revised then. But once a thing has been decided on, it is not so easy to have it altered." The initial reforms may have been ordered by the Americans, but they quickly found a Japanese constituency.[15]

Landlocked Iraq was not merely the opposite of an island but also, by the Bush administration's own choice, the bull's-eye of world attention—central to U.S. strategy for controlling the Middle East and its natural resources, and central to what the present would portend politically for the future (liberalization and U.S. hegemony in theory, violence and accelerated instability in practice). There was neither physical security nor time to spare. At the topmost level where policy was actually formulated, however—or not formulated, as it turned out—very little of this registered.

## Planning Postwar Japan

Japan's capitulation in the summer of 1945 caught most planners in Washington by surprise. Only a handful of policy makers were aware of the top-secret development of nuclear weapons, and the prevailing assumption was that the war would drag on deep into 1946. Despite this, the transition from war to peace in Japan proceeded smoothly—more so than in Germany and occupied areas of Europe, where national and ethnic rivalries were intense and atrocities were perpetuated on all sides, including by the victorious Allied forces; more so than in China and Southeast Asia, where war carried on in new forms; and vastly more so than in Iraq over a half century later.[16]

In the refracted darkness of occupied Iraq, it became clearer just how competent the planners who dealt with defeated Japan had been. They initiated serious planning for the war's aftermath shortly after Pearl Harbor. They articulated U.S. and Allied intentions and objectives for the occupation quickly and clearly, announcing the terms of surrender before the atomic bombs were dropped and outlining the broad agenda of projected reforms within six weeks of the formal surrender on September 2. And they displayed a mature and generally pragmatic and bipartisan ability to bring a range of individuals, agencies, and political outlooks together in constructive ways from 1942 until 1947 or so, when domestic politics and Cold War fixations subjected Japan policy to an ideological litmus test. Throughout the entire period of occupation, moreover, the notion of social engineering—what would later be called nation building—was taken as a given. The state had an important role to play in civil affairs, tailored to the particular circumstances of time and place, and where Japan was concerned this applied to both the occupying power and the nation that was being occupied.[17]

Almost all of these seemingly straightforward assumptions and procedures became more noteworthy when set against what transpired in Iraq: the necessity of serious prior planning for the period after combat ended, the importance of articulating basic postwar objectives clearly and quickly, the benefits to be derived from engaging diverse opinions and encouraging genuine interagency collaboration, and the recognition that the state had a legitimate and essential role to play in realms beyond making or preventing war. What Iraq revealed was that these were not attitudes or procedures that could be taken for granted. To one degree or another, they were in fact repudiated in the run-up to invading Iraq.

From 1942 until 1947, much of the planning for postwar Japan was conducted under the aegis of "SWNCC," an acronym for the State-War-Navy Coordinating Committee. War and Navy were melded into the newly established Department of Defense in 1947, and thereafter grand policy affecting Japan carried the imprimatur of the also new National Security Council. General MacArthur's orders were channeled through the Joint Chiefs of Staff, which amplified them, and it was the documents he received from the Joint Chiefs that he took as definitive.

These were dense and reasonably orderly procedures, and before World War II ended, SWNCC had mobilized a great deal of expertise to assemble what was known about Japan and could be expected and accomplished once it was defeated. Interagency collaboration and division of labor were substantial rather than just nominal, with agencies such as the Office of Strategic Services, Office of War Information, and Foreign Economic Administration contributing to the process. Beginning in the fall of 1944,

82. *August 19, 1945: One of two specially marked Mitsubishi "Bettys" touches down in Ie Shima in the Ryukyu Islands en route to Manila, where the logistics of Japan's surrender and occupation were worked out at General MacArthur's headquarters.*

83. *August 30, 1945: MacArthur—unarmed, dressed in casual summer dress, and smoking his trademark corncob pipe—arrives at Japan's Atsugi airfield to assume control of the occupation as Supreme Commander of the Allied Powers.*

*84. September 29, 1945: A sensation at the time and the most famous occupation-era photograph ever since, MacArthur and Emperor Hirohito pose side by side at their cordial, historic first meeting. This single image captured the emperor's descent from his erstwhile "sacred and inviolable" eminence and MacArthur's dominance, while at the same time conveying the continuity of Japanese authority and governance that expedited a smooth transition to peace.*

for example, the Research and Analysis Branch of the Office of Strategic Services coordinated the compilation of twenty-five informational "hand-books" about Japan on subjects ranging from government and adminis-tration to money and banking to cultural institutions. Between the sum-mer of 1944 and summer of 1945, the Civil Affairs Division of the War Department assumed responsibility for an even more extensive series of "civil affairs guides" aimed at problems likely to be encountered in post-hostilities Japan. Some forty guides (of a projected seventy monographs) had been completed when Japan surrendered, and three in particular are regarded as having an impact on subsequent policy regarding labor, land reform, and local government. "Military government" training schools for both Germany and Japan were introduced under army and navy auspices in various locales in the United States beginning in 1942, and "civil affairs training schools" were established at Harvard, Yale, Chicago, Stanford, Michigan, and Northwestern in the summer of 1944.[18]

Many of the pre-surrender handbooks and guides did not have great impact, and many of the more than a thousand army and navy person-nel who received intensive training in Japanese language, culture, and civil affairs were poorly used after the surrender, or not even deployed to Japan at all. What mattered more was that major branches of the government were seriously engaged in the process. They agreed on MacArthur's appoint-ment as supreme commander, which was formalized a few days before Japan's mid-August capitulation. More significantly, despite the abruptness of Japan's defeat, the state, war, and navy departments were in a position to put together a solid blueprint titled "United States Initial Post-Surrender Policy for Japan." This was radioed to MacArthur on August 29, the day before he set foot in Japan. Most of the military officers and civilian offi-cials who staffed the occupation's general headquarters in Tokyo or were assigned to local duties were hastily recruited after the capitulation. At its peak, the staff at General Headquarters numbered around five thousand.

Japanese officials learned what surrender would entail beyond disar-mament and demobilization in a series of statements that began with the Potsdam Declaration of July 26, which laid down the terms of surrender under the names of the United States, United Kingdom, and China. The "Byrnes Note" of August 11 concerning the future status of the emperor was the first of these statements—ambiguous enough to hold out promise

*85. A casually attired GI distributing candy from his jeep attracts a lively crowd of children in Yokohama a few weeks after the first occupation forces arrived.*

that the throne would be respected, while at the same time unequivocal in affirming (as previously noted) that the authority of the emperor and Japanese government "shall be subject to the Supreme Commander of the Allied Powers who will take such steps as he deems proper to effectuate the surrender terms." How long would this take? It was impossible to say. On August 19 and 20, a high-level Japanese military team dispatched to Manila was given instructions by MacArthur's command about disarming the imperial forces and preparing the homeland for arrival of the massive land, sea, and air forces of the victorious Allied powers.[19]

The first small advance contingent of U.S. forces landed in Japan on August 27 (the day the minister of war issued his statement declaring that an orderly surrender was "our opportunity to display the magnificence of our nation"). MacArthur arrived three days later, taking care to be photographed disembarking from his plane at Atsugi airfield unarmed and with his trademark corncob pipe. Three days after that, on September 2, came the celebrated surrender ceremony in Tokyo Bay, which included a stunning display of the might of the forces that had crushed Japan—the sea choked with

*86. An American sailor on a borrowed bicycle passes a ruined building near Yokosuka naval base in the closing days of August 1945, virtually simultaneously with General MacArthur's serene arrival.*

warships, the sky slashed by endless flyovers of fighter planes. The emperor's representatives signed the instrument of surrender on this occasion, formally agreeing that the emperor and Japanese government were obliged to comply with the dictates of the Supreme Commander for the Allied Powers.

MacArthur's "message to the American people" on September 2 was comforting to the Japanese, for it spoke of redirecting "the energy of the Japanese race" and gave assurance that "if the talents of the race are turned into constructive channels, the country can lift itself from its present deplorable state into a position of dignity." There was, at the same time, neither promise nor expectation of a soft occupation policy. The lengthy "U.S. Initial Post-Surrender Policy for Japan" received on August 29 addressed punitive measures (war-crimes trials, reparations, etc.) but focused greatest attention on spelling out the broad, ambitious objectives of political and economic demilitarization and democratization. This basic

*87. In this snapshot of an American soldier from the opening days of 1946, the bicycle remains, but the parasol has been exchanged for an attractive young woman.*

policy statement was released to the public by the State Department on September 24, thus enabling the Japanese to read what only a few weeks earlier had been a secret internal U.S. government document.[20]

Almost overnight, "SCAP" became a ubiquitous acronym throughout Japan, signifying both MacArthur personally and the overall military government over which he presided. Prior to the end of the occupation in April 1952, SCAP issued around twenty-two hundred highly specific orders known as SCAPIN (from Supreme Commander of the Allied Powers Index), along with another seven thousand "administrative" directives (known as SCAPIN-A). As rechanneled through the Japanese government, these became transformed into over five hundred "Potsdam orders" (*potsudamu meirei*). Of particular influence in shaping public understanding early on was a SCAPIN issued on October 4 ordering the Japanese government to undertake "Removal of Restrictions on Political, Civil, and

*88. An astonished American photographer came upon this Japanese musical revue shortly after New Year's Day of 1946. Such Western-style productions were prohibited after Pearl Harbor. Their swift reappearance reflected both a sense of liberation and a light form of escapism from the hardships of daily life that continued, for most Japanese, for years after the surrender.*

Religious Liberties"; this included itemization of laws to be abrogated. One week later, MacArthur released a concise personal statement to the government concerning rapid implementation of "required reforms." Soon widely known as the "five fundamental rights" or "five great reforms," these involved (1) "emancipation of the women of Japan through their enfranchisement"; (2) "encouragement of the unionization of Labor"; (3) liberalization of the educational system; (4) creation of a "system of justice designed to afford the people protection against despotic, arbitrary and unjust methods"; and (5) "democratization of Japanese economic institutions" to ensure wide distribution of income and ownership. This October 11 statement was prefaced with the observation that these reforms would "unquestionably involve a liberalization of the Constitution."

Additional reforms were introduced in the next few months. Holding companies of the great *zaibatsu* conglomerates were ordered dissolved in

*89. In April 1947,* Life *ran a five-page photographic feature re-creating scenes from UPI correspondent Earnest Hoberecht's novel* Tokyo Romance, *a potboiler about an American journalist and Japanese movie star who fall in love. The book became a bestseller in Japan. In the scene staged here, the woman's father looks on approvingly as her suitor proposes marriage.*

November, for example, while December saw directives disestablishing "state religion" (State Shinto) and introducing a sweeping land reform that essentially appropriated property held by large landlords and redistributed it among a rural population that until then had high rates of tenancy and low levels of subsistence. The first postwar general election in April 1946 attracted over three hundred largely new (and ephemeral) political parties and saw the election of thirty-nine women to the lower house of the Diet. The ensuing session of the legislature spent many months discussing and tinkering with the radical constitutional revision that an impatient SCAP headquarters pressed on the Japanese government in February. (The new constitution was promulgated in September, came into effect in February 1947, and remained unrevised when the invasion of Iraq took place fifty-six years later.)

*90. In this conspicuously self-referential mise-en-scène from January 1946, Alfred Eisenstaedt photographs a pretender to the imperial throne and his family, posing outside the modest store they ran. The allure of such unthreatening subjects led illustrated magazines like* Life *to devote almost insatiable attention to picturesque aspects of traditional Japanese culture and society. Geisha, temples and shrines, imperial duck hunts, tea ceremony, flower arranging, ceramics, cultivated pearls, bonsai trees, tattoos, Ainu aborigines, Kabuki actors, sumo wrestlers, attractive rural and seaside locales, not to mention charming children and attentive women—all became magnets for media coverage of the erstwhile enemy.*

Japan remained confronted by formidable problems and challenges for several years after the occupation began. The armed forces numbered close to seven million men at the time of surrender, for example, most of whom were overseas. Repatriation of these physically and emotionally exhausted individuals, plus hundreds of thousands of civilians, carried into 1947—and for some, even later. People continued to die of malnutrition after the surrender, often in public places like railway stations where the homeless gathered, and the incidence of diseases such as tuberculosis was abnormally high. Unemployment and inflation made making ends meet a struggle for most urban families until at least 1948, and the economy remained extremely precarious through 1949. It took time for the ruins of

*91. This February 1946 self-portrait by Eisenstaedt, posing with three geishas, goes beyond the merely picturesque and exotic to suggest the feminized and often eroticized relationship between victor and vanquished that emerged almost overnight. In the process of "winning the peace," Japanese women cast a particular spell on non-Japanese males and contributed immeasurably to transforming the image of "Japan" that journalists and photographers transmitted back home. The wartime fixation on brutal Japanese fanatics—in President Truman's characterization, collective and essentially incorrigible "beasts"—was replaced by fascination with a seductive society steeped in the gentle arts.*

the burned-out cities to become replaced with new dwellings and workplaces, and dramatic recovery only arrived in the form of a war boom stimulated by the outbreak of conflict in Korea in June 1950 (prompting Yoshida to call the Korean War a "gift from the gods").

Certain reforms announced early on seemed slow to take hold, particularly at grassroots levels, and as time passed some occupation insiders held the democratization agenda up to critical public scrutiny. T. A. Bisson, an articulate left-wing participant in the implementation of economic democratization, addressed the shortcomings as well as accomplishments of the

92. Central Japan, *by Hans Mangelsdort, 1946.*

93. In a Temple Garden, *by Robert M. Graham, 1947.*

occupation in a 1949 book titled *Prospects for Democracy in Japan*, for instance, while two years later a more pessimistic American who had been involved in reforms at the local level produced a dour text titled *Failure in Japan*.[21]

At the same time, however, journalists churned out colorful and optimistic articles from the moment of MacArthur's arrival, and before long a parade of anecdotal books hit the market with jaunty titles like *The Conqueror Comes to Tea* (1946), *Star-Spangled Mikado* (1947), *MacArthur's Japan* (1948), *Fallen Sun* (1948), *Popcorn on the Ginza* (1949), *Kakemono: A Sketch Book of Postwar Japan* (1950), and *Over a Bamboo Fence* (1951, by the wife of a U.S. officer). Beginning in 1946, Earnest Hoberecht, a young UPI correspondent in Tokyo, became a minor celebrity by producing a few potboilers about love affairs between a Japanese woman and American man. Although written in English, these were immediately translated into Japanese and found an avid audience among female readers, who, it was reported, were particularly interested in his descriptions of kissing. Hoberecht's best-known offering, titled *Tokyo Romance*, had sold over two hundred thousand copies by April 1947 when *Life* magazine—even while describing it as "possibly the worst novel of modern times"—devoted a five-page photo feature to a reenactment of this "tale of interracial romance." (*Tokyo Romance* led a male Japanese reviewer to conclude that "the people of America must be intellectual midgets.")

While these various pleasantries were drawing attention, scores of thousands of postcards and letters from ordinary Japanese were pouring into U.S. occupation headquarters, addressed to MacArthur personally or his command more generally. The vast majority were positive and even effusive in tone, and more than a few were accompanied by small gifts. Japanese admirers assembled daily to see MacArthur stride out of his Tokyo headquarters at noon and walk to his limousine (he was going home for lunch and a nap), and it was only a matter of months after the surrender ceremony before higher-ranking military and civilian personnel were having their families join them for what turned out, for most of them, to be an exotic and warmly remembered interlude. Cordial and productive relations were established early on with a wide range of capable mid-level Japanese bureaucrats, and morale was generally high, at least until the reverse course was introduced. By the end of the first year, there was already a great deal of self-congratulation that the ambitious agenda of social engineering was successfully underway. By the end of the second year, virtually all of the reforms now regarded as central to Japan's emergence as a postwar democracy were in train—including not only the "five fundamental rights" but also other truly radical measures such as land reform.[22]

Discipline, moral legitimacy, well-defined and well-articulated objectives, a clear chain of command, tolerance and flexibility in policy formulation and implementation, confidence in the ability of the state to act constructively, the ability to operate abroad free of partisan politics back home, and the existence of a stable, resilient, sophisticated civil society on the receiving end of occupation policies—these political and civic virtues helped make it possible to move decisively during the brief window of a few years when defeated Japan itself was in flux and most receptive to radical change.

Much of this seemed routine and even mundane, until the absence of such attitudes and practices in occupied Iraq suddenly made them seem exceptional.

### Eyes Wide Shut: Occupying Iraq

Vignettes often epitomize grander circumstances, and in occupied Japan one of the most recurrent of such scenes involved candy. Among the photographs we have of conquerors and conquered encountering each other for the first time is a street scene of children in ragged clothing crowding around an unarmed GI who is passing out sweets, while other Japanese including adults look on from a distance. The date is September 1945 and the place Yokohama.

"Give me chocolate," one of the first English phrases Japanese children learned, has become indelibly associated with the occupation and still carries a multilayered ambiance. The killing had ended, and for good. Many GIs were friendly and kind. The Japanese were no longer the faceless, fanatical "beasts" that had to be, and deserved to be, indiscriminately incinerated. There was, moreover, more to the picture. Chocolate was also a symbol of the well-being, even the wealth, of the victors. Virtually all the children who clamored for candy and chewing gum then and for years after were malnourished, and sweets had disappeared from their lives. The Americans could (and did) provide what the nation's leaders and children's own parents could not.

Photographers accompanying the invasion forces usually dwelled on urban devastation, the awesome evidence of U.S. airborne destruction that had never been seen close-up by the bombers before. Destitute Japanese peopled these ruins, but photos only rarely dwelled on the burned or otherwise maimed; it was as if the bombs had destroyed only physical structures. In this setting, scenes of picture-perfect GIs surrounded by charming youngsters clamoring for candy reassured Americans back home about the innate gentleness of their fighting men—and more. Especially when set alongside another favorite subject of the earliest postwar foreign photographers—Japanese women—yesterday's enemy abruptly became nonthreatening. In American eyes, such images helped push aside the brutal immediate past and clarify the mission that lay ahead. The children were the future, the adults pliant, the culture exotic but fundamentally effeminate, peaceful, and receptive—and the new role of the victors was clear. They were now called on to be patient and paternalistic, teachers about democracy and agents of sweeping change.

In these resonant ways, the iconic little scene of GIs passing out chocolate was simultaneously sweet and bittersweet, as well as propagandistic. In any case it was peaceful, and in this respect a fair representation of the nation's interlude under American rule. The proclamations and preparations of Japan's leaders prior to the arrival of occupation forces were successful, and there was no violence against the foreigners when they moved in. Not a single American was killed, then or later. The street scene photographed in Yokohama just weeks after the first of the victors arrived could and would be taken at numerous other times and places during the long occupation period.[23]

Sweets also became a kind of synecdoche for occupied Iraq, albeit in this instance in an anecdotal and notorious way. Iraqi exiles assured President Bush that the invading force would be greeted with sweets and flowers, and no one at top levels seriously questioned this. Certainly no one imagined the flowering of improvised explosives instead, eventually in numbers almost beyond counting. There *was* relief and rejoicing that the dictator had been overthrown, and many Iraqis did extend warm greetings to the military forces that brought this about; but such gratefulness passed quickly. The imagined sweets and flowers survive as a dream, but in an unexpectedly disturbing way: for the Bush administration's planning—or, more accurately, negligible attention to serious planning— for postwar Iraq reflected the same dreamlike quality writ large. The planners who drafted and executed policy for postwar Japan would have found such almost romantic carelessness astonishing.[24]

The lessons that should have been drawn from postwar Japan—that occupations aimed at transforming an authoritarian society require not only clear legitimacy and enough space and time to innovate, but also administrative continuity, social cohesion, and experience in the workings of civil society on the part of the occupied—were not arcane or the special province of academic specialists. President Bush may have initially assumed that, like his own former sinful self, Iraq could and would be reborn overnight, but his advisers knew better—and then ignored what they knew. They disregarded not only forbidding social, political, and religious conditions that were taken seriously at the time of the first Gulf War, but also incisive warnings from lower-level officials as well as nongovernmental sources.

Postwar Japan was not really a serious model in anyone's thinking, but rather another example of the administration's penchant for using history ideologically. What should have been the red light of the "occupied Japan" example became instead one more green light aimed at speeding up the propaganda traffic; and leaders at the top became dazzled by their own spin.

■

IN A WORLD of less cognitive dissonance, two occupations that should have drawn attention were cases closer in time and place: the festering wound of territories occupied by Israeli settlers after 1967, and the Soviet intervention in Afghanistan from 1981 to 1989, which precipitated not merely the emergence of the mujahideen and subsequent rise of the Taliban but also the collapse of the Soviet Union. To lightly choose to invade and occupy yet another region in the Middle East in the face of such precedents, and without intense contingency planning, was hubris bordering on madness.

In theory, the war planners finally got around to formalizing thinking about post-combat challenges on January 20, 2003, two months before the invasion, when the president signed a secret directive establishing an "Iraq

Postwar Planning Office" within the Defense Department. Retired lieutenant general Jay Garner, to his surprise, was recruited a few weeks earlier to head this unit, which was rechristened Office of Reconstruction and Humanitarian Assistance (ORHA). Its mission was defined as "to help meet humanitarian, reconstruction, and administration challenges facing the country in the immediate aftermath of the combat operation"; its staffing was left largely to Garner, who prior to his recruitment had been CEO of a private company; and its projected budget was unspecified. There was nothing in these instructions about governance, and it was understood that Garner's appointment would be for a limited duration. L. Paul Bremer III, who replaced Garner and set up the more authoritative Coalition Provisional Authority (CPA) the following May, later characterized the ORHA as "a civilian rapid reaction force, a fire brigade, responsible for meeting immediate needs" that did not in fact immediately materialize, such as epidemics, food shortages, refugee flows, or damage to the oil fields by sabotage.[25]

One month after the presidential directive, Garner's team conducted what is known in army parlance as a "rock drill" at the National Defense College, attended by around two hundred individuals. The twenty-page report that emanated from this was not encouraging. "We risk letting much of the country descend into civil unrest [and] chaos whose magnitude may defeat our national strategy of a stable new Iraq," the report noted. And again: "We risk leaving behind a great unstable mess with potential to become a haven for terrorism." And again: "The conference did not take up the most basic issue: What sort of future government of Iraq do we have in mind, and how do we plan to get there?" While Garner's team was conducting its drill, officers in CENTCOM (U.S. Central Command, responsible for the Middle East and Central Asia) stationed in Doha on the Persian Gulf, on whom immediate post-invasion responsibilities would fall, issued a report pointing out that the war plans they were receiving were contradictory. Since the shock-and-awe offensive that preoccupied war planners was designed to "break all control mechanisms of the regime," they argued, it made no sense to talk about relying on Iraq's indigenous structures of command and control to ensure post-invasion stability. Absent a concrete U.S. plan for stabilization, Iraq faced the risk of disruptive activity by criminals and former regime members as well as "an influx of terrorists."[26]

These problems had been anticipated within the bureaucracy many months earlier, particularly among officials skeptical of the headlong rush to war. In September, for example, the Policy Planning Staff in the State Department finalized a fifteen-page, single-spaced memorandum titled "Reconstruction in Iraq—Lessons of the Past," based on over twenty cases of post-conflict reconstruction in the twentieth century. Unlike Afghanistan, this report argued, invading Iraq would require (in the retrospective summary words of Policy Planning Staff head Richard Haass) "a large-scale, long-term occupation." "Reconstruction in Iraq" opened with the timeworn cliché about winning the peace ("If we end up going to war with Iraq, we need to be prepared to win the ensuing peace"); called attention to deep indigenous challenges to national unity, and the need to "prevent a security vacuum after Saddam's ouster"; and offered a highly cautionary balance sheet of the baseline of "hardware" and "software" Iraq possessed that would be essential for its emergence as a stable and relatively democratic state.

In developing its analysis, the Policy Planning Staff introduced a buzz-word that was anathema in the conservative and neoconservative circles that influenced the administration's planning: *nation building*. Its country studies ran a gamut of possible post-conflict agendas ranging from "nation building lite" to "full-scale nation building," with the reconstruction of Europe and Japan after World War II being "examples par excellence" of the latter. In all likelihood, the invasion of Iraq would require "a more ambitious post-conflict reconstruction" than the administration appeared to be envisioning—even, despite obvious differences, something commensurate with what took place in Japan and a few other nation-states, such as South Korea, Greece, Italy, and postwar West Germany. (This thesis also was rendered in diagrammatic form in the report.) Easily imagined negative scenarios in a post-Saddam Iraq—a "chaotic post-conflict environment" domestically; the perils of living in a "troubled neighborhood" geographically; tensions between political players inside the country and a fractious "opposition in exile"; the absence of "recognized national figures—like Emperor Hirohito" who might provide a unifying symbol—all called for careful planning and intensive post-invasion engagement.

In conclusion, the report rejected the "MacArthur model" of occupied Japan as too costly as well as too vulnerable to being "perceived as a crude imperial grab for oil and power in the Middle East." What it endorsed instead was approaching reconstruction as a genuinely international effort involving nations, international organizations, and nongovernmental organizations—strongly led by the United States, but "operating typically under a UN mandate" and ideally headed by "an experienced and reliable non-American—and preferably non-Westerner"—with a UN title. Instead of one poison pill, the State Department's planners thus embedded two in their recipe for the occupation and reconstruction of Iraq ("nation building" and "internationalism"). Given the overwhelming fixation in the White House and Pentagon on a quick shock-and-awe, in-and-out war controlled start to finish by the United States, this was a document virtually guaranteed to sink quickly from sight. Secretary of State Colin Powell sent it to his counterparts in the Defense Department, the NSC, and the Office of the Vice President, but it never received a serious hearing in interagency deliberations.[27]

This was also the case with another, better-known initiative undertaken elsewhere in the State Department in the latter half of 2002: a "Future of Iraq Project" that eventually enlisted around a hundred mostly expatriate Iraqi experts (routinely identified as "free Iraqis") in various fields. This evolved into seventeen working groups and, by year's end, over a thousand pages of diffuse reports that might be very loosely compared to the handbooks and civil affairs guides for Japan produced under SWNCC during World War II. One report (by the working group on transitional justice) warned that "the period immediately after regime change might offer . . . criminals an opportunity to engage in acts of killing, plunder, looting, etc." Another (by the working group on transparency and anti-corruption measures) emphasized that "the people of Iraq are being promised a new future and they will expect immediate results. The credibility of the new regime and the United States will depend on how quickly these promises are translated to reality."[28]

Although the Future of Iraq Project mobilized considerable expertise, it did not pretend to offer a blueprint for occupation nor did it even succeed in offering a practical, coherent agenda. In the end, the reports became buried in the turf wars that set the State and Defense Departments in particular at loggerheads. The most "toxic" such fratricidal moment occurred in late February (the adjective is Douglas Feith's), just weeks before the invasion, when Rumsfeld abruptly rejected Jay Garner's concrete recommendations of senior U.S. advisers who could be immediately placed in Iraqi ministries to help stabilize and guide the transition to a post-Saddam government. The secretary of defense rejected the list out of hand primarily because it included too many specialists from the State Department. Even after the invasion was launched, Garner was essentially forced to fly blind. "I never knew what our plans were," he confessed after being replaced by Bremer. An inside joke had it that ORHA actually stood for "Organization of Really Hapless Americans." Black humor was irresistible, but it failed to capture the tragedy that resulted from such a stunted planning process, riddled by personal agendas and petty peevishness.[29]

As a consequence of such shortsightedness, post-invasion staffing and funding remained largely unresolved up to and through the point of invasion. Most of the debate on these matters remained in-house, but a few officers and officials—most famously General Eric Shinseki, the Army chief of staff, in late February—publicly challenged the low troop projections and low estimates of how costly the entire operation, including the endgame, would be. They were publicly rebuked for stepping out of line ("outlandish" and "wildly off the mark" was Deputy Defense Secretary Wolfowitz's response). When Bremer was appointed head of the Coalition Provisional Authority two months later, the RAND Corporation, which had a long track record of providing security studies to the government, handed him a lengthy study of previous occupations (including Japan and Germany) that concluded that ensuring security requires a ratio of twenty U.S. troops for every thousand people in the occupied country. Where Iraq was concerned, this translated into five hundred thousand troops—more than three times the number the White House planners assigned. Bremer passed this on to the president as he was leaving for his new post, and also to the secretary of defense. Although by this date occupied Baghdad was burning, he never received a response.[30]

Researchers accustomed to sifting through the old-fashioned typescript and carbon-copy documents of the World War II era encounter a conspicuous time warp when it comes to the fragmentary accessible documentation of planning "regime change" in Iraq. There are indeed cogent reports and papers. There is also an addiction to "bullet point" list making that reflects both the technical advances of a PowerPoint age and the scattershot thinking that too often accompanies this, confusing inventories of discrete "points" and queries with careful deliberation and clear conclusions. Lists, memos, working papers, and endless rounds of PowerPoint and slide presentations do not in themselves constitute coherent policy formulation. Nor do "plans" approved at high levels that in practice are ambiguous and even internally contradictory—the "bridging proposals" that Condoleezza Rice often crafted for the National Security Council to preserve an appearance of harmony and consensus. While the planning for combat operations was meticulous, the attention devoted to operational preparation for post-combat stabilization and reconstruction rarely went beyond the bullet-point level.[31]

The hoped-for scenario that ultimately guided the war-planning process was elemental to a fault: destroy Saddam's command and control, rely primarily on the Iraqi military and police for security, "bring new leadership . . . but keep the body in place" (in Rice's phrasing), hope that other nations would volunteer for postwar tasks, and withdraw most U.S. troops within two or three months. In Rumsfeld's Pentagon, the guiding mantra was to keep a light or small military "footprint" in Iraq—as already had been done in Afghanistan. As more cautious analysts in and outside the government were pointing out, however, if the despotic regime was decapitated, and looting and chaos were predictable, and it was dubious that the infrastructure would be intact, and it was uncertain where exactly new leadership would come from, and the situation in and around Iraq was already a tinderbox—then exactly who was to be primed to do what? No one knew. Garner's overwhelmed ORHA staff, at their late-February "inter-agency rehearsal and planning conference," observed that overshadowing questions of staffing and funding and what to do immediately to ensure law and order was the larger "critical issue" of civil administration: "Footprint to be small or large?"[32]

Virtually all critical accounts of preinvasion thinking about postwar Iraq, by both insiders and investigative journalists, reach the same conclusion: "There is a misconception that we were rehearsing a plan. There was no plan" (Colonel Paul Hughes, a member of the ORHA team). "There was no real plan. The thought was, you didn't need it. The assumption was that everything would be fine after the war, that they'd be happy they got rid of Saddam" (Lieutenant General Joseph Kellogg Jr., a senior member

of the Joint Chiefs of Staff). "The United States government didn't have
something ready to go the day after. It didn't have a clear-cut concept of
how it was going to proceed and that we could put in play immediately"
(Edward Walker, assistant secretary of state for Near Eastern affairs at the
time). "We did not have a well-developed theory of how best to produce
legitimate democracy in Iraq. Indeed, famously, when the war began, we
did not even have a plan" (Noah Feldman, senior constitutional adviser
to the CPA).[33]

Viewed from this larger perspective, the "occupied Japan" mirage
becomes just another small piece in the jigsaw of delusion and self-delusion
that marked the rush to war. Somehow there would simply be a happy
landing in Iraq, as there had been in Japan and Germany after World War
II—indeed, a happier landing, since the administration's projections envisioned withdrawing most troops quickly (while at the same time establishing, as in Japan and Germany, essentially permanent military bases). This
was not only faith-based policy making but also a reflection of something
else: a deep ideological aversion to the concept of social engineering or
nation building that lay at the heart of the earlier occupations of Japan
and Germany and had been central to the State Department's disregarded
September 2002 report.

The administration was trapped by rhetoric: how could one even use
the word, let alone plan the reality of an "occupation" of Iraq when what
was taking place was "liberation"? But beyond this, how could an administration whose core philosophy and core constituencies defined "freedom"
primarily in terms of unrestrained markets and optimal shrinking of the
role of the state commit itself to planning and promoting a reasonably
equitable and democratic new Iraq? Noah Feldman, who arrived in Baghdad at almost the same time Bremer did, put it succinctly. "This was an
administration that didn't want to do nation-building," he told an interviewer after returning. "Immediately on the fall of Saddam, they said, a
new government could emerge. Somewhat by magic."[34]

### Repudiating Nation Building

One of Rumsfeld's brusque habits as an administrator involved sending
staff and colleagues memos on whatever drew his attention at the moment.

These became known as "snowflakes," and the defense secretary produced between twenty and as many as one hundred of them daily. By the time he resigned following the congressional elections of 2006, the accumulated snowdrift amounted to around twenty thousand memos. One snowflake, dated March 10, 2006, reflected chagrin that opinion polls indicated two-thirds of Americans had concluded that the United States never had a plan for victory in postwar Iraq. "We need a better presentation to respond to this business that 'The Department of Defense had no plan,'" Rumsfeld fumed to his assistant secretary for public affairs. "That is just utter non-sense. We need to knock it down hard."

In a snowflake that fell earlier (in May 2004), Rumsfeld mused over whether terrorism should be redefined as a "worldwide insurgency" and went on to suggest that one of the reasons things were getting out of hand was that Muslims were lazy. Oil wealth often detached them "from the reality of the work, effort, and investment that leads to wealth for the rest of the world," he wrote. "Too often Muslims are against physical labor, so they bring in Koreans and Palestinians while their young people remain unemployed." How did this account for rising insurgency? "An unemployed population is easy to recruit to radicalism."[35]

Frivolous ideas of the latter sort usually melt before touching paper or the computer screen—but not in an administration unable to contemplate any possible relationship between its own actions and a spiraling incidence of terror and insurrection in Iraq and elsewhere. Rumsfeld's vexation at hearing the Pentagon accused of having had no postwar plans, on the other hand, is somewhat more understandable: surely there was a plan somewhere in that blizzard. Keeping a small footprint was a plan. So was supporting some sort of "Iraqi Interim Authority" dominated by exiles and "externals." President Bush actually signed such a plan emanating from the Pentagon on March 10, nine days before the invasion, after it had passed through the NSC—although this was kept secret even after U.S. forces entered Baghdad, and ultimately largely ignored by everyone, including the president, who briefed Bremer in May.[36]

Certainly, the question of post-hostilities "occupation" had been addressed on many occasions, albeit always with a double edge. On the one hand, the president's top advisers discussed the perils of foreign occupation. A State Department paper submitted to the NSC on July 25, 2002, under

*On May 1, 2003, some six weeks after launching Operation Iraqi Freedom, the Bush administration celebrated victory on the nuclear-powered aircraft carrier* Abraham Lincoln *"at sea" off San Diego. The president arrived by helicopter wearing full pilot's gear, before changing to civilian attire and announcing the end of major combat operations beneath a banner reading "Mission Accomplished." This celebration was modeled on the ceremony that took place on the battleship* Missouri *in Tokyo Bay on September 2, 1945, presided over by General MacArthur, but atmospheric similarities paled before the differences between the two occasions. The Japanese government formally surrendered beneath the* Missouri's *big guns, and representatives of all the victorious Allied powers were present. For Japan, the killing and dying was over. For Iraq, a spiral of instability, occupation, terror, and insurgency had just begun.*

*94. Japanese officials sign the instrument of surrender aboard the USS* Missouri, *September 2, 1945.*

95. *The nuclear-powered supercarrier* Abraham Lincoln *off San Diego, with the "Mission Accomplished" banner displayed on its superstructure.*

96. *This official group photograph with the carrier's deck crew nicely captures the Hollywood-style scripting of George W. Bush as a "war president."*

the title "Diplomatic Plan for the Day After," for example, warned that if the United States became depicted as an "occupying power," the result "would likely be delegitimized government; instability . . . and possibly terrorist acts—against U.S. forces." This was recycled shortly afterwards in a paper titled "Liberation Strategy for Iraq" that Rice's NSC submitted to the Principals Committee. Here the warning became "We do not want the world to view U.S. actions in Iraq as a new colonial occupation." State's September warning about the perils of imposing the "MacArthur model" in Iraq echoed this concern about avoiding any appearance of being engaged in an "imperial grab" for power and profits in the Middle East. Months later, when the machinery behind Operation Iraqi Freedom was almost in full train, the CIA raised the same warning, noting that "Iraq's history of foreign occupation . . . has left Iraqis with a deep dislike of occupiers. An indefinite foreign military occupation, with ultimate power in the hands of a non-Iraqi officer, would be widely unacceptable."[37]

At the same time, however—and often in the same discussions and reports—it was emphasized that once Saddam had been overthrown, the United States might find it necessary to remain deeply engaged in ensuring Iraqi stability, reform, and reconstruction for, not just a few months, but at least a year or more. Thus, the same August NSC paper on "Liberation Strategy for Iraq" that warned about the backlash if the invasion led to perception of the United States as "a new colonial occupation" also stated—without resolving or even highlighting the contradiction—that "the one option for regime change which gives the most confidence in achieving U.S. objectives is the employment of U.S. forces to accomplish regime change, *staying in significant numbers for many years to assist in a U.S.-led administration of the country*."[38]

These were not just practical issues that awaited resolution by pragmatic planners. They were deeply ideological, for ultimately they posed the question of the proper role of the military—and, beyond this, of the state. When Pentagon planners used the "light footprint" shorthand, they had in mind more than just the lean, high-tech military machine that mesmerized proponents of the "revolution in military affairs." This also was shorthand for avoiding deep engagement in nation building—that is, in the sort of wide-ranging and long-term social engineering that had been undertaken under military auspices in Japan and Germany. Opposition to nation building—

with all its connotations of the state playing an enormous role in development, and indeed in political, economic, and social development abroad—
was part of the agenda on which Bush ran for the presidency in 2000 (the
key speeches were in October), and Condoleezza Rice, his foreign-policy
adviser in the campaign, was instrumental in shaping this view.

Repudiation of nation building became one of the several rocks on which
post-hostilities planning was wrecked. (Whether to support Iraqi exiles
in a transitional government was another.) Two examples—an exchange
involving the national security adviser, and an eve-of-invasion speech by
the secretary of defense—graphically capture the attitude that ultimately
prevailed in ruling circles. In October 2002, several think tanks proposed
to Rice, as head of the NSC, that they work together to offer policy options
for postwar Iraq. The groups initially proposed—the Council on Foreign
Relations, Heritage Foundation, and Center for Strategic and International Studies—brought various political outlooks to the table, and Rice
responded positively. ("This is just what we need," one account quotes her
saying. "We'll be too busy to do it ourselves.") Rice was not supportive of
the Heritage Foundation, which was critical of the Iraq war idea, however,
and recommended bringing in the American Enterprise Institute (AEI)
instead. The latter was a strong supporter of the pending war.

Representatives of the think tanks met with Rice at her White House
office the following month in a meeting that marked the end rather than
the beginning of this initiative. After Leslie Gelb of the Council on Foreign Relations presented the case for laying out options for an overall post-
conflict policy, the president of the AEI intervened to chastise Rice for
even considering this. "Does Karl Rove [Bush's senior political adviser and
liaison to the political right] know about this?" Gelb quotes him saying.
"Does the president? Because I don't think they would approve. It sounds
like a nation-building exercise, and they—and you yourself, Condi—have
opposed such foolish Clintonesque policies time and again."

And that was more or less the end of it. As Gelb told a reporter later,
"They thought all those things would get in the way of going to war." The
episode survives as a snapshot of the self-proclaimed center of the world as
the war clock ran down: an influential conservative lobby that prided itself
on combining high ideals with tough-minded pragmatism assumed things
would fall into place after a decisive demonstration of military might, and

such credulity carried over to the president and his highest advisers. They were not predisposed to acknowledge that, in the real world, things fall apart more easily than they fall into place.[39]

Rumsfeld brought the administration's position to the public in an important speech titled "Beyond Nation Building" on February 14, 2003—a telling date in retrospect, for this was precisely when military and civilian officers at many levels were raising alarms about losing the peace. The occasion was an annual "salute to freedom" held at New York City's Sea, Air & Space Museum, which is housed in the decommissioned World War II battleship *Intrepid*. Rumsfeld began by unpacking the rhetorical shopping bag of now-familiar interlocking images. The *Intrepid* played a critical role in the Pacific after Pearl Harbor, he pointed out, and sailors on its deck had looked on in horror as Japanese suicide planes crashed into the U.S. fleet. The link to September 11 followed naturally: "More than a half century later this entire ship once again witnessed heroism and carnage. From the deck on a clear September morning Americans could watch with horror as suicide bombers struck again—this time crashing into the Twin Towers."

The analogies did not end there, of course. Rumsfeld described how the Americans fought back after Pearl Harbor and then went on and "helped the Japanese people rebuild from the rubble of war and establish institutions of democracy." The contemporary parallel was fighting-back in Afghanistan after September 11, and here the secretary introduced his "beyond nation building" theme. Without mentioning Japan again, he evoked Afghanistan as a model for behaving "not as a force of occupation but as a force of liberation." He spelled this out as follows: "The objective is not to engage in what some call nation building. . . . This is an important distinction. In some nation building exercises well-intentioned foreigners arrive on the scene, look at the problems and say let's fix it. This is well motivated to be sure, but it can really be a disservice . . . because when foreigners come in with international solutions to local problems, if not very careful they can create a dependency."

Lest the audience fail to understand this as a prescriptive rather than just descriptive observation, Rumsfeld proceeded to apply the lesson to "a post-Saddam Iraq." "As you know, the President has not made any decision with respect to the use of force in Iraq," he observed with a wink-wink coyness characteristic of administration pronouncements, "but if he were to do so that principle would hold true. Iraq belongs to the Iraqis and we do not aspire to own it or run it. We hope to eliminate Iraq's weapons of mass destruction and to help liberate the Iraqi people from oppression. . . . Stay as long as necessary and to leave as soon as possible." The audience greeted this with applause.[40]

These remarks were delivered a month after Rumsfeld had asserted decisive control over postwar planning. That the Pentagon assumed top place in the chain of command responsible for postwar Iraq was not in itself exceptional; the Joint Chiefs of Staff had performed the same role in the occupation of Japan. What was exceptional was that this affirmation of authority amounted to a petty victory in interdepartmental turf wars but was not followed by a concerted effort to exercise tight control over post-invasion planning. Although Rumsfeld was a notorious micromanager, postwar stabilization and civil affairs did not engage him to anywhere remotely near the degree that war planning did. The war machinery had been set in motion. An almost catatonic fixation on unleashing forces of massive destruction ruled the day, fully in keeping with the traditional "American way of war." And a cadre of planners addicted to concepts like shock and awe, system paralysis, decapitation, and regime change somehow managed to persuade themselves, Congress, the media, and most of the public that the results would be sweets and flowers rather than a truly decapitated, paralyzed, dysfunctional system.

The conspicuous loser in this bureaucratic infighting was the State Department, with its sprawling and inchoate "Future of Iraq Project." This may have been a small loss, but the practical as well as ideological dimension of the conflict was not buried among insiders at the time. This particular State Department project, for example, stated bluntly that "Iraq is not Afghanistan; U.S. should make commitment to Iraq like Japan and Germany."[41]

## Baghdad Burning

This was the situation Bremer confronted when he flew into Baghdad on May 12 to replace Garner's ORHA with the Coalition Provisional Authority. Before departing Washington, Bremer received briefings and papers from various military and civilian agencies but found the president and his national security team still without a comprehensive agenda. In his

97. *Iraqis at a rally in Baghdad demonstrate, in vain, against the terrorism that erupted in the wake of Operation Iraqi Freedom and establishment of the U.S.-led Coalition Provisional Authority, December 10, 2003.*

98. *Sunni Muslims protest the American presence after Friday prayers at Baghdad's Abu Hanifa mosque, 2003. The Arabic similarly reads, "Iraq Is Our Iraq, Not the Americans'."*

*99. Iraqis celebrate a roadside bomb that killed three American soldiers, January 17, 2004. The effectiveness of these "improvised explosive devices" (IEDs) against the massive might and high-tech sophistication of the U.S. military and its coalition allies—coupled with indigenous opposition to being occupied by the erstwhile "liberation" forces—stunned U.S. war planners.*

*100. Masked militants affiliated with the Mahdi Army loyal to the Shiite cleric Muqtada al-Sadr prepare for battle with U.S. forces in Baghdad's Sadr City, August 2003.*

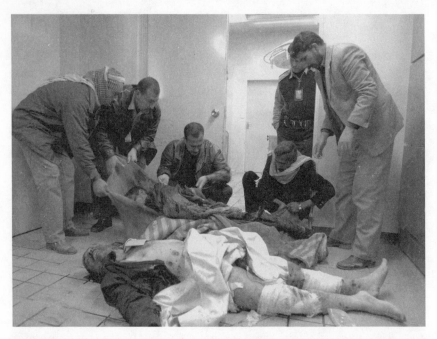

101. *Relatives gather to identify an Iraqi policeman killed by a suicide bomber in Kirkuk, February 23, 2004.*

102. *Mourners in Baghdad carry coffins for three slain Sunni Arab members of a committee working on a new constitution, July 20, 2005. The banner in the background reads, "No to federalism."*

loyal and courteous way, he later emphasized that the president's "direction was quite clear: that we were going to try to set the Iraqis on a path to democratic government and help them rebuild their country." Bremer immediately followed this caveat, however, by acknowledging that "none of us at that time" had any idea "what that would entail. The general guidance I had from the president and others was, 'Get over there and give us your recommendations.' "[42]

It was only at this late date that the word "occupation" became openly operative in official U.S. circles. (The formal moment was UN Resolution 1483, which was passed by the Security Council on May 22, 2003, and recognized the United States and United Kingdom "as occupying powers under unified command.") Bremer's first sight of Baghdad as his plane descended gave him the opening sentence of his later memoir: "Baghdad was burning." He hit the tarmac with nothing in his briefcase remotely comparable to the Potsdam Declaration or the detailed "Initial Post-Surrender Policy for Japan" that MacArthur received before setting foot in Japan, but this did not stop him from comparing (and contrasting) his assignment to the challenge the general had faced so many years before. "Yes, we're an 'occupying power,' " Bremer declared in concluding his first staff meeting on the evening of his arrival. "No getting around that." It was necessary to keep in mind "the relevant lessons of Germany and Japan," he told the exhausted team of ORHA workers and others who greeted him, and foremost among these was that democracy must rest on "a solid civil society . . . political parties, a free press, an independent judiciary, open accountability for public funds."[43]

Two months later, in July, as living conditions deteriorated and insurrection accelerated all around them, the CPA cobbled together a fifty-seven-page "Strategic Plan" for Iraq establishing benchmarks to be reached at different points within the next year. Bremer traveled to Washington to present this to the National Security Council at a meeting in the White House Situation Room, and was pleased with the response. "It's a good paper, Bremer!" Bush told him. "Your folks are sure thorough."[44]

The Iraqi press began calling Bremer the "MacArthur of Baghdad" within a few days, and Bremer himself compared his prerogatives to "the viceregal responsibilities" of MacArthur in Japan (and MacArthur's counterpart General Lucius Clay in occupied Germany). Iraq's new viceroy did not hesitate to tell recalcitrant Iraqi officials who balked at his orders that "I *am* the Iraqi government for now." And he was. The orders designating him administrator of the CPA that he received from the Pentagon on May 9 empowered him with "all executive, legislative, and judicial functions" in Iraq. Liberation had become foreign occupation, and occupation abruptly had turned into nation building of a sort—even as gunfire crackled outside the CPA's headquarters. "Liberated" Iraq was now deprived by fiat of sovereignty; and although this was nominally restored on June 28, 2004, when Bremer left and the CPA was dissolved, little changed thereafter. Occupation forces did not leave. The Americans remained ensconced—almost literally imprisoned—in the grotesque urban garrison known as the Green Zone. Violence and enormous human suffering continued.[45]

By almost all popular measures of evaluation, occupied Iraq became the antipode of occupied Japan—a spectacle of violence rather than peace, irreparable wounds and hatreds rather than healing and recovery, diminished rather than enhanced American security and prestige, overall failure as opposed to success. This is too simple, however. The reform and reconstruction projects eventually introduced under the CPA bore certain superficial resemblances to what transpired under MacArthur in Japan, and the occupation of Japan was hardly an unblemished exercise of "vice-regal" authority. Convergence "of a sort" occurred in many areas that are generally neglected by scholars, pundits, and policy makers—including the use and abuse of law and justice.

Bremer did not choose to dwell on the fundamental ideological differences that distinguished the social engineers of the mid-twentieth century from the reluctant, ill-prepared, conservative, and often profit-motivated private-sector "nation builders" he suddenly found himself overseeing. Nor did he pause to analyze the more disturbing ways in which his supreme command may have converged with or diverged from what took place in occupied Japan. He did, however, acknowledge that Iraq was not Japan. After reflecting a moment about his "MacArthur in Baghdad" sobriquet in the Arab press, he responded, "I'd settle for MacArthur's problems. Conditions weren't this complicated for him."[46]

# CONVERGENCE OF A SORT: LAW, JUSTICE, AND TRANSGRESSION

## *Jiggering the Law*

Almost exactly two years after the invasion of Iraq, the Defense Department released a major document—*The National Defense Strategy of the United States of America*—that contained a striking statement about U.S. "vulnerabilities" in the "changing security environment." "Our strength as a nation," this declared, "will continue to be challenged by those who employ a strategy of the weak using international fora, judicial processes, and terrorism."[47]

At first glance, international forums and judicial processes may seem to be odd bedfellows to pair with terrorism. In fact, this pairing reflected concerns that troubled conservatives long before September 11—challenges sometimes addressed in and outside the Pentagon under the rubric of "lawfare." After the Watergate scandal and Vietnam War, the lawfare argument maintained, political leaders, intelligence agencies, and military forces had become increasingly entangled in a web of laws promoted both domestically and internationally by human-rights groups and lawyers devoted to (as the critics saw it) the "criminalization of warfare." Law itself had become a battleground.

The fervent endeavors to strengthen presidential powers under the name of a "unitary executive" that peaked in the Bush administration reflected this gnawing perception of becoming "strangled by law." Predictably, 9-11 and the threat of future terrorist attacks propelled these concerns to almost frantic levels. The response—as expedited by the informal "War Council" of ultraconservative lawyers who secretly drafted the initial Office of Legal Counsel (OLC) opinions subsequently known as "torture memos"—was extreme, and ultimately left an indelible stain on both the presidency and the reputation of the United States. When Jack Goldsmith, a conservative lawyer who supported strengthening presidential power and endorsed declaring "war" on terror and denying "POW" status to prisoners, became head of the OLC in October 2003, he was distraught to find that these classified opinions were "deeply flawed: sloppily reasoned, overbroad, and incautious in asserting extraordinary constitutional authorities on behalf of the President." Two months after assuming his post, Goldsmith recommended that the critical memos governing interrogation be withdrawn and reframed, but before this was done the ground shifted. The notorious photographs from Abu Ghraib prison made their way onto the Internet (in April 2004); the denial of habeas corpus to prisoners held at Guantánamo became a global scandal; "rendition" of terror suspects to countries where they would be brutally interrogated likewise became a scandal, as did the revelation of invasive electronic surveillance domestically; and some of the secret torture memos were leaked to the public (beginning in June 2004). It was too late to repair the damage; and, indeed, mostly too late to reel in the practices themselves.[48]

Jiggering the law is hardly new under the sun, and also took place at various levels in American and Allied conduct in World War II and its immediate aftermath. Legal constraints were looser then. Such manipulations and abuses received little negative publicity, and perhaps most decisively, thoroughgoing victory over atrocious enemies all but erased such transgressions from memory. By contrast, the many miscarriages of the war on terror made the Bush administration vulnerable to criticism of the sort that victors escape. So did the uncontrollable digital world of exposé, scandal, propaganda, polemics, and principled dissent. And so did the particularly arrogant swagger with which the Bush White House pursued its "unitary executive" vision of an imperial presidency free from external restraints, especially where national security and international affairs were concerned.

President Bush's coarse manner of expressing himself only served to deepen the impression of contempt for the law. Typical was his exclamation to staff gathered in the White House emergency operations center on the evening of the September 11 attacks, as recounted by the NSC's counterterrorism expert Richard Clarke: "I don't care what the international lawyers say, we are going to kick some ass." However precisely accurate this quotation may be, it was pitch-perfect in capturing the scorn for international treaties and the like that already had preceded 9-11, and the disdain for legal restraints that became even more intense thereafter. It was also pitch-perfect in capturing a disturbingly sophomoric response to an extraordinarily complex challenge.[49]

Even among a growing chorus of domestic critics, it usually was taken for granted that such reckless regard for the law was aberrant—a departure from the respect for rule of law that is supposedly a bedrock of American democracy. The perception of egregiousness was accurate, but it was not accurate to assume that America and its allies had been scrupulous in respecting human rights, civil rights, and international law in earlier conflicts. It took over four decades, for example, for Congress and the executive branch to acknowledge that the incarceration of some 110,000 Japanese Americans after Pearl Harbor was a perversion of justice. (President Reagan signed the legislation apologizing for this in 1988.) Other areas in which established law was disregarded, circumvented, bent, or arbitrarily and substantially revised in conjunction with World War II remain largely ignored.

Like the legally questionable occupation of Iraq, the sweeping reform agendas imposed earlier on Germany and Japan disregarded existing conventions governing post-conflict occupations. What became an example of successful "demilitarization and democratization" for many observers, then and decades later, had no precedent in law or practice.

Similarly, the war-crimes trials conducted in Nuremberg and Tokyo and at scores of little-remembered military proceedings against thousands of less prominent former Axis enemies involved charges and procedures that have left a contested legacy. On the one hand, these trials introduced idealistic norms of war responsibility and accountability—in ways, indeed, that have returned to haunt the United States. At the same time, the war-crimes tribunals were riddled with procedural flaws and vulnerable to the accusation that they amounted to hypocritical exercises in "victor's justice."

In yet another direction, in this instance remotely comparable to the Bush administration's legalistic subterfuges and subsequent maltreatment of prisoners, the leading nations that claimed victory in Asia in 1945—including France, the Netherlands, and the Soviet Union along with the United States, United Kingdom, and China—all engaged in one form or another of abuse of surrendered forces. Hundreds of thousands of Japanese were denied swift repatriation, often for extended periods and sometimes fatally. Many were forced to perform labor for the victors, and tens of thousands were enlisted to participate in China's civil war or the colonial struggles against indigenous independence movements that followed the collapse of Japan's short-lived occupation of Southeast Asia.

These earlier abuses do not replicate the Bush administration's evasions of the law, or mitigate them, but rather help place such transgression in a larger historical frame—and a larger, confounding milieu in which cynicism, pragmatism, "realism," and even professed idealism may politicize the law and obstruct just practices.

## Legal and Illegal Occupation

Before World War II entered its endgame, the United States and Britain declared that the enormity of Axis crimes was sufficient justification for imposing sweeping changes within the enemy nations once they had been defeated. This was the rationale behind the concept of unconditional surrender announced by Roosevelt and Churchill in 1943 and adhered to in the German and Japanese surrenders. Briefly put, unconditional surrender had no legal precedent, and the extensive reform imposed in the Allied occupations that followed likewise had (in the words of an American scholar writing in 1949) "no place in accepted law on the subject and was strictly forbidden." A standard text on occupation law published several decades later concurs that the acceptance of unconditional surrender "was critical to the Allies because it was generally accepted that the law of occupation did not condone the measures the Allies intended to implement in both Germany and Japan."[50]

The central provision in accepted law in this regard was Article 43 in the Hague Regulations of 1907, which reads in full as follows: "The authority of the legitimate power having in fact passed into the hands of the occupant, the latter shall take all the measures in his power to restore, and ensure, as far as possible, public order and safety, while respecting, unless absolutely prevented, the laws in force in the country." In practice, "the laws in force" in defeated Japan, including the constitution as well as civil and penal codes, were subjected to wholesale revision, while the reform agenda in its entirety went far beyond anything previously deemed permissible to a foreign occupant—and certainly far beyond what was required to ensure public order and safety. The Hague Regulations also stipulated that property must be respected by the occupant—a provision that was severely challenged in occupied Japan by the land reform, dissolution of family-held *zaibatsu* holding companies, confiscation of property owned by organizations deemed to have been militaristic or ultranationalistic, termination of pensions to individuals purged as militarists, and the requisitioning of private residences and office buildings for use by occupation personnel.[51]

The legal basis of the occupation of Japan was, in fact, addressed confidentially in some detail within the U.S. government, and the legal limbo of the draconian policies initially adopted was, if not publicly broadcast, at least publicly acknowledged. An unusually frank two-volume tome on the "political reorientation of Japan" prepared by MacArthur's staff and published by the U.S. government in 1949, while the occupation was still underway, observed that the occupation "presented a new problem in international law": the surrender was "total"; the Japanese government remained in power; the goal was to "ensure a peaceful Japan" once foreign forces were withdrawn; and—here frankly acknowledged and fully quoted—Article 43 of the "Hague rules" explicitly prohibited altering the basic domestic laws of the occupied nation. "It has very generally been accepted that the military occupant exercises military authority over the occupied country but does not have full rights of sovereignty," this analysis continued. "How far the total surrender, made with full knowledge of the intentions of the victors, would operate to change this rule has never been established."[52]

In Japan, as in Iraq decades later, establishing respect for "rule of law" was a cardinal tenet in rationalizing democratic reform. This extended, insofar as public relations was concerned, to international law. Thus, in mid-December 1945, four months into the occupation, the Public Relations Office of the Supreme Commander of the Allied Powers assured the Japanese that "the civilian population will be kept free from all unwarranted interference with their individual liberty and property rights. . . . The occupation forces will observe the obligations imposed upon them by international law and the rules of land warfare." When push came to shove in the exercise of actual authority, however, the latter piety in particular was really honored only in the breach. As previously noted, the decisive instructions in this regard had been submitted to MacArthur by Truman three months earlier, on September 6, and explicitly affirmed that "our relations with Japan do not rest on a contractual basis, but on an unconditional surrender. Since your sovereignty is supreme, you will not entertain any question on the part of the Japanese as to its scope."[53]

■

THERE WAS NO precise counterpart in Iraq to the wartime pronouncements and post-hostilities documents the Americans used to legitimize their nation building in Japan: no principle of unconditional surrender, no formal terms and signed understandings equivalent to the Potsdam Declaration and Instrument of Surrender. In the weeks after Operation Iraqi Freedom was launched, U.S. authorities still refused to acknowledge they were engaged in a "military occupation"; and even when the United States and United Kingdom designated themselves the Coalition Provisional Authority and solicited the support of the UN Security Council (on May 8, 2003), they avoided speaking of themselves explicitly as "occupying powers."

It was not until the Security Council responded with the enabling Resolution 1483 on May 22, two full months after the invasion, that the "occupying powers" phrase was first formally used—and, as shepherded through the United Nations by the two powers, the resolution only served to make the legal waters more rather than less opaque and problematic. It began by *"reaffirming* the sovereignty and territorial integrity of Iraq," and then proceeded—astonishingly and foolishly in the view of some legal scholars—to emphasize that occupation authorities must "comply fully with their obligations under international law including in particular the Geneva Conventions of 1949 and the Hague Regulations of 1907."[54]

In the appraisal of Eyal Benvenisti, author of a major text on the international law of occupation, Resolution 1483 awakened "from its slumber" a body of laws that had been formulated in the nineteenth and early twentieth century, and "required that politicians and lawyers revive an old doctrine that in the last half century almost reached the state of desuetude." In the view of David Scheffer, who served as the Clinton administration's first ambassador-at-large for war-crimes issues, this ill-conceived attempt to use the United Nations to essentially confirm Anglo-American dominance over that international body where Iraq was concerned invited legal blowback. Scheffer, who supported the need for "bold and transformational control" over post-Saddam Iraq, concluded that by assigning the responsibilities of being "occupying powers" to the United States and Britain while affirming the applicability of the Hague and Geneva laws, Resolution 1483 actually laid the two occupying powers open to no less than twelve different areas of potential "civil liability or criminal culpability under occupation laws."[55]

Scheffer, focusing purely on legal issues, was taken aback by the carelessness with which these consequential matters had been "left on the shelf" during the long period of U.S. war planning—and then, like so much else pertinent to post-invasion order and security, and post-Saddam "nation building," were belatedly addressed so incompetently. This sort of criticism never arose in a public way when the American-led occupiers in Japan were gliding over the "Hague rules" like skaters. Still, the cavalier ethos of seizing sovereign power even while affirming respect for existing law including the Hague Regulations was comparable. Thus, despite Resolution 1483's reassuring opening words about respecting the sovereignty of Iraq, when CPA head Paul Bremer convened his first meeting with newly appointed Iraqi ministers four months later (on September 16), he more or less reprised Truman's message to MacArthur almost sixty years earlier. "Like it or not," he told the new ministers, "the Coalition is still the sovereign power here." And so it remained, with crippling political and psychological consequences, for another nine months.[56]

## War Crimes and the Ricochet of Victor's Justice

In Japan, as later in Iraq, the legality of the occupation was at best of passing interest, since disregard of the Hague Regulations quickly became a *fait accompli* and the defeated nation eventually did regain sovereignty. More controversial was the prosecution of so-called Class A war criminals in Tokyo—the counterpart to Nuremberg formally known as the International Military Tribunal for the Far East. These celebrated trials of German and Japanese civilian and military leaders had several goals, apart from simply punishing men who had unleashed horrendous aggression and atrocity. One long-term objective concerned the historical record: the trials provided a vehicle for assembling a documentary and testimonial record of such breadth and detail that future nationalists and apologists would be hard pressed to deny the transgressions committed by Nazi Germany and imperial Japan.

The second, more compelling goal was nothing less than to establish a new realm of international law that would hold individual leaders accountable for egregious acts of state—and, thus, ideally deter future acts of aggression. Such "deterrence" thinking amounted to a nonviolent complement to the earlier argument among strategic planners that using the atomic bombs would help stimulate postwar arms control and prevent future wars. Like unconditional surrender, this activist conception of the war-crimes trials entailed ignoring precedent—and, it followed, indicting defendants for transgressions that did not exist as crimes when they were allegedly committed. Holding individual leaders accountable for acts of state before an international tribunal was itself precedent-setting. The German and Japanese trials also introduced two new categories of war crimes—against "peace" and against "humanity." For obvious reasons, the specific itemization of Axis war crimes, including violation of established regulations and conventions, excluded acts such as the deliberate bombardment of civilian populations.[57]

"Crimes against humanity" was introduced at Nuremberg primarily to address the Holocaust, and did not play a significant role in the Tokyo tribunal. "Crimes against peace," on the other hand, was translated into conspiracy to wage aggressive war and applied to everything the Japanese had done abroad militarily since 1928. The "conspiracy" charge also was unprecedented in international law, and amounted to a grossly simplistic explanation of the upheaval in Asia (and within Japan itself) from just before the Great Depression to the end of the war seventeen years later. No serious historian of prewar and wartime Japan today would endorse this argument.

Like Nuremberg, the Tokyo tribunal involved a great deal of juridical idealism. This trial of twenty-eight high-ranking defendants (twenty-five by the trial's end) dragged on from mid-1946 to the end of 1948, and the defense actually was allowed to take more time than the prosecution to present its case. Nonetheless, these proceedings predictably opened the door to charges of illegality, double standards, and victor's justice that never have ceased to outrage Japanese conservatives and nationalists. Imperial Japan's military operations were undertaken in response to Western imperialism as well as to "chaos and Communism" in China that threatened Japan's essential economic interests there, these critics insist, employing the argument of self-defense common to defenders of aggression everywhere. The rallying cries of liberating Asia from Western imperialism and colonialism were sincere, and not merely propaganda masking naked self-interest. And where atrocities occurred, these largely reflected the unplanned excesses that take place on all sides in all wars. They were—again in a formulaic argument familiar to most zealots and patriots when explaining away their own crimes—aberrations.

There was no real counterpart in Iraq to the war-crimes trials of Germans and Japanese—and no corresponding attempt to use such a platform to subpoena documents and assemble testimony that would help establish a dense and optimally comprehensive record of the transgressions of the regime now placed in the dock. The disorderly trial and execution of Saddam Hussein focused on a fragment of the dictator's crimes and amounted, in the end, to little more than political theater.[58]

At the same time, however, there was another side to the Tokyo-trial

*103. Defendants at the International Military Tribunal for the Far East sit in front of a rotating display of huge maps depicting the Japanese empire between 1928 and the surrender. Beyond introducing new standards for prosecuting war crimes, another objective of these elaborate proceedings was to compile a detailed documentary and testimonial record of Japan's military expansion and "crimes against peace."*

proceedings that did resonate, however obliquely, in the wake of the U.S.-led invasion of Iraq—namely, the ricochet effect of the premise that individual leaders can be held responsible for conspiring to engage in aggression. Many U.S. military officers in Japan, like MacArthur's intelligence chief Major General Charles Willoughby, privately opposed the Class A trials as "hypocrisy" and pointed out that the United States would have to make sure it won all its future wars. MacArthur himself was not so categorical, but also opposed the general indictment of Japan's leaders for "responsibility for war" and confidentially confided that he would have preferred a short trial focusing on the Pearl Harbor attack. In the Iraq invasion, as with the Vietnam War earlier, these broad charges that the American-led prosecution promoted so vigorously in Tokyo—conspiracy, aggression, holding individual leaders to account for unprovoked wars of

*104. The trial of Saddam Hussein and a small number of codefendants, conducted by the Iraqi Interim Government beginning in October 2005, ended in Saddam's execution on December 30, 2006. Proceedings focused on a few charges, most notably a massacre that took place in 1982. By contrast to the elaborate postwar trials of German and Japanese leaders, Saddam's trial was exceedingly modest in both setting and substance. It neither set nor confirmed high standards in jurisprudence, nor did it make the slightest pretense at establishing a thoroughgoing record of the dictator's deeds.*

choice—came home to Washington. So did other postwar trials of the Germans and Japanese that involved atrocities and conventional war crimes like the abuse of prisoners.[59]

∎

APART FROM THE showcase Class A trials, and long consigned to the black hole of memory, well over five thousand other Japanese officers and enlisted men were prosecuted for war crimes in "Class B" and "Class C" military tribunals conducted by the Allied victors in scores of locales throughout Asia. (The British, French, Dutch, and Americans all held such local trials in their restored or former colonial possessions.) Although Class C trials involved a relatively small number of high-ranking officers charged with responsibility for atrocities committed by troops under their command, they left an enduring mark on postwar military law. This derived primarily from the earliest and most famous of these military commissions, convened by the Americans in Manila and ending in the conviction of General Tomoyuki Yamashita. Yamashita was charged with having "unlawfully disregarded and failed to discharge his duty as commander to control the operations of the members of his command, permitting them to commit brutal atrocities and other high crimes against people of the United States and its allies and dependencies, particularly the Philippines." He was found guilty on December 7, 1945, and sentenced to death—the month and day could hardly have been serendipitous—and both General MacArthur and the U.S. Supreme Court upheld the correctness of the Manila proceedings, the latter by a majority rather than unanimous vote.[60]

Yamashita, who earned the sobriquet "Tiger of Malaya" after leading Japanese forces to victory against a numerically superior British force in Singapore in the opening months of the war, had been assigned command of the beleaguered Japanese military in the Philippines in early October 1944, only weeks before the Americans launched their offensive to retake the islands. The atrocities perpetuated against Filipino "guerrillas" and civilians between then and June 1945—the period covered in the Manila trial—were indisputably appalling. Some 25,000 civilians were slaughtered in Batangas province; 8,000 in Laguna province; and another 8,000 men, women, and children in Manila. More disputable, and the focus of the military trial, was Yamashita's responsibility for these crimes, which he claimed to have neither sanctioned nor even known about—a defense that prosecutors challenged with an indictment covering 123 particular charges. The prosecution argued, among other things, that while he was not personally present where the bulk of atrocities took place, Yamashita's communications with Manila remained intact until June 1945; that he personally endorsed the summary execution of some two thousand "guerrillas"; and that he actually resided for a period in close proximity to some of the notorious camps holding Allied POWs.

None of the five U.S. officers who comprised the military commission that sat in judgment in Manila was a lawyer, and legal critics argue that this "lay court" produced a misleading and "ill-worded opinion" that required clarification in subsequent war-crimes trials conducted by the Allied powers. Still, the judgment in the Yamashita trial was reasonably clear in summation. "The Commission concludes," it read, "(1) that a series of atrocities

*105. General Tomoyuki Yamashita, with his American defense attorneys, at the Manila military tribunal where he was found guilty of responsibility for atrocities committed by troops under his command. Yamashita was executed on February 23, 1946.*

and other high crimes have been committed by members of the Japanese armed forces under your command against people of the United States, their allies and dependencies throughout the Philippine Islands; that they were not sporadic in nature but in many cases were methodically supervised by Japanese officers and noncommissioned officers; (2) that during the period in question you failed to provide effective control of your troops as was required by the circumstances." Where later critics found this opinion wanting was its failure to make explicit that there was ample evidence that, contrary to his defense, Yamashita had knowledge of the high crimes that took place during his many months as military governor of the Philippines as well as commander of Japanese forces there.[61]

Although the charge of "command responsibility" was not unprecedented, it was rare in war-related legal practice until this time, making the "Yamashita precedent" noteworthy as a template for subsequent war-crimes proceedings against accused German as well as Japanese officers. In the Tokyo war-crimes trials, which did not get underway until four months after Yamashita's execution, "count 54" in the prosecution's indictment involved having "ordered, authorized, and permitted" conventional war crimes, while "count 55" picked up the Yamashita indictment of "deliber-

ately and recklessly" disregarding "their legal duty to take adequate steps
to secure the observance and prevent breaches" of the recognized laws and
customs of war. Five "Class A" Japanese defendants were found guilty of
the former count, and seven of the latter.[62]

Whatever the shortcomings of the loosely crafted Manila opinion,
the "Yamashita precedent" became postwar shorthand for the basic legal
principle of command responsibility. This received renewed media attention after the U.S. invasion of Afghanistan and the incarceration without trial or redress of "unlawful enemy combatants" following 9-11, and
vastly greater attention after the exposure of abuses in Abu Ghraib prison
was accompanied by accusations (and, subsequently, clear documentation)
that responsibility extended all the way up the line of command to the
White House, Justice Department, Pentagon, and Central Intelligence
Agency. The Yamashita case also calls attention to some of the same provisions in the 1907 Hague Regulations that are pertinent to legal debates
concerning the occupations of Japan in 1945 and Iraq in 2003—for as
military governor of the Japan-occupied Philippines, Yamashita was found
derelict and criminally negligent in having failed to maintain public order
and safety in the territory over which his authority as occupant extended.
Abuses that took place under his command also violated the Geneva Conventions pertaining to prisoners of war.[63]

THE GENEVA CONVENTIONS pertinent when the war in Asia ended dated
from 1929. The Japanese government had signed these provisions at the
time, but in 1934—under the influence of the military establishment—the
Japanese parliament refused to ratify them. Humane and solicitous treatment of prisoners, the argument went, was at variance with the military
codes and discipline the Imperial Army and Navy imposed on their own
fighting men where the disgrace of capture or surrender was concerned.
Japanese officials subsequently offered assurance that, although not formally bound by the 1929 convention, the government "would apply it,
*mutatis mutandis*, to all American, Australian, British, Canadian and New
Zealand prisoners of war"—but this was mere verbiage. In the eyes of
Japan's Caucasian antagonists, nothing was more revealing of the barbar-
ity of the Japanese than their abuse of Anglo POWs—and, framed legally,

nothing made this clearer than their disdain for the spirit as well as letter of the Geneva provisions governing humane treatment of prisoners.[64]

The most extensive and least remembered postwar trials of Japanese addressed conventional (Class B) war crimes, and a large percentage of these cases involved abuse of Caucasian prisoners. All told, the total number of individuals indicted for B and C crimes combined was around 5,700, of whom an estimated 920 were executed (including a number of Korean and Formosan prison guards). It is indisputable that the Japanese military behaved atrociously and that POWs in certain camps were treated abominably. It is also clear that many of these local trials were hasty and arbitrary. Low-level prison guards were convicted, while their higher-ups escaped; defendants faced hearings conducted in languages other than Japanese; as in all military trials, evidence was admitted that would not be acceptable in civilian courts. On the other hand, just as in the Tokyo tribunal and lower-level command-responsibility trials, defendants were provided counsel. Unlike in the Class A trials or Yamashita case, moreover, a number of convictions were overturned on appeal.

Miscarriages of justice occurred, just as with individuals arrested as terrorists or "unlawful enemy combatants" in the wake of September 11—but the stronger impression that still comes through from the B and C trials is the gruesomeness of Japanese atrocities and the dehumanization that did take place in the war theaters, occupied areas, and prison camps. These were war crimes plain and simple, and as appalling to contemplate as the atrocities perpetuated by Al Qaeda and other terrorists, as well as in the insurgency, religious violence, and plain thuggery that took place in post-invasion Iraq and Afghanistan.

As so often, however, there is another side to this. After it became unmistakably clear how the Bush administration was actually treating prisoners under the euphemisms of "unlawful enemy combatants," "enhanced interrogation," "rendition," and the like, the U.S. and Allied prosecution of Japanese crimes against POWs in particular took on a haunting, sometimes taunting aspect. Once again, current events drew attention to Japan's wartime past. Again—as with the boomerang of "Pearl Harbor" as code for a war of choice—this cast unwelcome light on the conduct of the war on terror and the American practice, more generally, of double standards.

There are obvious differences: Japanese atrocities took place overall on

*106. The release of photographs of U.S. torture at Baghdad's Abu Ghraib prison in the spring of 2004 prompted this wall painting by the Iraqi artist Salah Edine Sallat. His hooded Statue of Liberty with her hand on an electrical switchbox stands alongside the most famous of the torture images, of a hooded prisoner connected to electric wires.*

a greater scale, and many prisoners abused and killed by the Japanese were not regarded as potential sources of critical information. But torture and other inhumane treatment of prisoners then, unlike later when it became Americans and their supporters flagrantly engaged in such acts, were called by their names and denounced unequivocally. "Water torture" aimed at obtaining information was one of these practices, and a very small number of Japanese were indicted and convicted for this. The moral outrage provoked by brutal treatment of prisoners was much more general in nature, however, as conveyed in Truman's statement after Hiroshima and Nagasaki that the atomic bombs were used "against those who have starved and beaten and executed American prisoners of war." This, it was argued at the time, was integral to what distinguished civilized people from barbarians, and the democratic nations from their Axis adversaries.[65]

SOME FORTY-FIVE YEARS after the World War II war-crimes trials ended, the Dutch jurist B. V. A. Röling, who sat on the bench in Tokyo

107. *An Iranian couple walks past giant murals on a highway near Tehran reproducing two of the most notorious Abu Ghraib torture photographs. The Persian script reads, "Today Iraq."*

as its youngest and perhaps most thoughtful member, acknowledged that "it is true that both trials [in Nuremberg and Tokyo] had sinister origins; that they were misused for political purposes; and that they were somewhat unfair. But they also made a very constructive contribution to the outlawing of war and the world is badly in need of a fundamental change in the political and legal position of war in international relations." The Tokyo trial was thus "a kind of milestone in legal development, and the attitude on which the judgments were based is absolutely necessary in an atomic age."[66]

Much the same attitude was reflected in the emphasis on command responsibility highlighted by the Yamashita trial and refined in a small number of subsequent trials of German and Japanese officers. A lengthy analysis published in the U.S. Army's *Military Law Review* in 1973 thus closes with the summary observation that "out of the ashes of World War II there rose a desire to further define the responsibility of a commander for war crimes committed by his subordinates, a responsibility recognized by the earliest military scholars." The principle is complex, as this detailed analysis demonstrates—but also severe and exacting where "wanton, immoral disregard" of the acts of subordinates is demonstrable.

Military law makes clear that a nation's leaders must be held to the highest standards of duty and responsibility; and where this is wanting and reckless acquiescence in such behavior prevails, "criminal responsibility" must be attached to such disregard.[67]

The 1973 study was published after the My Lai massacre in Vietnam drew renewed attention to the issue of command responsibility. (My Lai involved the mass murder of hundreds of South Vietnamese civilians by U.S. troops in 1968, and provoked worldwide outrage when exposed in 1969.) Viewed in retrospect, this judicious analysis by a military lawyer stands chronologically roughly halfway between General Willoughby's whispered criticism of the war-crimes trials of Japanese and the war on terror that followed September 11; and it resonates with both.

Willoughby warned that the United States had to make sure it won all its future wars, which it failed to do in Vietnam and again in Iraq. "My Lai" became a graphic metaphor or trope for infamous, criminal behavior in the Vietnam War—much as "Nanking," "Pearl Harbor," and "Bataan" or "our prisoners of war" did vis-à-vis the Japanese in the earlier war, and "Guantánamo," "Abu Ghraib," and "waterboarding" did vis-à-vis U.S. war conduct after 9-11. When Willoughby called attention to Allied "hypocrisy," he was able to keep such heretical thoughts private. Such controls began to disappear in the 1960s and 1970s, when television reportage came of age, and by the twenty-first century had been almost completely blown away by the revolution in cyber-communication—and, as the conservative critics would emphasize, by the rising influence of international law and the human-rights and civil-rights movements.

Despite the revolution in communications, however, and despite "lawfare" and the legions of lawyers the military and federal bureaucracy have enlisted to address this, it is still sobering to observe how much did not change between the 1970s and the war on terror. For all practical purposes, the legal precedents and principles the United States itself promoted after World War II were repudiated almost as soon as the Nuremberg and Tokyo trials wound down. It was acceptable that the United States and its allies sit in judgment of others, naïve to expect them to hold themselves to the same standards, and inconceivable that Americans would ever allow themselves to be called legally to account by non-Americans. Even putting aside larger questions concerning just war (*jus ad bellum*) and just practice in war (*jus in bello*), there was no serious command responsibility for conventional atrocities in Vietnam—or in the wars in Afghanistan and Iraq. Unaccountability consistently trumped "lawfare"—to the point where "international fora" and "judicial processes" could be officially aligned with "terrorism" as simply additional weapons of the weak.

## Spheres of Influence and the Limbo of Defeated Armies

Both the dubious legality of root-and-branch reform in occupied Japan and the convoluted legacies of the Japanese war-crimes trials are neglected in most accounts, since so much else in the way of constructive accomplishments was taking place in that defeated and isolated nation. Also neglected is the degree to which Allied victory and the putative end of a horrendous global conflagration was followed, almost seamlessly, by betrayals of wartime promises, insurrections, and new conflicts and crimes throughout Asia.

In theory, Japan's defeat liberated hundreds of millions of Asians who had been invaded, occupied, and oppressed by the emperor's men. In actuality, it paved the way for wars and occupations that involved the Allied victors themselves—and that hold a murky mirror, in their own way, to the invasion of Iraq and aspects of that later tragedy that are less unique than often claimed. Here the mirror reflects not only promises of liberation that were betrayed with terrible consequences, but also other persistent cultures of war as well: myopic "realism"; abuse of surrendered forces, and the legal contrivances that may abet this; lawlessness, terror, insurrection, and nationalisms capable of paralyzing materially superior military forces.

In his "message to the American people" delivered on September 2, 1945, MacArthur had declared that "today the guns are silent. . . . Men everywhere walk upright in the sunlight. The entire world lies quietly at peace."[68] For millions of war survivors in Asia, as in Europe, this was fiction: false light rather than sunlight, a fleeting lull at best. Suffering did not end for them, just as it did not end for the people of Iraq after the overthrow of Saddam Hussein; and much of this suffering involved callousness on the part of the victors. In place after place, country after country, men who did now walk tall in the sunlight often did not hesitate to hold others down, be they surrendered Japanese or Japan's former Asian victims. For those consigned to this fate, it was cruel to speak of the world lying quietly at peace—much as, in comparable ways, it was bitter for Iraqis decades later to have to listen to the American invaders constantly speaking about "liberation" and how they should be grateful to the United States as their country fell under foreign control and their personal lives became caught in a vortex of violence.

Japan's militaristic rise and fall rang the knell for old-style colonialism in Asia. The death throes were protracted, however, and the disconnect between rhetoric and reality remained little changed after MacArthur declared that the world at last lay quietly at peace. In 1941 and early 1942, Japan had usurped the place of the British, French, Dutch, and U.S. colonial powers in Southeast Asia and the Philippines in the name of "coexistence and coprosperity," proclaiming the dawn of a new era in which Great Nippon would serve as "the Leader of Asia . . . the Protector of Asia . . . the Light of Asia."[69] Many natives in this vast "southern region," extending across an area of over a million square miles, initially embraced these proclaimed anti-imperialist goals. They observed the rout of the Western colonial powers with astonishment, and in many instances welcomed the emperor's men as liberators; but the embrace rarely lasted. Economic exploitation and political oppression eclipsed initial hopes and promises, and outside the ranks of close collaborators no one mourned Japan's demise.

The American and British counter-proclamation of a new dawn for Asia and, indeed, the world was articulated early on in the "Atlantic Charter" jointly issued by Roosevelt and Churchill on August 14, 1941. This pledged, among other things, to "respect the right of all peoples to choose the form of government under which they will live." Although issued before Pearl Harbor and U.S. entry into the war, with Germany's aggression uppermost in mind, these ideals were reaffirmed in a "Declaration by the United Nations" (at that date, the term referred to the Allied powers) issued on January 1, 1942, in the name of twenty-six anti-Axis nations. Signatories included the four governments that would assume responsibility for overseeing Japanese military surrenders in the field throughout Asia: the United States, United Kingdom, Soviet Union, and China. The declaration began by citing the Atlantic Charter, and then rephrased this as a conviction "that complete victory over their enemies is essential to defend life, liberty, independence and religious freedom, and to preserve human rights and justice in their own lands as well as in other lands." It was for this reason that they were "now engaged in a common struggle against savage and brutal forces seeking to subjugate the world."

Nationalists throughout Asia took such declarations seriously as a promise that a victorious United States would take the lead in promoting a postcolonial world. From the moment Japan surrendered, these hopes and expectations were expressed with an intensity that caught Washington and London (and Paris and The Hague as well) by surprise. The phrase-makers obviously had not really paid much mind to their real-world audiences in distant and culturally alien lands. A British officer in the first contingent of U.K. troops that arrived to take the Japanese surrender in Java in September 1945, for example, later wrote with some wonder about the fervor for independence that greeted them. All around, when they entered Batavia, they beheld "huge slogans daubed in sprawling characters on the sides of vehicles and carriages. 'Atlantic Charter means freedom from Dutch Imperialism,' shouted one. 'America for the Americans— Monroe. Indonesia for the Indonesians,' screamed another. Everywhere the signs of rampant nationalism abounded. A caller lifting up a telephone receiver would be greeted by a bark of 'Merdeka' (Freedom) from the exchange."[70]

Some former colonies of the Western powers did gain independence soon after Japan's defeat, the Philippines and India notable among them. For millions of Asian nationalists elsewhere, however, wartime rhetoric about self-determination had little more substance than Japan's posturing as the Protector and Light of Asia. Throughout the length and breadth of Japan's crumbling empire, moreover, the assignment of responsibility for taking military surrenders in the field amounted to confirmation of Allied spheres of influence: the Soviet Union in Manchuria and half of Korea; Chiang Kai-shek's corrupt Nationalist regime throughout China, thoroughly dependent on U.S. military support; the United States in the Philippines, Japan, southern half of Korea, and entire Pacific Ocean area (newly christened an "American Lake" by some U.S. planners and pundits at the time); and the United Kingdom in Southeast Asia, where it was understood the British would reestablish their former territorial domina-

108. *Allied POWs liberated at Japan's Aomori prison wave U.S., British, and Dutch flags, August 29, 1945.*

109. *Emaciated American POWs liberated at Manila's Bilibid prison, February 1945.*

110. *Japanese POWs in Guam listen to the emperor's announcement of Japan's capitulation. Over six million Japanese awaited repatriation from overseas at war's end, and the return of scores of thousands was delayed for months and even a year or more.*

111. *Starving Japanese sailors rescued from the Marshall Islands after being stranded by the U.S. island-hopping campaign, September 1945. Much of the strong antimilitary sentiment in postwar Japan derived from the suffering that both military personnel and civilians experienced once the war turned against them.*

tion while also paving the way for the return of French and Dutch colonial authority. When forces led by the United Kingdom followed Japan's formal surrender in Tokyo Bay with their own ceremony in Singapore on September 12, accepting the surrender of all Japanese troops in Southeast Asia, the massed bands of the fleet captured the hubris of the moment with a spirited rendering of "Rule, Britannia!"[71]

Much of this division of labor and influence was practical. Some of it was accompanied by intense debates concerning if, when, and how old-style Western imperialism and colonialism could be eliminated or at least gradually phased out (through some sort of international trusteeship, for example, or pledges of eventual independence). The entire grand undertaking of moving from war to a hoped-for peace—a more intractable challenge than driving the great war machines forward had been—was undercut at almost every step by sharp disagreements among the erstwhile American, British, French, and Dutch allies.

The upshot of such complexity and contention, in any case, was fairly simple. Power politics governed postwar policy—and, just as had been the case in the war itself, Europe and the West took priority over Asia in U.S. planning. Why, despite strong public and private condemnations of the evils of the old imperialist system that Japan had uprooted, did U.S. policy makers ultimately extend political and material support to the British, French, and Dutch reoccupation of Southeast Asia? Secretary of State Cordell Hull minced few words about this. "We could not alienate them in the Orient," he explained in his memoirs, "and expect to work with them in Europe."[72]

This Europe-centrism was compounded by the fact that the vast majority of Allied military and civilian planners, both in the capital cities and in the field, had no prior knowledge of the atomic bomb and were caught by surprise by Japan's sudden surrender. Preoccupation with war strategy far outweighed intelligence gathering and planning for postwar challenges, and almost no one anticipated how formidable nationalistic and revolutionary agitation would prove to be everywhere from Korea through China to Southeast Asia. What in retrospect should have been predictable was not predicted—neither for the first time nor for the last.

The role played by Japan and many Japanese in this immediate postwar confusion and chaos was ironic. The defeated nation itself, instigator of so much death and destruction, was cocooned by the occupation and isolated from this violence and, indeed, from the world at large. Huge numbers of surrendered Japanese overseas, on the other hand, became an unwitting part of the upheavals that now convulsed the continent. Some military units were ordered to retain their weapons and participate actively in maintaining local "law and order," while other fighting men and technical personnel joined, or were coerced into joining, indigenous nationalist and communist movements. Scores of thousands of the emperor's loyal men thus found themselves engaged in new wars side by side with yesterday's adversaries. Hundreds of thousands who were spared this fate, moreover, still found themselves in a limbo of a different sort, as the victors delayed their evacuation and used them as forced labor. Protections conventionally guaranteed prisoners under the laws of war were withdrawn—extensively, arbitrarily, and with little public notice or outcry.

CLOSE TO 6.5 million Japanese fighting men and civilians awaited repatriation from overseas after August 1945, while slightly less than 1.2 million non-Japanese—mostly Koreans—desired repatriation *from* Japan to their native lands. The logistics were daunting, the process was complex and protracted, and in most cases the speed of return was impressive.

MacArthur's headquarters in Tokyo, which organized the shipping and domestic processing involved, took pride in its handling of these huge numbers. Roughly 1.5 million Japanese had been returned to the home islands by the end of February 1946, and another 1.6 million followed between March and mid-July. By the end of 1946, SCAP placed the total number repatriated back to Japan at 5.1 million. Before as well as after December 1946, however, it is difficult to trace the exact disposition of large numbers of military personnel and civilians. The Soviet Union engaged in the most notorious and prolonged abuse of surrendered Japanese, but was not alone in delaying the return of many whose only crime was being on the losing side.[73]

Although the Soviet Union did not enter the war against Japan until its final week, the number of Japanese troops and civilians that fell under its nominal control in Manchuria and northern Korea was huge, possibly in the neighborhood of 1.6 million. Some 293,000 managed to make their own way from northern Korea to the south, and around 625,000 others were repatriated by the Soviets by the end of 1947. The Japanese government calculated that as many as 700,000 were transferred to Siberia and interned as laborers. Although the Soviet Union resumed repatriation in May 1948, by the spring of 1949 Japanese and U.S. officials put the number still detained at over 400,000 and possibly as high as 469,000. They were shocked when the Russians claimed only 95,000 remained.

The last Japanese did not return from Siberia until the early 1950s; and it was not until 1991, after the collapse of the Soviet Union, that Russian records were released giving the names of some 46,000 Japanese who perished in Soviet hands. The precise numbers interned, and deceased, remain uncertain. Those detained the longest in the Soviet Union also were subjected to intense communist and anti-American indoctrination, and some of this was manifested in strident behavior by returning repatriates beginning in 1948. Postwar murder, abuse, and indoctrination by the Russians took place on a much greater scale where captured Germans were concerned; and all this naturally fed the Cold War propaganda machine in as well as outside Japan, where it was offered as one more confirmation of the brutal nature of the Soviet regime.[74]

IN CHINA, WHICH unlike the Soviet Union had suffered grievously at the hands of the Japanese, mass repatriation generally moved as quickly as could be expected—but with exceptions that were noteworthy in almost counterintuitive ways. For the duration of the long war that followed Japan's invasion in 1937, China was also at war with itself: an unoccupied interior counterpoised against a vast seaboard administered by collaborators under Japanese control, and a pent-up civil war pitting the Guomindang or Nationalists against Communists that was only superficially suppressed in the name of presenting a united front against Japanese aggression.

With Japan's capitulation, the Nationalists under Chiang Kai-shek enlisted U.S. military support to extend their authority nationwide. In fighting this reignited civil war, they not only delayed the evacuation of thousands of skilled Japanese technicians (and their dependents) but also enlisted the support of armed Japanese, particularly in the north where the Communists were strongest. Scores of thousands of Japanese troops remained active under Nationalist command for well over a year after the surrender—in some cases up to the time of the Communist victory in 1949.[75]

Because these uses and abuses of Japanese troops and technicians were embarrassing for all parties concerned, they received grudging acknowledgment at best. Much of what we rely on to reconstruct what took place thus remains disjointed and anecdotal. In November 1946, fifteen months after the surrender, for example, U.S. General Albert Wedemeyer complained about the slowness of the Nationalists in disarming the Japanese and concluded there were upwards of seventy thousand such troops in and around Beijing. At the very end of January 1947, a seasoned American diplomat in Nanjing calculated that around eighty thousand fully equipped Japanese troops were operating under Chiang's command in Manchuria. One of Chiang's closest collaborators in these activities was General Yasuji Okamura, the Japanese commander in chief in China when the war ended. In 1942 and 1943, Okamura had carried out a notorious "kill all, burn all, loot all" scorched-earth offensive against the Communists and their peasant supporters in north China that, by some accounts, killed over two million civilians. Okamura remained in China until 1949 as an adviser to Chiang, who protected him from indictment for war crimes. The Nationalist government also delayed the repatriation of thousands of Japanese administrators and technicians in Japan's former colony Formosa (Taiwan).[76]

Chiang's government was not the only force in China that both cultivated Japanese officers and exploited Japanese fighting men after the surrender. Some fifteen thousand Japanese troops, including officers, were commandeered to serve under the warlord Yan Xishan (Yen Hsi-shan) in Shanxi province in his doomed struggles against the Communists, with somewhere around seven thousand perishing by the time Yan was militarily crushed in 1949. (Their Japanese general, Hōsaku Imamura, committed suicide when Yan capitulated.) The Chinese Communists, on their part, also both enticed and coerced many thousands of Japanese soldiers and technicians into joining their side in the civil war—with the result that on a number of occasions "post surrender" Japanese pawns found themselves fighting each other in China's internecine bloodbath. The numbers concerning surrendered Japanese and delayed evacuation from China are as slippery as for the Soviet Union, but in April 1949, with Chiang and his tattered forces having fled to Taiwan and the Communists poised to declare the establishment of the People's Republic of China, U.S. intelligence estimated that upwards of sixty thousand Japanese still remained in Manchuria.[77]

■

IN SOUTHEAST ASIA, responsibility for taking the Japanese military surrender was delegated to the U.K.-led Southeast Asia Command (SEAC) under Admiral Lord Louis Mountbatten. Mountbatten's instructions, received before Emperor Hirohito actually broadcast Japan's capitulation, made London's priorities clear: reoccupation of Burma, Singapore, and major parts of Malaya; then Hong Kong, followed by "French Indo-China," where SEAC would prepare the way for the return of "French forces and civil affairs personnel"; then Siam (Thailand); and finally Java and Sumatra, where the mission was "to accept the surrender of Japanese forces and to prepare for the eventual handing over of this country to the Dutch civil authorities."

In forcing their return, the British, French, and Dutch received largely unpublicized political, economic, and material support from the United States—and military support from the newly baptized "JSP," or Japanese Surrendered Personnel. The JSP, as it happened, were not the only Asian military who were enlisted to help suppress local independence movements. Most of the troops in Mountbatten's SEAC, and most of the casualties that command sustained, came from India.[78]

With the support of their about-to-be-deposed Japanese overlords, indigenous forces led by Sukarno declared Indonesia's independence on August 17, while Vietminh forces under Ho Chi Minh in Indochina, having established what appeared to be firm control in both the north and the south, declared an independent Democratic Republic of Vietnam on September 2. These nationalist movements posed formidable challenges to reestablishing European colonial control—and, where Indonesia in particular was concerned, left the British, Americans, and Dutch momentarily thunderstruck. The latter, speaking largely through their colonial officials in exile (mostly in Australia), had assured everyone that their return would be welcomed; and both Mountbatten's SEAC and planners in Washington took such assurances at face value.

A State Department memorandum shortly after the surrender, for example, paraphrased the Dutch commander in chief of the Netherlands Indies Army as reporting earlier "that the people of the NEI [Netherlands East Indies] except for a few dissidents would generally support the former NEI Government and that it was the general impression that Japanese propaganda in the NEI had influenced about one tenth of 1% of the population." In June 1945, the State Department itself finalized a major report predicting that "the great mass of the natives will welcome the expulsion of the Japanese and the return of the Dutch to control."

As the official British military history of these developments put it—in language that easily can be transposed to criticisms directed against the Bush administration's wishful thinking about Iraq almost sixty years later—it quickly became "quite clear that the situation as described to Mountbatten when he was made responsible for the whole of the Netherlands East Indies had been a supreme example of wishful thinking. Instead of willing co-operation by the Indonesians, there was not only an open threat of war but also a considerable Indonesian force trained and equipped by the Japanese and ready to fight anyone attempting to restore Dutch dominion."[79]

Despite Japan's hasty support for Sukarno's declaration of independence on August 17, and despite the provision of weapons and supplies to the nationalists and desertion of some Japanese soldiers to their side, the bulk of Japanese forces dutifully complied with SEAC's orders. And despite Allied denunciations of the "inhuman, bestial practices" (Mountbatten's words) of the Japanese *vis-à-vis* their prisoners that the victors were discovering in many different locales, this did not prevent SEAC from ordering the defeated enemy to remain armed and to enforce "law and order" against the native nationalists until Dutch forces arrived and proved capable of taking over.

Some but not all of this was police work. In an eloquent "Christmas Day" letter submitted to President Truman in the closing days of 1945, the prime minister of the contested Republic of Indonesia wrote of air and naval bombardment by the British and went on to note that "the British and the Japanese acting under British orders have put many of our villages to the torch as punitive measures. Surabaya and Semarang are almost in ruins in consequence of the fighting that has taken place there." He then proceeded to invoke the particular faith that Asian nationalists placed in the United States as the last hope for defending the Atlantic Charter ideals: "We look to you, as the head of a country that has always been in the forefront of the fight for liberty, justice and self-determination, to use the benefit of your influence to stop the present bloodshed in Indonesia."[80]

An incisive essay on the SEAC policy of "sleeping with the enemy" puts the number of surrendered Japanese used militarily by the British and Dutch at upwards of 10,000 in Java, and "24,000 crack Japanese troops" (in the May 1946 words of the British Foreign Office) in Sumatra, with the total number of Japanese casualties placed at 717 dead, 387 wounded, and 205 missing in action. The United States followed these developments closely, especially in Sumatra where the primary objective was to defend oil refineries in which the Americans as well as Dutch and British had substantial vested interests. When Dutch forces finally arrived in sufficient force in mid-1946, the British transferred 13,500 surrendered Japanese to them, most of whom were not repatriated until May 1947.[81]

THE INDONESIAN STRUGGLE for independence continued until late 1949, when the Dutch finally abandoned their dream of a restored empire. (This was a hard dream to let go, since they had been ensconced in the East Indies since the seventeenth century.) In Indochina, the Allied betrayal was more tragic. Under the surrender arrangements agreed upon by the "Big Four" Allied powers at Potsdam in July, the Chinese Nationalists were responsible for taking the Japanese surrender in the northern half of Indochina, with SEAC taking charge in the south. The Chinese eventually acknowledged the sovereignty of the newly declared Republic of Vietnam, while the British, with U.S. support, did not. In facilitating the return of the French to the south, London and Washington ensured civil war and pursued a policy that eventually culminated in the Vietnam War. After the collaborationist disgrace of the wartime Vichy regime, France moved quickly to become, once again, occupier rather than occupied and (as a State Department report predicted even before Japan's surrender) to "reassert her prestige in the world as a great power." SEAC turned control over to French authorities in Saigon on December 19, 1945. Until then, however, much of the initial responsibility for maintaining law and order in the south was, again, delegated to the Japanese.[82]

British representatives did not arrive in Saigon until the last days of August, and upon surveying the scene they ordered the roughly seventy thousand Japanese military in the south to remain armed and garrisoned until SEAC and ultimately the French could take over. The Japanese performed critical logistics operations over the next few months. Their air force flew an estimated one hundred thousand miles under British orders, for example, carrying tens of thousands of pounds of supplies and ferrying some one thousand French and Indian troops. In mid-October, two months after the emperor announced Japan's capitulation, Japanese forces assisted U.K. and French troops in securing Saigon and its environs.

It was not until mid-November that SEAC finally announced locally that the disarmament of Japanese forces in Vietnam "will now begin," and not until the final days of November that the formal military surrender was completed and the British began to concentrate Japanese troops for repatriation and prepare for their own departure as sufficient French forces to take over arrived. Around the beginning of December, the Japanese calculated that they had suffered 406 casualties, including 126 killed, in fighting the Vietminh for their new masters.[83]

### Dissipating Intangible Assets

Article 6 of the Hague Regulations reads, "The State may utilize the labour of prisoners of war according to their rank and aptitude, officers excepted. The tasks shall not be excessive and shall have no connection with the operations of the war." The laws of war clearly did not sanction the use of prisoners in new wars entered into by their captors—nor did these regulations and conventions permit using surrendered fighting men as laborers long after the original conflict had ended. Nor, of course, did they condone their neglectful treatment. In one form or another, all of the victors in Asia engaged in such transgressions.

Japanese who surrendered to Mountbatten's SEAC were sometimes concentrated for extended periods in conditions that contributed to malnutrition and illness, for example, while scores of thousands who were physically fit were held back to perform labor tasks. When in mid-1946 MacArthur's headquarters requested that all Japanese be repatriated by the end of that year, the British announced their intention to retain

113,500 beyond then. As it transpired, they kept over 80,000 JSP for labor in Malaya and Burma into 1947, with the last of them not being returned to Japan until the end of that year—over two years after the war ended.[84]

The Americans, on their part, made no bones about evacuating "sick and other ineffectives" or "unproductive laborers" as promptly as possible while retaining more able-bodied Japanese as workforces in areas under their military control ("maintenance and repair of essential installations" was one descriptive phrase). This included at least 69,000 prisoners whose return home was delayed until the last three months of 1946—fourteen to sixteen months after the surrender (45,000 in the Philippines, 12,000 or more in Okinawa, 7,000 in the Pacific Ocean Area, and 5,000 in Hawaii). Masaki Kobayashi, who later became one of postwar Japan's most distinguished film directors, admired for his uncompromising depictions of war and oppression, was among the surrendered soldiers detained to labor in Okinawa until the end of 1946.[85]

Legalistic and euphemistic manipulations abetted these uses and abuses of surrendered enemy. Before the Allied victory over Germany was consummated, the British government introduced a legal turn of phrase to categorize German military taken prisoner under the unconditional surrender in a way that would remove them from the protection of international law. They were identified as "surrendered enemy persons" or "disarmed enemy persons"—and, as such, consigned to a status that presumably was not covered by the Hague and Geneva provisions, thus allowing them to be exploited as laborers and deprived of other rights and protections such as a guaranteed level of daily nutrition. Much the same linguistic subterfuge—"disarmed military personnel," "Japanese Surrendered Personnel"—was employed to similar ends in Asia. Seen in the light of such earlier maneuvering around humane laws and conventions, the Bush administration's later constructions of "unlawful enemy combatants" and the like, together with the abuse of captured individuals this facilitated, seem less exceptional than critics often claim them to be.[86]

WHILE THE FORMER victims and enemies of the Axis powers were largely indifferent to the fate of surrendered troops, in Southeast Asia the betrayal of promises of liberation was shocking and ultimately tragic.

Britain's unflagging imperial ardor was apparent for all to see. (In more Anglophobe U.S. circles, SEAC was said to stand for "Save England's Asian Colonies.") So was the colonial or neocolonial fervor of France and the Netherlands, whose return to Southeast Asia was openly supported by SEAC. The United States was more disingenuous—proclaiming its commitment to the ultimate goal of "self-government" even as it transported French forces from Marseilles to Saigon and urged the Dutch to remove the "U.S.A." Lend-Lease insignia from the military vehicles and weapons they relied on in reoccupying Indonesia. Without political and material U.S. support, the colonial reoccupations in Southeast Asia would have been impossible.[87]

As would happen repeatedly in later years and decades, the Western powers undertook these attempts to forcefully impose their authority without appreciating the pride, hope, humiliation, and ultimately rage that lay behind the indigenous movements—and with scant self-reflection about how their white man's arrogance was perceived. One of the few Westerners who did try to see Asia through Asian eyes was the American journalist Harold Isaacs, who witnessed these tumultuous developments and published his observations in a scathing 1947 book titled *No Peace for Asia*. In one vignette, Isaacs quoted a Dutch news release in Batavia titled "Collective Amok in Java," based on an analysis by a Dutch doctor. Indonesians agitating for independence and self-determination, in this diagnosis, were suffering from a bad case of "wish-fulfillment as regards Eastern superiority," and had been overcome by "a kind of dream life, a trance, a spiritual madness." He had, the doctor declared—shades of Joseph Grew on the Japanese during World War II, and L. Paul Bremer on Iraqis after the invasion in 2003, and uncountable other Westerners in between—observed this dream life taking "the place of rationalism brought by Western education, yes, even in highly educated individuals." "The hordes live in a mystic world of makebelieve," the analysis continued, and "carry on right in front of machine guns and beneath thundering planes. Still, the military answer is the only answer available to these hordes of fanatics."[88]

This is the imagined dichotomy between rational Westerners and irrational hordes of people of color that, for most Caucasians, never ceases to be gospel. When the commander in chief of the Dutch colonial forces had a moderately cordial conversation with nationalist leaders, for example, he reported with some surprise that "native delegates showed understanding and common sense." A few days earlier, his political adviser had informed the U.S. consul in Batavia (as cabled to Washington) that the "Indos" were "living in dream world of their making in which realistic arguments and actual facts are nearly excluded." These, of course, were the same Western officials that historians look back on as living in untenable dream worlds of their own; and those on the receiving end of such condescension were aware of this from the start.

An Islamic scholar responding to the "Collective Amok in Java" report, for example, politely observed that "it is the Dutch who are much more seriously afflicted with the hysteria of which this doctor writes." Apart from rare exceptions like Isaacs, the Westerners themselves were rarely capable of such irony, certainly not if it involved self-perception. Thus, hard-nosed negotiating of the sort the Europeans and Americans themselves had perfected became underhanded when proud and assertive non-Westerners practiced it. When the moderate president of the newly proclaimed Republic of Indonesia stated he would deal with a Dutch official as an envoy of a foreign government rather than colonial authority, the U.S. acting secretary of state (Dean Acheson) dismissed this as "typical oriental bargaining."[89]

ALTHOUGH IT IS natural and almost irresistible to compare and contrast occupied Iraq with occupied Japan, in many respects the attempt to reimpose Western hegemony in Southeast Asia after Japan's defeat provides an equally telling analogy. Be that as it may, this panoramic spectacle of a vaster Asia being occupied and reoccupied and torn asunder by foreign intrusion and domestic upheaval casts what took place in occupied Japan in clearer light. Isaacs, for one, was not won over by the hosannas to demilitarization and democratization emanating from MacArthur's headquarters in Tokyo immediately after the war. He dismissed the occupation as "a preposterous and macabre comedy," and placed the defeated nation firmly in the context of planning for the next war. "Every correspondent in Tokyo," he reported, "heard officers of general rank describe Japan as 'the staging area for the next operation'" against Russia or—as he himself anticipated—a Communist China.[90]

To Asians everywhere (as to Isaacs himself), it looked "very much as if the Americans were ready to allow the hated Japanese more relative self-government, freedom, and independence, than they were willing to see granted to any of Japan's recent victims"—be they Koreans or Annamites or Javanese, all of whom saw themselves as being at least as capable of running their own affairs as the Japanese. It was the Japanese, after all, who had plundered Asia and plunged it into the agony of war; and it was not other Asians "but the Americans, the British, the Japanese, the French, and the Dutch who had proved incapable of organizing any kind of secure peace in the Far East." Yet despite all this, Japan was being allowed to retain "not only its national identity but the essence of its old regime, while in the colonies the efforts of subject peoples to achieve their national identities were uniformly frustrated."

That the victorious powers did not hesitate to use Japanese troops in suppressing the nationalist movements, in Isaacs's view, could only be seen as "a further shocking and cynical indignity. This was not quite the picture people had of what American victory over Japan would mean in Asia." Almost overnight, the United States had dissipated "the greatest political asset ever enjoyed by any nation anywhere in our time"—the promise of being a true champion of the Atlantic Charter ideals. For Isaacs, who did not ignore the shortcomings of the independence movements, this could only be regarded as "one of the most extravagant and prodigal examples of conspicuous waste ever recorded in the annals of the nations."[91]

Here, from yet another perspective, were more new evils in the world. In the great game of power politics, the occupation of Japan was but a piece in a larger agenda of "staging areas" and spheres of influence strategizing in Asia; the use of surrendered Japanese to maintain law and order became a telling, if unplanned, part of this game; and the paternalistic attentiveness directed toward the defeated Japanese emerged as a sharp contrast to U.S. and Allied policy and practice toward other Asians.

The only place in Asia where the guns were really stilled and peace prevailed was Japan.

# NATION BUILDING AND
# MARKET FUNDAMENTALISM

## Controls and Capitalisms

Apart from law and justice, there are other areas where rough similarities tell us something more complicated about wars and occupations than emerges in the usual perception of Japan and Iraq as antipodean examples of success and failure. Although there was little violence in occupied Japan, and none against the occupation forces, for example, crime and corruption were serious problems. Largely forgotten today, looting took place on a massive scale prior to the arrival of U.S. forces. The difference from the plunder and vandalism that followed Saddam Hussein's fall was qualitative: in Japan, the looting was quasi-official, clandestine, and almost fastidious—the work of efficient thieves in the night who did not dream of sacking ministries and museums.

In a different direction, seemingly draconian policies that proved disastrous in Iraq—particularly the elimination of the military establishment and categorical purge of former officeholders—were also integral to the policy of the Supreme Commander of the Allied Powers. What differed was the outcome: in Japan, these policies caused personal distress, but not chaos. As in Iraq, too, many policies central to the early occupation agenda—like reparations and drastic economic deconcentration in Japan's case—amounted to false starts. On the other hand, certain policies of lasting influence—most famously constitutional revision—came about as a result of essentially ad hoc initiatives on the part of MacArthur and his Tokyo headquarters, rather than careful planning in Washington.[92]

"Ad hoc" was the name of the game in Iraq, given the fact that prior planning for occupation and nation building was nil; and constitutional revision also became part of the reformist agenda hastily introduced by the Coalition Provisional Authority. For all the reasons that made defeated Japan a vastly different society than post-Saddam Iraq, however—social cohesion, a pervasive secular outlook, deep identity as a culture and country, and meaningful experience as a pluralistic civil society—"democracy" did not find the same solid constituency in Iraq.

Two of the most striking points of partial convergence in conduct of the occupations were simultaneously the most telling points of divergence. One was the usurpation of Japanese and later Iraqi sovereignty and imposition of near-absolute U.S. control. The second involved promoting capitalism. Taken together, these illuminate how greatly the American conduct of war and peace changed over the decades that followed World War II.

MacArthur exercised authority in Japan for almost six years (he was relieved of his command in April 1951), as opposed to Bremer and his traumatic "year in Iraq" (the title of his memoir). The differences, however, went far beyond this. MacArthur operated within a clear chain of command and exercised control over both security and civil affairs. Nonmilitary personnel helped staff his General Headquarters (GHQ) in Tokyo, but the sort of ideological litmus tests that took place in staffing the CPA in Iraq—where party affiliation and even religious convictions influenced

recruitment—did not take place in the critical early years. On the contrary, eclecticism and bipartisanship gave GHQ much of its early vitality. (Bias against liberals and leftists entered the picture around 1947–48,
with the intensification of the Cold War and introduction of the reverse
course.) MacArthur welcomed civilian task forces to investigate matters
requiring technical expertise, both before and after the reverse course, but
legions of private contractors did not invade the defeated country alongside his victorious forces.

The post–1945 task forces reflected an old-fashioned sense of public
duty on the part of the experts recruited that had all but disappeared by
the twenty-first century. By much the same measure, the old military operated under a broader definition of responsibilities and obligations, which
extended to engaging in civil affairs in occupied lands and taking care of
the daily needs of its troops. In the process, it maintained the appearance
and in large measure reality of not merely discipline and control, but also
integrity and accountability. No one will ever associate discipline, control,
integrity, or accountability with the occupation of Iraq, either during or
after the short life of the CPA.

Just as in Iraq, creating a sound capitalist economy was always a goal
in Japan. What was understood as "capitalism" (and "sound" as well) was
another matter entirely. Land reform, encouragement of organized labor,
and trust busting were central to SCAP's early reforms aimed at "economic democratization." Even after projections for Japan changed with
the Cold War, moreover, it was taken for granted that the state had to
play a major role in promoting economic development. This meant not
only the U.S. state as the occupying power, but the Japanese state as an
essential player in establishing and enforcing economic priorities and,
where deemed necessary, protecting vulnerable industries and enterprises
against foreign exploitation.

By contrast, once the Americans found themselves plunged willy-nilly
into reconstructing Iraq, they pursued this with a zealotry that reflected
the reigning dogmas of market fundamentalism. "Privatization" became
the catechism of these latecomers to nation building. At one critical early
point, much of occupied Iraq's economy appeared to have been put up
for sale. At every point, an immense portion of the tasks and functions
involved in planning and directing civil affairs in a shattered nation were

outsourced to private and largely American contractors—even "civil affairs," even intelligence gathering, even security, even reconstruction endeavors that in Japan had been left to the Japanese and could have been done by Iraqis with greater efficiency and far less expense. The result was a level of confusion, cronyism, non-transparency, and corruption that had no counterpart in Japan.[93]

## Corruption and Crime

In the interlude between the emperor's announcement of capitulation in mid-August and the arrival of U.S. forces two weeks later, Japanese military and civilian officials hastened to destroy as much as possible of the paper record of their war. As a popular hyperbole had it, smoke from the air raids was replaced by smoke from burning documents. More devastating—although not publicly exposed and investigated until well over a year later—politicians, national and local officials, military officers, local police, entrepreneurs, and gangsters throughout the nation managed to spirit away gigantic quantities of finished products and raw industrial goods that had been accumulated for the ongoing war effort.

In Iraq, the counterpart to burning documents was plundering or destroying government computers and entire ministry buildings, while the counterpart to sacking the warehouses was riotous looting and vandalism in broad daylight, extending even to Baghdad's great museums. Near the end of 2003, it was estimated that the economic cost of this pillage probably amounted to around $12 billion. The scale and impact of Japan's "hoarded goods scandal" was surely no less in relative terms, and probably much greater. Most of the stolen or concealed stockpiles, which ranged from everyday essentials like blankets, utensils, and medicines to machinery to industrial raw materials and precious metals, were funneled into a black market that spurred inflation and crippled industrial reconstruction for several years. Other, more conventional scandals also were exposed later, including the diversion of funds earmarked for economic recovery through the Japanese Reconstruction Finance Bank.[94]

Where the looting in the two countries differed markedly was in the realm of public performance. In Iraq, this coincided with the arrival of U.S. forces and signaled a breakdown of public order. The failure of the

Americans to even venture to suppress this was disastrous but predictable, given the absence of contingency planning. "Stuff happens" was Defense Secretary Rumsfeld's response at a Pentagon briefing early on (on April 11, 2003). Months later (August 9), he dismissed mounting violence and chaos in Iraq with similar impassiveness: "Democracy is untidy. Freedom is untidy. Liberation is untidy." Much of the mainstream U.S. media found press conferences of this sort entertaining. Such theater of the absurd was the beginning of the end of American credibility.

In Japan, on the other hand, the looting was quick and extraordinarily tidy, undertaken almost overnight with broad official complicity and negligible public notice. For all practical purposes, it ceased when the Allied forces arrived with their overwhelming show of might and MacArthur proceeded to make unmistakably clear who was in charge. Only a miniscule portion of the stolen or concealed goods, however, was ever recovered. Thereafter disruptive activity took other forms, such as stonewalling or heel dragging by Japanese politicians, bureaucrats, and capitalists when they could get away with it. (The phrase among students of the occupation for such practices, which were particularly conspicuous in economic affairs, is "negative sabotage.") This happened frequently, but less frequently than counterexamples of constructive collaboration—and, in the final analysis, it was the latter that made the difference.

Combined with the extensive physical destruction of the war and inevitable disorder that followed, the diverted stockpiles and "negative sabotage" fed both a ravenous hyperinflation and nationwide black market that dominated the Japanese economic scene into 1949. In theory, the black market was illegal. In practice, it amounted to the "real" economy and almost no one could avoid participating in it as seller or buyer or both. As both cynics and appalled observers noted at the time, virtually every adult Japanese became a lawbreaker out of necessity.[95]

LAWLESSNESS ON THE part of the occupation forces also occurred in Japan, although nowhere near the extent to which this took place in defeated Germany and elsewhere in postwar Europe. The iconic photographs portraying friendly GIs with lively Japanese children and courteous if cautious adults were an accurate reflection of the speed with which both sides placed a human face on yesterday's despised enemy. By both official fiat and the personal choice of conquerors with cameras in their hands, however, no one recorded crimes by the victorious forces. These were inevitable given the size of the foreign presence: the total number of U.S.-led Allied personnel in Japan was close to a half million when the occupation began, and still over a hundred thousand before the Korean War erupted almost five years later. Occupation censorship coupled with self-censorship, however, ensured that such transgressions were airbrushed out of the picture of a thoroughly benign exercise in reconciliation.

The incidence of GI (and Australian and British) crimes against Japanese nationals is impossible to quantify for several reasons. Many victims remained silent; the Japanese government had no jurisdiction over crimes by the foreigners; occupation authorities covered up incidents reported to them; and the victors rarely prosecuted such crimes. In the first two weeks of occupation, before formal censorship was imposed on September 10, hundreds of crimes and misdemeanors involving occupation forces were reported in the Japanese press. The incidence remained high for weeks to follow and ranged from drunken brawling and vandalism to theft, armed robbery, assault, and rape. Some postwar Japanese sources argue that rapes by occupation forces became more frequent as time passed.[96]

Criminal activity on the Japanese side increased following surrender, but in conventional ways incomparable with the bombings and ethnic cleansings that ravaged Iraq. Crime rates rose, most conspicuously in robbery, theft, and the handling of stolen goods. Unsurprisingly, many perpetrators were demobilized soldiers who returned home to find themselves unemployed and, in the burned-out cities, sometimes without homes or surviving kin. One provocative epithet—*Tokkōtai kuzure*, or "degenerate Special Forces"—even stigmatized repatriated members of the superpatriotic kamikaze units as behaving with particularly lawless swagger. It became fashionable to speak of a breakdown of public morality, and nothing symbolized this more than the rapacious black market and emergence of prostitutes called *panpan* who catered specifically to the occupation forces. To Japanese conservatives, the rise of a militant labor movement was another sign of the decay of law and order, although in fact violence did not taint the movement until 1948 and even then such incidents were isolated.[97]

After Japan returned to prosperity beginning in the 1960s, the hardship, turmoil, and uncertainty of these early postwar years receded from
view. People were dying of malnutrition; gangs controlled the black market; unemployment was high, and daily subsistence precarious for huge
numbers of urban residents. Unlike later in Iraq, however, zealots were
not running wild and no one was placing improvised explosives by the
roadsides. Overall, order prevailed. Japanese comedians and cartoonists
even ventured to find lame humor in the rise in burglary and petty theft.
(Says a cartoon housewife to a burglar in her home: Everything's been
stolen from the bureau already. You might as well take the bureau itself.)
It was even possible to look at the black market and the brazen *panpan*
as possessing a resilience and vigor that, however decadent, reflected the
feisty opposite of despair—and that clearly would, and did, soon end.
No comparable humor or optimism found expression in Iraq.

## Successful and Disastrous Demilitarization

The contrast between public order in Japan and disorder in Iraq calls
attention to the most conspicuous policy area in which seemingly similar
directives had vastly different outcomes: enactment of a categorical purge
and dissolution of the military. On May 16, 2003, four days after arriving in
Baghdad, Bremer issued "Order No. 1," titled "De-Baathification of Iraqi
Society." This purge affected scores of thousands of mostly Sunni members at the top level of the Baath Party, including bureaucrats, managers of
government-owned corporations, schoolteachers, and medical personnel.
"Order No. 2," which followed on May 23 under the imprecise heading
"Dissolution of Entities," abolished the defense ministry, related security
ministries and agencies, and all existing military formations. It was promised that a new multiethnic, nonpolitical army would be established.

Estimates vary concerning how many individuals these directives made
jobless (and in some cases deprived of pensions as well as salaries), but
several hundreds of thousands of men, most of them possessing military skills and weapons, became part of a labor force already running at
over 50 percent unemployment. Insurrectionary violence and open anti-
Americanism increased thereafter, and it was in these circumstances that
(on July 2) President Bush responded with taunting. "There are some who

*112. Shiite Muslims in Baghdad protest American intervention in the selection of post-Saddam political leaders on May 15, 2003, just days after L. Paul Bremer III arrived to assume command of the Coalition Provisional Authority. The small sign on the left reads, "No No No to the foreign government."*

feel like—that the conditions are such that they can attack us there," he declared. "My answer is, bring 'em on. We've got the force necessary to deal with the security situation." Pugnacious rhetoric took the place of serious policy reevaluation, and wishful thinking again prevailed even as things fell apart.[98]

In Japan, MacArthur also oversaw introduction of a political purge and the dismantling of the military. The former was not given immediate priority, and the lengthy directive ordering it—titled "Removal and Elimination of Undesirable Personnel from Public Office"—was only issued in the first week of 1946. The purge unfolded in stages thereafter, and eventually denied public employment to slightly over two hundred thousand individuals who had held positions defined by the victors as militaristic or ultranationalistic. (Allied purges in occupied Germany affected twice that number.) Although the purge in Japan resembled that imposed in Iraq in its categorical nature, as well as in offering a cumbersome appeal process, the differences were significant. Bremer described the objective of his first two orders as being to "reassure Iraqis that we are determined to eradicate Saddamism," and his explicit model derived from the occupation of Germany rather than Japan. The Baath Party was seen as analogous to the Nazi Party, and "de-Baathification" a counterpart to "de-Nazification."[99]

Policy in occupied Japan took a different direction, for there was no counterpart to the Nazi or Baath parties. The closest ideological analogue to "Nazism" or "Saddamism" was the more amorphous cult of emperor worship—the "Way of the Emperor" or "Imperial Way" (*Kōdō*) that played so central a role in wartime indoctrination. Rather than eradicate this, the Americans early on resolved to utilize it by wooing Emperor Hirohito to their side and divesting him of some of his more spiritual ornamentation. The contradiction between exonerating the emperor while purging his most fervid and loyal servants (and indicting some as war criminals) was ignored, and what prevailed instead was a cool political cynicism. In the emperor and imperial institution, the Americans possessed—and adroitly manipulated—a potent symbol of unity, continuity, and stability. In the process, they also endorsed and perpetuated a potent symbol of paternalism, patriarchy, and blood nationalism.

While generally regarded in retrospect as riding roughshod over many individuals whose major transgression had been patriotism, the categorical Japanese purge was not socially disruptive. Career military officers constituted roughly three-quarters of those denied public positions. Around six hundred conservative politicians were banned from running for office in the first postwar general election in April 1946, which pained them more than it did the voting public. Although over eight thousand members of the economic elite were purged—including "1,535 captains of industry, finance and commerce"—capable managerial talent was available to assume their functions. Purges within the bureaucracy were small and had negligible influence. There was no schismatic impact comparable to Iraq, where "de-Baathification" translated into eliminating the Sunni technocrats and officials who dominated the party that had run the government.[100]

Dissolution of the Iraqi military essentially capped the disestablishment of the Sunnis, who had also dominated the officer corps, and made the prospect of Sunni-Sh'ia conflict all the more inevitable. In Japan, by contrast, the dissolution of the military establishment was a truly sweeping act that, surprisingly at first glance, was carried out without causing domestic turbulence. This radical demilitarization had rhetorical roots in the war years. Beginning in 1943, the United States and United Kingdom declared the complete and permanent disarmament of Germany and Japan to be a major war aim of the Allied coalition, and this was reiterated in the instructions sent MacArthur before his arrival in Japan, which stated that "Japan will be completely disarmed and demilitarized." This was implemented incrementally, with the downgraded and renamed war and navy ministries handling demobilization as well as narrow tasks like minesweeping before being swept away themselves under the new constitution.[101]

At war's end, Japan had slightly over seven million men under arms. The task of demobilization was formidable, and carried over into 1947. Unlike in Iraq later, it was understood that no reconstructed military establishment was in the offing. Complementary directives prohibited Japanese industry from engaging in military-related production. In a stunning symbolic stroke that caught MacArthur's superiors in Washington by surprise, this severe antimilitary ethos was enshrined in the draft constitution that was pressed on the Japanese government by MacArthur's headquarters in February 1946 and became law in November, after lengthy deliberation in the Diet. The new charter came into effect in May 1947.

WITHIN A FEW years, as the Cold War intensified and Japan became identified as a potential strategic ally, Washington came to regret this thoroughgoing demilitarization. Both then and afterwards, however, the Japanese populace proved unwilling to simply jettison these early antiwar ideals. The constitution still remained unrevised when the invasion of Iraq took place over a half century later; and while Japan had built substantial "self-defense" forces in the interim, their function and acceptable overseas missions remained constrained and contested. This greatly restricted Japan's military role in the Bush administration's wars in Afghanistan and Iraq—and at the same time helps illuminate why elimination of the army and navy after the war did not prove disruptive. The nation was exhausted after its long war, which for the Japanese dated back to 1937. Sixty-six cities lay in ruins; around ten million people were homeless; the national death toll came to some two million fighting men and over a half-million civilians; and it was calculated that somewhere around 80 percent of the millions of servicemen being repatriated from overseas were injured or ill. In the wake of disastrous defeat, the once-revered imperial military had no constituency.

The pervasiveness of cynicism vis-à-vis the military and militarists was captured in a phrase that became popular after the surrender: *damasareta*, "we were deceived." The military had become ascendant in the 1930s in a society that was not inherently and incorrigibly militaristic, and its demise had little bearing on maintaining domestic law and order. Millions of demobilized servicemen returned to their homes in the largely unscathed countryside; several million joined the ranks of the burgeoning labor movement; and most officers found their technical and administrative skills adaptable to the tasks and challenges of reconstruction. The human resources hitherto devoted to war service and war production were agnostic and primed—both technically and psychologically—for redirection into nonmilitary pursuits.

Abolition of the war and navy ministries—and of many of the economic controls they had assumed in the process of mobilizing for "total war"— was also welcomed by most capitalists and had a profound effect on the central bureaucracy. After years of kowtowing to the militarists, civilian ministries assumed command, led initially by the Ministry of Finance. In this somewhat unexpected manner, MacArthur's version of the "dissolution of entities" strengthened the indigenous administrative structures through which the Americans promoted their agenda.

## *"Generalists" versus "Area Experts"*

One of the more popular canards about the U.S. failure in Iraq is that most of the Americans who planned or manned the post-invasion occupation knew little beforehand about that country or the Middle East more generally. This is exaggerated but largely true. It is also something of a red herring. Hundreds of articulate Iraqi exiles and Middle East specialists participated in the private as well as public discussions and debates that preceded the invasion. It can even be argued that their factionalism and disagreements should have been yet another clear warning of the problems that lay ahead. This never occurred in the case of planning for postwar Japan, primarily because there was no politically energized Japanese exile community.

The larger red herring, in any case, is revealed by the fact that the same criticism can be directed at most of the Americans later praised for promoting the reformist agenda in defeated Japan. Few spoke Japanese or knew anything about Japan beforehand, and "generalists" and technical specialists were the prized recruits. To a considerable degree, this reflected deliberate bias and not just the exceedingly small number of Westerners who could even qualify as knowledgeable about Japan. When the legal expert Alfred Oppler, born and educated in Germany, was recruited to take a leading role in revising Japan's entire legal system, his experience was the rule rather than an exception. Upon reporting to Tokyo (in February 1946), Oppler confessed that he "did not have any knowledge of things Japanese." "Oh that is quite all right," the colonel who greeted him replied. "If you knew too much about Japan, you might be prejudiced. We do not like old Japan hands."[102]

Martin Bronfenbrenner, who served as a young economist in the occupation and went on to a distinguished academic career, made much the same observation for his own area of expertise. "The American Occupation forces were ill prepared to deal with Japan's economic problems," he later wrote. "Most of its civilian and military personnel were temporary employees, with little prior training or interest in things Japanese. As the Occupation progressed, they were also subject to adverse selection, with many of the best and most promising people taking more permanent or prestigious 'stateside' jobs, or going into private trade or professional practice in Japan when permitted to do so."

"At the outset," Bronfenbrenner went on, "most SCAP employees had but vague notions of the workings of the Japanese economy, and these were colored by wartime propaganda. Two extremes were in evidence: one saw the Japanese as backward 'Asiatics' in need of the charity and enlightenment of the West; the other saw the country capable of high productivity and economic advance if freed from the 'exploitation' of the zaibatsu, large landlords, and the government bureaucracy. Early policy was guided by an amalgamation of these views, coupled with political considerations, punitive attitudes (sometimes racist), and incomplete or inaccurate knowledge."[103]

Area specialists—and Japan specialists in particular—were regarded with suspicion by occupation planners on the often plausible grounds that they were biased by their cultural fixations and frequently insensitive to the more universal aspirations people share in common. An "old Asia hand" of World War II vintage, that is, would often argue that for cultural or historical reasons democracy or meaningful popular self-governance could not be expected to take root in Japan or anywhere else in Asia for that matter. Joseph Grew and the wartime coterie of State Department specialists known as the "Japan Crowd" exemplified this, as Grew made clear on many occasions. Just weeks after Japan's surrender, for example, he wrote to an acquaintance (and later reproduced the letter in his memoirs) that "any attempt to impose an outright democracy on the Japanese would result in political chaos and would simply leave the field wide open for would-be dictators to get control. One can't live in a country for ten years without knowing these things."[104]

George Sansom, a British diplomat and widely admired cultural historian who was first posted to Japan in 1904 and spent many years preparing internal reports on Japan's economy, was even more disdainful of SCAP's early reformist agenda. In December 1948, more than three years after the surrender, he contributed a foreword that bristled with scorn to a book on the Japanese economy in war and reconstruction. "This is not the place for a discussion of the policy of democratization which has been energetically, if at times unrealistically, pursued," Sansom wrote, "but it is pertinent to observe that parliamentary democracy was born and nourished in the West in relatively favorable economic conditions. It may be that hungry, ill-clothed and worried men in some countries will pour their energies into a struggle for political freedoms; but it is extremely doubtful whether Japan is one of those countries."[105]

A liberal New Dealer, on the other hand, as well as a traditional Republican champion of petite entrepreneurship like MacArthur, would argue otherwise. Colonel Charles Kades, the highly respected Government Section lawyer who had been a New Dealer and led the team that drafted the new constitution, made this philosophy amply clear—drawing on principles of universal human rights and aspirations that were then finding expression in the fledging United Nations. MacArthur, on his part, expounded at one point that "history will clearly show that the entire human race, irrespective of geographical limitations or cultural tradition, is capable of absorbing, cherishing and defending liberty, tolerance and justice, and will have maximum strength and progress when so blessed."[106]

This was a provocative divide in which "generalists" on both the political left and right tended to argue the universal applicability of fundamental rights and principles, while the putative "area experts" were inclined to focus on historical and cultural peculiarities that made non-Western societies inhospitable to values like "democracy." Often this attitude reflected not merely the inclination of area specialists to zero in on ostensibly incompatible differences, but also the class consciousness and arrogance of a diplomatic cohort that spent its career associating professionally and socially with foreign elites who regarded the lower classes in their own countries as ignorant and incapable of governing themselves. No matter how incompetent, autocratic, or militaristic those native elites might prove to be, at least they had received higher schooling, attended the right clubs, and in most cases spoke English. (Grew's meticulous private diary covering his ten years in Japan is, among other things, a chronicle of upper-class snobbery, with many of his most admired Japanese acquaintances and informants associated in one way or another with court circles.)

At a superficial level, somewhat the same sort of disagreement played out in the Bush administration's war of choice against Iraq. On the one hand, a chorus of neoconservative ideologues in particular—as well as solo performers such as President Bush and Prime Minister Blair—argued not only that Iraq was ripe for democracy but also that bringing this about there by violent regime change would have a ripple or domino effect throughout the Middle East. Blair, for example, channeled the MacArthur-like language of universality in a much-applauded speech before a joint session of Congress on July 17, 2003, when the bloom was fading rapidly from Operation Iraq Freedom and it was clear "democracy" would have to replace nonexistent weapons of mass destruction as the major rationale for the invasion. "Ours are not Western values," Blair declared, "they are the universal values of the human spirit. And anywhere . . . anywhere, anytime ordinary people are given the chance to choose, the choice is the same: freedom, not tyranny; democracy, not dictatorship; the rule of law, not the rule of the secret police." Those who criticized the invasion were dismissed as being guilty of old-fashioned racism and ethnocentrism, and guiltiest of all in this polemic were "Arabists" in and outside the State Department.[107]

The disdain of White House and Pentagon planners for Middle East experts apart from those who endorsed the neoconservative argument runs as a leitmotif through much (not all) insider and investigative writing on the Iraq war. Timothy Carney, who served under Jay Garner in the short-lived Office of Reconstruction and Humanitarian Assistance, for example, later emphasized how lacking in critical personnel this office was when it arrived in Baghdad. "There were scarcely any Arabists in ORHA in the beginning" at a senior level, he observed. "Some of us had served in the Arab world, but we were not experts, or fluent Arabic speakers." This was deliberate in his view, for Pentagon officials "said that Arabists weren't welcome because they didn't think Iraq could be democratic."[108]

This approximated, almost to the word, what Alfred Oppler and other recruits in the occupation of Japan had been told about the "old Japan hands." Sometimes, however, the area experts do have knowledge and insights worth being heeded.

### Privatizing Nation Building

Early in 2004, some months after the ORHA had been replaced by Bremer's Coalition Provisional Authority, Jay Garner told an interviewer that when the ORHA found itself facing an enormous array of postwar challenges, with no blueprint in hand, it immediately concluded there was no alternative but to "bring in contractor teams, as fast we could do it." This was not merely a desperate makeshift reaction, but a modus operandi already being promoted in Washington. "Outsourcing" was the magic word—and perhaps the closest the government really came to having a "plan" for post-conflict Iraq. Whatever nation building took place would be privatized.[109]

In early occupied Japan, the counterpart economic mantra was very different: "economic democratization." As formulated in the Initial Post-Surrender Policy for Japan, and frequently repeated, this reflected a consensus that stability, prosperity, and future peace were best assured by promoting the reorganization of industry, finance, commerce, labor, and agriculture in ways that would "permit a wide distribution of income and of the ownership of the means of production and trade." Both land reform and a strong labor movement were rationalized as forms of liberation that would create a more dynamic domestic market—and, in the process, thwart any possible threat of communistic revolution from below while simultaneously eliminating future need to capture markets abroad. In a similar vein, MacArthur denounced the huge family-controlled *zaibatsu* conglomerates as both vestiges of "feudal lineage" and a perverse form of socialism in private hands—"a standing bid for State ownership," in his alarmist words, "and a fruitful target for Communist propaganda and collectivist purposes." Both the Republican supreme commander and his New Dealer trust busters believed that breaking up these great conglomerates would stimulate competition and hasten the emergence of a dynamic middle class.[110]

At the same time, MacArthur's reformers tolerated and even promoted the visible hand of the state. Certain measures and mechanisms that the Japanese government had introduced to stimulate the wartime economy were retained; ministries responsible for finance and industry were strengthened; new planning agencies and eventually (in 1949) an entirely new Ministry of International Trade and Industry were introduced. Particularly after 1948, SCAP's own bureaucracy became deeply involved in economic planning aimed at stimulating recovery and making Japan "self-sufficient" by giving priority to an export-oriented manufacturing sector. After war erupted in Korea in 1950, this intervention extended to introducing legislation that would continue to protect the economy from foreign carpetbaggers after Japan regained sovereignty. The other side of endorsing "self-sufficiency" was thus a consensus that capitalist economies require reasonable protection from international as well as domestic predators, particularly at early and vulnerable stages of development.[111]

Even after the Cold War prompted retreat from radical policies regarding capital and labor and the redistribution of wealth, Americans engaged in Japan policy would have found remarkable the free-market fundamentalism that saturated U.S. policy in Iraq—the notion, that is, that an unregulated marketplace is fundamentally rational, let alone invariably beneficial to societies or the global economy more generally. They would surely have been appalled at the notion of turning over basic reconstruction tasks to foreign, profit-driven private interests. Beyond an old-fashioned moral aversion to letting greed run rampant, this earlier generation was sensitive to the social disruptiveness and political blowback of unregulated capitalism. Where Japan in particular was concerned, they also were keenly aware of the necessity of maintaining the trust essential to stable long-term relations by avoiding even the appearance of exploitation or economic imperialism.

The practical benefits of adhering to such economic prescriptions in the crisis situation of the time were considerable. On the U.S. side, the occupation escaped becoming a host to mercenaries or feeding trough for profiteers, and the United States emerged with its reputation for integrity intact. Japan regained sovereignty as a capitalist democracy with a mixed economy and a level of protectionism that gave both the ruling groups and general populace a certain sense of security. And the nation was set on a path of reconstruction that ended, three decades later, in Japan's emergence as the second most powerful capitalist state in the world, with the great majority of its citizens identifying themselves as "middle class."

■

THERE WAS MORE than a little hypocrisy in the fanfare about "privatization" that became associated with the occupation of Iraq, for on the U.S. side the state and private sector became as close as hand and glove. Nation building was turned over to entrepreneurs, with contractors usually guaranteed cost-plus profits funded with taxpayers' money. In an article published on July 1, 2004, coincidental with the termination of the CPA, a Washington-based journal catering to civilian and military officials framed the contradiction succinctly: "From the outset, the only plan appears to have been to let the private sector manage nation-building, mostly on their own." Once this door was opened, effective governmental monitoring and oversight virtually disappeared. What was left was essentially an

American-style version of security-focused state capitalism, dominated by the rough equivalent of what Japanese in the 1930s and early 1940s had called "national policy companies."[112]

In practice, this reliance on the private sector to carry out post-combat responsibilities probably came as close to a preinvasion "plan" as existed. Because war planning was conducted in supersecrecy, however, and because this was accompanied by elaborate public-relations manipulation (including denying that the decision to go to war had been made), it was difficult to set such activity in motion. Interagency discussions about recruiting contractors for reconstruction tasks began around September 2002, but it was not until the following January that the first few contracts were awarded under the auspices of the U.S. Agency for International Development (USAID). On February 13, the agency produced a thirteen-page document titled "Vision for Post-Conflict Iraq" that was made available to the *Wall Street Journal*, which publicized its contents in detail on March 10.

The *Journal* article drew wide attention. It reported that contracts totaling $900 million had been extended to five U.S. infrastructure engineering firms whose work was projected to be completed in eighteen months, creating "a new framework for economic and governance institutions." The key reconstruction problems to be addressed were identified as water systems, roadways, seaports and airports, health services, schools, and electrical generation. (The oil industry was not mentioned, although this received close attention in other preinvasion reports and commentaries.) Other contractors were still being sought, and required security clearance to be eligible. Even before the U.S. military had set foot in Iraq, the target nation's own skilled workforce was obviously deemed incapable of handling such engineering projects. As one Iraqi businessman observed bitterly some months later, when these contracting arrangements were in full flood, "They claimed that we were smart enough to build weapons of mass destruction capable of threatening the world, but now they treat us like red Indians on a reservation at the end of the 19th century."[113]

The *Journal* described the USAID project as harbinger of "the largest government reconstruction effort since Americans helped to rebuild Germany and Japan after World War II"—a description that quickly became a golden fleece dangled by business lobbies, with visions of billions rather than hundreds of millions of dollars in the offing. On May 1, the same newspaper drew even greater attention to the privatization agenda, this time with a front-page article headlined "Bush Officials Draft Broad Plan for Free-Market Economy in Iraq." The basic source for this piece was a hundred-page document drafted largely under the Treasury Department titled "Moving the Iraqi Economy from Recovery to Sustainable Growth," which had been circulated among financial consultants in February, prior to the invasion. This text was quoted as promoting "a broad-based Mass Privatization Program"—and the *Journal*'s lead paragraph did away with any possible lingering notion that Iraq really belonged to the Iraqis, as Rumsfeld had declared to applause in his "Beyond Nation Building" speech, or that the United States really intended to leave quickly. The article began as follows: "The Bush administration has drafted sweeping plans to remake Iraq's economy in the U.S. image."[114]

The bipolarity reflected in this abrupt transformation from being "beyond nation building" to being engaged in "sweeping plans" to create a little America on the Tigris found institutional form in the hastily created Coalition Provisional Authority. It was not until UN Resolution 1483 of May 22 validated the U.S. and British-led CPA that the word "occupation" actually became operative. Almost simultaneously, "nation building" began coursing through conservative circles in unexpected and discordant ways. One of the early technical advisers recruited by the CPA recalled (with some alarm) that "without exception" his fellow passengers on the flight to Baghdad were reading books not about Iraq, but about the occupations of Japan and Germany. Some months later, the conservative intellectual Francis Fukuyama voiced concern that the United States was only engaging in "nation-building 'lite'" (the repudiated State Department language of almost a year earlier) and not going far enough. Other conservatives were concerned for contrary reasons. When Condoleezza Rice belatedly assumed greater responsibility for Iraq (in early October), for example, her trusted adviser Robert Blackwill was assigned to look into the situation and responded in keeping with earlier apprehensions regarding occupation and nation building. "I don't like the way things are going over there," he was quoted as saying. "I don't like the political vibration. I don't like this idea of occupation."[115]

## Rendering Iraq "Open for Business"

Like it or not, Iraq was, as Bremer declared a few weeks after arriving, "open for business again." He might have added: and as never before. The initial occasion for this often-repeated comment was Resolution 1483 and the subsequent lifting of the economic sanctions that had been imposed on Iraq in 1990, but there was no intention to simply return to the status quo ante. Iraq's protective trade restrictions were abolished as soon as possible, with the import tariff eventually fixed at only 5 percent, paving the way for a flood of foreign imports. Bremer never lost an opportunity to explain the reasoning behind the CPA's shock program of sweeping privatization. "A free economy and a free people go hand in hand," he explained, and what this meant more specifically was that "substantial and broadly held resources, protected by private property, private rights, are the best protection of political freedom." In this context, "de-Baathification" signaled a great deal more than carrying out a political purge of the top levels of Saddam's police state. It also signified thoroughgoing deregulation of what Bremer referred to as the "Baathist command economy" and Saddam's "cockeyed socialist economic theory." Rumsfeld's parallel phrasing as the CPA came into existence and occupation replaced liberation was "market systems will be favored—not Stalinist command systems."[116]

The CPA's privatization agenda peaked in September 2003, with issuance of several orders. Order No. 37 established a flat tax rate of 15 percent, drastically reducing the burden on corporations and wealthy individuals. (This was another contrast to occupied Japan, where serious tax reform was not even addressed until 1949. The sweeping changes introduced at that time followed recommendations by a mission headed by Carl Shoup, stressed equity, and provided various tax breaks for companies—but at the same time instituted new taxes on capital gains, interest, accessions, and net worth, as well as a value-added tax.)[117]

Bremer's Order No. 39, which provoked the most intense responses pro and con, called for privatizing state enterprises, permitting 100 percent foreign ownership of Iraqi firms, tax-free repatriation of all investment profits, and forty-year leases on contracts. Under Order No. 40, privatization was extended to the banking sector in keeping, again, with

*113. Demonstrators protesting occupation policies outside a "Doing Business in Iraq" conference and exhibition in London, October 13, 2003. The "Iraq for Sale" catchphrase became ubiquitous in the wake of CPA announcements of plans to drastically privatize the Iraqi economy and open it to foreign investment.*

the goal of "transition from a non-transparent centrally planned economy to a market economy characterized by sustainable economic growth through the establishment of a dynamic private sector." Rumsfeld praised these reforms in Senate testimony on September 24, 2003, for creating "some of the most enlightened—and inviting—tax and investment laws in the free world." The *Economist* described them as "a capitalist dream"— albeit not without cynicism, for this frequently quoted phrase appeared in an article titled "Let's All Go to the Yard Sale."

Such popular perception that Iraq was not merely occupied but now also for sale does not appear to have given pause to the Americans who temporarily exercised sovereignty there. Apart from the rationality or irrationality of the CPA's orders—and no one denied the inefficiency and corruption of most Baathist economic institutions—what was particularly ill-conceived about this free-market jihad was its disregard of politics, mass psychology, and public appearance. Dreamers and critics alike spoke of a gold rush—and the critics, more precisely, of "blood money," "a license to loot the land," "a carpetbaggers' free-for-all." Iraqis them-

*114. Bilingual banner at a Sunni demonstration in front of the Baghdad headquarters of the Coalition Provisional Government, November 7, 2003. The demand for autonomy is presented as a fatwa, or Islamic religious decree.*

selves, blue collar and bourgeois alike, were appalled, and for good reason. As a former State Department official recalled the atmosphere in official Washington, "There was little interest in bringing in governments and companies from countries that had not supported the war. What motivated this view was a sense that to the victor should go the spoils, and that French and Russian firms should not benefit in any way given their opposition. . . . It is extraordinary that many people throughout the U.S. government thought Iraq was a jewel to hoard and not a burden to share. But they did."[118]

The frenzy to get in on the spoils was remarkable. A two-day "Rebuilding Iraq Conference" convened in Virginia that attracted hundreds of potential contractors and investors in late August, just before the key privatization orders were issued, typified this. A former secretary of defense (William Cohen) and former secretary of commerce (Mickey Kantor) were featured speakers. Bremer's "Iraq is open for business" statement headlined one version of the online advertising for the conference. The *Wall Street Journal*'s quote about "the largest government reconstruction effort" since Germany and Japan was recycled. The Council on Foreign Relations was cited as estimating "it will cost nearly $100 billion to rebuild Iraq"—and this was immediately trumped by noting that the Center for Strategic Budgetary Assessments "has calculated that the non-military rebuilding costs could near $500 billion." Iraq was described as "the newest, most lucrative and fastest growing market," a land with "enormous business potential."[119]

By year's end this euphoria had largely crashed to ground, but warning signs were present from the outset. The *Wall Street Journal*'s preinvasion article comparing USAID plans for Iraq to rebuilding Japan and Germany quoted a respected international-affairs expert, Anthony Cordesman, cautioning that it was essential to "convince the world that this is not profiteering." Immediate responses in the foreign press confirmed this would be difficult and probably impossible to do. The *Asia Times*, for example, summoned the language of a bygone age of turn-of-the-century imperialism vis-à-vis China by observing that "needless to say, the 'scramble for Iraq' is on." Coming from a different direction, politicians as well as businessmen excluded from the initial contracting process decried the "crony capitalism" of secret deals with companies known to have close Republican connections.[120]

When the *Journal* later publicized "plans to remake Iraq's economy in the U.S. image," its own page-one article again warned that this would be "controversial" and "contentious." Such plans were likened to the shock policies free-market apostles had introduced a decade previously in Russia and other countries of the former Soviet bloc, which met with decidedly mixed success as, in the *Journal*'s words, "rapid privatization of state-run enterprises led to sharp disruptions in jobs and services, as well as rampant corruption." This seemed increasingly prophetic as U.S. contractors began rushing into Iraqi while state-run companies remained in limbo, unemployment increased, and the infrastructure continued to deteriorate—all the more so when the State Department sponsored a conference of "VIPs" in the fortressed Green Zone in Baghdad simultaneously with the September issuance of the CPA's privatization orders and included Yegor Gaidar, the architect of Russia's draconian economic reforms, as a featured speaker.[121]

Even as promotion of the free-market reforms was at its peak, moreover, specialists in international law were observing that drastic privatization was probably illegal. This, too, was predictable. On May 22, just as the CPA settled in for business, the British weekly *New Statesman* leaked a secret memorandum to Prime Minister Blair from Lord Peter Goldsmith, the attorney general (who had previously declared the military invasion itself lawful, given the danger of Saddam's alleged weapons of mass destruction). Dated March 26, a week after the invasion began, this questioned the legality of the occupation in general and warned in particular that "the imposition of major structural economic reforms would not be authorized by international law."[122]

This commotion over economic policy threw particularly harsh and focused light on the general issue of the legality of the occupation. Attorneys representing the U.S. government and CPA maintained that drastically altering the existing economic system had been legitimized by Resolution 1483, since this was necessary to promote "effective administration" and "economic reconstruction and the conditions for sustainable development"—objectives endorsed by the United Nations. Many legal experts, on the other hand, pointed out that the CPA's privatization orders violated not only the Hague and Geneva provisions cited in the poorly drafted UN resolution, but also the U.S. Army's own field manual *The Law of Land Warfare* (which also reiterated the Hague and Geneva guidelines), as well as the Iraqi constitution (which, among other things, declared constitutional revision without the consent of the Iraqi people unlawful, barred private ownership of "national" resources or "the basic means of production," and explicitly prohibited foreign ownership of real estate or the establishment of companies by non-Arabs).[123]

This debate quickly became moot, for by the time the CPA closed shop on June 28, 2004, the vision of a gold rush already seemed like an opium dream. The "lucrative and fastest growing market" did not materialize. Chaos prevailed instead. Although the occupation had ended in name, however, it was not over in practice. U.S. forces stayed on, as did the foreign contractors with their lucrative public contracts, but market fundamentalism was dead as a policy prescription for Iraq. Three years later, beginning with the crash of the U.S. economy, it was all but dead worldwide—and the privatization mania in occupied Iraq, so damaging in so many ways, became emblematic of a much broader epoch of ideological wishful thinking.

## *Aid in Two Eras*

In September 2003, as these economic controversies regarding Iraq peaked amidst mounting political and social turmoil, President Bush again found it appropriate to offer defeated Japan and Germany as bright mirrors for Iraq. "America has done this kind of work before," he told the nation on September 7. "Following World War II, we lifted up the defeated nations of Japan and Germany, and stood with them as they built representative governments. We committed years and resources to this cause." On September 23, speaking before the UN General Assembly, he spoke of approaching Congress for "additional funding for our work in Iraq—the greatest financial commitment of its kind since the Marshall Plan."

The Marshall Plan comparison was natural, even irresistible—and more or less accurate insofar as eventual ballpark aid figures are concerned. By one careful estimate, U.S. aid allocations appropriated for Iraq from 2003 to 2006 totaled $28.9 billion, out of which $17.6 billion (62 percent) was directed to economic and political reconstruction and the remainder to improving Iraq security. This report, issued in March 2006 by the Congressional Research Service of the Library of Congress, concluded that "total U.S. assistance to Iraq thus far is roughly equivalent to total assistance (adjusted for inflation) provided to Germany—and almost double that provided to Japan—from 1946–1952." Converted to 2005 dollars, overall U.S. aid to Germany translated into a total of $29.3 billion, of which the Marshall Plan accounted for $9.3 billion. Over the same 1946–52 period, total assistance to Japan (where the Marshall Plan did not apply) amounted to roughly $15.2 billion in 2005 dollars, although the bulk of this was not directed to rehabilitating the economy.[124]

Quantitative comparison alone, however, is misleading. As with so many other matters pertaining to World War II and its aftermath, Winston Churchill became the most quoted phrasemaker for the Marshall Plan, famously describing it as "the most unsordid act in history." This was plausible hyperbole for what amounted to enlightened self-interest. The Marshall Plan, and economic aid programs for Europe and Japan more generally, served America's interests in several ways—not least, by

# OCCUPIED IRAQ AND THE LONG WAR

*To the end of the Bush presidency in January 2009, the visual record of this long war conveys a terrible stasis—terror, insurgency, ceaseless insecurity on the part of both the occupied and the U.S.-led military forces that occupied and patrolled them. American and British troops remained as tense and combat ready in 2008 as they were during the early weeks of Operation Iraqi Freedom more than five years earlier. The generic snapshots treasured by foreign photographers in occupied Japan some six decades earlier, depicting friendly soldiers interacting with local children, are also present for Iraq—but the soldiers are always armed to the teeth, and the children often injured. There are no counterparts to the soft subjects that attracted Westerners in occupied Japan—no scenes of socialization and fraternization, no discovery of the picturesque, no infatuation with indigenous traditions, no evocation of the feminine, the exotic, the mildly erotic. Year after year, anxiety, pain, trauma, protest, and grief draw the camera's eye.*

*115. November 12, 2004: U.S. soldiers rush a wounded comrade to a helicopter during operations in Fallujah.*

116. *March 5, 2005: A few weeks short of the beginning of the third year of occupation, a GI stands guard over a mother with two children during a routine house search in the northern city of Mosul.*

117. *January 11, 2007: American soldiers conduct a joint cordon and search operation with Iraqi army personnel in Baghdad.*

118.  *December 27, 2008: A mother and her three-year-old daughter lie in a Baghdad hospital after being injured in a car bombing in which twenty-two people were reported killed and fifty-four injured.*

119.  *July 12, 2008: A woman in Baghdad's Sadr City protests the detention of men seized in a house raid jointly conducted by U.S. and Iraqi forces.*

## COSTS OF WAR

*120. November 1, 2008: A woman weeps at a rally in Karbala demanding government aid for those widowed or orphaned following the U.S.-led invasion in 2003. When the Bush presidency ended, the human costs for Iraqis of its war of choice defied exact measurement but were in every respect tragic. The number of documented civilian deaths caused by terror, insurrection, and military operations between the invasion and January 2009 was around a hundred thousand, while serious estimates of violent deaths beyond the official numbers ran into the many hundreds of thousands. Estimates by Iraqi agencies of the number of children who had lost one or both parents ranged from one million to as many as five million, with a report released in January 2008 putting the number of homeless orphans at a half million. Around two million Iraqis, including a significant portion of the middle class, fled abroad after the invasion, mostly to neighboring countries. More than two million additional Iraqis had been internally displaced.*

helping to reconstruct and eventually integrate foreign economies that would provide markets for U.S. exports. This was explicit in the crisis vocabulary of official Washington in those times, which emphasized not only the vulnerability to communism of economically weak states in Europe and Asia, but also looming overproduction in the United States and a "dollar gap" that prevented foreign markets from absorbing this.[125]

More striking are the temporal, temperamental, and ideological differences between the post–World War II reconstruction agendas and Iraq. Where the first of these—*timing*—is concerned, economic reconstruction did not become a priority in occupied Germany and Japan until two to three years after the war ended. In both defeated nations, initial U.S. economic objectives were overwhelmingly directed at "economic disarmament" and "permanently" eliminating economic domination of neighboring countries. Accordingly, occupation authorities were explicitly ordered to take no actions aimed at "economic rehabilitation."

The basic directive to the commander in chief of U.S. forces in occupied Germany (dated April 26, 1945) made this eminently clear. "Germany's ruthless warfare and the fanatical Nazi resistance have destroyed the German economy and made chaos and suffering inevitable," this guiding document declared, and "the Germans cannot escape responsibility for what they have brought upon themselves." The clear and pressing goal was "the industrial disarmament and demilitarization of Germany" through reparations and severe restrictions on industrial production, and to this end, the U.S. commander was told, "You will take no steps (a) looking toward the economic rehabilitation of Germany, or (b) designed to maintain or strengthen the German economy." Beyond economic disarmament per se, this severe policy aimed at ensuring that "basic living standards" in Germany did not exceed "that existing in any one of the neighboring United Nations." This was not rescinded until July 1947, when a new Joint Chiefs of Staff directive (JCS 1779) affirmed that "an orderly and prosperous Europe requires the economic contributions of a stable and productive Germany." Prior to then, a considerable part of German heavy industry was dismantled for reparations, and severe restrictions were placed on production in critical sectors such as steel.[126]

Economic policy in Japan followed a similar course. Like the precedent directive for Germany, the Initial Post-Surrender Policy for Japan
minced no words on this. "The policies of Japan have brought down
upon the people great economic destruction and confronted them with
the prospect of economic difficulty and suffering," this guiding document observed, and then immediately proceeded to declare that "the
plight of Japan is the direct outcome of its own behavior, and the Allies
will not undertake the burden of repairing the damage." In this same
punitive spirit, again following the model for Germany, initial reparations policy envisioned using the dismantling and overseas relocation of
factories and the like not merely to compensate Japan's victims, and not
merely to raise standards of living elsewhere in Asia, but also to ensure
that such standards within Japan did not exceed those of neighboring
countries.[127]

When one of the most disastrous harvests in decades followed hard on
the heels of Japan's surrender, the United States responded with aid in the
form of foodstuffs, fertilizer, and the like; the explicit objective of such
humanitarian aid was to prevent social unrest that might imperil the occupation agenda. It was not until 1948 that a series of economic missions
from Washington called for suspending reparations, lifting restraints on
industrial production, abandoning the economic deconcentration program, curbing labor-union activity, laying off workers in the public sector
in particular, and promoting production for export even at the cost of
a decline in already precarious living standards. The key document that
established economic reconstruction and production for export as the new
"prime objective" of the occupation in Japan (NSC 13/2) was approved
by the National Security Council that summer and not signed by Truman
until October.[128]

There was no rationale in Iraq for the punitive economic neglect originally mandated in Germany and Japan—and, more critically, no time for
such procrastination. The Germans and Japanese could be left for a while
to stew in their own juices, as the more vindictive language of the times
often put it, but this was not feasible in ostensibly liberated Iraq. By choice,
America's preemptive war placed Iraq at the center of the war on terror
and center of global policy, making it a touchstone for what the United
States could and would do as a great power politically and economically as

well as militarily. There was no time to lose in making Iraq stable in every way—and, in practice, year after year passed with such precious time lost beyond recall.

THE *TEMPERAMENTAL* DIFFERENCES between economic planners in the early Cold War years and later, in the post–Cold War invasion of Iraq, are as striking as the differing windows of time. The belated decision to become actively engaged in promoting economic reconstruction in Europe in particular was undertaken with scrupulous care to avoid any appearance of impropriety. Probity was taken seriously, and so was the psychological as well as practical necessity of ensuring that recipients of U.S. aid played major roles in prescribing as well as administering the funds involved. Some seventeen nations in Western Europe ultimately benefited from the Marshall Plan (with Germany ranking behind Britain, France, and Italy in total aid received); and the recipients themselves took the lead in determining how the money would be used, with the United States exercising veto power over spending plans. European participation was conducted through the Committee on European Economic Cooperation (later renamed the Organization for European Economic Cooperation), which laid the groundwork for subsequent advances toward European unity.

This multinational structure of policy making and administration proved to be pragmatic, creative, and psychologically shrewd. At the same time, it was flexible and eclectic in catering to a diversity of national, political, and cultural as well as economic circumstances—necessarily and obviously so, administrators would have said at the time, although such distinctions and qualifications would be largely derided by the later believers in one-size-fits-all market fundamentalism. The program was also transparent and accountable. Congress created an independent Economic Cooperation Administration (ECA) that lasted only for the four-year duration of the Marshall Plan and was subjected to annual review before additional funds were appropriated. Staffed throughout its short life by individuals of considerable distinction drawn from both the public and private sectors, the ECA was applauded for avoiding politicization and corruption.[129]

Economic aid earmarked explicitly for reconstruction in Japan was comparatively modest. Most of the aid directed to Japan between 1946 and 1952 was administered through the U.S. government's GARIOA (Government Aid and Relief in Occupied Areas) program. This took the form primarily of food, agricultural supplies and equipment, and small amounts of medical supplies and the like, and totaled roughly $1.2 billion in value in then-current dollars ($7.9 billion in 2005 dollars). Infrastructure aid per se did not commence until mid-1948, under the so-called EROA (Economic Rehabilitation in Occupied Areas) program. Consisting primarily of machinery, industrial raw materials, transportation-related aid, and the like, this came to a total value of around $785 million ($5.2 billion in 2005 dollars). Additionally, as a vehicle for increasing the impact of the aid packages, beginning in 1949 the Japanese government directed some $845 million in yen proceeds from the sale of U.S. aid goods into a Counterpart Fund mechanism (also implemented in Europe) that committed the Japanese government to providing matching domestic funds for industrial reconstruction.[130]

In both Europe and Japan, the bureaucratic promotion of reconstruction was largely disciplined and professional—and, of inestimable importance, involved intimate participation by the recipients. (It did not, at the same time, escape some corruption on the Japanese side.) This is particularly noteworthy when set against, first, the notorious degree to which Iraqis were excluded from serious policy making during the reign of the CPA; and, second, the privatization, cronyism, ideological litmus tests, failures of oversight and auditing, unfulfilled promises, and outright corruption that came to be associated with appropriations for reconstruction in Iraq. The latter practices did not merely make "sordid" rather than "unsordid" a commonplace description of what actually transpired. In the eyes of much of the world, including the Iraqis, they made a mockery of all the high language about the rationality, efficiency, and discipline of economies structured (borrowing the *Wall Street Journal*'s phrase) "in the U.S. image."

THIS TEMPERAMENTAL DISCONNECT between the early Cold War planners and their post–Cold War counterparts went hand in hand with disparate *ideological* attitudes regarding bureaucratic competence and responsibility on the one hand, and private-sector efficiency and rationality on the other. This is not to deny ideological resonance across the generations. Once the late-1940s planners in Washington concluded that Germany and Japan had to be rehabilitated as the major "workshops" of a noncommunist Europe and Asia, respectively, concerted attention was devoted to increasing their productivity, improving their managerial skills, and integrating them into regional and global market systems capable of resisting and containing Soviet (and, quickly, Chinese) communism. Where Asia in particular was concerned, from 1949 on U.S. planners became fixated on closing off trade with China and developing tight, hierarchical trade relations linking Japan, Southeast Asia, and the United States—a vision of market integration that some planners referred to privately as a little "Marshall Plan for Asia." Early preoccupation with creating a viable domestic Japanese market by liberating workers and peasants gave way to promoting the interests of capital and coupling production for export with enforcing domestic austerity, while simultaneously undermining the influence of organized labor and the political left.[131]

These revised policies for the former Axis enemy were explicitly framed in terms of the "serious international situation created by the Soviet Union's policy of aggressive Communist expansion" (in the opening words of NSC 13/2), and emphasized that in relaxing the earlier focus on reform "private enterprise should be encouraged." Even while endorsing this vision of a bipolar world pitting capitalism against communism, however, these late-1940s policy makers never came close to embracing the shrink-the-government, privilege-the-private-sector, eliminate-all-barriers-to-foreign-trade-and-investment ideology that had become gospel by the time of the Iraq war. On the contrary, the new agendas of anticommunist economic assistance enlisted the expertise of professionals who usually supported interventionist policies of the sort associated with Keynesian theories and the New Deal, and who consequently tolerated and even encouraged what later free-market fundamentalists would denounce as planned or mixed economies.

An important policy directive introduced in December 1948, two months after NSC 13/2 was adopted, thus emphasized the "urgency that the Supreme Commander require the Japanese Government immediately to put into effect a program of domestic economic stabilization, including measures leading to fiscal, monetary, price, and wage stability, and maximum production for export." In putting this in play, occupation authorities collaborated with the Japanese government in promoting institutions, laws, and practices that became central to the industrial policy Japan rode to prosperity over the next several decades. These measures went beyond creation of the powerful Ministry of International Trade and Industry (MITI) in 1949 and extended to the passage in 1949 and 1950 of legislation governing trade, foreign exchange, and foreign investment. This was accompanied by the institutionalization of pervasive extralegal bureaucratic practices that eventually became widely known as "administrative guidance" (*gyōsei shidō*).[132]

Creation of the Ministry of International Trade and Industry capped a striking development in Japan's transition from war to peace. Beginning in the 1930s, central planning became a fixation of leaders intent on mobilizing the nation for "total war." Consolidation of influence and authority followed in both the public and private sectors, with the military assuming ever greater control over the bureaucracy and top-level cabinet planning. Defeat and occupation eliminated the military establishment, but not the penetrating reach of centralized authority. Civilian ministries and agencies assumed greater autonomy than before, particularly where economic issues were involved—and, by both example and deliberate policy, U.S. occupation authorities strengthened such bureaucratic prestige and authority even further. MacArthur's headquarters itself was the perfect model of a hierarchical command structure, and by operating indirectly through the Japanese government it bolstered the influence of Japan's own bureaucrats. By contrast to the experienced administrators and technocrats who honed their skills in the war years and survived the passage through to peace unpurged, Japan's postwar politicians were a motley and inexperienced crew.

MITI, inaugurated in conjunction with the so-called Dodge line—a severe "disinflation" policy orchestrated by the conservative Detroit banker Joseph Dodge—became the centerpiece in the new agenda of guiding the private sector toward export-oriented production. Its influence extended beyond control over imports and exports to include energy policy, patents and technology transfers, loans and subsidies, strategic allotment of critical resources to designated key sectors (beginning with coal, steel, shipbuilding, and electric power), transfers of capital, and promotion of higher value-added manufactures. MITI worked in close and not always amiable collaboration with the business community, and became the acknowledged master of the art of exerting influence by "administrative guidance"—that is, by recommendations and warnings backed up by powers of persuasion other than the law.

The political scientist Chalmers Johnson later famously described the industrial policy associated with MITI as a "plan-oriented market economy," and postwar Japan itself as a "capitalist development state." It was certainly a hybrid; but what is notable in retrospect, particularly when set against the privatization craze associated with market fundamentalism, is that it was American planners alongside sharp Japanese technocrats and businessmen—rather than some sort of peculiar "cultural" or "traditional" Japanese propensity—that established this as a rational model for promoting economic growth in the dire circumstances in which defeated Japan found itself.[133]

## Combating Carpetbagging in an Earlier Time

Apart from serving as midwife to MITI and encouraging "administrative guidance," U.S. occupation authorities also introduced legislation that reflected thinking antithetical to the CPA's shock program aimed at opening Iraq's economy to unrestricted foreign trade and investment. The Americans who helped plan Japan's recovery endorsed protectionism as essential for moving toward meaningful "self-sufficiency." Like the later nation builders in Iraq, their ultimate goal was to integrate Japan in a global capitalist system—but with careful attention to indigenous needs and morale, and not overnight.

Protectionism was grounded in two laws: the "Foreign Exchange and Foreign Trade Control Law" enacted in February 1949, and "Foreign Investment Law" passed the following year. Both laws rested on legislation dating back to the early 1930s, and both survived until 1979, when the former was substantially revised and the latter abolished. Passage of the exchange and trade law enabled Japan to resume private trade for the first time since the occupation began, and endorsed relatively free trade in principle while permitting a high level of government control in practice. A standard reference source on Japan notes that it was "ironic that these 'reformed' controls came to resemble the prewar system in its complexity, coverage, and effectiveness," and then proceeds to summarize the rationale for this neatly: "Given the urgent task of recovery from World War II, the occupation authorities and the Japanese government felt it essential to regulate the flow and distribution of exports, imports, and foreign exchange. Every major resource was critically scarce, and the free market could hardly be relied upon to achieve an optimal allocation of resources for the reconstruction of the country."[134]

Where foreign investment was concerned, the contrast to Iraq was striking in ways beyond simple protectionism as opposed to a "capitalist dream" of free and unfettered foreign access. There was no initial "open for business" euphoria as promoted by the CPA and private-sector entrepreneurs, no early "gold rush" frenzy to get in on investment opportunities. Unlike Iraq's oil, there was nothing in the way of natural as opposed to human resources. On the contrary, Japan's economic prospects appeared dismal at the time and provoked negligible interest in U.S. business circles. Officials like Under Secretary of the Army William H. Draper Jr., who traveled the chambers-of-commerce circuit in the United States trying to drum up interest in Japan once the reverse course began in 1948, met a tepid response; and even into the mid-1950s, architects of the Cold War U.S.-Japan relationship such as John Foster Dulles had no vision at all of Japan ever producing sophisticated manufactures that might be competitive in the United States or other Western markets.[135]

Many capital-starved Japanese firms were anxious to attract foreign investors at this time, and U.S. planners deemed it necessary to protect them against themselves, lest they sell out controlling interest for a fraction of their company's worth. Robert Fearey, a State Department specialist on Japan, spelled out this reasoning in a little book about the new "second phase" of the occupation published in 1950. Investment in Japan required licensing by SCAP, Fearey explained, which took care to ensure that this involved only "projects which would improve Japan's foreign exchange position or otherwise positively aid Japan's economic rehabilitation."

Investment in Japanese enterprises, Fearey went on, "was made subject to the further condition that the investment must include provision of

additional assets for the enterprise in contradistinction to the mere purchase of stocks or securities from other investors. Even with observance
of these conditions, the depressed prices for Japanese securities since the
war have offered opportunities for acquisition of securities at prices so far
below their actual worth as to require careful review of each transaction by
SCAP and the Japanese Government to avoid carpetbagging." While the
Foreign Investment Law of 1950 was promulgated to facilitate an inflow
of foreign capital and guarantee protection for such investments, it thus
simultaneously permitted the government to control such investment by
overseeing borrowing and prohibiting full or majority foreign ownership.
Instead, the Japanese government and its American patrons promoted the
purchase of foreign, and mostly American, technologies.[136]

## *Mixed Legacies in an Age of Forgetting*[137]

The mixed economy was not, of course, peculiar to Japan or to the mid-
twentieth century or to countries struggling to recover from the ravages
of a war that shattered most of the world outside the United States. The
role of the state differed from place to place and time to time. It reflected
both doctrinaire and pragmatic outlooks, as well as keen historical awareness of the destruction caused by private wealth and power left free to
grind less powerful people and countries beneath its wheels.

In Japan's case, the postwar mixed economy obviously reflected particular historical and cultural circumstances. Just as obviously, it drew attention because the nation became so prosperous so quickly, outstripping
even its erstwhile Axis ally Germany as well as other mixed economies of
Europe. The mix, in any case, was more practical than cultural in a traditional sense—a product, in good part, of the exigencies and disasters of
war followed by the evolving circumstances of the post-defeat interlude of
occupation. Policy played a role, and so did happenstance like the Korean
War. And not one but two states, centered in Tokyo and Washington,
were involved in shaping this.

Over time, many aspects of the Japanese economy that emerged out
of war and occupation became anachronistic, even as certain myths concerning early postwar reconstruction survived. The impact of U.S. aid
was one such myth. In practice this came late where reconstruction was

concerned. It was helpful but not enormous—and, in the larger financial balance sheet, was offset by the much greater cost to the Japanese
treasury of providing logistic support for the U.S. occupation forces.
By one estimate, the latter—which, at U.S. insistence, was more or less
hidden in the annual Japanese budgets—amounted to more than 2.4
times the total of GARIOA and EROA aid combined. These are the
sort of "black hole" figures that are usually forgotten even in standard
histories.[138]

Beyond this, it was not so much occupation-period economic policy as
a new war in Asia—the conflict that erupted in Korea in June 1950—that
jump-started Japanese recovery and prompted Prime Minister Yoshida
and Japanese conservatives in general to welcome the conflagration next
door as a "gift from the gods." Japan's Korean War boom involved a huge
influx of "special procurements" (*tokujū*) of goods and services from the
U.S. military. As the occupation ended and the war next door tapered off,
such orders were perpetuated in the form of "new special procurements"
(*shintokujū*).

Between June 1950 and the end of 1953, these military-related dollar
infusions brought around $2.3 billion into Japan—more than the total
aid received between 1945 and 1951—with another $1.75 billion of "new
special procurements" from 1954 through 1956, constituting the major
portion of the newly sovereign nation's "export" income. This was the
stimulating milieu in which Japanese engineers and entrepreneurs introduced, among other things, the practices of "quality control" that became
a signal feature of the nation's economic takeoff in the 1960s and 1970s.
Often associated with Japan's tradition of fine craftsmanship, quality control actually was learned from American teachers, and one in particular:
W. Edwards Deming.[139]

Certain initial occupation reforms in the economic and social spheres
provided a sound foundation for reconstruction—and, beyond this, for the
relatively equitable distribution of subsequent postwar prosperity. Notable
among these were the sweeping land reform, strengthening of the rights
of organized labor, and diversification of shareholding through dissolution of family-controlled *zaibatsu* holding companies. Also of immeasurable influence were the early demilitarization policies that channeled the
talents of the huge cadres of engineers and skilled blue-collar workers who

had been trained during the mobilization for war into civilian sectors like electronics and transportation. Far more than the Americans realized at the time, the Japanese workforce was primed to turn out high value–added exports once it found an international market.

For two decades after the occupation ended in 1952, that international market was severely restricted by the Japanese government's reluctant acquiescence to irresistible U.S. pressure to participate in the containment of the People's Republic of China. The compensatory payoff came in the form of preferential access to American licenses and patents, U.S. aid and trade policies that promoted Japanese trade with Southeast Asia, and U.S. indulgence of Japan's protracted maintenance of the protectionist measures introduced in 1949 and 1950 to prevent "carpetbagging" and foreign exploitation. Here, in both negative and positive ways, the interventionist state was more conspicuously America rather than Japan, although such gross foreign intrusion rarely enters discussions of the economic role of the state.[140]

A parallel and inseparable Cold War trade-off involved granting the United States military bases throughout Japan, and in Okinawa in particular, in return for security guarantees under the so-called U.S. nuclear umbrella. The domestic costs of this to Okinawa, which became a distorted military-base economy, were particularly harsh. When the United States invaded Iraq in 2003, the U.S. military presence in Japan was approaching its sixth decade, with no end in sight. Extension of this American empire of bases, more or less assumed by U.S. policy makers to be a boundless and inalienable right, may well turn out to be one of the closest parallels between the two occupations.[141]

■

"DEMOCRACY" WAS CERTAINLY a legacy of the occupation period in Japan, alongside the mixed economy, however far from ideal this democracy may have been in practice given the persistence into the twenty-first century of what amounted to a largely one-party conservative domination of the government along the lines established by Yoshida and others in the late 1940s and early 1950s. Contrary to the arguments of the "old Asia hands" that the Japanese people were incapable of self-governance—and contrary to the parallel hopes and expectations of old-line conservatives like Yoshida—many of the liberal ideals codified in one form or another during the initial years of postwar reformism took root. These values and reforms may be excoriated by contemporary Japanese conservatives and neonationalists, and may be diluted as time passes, but the early ideals of antimilitarism and democratization entered the contemporary political bloodstream. This is the "occupation legacy" that propagandists for the war of choice against Iraq chose to pry out of context as a mirror for Iraq, ignoring the domestic and historical circumstances that made this possible.

Where the mixed economy is concerned, the misuse of the Japanese example is just as basic. In time, the visible hand of the state choked off growth and creative responses to new challenges. As it happened, the dramatic bursting of the Japanese bubble occurred at the very end of the 1980s, almost simultaneously with the collapse of the Soviet Union— thus contributing, in its own way, to the celebration of privatization and market fundamentalism that became the voguish economic groupthink in America well before September 11. In the new age of selective remembrance and collective forgetting, the pragmatic and positive accomplishments of Japan's mixed economy—and of much postwar U.S. and European policy and practice as well—were simply written out of the picture. Placing near-absolute trust in the rationality and discipline of the market was the new gospel, regulation and long-term planning the new taboos— and it followed that there was nothing positive to be learned from past or even contemporary circumstances that suggested that this too (like the other side of the coin, unquestioning faith in the state) was a delusion and potential disaster.

Economic planning and protectionism in postwar Japan may have outlived their usefulness, but in their heyday this was a reasonable way of allocating scarce resources, promoting long-term thinking, reconciling national needs and private interests, competing in a cut-throat global economy as an initially vulnerable participant, ensuring a generous measure of overall social welfare, and even stimulating intense internal competition. For several decades the results captured the world's attention and were commonly if erroneously heralded as a "miracle." Real economic growth averaged roughly 10 percent annually in the 1960s, and 4 to 6 percent in the 1970s and 1980s. The great majority of Japan's citizens, struggling to start over in a ruined land only thirty-some years earlier, shared in this prosperity.

Like so much else in the recent past, most of this had been consigned to the bone yard of unfashionable history well before 9-11 and the war of choice against Iraq. "Globalization," "privatization," "outsourcing," "shrinking the government," and kindred articles of faith replaced basic planning and performance tasks that had been central to the post–World War II military occupation of Japan. Contempt for bureaucratic planning—not to mention for divergent opinions or worst-case contingency planning—suffused the ranks of top policy makers and led to almost inevitable tactical and strategic imbecilities. Cronyism and corruption coupled with disdain for the technical capabilities—and immediate pressing needs—of the Iraqis resulted in the very opposite of what transpired in occupied Japan: reconstruction and recovery entrusted to foreign profit seekers rather than to the Iraqis themselves. Although the destructive psychological as well as material repercussions of this were predictable, this made no difference to either the ideologues or the profiteers. Almost any proposal that ran counter to privatization and promotion of U.S.-led international capitalism was dismissed as Stalinist, or Baathist, or some other form of totalitarian command economy. One-size-fits-all theories and metrics flushed history, culture, psychology, and common sense down the drain—all in the name of hard-headed rationality. Those who called attention to red flags or writings on the wall—and there were more than a few such voices at middle and lower levels of the civilian and military bureaucracies—were placed beyond the pale.

There were no by-the-number "lessons" in social engineering or nation building to be learned from occupied Japan and its particular mix of the state and private sector. That was a different time and place. At the same time, however, there were general lessons to be learned about framing issues, thinking historically, imagining how things looked through the eyes of others, maintaining legitimacy, avoiding the appearance (let alone reality) of incompetence and corruption, balancing public requirements and private interests, recognizing the need for long-term planning as well as restraints on exploitation and profiteering, and practicing rather than just preaching optimal transparency and accountability.

Where a culture of willful forgetfulness prevails instead—and history, like intelligence data, becomes little more than a supermarket in which to pick and choose whatever conforms to existing tastes—neither war nor occupation nor liberation nor peaceful reconciliation and reconstruction are likely to be carried out successfully.

# FOOLS' ERRANDS
# AND FOOLS' GOLD

## Secular Priesthoods and Faith-Based Policies

After 9-11, George W. Bush and Osama bin Laden came to personify holy war in the old-fashioned sense of a clash of faiths, cultures, and civilizations. They quoted scripture, posited a Manichaean world of good versus evil, and never ceased to evoke the Almighty and portray themselves as His righteous and wrathful agent. Both were deeply religious men who lived in realms of certitude fortified against doubt and criticism.

Faith-based thinking, however, transcends religion and conventional clash-of-cultures categories. Modern war itself is a culture—just as bureaucratic behavior is, or corporate behavior, or the "herd instinct." In theory, moral norms codified in the Hague Regulations and Geneva Conventions govern the conduct of war in the West. Again in theory, "rationality" of a fundamentally Western sort governs modern bureaucratic, political, and economic behavior. In practice, this is mostly wishful thinking. Modern war remains largely wholesale killing. Bureaucracies are congeries of contending fiefdoms. Political morality is as often as not an oxymoron. And as the closing months of the Bush presidency revealed, "market rational" capitalism is in great part a myth. Beliefs and behaviors that have nothing to do with traditional religion rule our days, propagated and enforced by secular priesthoods.

To think about priesthoods, dogmas, and profane behavior in this manner is unsettling. Religion does still matter. Great struggles over conflicting ideals do remain integral to some if not all wars: World War II remains
the proof positive of this. At the same time, however, war and the men and
machinery and motives that drive it are more susceptible to comparative
analysis than antagonists are willing to acknowledge.

Japan's *seishin* or holy war in Asia and the Pacific, for example, was
conducted in the name of the "sacred and inviolable" emperor and sacro-
sanct Imperial Way ideology he exemplified. No serious historian, however, regards this as the key to why the nation went to war, or how it
conducted its military operations, or why all ended in ruinous defeat. On
the contrary, historians look to politics and geopolitics; to socialization
and indoctrination in a Depression-era imperialist world; to both organizational and individual pathologies; to strategic planning and, as it turned
out, strategic imbecilities.

Similarly, no one quotes more messianic scripture than the Islamist terrorists who made jihad a word that requires no translation. By the end
of the Bush presidency, however, only the most obdurate solipsists in
and outside the White House could ignore the diverse local conditions
and territorial concerns that drove individuals to terror or insurrection
in the first place—increasingly so, as it transpired, after the invasions of
Afghanistan and Iraq. Observations that were all but unthinkable right
after 9-11—that terrorists are not merely rational in their military tactics, for instance, but may also be "modern" and even "postmodern" in
their propaganda and globalized appeals—had become commonplace six
or seven years later.

Each in their own way, bin Laden and the Washington planners who
failed to anticipate 9-11 and embarked on a ruinous "war on terror" in its
wake engaged in faith-based thinking of a secular nature. It was the sanctity of native ground, centering in his case on Saudi Arabia, that initially
propelled Al Qaeda's leader to declare war on the West. And it was an article of faith in bin Laden's military belief system that superpower America
would prove acutely vulnerable to nonstate, low-intensity, asymmetrical
warfare. This, he declared years before September 11, was the great lesson
of the Soviet Union's defeat in Afghanistan in the 1980s.

By contrast, despite having supported the Islamists who brought down the Russians, American leaders drew no serious lessons about irregular warfare from Afghanistan—or from the earlier U.S. quagmire in Vietnam. On the contrary, they continued to rest faith in the traditional "American way of war": possessing and deploying overwhelming military force. As a knowledgeable insider (David Kilcullen) later phrased it, "One particular high-technology *über-blitzkrieg* style of fighting . . . had become conventional orthodoxy." This faith in brute force goes far to explain the failures of intelligence and imagination that were exposed on September 11 and in the war of choice against Iraq. At the time, any reasoned criticism of this orthodoxy was dismissed as "subversion," "defeatism"—or, put in terms of secular theology, heresy.[1]

This American veneration of force commonly found expression in shorthand. "The revolution in military affairs" was one of the most seductive of such mantras. "Shock and awe" was another (with Hiroshima and Nagasaki as prototype examples from an age of cruder weapons). "Cakewalk" captured the euphoric certainty of the true believer: America's power, coupled with its virtue, guaranteed that Iraq and subsequently much of the rest of the Middle East would move under the eagle's wing with little difficulty. A critic writing in the early weeks of the Obama administration called attention to a companion strain of faith-based military strategizing: the almost surreal "shibboleths of cold war nuclear theology" that continued to enthrall "the mandarins of the nuclear establishment."[2]

Apart from an ever-evolving technological capacity to kill and destroy, there is nothing new in the phenomenon of military creeds promoted by a lay clergy and taken to heart by credulous disciples and acolytes. What shielded the Bush administration from accountability even after its policies were exposed as coarse and incompetent, however, had little to do with the undeniable threat of terrorism. Rather, this immunity was inherent in the inviolate nature of the national "security state" that was spawned by World War II and the Cold War. Forty years prior to September 11, the America historian and critic Lewis Mumford was already describing this Leviathan as a "priestly monopoly of secret knowledge, the multiplication of secret agencies, the suppression of open discussion, and even the insulation of error against public criticism and exposure through a 'bi-partisan' military and foreign policy, which in practice nullifies public reaction and makes rational dissent the equivalent of patriotic disaffection, if not trea-

*121. A memorial in San Francisco's Washington Square on the first anniversary of the September 11 attacks. A total of 3,037 small flags were planted, including the flags of fifty-seven nations representing non-American victims.*

son." The security state, with its holy writ and labyrinthine complexity, amounted to a profane theocracy.[3]

FAITH-BASED THINKING EXCLUDES whole worlds from close examination. Truly critical appraisal of one's own assumptions and acts is beyond the pale. At the same time, the circumstances, attitudes, and capabilities of others are given short shrift. This seems counterintuitive where policy making affecting war and peace is concerned, since the essence of strategic planning presumably is to know the enemy while also knowing and acknowledging one's own flaws and vulnerabilities. In practice this is accomplished imperfectly.

The failures of U.S. military intelligence in 1941 and 2001 reflect this hermitic mindset. So do the "strategic imbecilities" of Japan's war of choice in 1941 and America's war of choice against Iraq over sixty years

*122. As the fifth anniversary of the invasion of Iraq approached, a church in Miami created this display in honor of Americans killed to that date in Afghanistan and Iraq. The memorial, photographed on March 17, 2008, featured 4,454 small flags.*

later, which in both cases reflected wishful and delusory thinking. Over and over, dogma trumped unbiased analysis and prevented incisive criticism and self-criticism from penetrating the top levels of decision makers. Groupthink prevailed. Massive operations mesmerized Japanese war planners in 1941 and White House and Pentagon strategists after 9-11. In the process, policies not involving brute force were marginalized. Anticipating and planning for the endgame was shunted aside. Red lights that seem obvious in retrospect were ignored.

After it became clear there was no substance to the arguments offered for invading Iraq (Saddam Hussein's alleged collusion with Al Qaeda and possession of weapons of mass destruction that could fall into terrorist hands), "cherry-picking" became a popular metaphor among critics. The phrase is more suggestive than is apparent at first glance. Apart from the skewed culling of raw intelligence data, which was plain to see in retrospect, the more intractable question is whether this was witting or unwitting—whether it reflected plain mendacity, or rather planners seeking and seeing what they were predisposed to find. Cherry-picking extended, moreover, beyond intelligence analysis to the uses and abuses of history. Running red lights—even failing to see them at all—involved an almost disdainful disregard of modern times and the very recent past.

All holy warriors ransack history to make a case for their own virtue as opposed to the transgressions and double standards of their foes. Beginning in the 1930s, the Japanese presented their aggression as "liberation" from long decades of Western imperialism and colonialism in Asia. The oppression and exploitation that took place in the areas they themselves occupied were glossed as "coexistence and coprosperity." Much of the anti-Western rhetoric of Islamist fundamentalists is similar in calling attention to the negative legacies of Western intrusion in the Middle East, tracing back to World War I in particular. That such uses of history are not groundless makes them effective as propaganda. That this is also half-truth history, scapegoating history, mythmaking, an adroit camouflage of one's own failures, crimes, sins, and double standards is, of course, never acknowledged.

On the U.S. side—as unwittingly captured in the impromptu response to 9-11 announcing that "history begins today"—much recent history was simply erased. The negative legacies of decades of European and American involvement in the Middle East were airbrushed away, along with any recognition that such legacies were imbedded in the big picture most Muslims and Arabs saw. Terror bombing was presented as an atrocity by "nonstate" actors who did not share the respect for human life that lies at the heart of Western values—thus amputating the practice of targeting noncombatants to undermine enemy morale from the establishment of this as standard operating procedure in the British and American air war during World War II. The U.S. failure to engage in serious planning for post-hostilities Iraq reflected a deep ideological aversion to "occupation," and "nation building" more specifically, despite the fact that past experience fairly screamed this would be an inescapable and daunting challenge in a decapitated post-Saddam Iraq. Overriding all was a Great Power arrogance that erased history's many examples of the pride and power of aggrieved groups and nationalities, the destructiveness and resilience of grassroots insurgencies, and the effective weapons of the weak in asymmetrical conflict.

However the post-Saddam Iraqi state may eventually shake down, the Bush administration's conduct of the "war on terror"—including the invasions of Afghanistan and Iraq and reliance on brute force for years thereafter—will enter history primarily as the fools' errands of a fundamentally faith-based planning process.

## Fools' Errands

In the final months of the Bush presidency, reports by the inspector general's offices of two different federal agencies suggested that nothing much had changed since September 11 when it came to eliminating deep dysfunction. A few days after the November 2008 presidential election, the inspector general of the Office of the Director of National Intelligence (ODNI), an agency established in response to the recommendations of the 9-11 Commission, issued a short, harsh report. The federal intelligence community was now composed of seventeen separate organizations, this observed, and the ODNI itself, ostensibly created to impose order on the sprawl of agencies that impeded intelligence gathering prior to 9-11, was regarded by many insiders as "just an 'additional layer of bureaucracy.'"

The November report called attention to organizational pathologies that differed little in essence from investigative findings dating back to the Pearl Harbor hearings after World War II. "Confusion about lines of authority" prevailed, along with "poor internal communications and lack of transparency." Even the ODNI had become a site of "'turf battles' . . . causing information and activities to be 'stovepiped'"—leading to the dismal conclusion that "the culture of protecting 'turf' remains a problem and there are few, if any, consequences for failure to collaborate." Lawyers, the report observed, as often as not impeded rather than helped resolve these problems ("quite often . . . legal impediments ended up being either myths that overcautious lawyers had never debunked or policy choices swathed in pseudo-legal justification"). Where intelligence gathering now involved reliance on outside contractors, the process was "impeded by a perceived lack of trust, communication, and accountability."[4]

The following month, the Office of the Special Inspector General

for Iraq Reconstruction released a much lengthier and equally damning report. Five years and nine months had passed since the invasion.
Titled *Hard Lessons* and focused on relief and reconstruction operations,
this analysis amounted to a diagnosis of pervasive intellectual sloth and
bureaucratic incompetence. The report did not address war planning per
se, or the politicization of policy making, or the incompetence of specific individuals. Nonetheless, its findings clearly applied across the board
to the White House and Pentagon, Congress, the federal bureaucracy,
and the private sector to which so many Iraq-related tasks had been outsourced. Opening with criticism of "the blinkered and disjointed pre-war
planning for Iraq's reconstruction," the report ended nearly five hundred
pages later by observing that, even after five years of chaos, "the government as a whole has never developed a legislatively-sanctioned doctrine or
framework for planning, preparing, and executing contingency operations
in which diplomacy, development, and military action all figure."[5]

More precisely than in the ODNI report, *Hard Lessons* spelled out
how almost all the generic failures of intelligence, imagination, planning,
and execution that had been apparent and widely discussed since 9-11
remained uncorrected. These included "back-of-the-envelope" planning,
turf wars, and "colliding chains of command" exacerbated by a "bureaucratic inertia" that, in Iraq, involved at least sixty-two offices and agencies engaged in managing reconstruction funding alone. Coherent policy
making was impeded by the culture of bureaucratic secrecy, as well as
chronic understaffing and underfinancing. Planners remained fixated on
"best-case" scenarios, and the "good soldier" syndrome of going along
with whatever an inept leadership prescribed compounded such wishful
thinking. Disdain for the sensibilities and capabilities of non-Western
others took concrete form in repeated imposition of ill-considered "*fait
accompli*" on the supposedly liberated Iraqis.[6]

The adjective "ad hoc" peppers *Hard Lessons* like a favorite condiment.
In one summary passage, the inspectors even describe the entire public-
private management amalgam they were evaluating as an "adhocracy"—a
sardonic albeit still restrained label for the protracted strategic imbecility
that fell under their review. A less tempered appraisal was offered around
this same time by Ahmad Chalabi, the favorite native son of neoconservative hawks who had lobbied for Saddam's overthrow even before 9-11.

Chalabi viewed America's five-plus years in Iraq with bitter ambiguity and associated it with, among other things, "an utterly corrupt reconstruction program that oversaw one of the biggest financial crimes in history, which has left average Iraqis with little water, power, health care, education or even food."[7]

The prescriptive side of the inspector general's critique amounted to a predictable primer for would-be reformers, spelling out the familiar utopia of bureaucratic rationality: unity of command; integrated systems; interagency coordination to eliminate "stovepipes" and "logjams"; rigorous oversight, discipline, and transparency in outsourcing; smart balancing of hard and soft (or military and civilian) power; and so on. There was nothing new in this wish list. September 11 had prompted urgent calls for such reforms, but with superficial results at best. Bureaucratic dysfunction lubricated the delusory and destabilizing invasion of Iraq in 2003. If anything, it increased after the invasion revealed there were no plans for an endgame. Turf wars, indiscipline, and nontransparency were greater than ever when the U.S.-led Coalition Provisional Authority skulked out of Baghdad in mid-2004, after a year of floundering occupation. *Hard Lessons* amounted to an indictment of managerial and organizational pathologies that characterized the full course of the Bush presidency—even after insurgency threatened to tear Iraq apart in 2005 and 2006, and even after the military "surge" and buying off of Islamic (and largely Sunni) dissidents that began in 2007 lowered the level of violence.

SUCH CRITICISM CARRIED a particular irony in that it was directed against an administration whose top officials took pride in calling attention to their managerial experience and expertise. Although their legacy to the world, including their political successors at home, was negligence and disarray spilling into disaster, this of course was not how they themselves saw it as they exited the stage. In a brief "farewell address" broadcast on January 15, 2009, President Bush did little more than strike a few familiar chords. His presidency had been defined by September 11 ("the worst attack on America since Pearl Harbor"). Although his persistent reference to good and evil "has made some uncomfortable," it was important to recognize that "good and evil are present in this world, and between the

two of them there can be no compromise." Afghanistan had been transformed from a cruel Taliban regime that harbored Al Qaeda into "a young
democracy," he averred, and Iraq from a brutal dictatorship into "an Arab
democracy at the heart of the Middle East."[8]

There was no self-reflection in this or other valedictories by departing officials. No acknowledgment of the enormous suffering and tens
and hundreds of thousands of deaths that arrogant, careless, and cal-
lous decision making had caused. No recognition of hubris, or having
erred in placing inordinate faith in brute force. No regret at having
stumbled from year to year as an "adhocracy." No mention, naturally,
that the "war on terror" turned a necessary campaign against terrorism
into fools' errands that left the incoming administration confronted with
ongoing instability and conflict in Iraq and Afghanistan, a new generation of recruits to Islamist terrorism, a Middle East and Central Asia and
South Asia wracked with tension and bristling with lethal weapons, and
an America that had squandered the enormous goodwill it enjoyed in the
wake of September 11.

## Fools' Gold

In these waning days of a bankrupt presidency, president-elect Barack
Obama called passing attention to the critique of the Oval Office that had
been building up ever since the fiasco of Operation Iraqi Freedom and
the fatuous "Mission Accomplished" performance: *groupthink*. "One of
the dangers in a White House, based on my reading of history," he told
reporters, "is that you get wrapped up in groupthink, and everybody agrees
with everything, and there's no discussion and there are not dissenting
views."[9] By this date, however, groupthink had acquired connotations far
beyond just policy making at the highest level. It also was associated with
a staggering crisis in the private sector: nothing less than the meltdown
of the financial and economic order at home and abroad, triggered by the
bursting of the so-called subprime-mortgage bubble in the United States
beginning in 2007. The fundamentalist faith in unfettered markets that
had contributed so greatly to both non-planning and chaotic planning in
the Iraq war and occupation—repudiating "nation building" and embracing extreme privatization—had imploded. Like their White House and

Pentagon brethren, the erstwhile realists on Wall Street and in banking and investment circles throughout the world turned out to be riding on faith and incapable of anticipating catastrophic risk.

Almost no one of influence predicted this. The prescient few who did warn that the financial system was careening out of control were ignored and even belittled, much like those who warned about a terrorist attack on the United States before 9-11, or about chaos in Iraq before Operation Iraqi Freedom was launched. Only after things fell apart did chastened experts explain, still in unison, how the financial system had been jury-rigged and why its collapse was inevitable. What was one to make of the skyrocketing fortunes, the sophisticated computer models, the esoteric "instruments" and "vehicles" that supposedly dispersed risk to the point of virtually eliminating it, the complex transactions that free-market fundamentalists had proclaimed to be the key to national and global prosperity? Alas, all turned out to be largely fools' gold.[10]

The fools' errands associated with Bush's war and the fools' gold of the financial markets were products of a shared mindset. Facile explanations for these disasters are easy to come by: war making driven by politics and special interests on the one hand and a highly deregulated economy driven by avarice, fixated on short-term profits, and spooked by fear on the other. In the latter crisis, it took no time at all for yesterday's admired titans of finance to metamorphose into "incompetents and greedheads" in the public eye, or for yesterday's champions of extreme privatization to turn into supplicants for massive state intervention and rescue.

This simultaneous breakdown in strategic policy and capitalist operations was stunning above all, however, because it went beyond individual failures and exposed the degree to which faith-based thinking had taken possession of the private as well as governmental sector. Hallucination camouflaged in elaborate trappings of reason and rationality is not a simple matter. Take, for example, the imaginary weapons of mass destruction that were presented, in laborious detail, as a major reason for launching preemptive war against Iraq. If leaders in Washington genuinely believed these existed, they were deluded and incompetent. If they cooked raw intelligence to promote a war desired for other reasons (such as enhanced access to energy resources), their actions were criminal. The inquiry moves to a different plane, however, when we recognize that the rush to war involved illusions concerning not only military capabilities in general—including America's—but also the presumed beneficence and self-correcting resilience of a virtually unrestrained capitalism leveraged by unprecedented levels of debt. Illusory power and illusory profits went hand in hand. The disintegration of the financial system effectively dissolved the line between cultures of war and cultures of money—and in the process called attention to behavioral pathologies at every level.

In countless ways, observations percolating through the mass media reinforced this grim diagnosis that groupthink and herd behavior had become epidemic. High finance and capitalist economics in general were associated with a priesthood that embraced doctrines about an almighty market, claimed to possess special knowledge about how this worked, eschewed transparency, and ostracized or excommunicated heretics who questioned its dogmas. Secrecy reigned ("the shadow banking system," "black box" computer operations, "dark markets," "off-balance-sheet" transactions). Congregations of devout believers sang the hymns of so-called mathematical finance with scant understanding of what the words really meant: stochastic processes, alphas and betas, the bell curve and Gaussian copula model, the random walk hypothesis, even the venerated "collateralized debt obligations" that seemed intoxicating but turned out to be simply toxic. Acronyms and jargon were intoned like Latin in a medieval mass—VaR, SPV, and SIV, for example, and "super-senior CDO of ABS assets." Information and expertise were compartmentalized. Everyone talked about risk and risk management, due diligence, moral hazard, and the like—but no one in a position of decisive influence took this seriously enough. For all practical purposes, it was taboo to suggest that it was irrational to ignore the irrational. Neither worst-case scenarios, nor sober long-term projections, nor rigorous reading of the past, nor commonsense reflection and judgment had a place at the main table. Hubris— "euphoria" in economics-speak—ran rampant.[11]

The resonance with critiques of the Bush White House and its intelligence failures was often close to pitch-perfect. A commentator in the *New York Times* characterized the panic of 2008 as "a chronicle of the capacity of highly paid professionals for self-delusion." He was reviewing a book about "modern financial insanity"—apt analogue to "strategic imbecility" in the cultures of war. A *Washington Post* writer called the bubble "a kind of financial alchemy," and paraphrased a portfolio manager who blamed Wall Street for "relying on elaborate models that predicted that default rates would be low when common sense screamed otherwise." A lengthy article in the *New Yorker* concurred that "the mathematical models indicated that there was very little risk, even if common sense said otherwise." Common sense, of course, was the factor conspicuous by its absence in the Bush administration's response to terrorism before and after 9-11.[12]

In November 2008, while on a visit to the London School of Economics, no less a personage than the queen of England asked why those engaged in financial and economic matters had failed to anticipate and head off the market crisis. Some seven months later, in mid-June, she received an answer in the form of a three-page letter from the British Academy bearing the names of thirty-eight "experts from business, the City, its regulators, academia, and government" who had been gathered to discuss the subject. There had been diligence and warnings, the queen was informed; indeed, one major English bank "reputedly had 4000 risk managers." In the upshot, however, the "financial wizards" and "best mathematical minds in our country and abroad" focused on "slices" of financial activity. As a consequence, they "frequently lost sight of the bigger picture."

The letter to Queen Elizabeth amounted to yet one more diagnosis of the "psychology of denial." In a widely quoted (and hyperbolic) observation, the experts declared that "it is difficult to recall a greater example of wishful thinking combined with hubris." They attributed the fact that "a generation of bankers and financiers deceived themselves" to compartmentalization of expertise and authority "combined with the psychology of herding and the mantra of financial and policy gurus." "So in summary, Your Majesty," their letter concluded, the inability to see the system as a whole amounted to "a failure of the collective imagination of many bright people, both in this country and internationally."[13]

*The psychology of herding.* A participant in the creation of leveraged "swaps" in the early 1990s recalled that "the herd instinct was just amazing. Everyone was looking for yield. You could do almost anything you could dream of, and people would buy it." Over a decade later, when an expert in derivatives at the Royal Bank of Scotland expressed concern that risk was being underestimated, he was pressured to resign. "The problem," as he explained it, "is that in banks, you have this kind of mentality, this groupthink, and people just keep going with what they know, and they don't want to listen to bad news." The London-based *Economist* concurred in calling attention to "the 'herd' mentality that contributes to financial bubbles," and suggested that the surprising degree to which "human beings are not rational" probably called for Darwinian explanations.[14]

In a clear-eyed case study of the crash published in 2009, Gillian Tett, who covered global markets for the *Financial Times*, delineated how a complex system of derivatives initially worshipped for disbursing risk eventually created a "pernicious feedback loop" that ended up increasing risk catastrophically. Her disastrous loop calls to mind what Benazir Bhutto called the Frankenstein's monster of U.S. and European Middle East policy, and analysts of strategic geopolitics more generally refer to as blowback. All this, of course—the gurus, the groupthink, the hubris or euphoria, the compartmentalization and failure to see things whole, the pernicious feedback loops—also runs like a red line through intelligence failures and military disasters from Pearl Harbor to Iraq.[15]

BEGINNING IN THE closing decades of the twentieth century, advances in cyberspace revolutionized the gathering and analysis of data. In theory, computers and computer models provided decision makers with an agility and sophistication undreamed of by earlier generations. "Rationality," it was proclaimed, had been carried to phenomenal new levels. This, too, was a belief system—captured, where fools' gold was concerned, in the near-absolute faith that became rested in "cyberfinance."

In widely publicized testimony before Congress, Alan Greenspan, the former chair of the Federal Reserve who bore considerable responsibility for the bubble, expressed "shocked disbelief" at the meltdown of the supposedly rational and efficient financial system. In his view, "the whole intellectual edifice . . . collapsed in the summer of last year [2007] because the data inputted into the risk management models generally covered only the past two decades, a period of euphoria. Had instead the models been fitted more appropriately to historic periods of stress, capital requirements would have been much higher and the financial world would be in far better shape today." A critique in *Wired* magazine called attention, in more barbed language, to the "ingenious way" financial gurus managed to "model default correlation without even looking at historical default data." Such ex-post-facto enlightenment paralleled the U.S. military's shocked rediscovery, after Iraq disintegrated, of a deep history of insurgency and neglected body of counterinsurgency doctrine. In his mea culpa, Greenspan noted that the flawed models in question included work that had garnered a Nobel Prize.[16]

As such comments suggested, "quants" (experts in quantitative analysis) had become the high priests of the new rationality, their gospel reinforced with elaborate and esoteric formulas. "Risk" was the very focus of their analyses. Historical data sets were integrated into their calculations. Yet, in the final analysis, truly catastrophic risk was slighted and big-picture history mattered little—not merely the pre–World War II precedents of robber barons, the Great Depression, and crippling debt, but a parade of postwar scandals and financial collapses as well. Statistics pertaining to the nationwide fall in U.S. housing prices in the 1930s, for example, were not included in the samples on which the basic risk models for subprime mortgages and other complex transactions were based. Much closer in time, the "period of euphoria" that dazzled Greenspan and his cohort was pocked with over a hundred financial crises globally, more than forty of them occurring in high-income countries. As it happened, in financial insanity, as in strategic imbecility, Japan again offered a precedent. Its protracted economic crisis of the 1990s and early 2000s had been set off by toxic debt associated with a property bubble. Like the strategic myopia that underlay the tactical brilliance of imperial Japan's December 1941 attacks, this was, once again, widely regarded as peculiarly Japanese by the erstwhile rationalists who formulated or endorsed the Wall Street model.[17]

Monday-morning critics drew attention to other examples of what in retrospect would seem to be transparent flaws in these ostensibly ultra-rational operations. A cover story on "risk mismanagement" in the *New York Times Magazine*, for example, noted that the model most investors relied on "could be gamed." A critique in the journal of the American Enterprise Institute concurred, calling attention to "gaming the metrics" and "massaging the data." But why did such standard operating procedure come as a surprise? The shadow banking system and off-balance-sheet vehicles existed to expedite such gaming. Practices like manipulating

how financial products were rated were camouflaged with almost give-
away euphemisms—"ratings arbitrage" in this case. The obvious cognate
activity here is the way Bush administration planners gamed their war of
choice by cherry-picking both raw intelligence data and history. Along
related lines, a special report published by the *Economist* as the transition
from the Bush to the Obama administration was taking place observed
that disregarding extreme risk "eventually leads to self-censorship." In
that publication's characteristically learned fashion, this report quoted a
nineteenth-century banker (George Gilbert Williams) in support of this.
"The system," the quote ran, "filters out the thoughtful and replaces them
with the faithful."[18]

In a study published just after the Bush presidency ended, two well-
known economists, George Akerlof and Robert Shiller, tapped the emerging field of behavioral economics to criticize the faith-based mindset of
their profession. In the circumstances, their commonsense arguments
were iconoclastic. What appeared to be sophisticated models of how the
economy works, they observed, neglected the entire realm of unquantifiable human behavior or "animal spirits" that an earlier generation of
economists had recognized as inseparable from economic performance.
(The phrase comes from John Maynard Keynes's 1936 book *The General
Theory of Employment, Interest and Money*.) It was necessary to bring human
psychology back into the picture—to recognize, that is, the impact of
qualitative as well as quantitative facts, noneconomic as well as economic
motivations, irrational as well as rational behavior. Excluding this from
economic theorizing accounted for the "suspension of disbelief" that had
led to the current crisis.[19]

That this needed to be said is remarkable. That such delusory thinking
is not peculiar to economics, but rather reflects deeper psychological and
institutional pathologies, including the cultures of war that never disappear, is beyond question. And whether humankind worldwide will one day
find the ability to truly control and transcend this is, at best, highly uncertain. This requires faith and reason of a radically different sort. Constructive change and deep cultures of peace will come, if at all, incrementally;
and that is where hope must reside.

# NOTES

## Part I: "Pearl Harbor" as Code

### CHAPTER 1: INFAMY AND THE CRACKED MIRROR OF HISTORY

1. The marked copy of Roosevelt's speech was reproduced in a little booklet titled *America's Entry into World War II* (Awani Press, 1995), which is sometimes available in U.S. military museums. More recently, it has been reproduced in Emily S. Rosenberg, *A Date Which Will Live: Pearl Harbor in American Memory* (Duke University Press, 2003), 84–85. Rosenberg's well-documented study provides useful pre–9-11 background for the post–9-11 "uses" of Pearl Harbor addressed here. In the speech as delivered to Congress, the president also added the phrase "so help us God," which does not appear in the draft.
2. Bob Woodward, *Plan of Attack* (Simon & Schuster, 2004), 24. Krugman's column of September 10, 2002, is reprinted in Paul Krugman, *The Great Unraveling: Losing Our Way in the New Century* (Norton, 2003), 242.
3. A graphic example of this slogan—wrapped around an artist's rendering of a slant-eyed, buck-toothed, swastika-wearing Japanese soldier caught in crosshairs—appeared early in 1942 in *Leatherneck*, a monthly directed primarily to the Marines. This is reproduced in John W. Dower, "Race, Language, and War in Two Cultures: World War II in Asia," in Lewis A. Erenberg and Susan E. Hirsch, eds., *The War in American Culture: Society and Consciousness during World War II* (University of Chicago Press, 1996), 174.
4. The Chicago billboard is described by Bruce Cumings in Bruce Cumings, Ervand Abrahamian, and Moshe Ma'oz, *Inventing the Axis of Evil: The Truth about North Korea, Iran, and Syria* (New Press, 2004), 5.
5. Bush spoke of a "war against terrorism" in his address to the nation on the night

of the September 11 attacks. Individuals involved in crafting his public presentations, however, regard this initial speech as ineffective and argue that the president did not really articulate his role as a "war president" effectively until his September 20 address to Congress (where the phrase was "war on terror"); see, for example, David Frum, *The Right Man: The Surprise Presidency of George W. Bush* (Random House, 2003), ch. 8, esp. 127, 135, 141–42.

6. Among the many commentaries on the "axis of evil" speech, see Woodward, *Plan of Attack*, 86–88; James Mann, *Rise of the Vulcans: A History of Bush's War Cabinet* (Penguin, 2004), 242, 317–21; and David Frum's insider account in *The Right Man*, ch. 12. In earlier drafts, the key phrase was "axis of hatred"; Bush's chief speechwriter Michael Gerson, a deeply committed evangelical Christian, changed "hatred" to "evil." For religious and conservative Americans, this revision was triply effective. It evoked not only World War II, but also the theological thunder of the Old Testament as well as the Cold War echoes of President Ronald Reagan's denunciation of the Soviet Union as an "evil empire."

Before as well as after the invasion of Iraq, it became fashionable in conservative circles to denounce critics of the Bush administration's war policies as participants in an "axis of appeasement." The damning reference was to Neville Chamberlain's 1938 meeting with Hitler in Munich, at which the British prime minister agreed to Germany's annexation of Czechoslovakia's Sudetenland, paving the way for seizure of the rest of Czechoslovakia the following year. The "anti-appeasement" mindset was reinvigorated in the administration's response to the 2006 report of a group of distinguished public figures co-chaired by former secretary of state James Baker and former congressman Lee Hamilton (published as *The Iraq Study Group Report*). This report placed terrorism and Iraq in the context of broader Middle East problems, including Israel and its occupied territories, and called for "a new diplomatic offensive" and "broader international support structure" to bring Iran and Syria, among others, into the search for a comprehensive solution. These recommendations were largely ignored. On May 15, 2008, Bush took the occasion of the sixtieth anniversary of the founding of Israel to visit Jerusalem and reaffirm the appeasement analogy: "Some seem to believe we should negotiate with terrorists and radicals. We have an obligation to call this what it is—the false comfort of appeasement." This was reasonably interpreted as a political attack on the likely Democratic presidential candidate, Barack Obama, and drew wide media attention. More significant, however, was the fact that such pseudo-history was used to justify a hostility to creative diplomacy that characterized the administration's foreign policy from start to finish. For "axis of appeasement," see William Kristol, "The Axis of Appeasement," *Weekly Standard*, August 26–September 2, 2002; Daniel Pipes, "[Appeasement and] Why Europe Balks," *New York Post*, January 28, 2003; Thomas L. Friedman, "Axis of Appeasement," *New York Times*, March 18, 2004.

7. MacArthur's message of September 2, 1945, is reproduced in the interim official report on the occupation of Japan: *Political Reorientation of Japan, September 1945 to September 1948: Report of Government Section, Supreme Commander for the Allied Powers* (Government Printing Office, 1949), vol. 2: 737. Bob Woodward notes the influence of MacArthur's speech on Bush's speechwriters in *State of Denial: Bush at War, Part III* (Simon & Schuster, 2006), 186. Sheldon Wolin draws a pro-

vocative analogy between the cinematic aspects of the "Mission Accomplished" performance and opening scenes in Leni Riefenstahl's *Triumph of the Will*, her celebration of Hitler's 1934 Nazi Party rally in Nuremberg; see his *Democracy Incorporated: Managed Democracy and the Specter of Inverted Totalitarianism* (Princeton University Press, 2008), 1–3.

8. These quotations from the August 30, 2005 speech, like other citations from formal presidential presentations introduced here, come from the White House transcript released online. After the Bush presidency ended, these materials were transferred to "The Bush Record" at georgewbush-whitehouse.archives.gov. Some of the White House references to occupied Japan came from a book I wrote (*Embracing Defeat: Japan in the Wake of World War II*), and led to a response on my part when the president repeated them in an address to the Veterans of Foreign Wars National Convention on August 22, 2007. See, for example, "Historian: Bush Use of Quote 'Perverse'" on the politico.com website for August 23, 2007.

9. The February 23, 1998, fatwa is reproduced in Osama bin Laden, *Messages to the World: The Statements of Osama bin Laden*, ed. by Bruce Lawrence (Verso, 2005), 58–62. Official and quasi-official sources on the 9-11 intelligence failure include the following: *The 9/11 Commission Report: Final Report of the National Commission on Terrorist Attacks upon the United States* (Norton, 2004); the "House-Senate Joint Inquiry Report on 9/11" (*Report of the Joint Inquiry into the Terrorist Attacks of September 11, 2001—by the House Permanent Select Committee on Intelligence and the Senate Select Committee on Intelligence*, issued December 2002 and available online at, among other sites, gpoaccess.gov and news.findlaw.com/nytimes); Steven Strasser, ed., *The 9/11 Investigations* (PublicAffairs, 2004; this includes staff reports of the 9/11 Commission, excerpts from the House-Senate Joint Inquiry Report, and testimony from fourteen key witnesses); *OIG Report on CIA Accountability with Respect to the 9/11 Attacks* (a short, slightly redacted Office of the Inspector General report released in August 2007); Thomas H. Kean and Lee H. Hamilton (the co-chairs of the 9/11 Commission), *Without Precedent: The Inside Story of the 9/11 Commission* (Knopf, 2006); Bob Graham, *Intelligence Matters: The CIA, the FBI, Saudi Arabia, and the Failure of America's War on Terror* (Random House, 2004). Senator Graham was the Democratic co-chair of the House-Senate Joint Inquiry, and his recapitulation of findings goes beyond the official report of December 2002 in indicting the Bush administration. See also Philip Shenon, *The Commission: The Uncensored History of the 9/11 Investigation* (Twelve, 2008); Shenon covered the commission for the *New York Times*.

10. See especially the concise executive summary of *New World Coming: American Security in the 21st Century* available online at, among other sites, fas.org and au.af .mil. The U.S. Commission on National Security/21st Century that prepared this study was established in 1998 and chaired by former senators Gary Hart and Warren Rudman. Fairly concise checklists of pre–9-11 warnings appear in *The 9/11 Commission Report*, ch. 8 (esp. 254–64); Shenon, *The Commission*, 151–55; and Graham, *Intelligence Matters*, xv, 3–79, 113 (on "twelve points" where the plot might have been uncovered), and 112, 173, 204 (on "a terrorist desire to use planes as weapons"). The phrase "the system was blinking red" came from the testimony of the then-head of the CIA, George Tenet, to the 9-11 Commission and was used as a chapter title in the commission's report. Intelligence data that in retrospect

seemed to point to a Pearl Harbor attack was introduced in the lengthy postwar congressional hearings on the surprise attack, and received pointed summary in the minority report submitted in connection with those hearings; see *Report of the Joint Committee on the Investigation of the Pearl Harbor Attack, and Additional Views of Mr. Keefe Together with Minority Views of Mr. Ferguson and Mr. Brewster* (Government Printing Office, July 20, 1946), 493–580.

11. Excerpts from Rice's canceled speech were released to the *Washington Post* over two and a half years later; see the issue of April 1, 2004. Philip Shenon notes that it was Rice who prevented former senator Warren Rudman, co-chair of the *New World Coming* study, from meeting with the president, and also calls attention to the omission of terrorism from Justice Department priorities; *The Commission*, 56, 246–48.

12. "Today, It Is We Americans Who Live in Infamy," *Los Angeles Times*, March 23, 2003. Schlesinger repeated this analogy later in these words: "Looking back over the forty years of the cold war, we can be everlastingly grateful that the loonies on both sides were powerless. In 2003, however, they run the Pentagon, and preventive war—the Bush Doctrine—is now official policy. Sixty years ago the Japanese anticipated the Bush Doctrine in their attack on the US Navy at Pearl Harbor. This was, FDR observed, an exploit that would live in infamy—except now, evidently, when employed by the United States"; "Eyeless in Iraq," *New York Review of Books*, October 23, 2003. David Sanger, a former foreign correspondent in Japan who was covering the White House in 2002, drew much the same equation months earlier. To many scholars, he wrote, "Iraq looks less like a pre-emptive strike and more like a preventive war. And there the classic example is one the White House is unlikely to cite with approval: Dec. 7, 1941. Every schoolchild in Japan is taught that the United States–led embargo on Japan was slowly killing the country's economy and undermining its ability to defend itself. That's why Japan has kept a museum celebrating the heroes of Pearl Harbor"; "Beating Them to the Prewar," *New York Times*, September 28, 2002.

13. Samuel Eliot Morison, *History of United States Naval Operations in World War II*, vol. 3: *The Rising Sun in the Pacific* (Little, Brown, 1953), 132. Morison reiterated this conclusion later in an October 28, 1961, *Saturday Evening Post* article titled "The Lessons of Pearl Harbor": "One cannot help admiring the tactical skill, the secrecy and the precision with which the Japanese Navy performed its treacherous mission. Yet the strategy which dictated it was so bad as to be considered, after the event, almost imbecile."

14. U.S. Department of State, *Foreign Relations of the United States: Japan, 1931–1941* (Government Printing Office, 1943), vol. 2: 648, 704, 706; Joseph C. Grew, *Ten Years in Japan: A Contemporary Record Drawn from the Diaries and Private and Official Papers of Joseph C. Grew, United States Ambassador to Japan, 1932–1942* (Simon & Schuster, 1944), 439, 469, 470, 472, 479, 484. Grew's other major wartime publication was a short book titled *Report from Tokyo: A Message to the American People* (Simon & Schuster, 1942). In hearings pertinent to his appointment as under secretary of state in December 1944, Grew framed this favorite thesis as follows: "It must be remembered today, if we are not to repeat the errors of the past, that Japanese attitudes and reactions have not conformed in a single important respect to any universal pattern or standard of behavior"; this testimony is reproduced

in Grew, *Turbulent Era: A Diplomatic Record of Forty Years, 1904–1945* (Houghton Mifflin, 1952), 1417. The diplomatic documents released in 1943 did not include materials gleaned from the still-secret MAGIC intercepts of Japan's diplomatic traffic. For Grew as quoted in the postwar congressional hearings on the Pearl Harbor attack, see Roberta Wohlstetter, *Pearl Harbor: Warning and Decision* (Stanford University Press, 1962), 354. Morison zeroed in on the "Japanese sanity cannot be measured by our own standards of logic" observation in advancing his "strategic imbecility" argument. See his "Lessons of Pearl Harbor."

15. Fellers's analysis is discussed at length in John W. Dower, *Embracing Defeat: Japan in the Wake of World War II* (Norton and New Press, 1999), 280–86.

16. U. S. Department of State, *Foreign Relations of the United States: 1955–1957*, vol. 2: *China*, 285; cited in James Peck, *Washington's China: The National Security World, the Cold War, and the Origins of Globalism* (University of Massachusetts Press, 2006), 5.

17. L. Paul Bremer III, *My Year in Iraq: The Struggle to Build a Future of Hope* (Threshold Editions, 2006), 190.

18. Wohlstetter, *Pearl Harbor*, 69; see also 356–57, where Wohlstetter applies essentially the same observation to the Japanese.

19. Bush's fixation on body counts is well documented; see, for example, Bob Woodward, "10 Take Aways from the Bush Years," *Washington Post*, January 18, 2009, quoting General George W. Casey Jr., commander of U.S. forces in Iraq from 2004 to 2007; also Woodward's *State of Denial*, 319–20, 483–84.

20. Pearl Harbor as godsend is discussed in chapter 6 of this book.

## CHAPTER 2: THE FAILURE OF INTELLIGENCE

21. This is a highly abbreviated (not to say cavalier) compression of the U.S.-Japan relationship on the eve of Pearl Harbor. Major accessible sources for the road to war in 1941, and the Pearl Harbor attack in particular, include the following: Gordon W. Prange, in collaboration with Donald M. Goldstein and Katherine V. Dillon, *At Dawn We Slept: The Untold Story of Pearl Harbor* (McGraw-Hill, 1981); Gordon W. Prange, with Donald M. Goldstein and Katherine V. Dillon, *Pearl Harbor: The Verdict of History* (McGraw-Hill paperback edition, 1986); Wohlstetter, *Pearl Harbor*; Dorothy Borg and Shumpei Okamoto, eds., *Pearl Harbor as History: Japanese-American Relations, 1931–1941* (Columbia University Press, 1973); Akira Iriye, *The Origins of the Second World War in Asia and the Pacific* (Longman, 1987); Waldo Heinrichs, *Threshold of War: Franklin D. Roosevelt and American Entry into World War II* (Oxford University Press, 1988). These sources have extensive bibliographic references. For a basic bibliography that includes primary as well as secondary materials, see also John W. Dower with Timothy S. George, ed., *Japanese History and Culture from Ancient to Modern Times: Seven Basic Bibliographies*, 2nd edition (Markus Weiner, 1995), 249–372. Particularly valuable for the Japanese side are the translated top-secret deliberations in Nobutake Ike, transl. and ed., *Japan's Decision for War: Records of the 1941 Policy Conferences* (Stanford University Press, 1967); also Donald M. Goldstein and Katherine V. Dillon, eds., *The Pearl Harbor Papers: Inside the Japanese Plans* (Brassey's, 2000; originally published in 1993). A balanced military

history of the war itself is Ronald H. Spector, *Eagle against the Sun: The American War with Japan* (Vintage, 1985).

22. Wohlstetter, *Pearl Harbor*, 258, 265–66 (quoting the Stimson diary at length, as entered into postwar congressional hearings). The late-November breakdown of relations involved Secretary of State Hull's rejection of Japan's last-ditch proposals on November 26 in a "Ten Point Note" that, rather than responding to these proposals, presented the most extreme itemization of U.S. desiderata submitted to that date. The Ten Point Note—often, and reasonably, called an ultimatum—replaced a compromise proposal that had been worked out in the U.S. government but was inexplicably jettisoned by Hull at the last moment.

23. Prange points out that the "myth" that the Hawaii attack was a "supersecret" was nurtured by the Japanese at the postwar war-crimes trials in Tokyo; see *At Dawn We Slept*, 28; also 110, 184, 200, 225, 266, 284, 344, for concrete examples of the sharing of attack-plan information, which included conducting war games. The emperor's familiarity with the plan to attack Pearl Harbor was carefully covered up by U.S. occupation authorities in defeated Japan, who deemed it necessary to keep him on the throne in order to make acceptance of their policies more palatable. Prange notes that the emperor was briefed on the plan between October 20 and 25 (ibid., 309), and Japanese sources published later confirm this. After the emperor's death in 1989, the diary of his grand chamberlain was published and included a vivid entry on Hirohito's familiarity with the war plans; see Dower, *Embracing Defeat*, 291–92. For Tōjō, see Alvin D. Coox, *Tojo* (Ballantine's Illustrated History of the Violent Century, War Leader Book No. 30, Random House, 1975), 119. See also Wohlstetter, *Pearl Harbor*, 380.

24. On the breaking of Japan's diplomatic code, known as "Purple," see Prange, *At Dawn We Slept*, ch. 9.

25. Wohlstetter, *Pearl Harbor*, 341–43.

26. For Yamamoto, see Goldstein and Dillon, *The Pearl Harbor Papers*, 116; also, for similar comments, ibid., 118, 140, and Prange, *At Dawn We Slept*, 16, 21. The November 15, 1941, policy document is reproduced in Ike, *Japan's Decision for War*, 247–49.

27. Goldstein and Dillon, *The Pearl Harbor Papers*, 124 (October 1941 letter). Shortly after conclusion of the Tripartite Alliance of September 1940, Yamamoto, then commander in chief of the Combined Fleet, expressed his fears of a war between Japan and the United States to Prime Minister Fumimaro Konoe in these quite prophetic words (as later recorded by Konoe): "If I am told to fight regardless of the consequences, I shall run wild for the first six months or a year, but I have utterly no confidence for the second or third year. The Tripartite Pact has been concluded, and we cannot help it. Now that the situation has come to this pass, I hope you will endeavor to avoid a Japanese-American war"; *Reports of General MacArthur: Japanese Operations in the Southwest Pacific Area* (Government Printing Office, 1966; compiled from Japanese Demobilization Bureaux Records), vol. 2, part 1: 33. These were the circumstances in which he came up with the idea of the Pearl Harbor attack. As late as late September 1941, Yamamoto was still trying to persuade the navy to oppose war; Spector, *Eagle against the Sun*, 78.

28. Wohlstetter, *Pearl Harbor*, 371 (war games); Goldstein and Dillon, *The Pearl Harbor Papers*, 182–83 (crew and wills); *Kodansha Encyclopedia of Japan* (Kodan-

sha, 1983), vol. 6: 169 (Japanese losses). On the U.S. side, seven ships including four battleships were sunk and another eleven vessels damaged; 188 aircraft were destroyed and over 150 damaged; and total casualties were around 3,580.

29. William J. Casey, *Scouting the Future: The Public Speeches of William J. Casey* (Regnery Gateway, 1989), 11 (from a May 21, 1982, speech).

30. Translations of the two fatwas appear in bin Laden, *Messages to the World*, 23–30, 58–62.

31. Bin Laden's interview with ABC reporter John Miller following the February fatwa is accessible on pbs.org, May 1998. In December 1998, bin Laden gave a ninety-minute interview to Al Jazeera television disclaiming direct responsibility for the bombings in Africa apart from inciting such actions, but declaring, among other things, that "there is a duty on Muslims" to acquire chemical, biological, and nuclear weapons. He also belittled "the incredible weakness and cowardice of the American soldier" (as evidenced by the U.S. retreat from Somalia after the "Black Hawk down" incident in 1993), boasted of the victory of jihadi against the Soviet Union in Afghanistan, and flatly declared that "we believe that America is much weaker than Russia." After 9-11, Al Jazeera rebroadcast this long interview in full; see bin Laden, *Messages to the World*, 65–94.

32. Richard A. Clarke, *Against All Enemies: Inside America's War on Terror* (Free Press paperback edition with new foreword, 2004), 148.

33. Lawrence Wright, *The Looming Tower: Al-Qaeda and the Road to 9/11* (Knopf, 2006), 368. In the case of Pearl Harbor, the usual estimate of fatalities is 2,403, including 68 civilians. For September 11, legislation introduced to the U.S. Senate on December 20, 2001 (S.1867), put the numbers of deaths in New York including on the two hijacked planes at 2,823; at the Pentagon including the hijacked plane at 189; and on the fourth hijacked plane that crashed in Pennsylvania at 45. The number of non-Americans among those killed at the World Trade Center was around 235. Wright's account is an excellent introduction to developments on both the terrorist and U.S. sides prior to September 11. For illuminating, generally scathing insider accounts of U.S. intelligence prior to 9-11, see especially Clarke, *Against All Enemies*, and Michael Scheuer, *Imperial Hubris: Why the West Is Losing the War on Terror* (Potomac Books, 2004). From 1996 until his acrimonious dismissal in 1999, Scheuer headed the CIA's "bin Laden unit."

34. Bin Laden, *Messages to the World*, 104, 112.

35. *Hearings before the Joint Committee on the Investigation of the Pearl Harbor Attack*, 79th Congress (Government Printing Office, 1946), 39 volumes; and *Report of the Joint Committee on the Investigation of the Pearl Harbor Attack*. The various investigations are conveniently accessible on the Pearl Harbor History Associates, Inc. website at ibiblio.org/pha/pha.

36. On MacArthur in the Philippines, see chapter 5 (note 129) of this book.

37. John Toland, *Infamy: Pearl Harbor and Its Aftermath* (Doubleday, 1982). The revisionist literature and its critics are cited and briefly discussed in chapter 6 of this book.

38. Both Prange and Wohlstetter draw heavily on the congressional hearings. Prange, who served in the historical section of the U.S. occupation of Japan and, then and later, also conducted extensive interviews with Japanese participants

in the surprise attack, died in 1980 before his work was actually published; his collaborators (Donald Goldstein and Katherine Dillon) thus deserve particular credit for seeing these massive tomes into print. Prange's *At Dawn We Slept* (1981) devotes the lengthy third and final portion of the text (pp. 551–738) to the various U.S. hearings. His lesser-known *Pearl Harbor: The Verdict of History* (1986), also drawing extensively from Japanese as well as English sources, is particularly sharp in offering a balanced critical analysis of "the verdict of history." (The jointly produced U.S.-Japanese 1970 feature film *Tora! Tora! Tora!* was based largely on Prange's research.) Wohlstetter's *Pearl Harbor*, based entirely on the accessible English-language record, is regarded as a model of systems analysis that explains the primarily institutional reasons why U.S. diplomatic and military intelligence failed to provide adequate warning of the surprise attack. The "all made mistakes" observation appears in Prange, *Pearl Harbor*, xiv.

39. Wohlstetter, *Pearl Harbor*, 55. For Rice, see Seymour M. Hersh, *Chain of Command: The Road from 9/11 to Abu Ghraib* (Harper Perennial, 2005), 88; also 93, 97. "Chatter" receives close analysis in Patrick Radden Keefe, *Chatter: Dispatches from the Secret World of Global Eavesdropping* (Random House, 2005). See also Keefe's "Cat-and-Mouse Games," *New York Review of Books*, May 26, 2005 (reviewing William M. Arkin, *Code Names: Deciphering US Military Plans, Programs, and Operations in the 9/11 World*); also Michael Hirsh, "So Much Chatter, So Few Clues," *Washington Post National Weekly*, January 9–15, 2006. For an insightful review of Keefe's and other books on intelligence gathering, see Thomas Powers, "Black Arts," *New York Review of Books*, May 12, 2005, 21–25.

40. Wohlstetter, *Pearl Harbor*, 230. Priorities of the Bush administration prior to 9-11 included abandoning the Antiballistic Missile Treaty and promoting the controversial "Star Wars" defense system in outer space, detaching the United States from the so-called Kyoto environmental agreement and other international commitments, addressing China as the projected superpower replacement of the Soviet Union, and promoting "regime change" in Iraq.

41. *Report of the Joint Committee on the Investigation of the Pearl Harbor Attack*, 252–54, 264.

42. These arguments permeate the minority report, but see especially *Report of the Joint Committee on the Investigation of the Pearl Harbor Attack*, 523, 538, 572–73.

43. Wohlstetter, *Pearl Harbor*, 47, 105, 168, 186, 229, 246, 278, 393–95.

44. *Report of the Joint Committee on the Investigation of the Pearl Harbor Attack*, 261; Wohlstetter, *Pearl Harbor*, 186, 394. The perceived necessity of keeping Magic secret also complicated investigations of the Pearl Harbor disaster, since these materials were not made readily available to the first seven U.S. inquiries. Admiral Kimmel and General Short based much of their defense of their failure to anticipate the December 7 attack on the argument that they had been denied access to these crucial materials, and when transcripts of some important intercepts were introduced in the 1945–46 congressional hearings, it was without fully revealing where they had come from; see Prange, *At Dawn We Slept*, 628ff., 637, 670ff. The Magic materials were not declassified until 1977, when a substantial selection was made available in eight volumes by the Department of Defense under the title *The "Magic" Background to Pearl Harbor*. The same issue of classified materials has also impeded full investigation and disclosure of the intelligence failure of September 11.

45. See the "memoir" of the commission's co-chairs: Kean and Hamilton, *Without Precedent*. Although ostensibly endorsed by the White House, this was not an "official" investigation—a fact that hampered obtaining classified materials. *Without Precedent* thus conveys a double message: praising the executive branch and other agencies for their cooperation while simultaneously documenting the political pressures and obstacles the commission faced. This was standard operating procedure so long as the Republican Party controlled the White House and Congress. For a wide-ranging sample of critical commentary on the commission's findings, see the transcripts and written texts submitted at a one-day hearing in the House of Representatives on the July 22, 2005, anniversary of the publication of the 9-11 report. This bears the cumbersome title *The 9/11 Commission Report One Year Later—A Citizen's Response: Did the Commission Get It Right? 9/11 Families, Government Workers and Scholars Respond*. Philip Shenon similarly calls attention to stonewalling by various officials and agencies, as well as the scrupulous care taken by Kean and especially Hamilton to avoid assigning individual responsibility for the top-level failure to follow up on warnings of a terrorist threat that lower-level operatives were providing; on the latter, see Shenon, *The Commission*, esp. 38, 99, 130, 404–6. The most trenchant critique in this regard was provided by one of the major backstage contributors to the report, Professor Ernest May of Harvard; see his "Government Writes History," *New Republic*, May 23, 2005. The impediments faced by the 1945–46 joint congressional hearings were concisely summarized in the minority report in *Report of the Joint Committee on the Investigation of the Pearl Harbor Attack*, 497–502.

46. Thomas Powers, "Secret Intelligence and the 'War on Terror,'" *New York Review of Books*, December 16, 2004. Bob Graham details the same argument at length in his *Intelligence Matters*.

47. Clarke, *Against All Enemies*, ch. 10 (227–46); the Wolfowitz quote appears on 232.

48. The July 10 exchange was first emphasized by Bob Woodward in *State of Denial*, 49–52, 79–80. On the better-known President's Daily Brief of August 6, see *The 9/11 Commission Report*, 260–63; Kean and Hamilton, *Without Precedent*, 89–97. In addition to the detailed insider critiques by Clarke and Scheuer, there is an ever-growing literature that calls attention to specific "missed opportunities" due to turf wars, personal rivalries, and top-level inattentiveness to mid-level warnings. See, for example, Wright, *The Looming Tower*, esp. 279, 315, 329, 341–44, 350–51, 362. Graham itemizes twelve points at which the 9-11 plot might have been uncovered and possibly thwarted in his *Intelligence Matters*; see esp. xv, 3–79, 113.

49. *The 9/11 Commission Report*, 406. The numerous short quotes introduced in the text are scattered throughout the report; see in particular, however, 89, 95, 401–17.

## CHAPTER 3: THE FAILURE OF IMAGINATION

50. Prange, *Pearl Harbor*, 515. Morgan recounted this to Prange in an interview in October 1976.

51. *Report of the Joint Committee on the Investigation of the Pearl Harbor Attack*, 259; Prange, *At Dawn We Slept*, 689; Wohlstetter, *Pearl Harbor*, 392.

52. Prange, *Pearl Harbor*, 552; Goldstein and Dillon, *The Pearl Harbor Papers*, 121.

53. Goldstein and Dillon, *The Pearl Harbor Papers*, 122.

54. The conflicting images of Japan at the turn of the century emerge vividly in several lavishly illustrated units on the "Visualizing Cultures" website produced at the Massachusetts Institute of Technology by John W. Dower and Shigeru Miyagawa. See visualizingcultures.mit.edu, and particularly "Throwing Off Asia" (in three parts), "Asia Rising," and "Yellow Promise/Yellow Peril." The latter two units are based on Japanese and foreign postcards of the Russo-Japanese War in the Leonard Lauder Collection at the Museum of Fine Arts, Boston, and "Yellow Promise/Yellow Peril" is particularly illuminating on the ambiguous European response to Japan's stunning emergence as a powerful imperialist power.

55. *Business Week*, September 1, 1945. This ad is reproduced in John W. Dower, "Graphic Japanese, Graphic Americans: Coded Images in U.S.-Japanese Relations," in Akira Iriye and Robert A. Wampler, eds., *Partnership: The United States and Japan, 1951–2001* (Kodansha International, 2001), 304–5.

56. For general treatments of these matters, see Akira Iriye, *Pacific Estrangement: Japanese and American Expansion, 1897–1911* (Harvard University Press, 1972); also Spector, *Eagle against the Sun*, esp. chs. 1–5. The 127 tests and revisions of Orange are noted in ibid., 57.

57. On the B-17 bombers, see Prange, *Pearl Harbor*, 145–52, 290–93; also Spector, *Eagle against the Sun*, 74–75. The three Pearl Harbor alerts are described in detail in Wohlstetter, *Pearl Harbor*, 71–169.

58. See, for example, Michael A. Barnhart, *Japan Prepares for Total War: The Search for Economic Security, 1919–1941* (Cornell University Press, 1987).

59. Prange, *Pearl Harbor*, 537, 555–56; Wohlstetter, *Pearl Harbor*, 336–38; E. Kathleen Williams, "Air War, 1939–41," in Wesley Frank Craven and James Lea Cate, eds., *The Army Air Forces in World War II*, vol. 1: *Plans and Early Operations, January 1939 to August 1942* (University of Chicago Press, 1948), 79–80. On the development of the Mitsubishi Zero as seen from the Japanese side, see the translated account by the chief designer Jirō Horikoshi, *Eagles of Mitsubishi: The Story of the Zero Fighter* (Washington University Press, 1980); also Akira Yoshimura, *Zero Fighter* (Praeger, 1996).

60. Prange, *Pearl Harbor*, 550, 569; H. P. Willmott, *The Second World War in the Far East* (Smithsonian Books, 1999), 54, 66, 78, 83–84; Russell F. Weigley, *The American Way of War: A History of United States Military Strategy and Policy* (Indiana University Press, 1973), 276.

61. For an archives-based analysis of World War II in Asia that is acutely sensitive to (and quotable about) Anglo racism, see Christopher Thorne, *Allies of a Kind: The United States, Britain, and the War against Japan, 1941–1945* (Oxford University Press, 1979). American racism vis-à-vis Asians was complicated by the positive attitude many Americans had come to hold toward China by the late 1930s. Although "anti-Oriental" movements and legislation constitute a deep stain in U.S. history of the nineteenth and early twentieth century, sympathy toward the Chinese in their struggle against the Japanese was strong—a development that derived in considerable part from the exceedingly effective positive image of the Chinese purveyed by popular writers such as the Nobel Prize–winning Pearl Buck. I address these matters at length in *War Without Mercy: Race and Power in the Pacific War* (Pantheon, 1986).

62. It is worth keeping in mind that surprise attacks have been common in modern times. These include the attack by Germany on the Soviet Union in 1941; by North Korea on South Korea in 1950, and soon after this the entry of the People's Republic of China into the Korean War; and the Tet offensive in the Vietnam War in 1968.

63. For examples of the bedrock assumptions noted here, see Ike, *Japan's Decision for War*, 78, 80, 82, 148, 152, 160.

64. Ike, *Japan's Decision for War*, 238, 246.

65. Katharine Sansom, *Sir George Sansom and Japan: A Memoir* (Diplomatic Press, 1972), 156 (MacArthur's quote).

66. Goldstein and Dillon, *The Pearl Harbor Papers*, 155. For the *Missouri* surrender ceremony, see Samuel Eliot Morison, *History of United States Naval Operations in World War II*, vol. 14: *Victory in the Pacific* (Little, Brown, 1960), 362–63. The flag that had been flying over the Capitol on December 7 had previously been displayed at Casablanca (where the Allied policy of "unconditional surrender" was announced in February 1943), Rome, and Berlin.

67. Japan's vision of what was needed to be secure and self-sufficient escalated steadily after the Manchurian Incident of 1931, with huge leaps taking place in 1937, with the invasion of China; in mid-1940, with the movement of Japanese forces into northern French Indochina; and of course in 1941, when the "move South" precipitated the attack on Pearl Harbor. As the empire expanded, so inevitably did the political rhetoric that accompanied it. Thus, the proclaimed "New Order" of 1938 (embracing Japan, China, and the puppet state of Manchukuo) metamorphosed into the Greater East Asia Co-Prosperity Sphere in 1940. Until around 1936, advocates of the "move South" fought a vigorous internecine battle with proponents of a "move North" against the Soviet Union, aimed at seizing the strategic resources of the Soviet Far East. (The Japanese army was more inclined to "move North" than the navy.) The "move North" argument continued to be advocated up to the eve of the Pearl Harbor attack, and the Americans were well aware of this from their intercepts of the Japanese diplomatic code. This was yet one more distraction—one more example of "noise"—that compounded the analysis of Japan's intentions. Some high-level U.S. planners (such as Rear Admiral Richmond Turner of the War Plans Division) were so fixated on the "move North" possibility that, in the eyes of later critics, they seriously impeded balanced intelligence analysis; Prange, *Pearl Harbor*, 326–31, is strong on this. For a close analysis of the "rational" quest for autarky or autonomy that drove Japanese expansion from the Manchurian Incident to the war with China, see James B. Crowley, *Japan's Quest for Autonomy: National Security and Foreign Policy, 1930–1938* (Princeton University Press, 1966).

68. *The 9-11 Commission Report*, 341–42; Clarke, *Against All Enemies*, ch. 6 (133–54), esp. 148. Terrorist attacks on U.S. targets abroad also mark this period, of course, notably those in Beirut (1982), Libya ("Pan Am 103" in 1988), Somalia (1993, later identified as involving Al Qaeda), Saudi Arabia (1995–96), and Kenya and Tanzania (1998, instigated by Al Qaeda).

69. This timetable for planning the Pearl Harbor attack has been extracted from Prange, *At Dawn We Slept*, 15, 27–28, 101, 106, 157–58, 223–31, 299, 309, 324, 328, 345, 372. On Al Qaeda's planning, see *The 9-11 Commission Report*, 365.

70. Warren I. Cohen, "The Role of Private Groups in the United States," in Borg and Okamoto, *Pearl Harbor as History*, 421–58. The well-known scholars of Far Eastern affairs who urged conciliation with Japan included Payson Treat, A. Whitney Griswold, and Paul Clyde; ibid., 452–53. Cohen concludes his detailed study with the observation that "the American people remained overwhelmingly opposed to involvement in the Far Eastern conflict or in any war"; ibid., 456.

71. Grew abandoned his general policy of appeasing Japan in a famous "green light" cable to the State Department on September 10, 1940, but continued to maintain hope that U.S. responsiveness to Japan's perceived interests would strengthen the influence of "moderates" within the Japanese government. His September 1941 advocacy of "constructive conciliation" came in conjunction with proposals for a personal meeting between Roosevelt and Prime Minister Konoe.

72. Mira Wilkins, "The Role of U.S. Business," in Borg and Okamoto, *Pearl Harbor as History*, 341–76. This excellent analysis includes useful tables and charts. For the *Fortune* opinion poll, see 350–51; Wilkins speculates that the poll, published in September 1940, was probably conducted in early July—just before the Roosevelt administration imposed the first serious restrictions on strategic exports.

73. Steve Coll's *Ghost Wars: The Secret History of the CIA, Afghanistan, and Bin Laden, from the Soviet Invasion to September 10, 2001* (Penguin, 2004), won the Pulitzer Prize. See esp. 92–93, 97–98 on Casey; 90, 104 on translation of the Qur'an; 11, 125–37, 149–51, 175 on weapons and other support for the Afghan fighters; and 155 on moral support for the non-Afghan mujahideen. The U.S. role in playing midwife to the mujahideen is also documented in vivid detail in Robert Dreyfuss, *Devil's Game: How the United States Helped Unleash Fundamentalist Islam* (Metropolitan, 2005), esp. ch. 11. The photograph of President Reagan meeting with mujahideen "freedom fighters" from Afghanistan is reproduced on the cover of Eqbal Ahmad, *Terrorism: Theirs and Ours* (Seven Stories Press, 2002).

74. Benazir Bhutto, *Reconciliation: Islam, Democracy, and the West* (HarperCollins, 2008), ch. 3, esp. 81–85, 149–55. Bhutto's secret role in providing covert aid to the Taliban is noted in Coll, *Ghost Wars*, 289–94, 298–300.

75. Bin Laden, *Messages to the World*, 48 (March 1997), 65, 82 (December 1998), 109 (October 21, 2001), 192–93 (February 14, 2003). On the absence of counterinsurgency doctrine and training, see chapter 5 (notes 176–178 of this book).

76. Clifford J. Levy, "Poker-Faced, Russia Flaunts Its Afghan Card," *New York Times*, February 22, 2009.

77. Freeman is quoted in Dreyfuss, *Devil's Game*, 290–91 (from an April 2004 interview with the author).

78. Scheuer, *Imperial Hubris*, 197–98.

79. Clarke, *Against All Enemies*, 30–32, 232.

80. *The 9-11 Commission Report*, 339–48.

81. *The 9-11 Commission Report*, 364; Hersh, *Chain of Command*, 91–92; Michael A. Sheehan, *Crush the Cell: How to Defeat Terrorism without Terrorizing Ourselves* (Crown, 2008), 6, 14. Jack Goldsmith, a conservative lawyer who became head of the president's Office of Legal Counsel in October 2003, devotes an entire chapter of his book to the role of "fear bordering on obsession" in driving post–9-11 administration policies; *The Terror Presidency: Law and Judgment inside the Bush Administration* (Norton, 2007), ch. 3 (esp. 71–76), also 165–67.

82. Nathaniel Pfeffer, "Japanese Superman? That, Too, Is a Fallacy," *New York Times Magazine*, March 22, 1942. In a book written many years ago, I dwelled at length on images of the enemy from both sides of the war in the Pacific, including the metamorphoses of the Japanese from little men to supermen. See *War Without Mercy*, esp. ch. 5 ("Lesser Men and Supermen"). This is not a unique phenomenon, and need not involve race. A similar "little men to supermen" transformation took place, for example, in the so-called missile-gap crisis that followed the Soviet test of an intercontinental ballistic missile in 1957.

## CHAPTER 4: INNOCENCE, EVIL, AND AMNESIA

83. Ford's original eighty-two-minute version of *December 7th* was censored by the government as being "damaging to morale." The thirty-four-minute version that was released to theaters and won an Academy Award deleted all the sections involving actors—notably the long exchanges between "Sam" and "C" and the cemetery dialogue about a war to end all wars at the end—as well as the excruciatingly long opening section depicting Japanese Americans in every walk of life engaged in espionage and torn by divided loyalties. The equally excruciating depiction of chaos and carnage, on the other hand, remained intact.

84. The production of *December 7th* in 1942 coincided with Executive Order 9066 (issued in February) and consequent roundup and incarceration of ethnic Japanese citizens as well as Japanese aliens living in California, Oregon, and Washington. Like the scapegoating of Admiral Kimmel and General Short, this can be understood in part as a way of drawing attention away from Washington's own responsibility for the unpreparedness at Pearl Harbor (a central theme of the original Ford film). One of the more ironic aspects of this incarceration was that it did not extend to Japanese Americans living in Hawaii. For a good study of Executive Order 9066 that includes both useful historical background and close analysis of Roosevelt's role and racial attitudes, see Greg Robinson, *By Order of the President: FDR and the Internment of Japanese Americans* (Harvard University Press, 2001). For a DVD of the Ford film with many accompanying materials, see *December 7th: The Pearl Harbor Story* (Kit Parker Films, 2001).

85. Jeanine Basinger, *The World War II Combat Film: Anatomy of a Genre* (Wesleyan University Press, 2003).

86. Armitage recounted his comment to Inter-Services Intelligence chief Mahmoud Ahmad in a *Frontline* television program titled "Return of the Taliban," the transcript of which was posted at pbs.org/wgbh on October 3, 2006. Perle is quoted by George Packer in *The Assassins' Gate: America in Iraq* (Farrar, Straus & Giroux, 2005), 41. David Bromwich notes the prevalence of "history begins today" as a post–9-11 cliché in "Euphemism and American Violence," *New York Review of Books*, April 3, 2008.

87. Frum, *The Right Man*, 145. Michael Scheuer, who was removed from his position as head of the CIA's "bin Laden unit" prior to September 11, has offered an extended indictment of this head-in-the-sand refusal to see 9-11 and Osama bin Laden's anti-Americanism as a serious response to past and present U.S. policies. See the updated paperback edition of his *Imperial Hubris* (Potomac Books, 2005), esp. 11–14 and 261–74 (the "New Epilogue"). "Bin Laden has been precise

in telling America the reasons he is waging war on us," Scheuer writes in a typical passage. "None of the reasons have anything to do with our freedom, liberty,
and democracy, but have everything to do with U.S. policies and actions in the
Muslim world"; ibid., x.

88. The full provocative statement in the September 16 press conference was, "This
crusade, this war on terrorism is going to take a while." For a concise summary
of the alarm and criticism this provoked among Muslims generally as well as in
Europe, see the *Christian Science Monitor*, September 19, 2001; many commentators expressed concern that framing the crisis in terms of evil and a crusade would
inflame "clash of civilizations" attitudes. Shortly after this, the United States
again found itself forced to meliorate its language—in this case by changing the
announced code name for the war on terror from "Operation Infinite Justice" to
"Operation Enduring Freedom." The former was being retracted, Defense Secretary Rumsfeld announced on September 25, because Islamic believers regard
such finality as something provided only by God. A Lebanese scholar in Beirut
suggested that a more appropriate revision would have been "Operation Infinite
Injustice," while an Iranian newspaper proposed "Operation Infinite Imperialism"; BBC News (news.bbc.co.uk), September 25, 2001.

89. Lawrence Wright offers a fascinating appraisal of Fadl's subsequent recantation
of the violent doctrinal writings on jihad he originally produced for Al Qaeda;
"The Rebellion Within," *New Yorker*, June 2, 2008. For "no act of ours," see
the president's address to the National Endowment for Democracy on October
6, 2005. Bremer made his early observations in a panel discussion titled "The
Coming War" on the PBS NewsHour with Jim Lehrer, broadcast on August 25,
1998.

90. Victor Davis Hanson, "War Myths," *National Review*, September 20, 2001.

91. The West Point speech is an excellent example of the wedding of dire visions,
noble ideals, and resolute military prescriptions that Bush used effectively in
building up support for the Iraq war. For prescient criticism of the incipient militarism of the emerging Bush Doctrine, see the newspaper columns of James Carroll collected in *Crusade: Chronicles of an Unjust War* (Metropolitan, 2004), esp.
6–7 ("sacred violence"), 115 (the West Point speech). For another critique framed
more in military terms, see Andrew J. Bacevich, *The New American Militarism:
How Americans Are Seduced by War* (Oxford University Press, 2005), as well as
Bacevich's many subsequent essays and articles. The new-style militarism of these
developments, with particular attention given to the worldwide U.S. "empire of
bases," is addressed by Chalmers Johnson in *The Sorrows of Empire: Militarism,
Secrecy, and the End of the Republic* (Metropolitan, 2004). On the other side of these
debates, it is difficult to exaggerate the fixation on "evil" among those who in
one way or another supported the administration's militaristic policies. For example, David Frum, the speechwriter who was involved in writing the "axis of evil"
address, and Richard Perle, a leading spokesman for the neoconservative ideology,
titled a jointly authored book *An End to Evil: How to Win the War on Terror* (Random House, 2003). Michael Ignatieff, a liberal supporter of the war, entered the
fray with *The Lesser Evil: Political Ethics in an Age of Terror* (Princeton University
Press, 2004; reissued with a new preface in 2005).

92. *Report of the Defense Science Board Task Force on Strategic Communication* (Office of

the Under Secretary of Defense for Acquisition, Technology, and Logistics; September 2004), 2, 17, 29, 40 (available online at fas.org/irp/dod/dsb).

93. *Transition to and from Hostilities: Supporting Papers* (Defense Science Board 2004 Summer Study, Office of the Under Secretary of Defense for Acquisition, Technology, and Logistics; January 2005), 68. These "supporting papers" were made available online at books.google.com; no such language appears in the report of the same title issued in December 2004.

94. Bhutto, *Reconciliation*, 84; the "shadow" metaphor is repeated on 96.

95. Cemil Aydin has written on these matters in thoughtful detail. See his *Politics of Anti-Westernism in Asia: Visions of World Order in Pan-Islamic and Pan-Asian Thought* (Columbia University Press, 2007); also his lengthy online article "Japan's Pan-Asianism and the Legitimacy of Imperial World Order, 1931–45" and his interview with Michael Penn titled "Imperial Japan's Islamic Policies and Anti-Westernism," both on the website japanfocus.org as of 2008. See also Ian Buruma and Avishai Margalit, *Occidentalism: The West in the Eyes of Its Enemies* (Penguin, 2004), and John Gray's provocative *Al Qaeda and What It Means to Be Modern* (New Press, 2004).

96. Guantánamo came into U.S. hands in 1901 under the so-called Platt Amendment to the 1898 treaty with Spain that followed the Spanish-American War. Under these arrangements, Cuba, until then under Spanish control like the Philippines, gained nominal independence while actually becoming dependent on the United States. Guantánamo was given to the United States to use as a military base—ostensibly to protect the Panama Canal—with the proviso that it would revert to Cuba when *both* sides agreed to this. The decisive events in Japan's simultaneous emergence as an imperialist power were victory in the Sino-Japanese War of 1894–95 (by which Formosa, later known as Taiwan, became a Japanese colony) and the Russo-Japanese War of 1904–5 (which established a Japanese foothold on the Asian continent and paved the way for annexation of Korea in 1910). Akira Iriye has documented how large a role fear of Japanese expansion into the Pacific played in rationalizing the U.S. seizure of Hawaii in 1895 and its annexation three years later; see his *Pacific Estrangement*.

97. Such rhetoric saturates all accounts of turn-of-the-century U.S. imperialism. For a general treatment, including many of the quotes here, see Stanley Karnow, *In Our Image: America's Empire in the Philippines* (Random House, 1989), esp. 9–20, 87, 100, 104, 128–29, 134. For Beveridge and his fellow senator, see Julius Pratt, *Expansionists of 1898: The Acquisition of Hawaii and the Spanish Islands* (Quadrangle Books, 1964; originally published by the Johns Hopkins Press in 1936), 227–28, 314; the response to the takeover of the Philippines in U.S. religious circles is discussed in ibid., ch. 3. Other carefully annotated sources include Stuart Creighton Miller, *"Benevolent Assimilation": The American Conquest of the Philippines, 1899–1903* (Yale University Press, 1983); also Richard E. Welch Jr., *Response to Imperialism: The United States and the Philippine-American War, 1899–1902* (University of North Carolina Press, 1979). Kipling's "The White Man's Burden," published in 1899, was subtitled "The United States and the Philippines."

98. "Benevolent global hegemony" became a mantra among neoconservative foreign-policy pundits after being introduced in an influential article by William Kristol and Robert Kagan well before 9-11; see "Toward a Neo-Reaganite

Foreign Policy," *Foreign Affairs*, July/August 1996. The "white man's burden" conceit experienced a color-sanitized resurrection less than three months before the invasion of Iraq when the *New York Times Magazine* (January 5, 2003) titled a controversial defense of the preemptive-war policy by Michael Ignatieff "The American Empire: The Burden." Ignatieff spelled out his faith in a postimperial "humanitarian empire" led by the United States in a short collection of his essays published in 2003 under the title *Empire Lite: Nation-Building in Bosnia, Kosovo, and Afghanistan* (Penguin Canada).

99. When McKinley was informed of Admiral Dewey's victory over the Spanish fleet in Manila Bay in 1898, he pulled out a map and was later quoted as saying, "I could not have told where those darned islands were within 2,000 miles!"; Pratt, *Expansionists of 1898*, 326. On McKinley and God, see ibid., 316, 334–35, but also Lewis L. Gould, *The Presidency of William McKinley* (Regents Press of Kansas, 1980), 140–42. Gould traces the original source for the "Almighty God" vignette back to a recollection of the occasion first printed in January 1903, over three years after McKinley met with the Methodists, and concludes that the "famed religious context" of these comments is "very questionable." The "liberty and law, peace and progress" quotation appears in Iriye, *Pacific Estrangement*, 59–60.

100. Aguinaldo, who lived into his nineties, made peace with the Americans but collaborated with Japan's occupation of the Philippines in World War II.

101. Edmund Morris captures the inflammatory nature of the conquest of the Philippines in his biography of Theodore Roosevelt, *Theodore Rex* (Random, 2001); see 97–104, esp. 98–100 for the references here. Yates Stirling, *Sea Duty: The Memoirs of a Fighting Admiral* (Putnam's Sons, 1939), ch. 5, esp. 79. Stirling's account of "the Philippine insurrection" mentions the "water cure" and records that his commander referred to the burning of entire villages as applying "black paint." ("You know what 'black paint' is? I hope you use plenty of it.") The damning secret report, released on April 11, 1902, was by Major Cornelius Gardener, the military governor of one province in the Philippines, and became known as the Gardener Report.

102. Morris, *Theodore Rex*, 100–1; William Safire, "Waterboarding," *New York Times Magazine*, March 9, 2008.

103. For the full text of Root's letter, see "Cruelty Charges Denied," *New York Times*, February 20, 1902. For other quotes, see Morris, *Theodore Rex*, 97, 101–2, 604 (n. 102).

104. Karnow, *In Our Image*, 194; also 12, 140. Famine arose primarily because 90 percent of the water buffalo (Stirling's "carabaos") were killed, making it impossible to plant or harvest rice, the staple food in rural areas. Over 70,000 U.S. troops were mobilized to suppress the Filipino resistance, and Karnow puts the immediate U.S. war dead at 4,234 killed and 2,818 wounded, with additional thousands later dying at home from war-related causes. The monetary cost of the conflict to the United States was $600 million (equivalent to $4 billion at the time Karnow was writing, in the late 1980s), with many millions more going out in pensions to veterans and their families. Although the U.S. military command in the Philippines tried to control the cable traffic on the war, American journalists protested such censorship; reports of extreme brutality, as well as the difficulties the U.S. forces were facing, were widely circulated. The issue of whether the Americans

had dispatched enough troops also became a source of controversy; see ibid., 12, 148–50. Max Boot, an outspoken supporter of the Iraq war, devoted a chapter to the 1899–1902 Philippine war in *The Savage Wars of Peace: Small Wars and the Rise of American Power* (Basic Books, 2003). Boot is unsparing about atrocities on both sides in this "dirty" (100) and "inglorious" (119) war, but concludes that this was "one of the most successful counterinsurgencies waged by a Western army in modern times" (127–28). Such "lessons" from the colonial past became increasingly common among conservatives who saw "paying attention to the rudiments of counterinsurgency strategy" as the key to reversing U.S. disasters in Iraq. For obvious reasons, estimates of violent deaths among Iraqis after the invasion vary greatly. In a book published after the Bush presidency ended, Juan Cole provides annotations to various demographic reports and concludes that "300,000 excess Iraqi deaths . . . seems to me the lowest estimate that is plausible"; *Engaging the Muslim World* (Palgrave Macmillan, 2009), 127.

105. In Chalmers Johnson's calculation, "between 1898 and 1934, the United States sent Marines to Cuba four times, Honduras seven times, the Dominican Republic four times, Haiti twice, Guatemala once, Panama twice, Mexico three times, Colombia four times, and Nicaragua five times"; *The Sorrows of Empire*, 190–93. These military interventions were usually undertaken in the name of the "Monroe Doctrine" (introduced in 1823 as a declaration of U.S. opposition to further European colonization in the Americas, but subsequently reinterpreted—especially in the so-called Roosevelt Corollary of 1904—as affirming the right of the United States to intervene in the countries of Latin America). In the 1930s, when Japan was pursuing its escalating quest for military and economic security, Japanese propagandists often presented Japan's policy as a "Monroe Doctrine for Asia." Americans brushed this aside, and the Japanese in turn used this as one more example of Western double standards.

106. "Remarks by the President to the Philippine Congress," October 18, 2003; *New York Times*, October 19, 2003.

107. Robert Fisk, *The Great War for Civilization: The Conquest of the Middle East* (Knopf, 2005), xviii. Bin Laden, *Messages to the World*, 181. Bin Laden's litany includes American "soldiers of Satan" and "devil's supporters" (61); "devils and demons among mankind, and especially the Crusaders" (88); "global alliance of evil" (182; a belated spin on February 11, 2003, of President Bush's "axis of evil" speech); "hegemony of the infidels" (196); and "Zionist-Crusader chain of evil" (214). Japan's militarists similarly claimed to be fighting a holy war (*seisen*) against the "demonic Anglo-Americans" (*kichiku Ei-Bei*), with their own ineffable purity as a race and culture embodied in the emperor-centered Imperial Way (*Kōdō*); see the comparison of *seisen* and jihad in chapter 12 of this book.

108. Rashid Khalidi pairs the well-known Napoleon and Maude quotations with Rumsfeld's comforting but soon discredited words to U.S. troops in April 2003, a month after the capture of Baghdad: "Unlike many armies in the world, you came not to conquer, not to occupy, but to liberate, and the Iraqi people know this"; *Resurrecting Empire: Western Footprints and America's Perilous Path in the Middle East* (Beacon Press, 2004), 37, 43. Fixation on victimization by outside forces easily falls into scapegoating and simplistic conspiracy theories that ignore reasons for the failure of most Middle East countries apart from Israel to keep up with

"the rise of the West," and it goes without saying that neither the realities nor exaggerations of past and present victimization legitimize terrorist crimes against humanity. The historian Bernard Lewis is often quoted where this "scapegoating" argument is concerned, and a quotation from one of his most popular books, a selection of talks and essays issued in the wake of 9-11, conveys the essence of his argument. "Many regions have undergone the impact of the West, and suffered a similar loss of economic self-sufficiency, of cultural authenticity, and in some parts also of political independence," he observes in his concluding pages. "But some time has passed since Western domination ended in all these regions, including the Middle East. In some of them, notably in East and South Asia, the resurgent peoples of the region have begun to meet and beat the West on its own terms—in commerce and industry, in the projection of political and even military power, and, in many ways most remarkable of all, in the acceptance and internalization of Western achievement, notably in science. The Middle East still lags behind"; *What Went Wrong? Western Impact and Middle Eastern Response* (Oxford University Press, 2002), 148.

It was Lewis who, in 1956, first used the term "clash of civilizations," and in time he emerged as a guru in the neoconservative circles that so strongly influenced the policy of the Bush administration; see, for example, Dreyfuss, *Devil's Game*, 330–35. Dismay at the deep pathologies apparent almost everywhere in the Middle East does not necessarily or inevitably translate into support for outside military intervention, however. Historians like Khalidi, who opposed the war and is strongly critical of the negative legacies of Western intrusion, also are unsparing in their criticism of the nationalistic and authoritarian postcolonial Middle Eastern states; see, for example, *Resurrecting Empire*, 60–73.

109. More than four years before 9-11, bin Laden gave an interview to CNN denouncing Western "arrogance" as having "set a double standard, calling whoever goes against its injustice a terrorist"; bin Laden, *Messages to the World*, 51. He often referred to destructive acts outside the Middle East like the nuclear bombing of Japan in World War II; found it effective to turn his distinctive oracular style to rhetorical questions like "How many acts of oppression, tyranny, and injustice have you carried out, O callers to freedom?" (168); and took pleasure in admonishing Americans (and inciting his Muslim and Arab audience) with declarations like "to you, values and principles are something which you merely demand from others, not that which you yourself must adhere to" (170).

110. Eleven full-color coversheets from the "Worldwide Intelligence Update," beginning March 17 and ending April 11, were reproduced online for the first time in conjunction with Robert Draper, "And He Shall Be Judged," GQ.com, May 17, 2009. The article notes that the biblical quotations caused some unavailing internal opposition in the Pentagon.

111. Thomas E. Ricks, "The Dissenter," *Washington Post National Weekly Edition*, February 16–22, 2009 ("kill-or-capture" and "MAMs"); adapted from Ricks's *The Gamble: General David Petraeus and the American Military Adventure in Iraq, 2006–2008* (Penguin, 2008). See Cole, *Engaging the Muslim World*, 117–18, on "Al Qaeda" corpses and imprisoned Iraqis; Cole quotes a former Green Beret from the Vietnam War who recalled how, after firefights, all dead Vietnamese were routinely declared to be "Viet Cong." In February 2004, Red Cross investigators

reported that military intelligence officers associated with the Coalition Forces told them "that in their estimate between 70 percent and 90 percent of the persons deprived of their liberty in Iraq had been arrested by mistake"; *Report of the International Committee of the Red Cross (ICRC) on the Treatment by the Coalition Forces of Prisoners of War and Other Protected Persons by the Geneva Conventions in Iraq during Arrest, Internment and Interrogation* (available online at icrc.org).

112. Bin Laden, *Messages to the World*, 114, 128; see also 175 ("Just as you kill, so you shall be killed; just as you bomb, so you shall be bombed. And there will be more to come"). The October 20 interview was not aired until January 31, 2002. In speaking of "traitors," bin Laden was referring explicitly to Muslim and Arab nations and regimes that supported the United States.

113. Bin Laden, *Messages to the World*, 51; for other references to the nuclear bombing of Japan, see 40, 44, 66–67, 105, 168–69. On delivering a "Hiroshima" to the United States, see *The 9/11 Commission Report*, 116; also *New York Times*, October 14, 2001. The turn against Al Qaeda by former jihadi became particularly conspicuous around 2007 and is addressed in Peter Bergen and Paul Cruickshank, "The Unraveling: The Jihadist Revolt against bin Laden," *New Republic*, June 11, 2008, and Wright, "The Rebellion Within." The "my brother Osama" address, quoted by Bergen and Cruickshank, was by Sheikh Salman al-Oudah, "one of bin Laden's erstwhile heroes." Wright gives particular attention to the basic Al Qaeda doctrinal text *Compendium of the Pursuit of Divine Knowledge*, authored under a pseudonym by Sayyid Imam al-Sharif and later repudiated by him.

114. Bin Laden, *Messages to the World*, 113–20, 129, 239–40. For other direct or indirect iterations of the "balance of terror" argument, see 51, 73, 104, 134, 175, 234. In his "destroyed towers in Lebanon" account, delivered in October 2004, bin Laden almost seemed to be offering "Remember Lebanon" as code comparable to "Remember Pearl Harbor" and "9/11—We Will Never Forget" in the American idiom.

115. Bin Laden, *Messages to the World*, 40, 117, 164–65, 239–40, 266–68. In 1996, bin Laden called attention to "the death of more than 600,000 Iraqi children because of the shortage of food and medicine which resulted from the boycotts and sanctions." Every year thereafter, he added 100,000 deaths to that total—observing in his first major address after 9-11 that "more than 1,000,000 children died in Iraq, and they are still dying, so why do we not hear people [in the United States] that cry or protest, or anyone who reassures or anyone who extends condolences?" His inflated numbers apparently derived from a widely publicized estimate of a half-million "excess" newborn, infant, and child deaths between 1990 and 1995 (discussed in chapter 4 in this book), which amounted to 100,000 annually.

116. Bin Laden, *Messages to the World*, 255; Barton Gellman, "Allied Air War Struck Broadly in Iraq; Officials Acknowledge Strategy Went beyond Purely Military Targets," *Washington Post*, June 23, 1991; Paul Lewis, "After the War; U.N. Survey Calls Iraq's War Damage Near-Apocalyptic," *New York Times*, March 22, 1991; "Gulf War Is Said to Have Cost the Region $676 Billion in 1990–91," *New York Times*, April 25, 1993.

117. U.S. Defense Intelligence Agency, "Iraq Water Treatment Vulnerabilities as of 18 Jan 91" (available online at globalsecurity.org). Strategic-paralysis theorizing is addressed in David S. Fadok, *John Boyd and John Warden: Air Power's Quest for*

*Strategic Paralysis* (Maxwell Air Force Base, Alabama: Air University Press, 1995); see chapter 1 for a concise summary. For "long-term leverage" (a quote from Warden), see Gellman, "Allied Air War Struck Broadly in Iraq." In a seminal article on "strategic paralysis," emphasizing the necessity of targeting "the whole system," with primary focus on concentric circles emanating outward from "leadership" (through "organic essentials," "infrastructure," "population," and lastly "fielded military"), Warden himself emphasized that "we hold direct attacks on civilians to be morally reprehensible and militarily difficult"; Col. John A Warden III, "The Enemy as a System," *Airpower Journal*, vol. 9 (Spring 1995), 40–55, esp. 51. Sanctions amounted to an indirect attack on the civilian population.

118. Gellman, "Allied Air War Struck Broadly in Iraq" ("definition of innocents"); bin Laden, *Messages to the World*, 47.

119. For Saddam, see "Speech of His Excellency President Saddam Hussein on the 30th Anniversary of 17–30 July 1968 Revolution in the Name of God, the Compassionate, the Merciful," July 17, 1998. Saddam described Iraq's enemies as trying to "assassinate" the Iraqis, and declared that if the enemy just looked at the glorious history of the Arab people they would see that the embargo and other threats simply revealed the "abyss" between the Iraqi spirit and their own "evils and their souls inciting them to evil." In a frequently quoted speech on January 17, 2001, marking the tenth anniversary of the Gulf War, Saddam similarly posed the conflict in classic Manichaean terms as a clash between "the people of civilizations, the cradle of prophethood" and "those who are so much disposed to evil that they have become the representative type of Satan in their actions and in their lack of character." These formulaic speeches are accessible online through keyword searches.

120. Colin Powell with Joseph E. Persico, *My American Journey* (Random House, 1995), 519–28; Schwarzkopf made his 1996 comments on "The Gulf War," a *Frontline* documentary first aired on PBS on February 4, 1997 (the transcript is online at pbs.org/wgbh); George Bush and Brent Scowcroft, *A World Transformed* (Knopf, 1998), ch. 19 (488–92, esp. 489).

121. Transcript of *This Week with David Brinkley*, ABC News, April 7, 1991; "Interview with the Vice President by Jonathan Karl," ABC News, February 23, 2007. For other early Cheney statements explaining why invading Iraq at the time of the Gulf War would be a quagmire, also available online, see the following: "Address by Secretary of Defense Dick Cheney to the Electronic Industries Association," Federal News Service, April 9, 1991; Susanne M. Schafer, "Cheney: No Ground Troops to Assist Kurds," Associated Press, April 12, 1991; Patrick E. Tyler, "After the War; U.S. Juggling Iraq Policy," *New York Times*, April 13, 1991; Editorial, "And Again: Once More into the Breach," *Washington Times*, April 19, 1991; Richard Cheney, "The Gulf War: A First Assessment," address to the Washington Institute for Near East Policy, April 29, 1991. Cheney repeated this argument in a presentation to the American Enterprise Institute on April 15, 1994, that was taped by C-SPAN and widely rebroadcast online when rediscovered in 2007. Juan Cole ruminates at some length on Cheney's about-face in *Engaging the Muslim World*, 136–42.

122. "Effect of the Gulf War on Infant and Child Mortality in Iraq," *New England Journal of Medicine*, vol. 327, no. 13 (September 24, 1992), 931–36. For the contro-

versial high estimate, see Sarah Zaidi and Mary C. Smith Fawzi, "Health of Baghdad's Children," *Lancet*, vol. 346 (December 2, 1995), 1485; an editorial appears on page 1439 of the same issue. Zaidi revised this original estimate downward (in very technical terms) in a letter published by *Lancet* in October 1997 (vol. 350: 1105).

123. The 1991–2002 estimate, by the Columbia University public health specialist Richard Garfield, is cited in "Iraq—Truth and Lies in Baghdad: The Debate over U.N. Sanctions," on the PBS "Frontline/World" website, November 2002; this introduces a number of basic sources on the subject. In their joint press conference, Bush and Blair emphasized the stark contrast between the brutality and cruelty of Saddam's regime ("beyond the comprehension of anyone with an ounce of humanity in their souls," in Blair's phrasing) and the "humanitarian" concerns of Washington and London ("this urgent humanitarian issue must not be politicized," as the president put it); see the White House transcript "President Bush, Prime Minister Blair Hold Press Availability," March 27, 2003. The White House included Blair's comment on child mortality in a subsequent release on "Life under Saddam Hussein: Past Repression and Atrocities by Saddam Hussein's Regime," April 4, 2003. The online literature on this subject is enormous. Among useful overviews of the debate, see Rahul Mahajan, "'We Think the Price Is Worth It,'" the Fairness and Accuracy in Reporting website at fair.org, November/December 2001; David Cortright, "A Hard Look at Iraq Sanctions," *Nation*, November 15, 2001; Matt Welch, "The Politics of Dead Children," *Reason Magazine*, March 2002.

124. "Punishing Saddam; Sanctions against Iraq Not Hurting Leaders of the Country, but the Children Are Suffering and Dying," CBS News Transcripts, *60 Minutes*, May 12, 1996. The interviewer was Leslie Stahl, and her report won an Emmy as well as a journalism award from Columbia University. Albright addresses the episode in her memoir *Madame Secretary* (Miramax, 2003), 275; see also "Albright 'Apologizes,'" Future of Freedom Foundation online commentary at fff.org, November 7, 2003.

125. "Speech of His Holiness Pope John Paul II in Reply to the New Year Greetings of the Diplomatic Corps Accredited to the Holy See," January 10, 1998, on the official Vatican website (vatican.va). For Halliday, see Youssef M. Ibrahim, "Higher Hopes in Baghdad for Ending U.N. Embargo," *New York Times*, October 18, 1998; Stephen Kinzer, "The World; Smart Bombs, Dumb Sanctions," *New York Times*, January 3, 1999; Halliday's first public speech after resigning, titled "Why I Resigned My UN Post in Protest of Sanctions," presented at Harvard on November 5, 1998 (available online at leb.net/~iac/oldsite/harvard.html); and his "Iraq and the UN's Weapon of Mass Destruction," *Current History*, February 1999, 65–68. Halliday repeated the genocide charge on many occasions following his resignation. For the most quoted version, see "John Pilger on Why We Ignored Iraq in the 1990s," *Newstatesman*, October 4, 2004, at newstatesman .com, and Pilger's "The Media Culpability for Iraq," *Zmag*, October 11, 2004, at zmag.org. For von Sponeck, see BBC News, at news.bbc.co.uk, February 14, 2000.

126. William F. Donaher and Ross B. DeBlois, "Is the Current UN and US Policy toward Iraq Effective?" *Parameters: US Army War College Quarterly*, vol. 31, no. 4 (Winter 2001–2002), 112–25.

127. Bremer, *My Year in Iraq*, 17–18, 28, 34–38, 61–66.
128. Fisk, *The Great War for Civilization*, 702–3.

### CHAPTER 5: WARS OF CHOICE AND STRATEGIC IMBECILITIES

129. See, for example, Spector, *Eagle against the Sun*, 106–8, 117; John Costello, *The Pacific War, 1941–1945* (Quill, 1981), 651–54; Prange, *Pearl Harbor*, ch. 28 (518–30); Prange, *At Dawn We Slept*, 558, 583; Wohlstetter, *Pearl Harbor*, 357–67; Morison, "The Lessons of Pearl Harbor." On December 6, the eve of the Japanese attack, MacArthur explained why the Philippines did not have to fear an attack by Japan. "The inability of an enemy to launch his air attack on these islands is our greatest security," he declared. "Most fighters are short ranged. . . . Even with the improvised forces I now have, because of the inability of the enemy to bring not only air but mechanized and motorized elements, leaves me [*sic*] with a sense of complete security"; Prange, *Pearl Harbor*, 521. On December 9, Army Chief of Staff General George C. Marshall reported receiving a cable from MacArthur stating that "enemy airplanes have been handled with superior efficiency and there are some indications that his dive bombers are at least partially manned by white pilots"; ibid., 528. See also similar reports cited in Dower, *War Without Mercy*, 105–6 (n. 16).
130. Once insurrection erupted in Iraq, the "foreign pilots" mindset was perpetuated in the administration's protracted fixation on the role of diehard Baathists and foreign agitators while minimizing the sectarian conflict, nationalist rage, and plain criminality its own policies had unleashed.
131. Douglas Feith dwells at length on both the rationale for war with Iraq and the debilitating persistence of "interagency discord" in his memoir *War and Decision: Inside the Pentagon at the Dawn of the War on Terrorism* (Harper, 2008). On the case for war, see esp. ch. 3, and also the ten-page document dated September 12, 2002, and titled "Presentation—The Case for Action" that Feith prepared for his superiors; the latter is included in the useful website that accompanies *War and Decision* (waranddecision.com/documents_and_articles/).
132. Richard Haass, who served as director of policy planning in the State Department at the time, takes credit for introducing the "wars of choice" phrase in an op-ed piece in the *Washington Post* on November 23, 2003, five months after he left office. His insider's account of the run-up to war is frank on the practical and moral dilemmas good soldiers in the bureaucracy face; see Haass, *War of Necessity, War of Choice: A Memoir of Two Iraq Wars* (Simon & Schuster, 2009), esp. 11, 15, and 246–50 (on why he did not resign in protest at the time).
133. *Republic of Fear* is the title of Kanan Makiya's denunciation of Saddam Hussein's Iraq, originally published under a pseudonym in 1989. Makiya's influential role in calling for the liberation of Iraq is addressed at length in Packer, *The Assassins' Gate*, where Makiya emerges as something of a dark prince.
134. For but one of innumerable examples of the proclaimed values for which the United States was fighting, see the president's introduction to "The National Security Strategy of the United States of America," released by the White House on September 17, 2002. For basic documents expounding Japan's mission, see Joyce Lebra, ed., *Japan's Greater East Asia Co-Prosperity Sphere in World War II*

(Oxford University Press, 1975); also *Kokutai no Hongi: Cardinal Principles of the National Entity of Japan*, translated by John Owen Gauntlett and edited by Robert King Hall (Harvard University Press, 1949).

135. "At O'Hare, President Says 'Get On Board,'" September 27, 2001; "Press Conference by the President," December 20, 2006. Both addresses are posted on the White House website.

136. The "rightwing radicalism" that found expression in Japan's quest for a so-called East Asian New Order (*Tōa shin chitsujo*) was accompanied by attempts to engineer a political-economic "New Structure" (*Shin taisei*) domestically; and overseas policies of occupation and the like, especially in Manchuria, reflected a concerted attempt to transplant and promote policies and ideologies associated with the radical vision of domestic renovation. For points of comparison between these developments and the right-wing radicalism of the Bush administration, see Dower, "The Other Japanese Occupation," *Nation*, July 7, 2003.

137. Bush's "body language" receives a substantial index entry in Bob Woodward's *Plan of Attack*. For Tōjō, see Ike, *Japan's Decision for War*, 129–63, 208. The investigative journalist Ron Suskind argues, on the basis of an anonymous informant from the intelligence community, that a few months before the invasion the Bush administration received evidence from an internal Iraqi source that Saddam was not pursuing the weapons programs that were the ostensible rationale for invasion. This was dismissed out of hand as disinformation—the president's own response, as Suskind tells it, being "Fuck it. We're going in"; *The Way of the World: A Story of Truth and Hope in an Age of Extremism* (Harper, 2008), 179–84.

138. Mark R. Peattie, *Ishiwara Kanji and Japan's Confrontation with the West* (Princeton University Press, 1975); Earl H. Kinmonth, "The Mouse That Roared: Saitō Takao, Conservative Critic of Japan's 'Holy War' in China," *Journal of Japanese Studies*, vol. 25, no. 2 (Summer 1999), 331–60; Shigeo Misawa and Saburo Ninomiya, "The Role of the Diet and Political Parties," in Borg and Okamoto, eds., *Pearl Harbor as History*, 321–40, esp. 337–40. The U.S. House of Representatives passed the so-called Iraq War Resolution on October 11, 2002, by a vote of 296 to 133; in the Senate the following day the vote was 77 to 23.

139. These have been translated by Nobutake Ike in *Japan's Decision for War*.

140. Feith, *War and Decision*, 53–55, 531 (for a flow chart). Feith also notes in passing (305) that "in practice, the written summaries of conclusions of interagency meetings—of the Deputies, Principals, and National Security Council—were very general, stating little more than the topics that had been discussed."

141. Feith, *War and Decision*, 245, 385–86. For examples of Feith's sustained lament over turf wars, see chapter 8 ("Discord in Washington") and the following pages in particular: 171–78 (turf wars within the Defense Department), 245–50 (disagreement between the Defense and State departments), 249–50 (Condoleezza Rice's failure to address these turf wars in the NSC), 289–93 and 360–66 (friction between the Pentagon and CENTCOM), and 385–89 (the most "toxic" example of Rumsfeld sabotaging Iraq policy out of pique with the State Department). As an exposé of bureaucratic infighting and dysfunction, Feith's account reinforces and extends, from a very different perspective, accounts by counterterrorism specialists like Richard Clarke and Michael Scheuer. Packer dissects the politicization of the bureaucracy in detail in *The Assassins' Gate*, esp. ch. 4 (100–48).

142. Barton Gellman paraphrases a Justice Department lawyer involved in a 2004 confrontation over illegal domestic surveillance orchestrated out of the Office of the Vice President to the effect that Cheney and his chief counsel David Addington "were gaming the system, using secrecy and intimidation to prevent dissenters from conducting an independent review"; "From Dissent to Rebellion," *Washington Post National Weekly Edition*, September 22–28, 2008; this is an excerpt from Gellman's book *Angler: The Cheney Vice Presidency* (Penguin, 2008).

143. Wolin, *Democracy Incorporated*. In Wolin's thesis, "inverted totalitarianism is only in part a state-centered phenomenon. Primarily it represents the *political* coming of age of corporate power and the *political* demobilization of the citizenry"—a process that brings with it "the triumph of contemporaneity and of its accomplice, forgetting or collective amnesia" (x). The hardball politics involved in promoting unfettered presidential authority are addressed in detail in, among other sources, Gellman's *Angler* and Jane Mayer, *The Dark Side: The Inside Story of How the War on Terror Turned into a War on American Ideals* (Doubleday, 2008). The term "imperial presidency" became popular during the Nixon administration and was given scholarly elaboration by Arthur Schlesinger Jr. in an influential book published the year before Nixon resigned: *The Imperial Presidency* (Houghton Mifflin, 1973). Schlesinger revisited the thesis for the Bush administration in *War and the American Presidency* (Norton, 2004).

144. The impasse over the post-invasion role of Iraqi "externals," also noted in chapter 13 in this book, is a core theme in Feith's book, *War and Decision*. On the Vulcans, see Mann, *Rise of the Vulcans*.

145. On the "War Council," see Mayer, *The Dark Side*, 65–66; Goldsmith, *The Terror Presidency*, 22–23. Goldsmith became head of the Office of Legal Counsel seven months after the invasion, and writes at length about his shock at discovering the "sloppily reasoned, overbroad, and incautious" nature of the legal opinions written by his predecessors; ibid., 10. (His account, which dwells at length on the War Council members and their excesses, is also addressed later in this book, in chapter 14.) Feith's comment on policy making by speech writing runs as follows: "When it came to crafting the President's public statements—often his most important articulations of policy—even the most productive interagency policy discussions amounted to little more than suggestions to the speechwriters, that they could either take or leave"; *War and Decision*, 309. Bob Woodward similarly notes in passing that "policy was made in speeches" under Bush; *Plan of War*, 216.

146. Paul R. Pillar, "Intelligence, Policy and the War in Iraq," *Foreign Affairs*, March/April 2006; Pillar, "The Right Stuff," *National Interest*, September/October 2007. For Haass, see his *War of Necessity, War of Choice*, 234.

147. Colonel Wilkerson introduced the "Oval Office cabal" phrase in a presentation titled "Weighing the Uniqueness of the Bush Administration's National Security Decision-Making Process: Boon or Danger to American Democracy?" sponsored by the New America Foundation on October 19, 2005.

148. On the emperor's wartime role in general, see Dower, *Embracing Defeat*, ch. 10–12; Herbert Bix, *Hirohito and the Making of Modern Japan* (HarperCollins, 2000); Peter Wetzler, *Hirohito and War: Imperial Tradition and Military Decision Making in Prewar Japan* (University of Hawaii Press, 1998); Stephen Large, *Emperor Hirohito and Shōwa Japan: A Political Biography* (Routledge, 1992); Edward J. Drea, *In the*

*Service of the Emperor: Essays on the Imperial Japanese Army* (University of Nebraska Press, 1998), esp. ch. 12; Kentaro Awaya, "Emperor Shōwa's Accountability for War," *Japan Quarterly*, vol. 38, no. 4 (October–December 1991), 386–98. The emperor did make formal presentations to the Diet, but these were not broadcast to the general population.

149. Bob Woodward, "Portrait of a President Changed by His Wars," *Washington Post National Weekly Edition*, September 22–28, 2008.

150. Examples of Bush's colloquial language (and other high officials' also) are beyond counting. See, for samples, Clarke, *Against All Enemies*, 24; Packer, *The Assassins' Gate*, 45; Woodward, *State of Denial*, 73, 134, 221, 232 (most of which suggest a great deal of anal fixation in the executive branch); Suskind, *The Way of the World*, 184 (see n. 137 above). The president's notorious "bring 'em on" rhetoric came back to haunt him, and his early "dead or alive" swagger persuaded many foreign observers that he epitomized the Wild West traditions of Hollywood rather than any serious tradition of statesmanship. It is worth keeping in mind, however, that as the "Watergate tapes" and other materials that contributed to the downfall of President Nixon revealed, Bush was not exceptional in falling back on colloquial and even vulgar language when serious matters of policy were concerned. For the emperor's often-cited poem, see Ike, *Japan's Decision for War*, 151; delivered at the critical September 6 Imperial Conference, this read as follows: "All the seas in every quarter are as brothers to one another. Why, then, do the winds and waves of strife rage so turbulently throughout the world?" (*Yomo no umi / mina harakara to / omou yoni / nado namikaze no / tachisawaguramu*).

151. On the unsuccessful "Konoe Memorial" of February 1945 in which the former prime minister Fumimaro Konoe entreated the emperor to seek peace, see Dower, *Empire and Aftermath: Yoshida Shigeru and the Japanese Experience, 1878–1954* (Council on East Asian Studies, Harvard, 1979), ch. 7. The classic articulation of the "proximity to the throne" thesis was presented shortly after the war by Masao Maruyama, one of Japan's most influential political scientists; see his *Thought and Behaviour in Modern Japanese Politics* (Oxford University Press, 1963). It took the atomic bombs and Soviet entry into the war in August 1945 to shake the emperor out of his denial. In the case of the Bush administration, it was not until late in 2006, more than three years after the invasion, that the president and NSC even began to acknowledge that the violence in Iraq amounted to a civil war and inaugurated a serious review and revision of Iraq policy—resulting in the "surge" initiated under General David Petraeus the following year. Although violence declined under the surge, a June 2008 report by the Government Accountability Office, acknowledging "some progress," concluded the security environment in Iraq remained "volatile and dangerous," this progress was "fragile," and "many unmet goals and challenges remain"; United States Government Accountability Office Report to Congressional Committees, *Securing, Stabilizing, and Rebuilding Iraq—Progress Report: Some Gains Made, Updated Strategy Needed*, esp. the cover summary and 1, 3, 59.

152. The "tribal" paradigm is but one example of the propensity for advancing cultural explanations for behavior that is understandable without such baggage. As the quagmire in Iraq deepened, for example, the press introduced an American general who emphasized the need to focus less on killing insurgents and more on

rebuilding the shattered nation. "Every time we shoot at an Iraqi in this culture—a culture of revenge, a culture of honor—we stand the chance of taking someone who is sitting on the fence," he was quoted as saying, and pushing him toward "the terrorists and foreign fighters"; *New York Times*, April 1, 2006. It does not require a culture of revenge and honor, however, to react against being occupied and shot at and having one's home invaded and family members terrified by foreign soldiers who are usually frightened themselves. I have addressed the racist as well as pseudo-scientific "national character" labels attached to the Japanese enemy in World War II in considerable detail in *War Without Mercy*; see especially chapter 6 ("Primitives, Children, Madmen") and 7 ("Yellow, Red, and Black Men"). For often-quoted examples of the bee hive, swarm, and sheep, see Grew, *Turbulent Era*, 1409, 1418.

153. Bix, *Hirohito and the Making of Modern Japan*, 308–10. Bix cites a Japanese study advancing the thesis of "parallel arguments" in documents pertaining to war policy; ibid., 724, n. 66.

154. Feith, *War and Decision*, 143–44, 249–50; see also 439. Rice's essentially consensual modus operandi as national security adviser also emerges strongly in Elisabeth Bumiller's *Condoleezza Rice: An American Life* (Random House, 2007); see, for example, 134 (Rice's description of herself as a "transmission belt" for the president), 205, 217–18, 225. A similar portrait of Rice as an enabler who papered over issues in order to carry out the president's wishes emerges in the account of former White House press secretary Scott McClellan, *What Happened: Inside the Bush White House and Washington's Culture of Deception* (PublicAffairs, 2008); see, for example, 144–46. Richard Haass, writing from a State Department perspective, also is harsh in appraising Rice's interpretation of her role as national security adviser; see, for example, *War of Necessity, War of Choice*, 184–85, 209, 213–14. The papered-over disagreements that underlay the absence of serious planning for postwar Iraq are addressed in chapter 13 in this book.

155. Recognition of the strong strain of conformity or consensual thinking in America can be traced back to Tocqueville, and was amplified in the decades following World War II in a variety of academic and popular writings about the "company man," the "organization man," the "man in the grey flannel suit," and so on. The term "groupthink" itself was coined by the sociologist William Whyte in an article published in 1952 (he defined it as "rationalized conformity"), and was applied to case studies in U.S. foreign policy by the research psychologist Irving Janis in an influential 1972 book titled *Victims of Groupthink* (Houghton Mifflin). After *The 9/11 Commission Report* used the concept in explaining the September 11 intelligence failure, it became ubiquitous in critical (and self-critical) commentary about the invasion of Iraq as well. A 511-page unanimous report issued by the Senate Intelligence Committee in July 2004, over a year after the Iraq invasion, reinforced this by similarly speaking of a culture of "group think" in intelligence agencies that left the argument that Iraq possessed illicit weapons unchallenged. The *New York Times*, for one, seized on this for a "slug" or subtitle to its coverage of the latter report ("Panel Unanimous: 'Group Think' Backed Prewar Assumptions, Panel Concludes"), and followed this with a run of sociological, confessional, and etymological pieces. On July 15, the *Times* published a guest column by Barbara Ehrenreich titled "All Together Now," with

the subtitle "Groupthink, as American as Apple Pie." The next day, an editorial titled "A Pause for Hindsight" offered this mea culpa: "We did not listen carefully to the people who disagreed with us. Our certainty flowed from the fact that such an overwhelming majority of government officials, past and present, top intelligence officials and other experts were sure that the weapons were there. We had a groupthink of our own." Early the following month (August 8), William Safire devoted his regular "On Language" column to "Groupthink." On the second anniversary of the invasion of Iraq, the weekly *Economist*, which also supported the invasion, harkened back to *The 9-11 Commission Report* in attributing "the main intelligence failures concerning both Iraq and September 11th" to "a predilection to 'group-think'"; March 19, 2005. George Packer, who likewise supported the war, later wrote similarly of "the insidious effects of airtight groupthink" that made the Bush administration's intelligence projections concerning Iraq such a disaster; *The Assassins' Gate*, 116. "Groupthink" became so ubiquitous a phrase for explaining both 9-11 and Iraq that it almost seemed to become self-referential. As noteworthy as the ubiquity of such observations, however, is the fact that they never fundamentally alter the countervailing American mystique of an enduring spirit of rugged individualism. Despite countless examples to the contrary, "groupthink" is still deemed abnormal and aberrant where American individuals or institutions are concerned—an Orwellian pathology more properly associated with totalitarian societies like the Soviet Union, "consensual" societies like Japan, and alien "tribal" societies in general. Groupthink, herd behavior, and like pejoratives also later became *de rigueur* in explaining damaging conformist behavior in the economic and financial sector. This is briefly addressed in the epilogue of this book.

156. "National Security Strategy of the United States of America," September 17, 2002. This celebrated document is actually a thematically rearranged compilation of extracts from presidential statements issued between September 14, 2001, and September 17, 2002. The origin of the preemptive war doctrine is usually dated to defense guidelines drafted in 1992 by Paul Wolfowitz, then serving as under secretary of defense for policy under the presidency of George H. W. Bush; these guidelines were repudiated when they became known and provoked controversy.

157. The notes by Rumsfeld's aide, Stephen Cambone, were revealed by CBS News on September 4, 2002, and cited on CBSNews.com. The actual handwritten memo was made available online in photo form in 2006; see "DoD Staffer's Notes from 9/11 Obtained Under FOIA," on the outragedmoderates.org website, February 16, 2006. Rumsfeld's response is understandable when set against a four-page memorandum laying out the case for regime change in Iraq that he submitted to Condoleezza Rice on July 27, six weeks before 9-11; this is reproduced in Feith, *War and Decision*, 535–38, and on the book's ancillary website. Feith himself devotes many pages (esp. chapter 6 and 7) to the rationale for attacking Iraq. There is an enormous literature debating exactly when Bush decisively "decided on war" with Iraq, but this can easily obscure the fact that time and again formal decision making lags behind informal but irreversible commitments. A wealth of subsequent documentation supports George Packer's 2005 conclusion that the administration "was inexorably set on a course of war" by the spring of 2002, a full year before the invasion; *The Assassins' Gate*, 45, 61.

158. See, for example, Ike, *Japan's Decision for War*, 131, 132, 135, 152, 193, 202, 211, 272.

159. On the persistence of Japanese "move North" thinking even after the "move South" policy had gained ascendancy, see Ike, *Japan's Decision for War*, 79, 81, 87, 141–42, 158–59, 191–93, 207; also Prange, *At Dawn We Slept*, 235, 237. For the Hawaii plans, see John J. Stephan, *Hawaii under the Rising Sun: Japan's Plans for Conquest after Pearl Harbor* (University of Hawaii Press, 1984). In December 1942, researchers in Japan's Ministry of Health and Welfare completed a study titled *An Investigation of Global Policy with the Yamato Race as Nucleus* that imagined an "East Asia Cooperative Body" eventually extending over Soviet territory east of Lake Baikal in the north, Australia and New Zealand in the south, and India and much of the Middle East to the west—an almost literal realization of propaganda about placing "the whole world under one roof." This massive report (totaling some four thousand pages) is analyzed in Dower, *War Without Mercy*, ch. 7 (262–90; see esp. 273–74). U.S. projections concerning potential post-Iraq military action against the "axis of evil" and numerous additional possible targets are noted, among other sources, in Wesley K. Clark, *Winning Modern Wars: Iraq, Terrorism, and the American Empire* (PublicAffairs, 2003), 130 (he refers to this as a "draining the swamp" strategy); also Johnson, *The Sorrows of Empire*, 286. A little more than a month after September 11, Vice President Cheney told the BBC that there might be "as many as 40 or 50" nations harboring Al Qaeda cells that could be targeted for a range of actions ranging from financial to diplomatic to military; *Guardian International*, November 17, 2001.

160. Wohlstetter, *Pearl Harbor*, 341–43, on Japan's opening strikes. Although rapid U.S. advances in military technology put the Japanese to shame as the Pacific War unfolded, the Japanese military did embrace projects they hoped would give them an edge. They succeeded in launching not only the world's largest two battleships, the *Musashi* and *Yamato*, both sunk in 1945, but also the largest submarines ever built before the 1960s. The latter, known as the *Sen Toku* I-400 class, were essentially submarine aircraft carriers. Some four hundred feet in length, the I-400s were capable of sailing around the world one and a half times without refueling and carried three specially constructed fold-wing bombers capable of delivering a single eight-hundred-kilogram bomb. Another brainchild of Admiral Yamamoto, conceived in 1942 as the war turned against Japan, the I-400s were envisioned as launching attacks on the Panama Canal as well as major U.S. cities on either coast. Plans were also made, but never realized, to introduce a capability of using these bombs to deliver bacteriological agents on U.S. targets (by releasing rats and insects infected with bubonic plague, cholera, dengue fever, typhus, and other diseases). Three of the giant submarines were commissioned in 1944 and 1945, but the U.S. assault on the home islands thwarted plans to attack the Panama Canal. (There are many online entries for the "I-400-class submarine." See, for example, "UH Team Locates Huge Japanese Sub," on the *Star Bulletin* website [starbulletin.com], March 20, 2005; also Irwin J. Kappes, "Japan's WWII Monster Sub," on the MilitaryHistoryonline.com website, 2007.) The most notorious Japanese project to develop chemical and biological weapons was carried out by "Unit 731" in Manchuria from the late 1930s to the end of the war. Although this involved lethal experiments on prisoners, Unit 731's activities were covered up after the war by U.S. authorities in exchange for debriefing on the experiments;

see Peter Williams and David Wallace, *Unit 731: Japan's Secret Biological Warfare in World War II* (Free Press, 1989; this study derived from the authors' research for the 1985 British television documentary *Unit 731—Did the Emperor Know?*). Once the war was underway, Japanese scientists also seriously looked into the feasibility of developing an atomic bomb; see "'NI' and 'F': Japan's Wartime Atomic Bomb Research," in John W. Dower, *Japan in War and Peace: Selected Essays* (New Press, 1993), 55–100. They also looked into "death ray" (thermal ray) weapons and unmanned remote-control vehicles. In the final analysis, however, the most innovative Japanese military tactic was the crudest and most desperate: introduction of the suicidal kamikaze in the final year of the war. For a close analysis of the various weapons projects, see Walter E. Grunden, *Secret Weapons and World War II: Japan in the Shadow of Big Science* (University Press of Kansas, 2005). Grunden concludes that "the polycratic nature of the national government and the ubiquitous interservice rivalry" severely impeded Japan's attempts to mobilize science and technology behind the war effort, and biological-warfare research was "the weapons program that came closest to emerging as a Big Science project"; ibid., 10, 46–47. Contrary to the mythology of "one-hundred hearts beating as one," Japan at war was plagued by ferocious turf wars and organizational fiefdoms at almost every level. Another obverse side to "high-tech" sophistication on the part of the Japanese military was the persistence of traditional operational thinking. Yamamoto's utilization of naval airpower was the high point of innovation. Even before his death in 1943, the Imperial Navy fell back on the dream of a "decisive battle" conducted by battleships and failed to throw off "old, obsolete concepts from the days of Nelson and the Russo-Japanese War"; see former vice admiral Toshiyuki Yokoi's stinging "Thoughts on Japan's Naval Defeat" in David C. Evans, ed., *The Japanese Navy in World War II: In the Words of Former Japanese Naval Officers*, 2nd edition (Naval Institute Press, 1986), 499–515. For a scathing analysis of "inflexible" naval thinking as it affected one particular force, see Carl Boyd and Akihiko Yoshida, *The Japanese Submarine Force and World War II* (Naval Institute Press, 1995), esp. xi–xiii, 6–7, and ch. 6 (on "decisive battle" delusions in 1944).

161. *Congressional Record*, vol. 87, 9509–13 (these pages reprint editorials published on December 8, 1941).

162. *Congressional Record*, vol. 87, 10118 (for Churchill's full address).

163. Paul D. Eaton, "A Top-Down Review for the Pentagon," *New York Times*, March 19, 2006. On May 9, 2003, a week after Bush's "Mission Accomplished" speech, Eaton was abruptly and unexpectedly given responsibility for rebuilding the Iraqi military, but was never provided adequate resources to do so. "I was very surprised to receive a mission so vital to our exit strategy so late," he confided in an earlier press interview. "I would have expected this to have been done well before troops crossed the line of departure"; *New York Times*, February 11, 2006. Inside supporters of the war of choice against Iraq like the former speaker of the House of Representatives Newt Gingrich, who was a member of the influential Defense Policy Board, later agreed that the way the so-called post-hostilities operations were carried out was "one of the most amazing strategic mistakes I've ever seen." From this perspective, however, the original war plan was sound ("staying light, getting in, rebuilding the Iraqis quickly, and getting out"), and the amazing stra-

tegic mistakes could be attributed primarily to disastrous decisions by the Coalition Provisional Authority led by Paul Bremer in Iraq (disbanding the Iraqi army, purging Baath Party members, etc.) compounded by failures in the White House and Pentagon to move quickly and decisively to rectify these errors; Gingrich is quoted in Peter J. Boyer, "Downfall: How Donald Rumsfeld Reformed the Army and Lost Iraq," *New Yorker*, November 20, 2006. The conservative debating stance for future discussion of the Iraq disaster is clearly reflected here: good policy, inept execution.

164. For a very concise recent sample of literature on the Japanese side concerning the decision for war, which quotes some of these reservations, see Yomiuri Shimbun, *Who Was Responsible? From Marco Polo Bridge to Pearl Harbor*, ed. James E. Auer (Yomiuri Shimbun, 2006), esp. ch. 7. This is a translation of a year-long newspaper series by the Yomiuri Shimbun War Responsibility Reexamination Committee. The journalistic team concluded that primary responsibility for the war fell on two prime ministers: first, Tōjō, and second, Konoe. The emperor, by contrast, "was not seriously responsible"; ibid., 223–24.

165. Feith, *War and Decision*, 332–35; Woodward, *Plan of Attack*, 205–6; Woodward, *State of Denial*, 178–79. See also the December 2002 PowerPoint list produced by Feith's office titled "Discussion: Possible Contingencies," reproduced on his waranddecision.com website.

166. Powell made this comment in "GQ Icon: Colin Powell," an interview with Walter Isaacson in *GQ*, October 2007. The memo was brought up by Rumsfeld himself in an interview with Danielle Levitt in the same issue of *GQ*. Powell's futile attempt to persuade the president to face the problems war would pose is summarized in Woodward, *Plan of Attack*, 149–51. Even Feith acknowledges, almost in passing, that "it's fair to ask whether the [Defense] department and the Administration took the exercise [in potential post-conflict challenges] seriously enough and performed all the practical follow-up work that was called for"; *War and Decision*, 335.

167. Ike, *Japan's Decision for War*, 247–49. Former vice admiral Yokoi described this document as "the sole grand strategy ever made before the war began"; "Thoughts on Japan's Naval Defeat," 504. Fujiwara Akira, one of Japan's foremost military historians, similarly concluded that the outlook of Imperial Army planners was "often permeated by wishful thinking." Thus, the army "never drew up any plans for the defense of the areas under its occupation or for the type of amphibious operations that took place later in the Pacific theater," and "never made any attempt to estimate the outcome of a war with the United States"; see his "The Role of the Japanese Army," in Borg and Okamoto, *Pearl Harbor as History*, 194–95.

168. United States Strategic Bombing Survey, *The Effects of Strategic Bombing on Japan's War Economy* (December 1946), 5.

169. Jerome B. Cohen, *Japan's Economy in War and Reconstruction* (University of Minnesota Press, 1949), 104; Sansom's observations appear in the foreword to Cohen's dense study (viii).

170. W. F. Craven and J. L. Cate, eds., *The Army Air Forces in World War II*, vol. 1: *Plans and Early Operations, January 1939 to August 1942* (University of Chicago Press, 1958), 81.

171. Scott McClellan's *What Happened* created a momentary media frenzy of historical interest primarily because of the degree to which political "loyalty" was placed at

the center of the debate; Thomas Powers, "The Vanishing Case for War," *New York Review of Books*, December 4, 2003; Frank Rich, *The Greatest Story Ever Sold: The Decline and Fall of Truth from 9/11 to Katrina* (Penguin, 2006); Select Committee on Intelligence, United States Senate, *Report on Whether Public Statements Regarding Iraq by U.S. Government Officials Were Substantiated by Intelligence Information*, 110th Congress, June 2008, and the committee's press release accompanying this dated June 5, 2008.

172. Clark, *Winning Modern Wars*, 88–92. The "Downing Street Memorandum" received wide publicity when revealed in May 2005 and is widely available online. For incisive discussions of this by Mark Danner, see "The Secret Way to War," *New York Review of Books*, June 9, 2005, and subsequent discussion in the issues of July 14, 2005 ("The Iraq Pretext: Why the Memo Matters"), and August 11, 2005 ("Iraq's Buried History: The Memo, the Press and the War"). Danner's writings were subsequently collected in *The Secret Way to War: The Downing Street Memo and the Iraq War's Buried History* (New York Review Books, 2006).

173. Michael R. Gordon and General Bernard E. Trainor, *Cobra II: The Inside Story of the Invasion and Occupation of Iraq* (Pantheon, 2006), 157; Peter Galbraith, *The End of Iraq: How American Incompetence Created a War without End* (Simon & Schuster, 2007), 90–91.

174. Thomas F. Ricks, *Fiasco: The American Military Adventure in Iraq* (Penguin, 2006), 72 (Army War College); Pillar, "The Right Stuff." The two reports initiated at the urging of Paul Pillar were placed online at gpoaccess.gov in the closing days of May 2007 as appendices A and B in the Senate's lengthy *Report of the Select Committee on Intelligence on Prewar Intelligence Assessments about Postwar Iraq*, and were widely noted in the media at the time. Pillar departs from many other analysts in rejecting the argument that the Iraq war was "a good idea spoiled by poor execution," arguing that on the contrary it was "always a fool's errand" driven by ideologues who ignored the basic procedures of sound decision making.

175. Feith, *War and Decision*, 277, 284 (occupying power); 335, 361 (Principals Committee); 363–66 (action memo). See also Feith's waranddecision.com website (for "Day 1," a presentation by the Office of Reconstruction and Humanitarian Assistance).

176. General Jack Keane in a televised interview on *NewsHour with Jim Lehrer*, April 18, 2006; also quoted by John A. Nagl in his foreword to the University of Chicago Press edition of the *Counterinsurgency Field Manual* issued by the Army and Marine Corps in December 2006; see xiii–xv. In the introduction to this trade edition of the manual, Sarah Sewall similarly calls attention to the failure of U.S. military leaders after Vietnam "to disabuse the comforting but misleading explanatory folklore ('the politicians tied our hands' or 'the American people lost their nerve'). It was convenient to divert the blame and focus instead on the USSR"; ibid., xli–xlii. Nagl himself authored the most widely cited text on this subject; see his *Learning to Eat Soup with a Knife: Counterinsurgency Lessons from Malaya and Vietnam* (University of Chicago Press, 2005; originally published in 2002), esp. ch. 1, 3, 8, and 9. On the repudiation of counterinsurgency training, see also Peter Boyer's informative article "Downfall"; Steve Coll, "The General's Dilemma: David Petraeus, the Pressures of Politics, and the Road out of Iraq," *New Yorker*, September 8, 2008; and David Cloud and Greg Jaffe, *The Fourth Star: Four Generals and the Epic Struggle for the Future of the United States Army* (Crown, 2009).

Among their numerous examples of the military's fixation on winning short wars with "overwhelming firepower and superior technology," and its concomitant aversion to drawing lessons about guerrilla warfare from Vietnam, Cloud and Jaffe recount how Andrew Krepinevich, a lieutenant colonel with a Ph.D. from Harvard, was "banned . . . from speaking on campus" by the superintendent of West Point after publishing a critical book titled *The Army and Vietnam* in 1986; *The Fourth Star*, 48, 60–64.

177. David Kilcullen, *The Accidental Guerrilla: Fighting Small Wars in the Midst of a Big One* (Oxford University Press, 2009), xv–xvi; see also "Army, Marine Corps Unveil Counterinsurgency Field Manual," Army News Service, December 15, 2006. Michael Scheuer quotes an incisive after-action report on the Soviet-Afghan war prepared by the Soviet General Staff that was summarized for CIA officials in September 2001 and published in an English translation the following year, before the U.S. invasion of Iraq. Although naturally focused on Afghanistan, the report offers a strong and prescient warning against engaging in "impetuous" warfare without taking into consideration "historic, religious, and national peculiarities" of the enemy; *Imperial Hubris*, 30–32. Afghan fatalities in the anti-Soviet war are generally placed at over one million, with another four-plus million disabled, maimed, or wounded. Approximately one-third of the population (five million) fled to other countries, and another two million were internally displaced.

178. Nagl conveys the jargon of these conventional military attitudes very well; see, for a sample, *Eating Soup with a Knife*, 198–206.

179. Scott Shane, "China Inspired Interrogations at Guantánamo," *New York Times*, July 2, 2008. The *Times* article observed that "in what critics describe as a remarkable case of historical amnesia, officials who drew on the SERE program appear to have been unaware that it had been created as a result of concern about false confessions by American prisoners." (SERE is an acronym for "Survival, Evasion, Resistance and Escape," a decades-old military training program for pilots and soldiers who might be captured and tortured.) The *Times* revisited this subject over nine months later, after new Bush administration torture documents were released by the Obama administration; Scott Shane and Mark Mazzetti, "In Adopting Harsh Tactics, No Inquiry into Their Past Use," *New York Times*, April 22, 2009. In fact, almost all serious writings on torture address the issue of false "confessions."

180. Even critics of the Bush administration's response to 9-11 as outspoken as Noam Chomsky acknowledged they did not foresee the insurrection that followed the invasion of Iraq; see his *Imperial Ambitions: Conversations on the Post 9-11 World* (Metropolitan, 2005), 46–47. One can, of course, look further back in history to the modern "age of imperialism" itself, when small numbers of Europeans and Americans were able to maintain control over large populations in faraway lands with but a minimal military and administrative presence.

181. On the president's subsequently well-publicized January 10, 2003, meeting with Iraqi exiles, see Woodward, *Plan of Attack*, 258–60; Packer, *The Assassins' Gate*, 96–97. Packer's thoughtful study provides insight into the many different political and ideological perspectives that persuaded a wide range of individuals outside the so-called White House cabal to support the war. It is difficult to exaggerate the importance of such "sweets and flowers" reassurances, particularly since

the exile community and other supporters of a war of choice were lobbying a president and administration that heard only what they were predisposed to hear.

182. The chief of staff was Hajime Sugiyama, and the exchange took place on September 5, 1941, one day before the decisive Imperial Conference at which Hirohito read the poem by his grandfather, the Meiji emperor. This sharp exchange is well known; see, for example, Watanabe, *Who Was Responsible?*, 120.

183. The "gates of hell" statement was made by Amr Moussa, secretary general of the Arab League, and is quoted by Michael Slackman in "Chaos in Iraq Sends Shock Waves across Middle East and Elevates Iran's Influence," *New York Times*, February 27, 2006. Scowcroft is quoted in Jeffrey Goldberg, "Breaking Ranks," *New Yorker*, October 31, 2005, 57. In a retrospective comment on the mood in Washington in the fall of 2002, Paul Krugman wrote similarly: "Why were the elite so hawkish? Well, I heard a number of people express privately the argument that some influential commentators made publicly—that the war was a good idea, not because Iraq posed a real threat, but because beating up someone in the Middle East, never mind who, would show Muslims that we mean business. In other words, even alleged wise men bought into the idea of macho posturing as policy"; "Know-Nothing Politics," *New York Times*, August 8, 2002.

Seymour Hersh notes that "the bible of the neocons on Arab behavior" was a book by Raphael Patai titled *The Arab Mind*, originally published in 1973, that included a long section on sexual taboos—a treatment that Hersh suggests later influenced some of the methods of torture the United States adopted in dealing with Arab and Muslim prisoners. He then goes on to quote an unnamed informant to the effect that two themes dominated neoconservative discussions: "one, that Arabs only understand force and, two, that the biggest weakness of Arabs is shame and humiliation"; *Chain of Command*, 38–39. Drawing a distinction between "shame cultures" and "guilt cultures," it should be noted, is another old horse that anthropologists often ride to distinguish between the Judeo-Christian tradition and almost everyone else. During the Pacific War, the anthropologist Ruth Benedict and others argued that in Japan's "shame" culture individuals were not guided by allegiance to "universal" values (as in guilt cultures), but rather responded in accordance with the dictates of the particular situation; what mattered was "face."

At the same time, however, Hersh also quotes the influential neoconservative spokesman Richard Perle in a blunter assessment devoid of such cultural trappings: "Arabs are like most people. They like winners, and will go with the winners all the time"; *Chain of Command*, 182. Be that as it may, brandishing a big stick and demonstrating a willingness to use it is a staple of the colonialist mentality as well as deterrence theory, and often spills into unvarnished arrogance on the one hand and counterproductive reliance on force on the other. The belief that Muslims and Arabs would be intimidated by a show of force also has precedents in the reasoning behind U.S. and British "deterrence" and "economic strangulation" policies in the period leading up to Japan's initiation of war in 1941. Britain assumed its Singapore garrison and a few warships would do the trick, for example, while the United States placed faith in a combination of strategic embargoes and a show of force in Hawaii and the Philippines. In the months leading up to Pearl Harbor, General Marshall, the army chief of staff, frequently referred to the stationing of B-17 bombers in the Philippines as a "serious deterrent," while Secretary of War Stimson spoke of this as America's "big stick" and expressed hope that it would "keep the fear of God in Japan." In October 1941, when the British dispatched the battleship *Prince of Wales* and cruiser *Repulse* to the Indian Ocean, a Foreign Office official gushed in his diary that this would surely make a difference, for the Japanese were "so hysterical" that they might well "rush themselves off their feet." For these particular references, see Heinrichs, *Threshold of War*, 38, 148, 175–76, 193–98, 203–4. The U.S. economic embargo and positioning of military forces in Hawaii and the Philippines merely increased the desperation Japan's leaders felt, and reinforced the argument that "time is running out." Japanese aircraft sank both of the British warships off the coast of Malaya in the opening days of the war.

184. Jonah Goldberg, "Baghdad Delenda Est, Part Two," *National Review*, April 23, 2002. Goldberg's title derived from the notorious phrase "Carthage must be destroyed" with which the Roman senator Cato the Elder is said to have ended many of his speeches. He was paraphrasing Michael Ledeen, one of the American Enterprise Institute's well-known public intellectuals. It can be argued that there was an even more damning analogue to this support of muscle flexing in conservative and military circles: namely, that every ten years or so the United States needed to commit troops to action to try out the latest weaponry.

185. The much-discussed "cakewalk" idiom came from Ken Adelman, a neoconservative member of Rumsfeld's advisory Defense Policy Board, and involved op-ed pieces in the *Washington Post* on February 13, 2002 ("Cakewalk in Iraq"), and April 10, 2003 ("'Cakewalk' Revisited"). For "create our own reality," see Ron Suskind, "Without a Doubt," *New York Times Magazine*, October 17, 2004. This quotation, imbedded in a lengthy commentary on Bush's "faith-based presidency," provoked massive online polemical commentary. It was, in fact, boilerplate, albeit vividly painted. Speaking of the occupation of Iraq, for example, Rumsfeld similarly declared that "we will impose our reality on them"; quoted in Mark Danner, "Weapons of Mass Destruction and Other Imaginative Acts," *New York Times*, August 27, 2008 (in a review of Suskind's *The Way of the World*). This, in a nutshell, is what all strategic military thinking envisions; the problem here was the smugness and hubris.

186. For bin Laden on superpower vulnerability, see bin Laden, *Messages to the World*, 82; also 48, 109, 192–93. His "restorer of energies" speech was broadcast on Al Jazeera and translated by the Associated Press; see *New York Times*, January 19, 2006.

187. Lawrence Wright, "The Rebellion Within," *New Yorker*, June 2, 2008 ("catastrophe for Muslims"). The Internet comment appeared in an August 2002 posting quoted in Scheuer, *Imperial Hubris*, 22.

## CHAPTER 6: "PEARL HARBOR" AS GODSEND

188. "Rove Speaks at Penn," *The Bulletin: Philadelphia's Family Newspaper*, February 21, 2008.

189. *Congressional Record*, vol. 87, 9509–13, 9521.

190. *Henry Lewis Stimson Diaries, 1909–1945*, entry for November 25, 1941; Stimson's

diary and papers can be found at the Yale University Library and are available on microfilm. See also Prange, *Pearl Harbor*, 519.

191. *Report of the Joint Committee on the Investigation of the Pearl Harbor Attack*, 251–52.

192. The revisionist literature, which early on included several particularly influential writers (including Charles A. Beard, Charles Tansill, and Harry Elmer Barnes), is criticized at length by Prange in both *At Dawn We Slept* (839–50) and *Pearl Harbor* (38–49). In his October 1961 *Saturday Evening Post* article "The Lessons of Pearl Harbor," Morison offered a capsule version of the basic criticism of the backdoor-to-war argument: Roosevelt would have needed the connivance of at least eight top civilian and military aides, "all loyal and honest men who would never have lent themselves to such monstrous deception"; and even if there had been a desire to get the United States into the war, this purpose would have been better served by warning the commanders in Hawaii to get the fleet out of harm's way, since "even a frustrated attempt to strike Pearl Harbor would have been sufficient *casus belli* to satisfy the most isolationist congressman." For a more extended early appraisal of the controversy, see John McKechney, "The Pearl Harbor Controversy: A Debate among Historians," *Monumenta Nipponica*, vol. 18 (1963), 45–88. David Kahn, who studied what U.S. intelligence operatives presumably knew after the Magic intercepts were declassified in 1977, reached the strong conclusion that "not one datum of intelligence ever said a thing about an attack on Pearl Harbor." See Kahn's "The Intelligence Failure of Pearl Harbor," *Foreign Affairs*, vol. 70, no. 5 (Winter 1991–92), 138–52, esp. 147–50; also his earlier "Did FDR Invite the Pearl Harbor Attack?" *New York Review of Books*, May 27, 1982. Kahn's conclusion amounted to a critique of Wohlstetter and not just the revisionists. See also Spector, *Eagle against the Rising Sun*, 95–100, where John Toland's *Infamy* in particular is summarized and rejected. This debate still has a vigorous online existence.

193. The August 6 President's Daily Brief was acknowledged by Condoleezza Rice in testimony before the 9-11 Commission and declassified by the government on April 10, 2004. The July exchange was not widely known until Bob Woodward revealed it in *State of Denial*, 49–52, 79–80.

194. Project for the New American Century, *Rebuilding America's Defenses: Strategy, Forces, and Resources for a New Century* (September 2000), 51. Leading members of the PNAC included Dick Cheney, Donald Rumsfeld, Paul Wolfowitz, Richard Armitage, Zalmay Khalilzad, I. Lewis Libby, Elliott Abrams, and John Bolton—all of whom assumed positions in the Bush administration. Other influential PNAC members were Richard Perle, William Bennett, Robert Kagan, and William Kristol. As early as November 1998, shortly after its founding, the PNAC had petitioned President Clinton urging the removal of Saddam Hussein. The genesis of these expansive ideas is usually traced back to the controversial 1992 draft of a "Defense Planning Guidance" study written by Wolfowitz but subsequently shelved; see, for example, Packer, *The Assassins' Gate*, 12–15, 23–24. James Mann characterizes the PNAC as "the political arm of the neoconservative movement"; *Rise of the Vulcans*, 238.

   While "Pearl Harbor" is the favorite trope for a crisis that awakens the United States to the challenges of a forbidding world and makes possible a massive increase in military spending, it is not the only such example that conservatives draw from recent history. In an influential 1996 article in which they called for an assertive U.S. policy of "benevolent global hegemony," William Kristol and Robert Kagan emphasized the outbreak of the Korean War in 1950 (which enabled the Truman administration to implement the famous planning document known as NSC–68), and the Soviet invasion of Afghanistan and Iran hostage crisis (both dating from 1979), which prompted the military buildup of the 1980s for which conservatives had already laid the intellectual groundwork; "Toward a Neo-Reaganite Foreign Policy," 29–30.

195. Armitage is quoted in Samantha Power, "The Democrats and National Security," *New York Review of Books*, August 14, 2008.

196. *Report of the Commission to Assess United States National Security Space Management and Organization*, January 11, 2001 (submitted to members of the Committee on Armed Services of the Senate and House of Representatives), xv, 25. Elsewhere the report restated and highlighted this: "An attack on elements of U.S. space systems during a crisis or conflict should not be considered an improbable act. If the U.S. is to avoid a 'Space Pearl Harbor' it needs to take seriously the possibility of an attack on U.S. space systems"; viii–ix. Or again: "The U.S. is an attractive candidate for a 'Space Pearl Harbor'"; xiii, xiv, 22.

197. Excerpts from the *Nuclear Posture Review* were made public on January 8, 2002; this is accessible on globalsecurity.org. In May 2003, two months after the invasion of Iraq, the Senate Armed Services Committee approved the development of low-yield tactical nuclear weapons.

198. Air Force Space Command, *Strategic Master Plan FY06 and Beyond*, esp. i, 1, 6, 8, 23, 25 (made accessible online in October 2003). On "arms control" getting in the way of "space control," see Robert S. Dudney, "The Struggle for Space," *Air Force Magazine*, May 2004 (Dudney was editor in chief of the publication). Michael Krepon notes the subsequent watering down of the blunt language in this plan in his *Better Safe than Sorry: The Ironies of Living with the Bomb* (Stanford University Press, 2008), 186. The natural analogue to warnings about a "space Pearl Harbor" is fear of a "digital Pearl Harbor" in general, in which hackers or "cyberspies" cause mayhem by infiltrating electrical grids, air-traffic control systems, controls against overheating in nuclear power stations, etc. In and of themselves, such threats are disruptive—demanding huge expenditures to ensure cybersecurity, and leading to predictable turf wars over who will oversee this; see, for example, "Battle Is Joined," *Economist*, April 25, 2009.

199. Russell F. Weigley, *The American Way of War: A History of United States Military Strategy and Policy* (Indiana University Press, 1973), xxii. See note 157 above for Rumsfeld.

## Part II: *Ground Zero 1945 and Ground Zero 2001*

### CHAPTER 7: "HIROSHIMA" AS CODE

1. James Risen with Stephen Engelberg, "Signs of Change in Terror Goals Went Unheeded," *New York Times*, October 14, 2001. See also *The 9/11 Commission Report: Final Report of the National Commission on Terrorist Attacks upon the United*

*States* (Norton, 2004), 116 (around 1998, "Bin Laden had reportedly been heard to speak of wanting a 'Hiroshima' of at least 10,000 casualties"), 380.

2. Osama bin Laden, *Messages to the World: The Statements of Osama bin Laden*, ed. by Bruce Lawrence (Verso, 2005), 40 (November 1996), 51 (March 1997), 67 (December 1998).

3. Bin Laden, *Messages to the World*, 168–69 (October 2002); see also 105 (October 2001).

4. Rice introduced the mushroom-cloud imagery on CNN's *Late Edition with Wolf Blitzer*; the president picked it up in a major speech in Cincinnati.

5. Harlan Ullman and James P. Wade Jr., *Shock and Awe: Achieving Rapid Dominance* (National Defense University, December 1996), xxvi; see also xx, 13, 23–24, 47–48 (on how "Japan's surprise attack on Pearl Harbor produced the reverse effects of Shock and Awe and had the unintended consequences of galvanizing the U.S. into action"), 110. This influential doctrine, usually identified with Ullman in particular, is available online.

6. See, for example, the entry on "Just War Theory" by Alexander Moseley in the online *Internet Encyclopedia of Philosophy* (iep.utm.edu).

7. Douglas J. Feith, *War and Decision: Inside the Pentagon at the Dawn of the War on Terrorism* (Harper, 2008), 9, 163, 230; see also 177.

8. Even more than film and photographs, the most powerful images of the human dimension of the Hiroshima and Nagasaki bombings are drawings and paintings by survivors (*hibakusha*)—in which "mother and child" emerges as one of several pervasive themes. For an analysis of these graphics and database of several hundred representative renderings, see John W. Dower, "Ground Zero 1945" on the MIT Visualizing Cultures website at visualizingcultures.mit.edu.

9. On the use of "Zero" in the New Mexico test, see the eyewitness account by William L. Laurence in the *New York Times*, September 26, 1945.

10. See, for example, Sven Lindqvist, *A History of Bombing*, translated from the Swedish by Linda Haverty Rugg (New Press, 2000), 70–74, which includes the quotation from Bruno Mussolini.

11. Lindqvist, *A History of Bombing*, 71 (entry 152) for the Foreign Office quote; his source is *Indiscriminate Aerial Bombing of Non-Combatants in China by Japanese* (Shanghai, 1937). The famous *Life* photo is discussed by Daqing Yang in "War's Most Innocent Victim," *Media Studies Journal*, Winter 1999, 18–19. The Japanese had also bombed Shanghai in 1932, shortly after the so-called Manchurian Incident. Bombing civilians was not, in fact, beyond the pale of the so-called civilized nations at all. On the contrary, it was standard practice before the breakdown of the world order in the late 1930s. As Lindqvist notes, "The Italians did it in Libya, the French did it in Morocco, and the British did it throughout the Middle East, in India, and East Africa, while the South Africans did it in Southwest Africa." Bombing rebellious "natives" was, in fact, one of the ways in which the British demonstrated their virtue and superiority as the world's greatest imperial power. Just between 1916 and 1920, they bombed native populations in, among other places, Egypt, Afghanistan (Dacca, Jalalabad, and Kabul), Iran, Trans-Jordan, and Iraq (where the operation was called "control without occupation"); Lindqvist, *A History of Bombing*, 42–43 (entry 102), 74 (entry 160). The practice only became alarming to the self-described civilized nations when it spilled out from "bombing

natives" and came home. The double standards reflected here go beyond the discrepancy between rhetoric and practice, and were in fact canonized in the "rules of war" the great powers ostensibly endorsed at the time, for it was understood that these rules applied only to warfare between "civilized" nations and "similar" enemies. Slaughtering "uncivilized" tribes and peoples (with machine guns, for example, or in these instances bombs) was acceptable. Among just-war theorists, this is known as the practice of "asymmetrical morality"; see, for example, Alexander Moseley's entry on "Just War Theory" in the *Internet Encyclopedia of Philosophy*.

12. Roosevelt's well-known appeal can be easily accessed online. For foreign responses, see Tami Davis Biddle, *Rhetoric and Reality in Air Warfare: The Evolution of British and American Ideas about Strategic Bombing, 1914–1945* (Princeton University Press, 2002), 182–83. Additional examples of these fervent pleas for restraint in bombing, which continued up to 1941, are quoted in John W. Dower, *War Without Mercy: Race and Power in the Pacific War* (Pantheon, 1986), 38–40.

13. In its coverage of the atomic bombing of Hiroshima and Nagasaki, *Life* noted that this followed earlier air raids that "ripped the guts out of Japan's great cities." These raids, it was explained, relied on "newly developed 'jelly' bombs, which were aimed at different spots in a city and calculated to merge into one huge conflagration. Airmen called them 'burn jobs' and a good-sized 'burn job' did almost as much damage to property as the atomic bomb did and it also killed almost as many people"; "War's Ending: Atomic Bomb and Soviet Entry Bring Jap Surrender," *Life*, August 20, 1945, 25–31. Postwar reports of the U.S. Strategic Bombing Survey—a massive undertaking published by the U.S. government in the years immediately following the war—sometimes pick up the wartime rhetoric in referring to the saturation bombing of Japan as "dehousing"; see, for an example, *Effects of Incendiary Bomb Attacks on Japan: A Report on Eight Cities* (April 1947), 214.

14. The U.S. Strategic Bombing Survey (USSBS) placed estimated civilian German casualties from the air war at a minimum of "305,000 killed and 780,000 wounded," with 40 percent of the dwelling units in "some 50 cities that were primary targets" destroyed or heavily damaged, resulting in roughly 7.5 million Germans rendered homeless; see *Summary Report (European War)* (September 30, 1945), 1, 15–16. In 1956, the West German government estimated civilian deaths from strategic bombing at 410,000, while other estimates place fatalities at upwards of 600,000. W. G. Sebald, for example, opens his famous rumination on German war memory with the observation that "it is true that of the 131 towns and cities attacked, some only once and some repeatedly, many were almost entirely flattened, that about 600,000 German civilians fell victim to the air raids, and that three and a half million homes were destroyed, while at the end of the war seven and a half million people were left homeless, and there were 31.1 cubic meters of rubble for every person in Cologne and 42.8 cubic meters for every inhabitant of Dresden—but we do not grasp what it all actually meant"; *On the Natural History of Destruction* (Modern Library, 2004), 3–4. For Japan, the Survey calculated that "total civilian casualties . . . as a result of 9 months of air attack, including those from the atomic bombs, were approximately 806,000. Of these, approximately 330,000 were fatalities"; *Summary Report (Pacific War)* (July 1, 1946), 20. It is now generally acknowledged that the Survey's widely cited estimates—based on information provided by authorities in the two

defeated countries—were very conservative. Interestingly, one often-neglected USSBS report on Japan published in July 1947—over a year after the widely cited *Summary Report* of July 1946—rejected the generally agreed-upon figures and offered a drastically higher estimate of casualties, concluding that "approximately 1,300,000 people were injured and approximately 900,000 killed as a result of the bombings." In an appendix supporting these higher estimates, this report heaped scorn on the "rather shocking" and "almost unbelievable" investigations conducted by Japanese officials in this area, referring to the Japanese air-raid casualty estimates at one point as "mystic datum." See USSBS (Morale Division), *The Effects of Strategic Bombing on Japanese Morale* (July 1947), 1–2, 194–95. While the estimate of 900,000 fatalities seems extremely high, the harsh appraisal of Japanese data gathering, especially on such a sensitive subject, rings true.

CHAPTER 8: AIR WAR AND TERROR BOMBING IN WORLD WAR II

15. John Swope, *A Letter from Japan: The Photographs of John Swope*, ed. by Carolyn Peter (Grunwald Center for the Graphic Arts, Hammer Museum, University of California–Los Angeles, 2006). This exhibition catalog includes the full text of Swope's journal/letter covering the period from August 30 to September 20, 1945 (212–49) plus essays by Carolyn Peter and John W. Dower ("Picturing Peace: John Swope's Japan, August/September 1945").

16. Swope, *A Letter from Japan*, 220–21.

17. Wesley Frank Craven and James Lea Cate, eds., *The Army Air Forces in World War II*, vol. 5: *The Pacific: Matterhorn to Nagasaki, June 1944 to August 1945* (University of Chicago Press, 1953), 111–12, 144, 558–60. This semiofficial source, published shortly after the war, remains an invaluable study of U.S. air-war policy and practice; see especially the editors' foreword; ch. 18, 20, and 21 by James Lea Cate and James C. Olson (respectively titled "Precision Bombing Campaign," "Urban Area Attacks," and "The All-Out B-29 Attack"); and ch. 23, the editors' concluding chapter on the atomic bombs ("Victory"). In December 1944, U.S. air forces operating out of unoccupied China also launched a major attack on Japanese-held Hankow in which the B-29s were loaded only with incendiaries. General Claire Chennault later described this as "the first mass fire-bomb raid" attempted in the Asian theater, and suggested that "the results of this weapon against an Asiatic city" were influential as a model for subsequent firebomb raids against Japan. Authoritative sources including the Craven and Cate volume trace a more lengthy and formal background to the later incendiary raids against Japan; ibid., 144. Another little-remembered example of area bombing against the Japanese took place in the air war on Formosa (Taiwan) in the opening months of 1945. Of eleven principal cities on this fortified colonial archipelago, five were almost completely destroyed (Kiirun, Shinchiku, Kagi, Tainan, and Takao), four were 50 percent destroyed (Shoka, Heito, Giran, and Karenko), one was one-third destroyed (Taihoku), and only one escaped relatively undamaged (Taichu). U.S. bombers dropped over 62,000 gallons of napalm in the Formosa campaign; ibid., 485–89.

18. See quotations in A. C. Grayling, *Among the Dead Cities: The History and Moral Legacy of the WWII Bombing of Civilians in Germany and Japan* (Walker, 2006), 47, 119. The difference in construction materials meant that, unlike the air war

against Germany, the U.S. Army Air Forces (USAAF) relied almost exclusively on firebombs in their attacks on Japanese cities, "since the flimsily built dwellings grouped in densely populated and congested areas were extremely vulnerable to saturation attacks and required no high explosives to 'open them up'"; USSBS, *A Report on Physical Damage in Japan* (June 1947), 1, 67 (which puts the amount of high explosives used in the incendiary attacks on Japanese cities at a mere 1 percent). This accounts for why the photographer John Swope saw no bomb craters in the burned-out cities.

Debate concerning the Anglo-American air war against Germany has been much more extensive than that concerning the air war against Japan that preceded Hiroshima and Nagasaki, perhaps because the birth of the nuclear age and U.S. decision to actually use the atomic bombs has been so mesmerizing to commentators. The air war in the European theater was the prelude to that conducted against Japan, in any case, and for researchers it involves many of the same archival sources and strategic issues, and raises the same moral questions. Attention to the bombing of German cities was conspicuously sharpened by the writings of W. G. Sebald beginning in the 1990s, and became a point of particularly intense debate following Jörg Friedrich's detailed, anecdotal (and chaotic) account in *Der Brand: Deutschland im Bombenkrieg, 1940–45*, published in 2002 and available in translation as *The Fire: The Bombing of Germany, 1940–1945* (Columbia University Press, 2006). Scholarly writings prompted by Friedrich's book provide a useful introduction to the issues and general literature involved. See, for example, the November 2003 online forum on "World War II: Rethinking German Experiences," posted on the "h-german" website (h-net.org/~german), as well as the following well-annotated essays: Thomas Childers, "'*Facilis descensus averni est*': The Allied Bombing of Germany and the Issue of German Suffering," *Central European History*, vol. 38, no. 1 (2005), 75–105; Robert G. Moeller, "On the History of Man-Made Destruction: Loss, Death, Memory, and Germany in the Bombing War," *History Workshop Journal*, vol. 61 (2006), 103–34; Charles S. Maier, "Targeting the City: Debates and Silences about the Aerial Bombing of World War II," *International Review of the Red Cross*, no. 859 (2005), 429–44. Thoughtful monographs that give attention to moral as well as policy issues include Ronald Schaffer, *Wings of Judgment: American Bombing in World War II* (Oxford University Press, 1985); Michael S. Sherry, *The Rise of American Air Power: The Creation of Armageddon* (Yale University Press, 1987); Richard G. Davis, *Carl A. Spaatz and the Air War in Europe, 1940–1945* (Center for Air Force History, United States Air Force; distributed by Smithsonian Institution Press, 1993); Biddle, *Rhetoric and Reality in Air Warfare*; and Grayling, *Among the Dead Cities*. For two particularly incisive analyses of the military record as it pertains to U.S. bombing policy and practice in Germany, and in Japan up to March 1945, see Richard G. Davis, "German Rail Yards and Cities: U.S. Bombing Policy, 1944–1945," *Air Power History*, Summer 1995, 46–63; Thomas R. Searle, "'It Made a Lot of Sense to Kill Skilled Workers': The Firebombing of Tokyo in March 1945," *Journal of Military History*, vol. 66, no. 1 (January 2002), 103–33. For a valuable recent addition to this literature, see Yuki Tanaka and Marilyn B. Young, eds., *Bombing Civilians: A Twentieth-Century History* (New Press, 2009); this includes essays by both Ronald Schaffer and Robert Moeller on the air war in Europe, Mark Selden on the bombing of

Japan, Tsuyoshi Hasegawa on the atomic bombs, and Michael Sherry on strategic bombing, prophecy, and memory.

The intensive technical investigation of the air war against Germany and Japan conducted by the U.S. Strategic Bombing Survey produced some 200-plus individual reports on Germany and 108 on Japan. Of particular interest where Japan is concerned are the following: *Summary Report (Pacific War)* (July 1946); *Japan's Struggle to End the War* (July 1946); *The Effects of the Atomic Bombs on Hiroshima and Nagasaki* (June 1946); *The Effects of Strategic Bombing on Japanese Morale* (June 1947); *The Effects of Strategic Bombing on Japan's War Economy* (December 1946); *Effects of Incendiary Bomb Attacks on Japan: A Report on Eight Cities* (April 1947); and *A Report on Physical Damage in Japan* (June 1947).

19. On Imperial Army projections for a long-range bomber, named "Mount Fuji" and capable of carrying out an attack against the United States, see Maema Takenori, *Fugaku: Bei Hondo o Bakugeki Seyo* (The "Mount Fuji"—Let's Bomb the U.S. Mainland!) (Kodansha Bunko P600, 1995). The *Sen Toku* I-400-class submarine is noted in chapter 5 (note 160) in the present book. Within Japan's ferociously factionalized military establishment, the army and navy separately looked into the possibility of producing nuclear weapons; see John W. Dower, "'NI' and 'F': Japan's Wartime Atomic Bomb Research," in Dower, *Japan in War and Peace: Selected Essays* (New Press, 1993), 55–100.

20. Quoted and annotated in Sherry, *The Rise of American Air Power*, 31, 58. For truly original and vivid introductions to apocalyptic, racist visions as well as actual bombing practices prior to World War II, see Lindqvist's *A History of Bombing*, especially entries 45, 46, 55, 56, 59, 60, 69, 71, 72, 126, 127, 128, 132, 155; also H. Bruce Franklin's engrossing *War Stars: The Superweapon and the American Imagination* (Oxford University Press, 1988), especially chapter 1 through 7; a revised and expanded edition was published in 2008 by University of Massachusetts Press.

21. Schaffer, *Wings of Judgment*, 107–8. Measuring between 7.9 and 8.4 on the Richter scale, the Kanto earthquake occurred at lunchtime on September 1, when many people were cooking on charcoal braziers; the ensuing fires sucked in oxygen and merged to create a firestorm comparable to the great Tokyo air raid of March 1945. Total fatalities came to well over 100,000 individuals; some sources place the figure as high as 140,000. Photographs of the 1923 destruction, including masses of charred corpses, are virtually indistinguishable from photos of the March 9, 1945, U.S. air raid on Tokyo that killed a comparable number.

22. Larry I. Bland et al., eds., *The Papers of George Catlett Marshall*, vol. 2: *"We Cannot Delay," July 1, 1939–December 6, 1941* (Johns Hopkins University Press, 1986), 675–81; this report of the November 15 briefing was prepared by Robert L. Sherrod, the military affairs correspondent for *Time*. For the November 19 staff instructions, see John Costello, *The Pacific War, 1941–1945* (Quill, 1981), 105–6.

23. The *United States News* graphic is reproduced in a "visual essay" in Sherry, *The Rise of American Air Power*. See also the much earlier illustration of biplanes bombing Asian civilians that accompanied an article about air war in Asia by General William Mitchell in the January 30, 1932, issue of the weekly *Liberty*, addressing the significance of the Japanese takeover of Manchuria; reproduced in Franklin, *War Stars*, 77ff. This was highlighted with the following italicized quote: "What

Japan is in deadly fear of is our air forces. Her islands offer an ideal target for air operations."

24. On pre–Pearl Harbor bombing plans involving Japan, see Sherry, *The Rise of American Air Power*, 100–15, 383. Schaffer identifies some of the many private-sector participants enlisted in the "incendiary program" immediately after Pearl Harbor (including the Arthur D. Little Company, E. I. du Pont Company, Eastman Kodak, Standard Oil Development Company, various chemical suppliers and insurance experts, and professors at such institutions as the Massachusetts Institute of Technology and Harvard; *Wings of Judgment*, 108, 122.

25. Disney's *Victory Through Air Power* was released on DVD in 2004 as part of a larger collection of wartime Disney propaganda films titled *Walt Disney Treasures—On the Front Lines (1943)*. For discussions, see James Agee, *Agee on Film* (Grosset and Dunlap, 1958), vol. 1: 43–44 (from a review dated July 3, 1943); Richard Schickel, *The Disney Version: The Life, Times, Art and Commerce of Walt Disney*, 3rd edition (Ivan R. Dee, 1997; originally published by Simon & Schuster, 1968), 273–75; Sherry, *The Rise of American Air Power*, 127–31; Biddle, *Rhetoric and Reality in Air Warfare*, 264, 268; "The Globe Presents 'Victory Through Airpower,' a Disney Illustration of Major de Seversky's Book," *New York Times*, July 19, 1943.

26. The sixty-nine missions, which do not include Dresden, are itemized in Davis, "German Rail Yards and Cities," 48. Davis calculates that by the fourth quarter of 1944, roughly 80 percent of Eighth Air Force raids were carried out relying on the H2X "blind bombing" device. In his words, firebombs or incendiaries "had but one function—the destruction by fire of soft targets, such as barracks, houses, commercial buildings, and administrative and governmental offices. A heavy bomber raid dropping thousands of small incendiaries ignited fires that destroyed residences, made the population homeless, and caused debilitating burn injuries, which tied up medical services, disrupted production, and lowered morale"; ibid., 49. He also explicitly raises the *jus in bello* issue, stating that "in its consistent loading of large numbers of incendiary bombs for use against marshaling yards the Eighth did cross the line between rail yard and 'city area' attacks. The loading of incendiaries could be construed to violate the precept of 'proportionality' under the laws of war"; ibid., 56, 62n. Davis analyzes the air war in Europe in much greater detail in a book published two years before the 1995 article: see his *Carl A. Spaatz and the Air War in Europe*, especially 543–64 (on U.S. bombing policy from late 1944 through Dresden) and 564–71 (where he concisely summarizes the U.S. Eighth Air Force targeting of German cities, but at the same time takes issue with scholars such as Michael Sherry who speak of this in terms of technological fanaticism and outright "evil"). See also Searle, "'It Made a Lot of Sense to Kill Skilled Workers,'" 105–9; Biddle, *Rhetoric and Reality in Air Warfare*, 228–29, 239–40, 243–45, 253–54.

27. The percentage of incendiaries in the bomb load dropped by the Eighth Air Force on Dresden (40 percent) was in line with other U.S. raids on major German cities such as Cologne (27 percent), Nuremberg (30 percent), Berlin (37 percent), and Munich (41 percent). See Davis, *Carl A. Spaatz and the Air War in Europe*, 570; Davis, "German Rail Yards and Cities," 57–58. On the widely analyzed bombing of Dresden, see for example Davis, *Carl A. Spaatz and the Air War in Europe*, 556–64; also Biddle, *Rhetoric and Reality in Air Warfare*, 254–59. Davis accepts

35,000 fatalities as reasonable for the Dresden attack, with most fatalities deriving from the Royal Air Force raid, but notes that estimates run as high as 250,000 (543, 557); see also his "German Rail Yards and Cities," 59. Biddle endorses a low estimate of 25,000 fatalities.

28. Davis, *Carl A. Spaatz and the Air War in Europe*, 508, 568–71; Davis, "German Rail Yards and Cities," 49–53, 60, 61n; Biddle, *Rhetoric and Reality in Air Warfare*, 239–45. Such euphemisms not only misled the public but also provided a certain psychological cushion for the planners and air crews who were in fact engaged in killing civilians.

29. On the February 17 Associated Press dispatch (by Howard Cowan), which hit the U.S. media on February 18, see Davis, *Carl A. Spaatz and the Air War in Europe*, 558; Schaffer, *Wings of Judgment*, 98–103; Sherry, *The Rise of American Air Power*, 261; Biddle, *Rhetoric and Reality in Air Warfare*, 258; Grayling, *Among the Dead Cities*, 72 (which notes that "the words reached front pages in the United States, but were censored in England"); Charles Webster and Nobel Frankland, *The Strategic Air Offensive against Germany, 1939–1945* (Her Majesty's Stationery Office, 1961), vol. 3, part 5: 113 (which notes that despite media censorship, the quote was picked up in the House of Commons). Harris's comment, on March 29, actually came in response to the Churchill quotation that follows here at note 30 in the present text; Davis, *Carl A. Spaatz and the Air War in Europe*, 581.

30. Webster and Frankland, *The Strategic Air Offensive against Germany*, vol. 3: 112.

31. Webster and Frankland, *The Strategic Air Offensive against Germany*, vol. 3: 112–19; the authors of this official history characterize the March 28 minute as "the least felicitous of the Prime Minister's long series of war-time minutes."

32. Kenneth P. Werrell, *Blankets of Fire: U.S. Bombers over Japan during World War II* (Smithsonian Institution Press, 1996), 48–49; Craven and Cate, *The Army Air Forces in World War II*, vol. 5: 610; Schaffer, *Wings of Judgment*, 115. These experiments are discussed on the official website of the Dugway Proving Ground (dugway.army.mil), which also notes that the so-called German Village still exists in a deteriorated state and is "eligible for listing in the National Register of Historic Places." The "Japanese Village" has disappeared, apart from an observation bunker and some hydrants. Demolition tests of a related nature also were conducted at Eglin Field in Florida.

33. Antonin Raymond, *Antonin Raymond: An Autobiography* (Tuttle, 1973), 188–89. I was led to Raymond's memoir by Mike Davis, *Dead Cities, and Other Tales* (New Press, 2003), 65–69.

34. Searle, "'It Made a Lot of Sense to Kill Skilled Workers,'" 116–17; Craven and Cate, *The Army Air Forces in World War II*, vol. 5: 9, 26–28, 551–54, 610. For succinct summaries of U.S. bombing policy vis-à-vis Japan up to early 1945, see Schaffer, *Wings of Judgment*, 107–27; Biddle, *Rhetoric and Reality in Air Warfare*, 261–70.

35. Schaffer, *Wings of Judgment*, 116. Some sources conflate this remarkable fatality estimate to "casualties"; see Werrell, *Blankets of Fire*, 53; Biddle, *Rhetoric and Reality in Air Warfare*, 264–65.

36. Schaffer, *Wings of Judgment*, 124.

37. Searle, "'It Made a Lot of Sense to Kill Skilled Workers,'" 119 (on the meteorological considerations). As noted earlier, weather projections also influenced the

timing of Japan's initiation of war in 1941 and the Bush administration's invasion of Iraq in 2003.

38. Craven and Cate, *The Army Air Forces in World War II*, vol. 5: 4–9, 574, 613, 623; Searle, "'It Made a Lot of Sense to Kill Skilled Workers,'" 114. "Superfortress" was an official label for the B-29, often abbreviated as "Superfort." In coded messages, the B-29 was also called "Dreamboat," "Stork," and "Big Brother."

39. Searle, "'It Made a Lot of Sense to Kill Skilled Workers,'" 113–14, 117–18, 121.

40. Craven and Cate, *The Army Air Forces in World War II*, vol. 5: 614–17; Curtis E. LeMay with MacKinlay Kantor, *Mission with LeMay: My Story* (Doubleday, 1965), 387; USSBS, *A Report on Physical Damage in Japan*, 97 (on B-29s being turned upside down). Schaffer summarizes the descriptive literature on the on-the-ground experience of this first great Tokyo air raid in *Wings of Judgment*, 128–37. While all sources emphasize the ineffectiveness of Japanese antiaircraft defenses, and the particularly low rate of loss once the urban-area raids were initiated in March 1945, the B-29 losses that did occur in the air war against Japan, including for reasons of mechanical failure, should not be neglected. Several thousand U.S. airmen lost their lives. See, for example, Craven and Cate, *The Army Air Forces in World War II*, vol. 5: 574, 606, 616, 641, 644; also, for a thoughtful firsthand recollection, Wilbur H. Morrison, *Hellbirds: The Story of the B-29s in Combat* (Duell, Sloan & Pearce, 1960). According to Conrad C. Crane, Army Air Forces losses in the air war against Japan "were remarkably light, a tribute to the effectiveness of American tactics as well as to the weakness of Japanese defenses. Only 437 of the Very Heavy Bombers [B-29s] were lost in combat operations, mostly because of technical failures. In contrast, over 3,000 B-17s and 1,000 B-24s had been lost by the Eighth Air Force against Germany"; see Crane's *Bombs, Cities, and Civilians: American Airpower Strategy in World War II* (University Press of Kansas, 1993), 140–41.

41. Craven and Cate, *The Army Air Forces in World War II*, vol. 5: xix–xx, 618–23, 638 (on not targeting the imperial palace). For a more extended treatment of wartime U.S. thinking about the emperor, see John W. Dower, *Embracing Defeat: Japan in the Wake of World War II* (Norton and New Press, 1999), 280–86. For fuller technical treatments of the effects of the air war against Japan, see especially the following reports by the USSBS: *Effects of Incendiary Bomb Attacks on Japan*, esp. 65–117 on Tokyo; *A Report on Physical Damage in Japan*, esp. 38–115 on "Fire against Japan." On civilian deaths in Okinawa, see George Feifer, *The Battle of Okinawa: The Blood and the Bomb* (Lyons Press, 2001; originally published as *Tennozan: The Battle of Okinawa and the Atomic Bomb*, 1992), xi (150,000 civilian fatalities); Richard Frank, *Downfall: The End of the Imperial Japanese Empire* (Random House, 1999), 72, 188 ("at least 62,000 and perhaps as many as 100,000 to 150,000 civilians perished"); Ronald H. Spector, *Eagle against the Sun: The American War with Japan* (Vintage, 1985), 540 (80,000 civilian fatalities); Kodansha, *Japan: An Illustrated Encyclopedia* (Kodansha, 1993) vol. 2: 1141 ("a quarter million Japanese lives," which would put civilian as opposed to military fatalities at over 140,000). Most Japanese sources put the number of civilian deaths at between 100,000 and 150,000.

42. Craven and Cate, *The Army Air Forces in World War II*, vol. 5: 639, 643.

43. *New York Times*, May 30, 1945. Although the *Times* stated that fifty-one bombers had been lost (two in the March 9 raid, but a total of twenty-nine in the final two raids on May 23–24 and 24–25), its itemization of planes lost per raid only added up to forty-eight. The imperial palace was unintentionally, and slightly, damaged on one of the last raids.

44. "Secondary target" data here follows the chronologically arranged table of "Incendiary Missions against Secondary Cities" in Craven and Cate, *The Army Air Forces in World War II*, vol. 5: 674–75. This itemizes sixty air raids, with three "secondary cities" being bombed twice, making a total of fifty-seven cities incinerated after the opening offensive against the Big Six urban areas. As usual, there are discrepancies and uncertainties in the data, and conflicting alternative sources. The Strategic Bombing Survey (a major source for Craven and Cate) concluded that "in the aggregate, 104,000 tons of bombs were directed at 66 urban areas" (which leaves some room for misunderstanding whether this includes or excludes the atomic bombings), and that "some 44 percent of the built-up area of the 66 cities attacked was destroyed"; USSBS, *Summary Report*, 17. Although its tabular résumé itemizes only fifty-seven "secondary cities" (rather than fifty-eight), the Craven and Cate volume itself states that "in all, counting the 2 hit by atomic bombs, 66 cities suffered area attacks which burned out a total of 178 square miles" (vol. 5: xx). Some lists, however, put the total number of incendiary missions prior to Hiroshima and Nagasaki at sixty-seven; see, for example, the unsourced appendix in Martin Caidin, *A Torch to the Enemy: The Fire Raid on Tokyo* (Ballantine, 1960), 159–60, which is cited and reproduced (with one unexplained change of cities) in the Wikipedia entry on "Strategic Bombing in World War II" and has been picked up in other sources. In part, these disparities, which exist in Japanese sources as well, derive from different criteria used in identifying a bombing raid as an "incendiary mission." For the journal entry about the Toyama air raid being a "milk run," see "Sgt. Abe Spitzer Collection" on the Manhattan Project Heritage Preservation Association website at mphpa.org, 9–10.

45. USSBS, *Summary Report (Pacific War)*, 17–18. For the tonnage of bombs dropped, see USSBS, *The Effects of Strategic Bombing on Japan's War Economy*, 35; also R. J. Overy, *The Air War, 1939–1945* (Stein & Day, 1981), 128. The Strategic Bombing Survey calculated that the bomb load dropped on Japan proper was 161,425 tons, compared to 1,356,808 tons dropped on Germany.

46. On firestorms, see Freeman Dyson, "A Failure of Intelligence: Operational Research at RAF Bomber Command, 1943–1945," *Technology Review* (Massachusetts Institute of Technology), November/December 2006, 62–71. Dyson, who joined Bomber Command as a researcher in 1943 at the age of nineteen, notes that "every time Bomber Command attacked a city, we were trying to raise a firestorm, but we never learnt why we so seldom succeeded. Probably a firestorm could happen only when three things occurred together: first, a high concentration of old buildings at the target site; second, an attack with a high density of incendiary bombs in the target's central area; and, third, an atmospheric instability." For other contributing factors to the relatively low fatality estimates apart from Tokyo and the two atomic-bomb targets, see USSBS, *Summary Report (Pacific War)*, 20, 22.

47. Craven and Cate, *The Army Air Forces in World War II*, vol. 5: 653–58; USSBS, *The Effects of Strategic Bombing on Japan's War Economy*, 38; USSBS, *A Report on Physical*

*Damage in Japan*, 39. On "milk runs," see, for example, Morrison, *Hellbirds*, 140; Manhattan Project Heritage Preservation Association, "Sgt. Abe Spitzer Collection," 9–10; Edwin P. Hoyt, *The Kamikazes* (Arbor, 1983), 264.

48. SGM Herb Friedman (Ret.), "The Strategic Bomber and American PSYOP," 6–28, esp. 11, 24–27. This long (51-page) online article is densely illustrated in full color, and can be accessed at psywarrior.com. This is an outstanding website for graphic psychological warfare operations from World War II to the present. Three of Friedman's other contributions here also are highly illuminating: "Japanese PSYOP during WWII" (45 pages), "OWI Pacific PSYOP Six Decades Ago" (86 pages), and "U.S. Army PWB Leaflets for the Pacific War" (91 pages). See also Schaffer, *Wings of Judgment*, 140–42, on the twelve-city leaflet.

49. USSBS, *Summary Report (Pacific War)*, 20–22; Craven and Cate, *The Army Air Forces in World War II*, vol. 5: 754–56. The rural population provided the bulk of Imperial Army draftees, and already felt the impact of the war in the rapidly rising number of combat fatalities (which amounted, in the end, to some two million soldiers and sailors).

50. Crane, *Bombs, Cities, and Civilians*, 133.

51. In making the case that the bombing of civilians in Japan, as in Germany, was unnecessary, ineffective, and immoral, for example, A. C. Grayling relies strongly, in the Japanese instance, on the conclusion reached in a study by Robert A. Pape, to the effect that "the principal cause of Japan's surrender" was "the sea blockade, which crippled Japan's ability to produce and equip forces necessary to execute its strategy." Second in importance was the Soviet declaration of war that followed the bombing of Hiroshima, and third the mere threat of Allied invasion. In Pape's view—which essentially rejects the critical but more balanced appraisal of the Strategic Bombing Survey, and is by no means a majority one—the strategic bombing campaign was all but irrelevant; Grayling, *Among the Dead Cities*, 113–14, quoting Pape's *Bombing to Win: Air Power and Coercion in War* (Cornell University Press, 1996).

52. I have dealt in detail elsewhere with anxiety about popular morale and attitudes on the part of the Japanese police and upper classes. See "Sensational Rumors, Seditious Graffiti, and the Nightmares of the Thought Police" in Dower, *Japan in War and Peace*, 101–54; also *Empire and Aftermath: Yoshida Shigeru and the Japanese Experience, 1878–1954* (Council on East Asian Studies, Harvard University, 1979), especially chapters 7 and 8.

53. Craven and Cate, *The Army Air Forces in World War II*, vol. 5: 658.

54. Quoted in Biddle, *Rhetoric and Reality in Air Warfare*, 269 (from "Highlights of the Twentieth Air Force," Office of Information Services, Headquarters, Army Air Forces, 1945).

55. On this issue of targeting priorities, see USSBS, *The Effects of Strategic Bombing on Japan's War Economy*, 2–3, 63–65; also *Summary Report (Pacific War)*, 17, 19. The Strategic Bombing Survey neither denied nor criticized the effectiveness of urban-area attacks, but rather argued that combining these with a far more serious agenda of "rail attacks" probably would have brought about an earlier surrender. Whether this is a valid criticism or not is a matter of dispute.

56. Charles J. V. Murphy, "The Air War on Japan," *Fortune*, September/October 1945.

57. Cited in Dower, *Embracing Defeat*, 286.

58. *The Fog of War*, directed by Errol Morris; this won the Academy Award for Best Documentary (Feature) in 2003.

### CHAPTER 9: "THE MOST TERRIBLE BOMB IN THE HISTORY OF THE WORLD"

59. Otis Cary, "The Sparing of Kyoto, Mr. Stimson's 'Pet City,'" *Japan Quarterly*, vol. 11 (October–December 1975); Schaffer, *Wings of Judgment*, 143–46. Nagasaki, which was subjected to five small-scale air attacks before August 1945, was added to the Interim Committee list after the other cities had been designated; overall, these earlier air raids destroyed only a few hundred residences and some twenty industrial buildings. Thus, as the Strategic Bombing Survey noted, when the atomic bomb was dropped, Nagasaki also "was comparatively intact"; *The Effects of Atomic Bombs on Hiroshima and Nagasaki*, 9.

The literature on the development and use of the atomic bombs—based on archives, memoirs, and interviews—is enormous. Much of this is cited in the notes that follow. For densely annotated accounts, see in particular Martin Sherwin, *A World Destroyed: Hiroshima and Its Legacies*, 3rd edition (Stanford University Press, 2003; originally published in 1975 with a different subtitle), which includes valuable documentary appendices; Richard Rhodes, *The Making of the Atomic Bomb* (Simon & Schuster, 1986); Gar Alperovitz, *Atomic Diplomacy: Hiroshima and Potsdam—The Use of the Atomic Bomb and the American Confrontation with Soviet Power* (Simon & Schuster, 1965); Gar Alperovitz et al., *The Decision to Use the Atomic Bombs and the Architecture of an American Myth* (Knopf, 1995), which contains extensive long quotations; Gerard DeGroot, *The Bomb: A Life* (Harvard University Press, 2004); Franks, *Downfall*; Tsuyoshi Hasegawa, *Racing the Enemy: Stalin, Truman, and the Surrender of Japan* (Harvard University Press, 2006); Kai Bird and Martin J. Sherwin, *American Prometheus: The Triumph and Tragedy of J. Robert Oppenheimer* (Knopf, 2005); and the numerous articles by Barton Bernstein. Many of these issues came to a head in the 1994–95 controversy over the "*Enola Gay* exhibition" at the Smithsonian Institution. For responses to this, see Edward Tabor Linenthal and Tom Engelhardt, eds., *History Wars: The Enola Gay and Other Battles for the American Past* (Metropolitan, 1996; I contributed an essay to this volume on tragic and heroic narratives of the use of the bombs); also Kai Bird and Lawrence Lifschultz, eds., *Hiroshima's Shadow: Writings on the Denial of History and the Smithsonian Controversy* (Pamphleteer's Press, 1998), a wide-ranging anthology. J. Samuel Walker, a historian with the U.S. Nuclear Regulatory Commission, authored several summaries of the historiographical debates. See his contribution to Michael J. Hogan, ed., *America in the World: The Historiography of American Foreign Relations since 1941* (Cambridge University Press, 1995), 206–33; his concise study *Prompt and Utter Destruction: Truman and the Use of Atomic Bombs against Japan* (University of North Carolina Press, 1997); and "Recent Literature on Truman's Atomic Bomb Decision: A Search for a Middle Ground," *Diplomatic History*, vol. 29, no. 2 (April 2005), 311–24. For scholarly essays critical of or divergent from "revisionist" criticism of the use of the bombs, see Robert James Maddox, ed., *Hiroshima as History: The Myths of Revisionism* (University of Missouri Press, 2007); this includes articles by Sadao

Asada, Edward J. Drea, D. M. Giangreco, Robert P. Newman, and others. The online contribution to the debate is overwhelming; of particular value for primary sources and quotations are extensive sites posted by Doug Long (doug-long.com) and Gar Alperovitz and others (accessible under "'The Decision to Use the Atomic Bomb'—Gar Alperovitz and the H-Net Debate" at doug-long.com/debate.htm.).

60. The explosion of the second bomb above the Urakami cathedral became a central symbolic theme in the postwar writings of Nagai Takashi, a Catholic scientist whose wife was killed in the bombing and who died of radiation sickness himself in 1951. Nagai became known as the "saint of Nagasaki" in some circles for his intimate and prolific writings on the meaning of nuclear destruction, which he turned into a message from God; see Dower, *Embracing Defeat*, 196–98. The iconic postwar photography of the nuclear legacy in Nagasaki by Shōmei Tōmatsu includes several well-known images of the shattered, blackened marble statues of Christian saints. For a sample of Tōmatsu's Nagasaki photographs, see Leo Rubinfein and Sandra Phillips, eds., *Shomei Tomatsu: Skin of the Nation* (San Francisco Museum of Modern Art, in conjunction with Yale University Press, 2004). One of the best-known intimate survivor accounts of the Hiroshima bombing is the diary-memoir of Dr. Michihiko Hachiya: *Hiroshima Diary: The Journal of a Japanese Physician, August 6–September 30, 1945* (University of North Carolina Press, 1955). (I contributed essays to both the Tōmatsu catalog and the 1995 reissue of Hachiya's book.)

61. USSBS, *Effects of the Atomic Bombs on Hiroshima and Nagasaki*, 3, 5, 15, for fatality estimates, entire (23 pages) for the most influential early overview; Tadatoshi Akiba, "Atomic Bomb," *Kodansha Encyclopedia of Japan* (Kodansha, 1983), vol. 1: 107–11; Toshiyuki Kumatori, "Atomic Bomb Related Disease," *Kodansha Encyclopedia of Japan*, vol. 1: 111–14. See also the two-volume abridged version of Kodansha's invaluable nine-volume encyclopedia: *Japan: An Illustrated Encyclopedia* (1993), vol. 1: 74–79; for unexplained reasons, the entry on "Atomic Bombs" here does not include the high fatality estimates for 1950 that appear in the original 1983 edition. The most voluminous compendium of (sometimes conflicting) data on the effects of the atomic bombs was published in Japanese by the Iwanami publishing house in 1979 and subsequently issued in English translation; see Committee for the Compilation of Materials on Damage Caused by the Atomic Bombs in Hiroshima and Nagasaki, *Hiroshima and Nagasaki: The Physical, Medical, and Social Effects of the Atomic Bombings*, transl. by Eisei Ishikawa and David L. Swain (Basic Books, 1981). This 706-page tome is not an easy reference source to use, but it provides excellent insight into the challenge of assembling viable data on these matters. On gross casualty figures, see, for example, ibid., 113, 115, 349, 353–54, 367–69 (for the high fatality estimates as of 1950), 395, 406, 420, 457. Much of the information in the paragraphs that follow in the main text can be found in these several detailed sources.

62. See the two "Ground Zero 1945" websites at visualizingcultures.mit.edu. One of these features a text (by me) on drawings of the atomic-bomb experience by Hiroshima survivors and a database of over 400 such images from the Hiroshima Peace Memorial Museum; the index number of this particular drawing, by Masato Yamashita, is GE06-36. The second site reproduces in both English and Japanese the illustrated retrospective account of a survivor who was a schoolboy at the time.

63. USSBS, *Effects of the Atomic Bombs on Hiroshima and Nagasaki*, 19; *Kodansha Encyclopedia of Japan*, vol. 1: 110, 113; Committee for the Compilation of Materials, *Hiroshima and Nagasaki*, 154–56, 210–37, 449–54.

64. On the psychological impact of the bombs among survivors, see Robert Jay Lifton, *Death in Life: Survivors of Hiroshima* (Random House, 1967). I have addressed the bombs in Japanese memory in several publications, with particular focus on graphic or visual memory. See "Japanese Artists and the Atomic Bomb" in Dower, *Japan in War and Peace*, 242–56; "War, Peace, and Beauty," in Dower and John Junkerman, eds., *The Hiroshima Murals: The Art of Iri Maruki and Toshi Maruki* (Kodansha International, 1985); and "The Bombed: Hiroshimas and Nagasakis in Japanese Memory," in Michael J. Hogan, ed., *Hiroshima in History and Memory* (Cambridge University Press, 1996), 116–42. To date, fear that exposure to nuclear radiation might contribute to hereditary genetic pathologies has proved to be unfounded.

65. The training of the crew assigned to drop the bomb is discussed in General Leslie M. Groves, *Now It Can Be Told: The Story of the Manhattan Project* (Perseus, 1975), ch. 18 and 20 (see esp. 286), and at lively but unannotated length in Gordon Thomas and Max Morgan Witts, *Enola Gay* (Stein & Day, 1977); see also David Samuels, "Atomic John," *New Yorker*, December 15, 2008 (for 155 "test units"). On radiation projections, see Nuel Pharr Davis, *Lawrence and Oppenheimer* (Simon & Schuster, 1968), 166–67; Rhodes, *The Making of the Atomic Bomb*, 632; Bernstein, "The Atomic Bombings Reconsidered," *Foreign Affairs*, January/February 1995. Groves later claimed that after the Alamogordo test he concluded that "casualties resulting from direct radiation and fallout" would be minimal due to the considerable height above ground at which the atomic bomb would be detonated; *Now It Can Be Told*, 269, 286. They were not.

66. For the first eye-witness journalistic account of the Trinity test, by the only reporter authorized to be present, see the report by William Laurence belatedly released by the War Department and published in various newspapers including the *New York Times*, September 26, 1945. These details are well covered in the extensive secondary literature on the development of the atomic bomb; see, for example, the recent skillful summation in DeGroot, *The Bomb*, ch. 5; Rhodes, *The Making of the Atomic Bomb*, especially the long chapter 18 on Trinity. See also Robert Jungk's unannotated early study *Brighter than a Thousand Suns: A Personal History of the Atomic Scientists* (Harcourt Brace Jovanovich, 1956); Richard G. Hewlett, *The New World, 1939–1941* (Pennsylvania State University Press, 1962); and Margaret Gowing, *Britain and Atomic Energy, 1939–1945* (Macmillan, 1964). Gowing was a historian and archivist with the United Kingdom Atomic Energy Authority, and the Authority held the copyright to the manuscript. The "blinded by the flash" anecdote appears in "Sgt. Abe Spitzer Collection," 15.

67. For the Standardized Casualty Rate calculation, see Rhodes, *The Making of the Atomic Bomb*, 734.

68. Sherwin, *A World Destroyed*, 312 (appendix P, for Farrell); Laurence in *New York Times*, September 26, 1945 (for Kistiakowsky); Samuel Eliot Morison, *History of United States Naval Operations in World War II*, vol. 14: *Victory in the Pacific* (Little, Brown, 1960), 340 (for Churchill). Truman's "Potsdam diary" is reproduced in full in Robert H. Ferrell, ed., *Off the Record: The Private Papers of Harry S. Truman*

(Harper and Row, 1980), 46–59. This fascinating document—hastily written on twenty sheets of paper, and tucked away unknown for a quarter century in the papers of a minor U.S. official at Potsdam (Charles G. Ross)—was first published by Eduard Mark in *Diplomatic History*, vol. 4, no. 3 (Summer 1980), 317–26. Truman's apocalyptic language echoes the first serious briefing on the existence of the new weapon he received on April 25 from Secretary of War Stimson, who also expressed fear that "modern civilization might be completely destroyed"; see Sherwin, *A World Destroyed*, 291–92 (appendix I). Elting Morison notes that Stimson's wartime diary reveals a "running litany" of ominous adjectives whenever the secret weapon is referred to: "the dreadful," "the terrible," "the dire," "the awful," "the diabolical," and so on; see Morison, *Turmoil and Tradition: A Study of the Life and Times of Henry L. Stimson* (Houghton Mifflin, 1960), 618.

69. Bird and Sherwin, *American Prometheus*, 309; see also Len Giovannitti and Fred Freed, *The Decision to Drop the Bomb* (Coward-McCann, 1965), 197. Oppenheimer intones this frequently cited quotation in an excellent television documentary titled *The Day after Trinity* directed and produced by Jon Else in 1980. Bird and Sherwin indicate that he had made the same allusion at least as early as 1948, and possibly before this.

70. Groves, *Now It Can Be Told*, 267. The April 27, 1945, meeting of the Target Committee that established these criteria preceded the formation of the Interim Committee by three weeks. Truman became president on April 12, upon the death of President Roosevelt.

71. The minutes of the famous May 31 meeting of the Interim Committee are reproduced as appendix L in Sherwin, *A World Destroyed*, 295–304.

72. Bird and Sherwin, *American Prometheus*, 296 ("delicate euphemisms"); DeGroot, *The Bomb*, 73 ("In other words, the committee had approved terror bombing but called it something else"), 77–78 ("mere window dressing"); Ferrell, *Off the Record*, 55–56 (Truman's diary). For a sampling of Stimson's gyrations on the morality of bombing civilians, see Rhodes, *The Making of the Atomic Bomb*, 640, 647–48, 650.

73. *Public Papers of the Presidents of the United States: Harry S. Truman: 1945* (Government Printing Office, 1961), 97 (Truman's radio address of August 9, 1945); Harry S. Truman, *Memoirs*, vol. 1: *Year of Decisions, 1945* (Signet Books edition, 1965; originally published in 1955), 462–63. Even Curtis LeMay, who dismissed deliberating about the morality of Allied bombing of civilians in World War II with a curt "Nuts," acknowledged the necessity of psychological blocking or numbing. On the one hand, he rationalized killing even children as war workers: "All you had to do was visit one of those [Japanese] targets after we'd roasted it, and see the ruins of a multitude of tiny houses, with a drill press sticking up through the wreckage of every home. The entire population got into the act and worked to make those airplanes or munitions of war . . . men, women, children. We knew we were going to kill a lot of women and kids when we burned that town. Had to be done." Indeed, in his particularly rough way, he even went on to justify obliterating or erasing "the enemy's potential" by observing that "there is nothing new about this massacre of civilian populations. In ancient times, when an army laid siege to a city, everybody was in the fight. And when that city had fallen, and was sacked, just as often as not every single soul was murdered." At the same time, however, LeMay also wrote this in the same memoir, in a passing reference to

the air war in Germany: "You drop a load of bombs and, if you're cursed with any imagination at all, you have at least one quick horrid glimpse of a child lying in bed with a whole ton of masonry tumbling down on top of him; or a three-year-old girl wailing for *Mutter . . . Mutter . . .* because she has been burned. Then you have to turn away from the picture if you intend to retain your sanity. And also if you intend to keep on doing the work your Nation expects of you." See Curtis E. LeMay with MacKinlay Kantor, *Mission with LeMay: My Story* (Doubleday, 1949), 383–84, 425.

74. USSBS, *Effects of the Atomic Bombs on Hiroshima and Nagasaki*, 21; J. Robert Oppenheimer, "Atomic Weapons and the Crisis in Science," *Saturday Review of Literature*, November 24, 1945, 10 (quoted in Bernard Brodie, ed., *The Absolute Weapon: Atomic Power and World Order* [Harcourt, Brace, 1946], 73).

75. Truman, *Memoirs*, vol. 1: 295 ("at least five hundred thousand American casualties"), 460 ("General Marshall told me that it might cost half a million American lives to force the enemy's surrender on his home grounds"). For the exchange at Columbia, which took place in 1959, see Robert H. Ferrell, *Truman: A Centenary Remembrance* (Viking, 1984), 146.

76. Barton Bernstein, "A Postwar Myth: 500,000 U.S. Lives Saved," *Bulletin of the Atomic Scientists*, June/July 1986, 38 (for Churchill's estimate); Winston Churchill, *The Second World War: Triumph and Tragedy* (Houghton Mifflin, 1953), 639.

77. Henry Stimson, "The Decision to Use the Bomb," *Harper's Magazine*, February 1947; Henry Stimson and McGeorge Bundy, *On Active Service in War and Peace* (Harper and Brothers, 1948), 632. The Stimson article has been widely reprinted, and was reproduced with additional commentary in ch. 23 of the latter.

78. Rhodes, *The Making of the Atomic Bomb*, 687–88; see also Groves, *Now It Can Be Told*, 264.

79. A translation and analysis of *Ketsu-Go* is included in *Reports of General MacArthur* (compiled from Japanese Demobilization Bureaux Records), vol. 2, part 2: *Japanese Operations in the Southwest Pacific Area* (Government Printing Office, 1966), 601–9.

80. D. M. Giangreco, "Casualty Projections for the U.S. Invasion of Japan, 1945–46: Planning and Policy Implications," *Journal of Military History*, vol. 61 (July 1997), 521–82, esp. 535–39, 561, 567. In his memoirs, General LeMay recalled that when he was assigned to take over the bombing of Japan, Twentieth Air Force Chief of Staff General Lauris Norstad "in effect" had told him, "You go ahead and get results with the B-29. If you don't get results, you'll be fired. . . . If you don't get results it will mean eventually a mass amphibious invasion of Japan, to cost probably half a million more American lives"; LeMay and Kantor, *Mission with LeMay*, 347. Since this as-told-to memoir deliberately adopts a corner-of-the-mouth, cigar-in-hand style of storytelling, the quotation is suspect; but it conforms to the "Saipan ratio" thinking of the time.

Giangreco's analysis was written in critical response to the provocative argument advanced by Barton Bernstein that, prior to the atomic bombings, the U.S. military anticipated vastly lower fatalities (between 20,000 and 46,000) in its projected invasion; see especially Bernstein's 1986 article "A Postwar Myth," 38–40. The "fatalities" numbers game became a contentious issue (and destructive distraction) in the 1994–95 controversy over the *Enola Gay* exhibition at the

Smithsonian Institution's Air and Space Museum. It also provoked extensive and often acrimonious subsequent debate, much of which is accessible online. For responses and counterresponses involving Giangreco and Bernstein (who also challenges the significance of the "Saipan ratio"), see the following in subsequent issues of the *Journal of Military History*: Bernstein's long review essay "Truman and the A-Bombs: Targeting Noncombatants, Using the Bomb, and His Defending the 'Decision,'" vol. 62, no. 3 (July 1998), 547–70; exchange of letters, vol. 63, no. 1 (January 1999), 243–51; letters, vol. 63, no. 4 (October 1999), 1067–70. A lengthier restatement of Giangreco's position in the debate, originally dated July 31, 1998, was later posted online as "Casualty Estimates: D. M. Giangreco's Rebuttal of Barton J. Bernstein" (accessible through the "nuclear weapons" listing at endusmilitarism.org). For samples of the protracted tempest, see Michael Kort, "Casualty Projections for the Invasion of Japan, Phantom Estimates, and the Math of Barton Bernstein," *Passport* (Newsletter of the Society for Historians of American Foreign Relations), December 2003, and Bernstein's lengthy counterargument ("Marshall, Leahy, and Casualty Issues—A Reply to Kort's Flawed Critique") in *Passport*, August 2004; also Alperovitz, *The Decision to Use the Atomic Bomb*, 466–71.

81. Giangreco, "Casualty Projections," 564–67.

82. Giangreco, "Casualty Projections," 541–50; Giangreco focuses on the Hoover report in his October 1999 letter in *Journal of Military History*. Eisenhower's recollection, cited by Giangreco, appears in a 1965 letter to John J. McCloy. Giangreco also cites an internal Army study prepared in the closing months of the war by Dr. William Shockley, who later won a Nobel Prize in Physics for his work on the transistor, that analyzed available casualty data but was not completed in time to have any influence. Like the Hoover report, this anticipated enormous losses in an invasion, concluding that "we shall probably have to kill at least 5 to 10 million Japanese. This might cost us between 1.7 and 4 million casualties including [between] 400,000 and 800,000 dead"; Giangreco, "Casualty Projections," 568. For key primary documents concerning discussion of casualty projections at the highest levels as of June 1945, including the Hoover memorandum (although this is not identified as such), see appendices U, V, W in Sherwin, *A World Destroyed*, 335–63.

83. See the discussion of the May 30 *New York Times* article in chapter 8. The obverse side of postwar exaggeration of probable American fatalities in an invasion was gross underestimation of actual fatalities in Hiroshima and Nagasaki. This was not necessarily deliberate, and in considerable part reflected reliance on inaccurate evaluations by Japanese officials. At the same time, however, much concrete knowledge about the effects of the bombs, including radiation poisoning, *was* deliberately censored in the wake of the war; major attention on the part of postwar U.S. scientists and investigators was devoted to structural, physical damage; and, fundamentally, neither the victors nor the postwar Japanese government were particularly interested in the victims apart from what survivors might reveal about radiation effects.

84. Appendix M in Sherwin, *A World Destroyed*, 304–5.

85. The partial record of the June 18 meeting is accessible in various forms and sources. See U.S. Department of State, *Foreign Relations of the United States: The*

*Conference of Berlin (The Potsdam Conference), 1945* (Government Printing Office, 1960), vol. 1: 903–10 (hereafter cited as *FRUS: Conference of Berlin*); appendix W in Sherwin, *A World Destroyed*, 355–63; also Giangreco, "Casualty Projections," 552–60.

86. Rhodes, *The Making of the Atomic Bomb*, 676, 701; Peter J. Kuznik, "Defending the Indefensible: A Meditation on the Life of Hiroshima Pilot Paul Tibbets, Jr.," posted online at *The Asia Pacific Journal: Japan Focus* (japanfocus.org), January 2008 (the quote about Tibbetts is by Abe Spitzer).

87. *Public Papers of the Presidents of the United States: Harry S. Truman, 1945*, 212, 362.

## CHAPTER 10: THE IRRESISTIBLE LOGIC OF MASS DESTRUCTION

88. The Korean War probably saw the deaths of more than a million South Koreans, some 85 percent of them civilians, and a like number of North Koreans (over 10 percent of the total population of the north). In Vietnam, plausible estimates put the number killed between 1954 and 1975 at over three million, including around two million civilians in the north and south combined.

89. Tom Engelhardt addresses this cultural tension imaginatively in *The End of Victory Culture: Cold War America and the Disillusioning of a Generation* (Basic Books, 1995), and added an insightful postscript on the fifth anniversary of September 11; see his "9-11 in a Movie-Made World," *Nation*, September 25, 2006.

90. The comment in Truman's diary entry is prefaced with the observation that "it is certainly a good thing for the world that Hitler's crowd or Stalin's did not discover this atomic bomb"; Ferrell, *Off the Record*, 56. Leahy's famous quote appears in his memoir *I Was There: The Personal Story of the Chief of Staff to Presidents Roosevelt and Truman. Based on His Notes and Diaries Made at the Time* (Whittlesey House, 1950), 441. For Rabi, see Alice Kimball Smith, *A Peril and a Hope: The Scientists' Movement in America, 1945–47* (University of Chicago Press, 1965), ii. For close analysis of ambivalence and anxiety in the decades following World War II, see also Paul Boyer, *By the Bomb's Early Light: American Thought and Culture at the Dawn of the Atomic Age* (Pantheon, 1985).

91. Oppenheimer's often-quoted observation, made in a talk at MIT in November 1947, was, "In some sort of crude sense which no vulgarity, no humor, no over-statement can quite extinguish, the physicists have known sin; and this is a knowledge which they cannot lose."

92. For MacArthur, see *FRUS: Conference of Berlin*, vol. 1: 906. An Allied invasion of the home islands might have involved horrors beyond the kind of mayhem seen in Okinawa. U.S. planners, for example, gave passing consideration to using poison gas to incapacitate the defenders, and apparently were seriously considering using chemical and biological agents to destroy the Japanese rice crop and even ocean fisheries around Japan; see Crane, *Bombs, Cities, and Civilians*, 137–38.

93. Sherwin, *A World Destroyed*, 207–8; this almost casual exchange was recalled by Ernest O. Lawrence.

94. Grew's lobbying on the unconditional-surrender issue began with a key memo to the president on May 28 and is discussed in his voluminous memoir *Turbulent Era: A Diplomatic Record of Forty Years, 1904–1945* (Houghton Mifflin, 1952); see esp. ch. 36 ("The Emperor of Japan and Japan's Surrender"), 1406–42, which reproduces

some of the key memos. For an annotated analysis, see Waldo H. Heinrichs Jr., *American Ambassador: Joseph C. Grew and the Development of the United States Diplomatic Tradition* (Little, Brown, 1966), 372–80; also Alperovitz et al., *The Decision to Use the Atomic Bomb*, esp. 45–49, 58–61. For intercepted "peace feelers through the Soviet Union," see *FRUS: Conference of Berlin*, vol. 1: 873–883, and vol. 2: 1248–64, 1291–98. The most striking cable from Foreign Minister Shigenori Tōgō to the Japanese ambassador in Moscow was dated July 12, decoded by the United States on July 13, and known to top U.S. officials including Truman. For earlier drafts of the Potsdam Declaration, see *FRUS: Conference of Berlin*, vol. 1: 889–99 and vol. 2: 1265–90, especially vol. 1: 894, 899 and vol. 2: 1269; the final draft is accessible in many sources, including the excellent surrender-related appendices in Robert J. C. Butow, *Japan's Decision to Surrender* (Stanford University Press, 1954), 243–44. Much of the more critical commentary on these issues is quoted and annotated in Alperovitz et al., *The Decision to Use the Atomic Bomb*; see esp. 31–79 (unconditional surrender); 81–184 (the Russian option); 221–317 (Potsdam, including the intercepted Japanese diplomatic cables).

The deleted "paragraph twelve" was preceded by a stern itemization of the nonnegotiable terms of surrender. These terms included eliminating "for all time the authority and influence of those who have deceived and misled the people of Japan into embarking on world conquest" (paragraph six); indefinite occupation by the victors (paragraph seven); limiting Japanese sovereignty to the four main home islands plus unspecified "minor islands" (paragraph eight); "completely" disarming Japanese military forces (paragraph nine); meting out "stern justice . . . to all war criminals," while supporting and strengthening "democratic tendencies among the Japanese people," including guarantees of freedom of speech, religion, and thought, and respect for fundamental human rights (paragraph ten); and restrictions on war-related industrial production, but not on peaceful industries or trade essential to sustain the economy and also to pay reparations (paragraph eleven). As of July 18, the draft version of paragraph twelve in the hands of the Joint Chiefs of Staff read as follows: "The occupying forces of the Allies shall be withdrawn from Japan as soon as our objectives are accomplished and there has been established beyond doubt a peacefully inclined, responsible government of a character representative of the Japanese people. This may include a constitutional monarchy under the present dynasty if it be shown to the complete satisfaction of the world that such a government will never again aspire to aggression." The critical second sentence was deleted at this point, largely at the insistence of James Byrnes, Truman's new secretary of state (beginning July 3) and the Joint Chiefs of Staff. In the proclamation issued from Potsdam on July 26, paragraph twelve read in full as follows: "The occupying forces of the Allies shall be withdrawn from Japan as soon as these objectives have been accomplished and there has been established in accordance with the freely expressed will of the Japanese people a peacefully inclined and responsible government."

95. USSBS, *Summary Report (Pacific War)*, 26; also USSBS, *Japan's Struggle to End the War*, 12–13. J. Robert Oppenheimer, "The International Control of Atomic Energy," *Bulletin of the Atomic Scientists*, vol. 1, no. 12 (June 1, 1946), 1; see also Bird and Sherwin, *American Prometheus*, 324, 348. For an extended analysis of the Survey's conclusion regarding the imminence of Japan's collapse, see Barton

Bernstein, "Compelling Japan's Surrender without the A-Bomb, Soviet Entry, or Invasion: Reconsidering the U.S. Bombing Survey's Early-Surrender Conclusion," *Journal of Strategic Studies*, vol. 18, no. 2 (June 1995), 101–48.

96. On September 20, 1945, LeMay flatly told a press conference that the atomic bomb "had nothing to do with the end of the war," which would have ended in two weeks anyway without either the bombs or a Soviet declaration of war. LeMay had no input into the development or use of the bombs, and in making this blunt observation was, of course, plugging the decisive role of his own B-29 air raids in precipitating Japan's capitulation. Halsey's ulterior agenda, if he had one, would have been making the case for the decisive role of the U.S. Navy in cutting off Japanese access to resources. See Alperovitz et al., *The Decision to Use the Bomb*, 336 (LeMay), 331, 720 (Halsey), plus the more general overview of military critics of the use of the bombs in ibid., 319–71. Many years later, LeMay told an interviewer that in June 1945 he had briefed the Joint Chiefs of Staff in Washington and told them his planners calculated they could force Japan to surrender by September. The presentation made no impression (in LeMay's recollection, "General Marshall slept through most of the briefing. I can't blame him; he was probably worn down to a nub"). In the same interview, he reiterated the argument that "the war was over before the atomic bomb was dropped," but at the same time said that, all things considered, "use of the atomic bomb was a wise decision"; Richard H. Kohn and Joseph P. Harahan, eds., *Strategic Air Warfare: An Interview with Generals Curtis E. LeMay, Leon W. Johnson, David A. Burchinal, and Jack J. Catton* (Office of Air Force History, United States Air Force, 1988), 63–65, 69–70. Halsey's notorious racism and "kill Japs" rhetoric is annotated in Dower, *War Without Mercy*, 36, 79, 85. For Eisenhower's often-quoted criticism, see his *Mandate for Change, 1953–1956: The White House Years* (Doubleday, 1963), 312–13. For Leahy, see *FRUS: Conference of Berlin*, vol. 1: 909; Leahy, *I Was There*, ch. 23, esp. 441.

97. The Jefferies Report, so called after its chairman Zay Jefferies, a distinguished metallurgist from General Electric, is excerpted as appendix R in Sherwin, *A World Destroyed*, 315–22; see also chapter 12 (note 176 in this book). There is a voluminous literature on apprehension concerning use of the bomb among scientists before as well as after Hiroshima. See especially Smith, *A Peril and a Hope*, esp. ch. 1 (3–72) on the war years. Most of this concern focused on early establishment of international controls to prevent a nuclear arms race, an issue to which Niels Bohr had devoted particular, and conspicuously vain, efforts in personal approaches to both Roosevelt and Churchill. The literature on Bohr's futile endeavors is a subject in itself. See, for good samples, Rhodes, *The Making of the Atomic Bomb*, 523–38, 620–21, 644–45, 782–88; Sherwin, *A World Destroyed*, ch. 4.

98. The Franck Report, dated June 11, 1945, is reprinted in full as an appendix in Smith, *A Peril and a Hope*, 371–83, and in slightly abridged form as appendix S in Sherwin, *A World Destroyed*, 323–33. It was declassified by the Department of War in 1946 and first made public in the May 1946 issue of the *Bulletin of Atomic Scientists*. The "rocket bomb" referred to the "V–2" missile the Germans deployed for several months beginning in November 1944, which killed over 3,000 civilians, mostly in England and Belgium.

99. Smith, *A Peril and a Hope*, 53–59; see also Alperovitz et al., *The Decision to Use the*

*Atomic Bomb*, 185–91. The poll, dated July 12, 1945, was first made public in the February 1948 issue of *Bulletin of the Atomic Scientists*. Smith's overall discussion is particularly helpful in profiling the scientists involved in these initiatives and spelling out their concerns. Like other commentators, she notes that the Chicago scientists had focused on theoretical problems and essentially completed their work well before the Trinity test, whereas Oppenheimer and his Los Alamos team were intensely involved right up to the last minute in making the bomb work. This helps explain why the most incisive wartime focus on the political implications of the new weapon emanated from Chicago rather than Los Alamos: participants there had more time to reflect on such matters. The presence in Chicago of esteemed scientists like Franck and Leo Szilard, who were keenly sensitive to moral and political issues—and less trusting of "statesmen" in Washington than Oppenheimer—also made a difference.

100. Sherwin, *A World Destroyed*, 301 (appendix L for Marshall on May 31) and 307–8 (appendix O for Bard); Herbert Feis, *The Atomic Bomb and the End of World War II* (Princeton University Press, 1966), 201. For a lengthy compilation of often-quoted U.S. military figures who criticized the use of the bombs, see Alperovitz et al., *The Decision to Use the Atomic Bomb*, 319–71.

101. Truman, *Memoirs*, 462; Churchill, *The Second World War*, 638–39. Churchill was well aware of the scientists' concerns about immediately addressing the political issue of postwar arms control, having had among other things an exceedingly abrasive personal meeting with Niels Bohr on the subject (see note 97 above). The official British history of these matters phrased the issue more carefully and accurately, noting that "whatever doubts there were among the British did not receive expression at the highest level"; Margaret Gowing, *Britain and Atomic Energy, 1939–1945* (Macmillan, 1964), 370–71. Of "thousands" of British documents studied, however, Gowing found "only two that express doubt whether an atomic bomb should be used" and contrasts this to debates on the U.S. side.

102. See appendix M in Sherwin, *A World Destroyed*, 304–5 (the June 16, 1945, minutes of the Science Panel). The many arguments marshaled in rejecting a prior "demonstration" of the new weapon are documented in various sources; see, for example, Feis, *The Atomic Bomb and the End of World War II*, 196–99; Gowing, *Britain and Atomic Energy*, 373; Rhodes, *The Making of the Atomic Bomb*, 647–48; Sherwin, *A World Destroyed*, 207–8; Bird and Sherwin, *American Prometheus*, 298–99; Alperovitz et al., *The Decision to Use the Bomb*, 163–64. The Trinity test itself tended to strengthen skepticism concerning the effectiveness of a demonstration in an unpopulated locale. What, after all, was really left after the test explosion to confirm the awful destructiveness of the new weapon? Little more than desert sand turned into glass. As Oppenheimer later put it, "We did not think exploding one of these things as a firecracker over a desert was likely to be very impressive. ... The destruction on the desert is zero"; United States Atomic Energy Commission, *In the Matter of J. Robert Oppenheimer: Transcript of Hearing before Personnel Security Board, Washington, D.C., April 12, 1954 through May 6, 1954* (Government Printing Office, 1954; reprinted by MIT Press, 1971), 34.

103. Alperovitz et al., *The Decision to Use the Atomic Bomb*, 243–47, 300–1. This is a major critical theme in the scholarship of Alperovitz, Martin Sherwin, Kai Bird, and other influential critics of the decision to use the bomb.

104. In addition to citations in note 94 above, see Grew's February 12, 1947, letter to Stimson excerpted in Barton J. Bernstein, ed., *The Atomic Bomb: The Critical Issues* (Little, Brown, 1976), 29–32.

105. *FRUS: Conference of Berlin*, vol. 1: 909.

106. *FRUS: Conference of Berlin*, vol. 1: 895–97 and, for Grew's brief rejoinder, 900–1.

107. See the discussion of "'Generalists' *Versus* 'Area Experts'" in chapter 15 of this book for the arguments of Grew and others that the Japanese were incapable of Western-style democracy. Grew's personal associations with, and knowledge of, "the Japanese" during his ten-year tenure as ambassador were almost exclusively focused on upper-class individuals, including intimates of the emperor such as the fervent loyalist Count Nobuaki Makino, who served at one point as lord keeper of the privy seal; Dower, *Empire and Aftermath*, 108–12. For the "Japan Crowd" and its political and ideological critics in and outside the State Department, see Howard B. Schonberger, *Aftermath of War: Americans and the Remaking of Japan, 1945–1952* (Kent State University Press, 1989), especially chapter 1 (on Grew) and chapter 3 (on T. A. Bisson). The critique of the Japan Crowd's soft line on the emperor and projected postwar policy toward Japan more generally reached the public at the time through small liberal and left-wing periodicals such as *Amerasia* and *Far Eastern Survey*. It was conveyed with particular scorn in a little book by Owen Lattimore, in which the well-known Asia expert belittled "the sacred cows of our cheaper Japan-expert Brahmins," and went on to declare that "Sacred Cow Number One, and in fact the cows to end all cows, is the Japanese Emperor" (cow number two was the moderates or "liberals" whom the Brahmins saw as a force for peace); *Solution in Asia* (Little, Brown, 1945), especially 29, 46, 187–91. Andrew Roth, a strong supporter of the China Crowd position, captured these arguments in a book published just after the surrender that came to be called "the Bible" among liberal reformers in early occupied Japan; see his *Dilemma in Japan* (Little, Brown, 1945), which includes a chapter on "The State Department and Japan's 'Old Gang,'" and another titled "Can We Do Business with Hirohito?" In addition to MacLeish and Acheson, influential State Department officials associated with the China Crowd position included Stanley Hornbeck and John Carter Vincent.

Cordell Hull, the former secretary of state under Roosevelt, devoted a chapter to "Unconditional Surrender" in his lengthy memoirs. Although sympathetic to arguments that letting the emperor retain some of his functions was desirable, he opposed the paragraph-twelve modification of the unconditional-surrender formula when Byrnes contacted him about this just before Potsdam, on the grounds that "the statement seemed too much like appeasement of Japan"; see *FRUS: Conference of Berlin*, vol. 2: 1267–69; Cordell Hull, *The Memoirs of Cordell Hull* (Macmillan, 1948), vol. 2, ch. 113, esp. 1591–94. Hull and other critics at the time were out of the loop where atomic-bomb policy was concerned, and it is unclear how much influence their thinking had on Byrnes, the new secretary of state, who is generally regarded as the decisive figure behind dropping the "constitutional monarchy" language in paragraph twelve. In postwar recollections, however, Byrnes spoke of knowing about "differences of opinion in the State Department as to whether, at the time of surrender, we should insist on the removal of the Emperor," and for all practical purposes, on this particular issue his opposition coincided with theirs; James F. Byrnes, *Speaking Frankly* (Harper & Brothers, 1947), 204.

108. Naotake Satō, the Japanese ambassador in Moscow, also belittled the vacuous nature of the message he was instructed to convey to the Soviet government as full of beautiful phrases but "remote from the facts and empty in content." The chances of the Soviet Union or other Allied powers taking this seriously, he told Foreign Minister Tōgō right away, was "next to nothing"; *FRUS: Conference of Berlin*, vol. 1: 877–83. When the Foreign Ministry persisted in insisting that Satō pursue these overtures to Moscow even after the Potsdam Declaration was issued on July 26, Satō was again unable to restrain his scorn. All these gestures, he cabled Tōgō, "will be futile, regardless of how we explain that our desire to ter-minate the miserable war is in accordance with the will of our gracious Emperor and that Stalin will be called the advocate of world peace, etc." He audaciously told his superior that "I see a serious discrepancy between your views and the actual state of affairs"; ibid., vol. 2: 1296–97. The ineptitude and vacillation of the emperor even at this crucial juncture is addressed in Herbert Bix, "Japan's Delayed Surrender: A Reinterpretation," *Diplomatic History*, vol. 19, no. 2 (Spring 1995), 197–225, and, slightly revised, in Bix's *Hirohito and the Making of Modern Japan*, ch. 13 (487–530). See also Tsuyoshi Hasegawa, *Racing the Enemy: Stalin, Truman, and the Surrender of Japan* (Harvard University Press, 2005), esp. 106–10, where Hasegawa describes the overtures to Moscow as "wasting precious time by conducting inept diplomacy," a reflection of "the fantasy world in which the Japanese government was living," a "dismal failure," and a "pipedream."

109. I have noted the persistence of wartime demands for the "complete and perma-nent" disarmament of Germany and Japan in "Occupied Japan and the Cold War in Asia," in Dower, *Japan in War and Peace*, 164–65 (esp. n. 10). As early as the Cairo Declaration of December 1, 1943, the leaders of the United States, Great Britain, and unoccupied China made clear that Japan would be stripped of its colonies and "expelled from all other territories which she has taken by violence and greed," with its sovereignty confined primarily to the four main islands of the homeland; *FRUS: Conference of Berlin*, vol. 1: 926.

110. Truman, *Memoirs*, 472–76, 481, 484, 503–4; *Public Papers of the Presidents of the United States: Harry S. Truman, 1945*, 216–18; Butow, *Japan's Decision to Surrender*, 241–50 (for documents pertaining to Japan's capitulation). See also chapter 13 in the present book on the Byrnes Note.

111. I address the "imperial democracy" of the occupation period at length in *Embrac-ing Defeat*, ch. 9 through 11 (277–345), and the new constitution in chapter 12 and 13 (346–404). On the initial reformist agenda imposed by MacArthur, which went considerably beyond what even the stern Potsdam Declaration had intimated, see ibid., ch. 2 (65–84). The occupation of Japan is addressed in Part III of the pres-ent book, and contrasted to the U.S. occupation of Iraq that followed the 2003 invasion.

112. *FRUS: Conference of Berlin*, vol. 1: 905, 930 (June 1945 evaluation); Truman, *Mem-oirs*, vol. 1: 458 (on "casually" informing Stalin of a new weapon). On April 13, 1941, Japan and the Soviet Union signed a neutrality pact pledging nonaggression against one another for five years; on April 5, 1944, the Soviet Union announced it would not renew this when it expired. This was an augury of things to come, but

the Soviet declaration of war against Japan on August 8, 1945, was nonetheless a violation of the pact.

113. The breadth and intensity of this anticommunist, anti-Soviet counterintelligence was vividly revealed to the public in the 1954 Atomic Energy Commission inquiry into the loyalty and trustworthiness of Oppenheimer, who was subsequently denied his security clearance. Although the rationale for this inquisition dealt at length with Oppenheimer's postwar opinions concerning nuclear issues such as development of a thermonuclear (hydrogen) bomb, large portions of the hearings addressed his activities, political concerns, and personal acquaintances as a so-called fellow traveler beginning in the mid-1930s. See *In the Matter of J. Robert Oppenheimer*; also Groves, *Now It Can Be Told*, esp. ch. 10. Kai Bird and Martin Sherwin address this at length in their prize-winning *American Prometheus*.

114. Yonai is quoted at greater length by Bix in "Japan's Delayed Surrender," 217–18, and in *Hirohito and the Making of Modern Japan* (HarperCollins, 2000), 509–10. For Konoe, see Hasegawa, *Racing the Enemy*, 198.

115. Alperovitz et al., *The Decision to Use the Atomic Bomb*, 418 (the decoded August 12 cable); Hasegawa, *Racing the Enemy*, 3, 5, 198–99, 295–98. For a contrary argument by a Japanese scholar, emphasizing the impact of the bombs, see Sadao Asada, "The Shocks of the Atomic Bomb and Japan's Decision to Surrender: A Reconsideration," *Pacific Historical Review*, vol. 67, no. 4 (1998). Hasegawa rejects this argument and exchanged letters with Asada in "Tsuyoshi Hasegawa vs. Sadao Asada: Debating Hiroshima," *Journal of Strategic Studies*, vol. 29, no. 3 (June 2006), 565–69.

116. The argument that the Soviet declaration of war *rather than* the atomic bombs was decisive in prompting Japan's capitulation actually found almost immediate expression in U.S. circles. On August 15, 1945, for example, the *New York Times* ran an article on Claire Chennault, the near-legendary leader of the U.S. "Flying Tigers" air squadron in China, under this two-tier headline: "Chennault Holds Soviet Forced End / Russia's Entry Decided War With Japan Despite Atomic Bomb, Air General Says." The lead paragraph read as follows: "Russia's entry into the Japanese war was the decisive factor in speeding its end and would have been so even if no atomic bombs had been dropped, is the opinion of Maj. Gen. Claire Chennault, who arrived [in Rome] today en route home via Germany." (Buried in the article was also a glancing reference to Chennault's position on the emperor, which would not have pleased Joseph Grew. "General Chennault," this paragraph read, "is unsympathetic with the Japanese royal house and feels that it might have been better if the situation had produced a popular uprising that would have eliminated it.")

117. P. M. S. Blackett, *Fear, War, and the Bomb: Military and Political Consequences of Atomic Energy* (Wittlesey House, McGraw-Hill, 1948), 139–40. The title of the book in Britain was *Military and Political Consequences of Nuclear Energy*. Blackett was extrapolating, among other postwar sources, from the information provided and conclusions reached by the U.S. Strategic Bombing Survey.

118. Atomic Energy Commission, *In the Matter of J. Robert Oppenheimer*, 561; see also Oppenheimer's coupling of war and postwar considerations in ibid., 34.

119. Truman, *Memoirs*, vol. 1: 87; appendix I in Sherwin, *A World Destroyed*, 291–92, for Stimson's report. The so-called revisionist scholarship on these matters was lifted

to a new level of documentary support and public attention with the publication of Gar Alperovitz's *Atomic Diplomacy: Hiroshima and Potsdam*, originally published in 1965 and issued in a new edition two decades later (Penguin, 1985). Martin Sherwin, Kai Bird, Richard Rhodes, Barton Bernstein, Tsuyoshi Hasegawa, and others have likewise documented the linkage between the bombs and Soviet policy in persuasive detail. For the fiftieth anniversary of the bombings in 1995, Alperovitz and several collaborators reassembled and reappraised the available documentation in the almost encyclopedic *The Decision to Use the Atomic Bomb*.

120. Rotblat recalled Groves's comment in a 1989 interview with Martin Sherwin; see Bird and Sherwin, *American Prometheus*, 284–85. Dismayed by the redefined purpose of the new weapon, Rotblat resigned from the Manhattan Project in December 1944, one of the very few scientists to act decisively in this manner, and devoted himself to promoting nuclear disarmament after the war. He received the Nobel Peace Prize in 1995 for his efforts in the cause of nuclear disarmament as secretary general of the Pugwash Conferences on Science and World Affairs. For Groves, see Atomic Energy Commission, *In the Matter of J. Robert Oppenheimer*, 173; the comment was made in the context of delineating the vigilant anticommunist counterintelligence surveillance conducted against participants in the Manhattan Project. See also Groves's memoir *Now It Can Be Told*, 132, 141.

121. Spencer R. Weart and Gertrud Weiss Szilard, eds., *Leonard Szilard: His Version of the Facts* (MIT Press, 1978), 184; James F. Byrnes, *All in One Lifetime* (Harper, 1958), 284. See also Rhodes, *The Making of the Atomic Bomb*, 636–38; Smith, *A Peril and a Hope*, 29–30. From the outset of the Manhattan Project, scientists suspected of being soft on the Soviet Union were followed, taped, and in all other possible ways closely scrutinized by counterintelligence agents reporting to Groves. In addition to the 1954 Atomic Energy Commission hearings on Oppenheimer, see Bird and Sherwin, *American Prometheus*. Szilard and his colleagues were typically shadowed by agents on this futile visit to Byrnes.

122. Stimson diary entries for May 14, 15, 16 and June 6, 1945; accessible at "Hiroshima: Henry Stimson's Diary and Papers" at doug-long.com/stimson. James Conant, president of Harvard and a member of the Interim Committee, introduced the notion of U.S. possession of the new weapon as a "bargaining chip" in future arms control negotiations with the Russians as early as 1944; Sherwin, *A World Destroyed*, xxiii.

123. Truman, *Memoirs*, vol. 1: 295, 454–55, 469, 475–76, 501.

124. Byrnes, *Speaking Frankly*, 208; Gregg Herken, *The Winning Weapon: The Atomic Bomb in the Cold War, 1945–1950* (Vintage, 1982), 44 (quoting the journal of Walter Brown for July 24).

125. Morison, *Turmoil and Tradition*, 615–16; Groves, *Now It Can Be Told*, 135; Sherwin, *A World Destroyed*, 138, 199–200; Thomas and Witts, *Enola Gay*, 90–92. In his last meeting with Roosevelt on March 15, 1945, Stimson discussed a memo the president had sent him from a "distinguished public servant . . . who had been alarmed at the rumors of extravagance in the Manhattan project" and was fearful that it would turn out to "be a lemon." Stimson told him things were proceeding well, but there were matters concerning "future control after the war" that had to be resolved "before the first projectile is used"; Stimson and Bundy, *On Active Service in Peace and War*, 615–16.

126. Weart and Szilard, *Leonard Szilard*, 184. See also Sherwin, *A World Destroyed*, 138, 330 (in appendix S, the Franck Report). Herbert Feis quotes a wartime adviser to the under secretary of war who visited Oak Ridge and dryly assured his superior that "you have really nothing to worry about. If the project succeeds, no one will investigate what was done, and if it does not succeed, every one will investigate nothing else the rest of your life"; *The Atomic Bomb and the End of World War II*, 198. Two billion dollars in 1945 was the equivalent of over twenty billion dollars in 2008.

127. Blackett, *Fear, War, and the Bomb*, 138.

128. The diary of Walter Brown, Byrnes's associate, is included in the James F. Byrnes Papers at the University of South Carolina; see the fuller citation in Wilson D. Miscamble, *From Roosevelt to Truman: Potsdam, Hiroshima, and the Cold War* (Cambridge University Press, 2007), 232. In the June 29 *Washington Post* poll on the emperor, the remaining 23 percent of responses was identified as "Miscellaneous and no opinion"; see also George H. Gallup, *The Gallup Public Opinion, 1935–1971* (Random House, 1972), vol. 1: 488–89.

## CHAPTER 11: SWEETNESS, BEAUTY, AND IDEALISTIC ANNIHILATION

129. Rhodes, *The Making of the Atomic Bomb*, 734.

130. Joseph Rotblat, "Leaving the Bomb Project," *Bulletin of the Atomic Scientists*, vol. 41, no. 7 (August 1985), 18.

131. Kenneth D. Campbell, "Sweetness, Shame of the A-Bomb," *MIT Tech Talk*, October 2, 1991 (quoting from a lecture by Weisskopf at MIT). Many scientists shared Weisskopf's belief that the Nagasaki bomb was unnecessary; see Smith, *A Peril and a Hope*, 78. For a similar argument by a Japanese scientist with inside connections at the time, see Taro Takemi, "Remembrances of the War and the Bomb," *Journal of the American Medical Association*, vol. 250, no. 5 (August 5, 1983), 618–19. Hans Bethe, who headed the theoretical physics unit at Los Alamos, expressed retrospective regret in terms similar to Weisskopf's. Asked how the scientists viewed "the moral or humane problems that many people have discerned in the atomic bomb program at Los Alamos," he replied as follows: "I am unhappy to report that during the war—at least—I did not pay much attention to this. We had a job to do and a very hard one. The first thing we wanted to do was get the job done. It seemed to us most important to contribute to victory in the way we could. Only when our labors were finally completed when the bomb dropped on Japan, only then or a little bit before then maybe, did we start thinking about the moral implications"; Atomic Energy Commission, *In the Matter of J. Robert Oppenheimer*, 326.

132. Teller and Tuck are quoted in Nuel Pharr Davis, *Lawrence and Oppenheimer* (Simon & Schuster, 1968), 177, 185–87; for Oppenheimer, see Atomic Energy Commission, *In the Matter of J. Robert Oppenheimer*, 14. Although the 1954 hearings on Oppenheimer's loyalty derived in considerable part from his initial opposition to a postwar crash program to develop the "dreadful" hydrogen bomb, at the same time he acknowledged that "it was a sweet and lovely and beautiful job," and "technically so sweet that you could not argue about that," and eventually went along with it; see ibid., 229, 251. General Groves's comment on these matters to the 1954

inquisitors was dry and almost droll. When the war ended, the academic scientists all "wanted out," he observed, "but after they had this extreme freedom for about 6 months, they all started to get itchy feet, and as you know almost every one of them has come back into Government research, because it was just too exciting, and I think still is exciting"; ibid., 178.

133. Atomic Energy Commission, *In the Matter of J. Robert Oppenheimer*, 13, 81.

134. Alice Kimball Smith and Charles Weiner, eds., *Robert Oppenheimer: Letters and Recollections* (Harvard University Press, 1980), 315–25, esp. 317.

135. The *High Noon* analogy was offered by I. I. Rabi in Jon Else's 1980 documentary film *The Day after Trinity*; also quoted in Rhodes, *The Making of the Atomic Bomb*, 676. For Fermi, see Robert Junck, *Brighter than a Thousand Suns*, 202. Fermi's jibes vis-à-vis his American colleagues cut two ways, for in 1943, in one of his first meetings with scientists at Los Alamos, he is quoted as having exclaimed to Oppenheimer, in what the latter described as a "surprised" voice, "I believe your people actually *want* to make a bomb"; Davis, *Lawrence and Oppenheimer*, 182.

136. Stimson Diary, April 6–11, 1945; June 6, 1945. One of the few issues on which Groves and Stimson disagreed was the inclusion of Kyoto on the initial list of projected bomb targets drawn up in April. Groves strongly supported this on the grounds that Kyoto, by far the most populous city on the list, "was large enough in area for us to gain complete knowledge of the effects of an atomic bomb. Hiroshima was not nearly so satisfactory in this respect." Stimson, who had visited the old capital before the war and been impressed with its cultural and historic significance, believed its destruction might backfire psychologically; see Groves, *Now It Can Be Told*, 273–76.

137. Truman, *Memoirs*, vol. 1: 460; Gowing, *Britain and Atomic Energy*, 367–68. The secondary literature on the Alsos operation to determine the extent of Germany's nuclear activities is extensive; Groves devotes several chapters to this in his recollections.

138. Richard G. Hewlett and Oscar E. Anderson Jr., *A History of the United States Atomic Energy Commission*, vol. 1: *The New World, 1939/1946* (Pennsylvania State University Press, 1962), 252–54; Sherwin, *A World Destroyed*, 209–10, 284 (appendix C for the September 18 Hyde Park *aide-mémoire*); Arjun Makhijani, "'Always' the Target?" *Bulletin of the Atomic Scientists*, vol. 51, no. 3 (May/June 1995), 23–27; Makhijani, "Nuclear Targeting: The First 60 Years," *Bulletin of the Atomic Scientists*, vol. 59, no. 3 (May/June 2003), 60–65. Sherwin also notes that a month after the May 1943 meeting, Vannevar Bush recorded that he and Roosevelt "spoke briefly of the possible use" of the bomb "against Japan, or the Japanese fleet," with Bush going on to note, somewhat ambiguously, that this reflected a shift in thinking from Germany to Japan. Sherwin offers the following additional factors as probably contributing to this shift of targets, clear by the spring of 1944: "(1) the war in Europe was expected to end first; (2) it was safer to assemble the bomb on a Pacific island than in England; (3) delivery against a target in a U.S. theater of war by a U.S. aircraft (B-29) emphasized 'American' primacy in this Anglo-American development."

139. Groves acknowledged that there was no concern whatsoever about a possible Japanese bomb, since it was clear the Japanese lacked the uranium or industrial capacity to produce a nuclear weapon; *Now It Can Be Told*, 187. Japan's desultory

wartime nuclear projects are examined in "'NI' and 'F': Japan's Wartime Atomic Bomb Research," in Dower, *Japan in War and Peace*, 55–100; also Walter F. Grunden, *Secret Weapons and World War II: Japan in the Shadow of Big Science* (University Press of Kansas, 2005), ch. 2 (48–82).

140. Agee, *Agee on Film*, 43–44; see also chapter 8 (note 25) above.

141. Morrison, *Hellbirds*, 146.

142. Stimson and Bundy, *On Active Service in War and Peace*, 613 (for the quotation here); Groves, *Now It Can Be Told*, 253, 265–66, and also 140 ("Our mission was to develop an atomic bomb of such power that it would bring the war to an end at the earliest possible date"). See also Groves's testimony in Atomic Energy Commission, *In the Matter of J. Robert Oppenheimer*, 163. George Kennan, the most articulate "realist" of the immediate postwar period, expressed the prevailing outlook involved here in the 1954 Oppenheimer hearings. Although speaking specifically about the hydrogen bomb (rather than the nuclear fission bomb of 1945), his observation amounted to a widely shared generality: "After all, we are dealing with weapons here, and when you are dealing with weapons you are dealing with things to kill people, and I don't think the considerations of morality are relevant"; Atomic Energy Commission, *In the Matter of J. Robert Oppenheimer*, 368.

143. Atomic Energy Commission, *In the Matter of J. Robert Oppenheimer*, 11, 31–33.

144. Arthur H. Compton, *Atomic Quest: A Personal Narrative* (Oxford University Press, 1956), 238; Groves, *Now It Can Be Told*, 253, 260, 279, 283; Atomic Energy Commission, *In the Matter of J. Robert Oppenheimer*, 773 (for Alvarez); Smith, *A Peril and a Hope*, 37, 63, 65.

145. Smith, *A Peril and a Hope*, 49; Gowing, *Britain and Atomic Energy*, 368–73. In his influential essay on the air war against Germany, W. G. Sebald cited estimates that England's bombing offensive "swallowed up" one-third of the nation's entire production of war matériel, and went on to observe that an enterprise of such "material and organizational dimensions . . . had such a momentum of its own that short-term corrections in course and restrictions were more or less ruled out, especially when, after three years of the intensive expansion of factories and production plants, that enterprise had reached the peak of its development—in other words, its maximum destructiveness." Many forces drove this momentum as Sebald saw it: economic imperatives, bolstering home-front morale, retribution, and "sympathy with the innermost principle of every war, which is to aim for as wholesale an annihilation of the enemy with his dwellings, his history, and his natural environment as can possibly be achieved"; *On the Natural History of Destruction*, 18–19; see also 65 on bombs being "expensive items" that couldn't be wasted.

146. Sherry, *The Rise of American Air Power*, esp. ch. 6 ("The Dynamics of Escalation"), 7 ("The Sociology of Air War"), 8 ("The Sources of Technological Fanaticism"), and 9 ("The Triumphs of Technological Fanaticism"); the workforce is noted on 190, and "laboratory in destruction" observation appears on 234–35.

147. In recounting his role in the development and use of the bombs, Groves consistently placed prime emphasis on his "compartmentalization rules"; see, for example, his *Now It Can Be Told*, 140; also testimony in Atomic Energy Commission, *In the Matter of J. Robert Oppenheimer*, 164, 175.

148. Teller's recollection is quoted in Smith, *A Peril and a Hope*, 56, from a 1962 pub-

lication by Teller. For the Oppenheimer quote, see Atomic Energy Commission, *In the Matter of J. Robert Oppenheimer*, 236. The 1954 Atomic Energy Commission hearings cast sharp light on bedrock principles and assumptions of patriotism and loyalty that predated the Cold War and onset of so-called McCarthyism. Any critical reflection, and certainly any expressed opinion, on "political, diplomatic and military considerations" or "strategic and tactical uses of weapons and all that" outside the technical mission of the scientists, for example, was deemed inappropriate and suspect; see, for example, ibid., 455, 958–60. Witnesses also were asked whether they would put "loyalty to your country" above "loyalty to a friend"; ibid., 624–25, 654.

149. Groves, *Now It Can Be Told*, 265, 271.

150. Morison, *Turmoil and Tradition*, 620–21. Writing before many official documents became declassified, Morison concluded that the major reason for using the bombs was "the closing of the Japanese war as an end in itself" (622). Based on his familiarity with Stimson's diaries and conversations with individuals close to these matters, he also made clear that he had found no evidence to support the argument that, despite all his agonizing, Stimson had real doubts about dropping the bomb (635).

151. Lincoln made these comments in a speech in the House of Representatives on January 12, 1848.

152. See Davis, *Lawrence and Oppenheimer*, 224–25, on the origin of the Trinity code name.

153. Sherry, *The Rise of American Air Power*, 195–96 (Bowles quotations).

154. Morison, *Hellbirds*, 126, 141.

155. Robert Guillain, *I Saw Tokyo Burning: An Eyewitness Narrative from Pearl Harbor to Hiroshima* (Doubleday, 1981; originally published in French), 181–82; Paul Abrahams, "Breathing Fire," *Financial Times*, March 4, 2000. For Tōmatsu and Takemitsu, see Dower, "Contested Ground: Shōmei Tōmatsu and the Search for Identity in Postwar Japan," in Rubinfein and Phillips, *Shomei Tomatsu*, 72–85. In the bigger picture, it can be argued that no one surpassed the Japanese when it came to aestheticizing war in the 1930s and early 1940s. This was true both literally (in graphic arts, films, popular music, and the like) and ideologically, as seen in the previously discussed "Imperial Way" indoctrination and the "socialization for death" that accompanied this. See, for example, Dower, "Japan's Beautiful Modern War," in the exhibition catalogue *Wearing Propaganda: Textiles on the Home Front in Japan, Britain, and the United States—1931–1945*, ed. by Jacqueline Atkins (Bard Graduate School and Yale University Press, 2005), 93–113.

156. Williamson Murray, *War in the Air, 1914–1945* (Smithsonian Books/HarperCollins, 2005; originally published in Great Britain in 1999), 73 (Tirpitz).

157. See appendix P in Sherwin, *A World Destroyed*, 312. For a more restrained firsthand description of the visual effects of the Trinity test by the British observer O. R. Frisch, one of the participants in the discovery of fission in 1938–39, see appendix 5 in Gowing, *Britain and Atomic Energy*, 441–42.

158. Laurence's August 9 report was published, among other newspapers, in the September 9, 1945, issue of the *New York Times*.

159. For quotations from the apocalyptic literature on future war with superweapons, see Franklin, *War Stars*, esp. 19, 32, 41, 76, 84. This fusion between the descriptive

language of science "fiction" and "reality" never disappeared. Thus, the obituary over six decades later of an airman who participated in both the Hiroshima and Nagasaki missions quotes him saying, of the former: "The top of that mushroom cloud was the most terrifying but also the most beautiful thing you've ever seen in your life. Every color in the rainbow seemed to be coming out of it"; "Charles Albury, 88, Co-Pilot of Nagasaki Bomber," *New York Times*, June 5, 2009.

160. On September 26, under the headline "Drama of the Atomic Bomb Found Climax in July 16 Test," the *New York Times* published Laurence's account of the Trinity test, at which he had again been the only journalistic observer. In this instance, he offered a remarkable, almost grotesquely anthropological picture of the ecstatic, primal, and tribal response to the spectacle of unprecedented man-made destructiveness among the scientists and other observers:

"The big boom came about 100 seconds after the Great Flash—the first cry of a new-born world. It brought the silent, motionless silhouettes to life, gave them a voice.

"A loud cry filled the air. The little groups that hitherto had stood rooted to the earth like desert plants broke into a dance, the rhythm of primitive man dancing at one of his fire festivals at the coming of spring.

"They clapped their hands as they leaped from the ground—earth-bound man symbolizing a new birth in freedom—the birth of a new force that for the first time gives man means to free himself from the gravitational pull of the earth that holds him down.

"The dance of the primitive man lasted but a few seconds, during which an evolutionary period of about 10,000 years had been telescoped. Primitive man was metamorphosed into modern man—shaking hands, slapping each other on the back, laughing like happy children."

For a critical analysis of Laurence's nuclear writings, and *New York Times* coverage of these matters more generally, see Beverly Ann Deepe Keever, *News Zero: 'The New York Times' and the Bomb* (Common Courage Press, 2004). In a 2004 online commentary titled "Hiroshima Cover-up: How the War Department's Timesman Won a Pulitzer," the journalists Amy Goodman and David Goodman called on the Pulitzer committee to retroactively rescind its award to Laurence; see commondreams.org for August 10, 2004.

161. Hadley Cantril and Mildred Strunk, *Public Opinion, 1935–1946* (Princeton University Press, 1951), 1067 (December 10, 1941 poll). These matters, including the differing attitudes towards the German and Japanese enemy, are treated in detail in Dower, *War Without Mercy*; see 53 for other polls. For the *Objective, Burma!* controversy, see Clayton R. Koppes and Gregory D. Black, *Hollywood Goes to War: How Politics, Profits and Propaganda Shaped World War II Movies* (University of California Press, 1988), 261–64. The internal memo (from Alvah Bessie to Jerry Wald) is reproduced in full in I. C. Jarvie, "Fanning the Flames: Anti-American Reaction to *Objective Burma* (1945)," *Historical Journal of Film, Radio, and Television*, vol. 1, no. 2 (1981), 117–37.

162. The lifting of censorship concerning Japanese atrocities is addressed in Dower, *War Without Mercy*; see esp. 41–57.

163. Groves, *Now It Can Be Told*, 324; *Public Papers of the Presidents of the United States: Harry S. Truman, 1945*, 212.

164. The full exchange between the general secretary of the Federal Council and Truman is reproduced online on the National Council of Churches USA website (ncccusa.org), under the heading "A moment in ecumenical history— August 1945: the churches and the bomb." For a subsequent (1946) public statement on "Atomic Warfare and the Christian Faith" by the Federal Council of Churches, see Bird and Lifschultz, *Hiroshima's Shadow*, 488–99. While public opinion supported using the bombs, early criticism by a range of prominent Americans (and others, like Albert Camus) is more widespread than usually remembered; for a good sampling, see "The First Critics" section in ibid., 237–311.

165. Craven and Cate, *The Army Air Forces in World War II*, vol. 5: 732–33 (this dry semiofficial source notes that "Arnold wanted as big a finale as possible," while General Carl Spaatz was hoping there would be time to drop a third atomic bomb); DeGroot, *The Bomb*, 102 (15,000 killed in raids after Nagasaki). Between August 8 and this "finale," fifteen U.S. bombing missions were conducted, without any losses; Kohn and Harahan, *Strategic Air Warfare*, 70.

166. "The Tokyo Express: A Life Photographer Takes a Ride to Hiroshima on Japan's Best Train," *Life*, October 8, 1945, 27–36. The same issue also included a photograph of a burned woman tending a male casualty with the caption "Atomic bomb victims in Hiroshima, suffering from burns and fractures, are cared for in filthy, fly-filled bank building. Instead of doctors, young, untrained Japanese girls dressed wounds." Not mentioned, even in the accompanying article, was that most doctors and nurses had been killed, and most hospitals and medical supplies destroyed. The often-cited poll on use of the bomb appeared in "The Fortune Survey," *Fortune*, December 1945, 305. Of the respondents, 53.5 percent agreed, "We should have used the two bombs on cities, just as we did"; only 4.5 percent believed, "We should not have used any atomic bombs at all"; 13.8 percent endorsed, "We should have dropped one first on some unpopulated region, to show the Japanese its power, and dropped the second one on a city only if they hadn't surrendered after the first one." The exact percentage supporting using more bombs before the Japanese had a chance to surrender was 22.7. This near-genocidal sense of revenge was not peculiar to Americans vis-à-vis the Japanese. Freeman Dyson recalled talking to the "well-educated and intelligent" wife of a British officer after the Dresden bombing, and asking if she believed it was right to kill German women and babies in large numbers at that late stage in the war. "Oh yes," she replied. "It is good to kill the babies especially. I am not thinking of this war but of the next one, 20 years from now. The next time the Germans start a war and we have to fight them, those babies will be the soldiers"; "A Failure of Intelligence," 71.

167. Henry A. Wallace, *The Price of Vision: The Diary of Henry A. Wallace, 1942–1946*, ed. by John M. Blum (Houghton Mifflin, 1973), 473–74. For other suggestions of the complexity of Truman's thinking on these matters (as opposed to the untroubled and unrepentant public image he cultivated and his admirers have usually cherished), see Gar Alperovitz's interesting essay "The Truman Show," *Los Angeles Times Book Review*, August 9, 1998.

168. Quoted in Rhodes, *The Making of the Atomic Bomb*, 697; see also Sherwin, *A World Destroyed*, 217–18 and, for the Science Panel, appendix M (304–5).

169. Compton, *Atomic Quest*, 236; Sherwin, *A World Destroyed*, 200 (Stimson's quotation about Conant). See also Smith, *A Peril and a Hope*, 46.

170. Blackett, *Fear, War, and the Bomb*, 139.

171. To a degree they would have been loath to acknowledge, these drop-the-bomb idealists, just like William Laurence of the *Times*, were channeling ideas with firm roots in pulp fiction tracing back to the turn of the century, where apocalyptic visions of "aerial warfare" were presented as a utopian "war for peace" and prelude to universal disarmament. H. G. Welles's 1914 novel *The World Set Free*, for example, envisioned atomic bombs that "continue to explode" and made destruction "so facile that any little body of malcontents could use it." War, in Welles's prophecy, "was becoming impossible," and leaders now had no choice but to secure the world "universally from any fresh outbreak of atomic destruction, and . . . ensure a permanent and universal pacification." After World War I, the inventor Thomas Edison contributed to these scenarios with a 1921 essay titled "How to Make War Impossible" that envisioned intensive military exploitation of scientific progress (including "atomic energy") and urged all governments to "produce instruments of death so terrible that presently all men and every nation would well know that war would mean the end of civilization." For an engrossing overview of this literature, see Franklin, *War Stars*, esp. 32–33, 41–44, 75–76; he devotes a full chapter to Edison.

Old-fashioned poetry also reinforced the utopian vision, particularly Tennyson's famous (and, read critically, racist and misogynist) "Locksley Hall," published in 1842. Both Truman and Churchill expressed deep attraction to Tennyson's vision of "a ghastly dew" of bombs raining down "from the nations' airy navies grappling in the central blue" that becomes prelude to when "the war drum throbb'd no longer, and the battle-flags were furl'd / In the Parliament of man, the Federation of the world." Ever since he was in his mid-twenties, Truman had carried a copy of the key lines in his wallet, frequently quoting them in inaugural meetings that culminated in the creation of the United Nations in 1945; he even pulled the well-creased paper from his wallet and read the pertinent lines to a White House correspondent en route to Potsdam; A. Merriman Smith, *Thank You, Mr. President: A White House Notebook* (Harper and Brothers, 1946), 286. Churchill called these verses "the most wonderful of modern prophecies"; quoted in Arthur Schlesinger Jr., "Bye, Bye, Woodrow," *Wall Street Journal*, October 27, 1993. Witting or not, Oppenheimer was evoking the same terrible/useful coupling Tennyson had fantasized about a century earlier when, in a "farewell" speech to the newly formed Association of Los Alamos Scientists on November 2, 1945, he famously described the new world of nuclear weapons as "not only a great peril, but a great hope"; see Smith and Weiner, *Robert Oppenheimer*, 315–25, esp. 319. This resonance between the fantasizing of earlier generations of writers of science fiction and the supposedly deep thinking of the wise men who rationalized idealistic annihilation in 1945 is analogous to the kinship between the speeches that accompanied the bloody turn-of-the-century takeover of the Philippines and the idealistic language White House speechmakers used to support the war of choice against Iraq. What passes as heavy-duty original thinking turns out to be in good part popular boilerplate.

172. *Bulletin of the Atomic Scientists of Chicago*, vol. 1, no. 1 (December 10, 1945), 1; the

journal dropped "of Chicago" from its name shortly afterwards. This dramatic reconstruction of Pearl Harbor as a cautionary symbol for the nuclear age had already been articulated in the Franck Report of June 1945.

## CHAPTER 12: NEW EVILS IN THE WORLD, 1945/2001

173. Averill A. Liebow, "Encounter with Disaster—A Medical Diary of Hiroshima, 1945," *Yale Journal of Biology and Medicine*, vol. 38 (October 1965), 61–239; the quote appears on 64. This entire issue is devoted to Liebow's annotated diary.

174. Bird and Sherwin, *American Prometheus*, 290 (for Oppenheimer; see also 323, where Oppenheimer refers to the bomb after the war as an "evil thing"); *Public Papers of the Presidents of the United States: Harry S. Truman, 1945*, 223, 255.

175. Liebow, "Encounter with Disaster," 237–39. Dr. Liebow's concluding reflections read in full as follows: "The use of this weapon as we contemplated it, and then more when we saw its effects, and then even as we wrote of it, filled us with revulsion. We acquired a sympathy, not for those on the periphery who acquired a Prometheus complex and cried *mea culpa* as a means of proclaiming their own importance, but for the physicists who bore the real responsibility for the development of the atomic bomb and who suffered genuine torment of conscience. Were we, even in the aftermath, accessories to a crime against mankind? Surely death and injury of innocents is wickedness that can never be condoned. But even killing by hand, in combat, while honoring the traditions of 'chivalry' is still murder. The crime is of the same kind. Chivalry was crushed and burned when the first unseeing stones and firebrands were hurled. It had died centuries before Hiroshima. We thought also of the 15,000 hospital beds in the Marianas now never to be used, and of the hundreds of thousands of lives, American and Japanese, that would have been the cost of assault and conquest of the home islands of Japan. Had more been spared than were lost and maimed in the two cities? But why could not an atomic explosion near, but not upon, a living city, have been as persuasive? Even if it was 'necessary' to destroy one city, how could one justify the devastation of another? We could only hope that reasons based on morality as well as strategy dictated the decisions.

"When we saw the pitifully crippled and maimed we felt both guilt and shame. But was the absence of resentfulness [on the Japanese side] the stoicism of a brave and disciplined people or was this also some reflection of guilt on their own part? Perhaps there was an element of both. . . .

"When on September 6, 1946, the completed report of some 1,300 pages, bound in six substantial volumes, was handed to Col. Ash, there ended a still vivid chapter. But while the chapter came to an end we were left with the uneasy feeling that the book remains unfinished—and it continues as a haunting memory. May the evil of which it tells never come back!"

176. Sherwin, *A World Destroyed*, appendix R (Jefferies Report), 316. The report is discussed in chapter 10 (note 97) of the present book.

177. Vera Brittain, *Seed of Chaos: What Mass Bombing Really Means* (published in London for the Bombing Restriction Committee by New Vision Publishing, April 1944); the American version of this booklet, published by the pacifist Fellowship of Reconciliation, was titled *Massacre by Bombing: The Facts behind the British-*

*American Attack on Germany.* The second quotation Brittain used in introducing her book was a biblical query from Jeremiah 6:15: "Were they ashamed when they had committed abomination?" The response to Brittain included criticism by George Orwell in England, defense of the bombing policy by President Roosevelt, and generally adverse letters to the *New York Times*, which ran a story on the booklet. For responses, see Sherry, *The Rise of American Air Power*, 138–43; Crane, *Bombs, Cities, and Civilians*, 28–31.

178. Merle Miller, *Plain Speaking: An Oral Biography of Harry S. Truman* (Berkley, 1973), 248. Miller concluded that Truman's "private library at the Truman Memorial Library" contained "every book ever published on the Bomb." Truman had underlined this passage, the last line twice. (I have followed here the *Hamlet* text as it appears in the Clarendon Press edition of Shakespeare's complete works. Miller's transcription differs slightly editorially.)

179. Peter Baker, "Bush Tells Group He Sees a 'Third Awakening,'" *Washington Post*, September 13, 2006. In U.S. history, the First Great Awakening refers to a wave of Christian fervor in the colonies from around 1730 to 1760, and a Second Great Awakening is said to have occurred in the early decades of the nineteenth century. For a sample of journalistic commentary on the administration's good/evil dichotomy at the time of the fifth anniversary of 9-11, see "In the World of Good and Evil," *Economist*, September 16, 2006.

180. The careful evocation of the "wonder-working power" hymn in the State of the Union address is discussed in an online report of a conversation between CBS correspondent Lesley Stahl and David Kuo, an evangelical Christian who worked in the White House as a speechwriter but eventually resigned after concluding that the Republican slogan "compassionate conservatism" was mere rhetoric; "A Loss of Faith," CBSNews.com, October 15, 2006. The full lyrics are available online.

181. "The World Islamic Front," February 23, 1998, in bin Laden, *Messages to the World*, 58–62; "To Our Brothers in Pakistan," September 24, 2001, in ibid., 100–2; "The Winds of Faith," October 7, 2001 (or earlier), ibid., 103–5. Bin Laden continued to hammer the thesis of a righteous balance of terror in the weeks and months that followed; see, for example, "Terror for Terror," October 21, 2001 (106–29), and "Crusader Wars," November 3, 2001 (133–38).

182. "Terror for Terror," October 21, 2001, in bin Laden, *Messages to the World*, 121.

183. Japanese venerated the dead; placed flowers, rice, cigarettes, rice wine (saké), and other plain offerings by their graves or memorial tablets; even welcomed them back on the annual midsummer Ōbon or "All Souls Day" celebrations. For scattered examples of appeals to the divine by Japanese military men at the time of the Pearl Harbor attack, see Donald M. Goldstein and Katherine V. Dillon, eds., *The Pearl Harbor Papers: Inside Japanese Plans* (Brassey's, 2000), 195, 207, 215, 256–57; Gordon W. Prange, *At Dawn We Slept: The Untold Story of Pearl Harbor* (McGraw-Hill, 1981), 325, 345. Military hardliners who deemed it essential to attack the United States as soon as possible similarly responded to the so-called Hull Note of late November 1941, interpreted as an unacceptable ultimatum, as *tenyū*, or a godsend; Yomiuri Shimbun, *Who Was Responsible? From Marco Polo Bridge to Pearl Harbor*, ed. James E. Auer (Yomiuri Shimbun, 2006), 119.

184. On the intellectual and ideological underpinnings of anti-Western thought, see Cemil Aydin, *Politics of Anti-Westernism in Asia: Visions of World Order in Pan-*

*Islamic and Pan-Asian Thought* (Columbia University Press, 2007); Ian Buruma and Avishi Margalit, *Occidentalism: The West in the Eyes of Its Enemies* (Penguin, 2004); Tetsuo Najita and H. D. Harootunian, "Japanese Revolt against the West: Political and Cultural Criticism in the Twentieth Century," in Peter Duus, ed., *The Cambridge History of Japan*, vol. 6: *The Twentieth Century* (Cambridge University Press, 1988), 711–74. Accessible primary sources on the Islamist side include bin Laden's *Messages to the World*; Sayyid Qutb's enormously influential *Milestones*, originally published in 1964 and cited in note 193 of this chapter; and the voluminous online Muslim and Islamist literature on jihad and terror. Many Japanese primary materials are available in translation, including the following particularly valuable sources: Wm. Theodore de Bary, Carol Gluck, and Arthur Tiedemann, eds., *Sources of Japanese Tradition*, vol. 2: *1600–2000* (Columbia University Press, 2005), esp. sections on "Nationalism and Pan-Asianism" (789–820), "The Rise of Revolutionary Nationalism" (948–79), and "Empire and War" (980–1017); John Owen Gauntlett, transl. and Robert King Hall, ed., *Kokutai no Hongi: Cardinal Principles of the National Entity of Japan* (Harvard University Press, 1949); Robert King Hall, *Shūshin: The Ethics of a Defeated Nation* (Columbia University Press, 1949); "The Way of the Subject" (*Shimin no Michi*), included as an appendix in Otto Tolischus, *Tokyo Record* (Reynal & Hitchcock, 1943), 405–27; Joyce C. Lebra, ed., *Japan's Greater East Asia Co-Prosperity Sphere in World War II: Selected Readings and Documents* (Oxford University Press, 1975). For the exploitation of Shinto and Buddhism by Japanese ideologues and militarists, see D. C. Holtom, *Modern Japan and Shinto Nationalism* (University of Chicago Press, 1943); James W. Heisig and John C. Maraldo, eds., *Rude Awakenings: Zen, the Kyoto School and the Question of Nationalism* (University of Hawaii Press, 1994); Brian Victoria, *Zen at War* (Weatherhill, 1997). The basic source on Japanese anti-Semitism is David Goodman and Masanori Miyazawa, *Jews in the Japanese Mind: The History and Uses of a Cultural Stereotype* (Free Press, 1994). Donald Keene addresses Japanese writers and the war in several essays rich with quotations: "Japanese Writers and the Greater East Asia War," *Journal of Asian Studies*, vol. 23, no. 2 (1964), 209–25; "Japanese Literature and Politics in the 1930s," *Journal of Japanese Studies*, vol. 2, no. 2 (1976), 225–48; "The Barren Years: Japanese War Literature," *Monumenta Nipponica*, vol. 33, no. 1 (1978), 67–112; and "War Literature," in his book *Dawn to the West: Japanese Literature of the Modern Era* (Holt, Reinhart and Winston, 1984), 906–61. I analyze and quote at some length an internal Japanese wartime document titled "Global Policy with the Yamato Race as Nucleus," in *War Without Mercy*, ch. 10 (262–90).

185. The most focused analysis of socialization for death in imperial Japan is Kazuko Tsurumi, *Social Change and the Individual: Japan before and after Defeat in World War II* (Princeton University Press, 1970); see esp. chapter 2 ("The Army: The Emperor System in Microcosm") and chapter 3 ("Socialization for Death: Moral Education at School and in the Army"). Translations of the diaries and intimate last writings of kamikaze pilots and other young Japanese who died in the war include Nihon Senbotsu Gakusei Kinenkai, comp., *Listen to the Voices of the Sea (Kike Wadatsumi no Koe)*, transl. by Midori Yamanouchi and Joseph L. Quinn (University of Scranton Press, 2000); Hagoromo Society of Kamikaze Divine Thunderbolt Corps Survivors, ed., *Born to Die: The Cherry Blossom Squadrons* (Ohara,

1973); Emiko Ohnuki-Tierney, transl., *How Lonely Is the Sound of the Clock: Diaries of Japanese Soldiers in the Special Attack Force* (University of Chicago Press, 2006). Recollections by kamikaze who survived the war, or individuals intimately knowledgeable about them, include Yasuo Kuwahara and Gordon T. Allred, *Kamikaze* (Ballantine, 1957); Ryuji Nagatsuka, *I Was a Kamikaze* (Macmillan, 1974); Rikihei Inoguchi, Tadashi Nakajima, and Roger Pineau, *The Divine Wind: Japan's Kamikaze Forces in World War II* (Ballantine, 1958); essays by Rikihei Inoguchi and Tadashi Nakajima, Kennosuke Torisu and Masataka Chihara, Toshiyuki Yokoi, and Mitsuru Yoshida in David C. Evans, ed., *The Japanese Navy in World War II: In the Words of Former Japanese Naval Officers* (Naval Institute Press, 1969; second edition, 1986); Hatsuo Naito, *Thunder Gods* (Kodansha International, 1989); Yutaka Yokota with Joseph D. Harrington, *Kamikaze Submarine* (Leisure Books, 1962); and interviews in chapter 15 of Haruko Taya Cook and Theodore F. Cook, eds., *Japan at War: An Oral History* (New Press, 1992). For secondary sources, see Ivan Morris's excellent essay "If Only We Might Fall," in his *The Nobility of Failure: Tragic Heroes in the History of Japan* (New American Library, 1975), 276–334, 438–62; Denis Warner and Peggy Warner, with Commander Sadao Seno, *The Sacred Warriors: Japan's Suicide Legions* (Avon, 1984); Peter Hill, "Kamikaze, 1943–5," in Diego Gambetta, ed., *Making Sense of Suicide Missions* (Oxford University Press, 2005), 1–41; Richard O'Neill, *Suicide Squads: Axis and Allied Special Attack Weapons of World War II—Their Development and Their Missions* (Ballantine, 1981); Morison, *History of United States Naval Operations in World War II*, vol. 14; ch. 12 in Frank, *Downfall*. Emiko Ohnuki-Tierney brings the insights of symbolic anthropology to the subject in *Kamikaze, Cherry Blossoms, and Nationalisms: The Militarization of Aesthetics in Japanese History* (University of Chicago Press, 2002); see especially ch. 5. Professor Ohnuki-Tierney dwells at length on the ideologies of *pro patria mori* ("to die for the country," from Homer) and *pro rege et patria mori* (to die for sovereign and country), and the distinction between the patriotism of the former, which drove many of the highly educated pilots she studies, and cruder expressions of political nationalism.

186. My translation. *The Most Beautiful* is one of the earliest films directed by Kurosawa, and remains one of his least known and one of the very few never made easily accessible on video to foreign audiences—obviously because of its propagandistic nature. Donald Ritchie discusses *The Most Beautiful* in his invaluable guide *The Films of Akira Kurosawa* (University of California Press, 1984), 26–29. Kurosawa himself reflects fondly on it in his *Akira Kurosawa: Something Like an Autobiography* (Vintage, 1983), where he goes so far as to call it "not a major picture, but . . . the one dearest to me"; 132–35.

187. Insightful sources on terrorism and socialization for death that can be set against the Japanese experience to draw out similarities and differences include Louise Richardson, *What Terrorists Want: Understanding the Enemy, Containing the Threat* (Random House, 2006), and Jessica Stern, *Terror in the Name of God: Why Religious Militants Kill* (HarperCollins, 2003). For an often-cited study of terrorist suicide bombing that emphasizes defense of native land over religion, see Robert A. Pape, *Dying to Win: The Strategic Logic of Suicide Terrorism* (Random House, 2005); based largely on case studies through 2001, this appeared in an earlier, influential incarnation as "The Strategic Logic of Suicide Terrorism," *American Political Science*

*Review*, vol. 97, no. 3 (August 2003). See also Gambetta, *Making Sense of Suicide Missions*, especially essays by Gambetta and Luca Ricolfi. One of the provocative points of comparison between Japanese and Islamist suicide missions is that, in both cases, the number of incidents and "martyrdoms," and even immediate enemy casualties, is remarkably small compared to the panic produced among the targeted enemy.

188. In her excellent study, Louise Richardson explicitly defines terror as "the act of substate groups, not states," but acknowledges that this is controversial and accepts the argument that operations such as the Allied bombing campaign in World War II and the atomic bombings of Hiroshima and Nagasaki were "the moral equivalent of terrorism"; *What Terrorists Want*, 5. Her focus is understandable. The psychology, legitimizing language, and moral (or immoral) equivalence of state and substate terror are congruent on a great many points that invite closer comparative study, however, and many of the arguments Richardson advances in her overview of substate terrorism also help illuminate the holy war of imperial Japan as well as the Allied air war against Germany and Japan. "Revenge," for example, is one of the "three R's" of individual terrorist motivation she examines (along with renown and reaction); see, for example, ibid., 41–45, 88–94, 100. This congruence is not just a modern or postmodern issue. After the hypocrisy and double standards of the war on terror became obvious, the following lines by a pirate in Augustine's early fifth-century *City of God* became widely quoted online and in antiwar circles: "Because I do it with one small ship, I am called a terrorist. You do it with a whole fleet and are called an empire."

189. Numerous firsthand accounts testify to the psychological effectiveness of the kamikaze attacks. In a roundtable discussion in the 1980s, for instance, a high U.S. air force officer recalled how "one admiral said, 'Twenty-four more hours of this, and I quit.' He threatened to pull out of the Okinawa operation because of the kamikazes. That was why we had to attack the airfields on a daily basis"; Kohn and Harahan, *Strategic Air Warfare*, 49–50.

190. When Vice President Cheney told a television audience five days after September 11 that operations on "the dark side" were inevitable, what this meant in practice went beyond the clandestine operations most viewers and listeners imagined. This set the stage for systematic torture and other abuses of prisoners, a policy and practice exposed well before the Bush administration ended and illuminated in greater detail when hitherto secret documents were released under the succeeding administration. Mark Danner and Jane Mayer, among many other critics, have examined these transgressions extensively and incisively. See, for example, Danner's *Torture and Truth: America, Abu Ghraib, and the War on Terror* (New York Review of Books, 2004), his interview with Tom Engelhardt in Englehardt's *Mission Unaccomplished: Tomdispatch Interviews with American Iconoclasts and Dissenters* (Nation Books, 2006), and his numerous articles; Mayer's *The Dark Side: The Inside Story of How the War on Terror Turned into a War on American Ideals* (Doubleday, 2008), as well as subsequent reportage; Steven Strasser, ed., *The Abu Ghraib Investigations: The Official Reports of the Independent Panel and the Pentagon on the Shocking Prisoner Abuse in Iraq* (PublicAffairs, 2004); and Richard Falk, Irene Gendzier, and Robert Jay Lifton, eds., *Crimes of War: Iraq* (Nation Books, 2006).

191. Rimington's interview with Decca Aitkenhead appeared in the *Guardian*, October

18, 2008. For Macdonald's address, see "CPS Lecture—Coming Out of the Shadows," October 20, 2008, placed online by the Crown Prosecution Service at cps. gov.uk.

192. Abu Bakr Naji, *The Management of Savagery: The Most Critical Stage through Which the Umma Will Pass*, translated by William McCants for the John M. Olin Institute for Strategic Studies at Harvard University, May 2006. The original paper was published online in 2004, and the translation made available online, among other sites, through the Combating Terrorism Center at West Point (ctc.usma. edu), with which McCants is associated. For discussions, see Stephen Ulph, "New Online Book Lays Out Al-Qaeda's Military Strategy," *Terrorism Focus*, vol. 2, no. 6 (March 17, 2005); Jarret M. Brachman and William F. McCants, "Stealing Al-Qa'ida's Playbook," *CTC (Combating Terrorism Center) Report*, February 2006; William F. McCants, "Terror's Playbook," *New York Daily News*, July 29, 2006. "Abu Bakr Naji" publishes in an Al Qaeda online journal, and McCants has suggested that the name may actually be a collective pseudonym. For a sobering analysis that places *The Management of Savagery* in a broader overview of jihadi strategic thinking after 9-11, see Lawrence Wright, "The Master Plan," *New Yorker*, September 11, 2006.

193. Sayyid Qutb, *Milestones* (Cedar Rapids, Iowa: The Mother Mosque Foundation, n.d.). The vocabulary of "evil" emerges particularly strongly in chapter 10; for quotations cited here, see especially 9-11, 73, 129, 138-39. See also Paul Berman, "The Philosopher of Islamic Terror," *New York Times*, March 23, 2003. Berman, who supported the invasion of Iraq and published this lucid critical essay as it was being initiated, lavishes considerable praise on the seriousness and forcefulness of Qutb's writings, particularly prior to the more simplistic *Milestones*, even while finding them ultimately pathological and totalitarian. His argument is that this was indeed a serious war of ideas—and neither President Bush and his advisers nor the liberal community were facing it seriously. While Berman calls Qutb Al Qaeda's Karl Marx, other critics argue that *Milestones* amounted to the *Mein Kampf* of the Islamists' holy war; Jonathan Raban, "Truly, Madly, Deeply Devout," *Guardian*, March 2, 2002.

194. Nasir bin Hamid al-Fahd, *A Treatise on the Legal Status of Using Weapons of Mass Destruction against Infidels*, posted at jihadspin.com in May 2003. See also Michael Scheuer, *Imperial Hubris: Why the West Is Losing the War on Terror* (Potomac Books, 2004), 154-56. I have not attempted to reconcile al-Faud's references to the Qur'an with other translations, which give slightly different verse numbers. Al-Fahd was arrested by Saudi authorities shortly afterwards. The "blessed Tuesday" euphemism appears in an earlier extended rationalization by Ramzi bin al-Shibh, one of the planners of the September 11 attacks, who included a "Ruling on the Killing of Women and Children of the Non-Believers" in an extended message titled "The Truth about the New Crusade" that was found on the hard drive of a computer abandoned when Al Qaeda leaders fled Kabul with the routed Taliban after the U.S. invasion of Afghanistan. See Alan Cullison, "Inside Al Qaeda's Hard Drive," *Atlantic Monthly*, September 2004; Cullison quotes this message at length.

195. "Terror for Terror," October 21, 2001, in bin Laden, *Messages to the World*, 106-29, esp. 124-25.

196. Somewhat unexpectedly, I found myself exploring this at length in a study of defeated Japan; see chapter 5 (168–200), titled "Bridges of Language," in *Embracing Defeat*.

## Part III: Wars and Occupations

### CHAPTER 13: OCCUPIED JAPAN AND OCCUPIED IRAQ

1. I address Yoshida's career in several places: *Empire and Aftermath: Yoshida Shigeru and the Japanese Experience, 1876–1954* (Council on East Asian Studies, Harvard, 1988); "Yoshida in the Scales of History," in John W. Dower, *Japan in War and Peace: Selected Essays* (New Press, 1993), ch. 6 (208–41); and the "Yoshida Shigeru" entry in *Kodansha Encyclopedia of Japan* (Kodansha, 1983), vol. 8: 343–45. For his observation that "history provides examples of winning by diplomacy after losing in war," see *Empire and Aftermath*, 312.

2. Ali Allawi, *The Occupation of Iraq: Winning the War, Losing the Peace* (Yale University Press, 2007); Allawi's speech was sponsored by the Carnegie Council on April 11, 2007.

3. An incisive report based on a December 2002 workshop at the Army War College warned that "the possibility of the United States winning the war and losing the peace is real and serious"; see Conrad C. Crane and W. Andrew Terrill, *Reconstructing Iraq: Insights, Challenges, and Missions for Military Forces in a Post-Conflict Scenario* (Strategic Studies Institute, United States Army War College, February 2003), 42. A study cosponsored by the Council on Foreign Relations around the same time similarly stated in its opening paragraph that, "put simply, the United States may lose the peace, even if it wins the war"; Edward P. Djerejan and Frank G. Wisner, co-chairs, *Guiding Principles for U.S. Post-Conflict Policy in Iraq: Report of an Independent Working Group Co-sponsored by the Council on Foreign Relations and the James A. Baker III Institute for Public Policy of Rice University* (January 2003), 1. An "action memo" titled "Maintaining Public Order during Combat Operations in Iraq" submitted to Central Command (CENTCOM) by the Pentagon early in February likewise emphasized that the dangers of post-combat disorder were so great that the United States could "win the war but lose the peace"; Douglas J. Feith, *War and Decision: Inside the Pentagon at the Dawn of the War on Terrorism* (Harper, 2008), 364. Although not stated explicitly, this same perception animates another think-tank study initiated shortly before the invasion and finalized several months after; see James Dobbins et al., *America's Role in Nation-Building: From Germany to Iraq* (RAND, 2003), which presents case studies of Germany, Japan, Somalia, Haiti, Bosnia, Kosovo, and Afghanistan.

4. The CIA actually prepared a report titled *The Postwar Occupations of Germany and Japan: Implications for Iraq* as early as August 2002; see the brief summary on pages 102–3 in appendix C of the Senate's *Report of the Select Committee on Intelligence on Prewar Intelligence Assessments about Postwar Iraq*, May 25, 2007 (accessible online at intelligence.senate.gov/prewar). The first White House evocation of Japan and Germany as models for a possible occupation of Iraq occurred on October 10, 2002; see David E. Sanger and Eric Schmitt, "U.S. Has a Plan to Occupy

Iraq, Officials Report," *New York Times*, October 11, 2002. This led to a flurry of media reports in which spokesmen and officials were quoted as saying that the administration was still hoping there would be no war, but should it come to that there were "lots of different models from history that one can look at," including Japan and Germany (as Secretary of State Powell put it on National Public Radio on October 11). In an August 2007 speech to a Veterans of Foreign Wars audience, President Bush drew on an unnamed scholar of occupied Japan in attacking those who doubted that democracy was possible in Iraq; as it happens, I was the academic, and when contacted took public issue with the spin. See, for example, "Historian: Bush Use of Quote 'Perverse,'" politico.com, August 23, 2007.

5. "Convergence of a sort" between the occupations of Japan and Iraq is addressed in chapters 14 and 15 in this book.

6. The Japanese government did send some of its "self-defense forces" to assist in Afghanistan and Iraq, but their missions were constricted.

7. The late literary and social critic Jun Etō, who committed suicide in 1999, was particularly influential in displacing what postwar leftist scholars had effectively characterized as the "dark valley" of Japan's "fifteen-year war" (1931–45) with the argument that the truly dark period of modern Japanese history was the loss of sovereignty that followed the war and lasted from 1945 to 1952.

8. For an analysis by an astute longtime observer conversant with internal Japanese debates, see Gavan McCormack, *Client State: Japan in the American Embrace* (Verso, 2007).

9. I contributed to this in a very small way with two preinvasion articles: "Lessons from Japan about War's Aftermath," *New York Times*, October 27, 2002; also "A Warning from History: Why Iraq Is Not Japan," *Boston Review*, February 2003, 6–8. A version of the latter piece in the original question-and-answer form appeared as *JPRI Occasional Paper No. 30* (Japan Policy Research Institute, April 2003). See also Dower, "The Other Japanese Occupation," *Nation*, July 7, 2003 (11–14), which suggests that Japan's occupation of Manchuria and the right-wing radicalism behind this would be a better analogy to the U.S. occupation of Iraq. As the discussion that follows in this chapter indicates, however, more interesting in retrospect than such easily ignored criticism by outsiders is the fact that a great many civilian and military intelligence personnel were producing detailed internal reports that also pointed out the unique and formidable challenges Iraq posed—similarly, to no avail whatsoever.

10. For a detailed account of the closing stages of the war, compiled largely from records of the Japanese Demobilization Bureau, see *Reports of General MacArthur*, vol. 2, part 2: *Japanese Operations in the Southwest Pacific Area* (Government Printing Office, 1966), especially chapters 20 and 21, "Decision to Surrender" and "The Return to Peace." The quotations cited here appear on 728 and 743.

11. *Reports of General Macarthur*, vol. 2: 2; the quotations appear on 754 and 755.

12. The discrepancy between preinvasion government arguments justifying invasion and post-invasion U.S. intelligence findings is laid out in almost point-by-point detail in the lengthy report of the Select Committee on Intelligence, U.S. Senate, *Report on Whether Public Statements Regarding Iraq by U.S. Government Officials Were Substantiated by Intelligence Information, Together with Additional and Minority Views*, June 2008. The committee majority concluded that "the Administration's

public statements were *NOT supported by the intelligence*" on such critical issues as close relations between Iraq and Al Qaeda, Saddam's readiness to provide weapons of mass destruction to terrorists, statements by the president and vice president regarding the postwar situation in Iraq, intelligence uncertainties concerning Iraq's chemical weapons production, etc.

13. I have summarized these and other "transwar" legacies in "The Useful War" in Dower, *Japan in War and Peace*, ch. 1 (9–32).

14. The lawyer and scholar Noah Feldman, who worked on constitutional revision under the Coalition Provisional Authority following the invasion, called attention to the absence of meaningful civil society in Iraq in his *What We Owe Iraq: War and the Ethics of Nation Building* (Princeton University Press, 2004), 71–82.

15. Yoshida's lament is quoted at greater length in Dower, *Empire and Aftermath*, 313.

16. On the atrocities that accompanied the Allied victory in Europe, see Giles Mac-Donogh, *After the Reich: The Brutal History of the Allied Occupation* (Basic Books, 2007).

17. The best detailed analysis of occupation policies and practices is Eiji Takemae, *Inside GHQ: The Allied Occupation of Japan and Its Legacy* (Althone Press, 2002). I also have addressed the subject at length from various perspectives; see *Empire and Aftermath*; also *Embracing Defeat: Japan in the Wake of World War II* (Norton and New Press, 1999). All three of these books are densely annotated and rely heavily on Japanese as well as English-language resources. In 1949, MacArthur's command authored and edited a remarkable, massive two-volume publication of narrative and documents that remains basic to research on the occupation: *Political Reorientation of Japan: September 1945 to September 1948: Report of Government Section, Supreme Commander for the Allied Powers* (Government Printing Office, 1949).

18. Takemae, *Inside GHQ*; chapter 5 is especially good on pre-surrender preparations; see 206–9 for the schools, handbooks, and guides.

19. See the discussion of the Byrnes Note in chapter 10 in this book. Volume 2 of *Political Reorientation of Japan* is the most convenient source for U.S. documents pertinent to occupation policy. See 423–24 for the August 29 "Initial Post-Surrender Policy" stance on the emperor; also 427 for the September 6 clarification of MacArthur's authority as Supreme Commander for the Allied Powers, which reemphasized unconditional surrender and the absence of restrictions on MacArthur's authority.

20. The earliest drafts of this basic document traced back to 1944, with the final "SWNCC" revision approved on August 31 (as SWNCC 150/4). Truman's formal approval came on September 6. MacArthur was subsequently guided more closely by a more detailed version of the basic post-surrender policy by the Joint Chiefs of Staff dated November 3 (JCS 1380/15), which was not declassified until November 1948. See Edwin M. Martin, *The Allied Occupation of Japan* (American Institute of Pacific Relations, 1948), which includes the basic JCS text as an appendix.

21. T. A. Bisson, *Prospects for Democracy in Japan* (Macmillan, 1949); Robert B. Textor, *Failure in Japan: With Keystones for a Positive Policy* (John Day, 1951).

22. Popular American images of defeated Japan and the Japanese are addressed by Naoko Shibusawa in *America's Geisha Ally: Reimagining the Japanese Enemy* (Harvard University Press, 2006). For Hoberecht, see "Japanese Best-Seller: A

U.S. War Correspondent Tickles the Oriental Fancy with a Tale of Interracial Romance," *Life*, April 7, 1947 (107–11); "Nipponese Best-Seller," *Time*, October 28, 1946; "Earnest Hoberecht, Popular Novelist in Occupied Japan, Is Dead at 81," *New York Times*, September 26, 1999. For letters to MacArthur, see Rinjiro Sodei, *Dear General MacArthur: Letters from the Japanese during the American Occupation* (Rowman & Littlefield, 2001). My own book *Embracing Defeat* focuses on the Japanese side of the occupation, especially at the popular and grassroots levels.

23. See Dower, *Embracing Defeat*, for photographs (the revised edition of the Japanese translation of this book also contains photo-essays in each chapter that do not appear in the English edition). The centrality of "women and children" in U.S. images of occupied Japan is discussed in Shibusawa, *America's Geisha Ally*, ch. 1. The RAND study published at the time of the Iraq invasion notes that, of its seven case studies of U.S.-led occupations, there were "no postconflict combat deaths" in Japan, Germany, Bosnia, and Kosovo; Dobbins et al., *America's Role in Nation-Building*, 153.

24. The first IED—the "improvised explosive devices" which soon became the signature weapon of an insurgency that destroyed all early hopes for stability—appears to have been set off on March 29, 2003, a week before coalition forces entered Baghdad; *Washington Post National Weekly Edition*, October 8–14, 2007.

25. L. Paul Bremer III, *My Year in Iraq: The Struggle to Build a Future of Hope* (Threshold Editions, 2006), 24–25; see also Feith, *War and Decision*, 347–50.

26. Bob Woodward, *State of Denial: Bush at War, Part III* (Simon & Schuster, 2006), 112–13, 124–26 (ORHA and the rock drill); Office of Reconstruction and Humanitarian Assistance, "Inter-Agency Rehearsal and Planning Conference," February 21–22, 2003, on the Douglas Feith website waranddecision.com (for the bullet-point agenda prepared on February 20); Michael R. Gordon and General Bernard E. Trainor, *Cobra II: The Inside Story of the Invasion and Occupation of Iraq* (Pantheon, 2006), 145–46 (the Doha report). Jay Garner later noted in passing that his ORHA team concluded they would have to rely on twenty of Iraq's ministries to set the country back on its feet, but looters destroyed seventeen ministry buildings; edited online transcript of an August 11, 2006, interview on PBS television's *Frontline* (posted as "The Last Year in Iraq" at pbs.org/wgbh on October 17, 2006).

27. The document, dated September 26, 2002, is reproduced in full (but without case-study appendices) in Richard Haass, *War of Necessity, War of Choice: A Memoir of Two Iraq Wars* (Simon & Schuster, 2009), 279–93, and discussed on 226–28.

28. The Future of Iraq Project was placed online by the National Security Archive at George Washington University (gwu.edu/~nsarchiv/) in September 2006; see especially the September 1 posting titled "New State Department Releases on the 'Future of Iraq' Project" and the PowerPoint "Overview" summary. For a 102-page report by the "Conference of the Iraqi Opposition" working under the auspices of this project, see "Final Report on the Transition to Democracy in Iraq" (November 2002) on the Feith website waranddecision.com. See also James Fallows, "Blind into Baghdad," *Atlantic Monthly*, January–February 2004; Packer, *The Assassins' Gate: America in Iraq* (Farrar, Straus & Giroux). For dismissals of the value of the project, see Feith, *War and Decision*, 375–78; Bremer, *My Year in Iraq*, 25. The Future of Iraq Project had detractors even within the State Department.

In his memoir, Richard Haass, then head of the Policy Planning Staff, writes that "the reality was considerably less than the hype. These reports were long in detail but for the most part lacked practicality or relevance in the field. They were not taken seriously (for good reason I thought) by planners in the Defense Department"; *War of Necessity, War of Choice*, 257.

29. Feith, generally a great admirer of Rumsfeld, describes this "toxic" episode in *War and Decision*, 385–89. The Garner quotation and ORHA acronym joke appear in Rajiv Chandrasekaran's lively *Imperial Life in the Emerald City: Inside Iraq's Green Zone* (Knopf, 2006), 30, 52.

30. For Shinseki, see Eric Schmitt, "Pentagon Contradicts General on Iraq Occupation Force Size," *New York Times*, February 28, 2003; also the online transcript of the PBS *Frontline* documentary "Rumsfeld's War" (posted October 26, 2004, at pbs.org/wgbh). For the RAND study, see Bremer, *My Year in Iraq*, 8–12; Dobbins et al., *America's Role in Nation-Building*.

31. I am taking issue with Feith here, who in his memoir and public presentations argues vehemently that there *was* a plan. Feith himself, however, also emphasizes the failure of top leaders, especially Rice, to resolve antagonistic positions.

32. Gordon and Trainor, *Cobra II*, 142 (Rice); Feith, *War and Decision*, 142, 149, 393–94 (small footprint and Afghanistan); Office of Reconstruction and Humanitarian Assistance, "Inter-Agency Rehearsal and Planning Conference," February 21–22, 2003, on the Feith website waranddecision.com.

33. Gordon and Trainor, *Cobra II*, 152 (Hughes); Thomas F. Ricks, *Fiasco: The American Military Adventure in Iraq* (Penguin, 2006), 109–10 (Kellogg); "Turf Wars and the Future of Iraq," online transcript of a PBS *Frontline* broadcast on October 9, 2003, at pbs.org/wgbh (Walker); Feldman, *What We Owe Iraq*, 32. George Packer put it bluntly in *The Assassins' Gate*: "There was no Plan B" (118). Ricks comes to the same conclusion that Pentagon planners "never actually produced a usable blueprint for running postwar Iraq" (*Fiasco*, 80); and again: "There was no discussion of a fallback plan" (162).

34. Noah Feldman interview with Bradford Plumer on *Mother Jones* online (motherjones.com), posted January 16, 2005.

35. Robin Wright, "From the Desk of Donald Rumsfeld," *Washington Post National Weekly Edition*, November 5–11, 2007; Feith, *War and Decision*, 57–58; see also 110–15 on Rumsfeld's style.

36. The "Iraqi Interim Authority" plan is basic to Feith's strenuous argument that "the common accusation that the Administration neglected to conduct postwar planning for Iraq is wrong," and he dwells on this at length in *War and Decision*. See especially 275, 401–13, 423–24, 435–41, 549–51 (plus other Index references); also the three short documents on the "IIA" in the book's complementary website, waranddecision.com. Feith summarizes his arguments concisely in "War and Decision: Inside the Pentagon at the Dawn of the War on Terrorism," a book launch at the Center for Strategic and International Studies on April 24, 2008 (available in video at csis.org and transcript at waranddecision.com). Even by Feith's own account, however, it is difficult to take this exceedingly wishful "plan" seriously; and he himself regrets that few at top levels really did either. At the heart of the issue was fierce controversy over the role to be played by the Iraqi "externals" in any U.S.-led transitional government—the Pentagon being

strongly in support of this, while the State Department argued that such a transitional government would not have "legitimacy" in the eyes of most Iraqis. Posthostilities planning foundered on this.

37. Feith, *War and Decision*, 277–79, 283–86, 605. A slightly redacted version of the CIA report, titled "National Intelligence Council: Principal Challenges in Post-Saddam Iraq" and dated January 2003, is reprinted as appendix B (pages 52–91) in *Report of the Select Committee on Intelligence on Prewar Intelligence Assessments about Postwar Iraq*; the quotation appears on page 10 of this report (61 on the digitized text).

38. Feith, *War and Decision*, 285; see also 278, 409–10, 453. The largely ignored ORHA report of February also spoke at various points of undertakings that—even assuming stability—would require major U.S. input for a year or more; "Inter-agency Rehearsal and Planning Conference."

39. Leslie H. Gelb, *Power Rules: How Common Sense Can Rescue American Foreign Policy* (HarperCollins, 2009), 237–39; George Packer re-created this episode earlier in his *Assassins' Gate*, 111–12. The Council on Foreign Relations subsequently published two preinvasion reports on Iraq: *Guiding Principles for U.S. Post-Conflict Policy in Iraq* (January 1, 2003) and *Iraq: The Day After* (March 12, 2003). The first of these in particular endorses the basic objective of upholding "fundamental human rights and free-market economics" in Iraq, but advances a number of commonsense arguments that the administration failed to heed. These include the "need to pivot quickly from combat to peacekeeping operations in order to prevent post-conflict Iraq from descending into anarchy"; the importance of letting the Iraqis themselves run the country, and making clear "that the United States has no desire to become the de facto ruler of Iraq"; emphasis on a strong, short-term international and UN role in administering the invaded country, with U.S. influence "best played in the background"; resisting the temptation to promote "exiled Iraqi leaders" in any interim provisional government; and so on. This report also emphasized that "the continued public discussion of a U.S. military government along the lines of postwar Japan or Germany is unhelpful."

40. Rumsfeld's "Beyond Nation Building" speech was posted online by the Department of Defense at defense.gov/speeches. On another preinvasion occasion, Rumsfeld similarly declared, contrary to all that followed, that Iraq's future government "is not for the United States, indeed not even for the United Nations to prescribe. It will be something that's distinctively Iraqi"; quoted in the Council on Foreign Relations report *Guiding Principles for U.S. Post-Conflict Policy in Iraq*, 4. Afghanistan was the favorite example of a "light footprint" in the Pentagon, and Feith repeatedly cites this precedent—both the negative example of the Soviet experience and positive example of the post–9-11 U.S. incursion—in arguing that nation building was "bad baggage"; *War and Decision*, 76, 89, 101–2, 134, 139, 145, 149. This reflected the sanguine appraisal of post-Taliban developments that prevailed in the White House and Pentagon at the time of the Iraq invasion, albeit not necessarily elsewhere in the bureaucracy; see, for example, Haass, *War of Necessity, War of Choice*, 196–201, on reservations in the State Department. By the time the Bush administration approached its end in 2008, this too was widely recognized to be delusory. The Taliban was on the rise again, and publications like the *Washington Post* were referring to the mistaken decision "to eschew 'nation

building' and rely on Afghan warlords to keep order in the hinterlands"; *Washington Post National Weekly Edition*, August 18–24, 2008, in a book review of Ahmed Rashid, *Descent into Chaos: The U.S. and the Failure of Nation Building in Pakistan, Afghanistan, and Central Asia* (Viking, 2008).

41. See the National Security Archive online postings (at gwu.edu/~nsarchive/) of "Future of Iraq Project" documents, especially that of September 1, 2006, titled "New State Department Releases on the 'Future of Iraq' Project." Gordon and Trainor highlight this hostility to nation building as one of the Bush administration's "five grievous errors" in the epilogue to their *Cobra II*; see esp. 503–4.

42. For Bremer interview, see "The Lost Year in Iraq," an October 17, 2006, *Frontline* broadcast posted at pbs.org/wgbh; see also Bremer, *My Year in Iraq*, 7–13, 117. Even as his disastrous year exercising "viceregal responsibilities" was drawing to a close amidst mounting violence and insurrection, Bremer notes that Bush was particularly emphatic on the importance of having an Iraqi leader "who's willing to stand up and thank the American people for their sacrifice in liberating Iraq"; ibid., 359.

43. Bremer, *My Year in Iraq*, 19–20.

44. Bremer, *My Year in Iraq*, 114–19.

45. Bremer, *My Year in Iraq*, 13, 36–37.

46. Bremer, *My Year in Iraq*, 37.

## CHAPTER 14: CONVERGENCE OF A SORT: LAW, JUSTICE, AND TRANSGRESSION

47. Department of Defense, *The National Defense Strategy of the United States of America* (March 2005), 2, 5.

48. Jack Goldsmith devotes considerable attention to the conservative position on "lawfare," as well as his own disenchantment with the basic legal opinions used to legitimize torture, in his memoir *The Terror Presidency: Law and Judgment inside the Bush Administration* (Norton, 2007). See esp. 53–70 (on lawfare), 85–89 (on "unitary executive" thinking), and 10, 141–51 (his legal critique of the original basic opinions governing interrogation). For a detailed summary of Goldsmith's arguments, see Jeffrey Rosen, "Conscience of a Conservative," *New York Times*, September 9, 2007.

49. Richard A. Clarke, *Against All Enemies: Inside America's War on Terror* (Free Press, 2004), 24. The published and online literature on legal issues including the invasion and occupation of Iraq is vast. For assessments by a number of legal scholars, both supporting and criticizing the Bush administration, see *Future Implications of the Iraq Conflict: Selections from the "American Journal of International Law"* (American Society of International Law, January 2004). This focuses on the legality of the use of force in Iraq and subsequent occupation measures, and includes appendices of pertinent UN Security Council resolutions. Of particular interest pertaining to the legal status of the occupation are David J. Scheffer, "Beyond Occupation Law," 130–48; also the opening section of Eyal Benvenisti, "Water Conflicts during the Occupation of Iraq," 148–52. For a semiofficial British analysis including the UN's critical Resolution 1483, see Paul Bowers, "Iraq: Law of Occupation" (International Affairs and Defense Section, House of Com-

mons Library, Research Paper 03/51, June 2, 2003). See also Center for Economic and Social Rights, *Beyond Torture: U.S. Violation of Occupation Law in Iraq*. Initially posted online at cesr.org around July 2004, following termination of the Coalition Provisional Authority, this itemizes the various categories in international law that critics accuse the administration of violating and includes many crosslinks. A later short categorical itemization of violations was submitted to the UN Security Council on May 19, 2006, under the title "NGO Letter to the Security Council on Iraq."

50. Pitman B. Potter, "Legal Basis and Character of Military Occupation in Germany and Japan," *American Journal of International Law*, vol. 43, no. 2 (April 1949), 323–25; Eyal Benvenisti, *The International Law of Occupation* (Princeton University Press, 1993), 59–63, 91–96 (the quotation appears on 91).

51. The most extended study of legal aspects of the occupation of Japan is Nisuke Ando, *Surrender, Occupation, and Private Property in International Law: An Evaluation of US Practice in Japan* (Clarendon Press, 1991), which concludes that given the peculiar conditions created by unconditional surrender, as formulated in the Potsdam Declaration and Instrument of Surrender, the economic losses incurred under both the *zaibatsu* liquidation policies and land reform were in fact not illegal, whereas the nonpayment of pensions amounted to an abuse of the power of the occupant; see esp. 111–15. Ando's often turgid analysis notes the significant ways in which the occupation of Germany differed from that of Japan (there was no existing government when Germany surrendered, and the victors ruled directly through military governance). He suggests that there was a vaguely contractual dimension to the Japanese surrender—which an intact Japanese government agreed to in signing the Instrument of Surrender (which reiterated the terms of the Potsdam Declaration); that this presumed the continuity of the Japanese government; that at the same time this also permitted the United States to undertake measures that transgressed the Hague Regulations on occupation; and that, in practice, the Japanese government was left with very little authority indeed. This is a difficult book to parse, but see some of the more general statements on 81, 101–2, 108, 123–24.

52. *Political Reorientation of Japan*, vol. 1: 88–89.

53. Ando, *Surrender, Occupation, and Private Property in International Law*, 31 (the December public-relations release); *Political Reorientation of Japan*, vol. 2: 427. This was stated as follows earlier in a policy paper submitted to Secretary of War Stimson by the State Department weeks before the war ended: "By the instrument of unconditional surrender the emperor of Japan renounces his power and authority and the supreme allied commander acquires supreme legislative, judicial and executive authority"; U.S. Department of State, *Foreign Relations of the United States, 1945*, vol. 6: *The British Commonwealth, the Far East*, 560. Hereafter, this basic series of official State Department documents is cited as *FRUS*.

54. Benvenisti, "Water Conflicts," 149 (initial denial of military occupation). Resolution 1483 is reproduced, among many other places, in *Future Implications of the Iraq Conflict*.

55. Benvenisti, "Water Conflicts," 149, 152; Scheffer, "Beyond Occupation Law," esp. 135n for the precise Hague and Geneva "instruments" applicable to Iraq, and 142–44 for the itemized "liability trap." See also Scheffer's abbreviated presenta-

tion of his critique in "A Legal Minefield for Iraq's Occupiers," *Financial Times*, July 24, 2003.

56. Bremer, *My Year in Iraq*, 158.

57. The U.S.-led prosecution at the Class A Tokyo trials also excluded one of the most heinous of high-level Japanese war crimes: the lethal "Unit 731" medical experiments involving some three thousand prisoners in Manchuria. These crimes were suppressed, and the known criminals granted exemption from prosecution, in exchange for sharing their scientific findings with U.S. military researchers. For an annotated treatment of this and other aspects of these trials, see Dower, *Embracing Defeat*, ch. 15 ("Victor's Justice, Loser's Justice"), 443–84. The most interesting departure from the "victor's justice" aspect of the war-crimes prosecutions of Japanese was probably the trial of Lieutenant General Tasuku Okada in the subsidiary "Class B and C" tribunals held in Yokohama. Okada was accused of summarily executing thirty-eight American aircrew who bailed out and were captured after air raids against Nagoya in the closing months of the war. He did not contest the charges, but on the contrary argued that the airmen were not prisoners of war as defined in the Geneva Conventions but rather war criminals who violated international law by bombing noncombatants. Okada, supported by his U.S. defense attorney, Joseph Featherstone, adopted this defense—and argued that the executions of the airmen were his responsibility, and his alone—knowing that this meant his certain conviction. He wished to make a sustained case against indiscriminate air war; and the unusual aspect of the Yokohama proceedings was that both the prosecution and the bench allowed him to do so. A surprising level of mutual respect was generated in the course of Okada's trial, and after the death sentence was passed, both the chief prosecutor and the U.S. officers who sat in judgment recommended clemency, which General MacArthur rejected. Okada himself praised the fairness of the proceedings. The eminent writer Shōhei Ōoka later devoted a nonfiction book to the Okada trial, and a well-received movie based on Ōoka's book and titled *Best Wishes for Tomorrow*—which opens with the image of Picasso's *Guernica* and scenes from Japanese air strikes in China, as well as the Luftwaffe's bombing of London and the British RAF air war in Europe—was released in Japan in 2008. See, for example, Roger Pulvers, "A New Movie about WWII Japanese Asks Where the War-Crimes Buck Stops," *Japan Times*, May 20, 2007; Norio Murio, "Japanese Film a Poetic Look at a WWII War Crime Trial," *Stars and Stripes*, March 9, 2008. The Okada trial was the exception that proved the rule. More generally, where one's own side may have committed like crimes, a study of post–World War II war-crimes trials published by the U.S. Army notes that "no nation is going to charge its own citizen with the commission of a war crime for obvious political reasons"; Major William H. Parks, "Command Responsibility for War Crimes," *Military Law Review*, vol. 62 (Headquarters, Department of the Army: Fall 1973; also issued as Department of the Army Pamphlet 27–100–6), 100.

58. A truly serious and thoroughgoing prosecution of Saddam Hussein and his Iraqi confederates for crimes committed over the long course of his brutal Baathist regime—aimed, as both Nuremberg and the Tokyo tribunal were, at establishing a massive documentary record of the transgressions of the accused regimes—would have given defense attorneys the opportunity to document the early support of Saddam by the United States and other major powers, their role in building up

his war machine, their assistance to Iraq in its war with Iran from 1980 to 1988, and the tacit support of the United States (including from later key members of the George W. Bush administration such as Rumsfeld) in suppressing vigorous international denunciation of atrocities such as the later-notorious gassing of the Iraqi Kurdish town of Halabja in 1988.

59. B. V. A. Röling and Antonio Cassese, *The Tokyo Trial and Beyond* (Polity Press, 1993), 80 (MacArthur), 85 (Willoughby). The war-crimes trials of the Japanese, and the issue of war guilt more generally, are addressed in Dower, *Embracing Defeat*, ch. 15 and 16; see 451–54 for Allied criticisms of the Tokyo tribunal at the time. The most extended point-by-point critique of the majority "Judgment of the International Military Tribunal for the Far East" is the dissenting opinion by the Indian justice Radhabinod Pal. The best-known scholarly criticism is Richard Minear's *Victors' Justice: The Tokyo War Crimes Trial* (Princeton University Press, 1971); for a succinct critical summary by Minear, see his entry on "War Crimes Trials" in *Kodansha Encyclopedia of Japan*, vol. 8: 223–25. For another concise, critical overview, see Stephen Large, "Far East War Crimes Trials" in I. C. B. Dear and M. R. D. Foot, eds., *The Oxford Companion to World War II* (Oxford University Press, 1995), 347–51. The "conspiracy" premise, which was the key to the indictment of Class A leaders at the Tokyo tribunal, is also the premise of a mock war-crimes trial of President Bush and his top aides offered by a former U.S. prosecutor in 2006—the conspiracy in this case being to defraud the American public with knowingly false arguments concerning the necessity of preemptive war against Iraq; see Elizabeth de la Vega, *United States v. George W. Bush et al.* (Seven Stories Press, 2006).

60. For an incisive study that devotes critical attention to the Yamashita case, see Parks, "Command Responsibility for War Crimes," 1–104. Later thoughtful appraisals include Richard L. Lael, *The Yamashita Precedent: War Crimes and Command Responsibility* (Scholarly Resources, 1982); also, for a short summary, Bruce D. Landrum, "The Yamashita War Crimes Trial: Command Responsibility Then and Now," *Military Law Review*, vol. 149 (Summer 1995), 293–301. A detailed reprise of the Yamashita trial is accessible online at ess.uwc.ac.uk as "Case No. 21: Trial of General Tomoyuki Yamashita" from *Law Reports of Trials of War Criminals, Selected and Prepared by the United Nations War Crimes Commission*, vol. 4 (Her Majesty's Stationery Office, 1948). The dissent of Supreme Court Justice Frank Murphy is particularly well known in this case; on this as well as MacArthur's denial of the Yamashita appeal, see Parks, 35–37. Yamashita's American defense lawyer A. Frank Reel brought the case for his client's innocence to a broader public in *The Case of General Yamashita*, a trade book published in 1949 that has retained considerable (and considerably misleading) influence despite subsequent substantive critiques such as those by Parks and Lael. The distribution or translation of Reel's published defense of Yamashita was banned by U.S. authorities in occupied Japan; Parks, 70.

61. Parks, "Command Responsibility for War Crimes," 22, 70–71, 87–88 (on the poorly crafted opinion); ibid., 30 (for the opinion itself).

62. Parks dwells at length on subsequent "command responsibility" trials of both German and Japanese officers, in which the infelicities in the *Yamashita* opinion were eliminated.

63. On command responsibility under the Hague Regulations, see Parks, "Command Responsibility for War Crimes," 10, 14, 23, 34, 43, 49, 56, 83.

64. For a concise summary of these differing attitudes toward POWs, see Charlotte Carr-Gregg, *Japanese Prisoners of War in Revolt: The Outbreaks at Featherston and Cowra during World War II* (St. Martin's Press, 1978), esp. ch. 1 ("The Status of Prisoners of War in Western and Japanese Society"). The Japanese military's categorical denunciation of surrender by Japanese fighting men received consummate expression in the imperial army's *Senjinkun* or "Field Code" issued in January 1941, less than a year before the initiation of war with the Allied powers.

65. For searing case studies of Japanese war crimes based on trial records, see Yuki Tanaka, *Hidden Horrors: Japanese War Crimes in World War II* (Westview Press, 1996). Gavin Dawes focuses on abuse of POWs in *Prisoners of the Japanese* (Morrow, 1993). Variations in prison conditions emerge in John A. Glusman, *Conduct under Fire: Four American Doctors and Their Fight for Life as Prisoners of the Japanese, 1941–1945* (Viking, 2005). John Swope mentions how liberated POWs called attention to a range of prison-guard behavior, including attempts to be as humane as possible, in Carolyn Peter, ed., *A Letter from Japan: The Photographs of John Swope* (Hammer Museum at UCLA, 2006). Beginning around 2006, and with increasing intensity thereafter, the Japanese use of waterboarding became a focus of media controversy in the United States. For samples, see Evan Wallach, "Waterboarding Used to Be a Crime," *Washington Post*, November 4, 2007; Kinue Tokudome, "Waterboarding: The Meaning for Japan," *Asia-Pacific Journal*, January 24, 2009 (posted on japanfocus.org); Paul Begala, "Yes, *National Review*, We Did Execute Japanese for Waterboarding," widely posted online on April 24, 2009 (see, for example, huffingtonpost.com). For the fuller context of Truman's comments, see chapter 11 at note 163 in this book.

66. Röling and Cassese, *The Tokyo Trial and Beyond*, 86, 89.

67. Parks, "Command Responsibility for War Crimes," 101–4.

68. *Political Reorientation of Japan*, vol. 2: 737.

69. This particular Japanese slogan—commonly rendered as "Nippon, the Leader of Asia; Nippon, the Protector of Asia; Nippon, the Light of Asia"—was introduced in Indonesia in March 1942 and known as the Triple A (or AAA) movement. See, for example, Benedict R. O'G. Anderson, *Java in a Time of Revolution: Occupation and Resistance, 1944–1945* (Cornell University Press, 1972), 27.

70. Lieutenant-Colonel A. J. F. Doulton, *The Fighting Cock: Being the History of the 23rd Indian Division, 1942–1947* (Gale and Polden, 1951), 232. Doulton's description of looting, insurgency, and terror in Java—as well as his condescension toward Indonesian politicians and their lack of "any understanding of modern political thought"—often reads in retrospect like accounts emanating from Baghdad in the aftermath of the U.S. invasion in 2003; see, for example, 233, 241, 277.

71. John W. Dower, "Occupied Japan and the American Lake, 1945–50," in Edward Friedman and Mark Selden, eds., *America's Asia: Dissenting Essays on Asian-American Relations* (Pantheon, 1971), 145–206; Dower, "Occupied Japan and the Cold War in Asia," in Michael J. Lacey, ed., *The Truman Presidency* (Woodrow Wilson International Center for Scholars and Cambridge University Press, 1989), reprinted as chapter 5 in Dower, *Japan in War and Peace* (155–207); Major-General S. Woodburn Kirby et al., *The War against Japan*, vol. 5: *The Surrender of Japan*

(Her Majesty's Stationery Office, 1969), 271 ("Rule, Britannia!"). Metaphoric flights by U.S. strategic planners also included describing Japan as "the 'Grand Central station' of the Far East" insofar as postwar military and commercial airbases were concerned; see Wm. Roger Louis, *Imperialism at Bay: The United States and the Decolonization of the British Empire, 1941–1945* (Oxford University Press, 1978), 74 and 75 (on the Pacific as "our lake").

72. Cordell Hull, *The Memoirs of Cordell Hull* (Macmillan, 1948), vol. 2, ch. 114, esp. 1599. A lengthy policy paper submitted by the Department of State to Secretary of War Stimson on June 22, 1945, makes the same point in these words: "The United States Government may properly continue to state the political principle which it has frequently announced, that dependent peoples should be given the opportunity, if necessary after an adequate period of preparation, to achieve an increased measure of self-government, but it should avoid any course of action which would seriously impair the unity of the major United Nations"; *FRUS, 1945*, vol. 6: 558. For detailed archives-based analyses of these debates, see Louis, *Imperialism at Bay*; also Christopher Thorne, *Allies of a Kind: The United States, Britain and the War against Japan, 1941–1945* (Oxford University Press, 1978), esp. ch. 27 and 30. The protracted give-and-take involving State Department personnel can be followed in numerous pre- and post-surrender volumes of the department's *FRUS* documentary series. Well-regarded case studies include Robert J. McMahon, "Toward a Post-colonial Order: Truman Administration Policies toward South and Southeast Asia," in Lacey, *The Truman Presidency*, 339–65; George McT. Kahin, "The United States and the Anticolonial Revolutions in Southeast Asia, 1945–1950," in Yonosuke Nagai and Akira Iriye, eds., *The Origins of the Cold War in Asia* (Columbia University Press, 1977), 338–63; George C. Herring, "The Truman Administration and the Restoration of French Sovereignty in Indochina," *Diplomatic History*, vol. 1 (Spring 1977), 97–117. A recent overview is provided in Ronald H. Spector, *In the Ruins of Empire: The Japanese Surrender and the Battle for Postwar Asia* (Random House, 2007).

73. The major accessible account of repatriation from the U.S. perspective appears in *Reports of General MacArthur*, vol. 1, Supplement: *MacArthur in Japan: The Occupation: Military Phase* (Government Printing Office, 1966; this was actually prepared by MacArthur's General Staff around 1949), ch. 6 (149–91). Many of the cumulative figures cited in this present discussion come from this official source, although the data presented (like so many other numerical estimates from these years) are cumbersome and often confusing and even contradictory. See 148 for an annotated map that provides the only cumulative assemblage of the official numbers and locales of Japanese awaiting repatriation shortly after the war's end; this breakdown is as follows: 372,000 in Karafuto and the Kuriles; 700,000 in Siberia; 1,105,800 in Manchuria; 223,100 in Darien and Port Arthur; 322,550 in northern Korea; 594,800 in southern Korea; 62,400 in northern islands near Japan; 1,501,200 in China; 479,050 in Formosa; 69,000 in the Ryukyus; 19,200 in Hong Kong; 32,000 in northern Indochina; 130,900 in the Pacific Ocean areas; 710,650 in Southeast Asia; 15,550 in the Netherlands East Indies; 138,700 in "Australian Areas"; 3,600 in Hawaii; 800 in New Zealand. This totals 6,481,300 individuals.

The challenges that confronted the U.K.-led Southeast Asia Command, which was responsible for overseeing Japanese military surrenders throughout Southeast

Asia (excluding the Philippines and northern Indochina), are addressed in detail in the final volume of the official British war history; see Kirby et al., *The War against Japan*, vol. 5, part 3 (223–375) and appendix 27 (504–6). The general subject of repatriation invites future close scrutiny. Among other things, this will require distinguishing between civilian and military personnel; addressing the plight and fates of tens of thousands of Koreans and Formosans who had been enlisted in the Japanese military; identifying the thousands of overseas military separated out for possible prosecution for war crimes; tracing various patterns of post-surrender desertion; identifying the huge numbers who fell through the cracks of the formal repatriation procedures (as in Manchuria, where as many as 100,000 civilians died trying to make their way back to Japan); identifying more precisely the hundreds of thousands dragooned by the victors for labor, technical, and military tasks; and, most challenging, analyzing to the extent possible the incidence of illness and mortality among the millions who awaited repatriation.

74. *Reports of General MacArthur*, vol. 1: Supplement: 159–61, 179–91; Dower, *Embracing Defeat*, 52–53. As in defeated Germany and other "liberated" areas in the West, the Soviet armies also engaged in rampant rape and looting in Manchuria and elsewhere. Giles MacDonogh addresses Soviet (and other Allied) rape and plunder in *After the Reich: The Brutal History of the Occupation* (Basic Books, 2007; the subtitle of the original British edition is "From the Liberation of Vienna to the Berlin Airlift"). MacDonogh estimates that as of June 1945 somewhere between four and five million German prisoners had been put to work in the Soviet Union, "helping to rebuild its cities," and follows German sources in placing the total number of German prisoners who died in Soviet hands at 1,094,250—with half of these deaths occurring after the German surrender in April 1945; ibid., 420–25. Elsewhere, MacDonogh observes that the Germans, on their part, "had systematically killed three million of their Russian prisoners"; ibid., 394.

75. Much of the China-related data that follows derives from Donald G. Gillin and Charles Etter, "Staying On: Japanese Soldiers and Civilians in China, 1945–1949," *Journal of Asian Studies*, vol. 42, no. 3 (May 1983), 497–518. This illuminating article complements and offsets the sanitized official account of repatriations from China in *Reports of General MacArthur*, vol. 1: Supplement: 170–76. For a vivid journalistic account of the political situation in China in the immediate wake of Japan's surrender that captures some of the turmoil of these months and years, see Theodore H. White and Annalee Jacoby, *Thunder Out of China* (William Sloane, 1946), ch. 19 (279–97).

76. Gillen and Etter, "Staying On," 499–503; *Reports of General MacArthur*, vol. 1: Supplement: 173–74 (Japanese in Formosa). For other estimates, see White and Jacoby, *Thunder Out of China*, 284, 289.

77. Gillen and Etter, "Staying On," 506–8, 511–15; *Reports of General MacArthur*, vol. 1: Supplement: 176. The delayed repatriation of Japanese from China is also addressed in diplomatic exchanges in the State Department's *FRUS* volumes. In December 1946, for example, U.S. military authorities in China estimated that there were still some 70,000 Japanese "so-called technicians and members of their families withheld from repatriation in Manchuria"; *FRUS 1946*, vol. 10: *The Far East: China*, 909. The following April, the Japanese government informed the Americans that at least 87,000 Japanese still remained in China, most of them also

apparently comprising technical experts and their families; *FRUS 1947*, vol. 7: *The Far East: China*, 993–95. In September 1947, the Chinese government put the number of Japanese remaining to be repatriated at over 76,000, with the majority in Manchuria under the control of the Nationalists (18,000) and Communists (50,000). The Americans noted that the numbers for Manchuria were not necessarily reliable; *FRUS 1947*, vol. 7: 998.

78. Priorities of the Southeast Asia Command were conveyed to Mountbatten in a directive dated August 13; Kirby et al., *The War against Japan*, vol. 5: 228–30. See also Peter Dennis, *Troubled Days of Peace: Mountbatten and South East Asia Command, 1945–46* (St. Martin's Press, 1987), which complements Kirby's official history as a close recounting of the challenges Mountbatten's command faced.

79. *FRUS 1945*, vol. 6: 573, 1158, 1178; Kirby et al., *The War against Japan*, vol. 5: 311, 316. Dennis similarly observes that "ignorance, self-delusion and neglect marked the allies' understanding of the realities of the situation in the NEI"; *Troubled Days of Peace*, 68, 75–78. See also Thorne, *Allies of a Kind*, 613, 625, 681. For good general accounts of Indonesia during and immediately after the Japanese occupation, see Anderson, *Java in a Time of Revolution*, esp. ch. 2 and 3 (16–60) on the occupation and emergence of the independence movement, and chapter 7 on the militant *pemuda* or politicized Indonesian youth groups, and the most savage early postwar clashes in Java involving Japanese troops. For Sumatra, see Anthony Reid, *The Blood of the People: Revolution and the End of Traditional Rule in Northern Sumatra* (Oxford University Press, 1979), esp. ch. 5 (104–47) on developments under Japanese occupation and 165–69 on the most violent clashes involving "Japanese Surrendered Personnel." Reid also offers a case study (in chapter 7) of Japanese who supported the Indonesian independence movement.

80. *FRUS 1945*, vol. 6: 1186–88; see also *FRUS 1946*, vol. 8: *The Far East*, 797–98. Harold Isaacs cites an official communiqué stating that RAF Mosquitoes and "lend-lease P–47s" flew 148 sorties against Indonesian villages in November 1945 alone and, among other accomplishments, wiped the village of Tjibadak "off the map"; Harold R. Isaacs, *No Peace for Asia* (Macmillan, 1947), 132. On the particularly notorious Semarang clash of mid-October, see Anderson, *Java in a Time of Revolution*, 146–49.

81. Andrew Roadnight, "Sleeping with the Enemy: Britain, Japanese Troops and the Netherlands East Indies, 1945–1946," *History*, vol. 87 (April 2002), 245–68. Roadnight notes that a Japanese major who commanded the "Kido Butai" that participated in some of the bloodiest encounters in Java was recommended by local British officers for the Distinguished Service Order, although higher-ups shrank from going beyond words of appreciation. The official British history puts the number of armed Japanese troops as of May 1946 at 10,300 in west Java and around 28,100 in Sumatra, and notes that an additional 25,000 (15,000 of them disarmed) were "in Indonesian hands" in central and east Java. SEAC also ordered some 2,700 armed Japanese to patrol the notorious Burma-Siam Railway in Thailand; Kirby et al., *The War against Japan*, vol. 5: 296, 504. On the transfer of Japanese from British to Dutch hands, see *Reports of General MacArthur*, vol. 1: Supplement: 179, 191; Kirby et al., *The War against Japan*, vol. 5: 506. Concerning postwar Japanese casualties in Indonesia, Ken'ichi Goto gives the total number of Japanese killed in the first six postwar months as 627; see his *Tensions of Empire:*

*Japan and Southeast Asia in the Colonial and Postcolonial World* (Ohio University Press, 2003), 171. Anderson gives estimates of Japanese killed in the Semarang clash alone as 500, and cites other sources that place the number as high as 850; *Java in a Time of Revolution*, 146–49.

82. *FRUS 1945*, vol. 6: 568.

83. Isaacs, *No Peace for Asia*, 150–62; Spector, *In the Ruins of Empire*, 128–29 (casualties), 129–30 (deserters), 134, 137. On Japanese who deserted to the Communist-led Vietminh, see Christopher Goscha, "Belated Asian Allies: The Technical and Military Contributions of Japanese Deserters (1945–1946)," in Marilyn Young and Robert Buzzanco, eds., *A Companion to the Vietnam War* (Blackwell, 2002), 37–64, esp. 42–44. Goscha puts the probable number at between 1,000 to 2,000 in the north and 500 to 1,000 in the south.

84. See Spector, *In the Ruins of Empire*, 86, for an example of surrendered Japanese being consigned to conditions that would have been deemed criminal had the situation been reversed. He notes that in Malaya and Singapore, where the Japanese surprise attack in 1941–42 had humiliated the United Kingdom, some 59,000 Japanese awaiting repatriation were initially transferred to the sparsely populated island of Rempang, where they were forced to clear the jungle, build shelters, and produce vegetables and other nourishment. During the first two months of their incarceration, daily provisions provided by SEAC amounted to 1,100 calories per person, and by 1946 around 20 percent were suffering from maladies including malaria, dysentery, and beriberi. The last Japanese were not repatriated from Rempang until over a year after the surrender. For delayed evacuation from Malaya and Burma, see *Reports of General MacArthur*, vol. 1: Supplement: 158–59, 178, 191. The official British history puts the total number of "Japanese retained for labour" after December 1946 at 98,000 (including the 13,500 consigned to the Dutch), and describes their evacuation as taking place in "monthly lifts" from June to December 1947; Kirby et al., *The War against Japan*, vol. 5: 506.

85. *Reports of General MacArthur*, vol. 1: Supplement: 158, 166–70. Kobayashi mentioned his detention in passing in an interview with Peter Grilli conducted in conjunction with the 1994 documentary film *Music for the Movies: Toru Takemitsu*; see the translation by Linda Hoaglund in *Positions*, vol. 2, no. 2 (Fall 1994), 382–405.

86. On the German surrenders, see MacDonogh, *After the Reich*, ch. 15, esp. 392–96. The Allied decision to use surrendered Germans as a post-surrender "workforce" dated from the Yalta conference and was supported with particular keenness by the British. While the United States did not use German prisoners extensively for post-surrender heavy labor, they turned over huge numbers of them to other nations that did, especially France; ibid., 397, 416, 419. On the new terminology for post-combat prisoners as applicable in the handling of Japanese surrenders, see Roadnight, "Sleeping with the Enemy," 265–68. The official British history offers a benign explanation for the "Japanese Surrendered Personnel" designation, suggesting that it derived from the Japanese military's own requests that surrendered troops not be treated as POWs, given the taint such status carried in Japan; Kirby et al., *The War against Japan*, vol. 5: 218, 252. This is not persuasive, for it contradicts the consistent Allied insistence on the "non-negotiated" nature of the surrender and does not take into account the Allied precedent vis-à-vis surrendered Germans or the abuses such nomenclature facilitated. Moreover,

in Japanese military indoctrination, "surrender" itself was a great onus, and the government carefully avoided using the term in addressing its capitulation.

87. Dennis, *Troubled Days of Peace*, 27 (the reinterpreted SEAC acronym); Isaacs, *No Peace for Asia*, 161 (U.S. material support for the French return to Indochina); *FRUS 1945*, vol. 6: 1164 (the formal U.S. request that the Dutch remove "U.S.A." insignia).

88. Isaacs, *No Peace for Asia*, 129.

89. *FRUS 1946*, vol. 8: 816 ("native delegates"), 839 ("Indos"), 801 (Acheson); Issacs, *No Peace for Asia*, 129 (Islamic scholar). Christopher Thorne is particularly sensitive to the race issue, and the index to his massive *Allies of a Kind* is unusually helpful in this regard; see "Race; racialism; racism," and also the "racism of" index subentry for Winston Churchill, whose utterances alone provide a little lexicon of derogatory nomenclature for Asians. Isaacs's book opens with a graphic chapter on "Wogs," "Niggers," and "Slopeys" in the eyes of American soldiers in China and Southeast Asia.

90. Isaacs, *No Peace for Asia*, 39, 187–200, esp. 199. The resonance between seeing Japan as a "staging area for the next operation" and the war drums many high officials in the Bush administration initially beat in seeing invasion and occupation of Iraq as but the first operation in a sequence of preemptive strategic offensives in the Middle East is, again, suggestive.

91. Isaacs, *No Peace for Asia*, 231–42, esp. 233 and 239.

## CHAPTER 15: NATION BUILDING AND MARKET FUNDAMENTALISM

92. I address constitutional revision at length in *Empire and Aftermath* (318–29) and *Embracing Defeat* (ch. 12 and 13).

93. In mid-2008, as the Bush presidency was drawing to a close, a BBC investigation estimated that "as much as $23 billion in US aid allocated to contractors working in Iraq may have been lost, stolen, or not properly accounted for"; see Michael Massing, "Embedded in Iraq," *New York Review of Books*, July 17, 2008. For a critical official evaluation of the reconstruction process, see Office of the Special Inspector General for Iraq Reconstruction, *Hard Lessons: The Iraq Reconstruction Experience*, released online in December 2008 and discussed in the Epilogue of the present book. The full report can be accessed at sigir.mil.

94. The November 24, 2003, issue of the *New Yorker* placed the estimated economic cost of the looting in Iraq at 12 billion dollars. The cost to the economy of the "hoarded goods scandal" in Japan was incalculable, but a rough calculation in 1947, when the looting was exposed, put the total of stolen goods at 300 billion yen at a time when the regular national budget for that same year was 205 billion yen; see Dower, *Embracing Defeat*, 112–20, and also 535 on the notorious later "Shōwa Denkō scandal" involving government reconstruction funds.

95. Dower, *Embracing Defeat*, 97–100. For a lively journalistic case study of American involvement in these activities, see Robert Whiting, *Tokyo Underworld: The Fast Times and Hard Life of an American Gangster in Japan* (Pantheon, 1999), esp. ch. 1 and 2.

96. In the first ten days of occupation in Kanagawa prefecture, where Yokohama is located, the number of reported rapes was 1,336. The Japanese government, aware

of the predatory behavior of its own forces in China and elsewhere, anticipated sexual assaults and prepared for the occupation by establishing a "Recreation and Amusement Association" that provided female companionship, including sex, for the conquerors. (An internal Japanese police report addressing early concerns frankly observed that "many of those who speak of pillage and rape, unsettling people's minds, are returnees from the war front.") Sexual crimes increased, it is argued, when this service was disbanded in 1946 at SCAP's orders. See, for example, Takemae, *Inside GHQ*, 67, 441; Dower, *Embracing Defeat*, 124, 130, 211, 412, and 579 (n. 16); Yuki Tanaka, *Japan's Comfort Women: Sexual Slavery and Prostitution during World War II and the U.S. Occupation* (Routledge, 2002); and the disturbing account of rape and assault by Australian forces in occupied Hiroshima in Allan S. Clifton, *Time of Fallen Blossoms* (Cassell, 1950), ch. 20. GI rapes in Okinawa are noted in George Feifer, *Tennozan: The Battle of Okinawa and the Atomic Bomb* (Ticknor and Fields, 1992), 178, 338, 495–99, 555. Abuses by the victorious Allied forces in Europe have generally focused on Soviet troops, but are more broadly assessed in MacDonogh, *After the Reich*, and William I. Hitchcock, *The Bitter Road to Freedom: A New History of the Liberation of Europe* (Free Press, 2008). Hitchcock acknowledges that Anglo-American forces in occupied Germany were generally "magnanimous in victory," while at the same time documenting how "liberation came hand in hand with unprecedented violence and brutality" not only in the final phase of combat but also afterwards in Germany, France, Belgium, the Netherlands, and Italy; see his brief preface for a thematic summary. Violence by the so-called liberation armies of World War II was of a different nature altogether than the behavior of U.S. forces in "liberated" Iraq, where occupation personnel were compelled to live on the knife's edge of panic, armed to the teeth in an alien world with no visible line between friendly civilians and lethal adversaries. Where comparability lies is in the cover-up of crimes and the immunity routinely given offenders on one's own side.

97. Dower, *Embracing Defeat*, esp. 107–10 (crime), 123–39 (prostitution), and 97–102, 139–48 (black-market activity).

98. See Gordon and Trainor, *Cobra II*, 479–85; Ricks, *Fiasco*, 158–66; Packer, *The Assassins' Gate*, 189–96; Bremer, *My Year in Iraq*, 54–58. Once these two initial orders became fair game, which happened quickly, war supporters attempted to distance the Bush administration by intimating that Bremer acted largely on his own. Where the army was concerned, Bremer argued that it had disintegrated by April 2003 and attempting to reassemble it would have been both foolish and impossible. His directive, he emphasized, was in any case processed through the murky channels of Washington. This issue was revisited in the media in the summer of 2007; see *New York Times*, September 4, 2007 ("Envoy's Letter Counters Bush on Dismantling of Iraq Army"), and Bremer's op-ed essay published two days later ("How I Didn't Dismantle Iraq's Army"). The official transcript of Bush's July 2 comment reads "bring them on," but the video of this exchange confirms that the president's phrasing was the more colloquial "bring 'em on."

99. For Bremer's "Saddamism" quote, see Michael R. Gordon, "The Conflict in Iraq: Winning the Peace; Debate Lingering on Decision to Dissolve the Iraqi Military," *New York Times*, October 21, 2004.

100. For the purge in Japan, see *Political Reorientation of Japan*, vol. 1: 8–81 ("Removal

of Ultranationalists"); Takemae, *Inside GHQ*, 266–70; Hans H. Baerwald, "Occupation Purge," in *Kodansha Encyclopedia of Japan*, vol. 6: 57–58. The knowledgeable occupation participant Martin Bronfenbrenner observed that although the purge of businessmen provoked alarmist outcry by some Americans about stripping Japan of its economic leadership, "its effect on economic recovery was questionable. . . . Many purgees continued to direct their enterprises unofficially as 'advisers.' In other cases, active young men replaced superannuated businessmen less capable of adapting to new conditions"; see his "Occupation-Period Economy (1945–1952)," in *Kodansha Encyclopedia of Japan*, vol. 2: 155. Bronfenbrenner puts the number of "members of the economic elite" purged at 8,309, as opposed to the more usual figure of 1,535 "captains" of industry, etc. used by Takemae (269).

101. "United States Post-Surrender Policy for Japan," in *Political Reorientation of Japan*, vol. 2: 423. Japan's war and navy ministries were renamed the First and Second Demobilization Ministries on November 30, 1945, and eventually demoted to a bureau under a civilian Demobilization Board that functioned until October 1947. Veterans' and survivors' benefits were terminated in February 1946; Takemae, *Inside GHQ*, 107–8.

102. Alfred Oppler, *Legal Reform in Occupied Japan: A Participant Looks Back* (Princeton University Press, 1976), 12.

103. Bronfenbrenner, "Occupation-Period Economy," 154. Bronfenbrenner, who worked in SCAP's influential Economic and Scientific Section, was one of the few Americans who was trained in Japanese language during the war and actually ended up working in occupied Japan.

104. Joseph C. Grew, *Turbulent Era: A Diplomatic Record of Forty Years, 1904–1945* (Houghton Mifflin, 1952), 1440–41; see also 1420, quoting a letter he wrote in April 1945 ("I am certain that we could not graft our type of democracy on Japan because I know very well that they are not fitted for it and that it could not possibly work"). See also Dower, *Embracing Defeat*, 217–24 (on "The Experts and the Obedient Herd"), and the lengthy citation on these contentious debates in chapter 10 (note 107) of the present book.

105. Sansom's comment appears, along with other disparaging remarks about occupation policy, in Jerome B. Cohen, *Japan's Economy in War and Reconstruction* (University of Minnesota Press, 1949), vii–x. In May 1945, when Sansom was shown an outline of State Department occupation plans for Japan at Grew's insistence, he questioned the projected reformist agenda on the grounds that "it is extremely doubtful whether, even if the Allies had at their disposal a host of erudite archangels, the Japanese people would respond to their teaching"; Thorne, *Allies of a Kind*, 655–56. For Sansom's confidential impressions of the situation in Japan as of January 1946, see Katharine Sansom, *Sir George Sansom and Japan: A Memoir* (Diplomatic Press, 1972), ch. 12 (144–59). He found MacArthur impressive; the American staff in Counterintelligence, charged with investigating war crimes and ultranationalism, "a lot of eager and well-intentioned young men who were not aware of the facts of political life"; the "theoretical proponents of democracy" who criticized the *zaibatsu* "fantastic and mistaken" in seeing these financial interests as fundamentally different from "similar combinations in the U.S. and other highly industrialized countries"; and reparations policy "merely vindictive." The "cheerful optimism" of Americans responsible for civil information and education

alarmed him ("they seemed to think that Japan can be supplied with a new system of education as a tailor might furnish a new suit"), while a conversation with two ostensibly liberal Japanese acquaintances versed in economics reminded him of the "fundamentally anti-white" prejudice of the intelligentsia, and the fact that "we could not count upon the Intellectuals to promote the objects of the occupation." On January 15, roughly two weeks after setting foot in occupied Japan, he was already raising a familiar conservative bogey: "I am not sure that the Americans realize what they are doing in their enthusiasm for freedom. It would be an ironical outcome of the occupation if Japan should be pushed into the arms of the U.S.S.R."

106. MacArthur is quoted by Oppler in *Legal Reform in Occupied Japan*, viii. For Kades and the internal debates on these issues, see Dower, *Embracing Defeat*, 370–73 (on "Thinking about Idealism and Cultural Imperialism").

107. The transcript of Blair's address was posted online by CNN at cnn.com.

108. Carney is quoted in David Rieff, "Blueprint for a Mess," *New York Times Magazine*, November 2, 2003. For a typical observation by careful reporters, see Gordon and Trainor, *Cobra II*, 475: "Bremer auditioned for the job by meeting with Rumsfeld, whom he knew from the Ford administration three decades earlier. Bremer was not an expert on the Middle East and in his years as a diplomat had never been posted in the region, but in Rumsfeld's Pentagon that was considered a plus. Rumsfeld had sought to block some of Jay Garner's picks because they were State Department Arabists who might be less than ardent supporters of Bush's bold plan to remake Iraq. With Bremer, he would not have that problem." In his memoir *My Year in Iraq*, Bremer took repeated care to challenge this argument by emphasizing the area skills, including language fluency, of some of his top CPA aides.

109. Shane Harris, "Outsourcing Iraq," *Government Executive*, July 1, 2004.

110. *Political Reorientation of Japan*, vol. 2: 435 (initial policy), 565 (*zaibatsu* deconcentration), 741 (distribution of income and ownership reiterated), 760 (land reform), 780 (*zaibatsu*).

111. This is placed in broad historical context by Chalmers Johnson in *MITI and the Japanese Miracle: The Growth of Industrial Policy, 1925–1975* (Stanford University Press, 1982).

112. Harris, "Outsourcing Iraq." Near the end of 2003, Juan Cole observed that "one could forgive the Iraqis if they conclude that the American system in Iraq is a form of state socialism, with Bremer playing the Politburo, giving orders and exercising a veto even though no one elected him to office, and Halliburton and Bechtel playing state-supported industries. Perhaps it looks more like Cuba so far than like capitalist democracy"; posted on Professor Cole's *Informed Comment* website (juancole.com), October 31, 2003.

113. Neil King Jr., "U.S. Prepares for Rebuilding of Iraq—Initial Plan Could Spend as Much as $900 Million on Repairs after a War," *Wall Street Journal*, March 10, 2003. (The five initial construction companies were Bechtel, Fluor, Kellogg Brown and Root, Louis Berger Group, and Parsons.) Patrick Cockburn, "From Triumph Has Sprung Murderous Fiasco," *Independent*, October 9, 2003 (red Indians). In August 2003, an anonymous woman blogger in Baghdad who became well known under the name "Riverbend" posted an entry about her cousin, an engineer in Baghdad, whose company had restored twenty of the

bridges destroyed in the first Gulf War. In May, when the CPA asked for estimates to rebuild a single bridge (the New Diyala Bridge), his company submitted a bid of $300,000 and was turned down. A week later, the contract went to an American company whose estimate was reported to be $50 million. Riverbend went on to note that Iraq had over 130,000 engineers, many thousands of whom were trained "in Germany, Japan, America, Britain and other countries"; Riverbend, *Baghdad Burning: Girl Blog from Iraq* (Feminist Press at the City University of New York, 2005), 34–37. At the start of the occupation, the ratio of private contractors to U.S. soldiers in Iraq was 1:10. By the end of 2006, it was roughly 1:1.4, with approximately 100,000 contractors including close to 50,000 private soldiers alongside 140,000 U.S. troops. See Renae Merle, "Hired Boots on the Ground," *Washington Post National Weekly Edition*, December 11–17, 2006; also Naomi Klein, *The Shock Doctrine: The Rise of Disaster Capitalism* (Metropolitan, 2007), 378–80. Klein's critique of the market fundamentalism of the so-called Chicago School places the privatization agenda firmly in a program of "shock therapy" dating back to the 1970s or earlier; see chapters 16, 17, and 18 on Iraq.

114. Neil King Jr., "Bush Officials Draft Broad Plan for Free-Market Economy in Iraq," *Wall Street Journal*, May 1, 2003. For a cogent sample of the privatization arguments that were being promoted in influential conservative circles prior to the invasion, see Ariel Cohen and Gerald P. O'Driscoll Jr., "Privatization and the Oil Industry: A Strategy for Postwar Iraqi Reconstruction," *National Interest*, January 22, 2003.

115. Noah Feldman, *What We Owe Iraq*, 1; Francis Fukuyama, "Nation-Building 'Lite,'" *Wall Street Journal*, October 1, 2003. Blackwill is quoted in "The Lost Year in Iraq," a *Frontline* interview with Bremer and others posted online at pbs.org/wgbh on October 17, 2006. For interesting takes on the clash between traditional conservatism exemplified by Rumsfeld's invade-and-leave views and a neoconservatism focused on remaking Iraq as a model democracy, see Marina Ottaway, "Iraq: One Country, Two Plans," *Foreign Policy*, July/August 2003 (also posted by the Carnegie Endowment for International Peace at carnegieendowment.org).

116. For Bremer quotes, see the online Voice of America transcript for June 1, 2003, at globalsecurity.org; also his characterizations of the Baathist economy in *My Year in Iraq*, 28, 61–66. The often-quoted "Iraq is open for business again" was delivered on May 27. Rumsfeld's formulation was made in a presentation to the Council on Foreign Relations on May 27, 2003. Juan Cole notes that the fixed 5 percent tariff "is exactly the level imposed by Great Britain on the Ottoman empire in the Treaty of 1838 and on a defeated Egypt at the Treaty of London in 1840"; posted on Cole's *Informed Comment* website (juancole.com), September 22, 2003.

117. Under the "Shoup Plan" in occupied Japan, maximum marginal taxes were lowered to 55 percent for individuals and 35 percent for corporations; see, for example, the online commentary on Carl Sumner Shoup by David Weinstein at columbia.edu/cu/economics; also Dick K. Nanto, "Shoup Mission," in *Kodansha Encyclopedia of Japan*, vol. 7: 172–73.

118. Donald Rumsfeld, "Prepared Statement for the Senate Appropriations Committee," September 24, 2003, quoted in Klein, *The Shock Doctrine*, 346. "Let's All Go to the Yard Sale," *Economist*, September 25, 2003; this same article characterized

the CPA agenda as a "shock programme." The *Economist* subsequently called attention to how this alienated even "the country's initially enthusiastic bourgeoisie"; see "Cleaner, but Still Bare: Iraq's Reconstruction" in the October 4, 2003, issue. The largely critical public response is voluminous. For samples quoted here, see T. Christian Miller, *Blood Money: Wasted Billions, Lost Lives, and Corporate Greed in Iraq* (Little, Brown, 2006); Jonathan Weisman and Anitha Reddy, "Spending on Iraq Sets Off Gold Rush: Lawmakers Fear U.S. Is Losing Control of Funds," *Washington Post*, October 9, 2003; Ibrahim Warde, "Iraq: A License to Loot the Land," *Le Monde diplomatique*, May 2004; David Usborne, Rupert Cornwell, and Phil Reeves, "Iraq Inc: A Joint Venture Built on Broken Promises," *Independent*, May 10, 2003 ("a carpetbaggers' free-for-all"). The September 24, 2003, entry in the published blogs of Riverbend is titled "For Sale: Iraq"; *Baghdad Burning*, 76–81. For spoils-to-the-victor, see Haass, *War of Choice, War of Necessity*, 251–52.

Diagnoses of the economic and financial crisis in Iraq differed on the causes of as well as solutions to the crisis. Thus, proponents of free-market "shock therapy" like Bremer spoke almost exclusively about the fatal combination of Baathist socialism and Saddam's war-mongering and corruption, while more liberal and leftist commentators acknowledged this but also emphasized (1) the massive destruction of Iraqi infrastructure in the 1991 Gulf War; (2) the devastating effects of the U.S.-led UN economic sanctions that followed; and (3) the chaos, incompetence, and corruption of the outsourcing frenzy that followed the invasion. Only belatedly, after the CPA was dissolved, did U.S. officials acknowledge that at least a portion of Iraq's state-run companies could in fact be rehabilitated to the extent of getting Iraqis back to work.

119. "Rebuilding Iraq Conference," at new-fields.com/iraq/agenda.htm. These conferences continued over several years. The "$100 billion" figure attributed to the Council on Foreign Relations derived from the Council's January 1, 2003, report *Guiding Principles for U.S. Post-Conflict Policy in Iraq*, which projected that "leaving aside immediate humanitarian needs, experts estimate that reconstruction will cost between $25 billion and $100 billion."

120. "U.S. Prepares for Rebuilding of Iraq," *Wall Street Journal*, March 10, 2003; Ehsan Ahrai, "The Lucrative Business of Rebuilding Iraq," *Asia Times*, March 26, 2003.

121. "Bush Officials Draft Broad Plan for Free-Market Economy in Iraq," *Wall Street Journal*, May 1, 2003; Klein, *The Shock Doctrine*, 341–43.

122. The full Goldsmith memorandum is included in John Kampfner, "Blair Was Told It Would Be Illegal to Occupy Iraq," *New Statesman*, May 26, 2003 (the weekly actually appeared on newsstands on May 22). See also Clare Dyer, "Occupation of Iraq Illegal, Blair Told," *Guardian*, May 22, 2003; John Innes, "US and UK Action in Post-War Iraq May Be Illegal," *Scotsman*, May 22, 2003.

123. The general issue of "law, justice, and transgression" in occupation policy is addressed in chapter 14 in the present book; for detailed analyses, including conflicting opinions and documentary appendices, see *Future Implications of the Iraq Conflict: Selections from the "American Journal of International Law"* (2004). For succinct summaries focusing on the privatization agenda, see Thomas Catan, "Iraq Business Deals May Be Invalid, Law Experts Warn," *Financial Times*, October 30, 2003; Daphne Eviatar, "Free-Market Iraq? Not So Fast," *New York Times*, January 10, 2004.

124. Nina Serafino, Curt Tarnoff, and Dick Nanto, *U.S. Occupation Assistance: Iraq, Germany and Japan Compared* (Congressional Research Service, Library of Congress, March 23, 2006). In current dollars over the 1946–52 period, total U.S. aid amounted to $4.3 billion to Germany and $2.2 billion to Japan. There are many fine distinctions to be made concerning such gross data: grants versus loans, humanitarian aid including food as opposed to economic reconstruction and other infrastructure projects, the recycling of aid in the form of "counterpart" funds administered in the recipient country, aid for explicitly military purposes, and so forth.

125. When the Marshall Plan analogy was being evoked in connection with reconstruction aid for Iraq, the editor of Marshall's papers (Larry Bland) took care to tell reporters that "the primary emphasis of the Marshall Plan was on restimulating trade"; David Firestone, "The Struggle for Iraq: The Cost—Debate Rises Where Bush and Marshall Plans Diverge," *New York Times*, September 27, 2003. See also the three retrospective articles authorized by Vince Crawley and widely distributed by the Department of State's Bureau of International Information Programs on May 21, 22, and 23, 2007—on the sixtieth anniversary of Marshall's famous speech; these can be conveniently accessed, for example, at the United States Mission to the European Union website: useu.usmission.gov. "The offer was generous," the third of these essays notes, "but the United States had a high degree of self-interest as well. An economically strong Europe no longer would require U.S. assistance, would be able to resume buying American products and could prevent a Communist takeover of the Continent"; Crawley, "Marshall Plan Seen as Model for Well-Run, Short-lived Program." In responding to Bush's request for reconstruction aid for Iraq, Democrats in the House of Representatives introduced a resolution that cited his September 23 speech to the United Nations and declared "make no mistake, this is not the Marshall Plan." They described the administration's appropriations request as "a laundry list of economic development projects," warned of the danger of "war profiteering," and called for greater accountability, transparency, State Department leadership, and active Iraqi input in setting priorities and administering the program. This resolution was introduced by Congresswoman Rosa DeLauro and sixty-one cosponsors on October 16, 2003.

126. The basic directive for Germany is reproduced in *FRUS 1945*, vol. 3: *European Advisory Commission, Austria, Germany*, 484–503; see esp. 487–88 and 493–94 on economic objectives. For earlier enunciations of these objectives, see ibid., 378–88 (January 6, 1945), 432–38 (March 10), and 471–73 (March 28); also *FRUS 1944*, vol. 1: *General*, 344–46 (September 29, 1944). The revised "level-of-industry" policy for Germany was issued as a military directive (JCS 1779) on July 11, 1947, and is reproduced in *Department of State Bulletin*, July 27, 1947 (186–93); see also ibid., September 7, 1947 (468–72).

127. *Political Reorientation of Japan*, vol. 2: 424. For an overview of reparations policy in Japan, see William S. Borden, *The Pacific Alliance: United States Foreign Economic Policy and Japanese Trade Recovery, 1947–1955* (University of Wisconsin Press, 1984), 71–83.

128. *FRUS 1948*, vol. 6: *The Far East and Australasia*, 857–62 (NSC 13/2). NSC 13/2 emphasized that "second only to U.S. security interests, economic recovery should be made the primary objective of United States policy in Japan," and that "we

should make it clear to the Japanese Government that the success of the recovery program will in large part depend on Japanese efforts to raise production and to maintain high exports through hard work, a minimum of work stoppages, internal austerity measures and the stern combating of inflationary trends including efforts to achieve a balanced internal budget as rapidly as possible."

129. See Barry Machado, *In Search of a Usable Past: The Marshall Plan and Postwar Reconstruction Today* (George C. Marshall Foundation, 2007) for a concise, well-annotated overview of the Marshall Plan written against the background of the occupation of Iraq. A confessed admirer of the "Marshall Planners," Machado identifies only two areas in which the Economic Cooperation Administration's ethos of resisting domestic corporate lobbying did not hold: in shipping and "Big Oil"; ibid., 122–23. His conclusion amounts to an indirect critique of the aid program in Iraq, in which temperament assumes a large role. Machado quotes Ralph Waldo Emerson's observation that "character is higher than intellect," and concludes that "today, character seems in much shorter supply than in the late 1940s."

130. These breakdowns vary somewhat depending on the source. In addition to the *U.S. Occupation Assistance* report issued by the Congressional Research Service in 2006, see Shinji Takagi, "From Recipient to Donor: Japan's Official Aid Flows, 1945 to 1990 and Beyond," *Essays in International Finance*, no. 196 (March 1995), esp. 1–8; and Robert A. Fearey, *The Occupation of Japan: Second Phase, 1948–1950* (Macmillan, 1950), 218–19.

131. For archives-based overviews of the economic reverse course in occupied Japan, see Dower, *Empire and Aftermath*, chapters 10, 11, and 12; Dower, "Occupied Japan and the Cold War in Asia," in Dower, *Japan in War and Peace*, 155–207; Borden, *Pacific Alliance*; Howard B. Schonberger, *Aftermath of War: Americans and the Remaking of Japan, 1945–1952* (Kent State University Press, 1989), esp. chs. 5, 6, and 7; Michael Schaller, *The American Occupation of Japan: The Origins of the Cold War in Asia* (Oxford University Press, 1987); Schaller, *Altered States: The United States and Japan since the Occupation* (Oxford University Press, 1997), esp. chapter 1; Schaller, "Securing the Great Crescent: Occupied Japan and the Origins of Containment in Southeast Asia," *Journal of American History*, vol. 69, no. 2 (September 1982), 392–414; Yutaka Kosai, "The Postwar Japanese Economy, 1945–1973," in Michael Smitka, ed., *Japan's Economic Ascent: International Trade, Growth, and Postwar Reconstruction* (Garland, 1998), 72–116.

132. "Economic Stabilization in Japan," December 10, 1948, *FRUS 1948*, vol. 6: 1059–60. For an annotated overview of "the blurring of state and society" in postwar Japan, see Brian J. McViegh, *The Nature of the Japanese State: Rationality and Rituality* (Nissan Institute/Routledge, 1998), esp. chapter 4. Legal commentaries on administrative guidance are excerpted in Meryll Dean, ed., *Japanese Legal System*, 2nd edition (Cavendish, 2002), 168–91.

133. Chalmers Johnson concludes that by the end of the occupation the Japanese bureaucracy was even more powerful than it had been during the war; see his *MITI and the Japanese Miracle*.

134. Robert S. Ozaki, "Foreign Exchange Control," in *Kodansha Encyclopedia of Japan*, vol. 2: 314–16.

135. See Schonberger, *Aftermath of War*, chapter 6 (on Draper), and Dower, *Embracing Defeat*, 537 (for Dulles).

136. Fearey, *The Occupation of Japan*, 149–50. Martin Bronfenbrenner also notes that the key laws on foreign exchange, trade, and investment "were intended to prevent capital flight from Japan, and to prevent foreign 'carpetbaggers' from buying up Japanese assets cheaply"; "Occupation-Period Economy," 157.

137. Tony Judt emphasizes "the place of recent history in an age of forgetting" in the introduction to his Europe-focused essays collected in *Reflections on the Forgotten Twentieth Century* (Penguin Press, 2008). Japan and Asia more generally, of course, pose the same challenge for historians and policy makers and make the task of comparative analysis all the more difficult and potentially illuminating.

138. Bronfenbrenner, "Occupation-Period Economy," 158.

139. Dower, *Embracing Defeat*, 540–46 (for special procurements, the Korean War boom, and Deming).

140. See, for a concise overview, Gary R. Saxonhouse, "United States, economic relations with, 1945–1973, in *Kodansha Encyclopedia of Japan*, vol. 8: 161–64.

141. Chalmers Johnson has developed the most extensive critical analysis of the U.S. "empire of bases" in a well-known trilogy: *Blowback: The Costs and Consequences of American Empire*, 2nd edition (Holt Paperbacks, 2004); *The Sorrows of Empire: Militarism, Secrecy, and the End of the Republic* (Metropolitan, 2004); and *Nemesis: The Last Days of the American Republic* (Metropolitan, 2006). By his careful reckoning, not including numerous secret bases, the United States maintains over 700 military bases outside the country and over 950 in the fifty states. Okinawa receives particularly close attention in *Blowback*, the first volume in the trilogy.

## EPILOGUE

1. David Kilcullen, *The Accidental Guerrilla: Fighting Small Wars in the Midst of a Big One* (Oxford University Press, 2009), 3. Kilcullen, among many others, also uses the concepts of "postmodern" and "globalized" to characterize contemporary terror and insurgency; see, for example, ibid., xvii, xxviii.

2. Philip Taubman, "Learning Not to Love the Bomb," *New York Times*, February 19, 2009.

3. Lewis Mumford, *The City in History* (Harcourt, Brace and World, 1961), 432f. ("Caption 49," accompanying a photograph of the Pentagon). My attention was drawn to Mumford by Andrew J. Bacevich, *The Limits of Power: The End of American Exceptionalism* (Metropolitan, 2008), 85–86.

4. Office of the Inspector General, Office of the Director of National Intelligence, *Critical Intelligence Community Management Challenges*, November 12, 2008. An unclassified version of this sixteen-page report was released on April 2, 2009, and can be accessed at globalsecurity.org; the quotations appear on 2, 6, 10, 12.

5. Office of the Special Inspector General for Iraq Reconstruction, *Hard Lessons: The Iraq Reconstruction Experience* (508-page "draft" report released on sigir.mil, December 2008), 5, 478. (Note: the pagination on this document is jumbled, and these citations refer to the sequential pagination of the online presentation.)

6. Turf wars is a persistent subject through the report, as are most of these themes. For specific passing references here, see *Hard Lessons*, 17 ("back-of-the-envelope"), 19 (working in secret), 28 ("bureaucratic inertia"), 47, 461 ("best-case" scenarios), 61 ("colliding chains of command"), 66 ("good soldier"), 145 ("*fait accompli*"),

307–8, 314, 338 (disdain for Iraqi sensibilities), 472–73 (sixty-two agencies). Suggestively, two of the nine chapters in John Nagl's influential critique of the U.S. Army's failure to draw basic lessons about counterinsurgency from the Vietnam War experience also use the concept of "hard lessons" ignored with disastrous consequences; see his *Learning to Eat Soup with a Knife: Counterinsurgency Lessons from Malaya and Vietnam* (University of Chicago Press, 2005; originally published in 2002).

7. For concrete examples of baneful "ad hoc" planning, see *Hard Lessons*, 59, 121, 124, 170, 187, 238, 336, 460, 466 ("adhocracy"). Chalabi's comments appear in an op-ed essay titled "Thanks, But You Can Go Now," *New York Times*, November 23, 2008. U.S. government auditors evaluating reconstruction programs in Afghanistan reached the same critical conclusions, noting that these programs remained "fragmented" and "lack coherence." By the end of the Bush presidency, funds expended for Afghanistan actually exceeded those for Iraq (totaling $60 billion, of which $32 billion came from the United States); see Karen DeYoung, "It's Worse Than They Realized," *Washington Post National Weekly Edition*, February 9–15, 2009.

8. Online text of "President George W. Bush's farewell address," January 15, 2009, as transcribed by the White House; this can be accessed under "The Bush Record" at georgewbush-whitehouse.archives.gov.

9. This was widely reported. See, for example, David Sanger, "'Political Anthropologists' Find Surprises during the Transition," *New York Times*, December 2, 2008.

10. After the meltdown, the early warnings of the chair of the Commodity Futures Trading Commission from 1996 to 1999 drew attention as representative of the way those who predicted catastrophe were marginalized. See, for example, Manuel Roig-Franzia, "Credit Crisis Cassandra—Brooksley Born's Unheeded Warning Is a Rueful Echo 10 Years On," *Washington Post*, May 26, 2009. For a persuasive argument that a system of derivatives originally conceived as a way of dispersing and minimizing risk was abused by subsequent practitioners, see Gilliam Tett, *Fool's Gold: How the Bold Dream of a Small Tribe at J.P. Morgan Was Corrupted by Wall Street Greed and Unleashed a Catastrophe* (Free Press, 2009).

11. On the opaque "pseudoscience" or "pseudo-objectivity" of financial modeling, see the early warning by Benoit Mandelbrot and Nassim Nicholas Taleb, "How the Finance Gurus Get Risk All Wrong," *Fortune*, July 11, 2005; also Jerry Z. Muller, "Our Epistemological Depression," *American*, January 29, 2009; Felix Salmon, "Recipe for Disaster: The Formula That Killed Wall Street," *Wired*, February 23, 2009. Tett's study necessarily introduces the opaque jargon and "alphabet soup" of acronyms; see, for example, *Fool's Gold*, 32–33 ("VaR") and 215 ("super-senior CDO of ABS assets").

12. Daniel Gross, "Boom, Bust, Repeat," *New York Times Book Review*, December 28, 2008 (reviewing Michael Lewis, ed., *Panic: The Story of Modern Financial Insanity*); Jill Drew, "Frenzy," *Washington Post*, December 16, 2008; Nick Paumgarten, "The Death of Kings: Notes from a Meltdown," *New Yorker*, May 18, 2009.

13. For access to the July 29, 2009, letter to Queen Elizabeth, see "The Global Financial Crisis—Why Didn't Anybody Notice?" on the website of the British Academy

at britac.ac.uk. An indirect route of access is through Matthew Lynn, "Royal Reasons for Overlooking Financial Meltdown," at bloomberg.com.

14. Simon Johnson, "The Quiet Coup," *Atlantic*, May 2009; Tett, *Fool's Gold*, 31, 137; "Unfinished Business," *Economist*, February 7, 2009. "Groupthink" and herd behavior in capitalist and corporate behavior drew considerable media attention after the sensational collapse of Enron in 2002, and in fact has an extensive genealogy in economic writings. For entrée to the scholarly literature, see Abhijit V. Bannerjee, "A Simple Model of Herd Behavior," *Quarterly Journal of Economics*, vol. 107, no. 3 (August 1992), 797–817; also Laurens Rook's extensively annotated "An Economic Psychological Approach to Herd Behavior," *Journal of Economic Issues*, vol. 40 (2006), 75–95. Why this failed to temper the "irrational exuberance" that ended in catastrophe is a subject in itself.

15. Tett, *Fool's Gold*, 210, 217, 225–26.

16. Salmon, "Recipe for Disaster." Greenspan's observations on the causes of the financial crisis, widely reproduced online, were presented before the House Committee of Government Oversight and Reform on October 23, 2008; his prepared remarks can be accessed under "Greenspan Testimony on Sources of Financial Crisis" at the *Wall Street Journal* website, wsj.com.

17. Edward Carr, "Greed—and Fear: A Special Report on the Future of Finance," *Economist*, January 22, 2009. Carr refers to an academic study identifying "139 financial crises between 1973 and 1997 (of which 44 took place in high-income countries), compared with a total of only 38 between 1945 and 1971." On the rejected Japan analogy, see Tett, *Fool's Gold*, 180–81.

18. Joe Nocera, "Risk Mismanagement," *New York Times Magazine*, January 4, 2009; Muller, "Our Epistemological Depression"; Carr, "Greed—and Fear"; Tett, *Fool's Gold*, 100 ("ratings arbitrage"), 131. See also Paumgarten, "The Death of Kings" (on "statistical legerdemain" and "tweaking the data and models until they said what you wanted").

19. George A. Akerlof and Robert J. Shiller, *Animal Spirits: How Human Psychology Drives the Economy, and Why It Matters for Global Capitalism* (Princeton University Press, 2009); see esp. 1–5, 167–74. For incisive reviews, see Benjamin M. Friedman, "The Failure of the Economy and the Economists," *New York Review of Books*, May 28, 2009; Louis Uchitelle, "Irrational Exuberance," *New York Times*, April 19, 2009. For another extended critique published after the financial crash, see Justin Fox, *The Myth of the Rational Market: A History of Risk, Reward, and Delusion on Wall Street* (HarperBusiness, 2009), which traces the genealogy of the efficient-market hypothesis. The spirit of rediscovered skepticism was nicely captured in a review of Fox's book in the *Economist* (June 13, 2009), which described the failed orthodoxy as "the Nicene Creed of the market rationalists" and traced its origins to "Nobel-laureate preachers" who "proclaimed from the pulpits of the University of Chicago that the market could do no wrong."

# ILLUSTRATION CREDITS

1. Naval Historical Foundation
2. Naval Historical Foundation
3. Naval Historical Foundation
4. Naval Historical Foundation
5. Naval Historical Foundation
6. Naval Historical Foundation
7. National Archives
8. Office of War Information / National Archives
9. National Archives
10. Original photo by Joe Rosenthal / Associated Press Photo
11. Original photo by Jeff Bush / *Connecticut Post* / Associated Press Photo
12. Rob Howard / Corbis
13. Sean Adair / Reuters / Corbis
14. Richard Drew / Associated Press Photo
15. Preston Keres / U.S. Navy
16. Naval Historical Foundation (from a Japanese photograph)
17. Naval Historical Foundation (from a Japanese photograph)
18. Naval Historical Foundation (from a Japanese photograph)
19. Naval Historical Foundation (from a Japanese photograph)
20. Clem Albers / National Archives
21. Dorothy Lange / National Archives
22. Russell Boyce / Reuters / Corbis
23. David A. O'Haver / U.S. Navy
24. Reuters / Corbis
25. Gerry Penny / EPA / Corbis
26. Reuters / Corbis
27. Saeed Ali Achakzai / Reuters / Corbis

28. Author's collection
29. Author's collection
30. Author's collection
31. Hoover Archives at Stanford University
32. Quotations excerpted from a slideshow of coversheets accompanying Richard Draper, "And He Shall Be Judged," gq.com, June 2009
33. Christopher Seneko / U.S. Navy
34. Ramzi Haidar / Getty Images
35. Andrew Parsons / Reuters / Corbis
36. Jean-Marc Bouju / Associated Press Photo
37. Kevin C. Quihuis Jr. / U.S. Marine Corps / DefenseImagery.mil
38. Jerome Delay / Associated Press Photo
39. Ramzi Haidar / AFP / Getty Images
40. David Leeson / *Dallas Morning News* / Corbis
41. Elliott Erwitt / Magnum Photos
42. National Archives (from a newsreel by H. S. Wong)
43. John Swope Collection / Corbis
44. John Swope Collection / Corbis
45. Bundesarchiv / wikimedia.org/wikipedia/commons
46. Imperial War Museum
47. Dugway Proving Ground / U.S. Army
48. Koyou Ishikawa / wikimedia.org/wikipedia/commons
49. Library of Congress
50. Courtesy Herb Friedman, retired U.S. Army Sergeant Major / psywarrior.com
51. Courtesy Herb Friedman, retired U.S. Army Sergeant Major / psywarrior.com
52. Courtesy Herb Friedman, retired U.S. Army Sergeant Major / psywarrior.com
53. Courtesy Herb Friedman, retired U.S. Army Sergeant Major / psywarrior.com
54. Courtesy Herb Friedman, retired U.S. Army Sergeant Major / psywarrior.com
55. Courtesy Herb Friedman, retired U.S. Army Sergeant Major / psywarrior.com
56. *Reports of General MacArthur* (vol. 2, part 2) / U.S. Government Printing Office
57. Associated Press Photo
58. National Archives
59. Harry S. Truman Library and Museum
60. National Archives
61. Courtesy Los Alamos National Lab
62. Courtesy Los Alamos National Lab
63. Courtesy Los Alamos National Lab
64. Courtesy Los Alamos National Lab
65. George Strock /Time & Life Pictures / Getty Images
66. W. Eugene Smith / Time & Life Pictures / Getty Images
67. Hulton-Deutsch Collection / Corbis
68. Naval Historical Foundation
69. Naval Historical Foundation
70. Naval Historical Foundation
71. Courtesy Los Alamos National Lab
72. Courtesy Los Alamos National Lab
73. Courtesy Los Alamos National Lab
74. Ed Westcot / courtesy Los Alamos National Lab
75. Department of Energy / courtesy Los Alamos National Lab

76. U.S. Army Corps of Engineers / courtesy Los Alamos National Lab
77. Courtesy Los Alamos National Lab
78. National Archives
79. Keystone / Hulton Archive / Getty Images
80. Alfred Eisenstaedt / Time & Life Pictures / Getty Images
81. Yōsuke Yamahata © Shogo Yamahata / courtesy IDG Films
82. Naval Historical Foundation
83. National Archives
84. Harry S. Truman Library and Museum
85. Courtesy of the U.S. Army
86. Naval Historical Foundation
87. John Florea / Time & Life Pictures / Getty Images
88. Tom Shafer / Bettmann / Corbis
89. John Florea / Time & Life Pictures / Getty Images
90. Alfred Eisenstaedt / Time & Life Pictures / Getty Images
91. Alfred Eisenstaedt / Time & Life Pictures / Getty Images
92. Courtesy of the U.S. Army Center of Military History
93. Courtesy of the U.S. Army Center of Military History
94. Associated Press Photo
95. Juan E. Diaz / U.S. Navy
96. Paul Morse / courtesy George W. Bush Presidential Library
97. Joe Radle / Getty Images
98. Abbas / Magnum Photos
99. Mario Tama / Getty Images
100. Joe Raedle / Getty Images
101. Marco Di Lauro / Getty Images
102. Ceerwan Aziz / Reuters / Corbis
103. Bettmann / Corbis
104. David Furst / AFP / Getty Images
105. National Archives
106. Ramzi Haidar / AFP / Getty Images
107. Gerry Penny / EPA / Corbis
108. John Swope / Naval Historical Foundation
109. Bettmann / Corbis
110. Naval Historical Foundation
111. Naval Historical Foundation
112. Marcel Mettelsiefen / EPA / Corbis
113. Scott Barbour / Getty Images
114. Paula Bronstein / Getty Images
115. Johancharles van Boers / U.S. Army / DefenseImagery.mil
116. Ghaith Abdul-Ahab / Getty Images
117. Davis Pridgen / U.S. Army / DefenseImagery.mil
118. Hadi Mizban / Associated Press Photo
119. Damir Sagolj / Reuters / Corbis
120. Ahmed Alhussainey / Associated Press Photo
121. Thomas Hoepker / Magnum Photos
122. Joe Raedle / Getty Images

# INDEX

Page numbers in *italics* refer to illustrations.

# ABOUT THE AUTHOR

John W. Dower was Ford International Professor of History at the Massachusetts Institute of Technology when *Cultures of War* was written, and retired to become professor emeritus in June 2010, as the book was in press. Prior to MIT, he taught at the University of Nebraska (1970–71), University of Wisconsin–Madison (1971–86), and University of California–San Diego (1986–91). He worked for several years as an editor and book designer in Tokyo in the early 1960s, and as an academic later spent a number of research years living in Tokyo, Kyoto, and Kamakura with his wife, Yasuko, and their children.

His scholarly work on modern Japanese history and U.S.-Japan relations has been attentive to several interrelated areas of concern. One is Japan and Asia in the turbulent modern world; another, the links as well as discontinuities between the years prior to and after the end of World War II in 1945; and another, overriding all, the dynamics of war, peace, and power observed from multiple perspectives. Professor Dower first addressed these themes in the dissertation research that became the baseline for his first scholarly book, *Empire and Aftermath: Yoshida Shigeru and the Japanese Experience, 1878–1954* (1979). In two later books on war and peace—*War Without Mercy: Race and Power in the Pacific War* (1986) and

*Embracing Defeat: Japan in the Wake of World War II* (1999)—he devoted increasing attention to social, cultural, and psychological developments at grassroots levels, drawing on Japanese- and English-language materials ranging from films and political cartoons to popular songs and publications to vernacular slogans and slurs. *War Without Mercy* won the National Book Critics Circle Award for Nonfiction and, in Japan, the Masayoshi Ōhira Memorial Prize for distinguished scholarship on Asia and the Pacific. *Embracing Defeat* won two book prizes in Japan and seven in the United States. The latter included the Pulitzer Prize, National Book Award, Bancroft Prize for work in American history and diplomacy, and Fairbank Prize for a scholarly book on Asia since 1800. Twelve of his early essays on a range of prewar and postwar topics were collected in the 1993 book *Japan in War and Peace*.

The graphics in *Cultures of War* reflect another of Professor Dower's abiding interests: visual images that invite close reading and may open new windows of perception. His first published book, drawing on his sojourn as a book designer, was *The Elements of Japanese Design* (1971). In 1980, he edited *A Century of Japanese Photography, 1840–1945*, an English edition of a major Japanese sampling of the first hundred years of photography in Japan, and in 1985 he and John Junkerman published *The Hiroshima Murals*, on the collaborative political art of the painters Iri and Toshi Maruki. The following year, he was executive producer of a documentary film on the Marukis, directed by John Junkerman and titled *Hellfire—A Journey from Hiroshima*, which was nominated for an Academy Award. In 2002, Professor Dower and Shigeru Miyagawa established the Visualizing Cultures project at MIT (visualizingcultures.mit.edu), a pioneer venture in image-driven scholarship and public education focused on Asia in the modern world.